AGAINST THE MAINSTREAM

MEDIA & CULTURE

Sut Jhally & Justin Lewis
General Editors

Vol. 1

PETER LANG
New York • Washington, D.C./Baltimore • Bern
Frankfurt am Main • Berlin • Brussels • Vienna • Oxford

AGAINST THE MAINSTREAM

The Selected Works of
GEORGE GERBNER

EDITED BY
Michael Morgan

PETER LANG
New York • Washington, D.C./Baltimore • Bern
Frankfurt am Main • Berlin • Brussels • Vienna • Oxford

Library of Congress Cataloging-in-Publication Data

Gerbner, George.
Against the mainstream: the selected works of George Gerbner /
George Gerbner; [edited by] Michael Morgan.
p. cm. — (Media & culture; vol. 1)
Collection of articles, essays, etc. originally published 1958–1999.
Includes bibliographical references.
1. Mass media. I. Morgan, Michael. II. Title.
III. Media & culture (New York, N.Y.); vol. 1.
P91.25 .G47 302.23—dc21 2001038381
ISBN 978-0-8204-4163-4 (paperback)
ISBN 978-0-8204-6163-2 (hardcover)
ISSN 1098-4208

Bibliographic information published by **Die Deutsche Nationalbibliothek.**
Die Deutsche Nationalbibliothek lists this publication in the "Deutsche Nationalbibliografie"; detailed bibliographic data are available on the Internet at http://dnb.d-nb.de/.

Cover design by Dutton & Sherman Design

29 Broadway, 18th floor, New York, NY 10006
www.peterlang.com

ACKNOWLEDGMENTS

Every attempt has been made to secure permission for all material that has been used in this volume. If any party should have any questions about usage of material, please contact the publisher.

INTRODUCTIONS

Table of Contents

VII. HIGHLIGHTS, EXCERPTS, AND BRIEF REPORTS

VIII. CRITICAL CONTRIBUTIONS

IX. OP-EDS AND SHORT TAKES

CHAPTER 1

ON GEORGE GERBNER'S CONTRIBUTIONS TO COMMUNICATION THEORY, RESEARCH, AND SOCIAL ACTION

BY MICHAEL MORGAN

"Hungarians Think the Darndest Things."
—Headline, *New York Times Book Review*, January 24, 1993

In an academic and professional career spanning nearly five decades, George Gerbner has published hundreds of articles and research reports and edited over a dozen books. Yet, remarkably, although his theories, his research, and his activism have had immense impacts, there exists no single volume devoted to his own writing. That is the very significant gap that this book is intended to fill.

In extremely broad strokes, we can sum up George Gerbner's biography to date in five basic periods:

1919–1939: Gerbner grows up in Hungary, has promising future as a poet, and is drawn to the study of rural folklore; leaves Hungary to avoid conscription to Nazi side of impending war

1939–1956: becomes U.S. citizen and soldier, has exploits as paratrooper; in California, works as journalist and writer, shifts into education and obtains graduate degrees

1956–1964: Assistant (and associate) professor at the Institute for Communication Research at the University of Illinois; he focuses on theory building and conducts a wide variety of research projects on media content and institutions

1964–1989: Professor and dean of the Annenberg School for Communication, University of Pennsylvania; directs the Cultural Indicators Project in long-term, large-scale studies of television content and effects

1990–onwards: Founder and president of the Cultural Environment Movement, building a global coalition of activists and organizations devoted to changing media policy and practices

This very brief sketch is fleshed out in Chapter 2 of this book, a 1995 interview with Gerbner conducted by John Lent. In the interview, Gerbner recounts the "curious journey" he has followed through his many roles as poet, folklorist, journalist, soldier, teacher, academic, researcher, writer, activist, and more.

Gerbner has worn many hats and pursued a wide range of projects over the years. His *Vita* lists nearly three dozen major research projects he has directed over a 40-year period, with funding from the National Institute of Mental Health, the Screen Actors Guild, UNESCO, and many other agencies and foundations. He has been a visiting professor in Athens, Budapest, Cairo, and elsewhere. He has served on a wide range of councils and boards and has consulted with dozens of organizations, ranging from the Indian Institute for Mass Communication to the U.S. Office for Substance Abuse Prevention. He has provided frequent expert testimony at congressional and other hearings. From 1973 to 1991, he served as editor or executive editor of the *Journal of Communication*, the discipline's most important scholarly publication (the norm for holding such a position is three years). During his 25-year tenure as dean of the Annenberg School for Communication at the University of Pennsylvania, he organized numerous national and international conferences, on topics such as Communications Technology and Social Policy, Child Abuse, and Doctors and Lawyers in the Media, bringing together scholars, practitioners, lawmakers, and noted public figures. He spearheaded the massive, four-volume *International Encyclopedia of Communication* (1989). He has received a large number of awards and honors, and his work has been the subject of video series produced by the Media Education Foundation and others.

These and numerous other distinguished endeavors have had considerable repercussions on the field. They are not, however, the central focus of this book. Instead, the purpose of this book is to compile, for the first time, a hearty sampling of Gerbner's voluminous academic (and popular) writings.

Although it has not always been the case, the work of George Gerbner has increasingly come to be seen as "critical." There is a touch of irony in this, in that at some times and in some quarters his theories (and especially his methodological approaches) have been seen as the *antithesis* of a critical perspective. This perception stemmed from a false assumption, endemic in the early 1980s, that the use of empirical research methods was somehow incompatible with the adoption of a critical stance. This presumed dichotomy seems to have pretty much disappeared in current scholarship; arguably, Gerbner's work has been a major impetus for this intellectually healthy development.

INTELLECTUAL ROOTS

In 1957, Robert Merton sketched out what he saw as differences between "European" and "American" approaches to social research, the sociology of knowledge, and mass communication. For example, while European scholars sought "knowledge," their American counterparts amassed "information." While the Europeans studied the ideology of social movements, the Americans surveyed the opinions of voters. Europeans tackled Very Important Matters in empirically questionable ways, with little concern for "reliability"; Americans brought great empirical precision to bear on trivial issues, with much emphasis on reliability. Europeans, working as lone scholars (presumably in dingy garrets, by candlelight), pondered incomprehensible theories about how ideas emerge; Americans, working in research teams (presumably in labs, wearing white coats), investigated overly simplistic models of how to change attitudes and affect behavior. The Europeans could conclude, "At least it's true"; the Americans could claim, "At least it's (statistically) significant." And so on.

These were generalized caricatures even in the 1950s, and while they are perhaps still recognizable today, the geographic distinctions are certainly less sharp than they may have been in the past. But because of historical happenstance, Gerbner was shaped by and trained in *both* traditions, and his work has always embraced both. (As *Newsweek* put it in 1982, his methodology "meshes scholarly observation with mundane legwork.") It encompasses, in some ways, the best of both worlds (which inevitably means it must suffer from some of the weaknesses of both as well). He understood the special power of empirical methods (why else would they be appropriated by powerful groups?), but he was aware of the dangers of being limited by them.

Thus, Gerbner's work reflects a vital, lively, and unusual synthesis of diverse scholarly traditions. There are many manifestations of this productive mix. For example, Merton also claimed that the Europeans took the audience for granted and neglected any systematic analysis of it, whereas for the Americans the audience was the uppermost concern. Also, Europeans were obsessed with broad patterns in the long run while American research was often ahistorical. In all these and other dimensions, Gerbner's work has (mostly) avoided either extreme; but instead of simply finding some comfortable compromise between them, it has dynamically integrated them to forge new ground.

THREE MAJOR PHASES

In 1956, Gerbner wrote "The structure of freedom is *organized* diversity whether it pleases or not" (p. 188). (The emphasis is in the original, and its ramifications should become clear as we proceed.) If any single statement could sum up the point of the work he has pursued over the decades as an academic and a public intellectual, that one would pretty much do the trick. We can identify three major intellectual phases in which Gerbner has worked to develop the implications of that statement, in different ways.

First, in the 1950s and '60s, he developed multidimensional theoretical models of the communication process, in mediated and unmediated forms, and at micro and macro levels; this work both led to and elaborated the ideas about organized diversity and freedom expressed in the above statement. This phase included a series of wide-ranging content analyses (e.g., of confession magazines, of film heroes, and others) that were often international in scope, along with several cross-national studies of media institutions. These studies formed a bridge to the second phase in which, in the 1970s and '80s (and beyond), he developed and directed a long-term research program known as the Cultural Indicators Project. Through the Cultural Indicators research paradigm, focusing especially on television content and effects, he brought a massive amount of empirical evidence to bear on the nature and consequences of the absence of this "organized diversity." Third, since the 1990s, he has been striving to mobilize a new social and political movement, made up of public groups, academics, unions, and professional and minority organizations, and dedicated to the transformation of the cultural environment so that it might someday achieve that diversity and, by extension, become a liberating rather than a repressive force.

Gerbner (1990, p. 249) has noted, "Research rarely advances in a straight line," and the thumbnail sketch above may give the impression of a more linear scholarly itinerary than is in fact the case. Nevertheless, as this volume demonstrates, there is both growth and continuity in his work over the years, and some recurrent guiding themes; in retrospect, his work, for all its diversity, indeed seems to reflect some "natural" and coherent intellectual progressions.

Much of Gerbner's work has sparked controversy. This is fortunate; it would be far worse to be ignored. As he put it in the interview that closes this book (conducted by Closepet and Tsui in 1992), "If nobody screams, you are not doing anything." There were, for example, heated debates in the 1970s with researchers from the television networks over the methods and findings of his studies of the portrayal of violence on television. Since the 1980s, his ideas and the research findings about television's impact on social beliefs—what he calls *cultivation analysis*—have continued to attract enormous amounts of attention, both positive and negative, within and without the academic community.

How influential is Gerbner's Cultural Indicators paradigm and his "cultivation analyses" of media effects? The 2000 version of the full bibliography of "Publications Relating to the Cultural Indicators Project" runs nearly 30 single-spaced pages. Bryant quipped that studies of cultivation seem "almost as ubiquitous as television itself" (1986, p. 231). At the time, Bryant noted that a systematic study of over 100 "Mass Media and Society" courses in U.S. colleges and universities showed that "cultivation was one of only three topics receiving detailed examination in more than half the courses" (p. 232). Further, he argued, "cultivation research is one of the few contributions by mass communication scholars to infiltrate" textbooks in such fields as social psychology and sociology "with some regularity" (p. 232). Clearly, Gerbner's theories have been the object of considerable attention. Moreover, it is not simply his ideas in and of themselves that account for the attention they have received. It is, at least in part, due to Gerbner's skill in "packaging" concepts, in framing them in memorable, and often alliterative, terms (e.g., "risk ratios," or the Three B's: "blurring, blending, and bending," among others).

The simplified and most commonly encountered version of cultivation goes something to the effect that "watching a lot of television makes people afraid." This is the sort of description one might expect to find in the popular press, but all too often it appears in mass communication, sociology, and psychology textbooks as well as in scholarly articles. Indeed, results from cultivation analyses are often erroneously referred to as "cultivation effects," an unfortunately sloppy twist that tends to equate cultivation with the very assumptions, inadequacies, and problems it was designed to go beyond. By stepping back and looking at where the idea came from, it may be possible to re-infuse some of the richness of Gerbner's early ideas and theories into the current debates.

MASS COMMUNICATION AND MESSAGES

Gerbner attempted to alter the nature of the conventional discourse about the social and cultural implications of mass communication. His first struggle was to develop an approach to mass communication that saw it in terms different from those of persuasion and propaganda research and to escape the scientism and positivism of that research. Later, he applied similar criticisms to common public concerns about media violence and the experimental work it inspired. He also argued for the need to dispense with traditional formal aesthetic categories along with conventional concerns about style, artistic quality, high culture vs. low culture, and selective judgments and interpretations. He tried to draw attention to the interplay of *systems* of messages, in the aggregate, and of the institutional structures that produced those systems. In most of his writings over almost 50 years, he has expressed fundamental disagreements with whatever dominant paradigms were currently in vogue. Any assumption, approach, or procedure that seemed widely accepted as the "normal way of doing things" was, by definition, suspect.

As did many others at the time, Gerbner focused heavily on "messages" in his early work, but he imbued them with some particular characteristics and functions. He acknowledged that messages were the "what" in Lasswell's famous formula, but as early as 1958 he dismissed that conceptualization as "too restrictive and too one-directional for a general theoretical communications model, or for a framework for critical research" (see Chapter 4). From the start, he sought to develop models of the communication process that distinguished it from other forms of social interaction; and he sought to develop approaches to communication research—cast, importantly, as a form of *basic cultural inquiry*—that were distinct from dominant concerns with prediction and control. He argued that this was, by definition, a critical turn. In doing so, he drew heavily in those days on Lazarsfeld's notions of critical vs. administrative research; in that context, his goal was to free the analysis of media content from the narrow limits of administrative research, and also to ground it in institutional policies and processes (see Chapter 4).

Gerbner argues that any message is a socially and historically determined expression of concrete physical and social relationships. Messages imply propositions, assumptions, and points of view that are understandable only in terms of the social relationships and contexts in which they are produced. Yet they also reconstitute those relationships and contexts. They thus function recursively, sustaining and giving meaning to the structures and practices that produce them.

Communication to Gerbner is "interaction through messages," a distinctly human (and humanizing) process that both creates and is driven by the symbolic environment that constitutes culture. The symbolic environment reveals social and institutional dynamics, and because it expresses social patterns it also cultivates them. This, then, is how Gerbner originally conceived of "cultivation": the process within which interaction through messages shapes and sustains the terms on which the messages are premised.

The production of messages then takes on special significance, since the resulting social patterns imply cultural and political power—namely, the right to create the messages that cultivate collective consciousness. With *mass* communication we have the mass production of messages, the cultural manifestation of the industrial revolution. Given the social functions of messages, the mass production of messages and of the symbolic environment then represents a profound transformation in social relationships and power. He summed this up in 1963:

> Message-systems which provide many of the raw materials of our consciousness (and of the terms of our perceptions) have become mass-produced, institutionalized commodities. Bigness, fewness, and costliness in cultural, as in any other, mass production brought centralization of control, standardization of product, streamlined efficiency of technique. These changes meant increasing penetration of influence into many spheres of life and across many previous boundaries of place, time, and social status. (p. 39)

Since messages reflect social relationships, mass-produced messages then bear the assumptions of the organizations (though not necessarily of the individuals) that produce them. Early on, Gerbner found it problematic that the major message-producing organizations tended to be profit-oriented, commercial corporations: "Industrial and market conditions and the corporate positions of cultural enterprises ... implicitly shape the assumptions, contexts, and points of view embedded in mass media products" (Gerbner, 1959, p. 271).

Thus, the transformation of message production by the process of industrialization is only part of the story; the more critical point is that message production became dominated by commercial interests. Gerbner quoted Van Den Haag's (1957) observation that "unless the requirements and effects of industrialization are fully grasped, popular culture does not become intelligible," and then added: "Even more specifically, unless the requirements and effects of a specific system of industrial and market relationships (such as the corporate structure) are fully grasped, mass media content analysis remains superficial" (Gerbner, 1958, p. 90). This warning has been lost on all too many of those who have conducted content analyses of media output.

Even in the 1950s, of course, it did not take any unusual observational skills to realize that the mass media—and therefore popular culture—were dominated by advertiser-supported, profit-seeking businesses. What Gerbner did was to point out some of the less obvious implications of this arrangement in novel ways, and to keep hammering the point home for almost 50 years.

STORYTELLING AND CULTIVATION

The key to his analysis was to place special emphasis on the cultural process of storytelling. He drew on Lowenthal's (1957) notion that "Man is born, strives, loves, suffers, and dies in any society, but it is the portrayal of *how* he reacts to these common experiences that matters since they almost invariably have a social nexus" (Gerbner, 1958, p. 88). (Presumably, Lowenthal did not mean to imply that these processes did not apply to women, although females certainly figure less prominently in the stories of Western societies.) Some years later, he argued "Whatever else they do, stories confirm authority and distribute power in specific ways. Story-telling fits human reality to the social order" (Gerbner, 1986, p. 255).

Gerbner contends that the basic difference between human beings and other species is that we live in a world that is created by the stories we tell. (I am quoting and paraphrasing rather liberally here from a variety of his writings.) All living organisms exchange energy with their environments. Many creatures process and exchange information, store impressions, and change their behavior as a result of learning. But only humans *communicate* by the manipulation of complex symbol systems. Humans therefore uniquely live in a world experienced and conducted largely through many forms and modes of storytelling. Most of what we know, or think we know, we have never personally experienced; we "know" about things based on the stories we hear and the stories we tell. We are, he claims, the stories we tell.

He identifies three types of stories. There are stories about how things *work*, in which the invisible dynamics of human life are illuminated. These stories are called *fiction*, and they build a fantasy we call reality. There are also stories about how things *are*; today, we mostly call them *news*, and they tend to confirm the visions, rules, and goals of a particular society. And there are stories of value and choice, of what to *do*. These have been called sermons, or instruction, or law; today they are called *commercials*. Together, all three kinds of stories, organically related, constitute culture; they are expressed and enacted through mythology, religion, legends, education, art, science, laws, fairy tales, and politics—and all of these, increasingly, are packaged and disseminated by television.

Gerbner is especially fond of quoting Andrew Fletcher of Saltoun (1655–1716), who wrote in a letter to the Marquise of Montrose: "If a man were permitted to make all the ballads, he need not care who should make the laws of a nation." Such a romantic notion is not easily testable by empirical methods, but that makes it no less compelling. Storytelling occupies a crucial role in human existence, and it is being increasingly monopolized by a small and shrinking group of global conglomerates whose attention does not extend beyond the bottom line and quarterly reports to stockholders. Therefore, the world we are inhabiting and (re)creating is one designed according to the specifications of marketing strategies.

A NEW VIEW OF "EFFECTS"

The impacts on those who consume messages and stories are not linear, mechanical, or hypodermic. Because this is a dialectical process (Gerbner, 1958), the "effects" of messages are relatively *indirect*. Uncovering aggregate and implicit patterns in mass-produced messages "will not necessarily tell us what people think or do. But they will tell us what most people think or do something *about* and in *common*" (Gerbner, 1970, p. 81). This argument has some affinity to the notion of agenda-setting, but it is cast on a deeper and more fundamental level. It is not so much the specific, day-to-day agenda of public issue salience that culture (and cultural media) sets as it is the more hidden and pervasive boundary conditions for social discourse, wherein the cultural ground rules for what exists, what is important, what is right, and so on, are repeated (and ritualistically consumed) so often that they are invisible.

In its earliest forms, then, the idea of "cultivation" had little to do with percentage differences shown between heavy and light television viewers in response to survey questions about social reality, which became the most common methodological strategy of cultivation analysis. Instead, in its early stages, Gerbner sought to describe the process by which mass communication creates publics and defines the perspectives and assumptions that are most broadly shared among those publics. In "Toward 'Cultural Indicators'" (1969), Gerbner wrote:

> A message (or message system) cultivates consciousness of the terms required for its meaningful perception. Whether I accept its 'meaning' or not, like it or not, or agree or disagree, is another problem. First I must attend to it and grasp what it is about. Just how that occurs, how items of information are integrated into given frameworks of cognition, is also another problem. My interest here centers on the fact that any attention and understanding cultivates the terms upon which it is achieved. And to the considerable extent to which these terms are common to large groups, the cultivation of shared terms provides the basis for public interaction. (p. 139)

Since the symbolic environment gives direction and meaning to human thought and action, cultivation is then the (continuous) outcome of interaction within the symbolic environment, assuring shared terms of discourse and behavior. The cultivation of "shared terms" and "collective consciousness," however, is not to be mistaken for consensus:

> On the contrary, the public recognition of subcultural, class, generational, and ideological differences and even conflicts among scattered groups of people

requires some common awareness and cultivation of the issues, styles, and points of divergence that make public contention and contest possible (Gerbner, 1969, p. 138).

Moreover, cultivation is not in itself the punchline. Again, the point is not so much that it occurs at all (it is after all the historic and universal function of all socio-cultural institutions and the stories they tell), but that the cultivation of collective consciousness is now institutionalized and corporately managed to an unprecedented degree. As mass communication creates publics, it can also dissolve (or blur and blend?) them. The *critical* point is that the "dissolution of publics into markets for mass media conceived and conducted in the increasingly demanding framework of commodity merchandising is the cultural (and political) specter of our age" (Gerbner, 1958, p. 108). Or, as he put it elsewhere:

> The rise of cultural mass production, creating audiences, subjecting tastes, views, and desires to the laws of the market, and inherently tending toward the standardized and the safe rather than the diversified or critical, creates new problems in the theory and practice of self-government. (Gerbner, 1959, pp. 276–277)

The consistent findings of subsequent decades of research, analysis, and theory-building have only made that statement stronger. These problems, and the challenges to democracy they pose, may not be as "new" as they were in the 1950s, but we do not seem to be any closer to solving them.

CULTURAL INDICATORS AND THE VIOLENCE PROFILES

Through a variety of distinct but loosely related studies of media industries, content, and functions (some of which are represented in Sections II and III), Gerbner began to develop what he called an "institutional approach" to mass communication. This called for the study of relationships among social structures, media message systems, corporate structures and processes, collective image formation, and public policy. These ideas soon thereafter came together in a more formalized way under the conceptual umbrella of the Cultural Indicators paradigm (see Chapter 14), which called for a three-pronged approach consisting of the study of media industries (institutional process analysis), media content (message system analysis), and media effects (cultivation analysis). The Cultural Indicators Project's first (and in many ways, primary) focus was on the problem of television violence.

The issue of television violence, never far off the public (and political) radar screen, was receiving a great deal of attention in the late 1960s and early '70s. At that time, Gerbner was selected by the National Commission on the Causes and Prevention of Violence (the "Eisenhower Commission"), and later by the Surgeon General's Scientific Advisory Committee on Television and Social Behavior, to conduct content analyses of the representation of violence on network television. This was the birth of the yearly "Violence Profiles," developed according to the theoretical parameters and methodological prescriptions of the Cultural Indicators paradigm. With funding from many different sources over the years, these profiles have provided 30 years of continuous monitoring of violence and many other recurrent features of the symbolic environment.

Gerbner saw the problem of television violence in a different way than did most others. The message (content) data showed more victims than victimizers: They revealed a clear social pecking order, with some groups (minorities, women, old people) consistently more likely to be victimized. He hypothesized that rather than imitating the acts of violence they see, most viewers might be more likely to identify with *victims*—that rather than disrupting the social order, television violence maintains the status quo by demonstrating and protecting the power of the powerful. By cultivating fear, apprehension, and mistrust, television might well contribute to a climate in which demands for security outweigh any remnants of concern about repression and violation of civil liberties. By cultivating "traditional" conceptions of women, minorities, older people, occupations, and so on, television's messages contribute to the maintenance of specific power hierarchies. The connection with the early version of cultivation is that in both cases mass-produced messages are seen as fundamental mechanisms of social control.

Violence played a special role in these theoretical developments, both because it was (and is) such a salient public issue, and because of the remarkable and consistent frequency with which it is portrayed on television. Gerbner often notes that stories from mythology to fairy tales to the Bible to Shakespeare have of course prominently featured violence. But the sheer amount of violence that television brings into every home on a daily basis is historically unprecedented.

Moreover, what we are "awash" in (his use of water metaphors is discussed below) is entertaining, thrilling, happy violence, quite useful and efficient for solving conflicts, for upholding the social order, and for demonstrating the consequences of transgression. (I am again paraphrasing liberally here.) It is useful for mobilizing massive support for police action at home, and for military action abroad, especially when enough of the audience (sorry, I mean "the public") can be convinced that some "vital interest" is threatened or that some villain "needs" to be punished. As a cheap production ingredient, it is useful for the creation of "product" (i.e., television programs) that can be more easily sold to media owners (broadcast, cable, satellite) in other countries; unlike humor, violence travels well. Most of all, it is useful for delivering to advertisers audiences who are in a "proper" mindset to be receptive to commercial messages.

As it developed, cultivation analysis, most simply, attempts to determine the contribution that differential amounts of television viewing make to people's conceptions of social reality. The main change from its earlier conceptualization was the incorporation of the empirical assessment of statistical differences in the beliefs, assumptions, and attitudes of lighter and heavier viewers. The specific, observable, independent contribution of television to conceptions of violence and other issues was assessed by analyses of data from many surveys, comparing responses and beliefs of heavy and light viewers, other things held constant.

Other techniques were explored, but cultivation analysis has almost entirely meant the analysis of survey data. It is not clear from the early writings exactly how this particular strategy developed; compared to institutional and message system analysis, the operational and analytical terms and procedures of cultivation *analysis* were relatively unspecified, and any number of empirical approaches might have emerged. Yet, through Gerbner's collaboration with Larry Gross (Gerbner & Gross, 1976; see Chapter 17), with some work on images of mental illness providing an interim conceptual model, that strategy became synonymous with cultivation analysis.

The trick was to investigate television's contributions to viewers' conceptions without directly asking people about television. Instead of asking people what they thought about television, people were simply asked about what they *thought*. Then, the question of whether or not amount of television viewing made a difference in conceptions could be addressed. This was not a minor methodological departure.

The more elaborated, data-based concept of cultivation was born in a time when over-the-air network broadcasting ruled people's media behavior essentially unchallenged. The term "broadcast" originally meant to sow seeds at random. In that context, "cultivation" was the perfect designation for his ideas of how media shape social conceptions, connoting "culture," which itself has deep etymological implications concerning the practices by which the basic human need for food can be nourished and sustained by means of livestock and agriculture (Williams, 1976).

In one sense, and despite its aptness for describing the primary functions of culture, "cultivation" is an uncharacteristically land-based metaphor for Gerbner. He has most often been drawn to *water-based* analogies to describe the "sea-change" of television and its role in redirecting the "flows" and "currents" of cultural "tides" (not to mention the notion of the "mainstream"). Interestingly, in the 1992 interview with Closepet and Tsui at the end of this book, Gerbner claimed to be unaware of his watery proclivities.

In any case, based on Gerbner's arguments about the cohesiveness of television content, cultivation analysis deals with overall, cumulative exposure to the total world of television. An individual story or program is simply "a drop in the ocean." This emphasis contrasted sharply with most previous research (and public debate), which tended to focus on individual programs, episodes, series, or genres, usually in terms of their short-term "effects" on viewers' attitudes and behavior. Such questions are not "wrong" and such effects are not unimportant; but they do not take into account what makes mass communication in general and television in particular different from earlier cultural media.

As Gerbner (1970, p. 71) put it, "most 'effects' research stemmed from theoretical perspectives that did not consider relevance to the mass-cultural process a principal criterion." When "effects" are defined as immediate "change" among individuals, we ignore the unique functions and distinctive features of contemporary mass communication—which means massive, long-term consumption of centrally produced, mass-distributed, repetitive stories among large and heterogeneous publics who never meet face to face and have little in common except the messages they share.

This issue—so central in all of Gerbner's work and at the forefront of many cultivation debates—continues to be important today, despite the development of new technologies, from the VCR to 500-channel cable systems to the Internet, which on the surface appear to offer more "choice" and "diversity." The original premise was that since similarities among different content "types" are more important than their differences, what counts most is overall exposure to and immersion in the world of television. Indeed, it is that global, aggregate, general focus that differentiates cultivation from mere "attitude change" studies.

Gerbner (1966, p. 102) defined the "effects" of communication as "the history and dynamics of continuities, as well as of change, in the reciprocal relationships between social structures, message systems, and image structures." The term "reciprocal" is important here, and is another indication that simplistic S-R models of cause and effect are insufficient and irrelevant to the idea of cultivation. A less unwieldy version of this formulation emerged in his "three-legged stool" notion of the relationships among (in effect) social patterns, media output, and public beliefs and ideologies; asking which of the three (i.e., media, culture, society) is the most important is like asking which leg holds up a three-legged stool. In this context, debates over the relationship between base and superstructure, or materialistic vs. idealistic explanations for social and cultural phenomena, seem a bit quaint. Communication is thus neither determinate nor symptomatic, but rather an essential cultural nutrient. The critical task is to reveal the dynamics of power in communications and of communications in society, in order to transform them.

EXTENSIONS OF CULTURAL INDICATORS

As the data piled up and the research reports were churned out, attention to Gerbner's ideas about cultivation was skyrocketing. Some of the attention took the form of independent replications and confirmations and refinements, and some took the form of harsh (and occasionally vituperous) criticism. Some of the criticism was helpful, some mildly annoying, and some beside the point. Some critics lost sight of the theory and became submerged in statistical minutiae. Shanahan and Morgan (1999) offer a lengthy treatment of these debates and controversies (see also Signorielli & Morgan, 1990), as well as a meta-analysis of hundreds of cultivation studies. In their (admittedly partisan) view, it turns out that Gerbner was right far more often than he was wrong.

Gerbner's original ideas and the intense work done in the late 1970s and 1980s have branched off in dozens of directions. Researchers have examined a variety of conditions and variations of cultivation analysis—for example, mainstreaming (homogenization), resonance (special susceptibility), the roles of cognitive processing, personal experience, selective viewing, perceived reality, new technologies, peer groups and the family, personal vs. society-level conceptions, and so on. Moreover, differences in cultivation patterns among different groups, and in numerous substantive and topical areas, have been investigated. Cultivation theory and analysis have continued to develop and progress, as new findings and conclusions have further extended and refined the theory (see Chapter 15).

An especially important outgrowth of Gerbner's work has been the attempt to carry out research under the Cultural Indicators paradigm in other countries and cultures. The development of cross-cultural, comparative analyses of message systems and cultivation patterns is a major challenge, in theoretical, methodological, and pragmatic terms. It provides the opportunity to investigate how relationships between television exposure and conceptions vary according to diverse policies, structures, message patterns, cultures, and audiences.

Again, cultivation means that the dominant modes of cultural production tend to generate messages and representations that nourish and sustain the ideologies, perspectives, and practices of the institutions and cultural contexts from which they arise. It does *not* simply mean that television viewing universally fosters fear, apprehension, sex-role stereotypes, or other related conceptions. If a particular message system (and culture) contains a great deal of violence, for example, then the media system of that society should cultivate corresponding conceptions; if the message system/culture does not contain a lot of violence, the media system should not cultivate such conceptions. The fact that U.S. television repeatedly portrays (and cultivates) a particular set of images of violence, sex roles, occupations, aging, health, science, social power, minorities, and so on, does not mean that other countries' television systems, which may or may not disseminate similar images, cultivate similar views. The fact that most other countries import so much of their programming further complicates the picture.

The early 1980s saw a flurry of attempts to replicate cultivation analysis in other countries, mostly in western Europe (England, the Netherlands, Sweden, and Germany), in Australia, and in Israel. Later, cultivation was explored in cultural, political, and historical contexts that are more different from those of the United States, such as in Asia (Taiwan, South Korea, the Philippines, and China) and in Latin America (Argentina and Brazil). Some of these studies confirmed general findings from the United States, and some did not (for overviews of these and other studies, see Melischek, Rosengren, & Stappers, 1984; Morgan, 1990; Morgan & Shanahan, 1992). Analyses of comparative message and/or cultivation data from Hungary, Japan, Finland, Russia (before and after the collapse of the USSR), and elsewhere were also undertaken (see, e.g., Chapter 32). Some of this international work stemmed from Gerbner's attempts in the late 1980s to organize a global project called "Television Around the World," whose purpose was to conduct parallel analyses of television policies, content, and effects with researchers in 26 participating countries. Unfortunately, due to the inability to obtain the funding needed to support such a massive project, and because of the scarcity of resources in many of the countries involved, the project accomplished far less than originally hoped.

The upheavals of old orders, and the transition to what had been nominally promoted as "democracy" in many countries in Latin America, Africa, and the former Eastern bloc, placed international cultivation analysis in a new context. In many countries, state-run media systems were privatized and quickly snatched up by multinational corporations. Veils of oppression were apparently lifted, only to be replaced by new ones. Gerbner saw the resulting media chaos in such places as Eastern Europe as leading to the resurgence of "neo-fascism, parochialism, and chauvinism"; while many cheered the prospect of new freedoms, Gerbner wanted to "warn them of uncritical acceptance" of commercial control of the media, since "they're mortgaging the socialization of their children to global conglomerates" (Closepet & Tsui, 1992).

In this context of widespread movement toward "democracy" (often conflated with "capitalism"), the critical implication of "organized diversity" in message production as a means of achieving cultural freedom has only become sharper. The state to Gerbner is not some benevolent grantor of such diversity, but it needs to become a force to promote it, to guarantee it, while, in contrast, it has usually worked, complicitly, to obstruct it. As the tyranny of the state is replaced by the tyranny of the market, it is falsely assumed that the *absence* of governmental controls and regulation somehow automatically means diversity and liberation. While Gerbner does not see state involvement or benignly paternalistic regulation as a panacea to the problem of the media, his point is that government has been anything but an innocent bystander.

ENTER CEM

All this brings us, not to the end of the story, but to the next installment, still being written. It is a new phase of activism on Gerbner's part, as a political organizer (and occasionally as an Op-Ed pundit). This episode is called the "Cultural Environment Movement" (CEM), and it is Gerbner's attempt to take things a step further, to go from a critique of existing cultural policy to its transformation: from research to action. It represents a shift from a critique of the practices of cultural industries to an attack on the very system that regulates, deregulates, and protects them. It is about how to turn a research project into a political project.

The Cultural Environment Movement is based on Gerbner's assertion that existing media structures in the United States are beyond the reach of democratic policy making. Since advertising is a tax-deductible business expense and since the costs of advertising are hidden in the price of the products that we buy (i.e., "We pay when we wash, not when we watch"), we have taxation without representation. But what can we *do* about it? The question is: "How can we work toward a freer, fairer, and more liberating cultural environment?" The answer, in part:

> We must reclaim the rights gained through centuries of struggle and conferred by law, the Constitution, and the basic principles of liberal education and self-government in a democracy. We must mobilize Americans to act as citizens as effectively as commercials mobilize us to act as consumers. (Gerbner, 1991, p. 2)

Through CEM, Gerbner has sought to build a broad-based coalition of media activists; educational, health, environmental, legal, and other professional associations; consumer groups and agencies; women's groups; religious and minority organizations; and many other groups and individuals who are "committed to broadening the freedom and diversity of the media mainstream that dominates U.S. and world cultures" (Gerbner, 1991, p. 3). CEM wants to have a broader range of voices and interests heard in cultural decision making, to assist grass-roots movements in the United States and elsewhere, to promote media literacy and critical viewing efforts, and to support media workers struggling within existing institutional constraints. Most of all, the goal is to put debate over cultural policy, with attention to media ownership, access, and diversity, on the sociopolitical agenda.

This is, of course, a tall order, and one that aims for far more than piecemeal reform. To date, Gerbner's CEM efforts have been directed more toward building a constituency and consolidating a coherent vision for the budding movement than toward specific legislative actions. (The bill authored by Sen. Paul Simon in the 1990s, which allowed the broadcast and cable networks and Hollywood producers to develop industry-wide standards on violence without fear of prosecution for violating antitrust statutes, was significantly bolstered by Cultural Indicators' Violence Profiles.)

One obvious problem is that "the public interest," historically and ostensibly the guiding principle in media regulation, in practice consists mainly of balancing competing *industry* interests. The "public" component of the interest equation is generally given short shrift by politicized administrative agencies (especially the FCC) and by those in Congress whose reelection campaigns are heavily financed by the various industries. Allowing other voices to be heard, much less making sure that they are heeded, will not be easy to accomplish.

An even more formidable task is to democratize the mechanisms and processes by which program production is funded. Production costs remain astronomical despite technical advances; advertisers are more than willing to invest in these efforts, while the idea of federal support is political anathema. This of course serves as the perennial justification for the present system. The few alternatives available have their own problems; PBS's are well-known, and the noncommercially supported cable channels (such as pay-cable and PPV) do not provide meaningfully alternative content. The problem of the lack of feasible alternatives to the current economic basis of program production is likely to be the major way to dismiss CEM's goals (by both governmental and media organizations); and CEM has not yet reached the stage where it has been able to propose specific, realistic, and workable alternatives that could help to develop the more democratic system it hopes to bring about.

CEM may be but a pipe dream, as much "a drop in the ocean" as any individual program or episode. But Gerbner's optimism is not Pollyanna-ish and can give one second thoughts about writing off the movement. As he put it in a 1994 video interview:

> To turn things around that almost everybody takes for granted is going to take a long time. And many people will consider it impossible. But then look around the world and see how many things that only five, ten years ago we considered impossible, are now reality. So I would say, if it's impossible, if it seems impossible, it means it's worth doing. (Gerbner, 1994)

He follows this admonition by asking us to remember the slogan of Soviet dissidents of the 1960s and '70s: When they offered a toast they said, "And here is to the success of our hopeless endeavor." Indeed.

OVERVIEW OF THE BOOK

We start off in Section I with Gerbner's early theories about communication as they emerged from his studies of folklore and literature at the University of Budapest and his studies of psychology and journalism at the University of California. Coupled with influences and arguments drawn from the works of Adorno, Fearing, Lazarsfeld, Lowenthal, and others, this provided a unique mix and produced novel and provocative syntheses of these perspectives, culminating in an ambitious and multidimensional model of communication. This early work also reflects his efforts to carve out a clear and compelling place for "Communications" as a new academic discipline, and it contains many ideas that were to launch him in a variety of directions in the decades to come. In the interests of historical authenticity, and to retain the original flavor, all uses of the generic "man" and "he" in these papers have been left in. (They are few and far between after the 1960s.)

As Gerbner explains in the Chapter 2 interview with John Lent, he came to education in a circuitous and somewhat serendipitous manner. In this context, the *study* of education was one of the first topical areas on which he focused. In the early 1950s, the educational potential of the new medium of television was being touted as much (or more) as its commercial or entertainment value; Gerbner notes that his master's thesis was perhaps the first ever written on educational television. Thus, it was natural that he would be drawn to investigate the relationship between education and the media, and the papers in Section II contain three diverse studies on the topic.

The first paper in this section ("Education about Education by Mass Media," 1966) considers what the media might be teaching us about education as an institution and as a process. The second, "Education in Newspaper Advertisements" (1964), is an early systematic content analysis of one aspect of the larger issue. The third, "Teacher Image in Mass Culture" (1972), is especially important in that it provides extensive elaboration of two concepts—"symbolic functions" and the "hidden curriculum"—that are absolutely central to the corpus of Gerbner's work. As his full bibliography shows, he authored over a dozen other studies and papers about education—including the immense "Mass Communications and Popular Conceptions of Education," a 10-nation international comparative research project conducted for the U.S. Office of Education in 1964—but these three give some of the flavor of his work in this area.

Section III includes a variety of studies he pursued in the 1950s and '60s, prior to developing the theoretical paradigm of Cultural Indicators (CI), yet they show him moving clearly toward that larger and more integrated model. There are systematic studies of media content (e.g., romance-confession magazines) using a variety of methods and approaches. There are institutional analyses of pressures and constraints affecting the production of media content, and examinations of the ideology of the organizations (and not necessarily of the individuals) that create that content. These studies are noteworthy for the range of topics they address. Interestingly, many of the studies Gerbner pursued in this period show a great emphasis on qualitative, interpretive research, sometimes abetted by content analysis and other quantitative techniques. These studies provide interesting data and offer valuable insights; although they are not entirely discrete efforts, they are not yet united by the common underlying conceptual framework of Cultural Indicators.

The CI framework is the specific focus of Section IV, which first presents an important theoretical piece from 1973, "The 3rd Voice." This paper sets out the full conceptual and operational definition of the Cultural Indicators model, along with its intellectual and political rationale. Gerbner clarifies and elaborates on the terms of analysis (and the interrelations among them) for the three-pronged study of institutional process analysis, message systems analysis, and cultivation analysis. Next, jumping ahead quite a bit, the 1994 paper on "Growing up with Television" extends the theoretical and methodological implications of the Cultural Indicators model and sums up 20 years worth of studies it inspired. The final entry in this section, "Advancing on the Path of Righteousness (Maybe)," from 1990, is perhaps Gerbner's most focused and explicit statement of what cultivation analysis is (and isn't).

Although the CI model stimulated research in an extremely wide variety of areas, it was first and foremost associated with the question of media violence. Section V presents a sampling of some of Gerbner's key writings about violence, over a 20-year period. "Living with Television," with Larry Gross (1976), was a report on the sixth year of monitoring media violence, and provided a much more detailed and specific explanation of the methodology of cultivation analysis. This paper also represents the first publication of cultivation data. It provided a template for many Violence Profiles that were to follow (and, often, to generate intense controversy).

The other papers in this section were chosen to touch on a range of issues related to media violence beyond those typically included in the Violence Profiles. The notion of "symbolic functions" is elaborated within an empirical focus on death ("Death in Prime Time," 1980), and the relationship of symbolic violence to real world terrorism is explored—in ways that go well beyond the usual terms of public discourse—in a 1990 paper on "Violence and Terror in and by the Media." The section also includes Gerbner's reflections, in a book review, of the role of the government vis-à-vis violence research ("Science or Ritual Dance," 1984), and a 1995 study of Anti-Violence Public Service Announcements. Given the very large number of papers and studies he has produced on the topic of media violence, this section could have become a book on its own.

As noted above, the 1980s saw Cultural Indicators studies branching off into many new directions, and the papers in Section VI reflect but a few samples of this variety. There are studies of television's contributions to political orientations, images of doctors and health, science and scientists, and the aging process. These studies show how message system and cultivation analysis can be applied in many areas besides violence, which is a theme that is continued into and amplified in Section VII. The entries in Section VII are highlights and excerpts from much longer data-based research reports on a wide variety of topics. These include studies of casting and fate (i.e., the representation of women and minorities on television) as well as the portrayal of alcohol and tobacco; even a study of the representation of animals is included. Other papers in this section present brief synopses of what were extremely large-scale studies, including an investigation of the content and effects of the Electronic Church, and comparative message and cultivation analyses of U.S. and Soviet television.

Gerbner's critical vision began to crystallize much more explicitly in the early 1990s. Certainly he began taking the gloves off more, stepping at least slightly away from the data (though grounding himself in them), and saying (in print) much more of what he really thought. The papers in Sections VIII and IX present diverse examples of this tendency. First, however, Section VIII starts out with a paper he wrote to cap off the 1983 double issue of the *Journal of Communication*, devoted to the topic of "Ferment in the Field." At the time, the "Ferment" that was shaking the field was the ascendance of critical studies, challenging the dominant and traditional paradigms and presuming (as noted above) that "critical/qualitative" research and "quantitative" research were mutually exclusive (and each a kind of litmus test of ideological purity). This paper puts the term "critical" in a new and different light, and seeks to turn the terms of that debate in more productive directions.

The other papers in Section VIII are crisp and hard-hitting attacks on assortments of myths, wishful thinking, and dangerous deceptions. Gerbner tears apart the conventional wisdom concerning the benefits of new technologies and illusions of diversity and choice. He exposes the narrow and misleading coverage of UNESCO in the U.S. press. He provides an especially thorough and comprehensive blast at the media coverage of the Persian Gulf War—and at the war itself. These papers anchor their critical contributions in painstaking and detailed scholarly work.

He also played with shorter and more "popular" forms, and especially since the 1990s he has been turning out pithy but meaty op-ed pieces, just as critical as those described above but less encumbered by academic conventions and cautions. Section IX offers brief opinion pieces on even more topics—cameras in the courtroom and O.J. Simpson, tobacco advertising, the invisibility of labor in the mainstream media, the new media ratings codes, and more.

Finally, Section X concludes the book with several brief but focused works that represent the shift from research to action in the form of the Cultural Environment Movement. It lays out the purposes and goals of CEM and includes the "Viewer's Declaration of Independence," designed to be a shot heard 'round the media world. The closing interview (from 1992) presents a compelling vision for the nascent movement.

TOWARD *ORGANIZED* DIVERSITY

From his earliest writings, Gerbner has argued that rigorous, replicable scientific methods should be harnessed for critical social uses, needs, and theory. His research has shown that the cultural process of storytelling, that most distinctly humanizing phenomenon, is being increasingly taken over by global commercial interests who have something to sell. As a result, government and public intervention in communication institutions and policy is necessary to insure equity and fairness, diversity and choice. CEM is a logical public manifestation of these arguments.

The traditional functions of the family, the school, the church, and other cultural institutions are being shaped by transnational corporations—a private government, run by people whom nobody knows and whom nobody elected. Through the Cultural Environment Movement, Gerbner hopes to consolidate and strengthen the work of diverse community, professional, and advocacy groups to "take back" the cultural environment, to provide a means of expression for those whose voices and interests do not fit commercial and market needs; that is, to harness the media to promote rather than undermine democracy. "Technological developments in communications hold out the possibility of greatly enhancing culture-power on behalf of existing social patterns—or of their transformation" (Gerbner, 1973, p. 572). In the problem may lie the solution. But it won't happen all by itself.

Again, "The structure of freedom is *organized* diversity whether it pleases or not." Whether one embraces or scorns his theories and research, and whether the Cultural Environment Movement succeeds or fails, the writings collected in this volume make it abundantly clear that George Gerbner has made profound, far-reaching, and critical contributions to the field of communication.

NOTE

Much of the material in this introduction is based on "The Critical Contribution of George Gerbner," by Michael Morgan, in J. Lent (ed.), *A Different Road Taken: Profiles in Critical Communication* (pp. 99–117). Boulder, CO: Westview, 1995.

REFERENCES

Bryant, Jennings. (1986). "The Road Most Traveled: Yet Another Cultivation Critique." *Journal of Broadcasting & Electronic Media*, *30*, 231–235.

Closepet, Ramesh, & Tsui, Lai-si. (1992). "An Interview with Professor George Gerbner." *Media Development*, *1*, 42–45.

Gerbner, George. (1956). "Toward a General Model of Communication." *AV Communication Review*, *4*, 171–199.

Gerbner, George. (1958). "On Content Analysis and Critical Research in Mass Communication." *AV Communication Review*, *6*, 85–108.

Gerbner, George. (1959). "Education and the Challenge of Mass Culture." *AV Communication Review*, *7*, 264–278.

Gerbner, George. (1960). "The Interaction Model: Perception and Communication." In J. Ball & F. C. Byrnes (eds.), *Research, Principles, and Practices in Visual Communication* (pp. 4–15). Washington: Dept. of Audiovisual Instruction, National Education Association.

Gerbner, George. (1963). "A Theory of Communication and Its Implications for Teaching." In *The Nature of Teaching*, University of Wisconsin-Milwaukee, School of Education. Reprinted in Ronald T. Hyman (ed.), *Teaching: Vantage Points for Study* (pp. 18–31). Philadelphia and New York: J.B. Lippincott, 1968.

Gerbner, George. (1966). "On Defining Communication: Still Another View." *Journal of Communication, 16*(2), 99–103.

Gerbner, George. (1969). "Toward 'Cultural Indicators': The Analysis of Mass Mediated Message Systems." *AV Communication Review*, *17*, 137–148.

Gerbner, George. (1970). "Cultural Indicators: The Case of Violence in Television Drama." *The Annals of the American Academy of Political and Social Science*, *388*, 69–81.

Gerbner, George. (1973). "Cultural Indicators: The Third Voice." In G. Gerbner, L. Gross, & W. H. Melody (Eds.), *Communications Technology and Social Policy* (pp. 555–573). New York: John Wiley & Sons.

Gerbner, George. (1986). "The Symbolic Context of Action and Communication." In R. L. Rosnow & M. Georgoudi (Eds.), *Contextualism and Understanding in Behavioral Science* (pp. 251–268). New York: Praeger.

Gerbner, George. (1990). "Epilogue: Advancing on the Path of Righteousness (Maybe)." In N. Signorielli & M. Morgan (Eds.), *Cultivation Analysis: New Directions in Media Effects Research* (pp. 249–262). Newbury Park, CA: Sage.

Gerbner, George. (1991). "Cultural Environmental Movement? What, Why and How." Unpublished "Mission Statement."

Gerbner, George. (1994). Interview in *The Killing Screens* (videotape). Northampton, MA: The Media Education Foundation, produced by Sut Jhally.

Gerbner, George, & Gross, Larry. (1976). "Living with Television: The Violence Profile." *Journal of Communication*, *26*(2), 173–199.

Lowenthal, Leo. (1957). *Literature and the Image of Man*. Boston: Beacon Press.

Melischek, Gabriele, Rosengren, Karl Erik, & Stappers, James (Eds.). (1984). *Cultural Indicators: An International Symposium*. Vienna, Austria: Verlag der Osterreichischen Akademie der Wissenschaften.

Merton, Robert. (1957). *Social Theory and Social Structure*. Glencoe, IL: The Free Press.

Morgan, Michael. (1990). "International Cultivation Analysis." In N. Signorielli & M. Morgan (Eds.), *Cultivation Analysis: New Directions in Media Effects Research* (pp. 225–248). Newbury Park, CA: Sage.

Morgan, Michael, & Shanahan, James. (1992). "Comparative Cultivation Analysis: Television and Adolescents in Argentina and Taiwan." In F. Korzenny & S. Ting-Toomey (Eds.), *Mass Media Effects Across Cultures: International and Intercultural Communication Annual*, Vol. 16 (pp. 173–197). Newbury Park, CA: Sage.

Shanahan, James, & Morgan, Michael. (1999). *Television and Its Viewers: Cultivation Theory and Research*. London: Cambridge University Press.

Signorielli, Nancy, & Morgan, Michael (Eds.). (1990). *Cultivation Analysis: New Directions in Media Effects Research*. Newbury Park, CA: Sage.

Van Den Haag, E. (1957). "Of Happiness and Despair We Have No Measure." In B. Rosenberg & D. M. White (Eds.), *Mass Culture: The Popular Arts in America*. Glencoe, IL: The Free Press.

Williams, Raymond. (1976). *Keywords: A Vocabulary of Culture and Society*. New York: Oxford University Press.

Chapter 2

INTERVIEW WITH GEORGE GERBNER

BY JOHN A. LENT

Guaruja, Brazil, August 19, 1992

George, tell me about your background, the days in Hungary, your education, your antifascist stands at various times, and your entrance into the American culture. At the same time, discuss the motivating factors that have guided you down a different path in scholarship—factors dealing with personal, institutional, and academic situations.

I was born in Budapest, Hungary, in 1919, during the last real Hungarian revolution, short-lived as it was. I grew up in the 1930s under the rise of fascism, which eventually reached and began to dominate Hungary and began to dominate and oppress much of my own life and thinking. I was educated in a very good gymnasium (high school) in Budapest and became very much involved in Hungarian literature and folklore. I spent probably the most rewarding months each year of my teens in various villages in Hungary, living and working with the peasants and trying to learn their culture, their language, their dialects, collecting folk songs, folktales. So my first academic interest upon entering the university was folklore and literature. I was fortunate since I was always good at what I was interested in but not in other things, so my grades were far from good enough for entrance into the university, which was a highly selective procedure. But is so happened that my school sent me, on the basis of a schoolwide competition and then a district wide competition, to a national literary competition. The representatives from each high school—the winners of high school competition—competed for the national prize in Hungarian literature. And it so happened that I won the first prize in Hungarian literature, which led to an amusing incident at the end of our baccalaureate, a week-long examination. The day before that final day of the baccalaureate, the results of this national competition came out and were published in the newspapers.

The principal of our school came to the classroom where the final session of the baccalaureate examination was held and looked at the records and lists of graduating students and looked at mine and said, "They have made a terrible mistake in not recognizing this Gerbner who's so good," and in the presence of everyone, including myself, corrected every one of my grades to an A. That assured my admission to the university. It's one of the series of accidents, if you could call them that, that in many ways provided turning points for my life.

Now my matriculation at the University of Budapest was short-lived. Toward the end of the first year, in the 1938–39 academic year, I was about to be drafted into the Hungarian army. Although I had no particular objections at that time about serving in the army, I had grave objections about serving in the Hungarian army. So, I left the country, and although I had no money, about five dollars, my parents bought a train ticket to Paris. I went to Paris (this was in the spring, I believe, May of 1939). I recall that just while I was on the train into Italy (I was going to Paris through Venice and Genoa, and then the Riviera, and then to Paris), the Italian army marched into Albania. (So we can fix the time by that particular event.)

I arrived in Paris without any money. There is no need now to recount interesting experiences of a penniless Hungarian arriving in Paris. But I did eventually meet some relatives of my parents who lent me the money for a passage to wherever I could go. Now by that time (I have to fill in a few minor details)—I had a half-brother, Laslo Benedek (we have the same mother, different fathers; his father, my mother's first husband, died; my mother remarried and then I was born). He was about fifteen or sixteen years older; he recently died. He was a film director, and by that time he had gone to Hollywood. So my ultimate objective was to come to the United States. It turned out that I could not get a visa to the United States; This was in 1939. The visa list for Hungarians under the American quota was filled for about twenty-five years and I was not about to wait twenty-five years for that visa. So I had to bribe a consulate official to give me a visa to Mexico, which I learned was not unusual; it was pretty much the common practice, and I got passage on the French ship, *Flanders* (a wonderful passenger liner), which was, incidentally, sunk in World War II. The only passage open at this time was a first-class passage. So I was traveling first class but had no money, which led to an embarrassment later on of not being able to tip the people who were kindly serving me. I arrived in Mexico on a tourist visa valid for six months.

My stay in Mexico was interesting, rather difficult, because again, I had no money. Within about two or three weeks, I became a guide, a tourist guide, even though I spoke very little Spanish. I was staying in a boarding house where mostly American tourists—particularly, for some reason, American schoolteachers—came in their cars. They know that I didn't speak good English, so they assumed that I spoke excellent Spanish, which I did not. I offered my services to be their guide in their cars and to take them to places that were "off the beaten path." That was very easy because I didn't know what the beaten path was. So almost everywhere we went—I picked out some places on the map—was off the beaten path. We drove into the main square of a small town or village and I said, "Now we'll stop right here while I go out and make arrangements." I had enough knowledge of Spanish to go to some fairly clean-cut, local native hotel and say here is a group of tourists and how much would it cost. The accommodations were extremely cheap. They were usually clean and dependable and secure, so I would go back to the car and say that everything was arranged. This way I got around Mexico, including Acapulco at a time when Acapulco had only one more or less modern hotel, and I basically had a wonderful time.

At the end of six months, my visa was up and by that time the war had broken out in Europe. I went to the American consulate and said, "I would like to go to Los Angeles where I have a half-brother." About six months before, I had applied for admission to UCLA as a foreign student and I was accepted, but I couldn't get there because I had no American visa. The consul said, "Well, I don't know exactly what to do with you. I'd like to help you, but you know there is an American law that says that if you arrive in an adjoining country to the United States, which could be either Mexico or Canada, you cannot enter even legally or in any way through the border." That is in order to avoid illegal entries, which is a joke, because thousands of people are making illegal entries every week and were then, but anyway, that was the law, and so he said, "My best advice is that you go to Havana which is separated by water. Go to the American consulate there and see what they can do for you." So again, begging and borrowing money for a passage, I went to Havana, went up to the American consulate, told them what the situation was, and the American consulate said, "I don't know exactly how to resolve your situation either, but it's not going to be on my conscience to send you back to Europe—the war is already on, and very clearly, you have no possibility of safely arriving in Hungary, so I'll give you permission to leave Cuba and to go to New Orleans on a ship that's going from Havana to New Orleans and see what they will do with you."

So I arrived in New Orleans. My half-brother had alerted some friends who lived in New Orleans to wait for me in the port of New Orleans. When I arrived at the port, we were lined up to examine documents but in addition to documents to examine the amount of money that we had with us. I didn't have enough money, so I was taken down to the Customs House. They had a hearing and I was ordered deported. As the hearing was over, a kind soul at the end of the table said, "You know, you can appeal." Nobody formally informed me of any rights. This was a person who had the decency to inform me at least after the hearing was over. So I raised my hand and I said, "Yes, I wish to appeal." That was considered a great nuisance by everybody because they had to sit down again and consider the appeal. Finally they said, "Okay, your appeal goes to Washington. It will take about two weeks. You have to stay here in New Orleans. Do you have any place to stay?" I said, "Yes, as far as I know there are people waiting. I hope they're still waiting for me outside."

I was discharged from this hearing to the custody of these friends, who happened to be the director of the Theatre Le Vieux Carre, a well-known community theater in New Orleans. So I was their house guest. They took me to their home, and there was another house guest staying at the same house, whom I met on my first day in the United States, and his name was Sinclair Lewis. So upon arrival I was a house guest along with Sinclair Lewis, most of whose books I had read in Hungarian, so that was a great experience.

After two weeks, the verdict came back that I could be admitted if I put up a bond of two hundred dollars. That's what this was all about; for only two hundred dollars, which was more in those days than it is today, they would have, without any pangs of conscience, deported me to a totally unknown destination. I cabled my brother, who borrowed two hundred dollars from friends and sent it to me.

I hitchhiked to Los Angeles, entered UCLA, but I was dissatisfied because, before I left Hungary, as I mentioned, I was interested in literature and writing, and the closest to that that I could get, my thought about that was journalism, and UCLA had no journalism, so soon thereafter, I transferred to Berkeley, and journalism.

A little-known fact of recent history is that in 1939 Hungary declared war on the United States, and that classified me as an enemy alien, which was no great problem, except that I had to report once a year. But what that meant was that I could not volunteer or be recruited into the American army.

I graduated in journalism from Berkeley. My stay at UCLA and to some extent even at Berkeley really consisted of trying to sort out my own experiences. The experience of living under fascism, of a certain amount of antifascist activity as much as a teenager can engage in, of knowing great people who sacrificed, struggled, who were jailed, who were martyred, many of whom were Communists, and of becoming very much interested in their lives, in their activities and their cause. My interest in joining the American army also stemmed from that.

After graduation, I got a job on the *San Francisco Chronicle*, where I was working in many capacities on the copy desk as a copy reader, headline writer, reporter, book reviewer, critic, and finally assistant editor, where I think I originated the first consumer column in the country, if not in the world. I was not an economist and not a financial expert, but I knew that during war conditions consumers required a great deal of knowledge about the regulations, the shortages, the quotas, and the various rationing, and I conceived of the idea of writing a column for the consumer about what the consumer needed to know.

Along about 1942, the American army needed men sufficiently to abolish the ban on foreigners, even enemy aliens, so at that point I was permitted to be inducted into the army, which I was. There was one option available. I was determined that if and when I got into the army, I didn't want to do a desk job or whatever I would be doing as a civilian because, you know, I felt that I could contribute to the war effort and to the antifascist effort as a civilian just as well as long as I was writing or editing or doing newspaper work—for that I didn't need the army. So when the inducting sergeant said, "There isn't much choice, but there is only one thing, if anybody wants to join the paratroops, step forward." I almost automatically stepped forward, and he said, "Well, you turn to the left, everybody else turn to the right." I went to the left and I was told to take a train to Fort Benning, Georgia, for paratroop training. So I underwent paratroop training, was assigned to the 541st Parachute Infantry in Camp Mackall, North Carolina.

When I heard that the regiment was about to be sent to the Pacific, I said, "Uh, uh! This is not my destination." So I went to Washington and visited with the OSS (Office of Strategic Services), which was the intelligence arm of the American army, who interviewed me and nodded and said, "Well, goodbye, don't call us. If we need you, we'll call you." In less than two weeks the order came down to my regiment saying, "Private First Class Gerbner report to Washington" at a certain place, which I did, and I was recruited into the OSS in the Operational Group called OG. There were two major field arms of the OSS. One was called OG, Operational Groups; the other one was called SI, Secret Intelligence. I was assigned to an Operational Group, which was a group of about fifteen trained to do small missions—sabotage, blowing up roads, bridges, etc.—and we underwent some training and were sent to North Africa. I had an extended and very pleasant period in Algiers and further training but basically was waiting for a mission.

Soon thereafter came the invasion, the landing in Normandy and Marseilles and soon. At one time we were supposed to go there, but that didn't materialize and we were taken to Italy, where the war was still going on. In Italy, since things went so slowly, I requested a transfer from OG to SI, which was granted, and I was sent to Bari, from Naples to Bari on the other side of Italy, for further training, and on, I believe, January 15, 1945, I parachuted with two others into occupied territory. The two others included an Austrian who was native to the area where we were supposed to land and another American soldier of German extraction, and I was an American soldier of Hungarian extraction, speaking some German, but no other of the related (Slavic) languages.

So on about the 15th of January, 1945, the three of us jumped by parachute in what originally was designated to be a target in southern Austria.[1] It so happens that the crew flying us—it was their fortieth (last) mission, and we ran into some flak, some anti-aircraft fire, and I guess, I can't blame them—they decided we were back in the hold, they didn't need us, they just knew that there were three guys who were sitting back there waiting for the target and their communication with us was simply a "green light." When they pressed the button, we were supposed to jump. Well, they pressed the button a little too soon, so they could turn back a little faster, and we landed in very strange territory—across the Drama River, actually in Slovenia, which was a surprise to us. We landed in very mountainous territory instead of a plateau, which was our original designated landing site. So we were separated in the air and never found the Austrian partner.

The other American and I found each other after some searching. We landed in seven feet of snow, in strange terrain. Soon after we found each other, only a few miles from us, all of a sudden the streetlights went on, which was a big surprise because we didn't know we were that close to inhabited territory. In fact, we were not far out of Maribor, and at that point we knew that something was very wrong and that the Germans by now were probably after us. So we started climbing the mountain as rapidly as we could, living on our emergency rations that we had in our pockets for about three or four or five days in big snow, occasionally singling out certain farmhouses and going in and asking for food, claiming—this was our cover story—that we were American flyers who had to bail out and asking about the partisans. At first, nobody knew anything about the partisans, but the higher we got—and the language we spoke was German and most of those people in that area, since it used to be part of the Austro-Hungarian empire, did speak it, especially the older people—so as we got higher and higher, they seemed to know more and more about the partisans. One night, they said, "Well, just go to sleep here on the floor and we'll see what we can do." The next morning there was a partisan courier who took us to one of the brigades operating in that area. For the rest of the duration of our stay, we were with the partisans. Germans were retreating from Greece and trying to secure their communication lines against the partisans working in the area and trying to cut off their rail and road transportation. So we were under severe attack. A brigade that started out with maybe 350 or 400 men, at that point, when we joined them, was down to about 60 or 70 or 80. And that kind of struggle for survival lasted, in fact, until VE Day.

When VE Day came, we changed places with the Germans—we went on the roads, the Germans went up to the hills because they did not want to surrender to the partisans, who fought the Germans furiously.

We in the meantime found our way to Trieste, and then back to Foggia in Italy, our headquarters, where we had been reported missing because they hadn't heard from us (through partisan radio) for quite a few weeks. We were sent to a rest camp, a very nice camp in Italy, where, after two days, I was paged and told that rest was over, there was a large army of about 250,000 Hungarians who had fled from the Russians and camped on the Austrian countryside. No one knew who they were, so would I mind going up and finding out who they were and trying to dispose of these people, or at least report what should be done. So I was flown to Salzburg and given all the necessary provisions—a jeep and a jail, which was what I needed. With an American sergeant also of Hungarian extraction, we started to explore the countryside to find out what this was about. We found the Hungarian prime minister, a pro-Nazi politician, his general staff, his high command, his cabinet, and about 250,000 men who were encamped under their command. So I had the privilege of arresting the prime minister under whom I left Hungary and his entire general staff and his high command and of taking them back to Budapest for war crimes trials. I followed some of these trials because soon thereafter I was assigned to the American military mission in Budapest. I was somewhat comforted by the impression that those were real trials; some of these people were acquitted, some of them were convicted, some of them were executed, including the prime minister.

During my stay at the American military mission in Budapest, another turning point in my life was meeting my wife. I used to go to the theater, which I liked very much, and one evening I was invited to a party under somewhat false pretenses. I was there to impersonate another American officer, also of Hungarian extraction, for whom this party had been arranged but who was unexpectedly transferred to Vienna and could not attend the party. But only the host knew him. Everybody else knew that there was an American officer coming but didn't know who it was, so they asked me to impersonate this friend of mine whose name was also George, so that's how I attended this party.

Upon arriving at the party I saw this beautiful young woman sitting on a couch and I sat down next to her and, what should I say, I've been sitting there next to her ever since. I said, "I've seen you somewhere before." She said, "Uh ha, I heard that before." And I said, "No, I really saw you on the stage in such and such a play," and

I remembered the part, which at least gave me some credibility. At the end of the party, I invited her to join me to go to the American officer's club not too far from there, just for a drink, and maybe a dance, and she said, "Well, I'm not accustomed to coming with two other young men and leaving with somebody else." Thereupon, given no choice, I invited the whole party to come and we all went to the officer's club, and that's how all of this began.

After a few months at the American mission in Hungary, I too was transferred to Vienna to edit a newspaper for the American occupation forces in Austria.

Ilona and I got married and she joined me in Vienna, and after a few months of that, we returned to the United States (to Los Angeles), where I had been registered as a member of the Newspaper Guild waiting for a newspaper job to turn up. While I was waiting, I got a call from the agency where I was registered and they said, "Mr. Gerbner, we don't have the job you are waiting for, but there is something else that came up which you may be interested, at least temporarily. There is a teaching job in journalism at John Muir"—which was at that time a junior college in Pasadena. "The journalism instructor left abruptly." This was on Thursday. "They need somebody to start on Monday. Would you mind doing that while you are waiting for what you really want?" "Well," I said, "I may as well do it." So I started teaching that Monday. I must say I've been teaching ever since because I discovered something that I had never really—this is another one of those so-called accidents that provides a turning point for one's life—I discovered that indeed, that was what I really wanted. Although I liked journalism, I always felt like a hired hand, basically did what other people told me to do, and found that as a teacher, and later on as a researcher, I found the style of life, the only style of life I know, in which you don't have to work for anybody else. Basically, you design your own program, and if you're lucky, you can conduct it with a minimum of interference and a certain amount of protection. The protection is never absolute. There is no such thing, but a least you have some claim to independence and freedom.

I started teaching, but I had no certification. In California at that time you could start on an emergency credential, provided that within two years you got the necessary credits and credential. So I started graduate work at the University of Southern California. I got my teaching credential, then went on to the master's. I wrote the first master's thesis ever, I believe, on education and television. That was completed in 1950, before there was even a national television service.

Then, I entered a Ph.D. program in the only place where communication was taken seriously, and that was in the Audiovisual Department of the School of Education at USC under Professor James D. Finn. He was one of the pioneers in educational technology and in the audiovisual movement. I was fortunate enough to be his student and, later on, his friend, and wrote a dissertation on "Toward a General Theory of Communication." That was simply an attempt to summarize what was written and known about communication in the fields of history, philosophy, social psychology, sociology, and cybernetics. Out of the exploration and that dissertation came what is sometimes called the Gerbner Model of Communication, which has served me pretty well since. So, putting it all together, I came to the conclusion that communication is really where the action is—the political action, the social action, the cultural action.

I was not able to follow my literary interests and my literary career, which led me to publish a book of poetry in Hungary before I left, because literature and poetry are like music. If you don't do it every day, if you don't live in it, if you're not totally into it, you lose it. Being uprooted meant isolation from the language, from everyday practice in the language and its dialects, and its subtleties. I have never been able to recapture that in any language. So partly my circumstances and partly my own interests led me to become more a researcher, an analyst, and social critic of cultural production. This led me, after Pasadena, first to a part-time teaching position while I was a doctoral student at USC; then I was recruited to the University of Illinois by Dallas Smythe. I met Dallas while he was a visiting professor in the summer teaching in the Department of Cinema at USC.

I should come back, I think, to one significant episode. Even before I got my teaching job, while I was still looking for a job in Los Angeles, I became active in political life, as a volunteer worker and editor for a newspaper for the Independent Progressive party, the party that nominated Henry Wallace for president in 1948. This was the beginning of the McCarthy years, and the California State Un-American Activities Committee came to the city of Pasadena, not so much to get at me—I was small fry—but to get at the superintendent, Willard Goslin, because he committed the unforgivable offense of redistricting the totally gerrymandered school districts of Pasadena in order to alleviate, if not abolish, racial segregation. That must have been a Communist plot, in their opinion, and the Un-American Activities Committee came down to get rid of Willard Goslin. They subpoenaed me because I was appointed to edit a school district newsletter for the Goslin administration. They had me on the stand for about forty-five minutes, asking what I was teaching, asking if it was true (it was) that I showed in my class the documentary film called *Races of Mankind*, based on anthropologist Ruth Benedict's work. They asked me if I was a member of a Communist party. I was not, and said so. Then they excused me without any further ado.

The law in California says, or said at that time, that if you are not notified by the end of the working day on the 15th of May that you have or not been reappointed, you are automatically reappointed. The 15th of May arrived, and four o'clock passed, four-thirty, four-forty-five passed, and I was not notified, so I thought I must have been reappointed. Five minutes before five o'clock, the phone rang from the Board of Education, and someone said, "Mr. Gerbner, we have to inform you that you are not reappointed for the next year." So I lost my job, which was very fortunate, because I got a much better job, but in the summertime—since we just had a child, and I needed a job—in the summertime, I became a research assistant at the Cinema Department at USC. That's how I met Dallas Smythe, who visited there that summer. And Dallas and his wife, Jenny, and the family became friends, and when I completed my dissertation, he proposed my appointment to the Institute of Communication Research, University of Illinois. That's how we arrived in Urbana, Illinois, where we spent eight years, from 1956 to 1964. During that time, I established some of the basic applications of my dissertation ideas and some other ideas about the analysis of the everyday cultural climate of our societies, in the United States, and eventually on a cross-cultural comparative basis.

One of the term papers that Jim Finn asked me to write while I was a graduate student in his class was, "What would you do if you were appointed the dean of a graduate school of communications? What kind of a program would you propose?" Well, in 1964 I was invited to become the dean of the Annenberg School of Communication. There were no faculty and there was no program to speak of. So the first task was to get at least two or three key people with whom jointly we could start building a new curriculum, which we did.

We defined the field of communications as a discipline that is focused on the process of human and social interaction through messages. This is a process that is on the periphery of every other social science discipline but at the center of none. We divided it into three parts: the concern over messages that ranges from semiotics to content analysis; the concern over the relationships between communicating parties, mostly sociological-psychological types of approaches; and the concern over large social institutions that are in the business of producing and distributing messages. We built a strong faculty, established a Ph.D. program in addition to the initial masters' program, and I guess the rest is the history of the school. My own work has developed despite the administrative concerns because, although I was the dean, ours was by far the smallest school at the university, smaller than many departments. The reason we were a school and not a department had to do with the legal terms of the Annenberg grant, and that was purely extraneous but a fortuitous necessity, because it gave us a great deal of independence. A school of about ten to twenty faculty members had the same status as the medical school, the school of engineering, and the school of law, and so we were very independent and successful in trying to implement our own vision of our program, recruit our own faculty, and set up our own criteria and requirements for students. Since much of the administrative work in which I was involved was in my own field, unlike deans who administer a great variety of fields and disciplines, I was able merely to cultivate my own interests and use my own judgment as I worked with our faculty and students on building the school.

My own work then became an extension of a continuing attempt to analyze and try to understand the everyday symbolic environment in which we live and in which we develop our notions and mythologies about life and the world.

I was inevitably drawn into cross-cultural, comparative work because, in order to understand the cultural environment of your own, it's inevitable and necessary to compare it to others. My empirical work was always historically inspired and conceptually guided to test certain propositions about media and society.

More recently, I entered into and launched an activity that attempts to apply the conclusions, or at least the challenges, and many of the dilemmas that I found in my analysis, into a form of citizen action that my colleagues and I call the Cultural Environment Movement. It poses an enormous challenge and requires rethinking cultural policymaking.

George, you have gone a different path. There must have been some penalties over the years that you had to pay for doing that, and also for being politically active at various times. Could you talk about that?

Except for being uprooted from my family and native country, by and large, I've been very fortunate in that penalties were few, far between and relatively easily remedied, like losing my job in Pasadena and other relatively minor things. The major price that I had to pay is not being able to put it all together in book form, doing mostly fragmentary work that exposed certain aspects of a critical view but never in a totally coherent way. That still remains to be done. As dean for a whole faculty and school, I had to be fairly prudent in expressing personal points of view. So I worked mostly as a researcher supporting conclusions by a great deal of evidence that is publicly and methodologically defensible. It was, in a way, a kind of fortified way of proving or testing propositions in which I was interested. It turns out that it is a very good way because if you get to be too polemical your opinion against anybody else's opinion has no special value. But if you can support your arguments and your conclusions with publicly credible, repeatable evidence, you assume an authority that otherwise cannot be gained.

There have been a few instances of my political interest arousing the ire of more or less powerful academic individuals, even some benefactors, but they were not fatal. As I said, my early experiences under the McCarthy era, and a few incidents, and a certain degree of isolation, and a certain degree of having to rely on one's own like-minded friends and colleagues for collegiality, for critique, and of being known as an analyst and a critic of the mainstream, rather than a part of the mainstream, is a price that I would consider well worth paying.

As to what I consider to be my major contribution—it's hard to say. I'd like to think that my major contribution is still to come in an attempt to synthesize and to put together many of the things that I have done. I am heavily involved in research projects, mostly outside-funded, contractual, or grant type of research projects that have kept me going and kept me extremely busy in the past thirty or forty years. So, fighting brush fires and being involved in specific projects, applied to social issues, has in many ways fragmented my work into many parts. As I look at my work, if and when I have the opportunity to put it all together, I think I'll find that they are all organically connected.

How do you feel your research has been used by various sectors, and do you think it has been misused in some cases? Explain some of those. Also, what do you feel, in the field of mass communications studies, have been some of the important changes, let's say, since you began your research career?

Our research has been used in a great variety of ways, including misuse, but most of the misuse, so called, comes from people who have never read it, who read about it from newspaper accounts, or who read about it from other people's critiques, but who have never really taken the trouble to read it carefully. The major misrepresentation has been by the media. My research has always touched some issue of public policy. I am not really that interested in individual behavior. I think that if it were "totally understood," it could be more easily controlled. So I'm satisfied that that is a quest that's beyond, and perhaps should be beyond, our scope of interest. I'm interested in those aspects of culture that are policy governed, and governed by large-scale industrial, social, political interests. And for that reason, when my research gets into the industrial policy area, it is often distorted and used as ammunition for purposes other than those I intended. That is inevitable, but I try to resist or counter it as much as possible.

The best example is our violence research. We analyze violence as a demonstration of power and demonstrate its long-term consequences. There may have been more violent periods than the present, although I am not sure of that, but I'm sure that there has never been an era when every home was drenched with violent imagery. It is mass-produced, happily sanitized, violent imagery with which our children grow up.

When our violence research gets into the media, it is always interpreted in a law and order context. In other words, will it lead to or will it result in imitation, will it result in threats to the established order. The answer to that is yes, but on a relatively small scale. But that is a small price for the enormous pacifying effect of exposure to violence. Exposure to violence cultivates, in most people, a sense of insecurity, a sense of dependence, a sense of demanding protection, and a consequence of being more easily controlled. You make large parts of your population afraid and insecure and say, "Well I can help you and protect you," and you have the best historically developed and tested form of social control that anyone has devised. Media are simply not interested, and if they are, they would not want to look at violence from that point of view, as a way of terrorizing populations. They want to look at it only from the point of view of justifying further repression.

The theory of cultivation is different from effects as a kind of short-term change. Market-oriented communication research came to the conclusion that, well, media are not very effective; they just maintain preexisting ideas, but they really can't change people's ideas. The "limited effects" theory arose. It overlooks the fact that the reason why campaigns to persuade people to change their patterns of thinking and action are so limited is that the everyday cultivation of a consistent orientation is so strong. Those are the real effects of media. They are so strong that they are not easily changed. So I consider our cultivation research a strategic intelligence exercise. That doesn't tell you how best to mount a campaign, but it's going to tell you what you are up against. You're up against a daily long-term cultivation of stable tendencies that large communities absorb over long periods of time and that are not easily changed, unless there is a societal change. So the theory of cultivation has as its target the making of social policy. It demonstrates the difficulty of changing opinion and policy without structural change in society. Academics sometimes interpret this as assuming that there is a passive audience, that they are totally dependent. Of course, there are obvious individual and group differences, and cultivation analysis shows some of them. But it's the long-term continuities and commonalities that determine the formation of public policy, not all the individual variations that some people point to as a way of countering the implications of cultivation theory. I think that these reinterpretations and misinterpretations have a functional value of attempting to defuse or confuse the policy implications of our theories.

What do you feel are the most important changes in the field of mass communications that you've witnessed in the last generation or more? What do you think has changed in the area of critical studies in mass communication?

This is a difficult question to answer because there are so many different strands, and because the temptation and the risk of overgeneralizing from some selected examples are so great. So I approach this question with great hesitation.

On one hand, the study of mass communication and culture has moved to the center of social concerns. On the other hand, the trendy term "cultural studies" was often used to distract from the social policy focus. In many ways, it's a diversion and regression. But that trend has passed and systematic research of the media-dominated, increasingly commercialized, militarized, and globalize cultural environment is becoming the central arena of the national and international struggles for power and privilege and of the resistance to power and privilege and for a more equitable form of society. That the struggle is shifting from older arenas, including military, economic, and political, to the cultural arena. That this is where most of our battles are fought and going to be fought. So we find ourselves center stage, unprepared for our role, unrehearsed in our scripts, and not at all agreed as to what should be done. This is not unusual, especially for critical studies. But there are also very positive developments, such as in critical media literacy curriculum building. There is a demand for communication graduates to teach in liberal arts programs. There is anxiety among parent groups and citizen groups about our cultural environment. Indeed, the liberal arts today include, as an essential part of general education, an analytical view of the everyday cultural environment.

The more academic developments are going in several directions at once—some of them forward, some of them backward. The tendency of some theorists to become abstruse, involved in ideological terminology, or to quibble about "proper" methodology is inhibiting research, and it's a waste of time.

The inclination to look on research that is systematic, that is methodologically self-conscious, that looks at the real world and demands empirical evidence of a systematic and replicable nature as some kind of logical positivism is misplaced. It is both philosophically and historically incorrect. The encounter with the real world has been a liberating force. It liberated thinking from clericalism, from theocratic and other axiomatic propositions that were sacred and therefore not presumed to be available for critical scrutiny. That was the renaissance in art and science. I think it can and should continue to be a liberating force. It has the authority of systematic and representative views of reality behind it. There is no greater authority than the authority to be able to say, "You don't have to believe what I say. This is the way I make my observation. You do it for yourself and see what you find." That to me is the ultimate human authority. Anybody who throws that away because of some misplaced claim of ideological Puritanism simply throws away the best political, social, academic, and intellectual tool we have.

All in all, I think communication studies as a systematic critical exercise is becoming more centrally located than ever before. The key question we should ask is not what is respectable to do, what has been successful, what the leaders in the field have done, but simply, Is that right? Does it make any real difference? Would the world be any different if I didn't do it?

NOTE

1. Gerbner was assigned the name "George Wood" for the mission. The notes from the mission read: Top Secret: Wood, the team captain is 25 years old, speaks German, Hungarian, French and Spanish, intelligent, resourceful, splendid physical condition, has good judgment and has been intensively trained and briefed in intelligence matters. He is also a radio operator, and in case of emergency will come on the air with the Gila circuit. His main function, however, is to head the team and organize the collection of intelligence.

PART I

EARLY THEORIES

Building Communications as a Discipline

CHAPTER 3

TOWARD A GENERAL MODEL OF COMMUNICATION

BY GEORGE GERBNER

The field of communication study is having communication troubles. It has no clear idea of its subject matter. It has no framework for the discussion of its technical concerns. And it has no value orientation for making much sense of its findings in terms of urgently needed judgments. Vigorous search for a technique and value-oriented theoretical structure appears to be the major need in the progress toward a science of communication.

Our purpose is to make a contribution to that search by presenting a *general model* of communication. The model incorporates some features of previous models (see bibliography) and adds some new features of its own. It structures communication into ten related aspects and areas of study. These aspects are discussed and illustrated through the construction of a verbal and a graphic version. Construction of the model is followed by the demonstration of some technical applications, the discussion of theoretical and research implications, and the development of some normative social concepts and directions in communication theory.

CONSTRUCTION OF THE GENERAL MODEL

Students of communication theory and research have much in common with the physicists Weisskopf and Rosenbaum who, discussing "A Model of the Nucleus" in the December 1955 *Scientific American* complained:

> Modern physics is frequently accused of deserting the real world for abstract mathematics. Instead of attempting to explain nature in terms of what we can see and feel, the impeachment runs, theoretical physicists offer only an arid set of equations whose physical meaning they will not even think about, let alone interpret to the vulgar.

The physicists thought the reproach undeserved. Model building is a major concern in nuclear physics, they noted; nearly every theory began with some model representing events and relationships understandable in terms of a real world. "Every model we build," they wrote, "is an effort to make sense of some particular class of experimental results....Hence our different models are not mutually exclusive....They can often be combined to give more complete understanding."

Model building and combining is thus an attempt to view complex, and often disjointed, processes and studies in a unifying framework which suggests an approach to further investigation. It permits the structuring of an event, and a field of study, and the discussion of relationships, processes, and their implications, in understandable and graphic terms.

THE VERBAL MODEL

A good verbal model is a concise explanation which describes an event and at the same time identifies its chief parts or aspects. It is based upon a conscious theoretical approach to the event it describes; and it includes a word-by-word or phrase-by-phrase identification of those aspects of the event that have actually been the focal points of concern and investigation.

What might be a description of a communication event, of one link in the chain of a communication process, that could serve as such a model? We can start with a communicating agent (source or destination) designated as *someone.* This communicating agent must perceive or have *perceived an event* of some kind in order to initiate or receive communication, and must *react* to the perception in some way. The nature of this reaction is influenced by the *situation* in which it takes place. The communicative reaction must be made through some mediating agents (channels, media), in other words *through some means.* It is transmitted in order *to make available* some communication *materials.* Materials must be *in some form* or pattern in order to carry a message. As the reaction to materials takes place in a situation, so every message is perceived *in a context.* All these aspects enter into the formation of *content.* And, finally, we can assume that *some consequences* always follow perceived content, whether or not it achieved a desired reaction.

If we accept this general description, we can then proceed to construct the verbal model by putting together its salient characteristics, represented by the italicized and phrases. Such a verbal model follows below on the left. It is broken down, line by line, into the ten basic aspects of communication. These aspects are numbered for later reference. In each line, on the right, appear a few words briefly identifying in a preliminary fashion some types of study and research associated with each aspect.

A more detailed discussion of these aspects of communication will follow the construction and demonstration of the graphic model. It might be emphasized here, however, that while the ten aspects can serve to structure the field of communication study, they represent shifts of emphasis rather than tight compartments. In fact, nearly every aspect can be viewed in terms of any of the others.

Verbal Model	Areas of Study
1. Someone	Communicator and audience research
2. perceives an event	Perception research and theory
3. and reacts	Effectiveness measurement
4. in a situation	Study of physical, social setting
5. through some means	Investigation of channels, media, controls over facilities
6. to make available materials	Administration; distribution; freedom of access to materials
7. in some form	Structure, organization, style, pattern
8. and context	Study of communicative setting, sequence
9. conveying content	Content analysis; study of meaning
10. Of some consequence	Study of overall changes

THE GRAPHIC MODEL

The advantage of a schematic model is that it can represent positions, directions, and relationships graphically. Once the model is understood, it can be used to explain visually complex events and concepts. But a graphic model can be cluttered up in the attempt to schematize concepts more clearly explained in words. So we shall use the two models jointly, and consider them two representations of the same basic model, each expressing certain things not easily described by the other.

The graphic model can be best understood by following its construction along the steps of the verbal model. Let us assume that a man notices a house burning across the street and shouts "Fire!" We begin to schematize the aspects of this communication event by our man, someone, represented as Step 1 on Figure 1, a human head labeled M for man or machine.

Next, comes the event and its perception. The event, here a burning house, is shown as circle E. Its perception is indicated as Step 2, a line leading horizontally from circle E, the event, to a circle inside M; the inside circle is labeled E'—event E as perceived by M.

In step 3 of our model, M reacts to having perceived the event. Reaction as such cannot be represented on a generalized communication model. (If this reaction involves some use of some means to initiate a message, it will be represented under Step 5.)

Step 4 takes note of the fact that all perceptions and reactions occur in a situation. On Figure 1, M is shown observing E from behind a window, indicating one feature of the situation. It is usually impractical to schematize a situation on a generalized model.

Step 5 marks the communicative nature of the reaction. It designates the means, the mediating agent capable of transmitting a signal (here "voice"), as a line leading downward from the communicating agent, M, to the communication product, SE.

Figure 1. Steps in the Construction of the Graphic Model

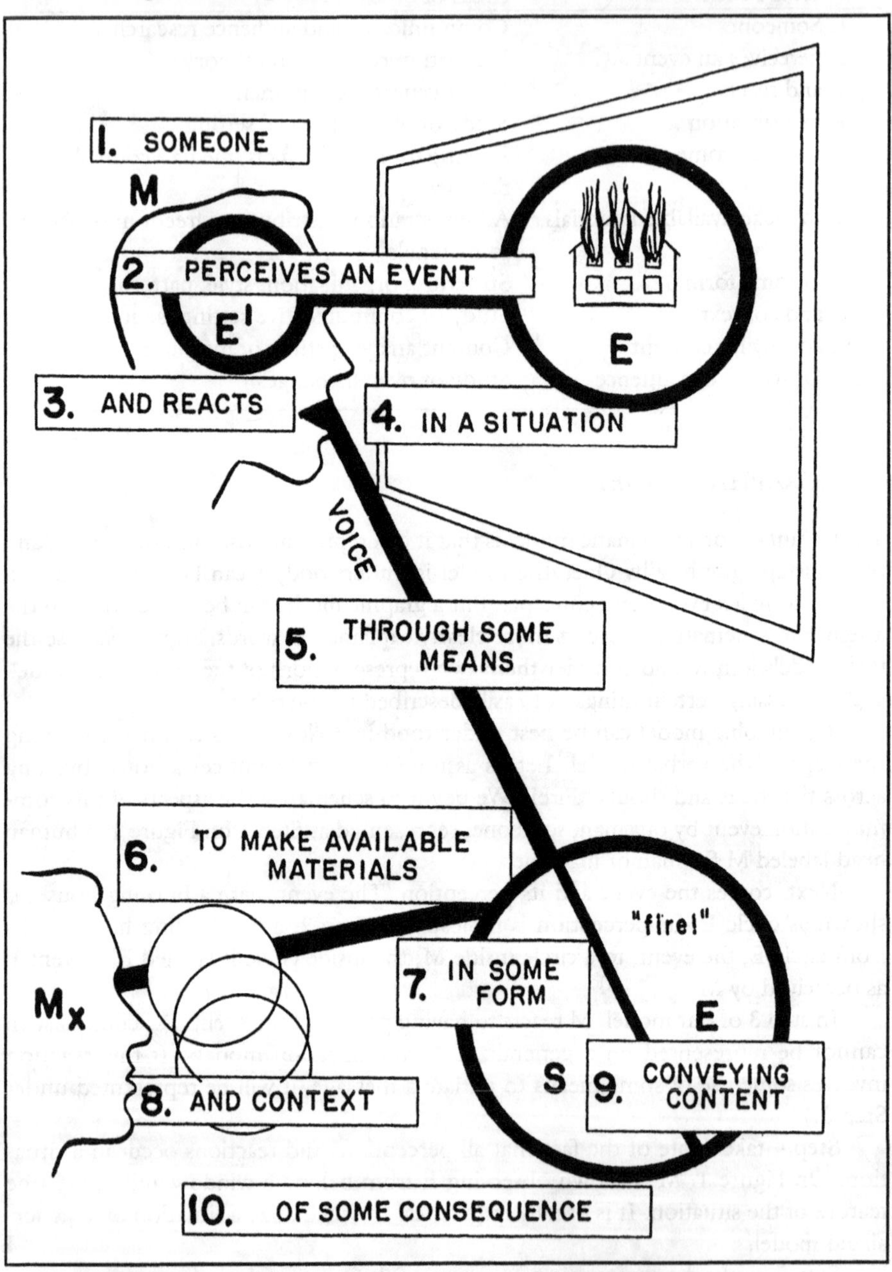

The means serve to make available materials to X destinations. Availability for perception is shown in Figure 1 as Step 6, a line leading horizontally from the communication product to another person, M_x.

Use of some means becomes a signal containing a message only if it is not random; that is, if it is in some form. Step 7 indicates the formal characteristics of the use of the means. It is represented as a half-circle attached to means, labeled S for signal or statement. (Here form might be denoted as a certain language sequence.)

Every signal exists in a context of other signals and statements. The three circles of Step 8 along the horizontal, perceptual, dimension denote context. Again, it is often impractical to schematize context on a generalized model, except by considering it an ever-present feature of the perceputal aspect.

The content qualities inherent in M's use of the means in S form are those aspects or attributes of the communication product capable of conveying a message. Step 9 represents content as a half-circle complementary to S, the signal. Content is marked E to denote those qualities of SE, the communication product, which reflect, represent, symbolize, or refer to the event. Thus the total communication product, SE, means signal or statement S about event E, in this case: "Fire!"

The consequences of this communication event can be appraised only in terms of all other aspects plus time; Step 10, therefore, cannot be adequately represented schematically.

Now we are ready to crystallize the generalized graphic model. We shall restrict it to those aspects and relationships best illustrated graphically, and let the verbal version express the rest.

GENERALIZED MODEL OF A COMMUNICATION EVENT

The basic generalized graphic model appears as Figure 2. We match it against the verbal model to illustrate those aspects of communication that lend themselves to schematic representation, to point out those aspects that cannot be easily diagramed, and to demonstrate some unique features of the graphic model.

1. *"Someone..."* The first variable of our model, shown as a human head on Figure 1, appears on the generalized graphic model (Figure 2) as a circle marked *M* for man or machine. *M* might be the destination of a message, or its originator, or both. *M's* relationship to the other elements in the diagram indicates its role (as on Figure 6). In a communication sequence involving both human and mechanical transmission, mechanical *M's* can be represented by squares (as, for example, on Figure 4).

2. "Someone *perceives an event...*" The perceptual aspect of communication forms the link between events and their reflection, or sensory, creative, cognitive reconstruction in and by the communicating agent, *M*. The event perceived can be a nonmediated, "natural" event, such as the burning house on Figure 1. In that case it is represented on the graphic model as an undivided circle marked *E* for event, as on Figure 2. Or it can be a mediated event, "surrogate," or communication product, as, for example, a description, picture, or television image of the burning house. In that case it is represented as a divided circle marked *SE* for "statement about event." (An example of that is shown on Figure 3 where a communication product, *SE*, is perceived by M_2 and M_3.)

Availability of the event (*E* or *SE*) for perception by *M* is shown by a line leading horizontally from the *E* (or *SE*) circle to the *M* circle. Its perception is indicated by leading this horizontal "selection-context-availability" line to a smaller circle inside *M*. This circle inside *M* is marked the same as the event plus a "prime" sign (′) for "event as perceived." Thus on Figure 2, event *E* is perceived by *M* as *E′*. On Figure 3 event *SE* is perceived as *SE′*.

3. "Someone perceives an event ***and reacts...***" There is no need to indicate the general nature of a reaction on a model of communication. The purpose of this aspect on the verbal model is to call attention to the area of effects study and effectiveness measurement. On the graphic model the communicative nature of the reaction will be dealt with under Point 5.

4. "Someone perceives an event and reacts ***in a situation...***" Every perception and reaction takes place in, and may be modified by, a situation which includes physiological, physical, and social dimensions. (The communicative setting of other statements, etc., will be referred to as context.) While this is an essential feature of the verbal model, it is impractical to schematize it on the graphic model. If necessary, salient features of the situation of perception and/or reaction may be noted anywhere on the field of the diagram, as was done on Step 4 of Figure 1.

Figure 2. The Basic Genealized Graphic Model

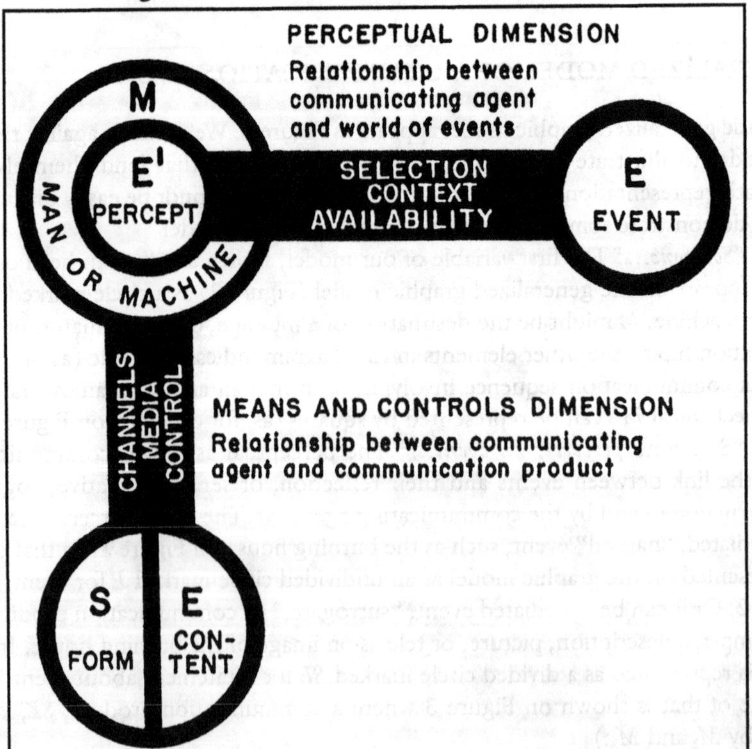

5. "Someone perceives an event and reacts in a situation *through some means...*" The means signify the agents, arrangements, controls, through which response can become communication product, and can be made available for perception. Thus *means* stands for channels; media; physical engineering; and administrative and institutional facilities for distribution and control. Under this aspect, the emphasis is on production and control; results in terms of actual distribution and availability for perception are examined below under the next heading, availability.

On our generalized graphic model *means* and controls appear as a vertical line relating *M*, the communicating agent, to *SE*, the communication product. Thus while the horizontal dimension indicates the perceptual process, the vertical axis denotes certain characteristics of the production and control aspect of communication: the *means* through which the communicating agent or agency creates, and distributes its communication products.

6. "Someone perceives an event and reacts in a situation through some means *to make available materials...*" *Availability* is the result of the creation, control, and distribution of communication products as it actually works out in a certain time and place. In a practical sense, something is *available* if it can be perceived. *Availability* is thus a feature of the horizontal, perceptual dimension relating the communicating agent to the world of events and statements *available* to him.

7. "Someone perceives an event and reacts in a situation through some means to make available materials *in some form...*" To carry a message, use of the means must be non-random. It must have some sequence, pattern, organization not found in single units or elements of its use; this is what we call its form. The formal characteristics of the communication product *SE* appear on the model as the half-circle *S*, for statement or signal, attached to the means axis and complemented by content *E*.

It might help at this point to introduce an example of a specific communication sequence diagramed along the lines of the general model. Such a sequence appears as Figure 3; it will be discussed along with continuing references to Figure 2, the basic generalized graphic model.

On Figure 3, a person, M_1, selects for perception event *E*, "condensation of moisture in the air." This is perceived as E' (recognized and mentally verbalized by M_1 as "rain"). M_1 reacts by using the sound channel to make his voice available for perception by M_2. His voice is modulated and patterned to form signal *S*, shown on Figure 3 as "language sequence."

8. "Someone perceives an event and reacts in a situation through some means to make available materials in some form *and context...*" The specific meaning in which *context* is used in our model is as the communicative setting of statements in space and time. Thus context, along with selection and availability, is a function of the perceptual, horizontal, dimension. (See Figure 2.) On Figure 3, context is not specifically marked. It would require other *E* or *SE* circles connected horizontally with E' to indicate that M_1*'s* statement about the rain is perceived and interpreted by M_2 in the context of other statements and perceptions about the weather.

9. "Someone perceives an event and reacts in a situation through some means to make available materials in some form and context *conveying content...*" Any nonran-

dom, structured transmission is some kind of signal; any form, or signal, carries some representational, symbolic, referential, or correspondence qualities or attributes. That is to say that an inherent and inseparable part of any signal is some *content*; when perceived and recognized we call this *meaning*. Thus signal or statement *S* never stands by itself. It is complemented by half circle *E*. The communication product *SE* has, therefore, signal, or formal qualities (the *S* part), and content qualities (the *E* part) marking the fact that every signal or statement is about, or is occasioned by, some event.

Figure 3 shows that the content attributes of the communication product *SE* are "about" (are occasioned by, and are in reference to) event *E*, that is, the change in weather. Statement *SE*, "It's raining," is in turn perceived by M_2 as *SE′*. Its "meaning" would be generally recognized by him as also calling attention to event *E*.

10. "Someone perceives an event and reacts in a situation through some means to make available materials in some form and context conveying content *with some consequences.*" Every perceived statement has some "effects." Our model divides "effects" into two types. The first is measured by the intent, or objectives of the communication. This type is better named *effectiveness* in reaching a desired objective; it is classified under Point 3 of the model, the *reaction*.

The second type of "effects" is independent of "success" on terms measurable by the intent or objective of the communication. These may not even be apparent in the awareness of either communicator or audience, or in the nature of the reaction at a

Figure 3. Aspects of a Communication Sequence Illustrated on the Graphic Model

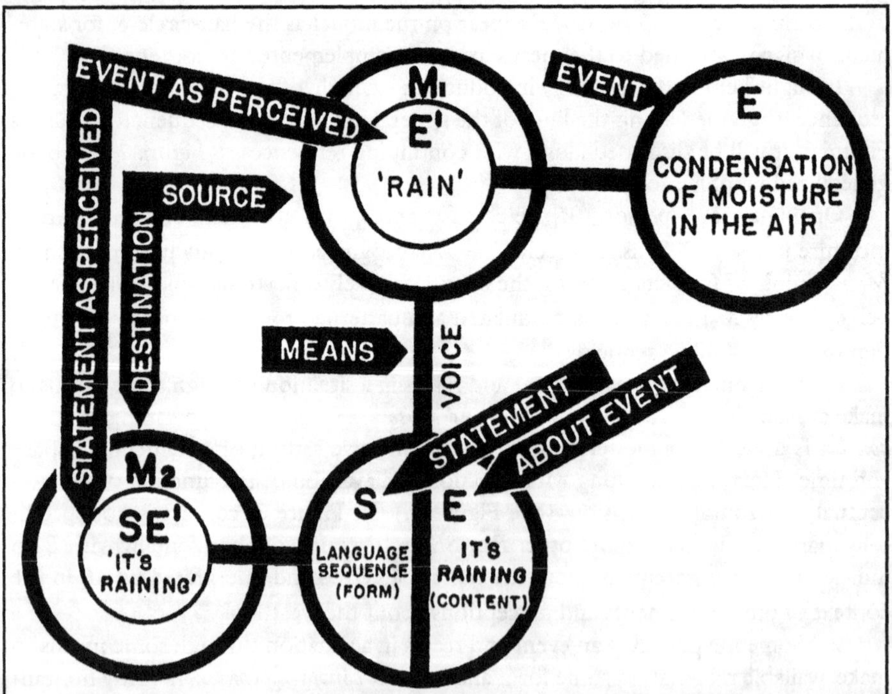

certain time. These are classified as *consequences.* They include all changes, intended or unintended, desirable or undesirable, that might take place consequent to the communication. For example, pedantic overemphasis on certain trivial details in a classroom might be "effective" as measured by a test on those details. But its *consequences* might also include loss of interest, hostility, and other undesirable attitudes.

SOME EXAMPLES: MIXED SEQUENCE, AND FEEDBACK

Figure 4 presents a mixed human and mechanical communication sequence. The communication event portrayed might be a telephone call, transmitting a single statement from one person to another. It is initiated by M_1, the source who perceives event *E*.

Let us assume that *E* is characterized as "disordered energy" or "rapid movement of air particles." M_1, sitting in his apartment, perceives this event as *E′*—physical discomfort associated with heat. He reacts by picking up the telephone receiver-transmitter, which is represented by the square M_2, and making statement *SE* by means of sound.

The original statement about the event, *SE*, is, "It's very hot here." This is "perceived" by M_2, as mechanical energy *SE′*, and is recoded by electronic means into an electrical energy signal pattern. This signal has been occasioned by the first statement about the event, and is, therefore, *SSE*, meaning signal about statement about event. *SSE*, the second communication product, is what is transmitted over the telephone wires.

Figure 4. Communication Sequence with Human and Mechanical Communicating Agents

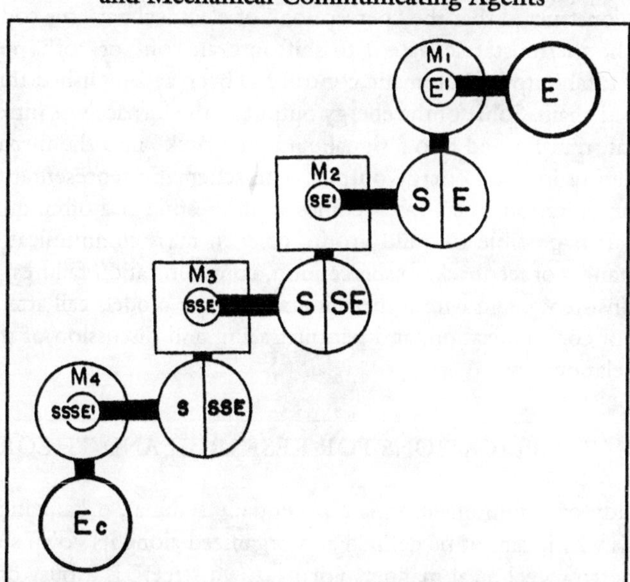

SSE, which is in the form of electrical energy patterns, is "perceived" by another telephone receiver-transmitter instrument M_3, as *SEE′* at the receiving end. M_3 recodes *SEE′* by electronic means into a mechanical energy signal pattern which is also a product of all previous statements, and is, therefore, communication product *SSSE*. This is the original statement about event *E*, namely *SE*, "It's very hot here," plus some accumulated residues of intervening signals, the spurious *SS*, usually called "noise." It is perceived by M_4 as *SSSE′*.

M_4, say a maintenance man in the building, reaches for the temperature control knob, and, without wasting another word, turns down the furnace, thereby bringing about E_c an event characterized by a more orderly, cooler, arrangement of energy in M_1*'s* apartment.

Figure 4 represents an "open sequence" of communication in the sense that the initiating event did not automatically activate the signal that eventually changed its state from *E* to E_c. Figure 5 represents a "closed sequence" accomplished by "feedback," as in an automatic control system.

M_1 on Figure 5 is a furnace. It reacts upon an undivided circle *E*, a nonmediated event, in this case again air temperature. In other words, the energy output of the furnace is coupled with the air surrounding it. Changes in this energy output are "perceived" by M_2, a thermostat. The perception is *E′*, probably on mechanical terms such as movement in a thermocouple due to changes in temperature. A small portion of the total energy output has thus been introduced into the thermostat, activating it. It reacts by recoding mechanical energy into an electrical signal, possibly coded in terms of changes in the flow of current, representing certain changes in the initial event *E* such as "too hot" or "too cold." This is signal *SE*. This signal, in the form of an electrical pattern, is "fed back" to the furnace, M_1, which "perceives" it as *SE′*. The furnace is so constructed that the "perception" of electrical patterns coded in a certain way by the thermostat activate it to shift into an "on" or "off" position, thus modifying its total output. Automatic control has been accomplished through feedback in a closed chain. Some of the energy output of the furnace was introduced into the thermostat, transformed into a signal, and "fed back" into the furnace as information regulating its total energy output. The schematic representation of more complex communication situations becomes an interesting and often quite involved undertaking. It is possible to build group, or even mass communication models, including instances of feedback, misperception, communication failures, etc. If used with some consistency, and within their limitations, the models call attention to the focal aspects of communication, and permit tracing and discussion of these aspects and of their relationships.

SOME IMPLICATIONS FOR RESEARCH AND THEORY

The study of communication is a potentially seminal, organizing discipline. That is why it cannot be defined and organized along its "own street" alone, in a narrow, technical manner. For its "own street" is a busy crossroads of

Figure 5. Automatic Control: Closed Communication Chain with Feedback

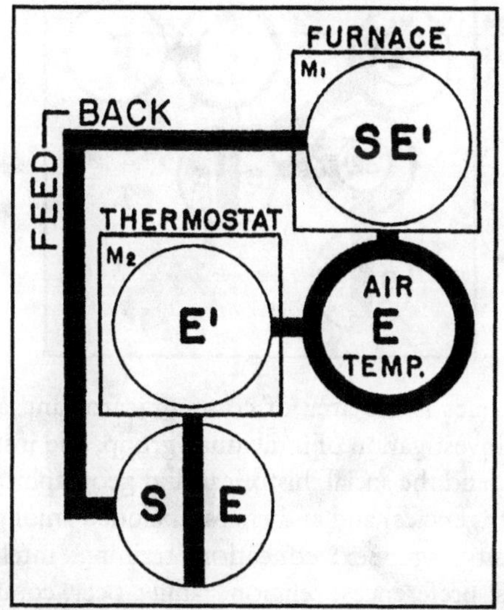

many disciplines in science, art, education, engineering, and of a great deal of social and philosophical concept-building. Organizing the traffic in this crossroads involves, in some sense, all who pass through. Along with the technical matters of setting up road signs and traffic lights, it involves some basic directions and orientations.

Any systematic approach to the study of communication is likely, therefore, not only to structure research and practice into manageable categories, but also to have far-reaching implications, often as broad and controversial as any set of basic scientific assumptions. These implications and assumptions should not be avoided in the discussion of any model, for they spell out the approach upon which the model is based, and the point of view from which it attempts to throw light on its subject matter.

The second part of this paper is devoted, therefore, to a discussion of our model following the sequence employed in the first part, but emphasizing the division of research and practice into the ten aspects, and some of the basic theoretical implications involved.

---

1. M ROLES: COMMUNICATOR AND AUDIENCE RESEARCH

The someone of the verbal model, the communicating agent, is the M element of the graphic model, represented by a circle (for man) or square (for machine), and always with a circle inside it standing for perception. Figure 6 portrays M in three of its roles. M_1 is a communication source; he perceives event E and makes statement SE about it. M_2 is a destination; he perceives statement SE but makes no communicative reaction. M_3 is both destination and source; he perceives statement SE and reacts by making statement SSE.

Figure 6. The Communicating Agent, M, in Three of Its Roles

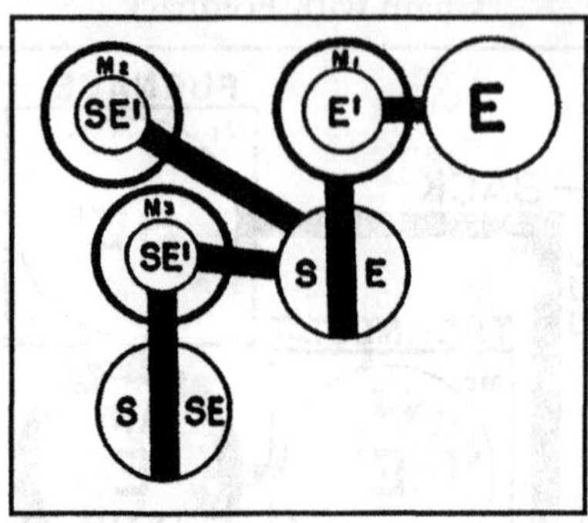

The study of M roles is the area of communicator and audience research. It involves primarily the investigation of individual, group, and institutional characteristics of communicators, and the social, historical, and geographical study of both communicating agents (or agencies) and audiences. Included among these characteristics are distribution; density; age; sex; education; training; intelligence; occupation; income; buying habits; preferences; religion; family, peer, community relationships; and social, cultural, or ethnic status; etc., as communication variables.

2. THE PERCEPTUAL ASPECTS OF COMMUNICATION

M "perceives an event"—but on what terms? This second aspect of our model involves the study of perception as an element of communication. The horizontal axis of the graphic model, linking *M* to the world of events, represents the perceptual process. The model also indicates that although perceptions are occasioned by events, and thus reflect events in some way, they also differ from events; that perceptions are functions of both *E*s and *M*s; and that statements about events stem from *M*'s way of perceiving events.

Different approaches to the study of perception range along the horizontal axis, according to relative emphasis given to the structuring or dominating effects of either *E* or *M* upon *E*′. For example, the transactional approach (13) stresses the structuring effects of *M*'s assumptions, point of view, experiential background, and other related factors, upon the perception, *E*′. Here, *E*, the event, is only "something out there," almost "created" in the act of perceiving it. The transactionalists demonstrate that in some situations different *M*s perceive different phenomena occasioned by the same event, or even "distorted" phenomena until and unless *M*'s point of view and assumptions about the event can be checked and modified through action.

The upper portion of Figure 7 shows a modification of the horizontal dimension of our diagram illustrating the transactional approach. It shows a man "transacting" through his "assumptive form world" (*M*), and through "something out there" (*E*), thus "creating" his perceptions.

Figure 7. Two Approaches to the Study of Perception

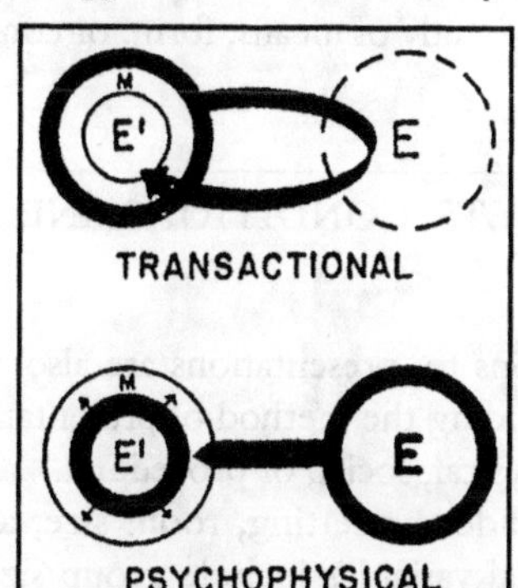

Equally familiar is the opposite, psychophysical, approach to perception (6). Here *E* is a firmer, independent variable; the world of material events, sounds, shapes, and forms is "in control," and perceptions are remarkable in their fidelity and adequacy under favorable conditions. The perceptual organization of *E'* corresponds to order and organization inherent in the universe of perceivable events. Learning and sharing more reliable perceptions is primarily a problem of becoming more sensitive and discriminating to stimuli.

The lower portion of Figure 7 illustrates the psychophysical approach in which the independent event, *E*, controls the dependent perception *E'*. The perception in turn acts upon the stimulus field, the organism *M*, making it more sensitive or "perceptive" to stimulation by *E*.

Our basic model also postulates the prior existence of independent reality *E*, giving rise to all perceptions. But it does not use any arrows; it attempts to take into account the creative, interactional nature of the perceptual process, avoiding any implications of either solipsism or mechanism.

---

3. REACTION TO COMMUNICATION: RESEARCH ON EFFECTIVENESS

Investigations of how *Ms* react to events or statements perceived are generally classified under study of "effects." Our model, as noted before, divides "effects" into two categories; the first is *effectiveness*, measured by the criteria of the objectives of presentation and classified under the present heading. The second is consequences, measured by criteria independent of the objectives of the presentation, and classified under point 10.

Effectiveness, then, is measured by specific objectives. If the objective is learning, did learning take place? Was it short- or long-range? If it is persuasion, did opinion change take place? If it is making a sale, did it result in sales? And so on. Such are the questions investigated under the *reaction-effectiveness* category.

When the emphasis shifts to the communicative nature of a reaction, then it comes under the heading of study of means, form, or content, and is classified under those aspects.

4. SITUATIONAL ASPECTS: CONDITIONS AND METHODS OF PRESENTATION

Perceptions of, and reactions to, presentations are also affected by the situation in which they take place, including the method of presentation. Situational variables in communication may be physical, social, or procedural.

Physical variables include the setting, room size, arrangement, light, sound, noise, heat level, etc. Social variables include group size, structure, composition, cohesiveness, and the like. Procedural variables refer to the manner of presentation and utilization. Investigations of such variables are classified under the situational aspect of communication study.

5. THE MEANS: CHANNELS AND MEDIA, DISTRIBUTION AND CONTROL

All communicative reactions are controlled by some *means*, facilitating the production and distribution of communication products. This aspect of communication is represented on the graphic model by the vertical dimension, relating the communicating agent or agency, *M*, through the *means* axis, to the communication product, *SE*.

Study of the *means* includes investigation of (a) material agents (channels and media) that facilitate the transmission of signals; (b) choices and combinations in the use of means; and (c) engineering, administrative, and institutional facilities controlling signals and their distribution.

The control and distributive phase of the study of means is closely related to the next aspect, availability of materials. The difference is that under *means*, research is centered on specified means and facilities producing communication, and controlling distribution, while under *availability* the problem is to determine what is actually available for perception at specified times and places.

This distinction becomes crucial especially in a discussion of the place of control, and of the relationship between control and freedom in social communication. It was inherent in the foregoing discussion that means of transmission must be controlled to produce nonrandom forms (that is, signals, statements), and to enhance economy, efficiency, and effectiveness in communication. It will be suggested under the next heading that facilities producing communication products may be controlled for the purpose of assuring equitable distribution, hence public availability, of statements reflecting all pertinent views about events of public concern.

6. AVAILABILITY: STUDY OF FREEDOM AND CONTROL IN COMMUNICATION

It has been noted that the aspect of ***availability*** has two related facets. One has to do with control of ***means*** and transmission facilities for the production of signals and for their ***adequate*** distribution. The other facet has to do with control of facilities for the purpose of ***equitable*** distribution, and with techniques for measuring the extent and nature of actual distribution of communication products ***available for perception.***

The problem of equitable distribution of all statements pertinent to decision making on public issues goes to the heart of the issue of freedom in an industrial society, where equitable distribution hinges upon control of the means of mass distribution, that is, of the mass media.

The case for freedom in communication rests upon the theory of self-government. The theory of self-government assumes that the majority of people are capable of making, and observing, correct rules and responsible controls in the public interest, if they can freely select and discuss diverse views and reasons in a representative context of the availability of all pertinent evidence. Self-government thus places the individual in two simultaneous roles. In his role as the governed, he is subject in his private actions to necessary rules and controls. But in his role as the governor, free citizen, of the self-governing society in which he lives, he is responsible for improving the laws; therefore his freedom of thought and speech must be unabridged, subject to no law but guaranteed bylaw, to promote free criticism and improvement of the laws that govern him.

The structure of our model of communication illustrates the relationship between control and freedom in a self-governing society. Controls are a feature of the vertical, and freedom of the horizontal dimension. The two are interrelated; there is no freedom of selection unless there is control over facilities to assure equitable distribution and availability.

Controls along the vertical (***means***) axis are thus essential both for the adequate transmission of signals, and for their equitable distribution. In a social sense, ***means*** is the sphere of private actions: access to and use of facilities to further individual views must be subject to rules and controls of law.

Freedom along the horizontal axis representing ***selection, context, and availability*** for ***perception*** is both an outcome of controls over the means of distribution, and a prerequisite for continuous improvement of means and controls. This is the sphere of public availability and perception, the communication requirements of free thought, speech, and decision making, whose abridgement in any way is proscribed by the First Amendment. The reason for the Constitutional guarantee of free press is thus to safeguard the ***thinking process*** of the community by making it responsible for assuring the equitable distribution (which means mass distribution) of all views and evidence pertinent to public issues. The attainment of freedom along the horizontal axis depends upon the positive exercise of that public responsibility for regulating private use of the facilities of communication along the vertical axis, in order to safeguard ***equitable*** availability.

Figure 8. The Interdependence of Regulation and Freedom in Mass Communication

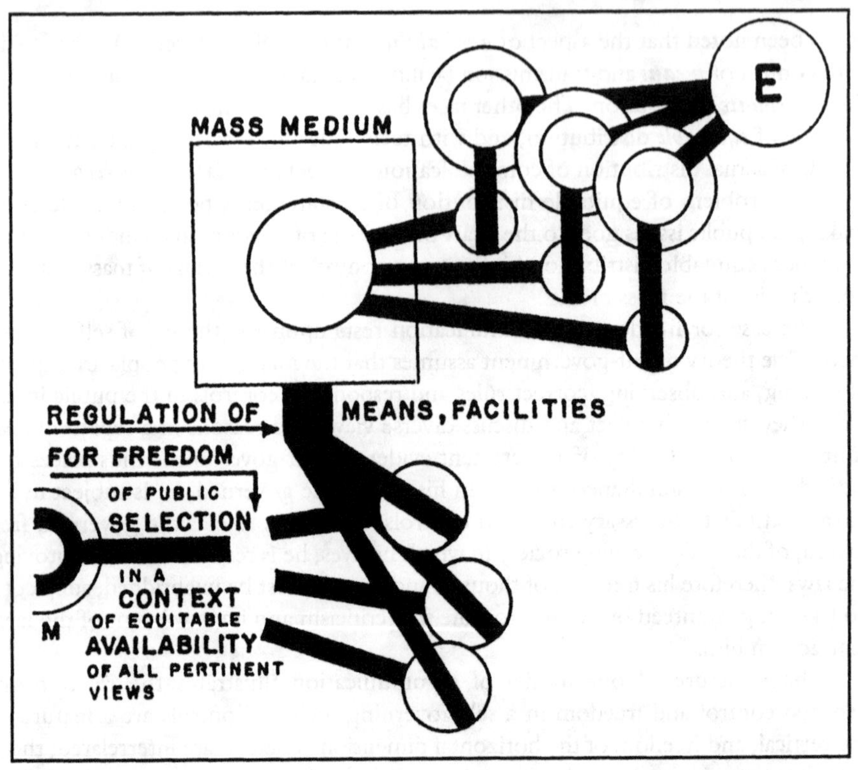

Figure 8 illustrates this reasoning. An event of public concern, *E*, is discussed or represented by three sources whose views can be made available to the public only by a mass medium, say a broadcasting network. The Federal Communications Commission exercises some control over the means of transmission to promote use of these facilities in the public interest, and to safeguard equitable availability of diverse views as in a political campaign. Regulation of the facilities is designed to assure that the public is free to select and discuss all pertinent views in a representative context.

Lacking an understanding of the place of controls and freedom in communication, the distinctions become confused. If freedom can be claimed to pertain to the vertical axis of private use of facilities, it can mean the freedom to distribute, suppress, or monopolize at will. Such "freedom" is a mutilation of the requirements of self-government through freedom of access, along the horizontal axis, to all communication products pertinent to public decision making.

It is only in this way that the issue of censorship can be dealt with without throwing out the baby along with the bathwater. Regulation over ***private actions*** and access to ***facilities*** is essential in order to assure ***public availability*** of ***diverse views*** and thus to prevent censorship through unregulated monopoly power, private or public.

The aspect of availability is thus a fruitful area of research into the institutional, social, and legislative theory and practice of communication. Included here are investigations attempting to measure distribution and availability of communication products, and freedom of selection (choice) by the communicating agent.

7. THE FORM OF SIGNALS; FROM STYLE TO STATISTICS

The transmitting agent must be formally structured in some way to carry a signal with representational, symbolic, or affective qualities, in other words, to convey a message. Formal qualities of statements are diverse, and have been studied in many ways. Some of these qualities are grammatical, rhetorical, graphic, or phonic structure, style, organization, color, dimensionality, design, complexity, and so on. They have been studied in terms of esthetic, functional, sales, and other criteria concerned with formal methodology.

Research into the formal aspects of large numbers of signals also includes mathematical and statistical approaches involving studies of probability of occurrence, frequency, redundancy, internal context, sequence, etc. Recent advances in the theory and mathematical treatment of information, developed mostly for purposes of electronic communication and automatic control by feedback, come under this heading. Shannon (17) constructed a model of a general communication system applicable to the mathematical theory and treatment of information. Figure 9 compares Shannon's diagram with the same communication system as portrayed in our general graphic model.

The problem of information theory has two aspects: selection and transmission. Information is defined at the source as the measure of one's freedom of choice in selecting a message. As freedom of choice increases, the probability of picking a certain message, something one already knows, decreases. The unknown, uncertain, improbable carries greater information value than the probable, commonplace, or easily predictable. Information at the receiving end, on the other hand, is something that reduces uncertainty. Random noises in transmission, however, add the kind of uncertainty that is undesirable because they did not come about through the sender's freedom of choice, and, instead of increasing information value, increase uncertainty about the messages at the receiving end.

Suppose now that the message, *SE*, sent by the source, has a certain formal information value in terms of freedom of choice at the source. (See Figure 9.) But in the course of coding and transmission, the signal deteriorates; it picks up spurious, random signals—"noise"—and comes out *SSSE.* The task of information theory is to subtract this undesirable element from received signals, and to obtain maximum dependability and economy (through reduction of noise, error, redundancy) in coding and in the use of channels.

So while information theory as such is not concerned with perceptual, cognitive, representational, or semantic aspects of signals (with content in the usual sense), it *is* concerned with the formal characteristics of signal systems as related to problems of

Figure 9. Shannon's Diagram of a General Communication System (Top) Compared with the Progress of a Signal in the Same System as Illustrated on the Graphic Model

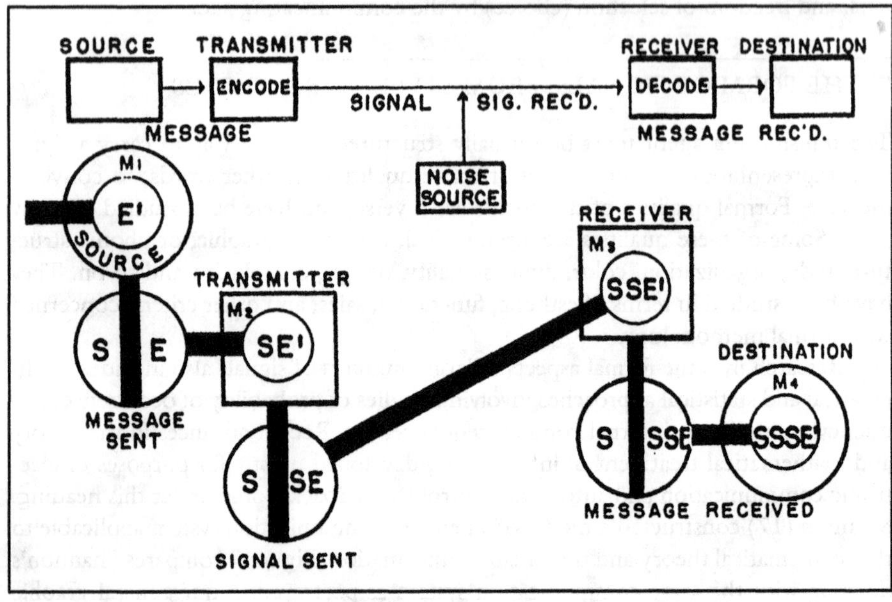

transmission and selection. Information theory may be pertinent, therefore, to problems of *availability* (selection) and *context,* as well as of *form* in communication.

8. CONTEXT: COMPOSITION OF THE COMMUNICATION FIELD

Context in our scheme refers primarily to the nature and composition of the communication field, in space and time, in which a certain event is selected for perception. (The internal composition of a signal or message has been classified under *form*; the physical and social setting of perception and/or reaction comes under the heading of *situation.*) Context, in this sense, is therefore an aspect of the perceptual dimension of the graphic model.

Figure 10 illustrates how studies of context can have a double-barreled significance. On one hand they shed light on distribution, on the pattern of availability of communication products in a specific instance and in regard to a specific message. On the other hand, they can help explain the nature of the selection process, or, at least, demonstrate the role of the composition of the communication field in bringing about certain ways of selecting, perceiving, and understanding statements.

Figure 10. Context: The Communication Field in Which the Selection Process Operates

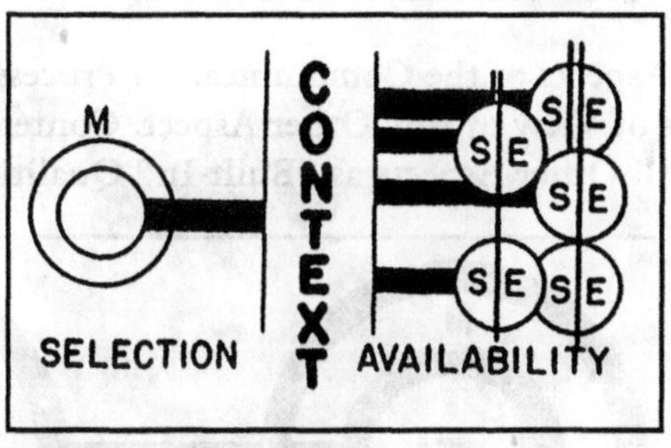

9. CONTENT: STUDY OF ALL RELATIONSHIPS AS REFLECTED IN THE STATEMENT

Any nonrandom communicative transmission is a signal. This means that it must be occasioned by some systematic use of some means. Therefore it reflects, represents, symbolizes, refers to, or corresponds to some pattern in some source. Thus every signal has *content,* even if one cannot tell its meaning at a certain instant. So on our graphic model, *S* never stands by itself, unless it signifies noise; it is always coupled with *E,* the representational, content qualities of the signal, to make up the communication product *SE.*

Content analysis is actually the investigation of a relational pattern, of the sum total of the attributes of all other aspects reflected as that quality of a statement which is not identical with its form. Strictly speaking, therefore, content analysis focuses not on how statements are perceived by certain individuals or groups, but on "built-in" qualities of communication products as they reflect aspects of the communication sequence of which they are a part.

So content can be studied from the point of view of any or all aspects and elements in our model. This is illustrated on our graphic diagram on Figure 11. We may find in our study of the *E* properties of statement *SE* that there are "built into" them some overt or implicit points of view, assumptions, etc., that were part of *M*'s way of perceiving events. These may even reflect *M*'s selection process, and the context of availability in which it operates. The situation in which *M* reacted, and the means he used to produce the signal, not only fashion its form but also affect its content qualities.

On the other side of the diagram, the content properties of statements may be related to the events that occasioned them. We may investigate content from the point of view of representational or symbolic adequacy, or correspondence; in other words, appraise its truth qualities.

Simple frequency counts, although they involve identification of content usually from the standpoint of form, would usually fall under the heading of availability or context study. On the other hand, semantic analysis, for example, focuses on content, especially on *M* versus *E* orientation of statements. The former is said to have intentional meaning, rooted in assumptions, inferences, etc. The latter is extensional orientation rooted in the world of events (or sense data). Philosophical, social, scientific criticism usually involves content analysis of some kind.

Figure 11. Any Aspects of the Communication Process May Be Studied from the Point of View of Any Other Aspect. Content (E part of SE) Might Reflect All Other Aspects as "Built-In" Qualities Inviting Study

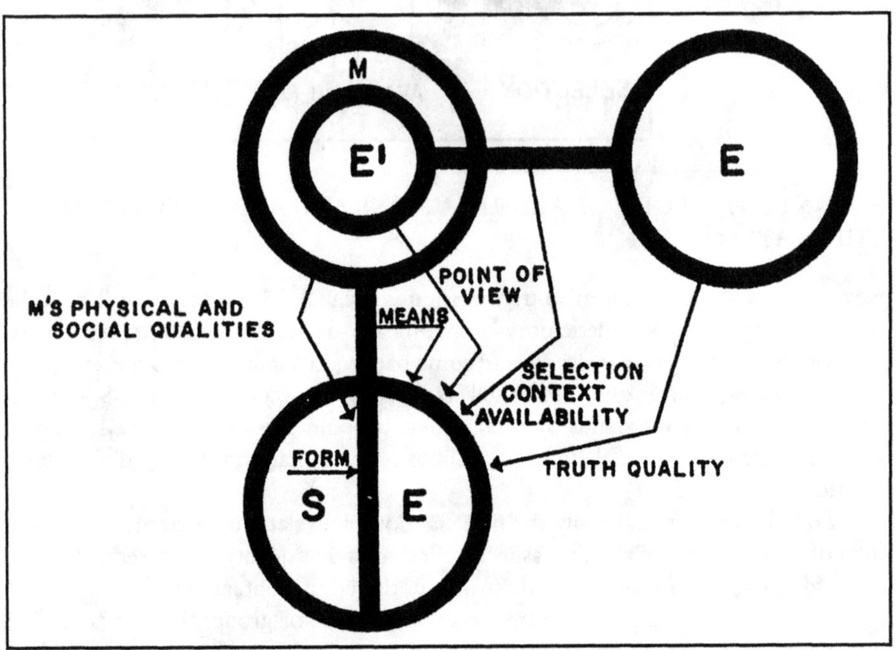

10. CONSEQUENCES: STUDY OF OVERALL CHANGES

When M's communicative reaction to event E produces SE, or when the perception of a statement produces another statement, a new event has come into being. This new event, the communication product, makes some irreversible contribution to some chain of events as it becomes part of that chain. If this contribution is measured by the yardstick of intent or objective inherent in the presentation which evoked it, it is classified as "effectiveness in reaching a desired objective," and comes under the heading of the reaction. If, however, we study the overall contribution, the tendency of communication to change a state of affairs or the state of some system independently of any preconceived objective, then we are dealing with consequences in terms of our model.

Robert K. Merton provided an example of this type of analysis in his study of mass persuasion when he contrasted the effectiveness of the Kate Smith war bond "talkathon" with some of its possible overall consequences in his last chapter on "The Moral Dimension."

Consequences may be studied through physical, social, or psychological analysis; they may be viewed in reference to changes in any or all aspects of communication over a period of time. They must be appraised, however, in the light of some normative concepts.

11. VALUE ORIENTATION: SOME NORMATIVE CONCEPTS ILLUSTRATED ON THE MODEL

The theory of communication can either find a scientific value orientation or remain the elaboration of manipulative techniques. A value-conscious approach is based on some normative standards and criteria. One possibility for a theory of communication is to formulate such value standards and criteria in terms of changes in knowledge. The following series of basic propositions about communication lead us to a value-oriented concept of knowledge.

Leading a fully human life is the principal goal of man. Making a human living is his principal activity. Both are possible only in a society; both require the production of goods and rendering of services by and through which we live and make a living.

A full human being is thus a member of the species Homo sapiens living in a society. Society is the pattern of productive and service relationships which create the conditions of human life and welfare. Social production involves the cooperative handling of materials on the basis of information; services involve the handling of information itself. Society is, therefore, cooperative living and labor through communication. It exists for the purpose of maximum human development.

Public knowledge is acquired through social communication, and describes the state of a social communicative system. The ultimate value of human welfare yields measures of value in social communication and of validity in public knowledge. Ideal social communication in terms of human welfare yields the greatest increase in valid public knowledge.

Knowledge is a communicative quality of man's social relationships with his world of events—of the horizontal dimension of our model—and a consequence of his communicative actions and products—represented on the vertical axis. The task is now to specify some normative characteristics of knowledge in terms of ideal communication.

Our model, as shown on Figure 12, suggests some normative aspects of knowledge, and forms a triangle defining a value-oriented concept of knowledge in communication terms. Along the horizontal side we find the perceptual dimension relating the individual, with his points of view and assumptions, to the world of events (and statements). The ideal along this dimension may be expressed as *valid perceptions freely selected from a representative context of all pertinent evidence.*

On the vertical axis we have added "beliefs" to "means" as a controlling aspect in communicative actions; the hypotenuse represents "truth" as the ideal quality relating statements to events. Reading along these two sides we find the ideal as *true beliefs reflecting valid points of view and presented through effective means and forms.*

Figure 12. A Conceptual Application of the Model to Illustrate a Definition of Knowledge as the Result of Ideal Social Communication

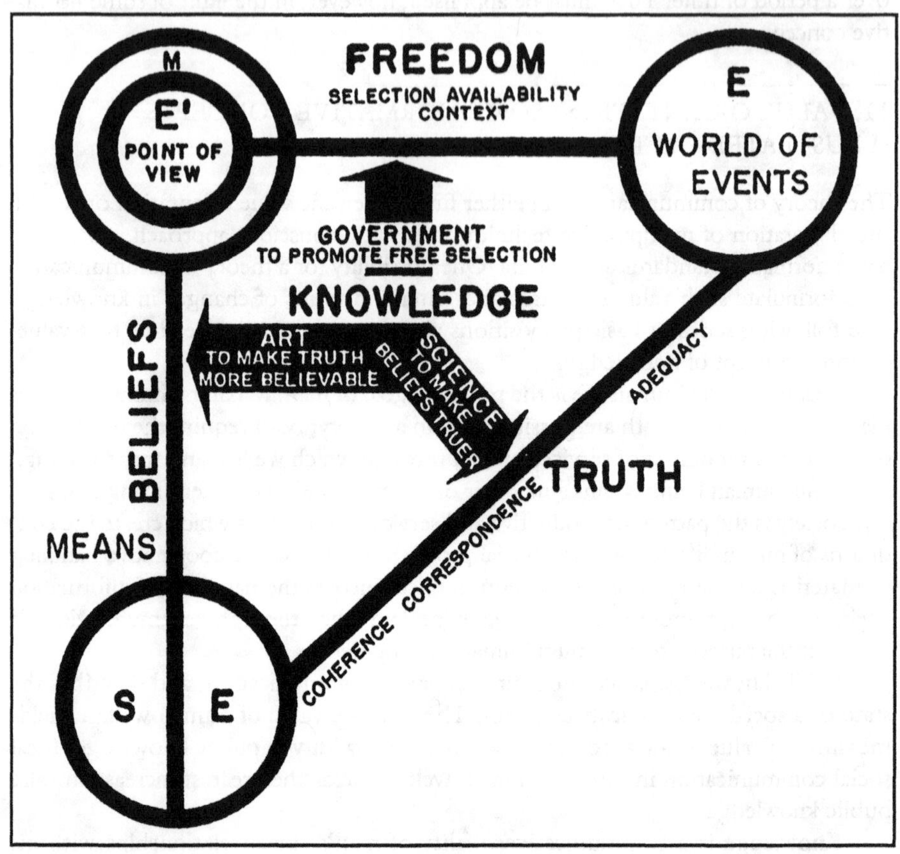

Human welfare is, of course, the criterion of validity, and the ultimate value which makes freedom, truth, and controls necessary. Its specific place on the model is along the vertical dimension, as it is the controlling value, or belief, that regulates man's ideal social actions and communications. Thus it is with human welfare as the paramount goal and controlling value that, contracting the above propositions for a briefer statement, we formulate our normative concept of knowledge in communication as *true beliefs freely acquired and clearly presented.*

In a self-governing society all citizens benefit by, and are responsible for, the promotion of public knowledge on such terms. Each advance in standards and expectations of human development imposes upon the major communicative institutions of society increasing demands for the freer acquisition and more effective presentation of a truer set of beliefs. Such have been the historic ideals, and growing functions, of democratic government, science, and art.

Government in a democracy is responsible for safeguarding the freedom of selection and the equitable availability of diverse views and evidence in matters of public concern. Otherwise there is no self-government, only manipulation of citizens, or as more elegantly phrased, "engineering of consent."

Science is the systematic examination of the truth quality of statements and beliefs in the light of reason and freely acquired independent evidence. It arises in response to real human needs, and it attempts to serve them by forming truer statements and more valid ways of perceiving. Standards of validity evolve through historical and scientific processes; they are expressed in terms relating value to human welfare, and are embodied in the governing principles of democratic society.

Art also serves real human needs. It is the creative effort to express, by the most moving and powerful means, true and significant propositions perceived from a valid point of view. The "beauty," the "emotional quality," of art (not wholly foreign to science!) rests in the excitement of *discovery* upon the perception of a convincing, true, significant, and valid statement. Art sensitizes us to the perception of human potentialities whose development society and science make possible.

Government, science, and art thus complement one another in communication as they function to make knowledge freer, beliefs truer, and truth more believable.

It might be argued that the discussion of such broad concepts is not the task of model building in communication theory. But if that is so, the study of communication must abandon hope of any scientific value orientation as an organized discipline, and remain torn by particular rationales behind specific research techniques. For scientific value orientation does not rest in technological efficiency on behalf of unscrutinized objectives; it rests in the concern with overall human needs and consequences behind all attempts to organize a field and map out an approach for further study.

This paper has not presumed to furnish a blueprint, but hopes to stimulate the search for one. It has attempted to present a unified approach to diverse aspects of the study of communication in terms of a model that might serve the triple functions of description, classification, and discussion. Above all, it tried to provoke the kind of model building in communication theory which can help us communicate about specialized technical matters and broad conceptual issues on related terms. If it succeeds in that, it has achieved its major purpose of helping to bridge that unnecessary gap between "arid equations" and the world of urgent questions.

REFERENCES

1. Cherry, E. C. "The Communication of Information." *American Scientist* 40:640–664, October 1952.
2. Dennis, W., editor. *Current Trends in Information Theory.* Pittsburgh: The University of Pittsburgh Press, 1953.
3. Deutsch, K. W. "On Communication Models in the Social Sciences." *Public Opinion Quarterly* 16:356–380, 1952.
4. Fearing, F. "Toward a Psychological Theory of Human Communication." *Journal of Personality* 22:71–88, September 1953.
5. Fearing, F. *Human Communication: An Introduction.* Los Angeles: The University of California, 1954. (Mimeographed)

6. Gibson, J. J. "A Theory of Pictorial Perception." *Audio-Visual Communication Review*, 2:3–23, Winter 1954.
7. Harwood, K. and Cartier, F. "On a General Theory of Communication." *Audio-Visual Communication Review* 1:227–233, Fall 1953.
8. Hovland, C. I. "Social Communications." *Proceedings of the American Philosophical Society* 92:371–375, November 1948.
9. Lasswell, H. D. "The Structure and Function of Communication in Society." *The Communication of Ideas*, edited by Lyman Bryson. New York: Harper & Bros., 1948.
10. Lazarsfeld, P. F. "Social Functions of Communication." *The Communication of Ideas*, edited by Lyman Bryson. New York: Harper & Bros., 1948.
11. Morris, C. *Signs, Language, and Behavior*. New York: Prentice-Hall, 1946.
12. Newcomb, T. M. "An Approach to the Study of Communicative Acts." *Psychological Review*, 60:393–404, 1952.
13. Norberg, K. "The Perception of the Visual World." *Audio-Visual Communication Review*, 1:190–194, Summer 1953.
14. Ogden, C. K. and Richards, I. A. *The Meaning of Meaning*. Revised Edition. New York: Harcourt, Brace, 1947
15. Ruesch, J. and Bateson, G. *Communication, The Social Matrix of Psychiatry*. New York: W. W. Norton and Co., 1951.
16. Schramm, W. "How Communication Works," in *Process and Effects of Mass Communication*, edited by Wilbur Schramm. Urbana: The University of Illinois Press, 1954.
17. Shannon, C. E. and Weaver, W. *The Mathematical Theory of Communication*. Urbana: The University of Illinois Press, 1949.
18. Smythe, D. W. "Some Observations on Communications Theory." *Audio-Visual Communication Review*, 2:24–37, Winter 1954.
19. Teachers College, Columbia University. "Communication and the Communication Arts," *Teachers College Record*, Vol. 57, No. 2, Entire Issue. November 1955.
20. Westley, B. H. and Maclean, M. S., Jr. "A Conceptual Model for Communications Research." *Audio-Visual Communication Review*, 3:3–12, Winter 1955.
21. Wiener, N. *Cybernetics, or Control and Communication in the Animal and the Machine*. New York: John Wiley & Sons, 1948.

Chapter 4

On Content Analysis and Critical Research in Mass Communication

By George Gerbner

Content is the coin of the communication exchange. Its nature, functions, and study should be the subject of lively technical and philosophical debate. But they are not. Or perhaps it depends on one's focus; in the broader scope of social and physical sciences the issue of *what* is involved in observation and communication lies at the heart of fundamental controversies. But in the newer specialization that straddles this social-scientific battleground, in content analysis, the outstanding issues appear to have been settled by the authorities.

So one is compelled to tread warily for fear of either adding to the din of battle in the larger context, or of appearing to be bent on disturbing the dignity of established procedures in the specialized field. What prompts us to proceed, nevertheless, is our experience that (a) in both teaching and research it is necessary to raise—and ultimately impossible to avoid—the basic issues of social science within the field of content analysis, and (b) that established procedures tend to limit content analysis to administrative research.

When theory appears to rationalize advances in methodology rather than build a framework for critical discussion of aims, the time is ripe for a consideration of aims without prior commitment as to means. We propose to do that by advancing an approach to content analysis which raises basic issues through tackling them from its own vantage point, and by summarizing the case for critical research.

AN APPROACH TO CONTENT ANALYSIS

Any process may be viewed as a patterned exchange between systems. We make inferences about the nature of processes through observation of stages, or outcomes, or consequences of the exchange. We call these occasions *events*; they make it possible for the observer to infer some things about the states of systems engaged in the exchange, and about their relationships to one another.

If a party to an exchange records, represents, or encodes in conventional (social) forms some aspects of the pattern of the exchange between itself and other systems, an event has been produced which has special qualities. A hot cup of coffee is in the process of exchanging energy with its surroundings. We infer the pattern of this exchange through observation and measurement (or by taking a sip). Coffee cannot produce a formally coded communication event, isolated from that exchange, encoding the pattern of the exchange, and expressing its own state and relationship in the exchange, such as the words "I am losing heat." We, however, can produce such an event indicative of our relationship in the exchange; we can say, "The coffee is getting cold." From that statement one can make inferences both about the process in the cup, and about the process that gave rise to the statement, i.e., our relationship to the coffee.

A *communication* is, then, a specialized, formally coded or representative social event that makes possible inferences about states, relationships, and processes not directly observed. The *process* of communication is the transmission of such events and sharing of certain inferences. The *content* of communication is the sum total of warranted inferences that can be made about relationships involved in the communication event.

The inferences can be of two kinds. The first kind is the conventional associations we make when we view the communication as a generalized form or code. This is the conventional, formal meaning, such as we might find in a dictionary.

Underlying the "formal message" with its denotative and connotative associations and differential response capabilities, we see in content the basis for inference about specific functional relations between the communicating agent or agency and other events or systems, and about actual or potential consequences. The conventional face value of a dollar bill is not the same as its actual role value in a specific exchange. The latter will reflect the objective relationships of producer, product, buyer, and seller in the exchange, and some consequences of these relationships, whether or not the parties engaged in the exchange are aware of them. Similarly, the statement "It's hot here" is a linguistic type or "form" which can be isolated from its behavioral context, recorded, recoded, etc., with little or no distortion of its formal, conventional meaning. But it is not only that; once uttered—whether pleasant or unpleasant, good or bad, real or fancied—it is also a unique and irreversible event reflecting, perhaps unwittingly, an objective set of underlying relationships which prompted its utterance. The advertising slogan, "Smoke X cigarettes; they're milder," whether valid or invalid, true or false, effective or ineffective, implies a particular set of social and industrial relationships whose expression in that form leads to consequences fully understandable only in terms of these relationships and not of the explicit message alone.[1]

"MICRO" AND "MACRO" ANALYSIS

The "micro" analyst of communication content is interested in gathering information about persons and making predictions about their behavior. In his search for the hidden dynamics of individual behavior he utilizes communication content either as fruitful material expressive in some form of the state of an organism, or as a necessary source when information about a person is restricted to the messages produced by that individual (30).

The analyst who views content as asocial event goes beyond individual behavior. His search is for the social determinants and possible consequences of both personal and institutional dynamics reflected in cultural products. His focus may be the autonomous creations of great art—whether mass reproduced or not—or it may be the everyday commodities of cultural industry.

From the former focus comes a clear statement of those tasks of content analysis which have been sidestepped in the preoccupation with methodologies. It is from the introduction to Leo Lowenthal's *Literature and the Image of Man* (28):

> Creative literature conveys many levels of meaning, some intended by the author, some quite unintentional. An artist sets out to invent a plot, to describe actions, to depict the interrelationships of characters, to emphasize certain values; wittingly or unwittingly, he stamps his work with uniqueness through an imaginative selection of problems and personages. By this very imaginative selection...he presents an explicit or implicit picture of man's orientation to his society: privileges and responsibilities of classes; conceptions of work, love, and friendship, of religion, nature, and art. Through an analysis of [his] works...an image may be formed of man's changing relation to himself, to his family, and to his social and natural environment....
>
> ...The specific treatment which the creative writer gives to nature or to love, to gestures and moods, to gregariousness or solitude, is a primary source for a study of the penetration of the most intimate spheres of personal life by social forces.

The analyst of literary content, as a social scientist, "has to transform the private equation of themes and stylistic means into social equations," writes Lowenthal. "In fact," he asserts, "most generalized concepts about human nature found in literature prove on close inspection to be related to social and political change." And: "Man is born, strives, loves, suffers, and dies in any society, but it is the portrayal of *how* he reacts to these common experiences that matters, since they almost invariably have a social nexus."

The "macro" analyst of mass media content deals with broad regularities in large systems of mass-produced cultural commodities. As the "micro" analyst assumes that the underlying laws of human dynamics find expression in communicative behavior, the "macro" analyst assumes that institutions, societies, and cultures manifest laws and order beyond that apparent to large numbers of people at any one time, and that systems of artifacts express objective, even if subtle or implicit, manifestations of this order. In his quest for the *system* behind the facts and forms of mass communication, the media analyst regards content as expressive of social relationship and intuitional dynamics, and as formative of social patterns.

SOME TASKS OF THE MASS MEDIA CONTENT ANALYST

His task, analogous in certain respects to that of the cultural anthropologist, cannot be merely descriptive of his or other people's subjective impressions. For example, the anthropologist does not see an ax handle only as a stick one could put a blade on and start chopping. To him the meaning of a cave painting is not only that it has reference to buffalos, or even that it implies certain technical skills and individual attitudes, desires, or fantasies. The major significance of artifacts is that they reflect historical human approaches to certain events; that they signify and regulate social relationships in ways their users or creators may not consciously recognize.

Egyptian mythology of a certain period may be traced to reflect the conquest of the upper Nile Valley by the people of the Delta who superimposed upon the water-gods the theological primacy of their Sun. Ancient Mesopotamian culture and religion may be seen to record and facilitate in symbolic forms a system of social relations based on the need for elaborate irrigation networks. Movable type was made possible by a long chain of technological and social revolutions; the printing of the Gutenberg Bible was a social event reflecting cultural relationships and paving the way for future revolutions.

Communications media can be regarded as historical systems of social control, conferred monopolies of knowledge through built-in "biases" (18). Some go even further in claiming that new media are inherently revolutionary in their implications, "each codifying reality differently, each concealing a unique metaphysics" (8). Distinguished analysts of mass media content cite a legal historian to the effect that "The greatest and most far-reaching revolutions in history are not consciously observed at the time of their occurrence" (23). Be that as it may, it prompts the analysts to remark, "It is by the investigation of style that we may gain more insight into the currents of history which are usually below the threshold of consciousness."

Our contention is not so much that inherent physical characteristics of media as such, or that formal elements of style, vocabulary, syntax, are themselves of profound and direct significance. Rather it is that the nature and consequences of these elements and characteristics can be understood best if content is viewed as bearing the imprint of social needs and uses.

In the words of Leo Lowenthal (27), "...objective elements of the social whole are produced and reproduced in the mass media." And: "The stimulus in popular culture is itself a historical phenomenon...; the relation between stimulus and response is preformed and prestructured by the historical and social fate of the stimulus as well as of the respondent."

The historical and social fate common to large bodies of mass media content is that they are selected and designed to be mass produced for a market. They spring from complex technological production and market relationships; they are products of an exchange between systems in which the decisive communicating agent is a modern business enterprise. Van Den Haag (38) writes:

> Unlike any other type of culture, popular culture—a full fledged style of living with a distinct pattern of feeling, thinking, believing and acting—was made possible and in the end necessary by mass production. Unless the requirements and effects of industrialization are fully grasped, popular culture does not become intelligible.

Even more specifically, unless the requirements and effects of a specific system of industrial and market relationships (such as the corporate structure) are fully grasped, mass media content analysis remains superficial. Their intimate ties to the specific industrial marketing system from which they arise give mass media materials their institutional autonomy, their implicit role-value or consequential meaning, and their underlying frame of reference.

Aside from the formal, conventional "message," mass media content bears the imprint of concrete circumstances of its creation. This includes such things as external outlook and the internal dynamics of the producing industry; its relationship to competitors; its control over resources, facilities of production, and distribution; the position of its decision makers in the industrial structure; their relationships to audiences, markets, advertising sponsors. Out of these come a set of managerial assumptions—both implicit and rationalized—reflected in large systems of content, and performing some aspects of its perception. The social determinants of cultural industry thus find their way into the consequential meaning of the material. They are expressed not so much in conventional forms and "messages" as through patterns of selection, omission, juxtaposition, through just the way things are "looked at."

Of course, it is necessary to classify and clarify conventional meanings and widely recognized consistencies in formal content. But the full meaning of such analysis emerges through procedures which combine investigation of the objective social origin and role of the stimulus with that of the response, and which search for manifestations of processes whose consequences do not depend on conscious intentions and perceptions. The primary tasks of the mass media content analyst lie in his attempts to *scientifically gather and test* inferences about content that may involve generally unrecognized or unanticipated consequences, to isolate and investigate consequential properties of content which escape ordinary awareness or casual scrutiny, to bring to awareness those hidden regularities of content which record and reflect objective mechanisms of social order. The classical role of cultural scholarship as a testing ground of critical social theory is to be strengthened, broadened, and deepened—not abolished—in the analysis of mass media content through the newer, more systematic and refined methodologies.

SOME THEORETICAL CONSIDERATIONS

Berelson (5) defines communication content as "that a body of meanings through symbols (verbal, musical, pictorial, plastic, gestural) which makes up the communication itself. In the classic sentence identifying the process of communication—'*who* says *what* to *whom*, *how*, and *what effect*'—communication content is the what." His definition of content analysis is "a research technique for the objective, systematic, and quantitative description of the manifest content of communication." Lasswell, Lerner, and Pool (23) speak of "symbol" as a technical term for words that "stand for (symbolize) the attitudes of those who use them, as distinguished, for example, from 'signs,' which are words that point to (signalize) objects external to their user." In their "symbol studies" they define content analysis as "quantitative semantics" which aims at achieving objectivity, precision, and generality through the use of statistical methods.

This approach has stimulated a growing volume of output and increasing recognition. Our purpose here is not to attempt a detailed critique. The "stray man" elements in the restrictive use of quantitative versus qualitative and manifest versus latent dichotomies have been challenged elsewhere (22,23) as resulting neither in objectivity nor necessarily in precision but quite possibly in fundamentally uncritical "scientism." The present task is to extend the theoretical underpinnings of this approach beyond the limitations of its phenomenalistic framework, to harness its methodological insights to more critical social uses, and to amplify the role of the content analyst in a broader conception of the communication process.

The Lasswellian formula, "who says what to whom, how, and with what effect" proved useful for many practical purposes. But it is too restrictive and too one-directional for a general theoretical communications model, or for a framework for critical research. For example, it places content (the "what) in a severely limited sequence. It has been amply demonstrated that *what* is said by the *who* depends also on his role as a *whom*; i.e., the communicator builds into his statement consciously and unconsciously his terms of perception as a receiver of communications, which, in turn, reflect his relationships with events of his world. Even symbols stand for attitudes, feelings, inner experiences *about* (or expressed in terms of sensory experiences of) events of an objective world. This causal thread from systems of subject-object relations to systems of content and consequences leads through the communicating agent or agency, but not necessarily through his awareness, or that of the receiver. When it comes to measuring "effects," the criterion of effectiveness in the light of conscious intentions or explicit objectives becomes insufficient except for administrative purposes. From the point of view of critical research, more interested in understanding normative aspects of the communication exchange than in appraising effectiveness on behalf of taken-for-granted objectives, a model of communication should be broadened to include certain additional features.

A GENERAL MODEL OF COMMUNICATION

The construction and some uses of such a general model was the subject of a previous *AV Communication Review* article (Chapter 3). It is summarized here for the purpose of facilitating discussion in that framework. The model makes provision for (a) portraying the communicating agent in a dynamic role as both sender and receiver; (b) designating his relation with the world of events as the ultimate source of his perceptions and statements; (c) making the distinction between formal properties of the communication product, and other inferences about content; and (d) specifically designating the study of consequences (aside from effectiveness in terms of overt intentions or objectives) as an area of research.

The model has ten basic components, some of which can be illustrated graphically. The ten components, forming a sentence identifying the essential aspects of a communication act or sequence, appear in capital letters below, accompanied by a brief description.

1. SOMEONE (the communicating agent or agency M engaged in an exchange with events of his world)
2. PERCEIVES AN EVENT (the exchange—for our purposes primarily perceptual—between systems M and E; horizontal dimension of the graphic model leading from "event" E to "event as perceived" E′; including such critical consideration as M's *selection* in a certain *context* from what is *available* for perception either directly or through the mediation of communication events)
3. AND REACTS (M's general response, not on graphic model)
4. IN A SITUATION (social and physical setting, not on graphic model)
5. THROUGH SOME MEANS (communicative facilities, vehicles, controls, used to produce communication event; vertical dimension of the graphic model)
6. TO MAKE AVAILABLE MATERIALS (part of the horizontal dimension)
7. IN SOME FORM (formal state of communication event; signal system created by nonrandom use of means; conventionalized structure, representative or syntactic patterns; designated as the S—signal—portion of the communication events SE)
8. AND CONTEXT (field or sequence in which a communication event is perceived; part of horizontal dimension)
9. CONVEYING CONTENT (the social event portion of the communication SE; those inferences from content which reflect objective relationships independent of intentions, conventional meanings, conscious perceptions)
10. WITH SOME CONSEQUENCE (the actual role of the communication event in its further exchanges with other M's objective outcomes as measured by criteria independent from intentions, overt perception, or

"effectiveness" in terms of objectives of the communication; not represented on graphic model).

INVESTIGATION OF CONTENT

The investigation of content focuses attention on SE, the communication product. It proceeds as a relational analysis on two levels. Both "formal" and "content" aspects of the communication product are studied with respect to all other elements of the communication sequence of which SE is a part.

Study of the formal continuities traces the flow or configurations of conventional ("arbitrary") systems of signs and symbols through classification and measurement. It relates the state of specific signal systems to that of others for comparison, or to intentions, desires, behaviors of the source, or to the "effectiveness" of the responses they elicit, or to technical use of communicative means.

Study of the consequential continuities represented in content includes the above, but is not limited to it. Here the communication product is viewed as a specific social event whose consequential meaning may be constant through variation in form, or may vary when form is held constant.

What we are discussing here is not the fact that words have different denotative or connotative meanings; that the sounds "horse" may refer to an animal, or to a condition of the vocal chords; that situation and context alter conventional meanings; that individual responses vary; or even that words (or other signals) may be used for strategic reasons to mask rather than reveal intentions. Rather, we are discussing the fact that a communication event may reveal something about the systematic exchange that produced it, quite apart from what we think it means, or what we intend it to mean.

We may analyze a photograph not to get responses to its conventional forms, but to determine the position of the camera or angle of lighting recorded in it. We may study a series of whiskey advertisements, not to determine their effects on sales, or on ideas about whiskey, but to make some inferences about more subtle social relationships recorded and reflected in them (such as the frequency with which their image of the "good life" involves the services of Negro waiters or Filipino busboys).

Content as an expression of objective relationships may be implicit in selection, omission, context, juxtaposition, point of view, etc., or it may be inferred through circumstantial or situational association. In that sense, consequential meaning is far from being an "arbitrary" convention. It is the property of a specific event or system of events. Every utterance of the English word "horse" (animal) is a unique event, socially determined through a long chain of associations in a certain cultural context with a certain type of animal which became domesticated at a certain point in history, and has continued to be one of the events people communicate about. In doing so they express an objective historical relationship toward it. Semanticists and semioticians notwithstanding, there is, in this sense, something "horsy" about the word "horse." The "map" is not the "territory" but a map does involve a mapmaker's rela-

Figure 11. Illustration of Some of the Relationships Involved in Content Analysis

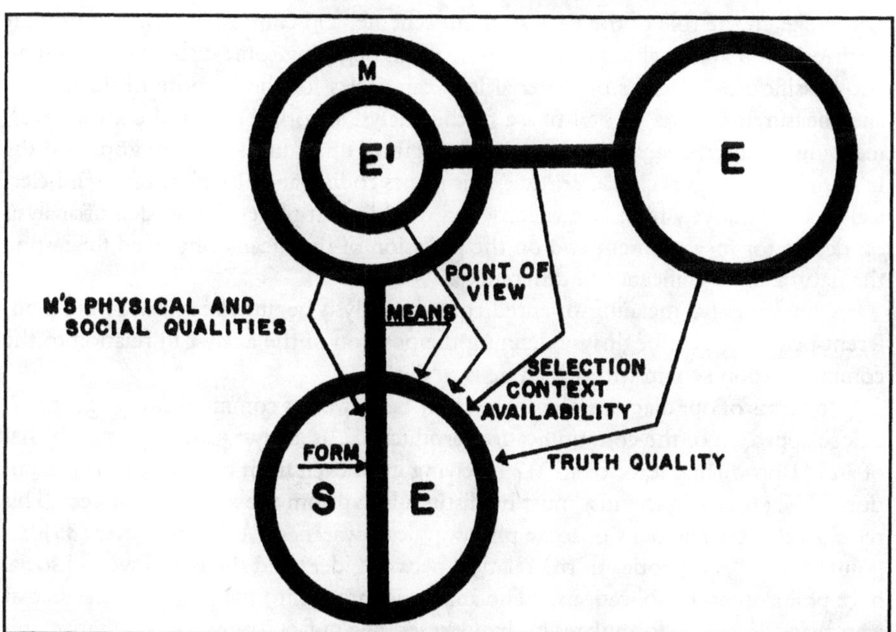

tionship to territory, determined socially and historically in terms of the territory as well as of the individual mapmaker.

Consider the study of a system of mass media products, e.g., male adventure magazine covers. Suppose formal analysis has indicated that the pattern of violent struggle with nature in juxtaposition with sex fears dominate most covers. Significant questions of content analysis might then be derived from our model by relating this communication event (SE) to the other aspects (see also Figure 11).

In what ways does this material reflect *physical and social qualities* of communicating agencies (publishers), and their relationships to other systems such as markets, advertisers, audiences, and their world of events? What *points of view* about life and the world as M sees them are implied and facilitated? What social arrangements of ownership and control of communicative *means* and facilities are revealed by the prevalence of this material? What patterns of *selection*, *context*, and *availability* are inferable from this body of content? How valid, adequate, and coherent is the correspondence of these representations to any actual system of events *(truth quality)*? What might be the *consequences* (aside from sales, likes and dislikes, conventional meanings, or "effectiveness" in terms of conscious objectives) of social relationships and points of view mediated through this content as a social event system? And so on. Each of these questions represents a way of relating the communication event system to other elements or relationships in the model; some of these can be illustrated on the graphic model as shown in Figure 11.

THE ROLE OF THE CONTENT ANALYST

Let us sketch the role of the analyst in our scheme, and contrast it with that in some form-oriented approaches for the purpose of highlighting some distinctions. Systematic classification of units of material into categories for the purpose of description and measurement is a pivotal phase of the analyst's work. Form and conventional-meaning oriented analysis begins with the setting up of units and categories on the basis of explicit signal characteristics. This makes coding and classification a semi-clerical task of relatively high face validity and reliability. It places the burden of analysis on design for measurement and on the precision of the means employed for testing the nature and significance of differences.

Consequential meaning-oriented content analysis begins elsewhere and in a different perspective. It begins by defining the position of the analyst in relation to the communication system with which he is to deal.

In terms of our diagram, the analyst may be viewed as communicating agent M2, whose approach to the communication product SE, as analyst, is different from that of an M1 producing it, or of an M2 receiving it, or even from his own casual perceptions. The analyst as scientist must be distinguished from the analyst as subject. This requires the development of some philosophical awareness. As Hans Speier (35) has pointed out, "All theories of the relation between ideas and the world we call social have philosophical implications." The analyst is forced into the philosophical area at least twice. When he formulates his hypotheses, "he in fact formulates a tentative philosophy which provides him with a frame of reference for his research....Again, when he comes to develop generalizations on the basis of his findings, he is taking a philosophical stand." The crucial issue is whether or not he is aware of the stand he is taking.

Awareness of one's own stand means that we react to our "naïve" perceptions of explicit manifestations in terms of a qualitatively different (more "objective") consciousness. As subjects we laugh when the hapless comic slips on the banana peel; as analysts we react to our own (and other subjects') laughter by tracing our own position (spatial, temporal, cultural, personal) in the exchange with that communication event, and by tracing the social history of the product. Our awareness of the known relationships in these two dimensions (along the horizontal and vertical axes of our model) suggests some of the most pertinent and least apparent questions to ask about unknown relationships in content.

Tentative answers to these questions may be thought of as the hypotheses of the analyst, usually stated in the form of content elements, categories, systematic functional relationships which may escape ordinary scrutiny.

Self-conscious hypothesis-making brings into content analysis a concern with the correctness of the analyst's entire approach to his material, with his philosophical stand, with his appraisal of the process out of which the material emerged—in other words, with the validity of a critical social theory implied in his hypotheses. Few of these hazards—and rewards—confront formal or administrative research in which ultimate goals and values are either given or assumed, and are not at stake in the research.

If the development of hypotheses through a scientific self-consciousness and critical value orientation is the first task of the content analyst, the second is the testing of his inferences through the un-self-conscious method and self-critical temper of science. Here critical, formal, and administrative researchers join in common concern over the development of research design and methodology sensitive to functional relationships of different types.

But before we advocate this union in methodology, it is necessary to explore further some crucial distinctions in aims and scope.

CRITICAL RESEARCH IN MASS COMMUNICATION

Paul Lazarsfeld (24) gave a lucid description of the distinctions between administrative and critical research in communication in an article written in 1941.

During the last two decades, he wrote, the media of mass communication have become some of the best known and best documented spheres of modern society. The reason for the rapid rise of communications research, he felt, was the notion that modern media of communication are tools handled by people or agencies for given purposes. As the communications investment of these agencies—both commercial and governmental—grew in size, and as the competitive stakes became higher, empirical research was called upon to help make administrative choices in communications strategy and method.

The objection of critical research is not directed against administrative tasks as such, but against limiting the theoretical scope of communications research to the aims which prevail in the majority of current studies, Lazarsfeld wrote. He summarized as a basic notion of critical research the contention that:

> ...one cannot pursue a single purpose and study the means of its realization isolated from the total historical situation in which such planning and study goes on. Modern media of communication have become such complex instruments that wherever they are used they do much more to people than those who administer them mean to do, and they may have a momentum of their own which leaves the administrative agencies much less choice than they believe they have. The idea of *critical research* is posed against the practice of administrative research, requiring that, prior and in addition to whatever special purpose is to be served, the general role of our media of communication in the present social system is to be studied.

SOME QUESTIONS AND HYPOTHESES

Lazarsfeld sketched the approach of the critical student. He will ask such questions as: "How are these media organized and controlled? How, in their institutional set-up, is the trend toward centralization, standardization, and promotional pressure expressed? In what form, however disguised, are they threatening human values?" He will feel that the prime task of research is "to uncover the unintentional (for the most part) and often very subtle ways in which these media contribute to living habits and social attitudes."

Lazarsfeld then indicated some steps in the formation of critical research hypotheses "by visualizing how a student would be trained to make observations in everyday life and to try to interpret them in terms of their social meaning." Note how these examples distinguish the role of the analyst as social scientist from his role as a subject:

> You sit in a movie and look at an old newsreel showing fashions of ten years ago. Many people laugh. Why do those things which we admired just a little while ago seem so ridiculous not?...Could it be that by laughing at past submissions, we gather strength to submit to the present pressure upon us? Thus, what looks to an ordinary observer like an incident in a movie theater, becomes, from this point of view, a symptom of great social significance.
>
> Or you find that a large brewery advertises its beer by showing a man disgustedly throwing aside a newspaper full of European war horrors while the caption says that in times like these the only place to find peace, strength, and courage is at your own fireside drinking beer. What will be the result if symbols referring to such basic human wants as that for peace become falsified into expressions of private comfort and are rendered habitual to millions of magazine readers as merchandising slogans? Why should people settle their social problems by action and sacrifice if they can serve the same ends by drinking a new brand of beer? To the casual observer the advertisement is nothing but a more or less clever sales trick. From the aspect of more critical analysis, it becomes a dangerous sign of what a promotional culture might end up with.

Could it be that the mass-produced portrayal of violent means for their own sake reflects social alienation and facilitates cynicism and apathy; that the "evil scientist" is an image of the hired intellectual, "neutral" in matters of human concern;' that, as has been suggested, "Peeping Tomism" is a "form of protest literature in prosperity"; that, as has also been suggested, conventional news values and front pages mirror market-orientation, a loss of historical perspective, and discontinuity of experience harmonious with positivistic science and philosophy? Neither administrative nor purely formal analysis will provide the answers to these and other questions striking at the roots of our uneasiness about popular culture in an age of mass production.

CONTENT AND SOCIAL REALITY

Franklin Fearing (12) expressed this view: "The hypothesis that the mass media reflect value-systems, satisfy needs of society, whether consciously or unconsciously held, furnishes the theoretical basis for extensive research in which the content of films and other mass media are analyzed in order to discover what the value-belief patterns of a given society are." But one cannot fully "discover" value-belief patterns without tracing them to their existential bases in the world of objective events, and without shedding some light on what and whose needs they really satisfy. Prewar German films, seen as reflecting "not so much explicit credos as psychological disposition—those deep layers of collective mentality which extend more or less below the dimensions of consciousness" (20), also reflect a system of concrete social and cultural operations which gave rise to Nazism. "Hollywood's Terror Films" can be seen not only in terms of their creating an "all-pervasive fear that threatens the psychic integrity of the average person"(21) but also in terms of a broader setting in which market-oriented social mechanisms of cultural industry shape this implicit function, and "need" such psychic consequences. In the last analysis no "state of mind" can be fully understood until its "discovery" is driven through to the objective social determinants that produce and require it.

Inner and external reality share common ground in content. Individual and institutional "perceptual frameworks"—with their implicit assumptions, need-value systems, experientially and historically developed vantage points—represent one side of the subject-object relation, structured in systematic unity and opposition with the other side—the events talked about, the social circumstances that shape our experience of meanings. Content arises out of the dialectical relation of subject and event. The nature of this relation depends on the realities of man's existence in, and struggle with, society and nature. Implicitly recorded in content, this relation becomes the property of a social event on whose terms the exchange continues.

Science is the penetration of human consciousness into the realities of existence. Content analysis can share in this enterprise through a critical awareness of social processes that shape both communication products and their perceptions and uses. Its hypotheses arise from the background of awareness of prevailing trends in cultural mass production. Specific studies focus on how content systems express these trends, and how they contribute or run counter to them. They culminate in the investigation of the range of implied consequences, in Lazarsfeld's words, "stamping human personalities in modern industrial society..., scrutinized from the viewpoint of more or less explicit ideas of what endangers and what preserves the dignity, freedom, and cultural values of human beings."

EDUCATION, MASS MEDIA, AND THE CHALLENGE OF CRITICAL CONTENT ANALYSIS

In the analysis of consequential meanings, educational research and content analysis have joint responsibilities. These responsibilities involve bringing to awareness mechanisms of psychic management masked in righteous overt forms, increasing conscious insight into tensions generated by the exposition of correct "facts" in an implicit structure which serves as an extension of the social process the "facts" purport to illuminate.

World War II Army orientation films come to mind as a fruitful subject for research from that point of view. There is already some evidence suggesting that perhaps the notable "boomerang effect" of some educational material was not so much a "failure" of communication as the implicit communication of built-in relationships superimposed upon formal content, expressing assumptions, points of view, etc., running counter to the explicit message.

A study of the home-front propaganda film *Don't Be a Sucker* (9) found, for example, that despite the "learning" of specific points by specific target audiences, the majority of the viewers identified with the German Hans rather than with the American Mike. A closer examination of the implicit content of the film revealed under the rather pedantic presentation of an anti-Nazi, pro-tolerance "message" the subtle imprint of a point of view from which fascism appeared dynamic, and democracy an invitation to weakness.

Another anti-bias film entitled *No Way Out* was subjected to searching content analysis (39). It was found that while on the level of verbal argument the film appeared to be a moving document, on a deeper level the producers could not escape the approach of an operationally racist society. The analysts wrote:

> There is of course no doubt of the good intentions of the makers of this film. But in order to show how wrong race hatred is, the film makers had to create a plot and characters and elaborate upon them in detailed images; here their fantasies from a less conscious level come to the surface: the Negro becomes a terrible burden that we must carry on our backs; a sacrifice of white corpses is required for his preservation; the image of the violated white woman forces its way to the screen; and so on. There is an effort to deny these unacknowledged nightmares about the Negro by locating race hatred exclusively in an exceptional, pathological character, but this attempt at denial remains, at bottom, ineffectual. The very title of the film, extremely puzzling in terms of the plot, expresses the basic ambiguity; though the Negro-hater is supposed to be defeated and the falsely accused Negro saved and vindicated, the title seems to state a deeper belief and draw a contrary "moral": there is no way out.

The Payne Fund studies of the early 1930s represented the first concerted attack by a group of investigators on broad social problems involved in cultural mass production. "Perhaps the most important conclusion concerning these data," wrote Edgar Dale (11) in his summary of the content analysis portion of that project, "is the fact that in large measure the characters, the problems, and the settings are removed from the lives of the persons who view [motion pictures]." And perhaps the most significant statement revealing the social implications of the "escapist" trend of overt themes was Dale's conclusion, "The good life is no longer a dream which can only be wished for. We now have at hand the machinery for making it a reality. This machinery for changing our current civilization is not commonly shown in the movies."

SOCIAL RELATIONS IN MASS MEDIA CONTENT

In the absence of continuing large-scale investigations the evidence concerning the implicit consequential meanings of mass media content is necessarily fragmentary. Berelson and Salter's (6) analysis of magazine fiction involving minority groups finds, under the overtly egalitarian "messages," the expression of stereotyped relationships and views of life that "serve to activate the predispositions of a hostile or even an indifferent audience." Smythe (34) observes similar implicit patterns in his study of television drama.

Head (17) concludes his study of television drama with the additional observation that as a conserver of the status quo television may be a prime contributor to growing cultural inertia. Lowenthal (26) notes in his study of magazine biographies an emphasis upon the private lives of "idols of consumption," indicating a shift from concern with social problems of production to uniformly individualized pressures of consumption. Implicit class bias is observed in the Bush and Bullock study of "Names in the News" (7); in Sussman's analysis of "Labor in the Radio News" (37); in Auster's "A Content Analysis of 'Little Orphan Annie'" (4); and in the Spiegelman, Terwilliger, Fearing research on comic strips (36). An audit (10) of 995 movies reviewed in *Variety* between 1953 and 1957 finds four of the five films dealing with organized labor presenting an unsavory view of unions (with the fifth banned from major theaters across the country).

Hamilton (16) traces the rise of pessimism in widely circulated Protestant sermons, especially in regard to the solution of social problems. Albig (3) finds similar value judgments implicit even in the current trend of opinion research, reflecting a "denigration of the average individual, a belaboring of his obvious lack of knowledge and information, and therefore, a skepticism concerning many aspects of political democracy."

Saenger (31) finds the undercurrent of hostility a dominant note in "Male and Female Relations to the American Comic Strip," and suggests the implicit message, "Love is dangerous because it leads to marriage in which...men lose their strength." Legman (25) wonders "whether the maniacal fixation on violence and death in all our mass-produced fantasies is a substitution for a censored sexuality, or is, to a greater degree, intended to siphon off—into avenues of perversion opened up by the censorship of sex—the aggression felt by children and adults against the social and economic structure."

Adorno (1) sees popular music joining in a response "manipulated not only by its promoters, but, as it were, by the inherent nature of the music itself, into a system of response-mechanisms wholly antagonistic to the ideal of individuality in a free, liberal society." In another connection (2) he writes: "Mass media...consists of various layers of meaning superimposed on one another....As a matter of fact, the hidden message may be more important than the overt since this hidden message will escape the controls of consciousness, will not be 'looked through', will not be warded off by sales resistance, but is likely to sink into the spectator's mind." He finds that the underlying " 'message' of adjustment and unreflecting obedience seems to be dominant and all-pervasive today." His analysis of popular fiction concludes that:

> ...The ideals of conformity and conventionalism were inherent in popular novels from the very beginning. Now, however, these ideals have been translated into rather clear-cut prescriptions of what to do and what not to do....True, conflicts of the nineteenth century type—such as women running away from their husbands, the drabness of provincial life, and daily chores—occur frequently in today's magazine stories. However, with a regularity which challenges quantitative treatment, these conflicts are decided in favor of the very

> same conditions from which these women want to break away. The stories teach their readers that one has to be "realistic," that one has to adjust oneself at any price.

Schramm's (32) quantitative analysis of the "World of the Confession Magazine" substantiates the observation of a punitive, puritanical code hidden in overtly rebellious themes. "It is very interesting," he notes, "to see how 'romance' magazines basically advise young women to shake the dew out of their eyes and the dreams out of their heads."

THE CHALLENGE FOR CRITICAL ANALYSIS

"The knowledgeable man in the genuine public is able to turn his personal troubles into social issues, to see their relevance for his community and his community's relevance for them," wrote Mills (29) in comparing the individual in a community of publics with members of audiences created as markets for cultural mass production. "The individual," he wrote,

> understands that what he thinks and feels as personal troubles are very often not only that but problems shared by others and indeed not subject to solution by one individual but only by modifications of the structure of the groups in which he lives and sometimes the structure of the entire society.
>
> Men in masses are gripped by personal troubles, but they are not aware of their true meaning and source. Men in public confront issues, and they are aware of their terms. It is the task of the liberal institution, as of liberally educated men, continually to translate troubles into issues and issues into the terms of their human meaning for the individual.

The case for self-government is predicated upon a community of publics. The dissolution of publics into markets for mass media conceived and conducted in the increasingly demanding framework of commodity merchandising is the cultural (and political) specter of our age. This fear is now joined by a growing concern over the trend of social science research, especially in the field of communications. More and more of this research is seen to succumb to the fate of mass media content itself in being implicitly tailored to the specifications of industrial and market operations. Concern "with questions of ethics in relation to the formation and effects of public opinion," wrote William Albig (3) in his review of the research of two decades, "...was largely absent, or at least unexpressed, in the writings of...contributors to opinion research in the past 20 years." Albig continued:

> Since 1920 a large professional class has developed to man the expanding activities of press, film, radio, television. At the same time, commercial and academic analysts of the communication process have proliferated. To a marked extent these professionals discuss this vast communications activity in terms of process, technique, stimuli, impact, effects, and semantic analysis, but not in terms of the ethical and value problems of communications content and effect.

It is, then, in this context of fragmentary evidence about the consequential meaning of mass media content, and of growing public and professional concern about its implications for a community of publics (including social scientists) that the challenge emerges. The challenge for mass communications research is this: to combine the empirical methods with the critical aims of social science, to join rigorous practice with value-conscious theory, and thus to gather the insight the knowledgeable individual in a genuine public must have if he is to come to grips (and not unconsciously to terms) with the sweeping undercurrents of his culture.

NOTE

1. It is evident that our distinctions are in contrast with those of the semioticians and "sign theorists" who see content as having reference *only* to semantic and syntactic characteristics of symbols. However, Kaplan (19) recognizes that content analysis "may, and indeed must take account of [pragmatic characteristics] in determining which aspects of content will be analyzed and in what ways."

REFERENCES

1. Adorno, T.W. "On Popular Music." *Studies in Philosophy and Social Science* 9:17–47; 1941.
2. Adorno, T.W. "How to Look at Television." *The Quarterly of Film, Radio, and Television* 8:213–36; 1954.
3. Albig, William. "Two Decades of Opinion Study: 1936–1956." *Public Opinion Quarterly* 21:14–22; 1957.
4. Auster, Donald. "A Content Analysis of 'Little Orphan Annie.'" *Social Problems* 2:26–33; July 1954.
5. Berelson, Bernard. *Content Analysis in Communication Research.* Glencoe, Illinois: The Free Press, 1952.
6. Berelson, Bernard and Salter, Patricia. "Majority and Minority Americans: An Analysis of Magazine Fiction." *Public Opinion Quarterly* 10:168–90; 1946.
7. Bush, Chilton R. and Bullock, Robert K. "Names in the News: A Study of Two Dailies." *Journalism Quarterly* 29:148–57; 1952.
8. Carpenter, E. "The New Languages." *Explorations* 7; March 1957.
9. Cooper, Eunice and Dinerman, Helen. "Analysis of the Film 'Don't Be a Sucker': A Study in Communication." *Public Opinion Quarterly* 15:243–64; 1951.
10. Cox, Carol A. "Labor in Motion Pictures." Unpublished research paper. Urbana: University of Illinois, College of Journalism and Communications, 1957.
11. Dale, Edgar. *The Content of Motion Pictures.* New York: The Macmillan Co., 1935.
12. Fearing, Franklin. "Social Impact of the Mass Media of Communication." *Mass Media and Education.* Fifty-Third Yearbook of the National Society for the Study of Education, Part II. Chicago: The University of Chicago Press, 1954. Chapter VIII, p. 165–92.
13. Gerbner, George. "Toward a General Model of Communication." *Audio-Visual Communication Review* 4:171–99; Summer 1956.
14. Gerbner, George. "The Social Anatomy of the Romance-Confession Cover Girl." *Journalism Quarterly* (in press).

15. Gerbner, George. "The Social Role of the Confession Magazine." *Social Problems* (in press).
16. Hamilton, Thomas. "Social Optimism in American Protestantism." *Public Opinion Quarterly* 6:280–83; 1942.
17. Head, Sidney W. "Content Analysis of Television Drama Programs." *The Quarterly of Film, Radio, and Television* 9:175–94; 1954.
18. Innis, H.A. *The Bias of Communication.* Toronto: University of Toronto Press, 1951.
19. Kaplan, A. "Content Analysis and the Theory of Signs." *Philosophy of Science* 10:230–47; 1943.
20. Kracauer, Siegfried. *From Caligari to Hitler: A Psychological History of the German Film.* Princeton, New Jersey: Princeton University Press, 1947.
21. Kracauer, Siegfried. "Hollywood's Terror Films; Do They Reflect an American State of Mind?" *Commentary* 2:132–36; 1946.
22. Kracauer, Siegfried. "The Challenge of Qualitative Content Analysis." *Public Opinion Quarterly* 16:631–41; Winter 1952–53.
23. Lasswell, H.D., Lerner, D., and Pool, I. De Sola. *The Comparative Study of Symbols.* Stanford, Calif.: Stanford University Press, 1952.
24. Lazarsfeld, Paul. "Remarks on Administrative and Critical Communications Research." *Studies in Philosophy and Social Science* 9:2–16; 1941.
25. Legman, Gerson. *Love and Death.* New York: Breaking Point, 1949.
26. Lowenthal, Leo. "Biographies in Popular Magazines." *Radio Research*, 1942–43. New York: Harper and Brothers, 1944.
27. Lowenthal, Leo. "Historical Perspectives in Popular Culture." *American Journal of Sociology* 55:323–33; 1950.
28. Lowenthal, Leo. *Literature and the Image of Man.* Boston: The Beacon Press, 1957.
29. Mills, C.W. *The Power Elite.* New York: Oxford University Press, 1956.
30. Osgood, C.E. "The Representational Model and Relevant Research Methods." *Content Analysis Today* (in press).
31. Saenger, Gerhardt. "Male and Female Relations to the American Comic Strip." *Public Opinion Quarterly* 19:195–205; 1955.
32. Schramm, Wilbur. "World of the Confession Magazine." Urbana: University of Illinois, Institute of Communications Research, 1955. (Mimeographed)
33. Smythe, D.W. "Some Observations on Communication Theory." *Audio-Visual Communication Review* 2:24–37; Winter 1954.
34. Smythe, D.W. "Reality as Presented by Television." *Public Opinion Quarterly* 18:143–56; 1954.
35. Speier, Hans. "The Social Determination of Ideas." *Social Research* 5:182–205; 1938.
36. Spiegelman, Marvin, Terwilliger, Carl, and Fearing, Franklin. "The Content of Comic Strips; A Study of a Mass Medium of 37. Communication," and "The Content of Comics: Goals and Means to Goals of Comic Strip Characters." In *The Journal of Social Psychology* 35:37–57; 1952, and 37:189–203; 1953, respectively.
37. Sussman, Leila. "Labor in the Radio News; An Analysis of Content." *Journalism Quarterly.* September 1945.
38. Van Den Haag, E. "Of Happiness and of Despair We Have No Measure." *Mass Culture, The Popular Arts in America.* (Edited by B. Rosenberg and D.M. White.) Glencoe, Ill.: The Free Press, 1957.
39. Wolfenstein, Martha and Leites, Nathan. "Two Social Scientists View 'No Way Out.'" *Commentary* 10:388–91; 1950.

CHAPTER 5

EDUCATION AND THE CHALLENGE OF MASS CULTURE

BY GEORGE GERBNER

For about the last 10 years, the study of mass communications and popular culture has come to be regarded increasingly as an educational responsibility. Attempts to meet this responsibility resulted in some useful publications. However, they made few inroads into the curriculum, and have scarcely been reflected in the preparation of teachers.

Perhaps the time is ripe to ask in what ways the educational response to the challenge of mass culture might bear fruit in the classroom. Our purpose is to pose this question by sketching the background of educational and scholarly attention, and by describing the assumptions, aims, and ideas guiding one approach to the study of the social aspects of mass communications.

BACKGROUND OF ATTENTION

The lessons of two world wars and the history of the 1930s impressed us with the power of "propaganda." More rigorous study and sober reflection showed, however, that the most potent sources of influence stem from the popular cultural context of a time and place rather than from single messages, campaigns, or personalities.

The myth of one man's "power to mold men's minds" gave way to the conception of a more complex, subtle, and more pervasive role of mass communications and the popular arts in human life. In that broadened context we attempted to sharpen and deepen our understanding of the cultural sources of our consciousness and actions. "Know thy communications to know thyself," a modern Socrates would have said, probably adding that "the unexamined culture is not worth living in."

Three-fourths of 100 basic references on research in mass communications compiled by Wilbur Schramm (9) were published since the end of World War II; half of them between 1948 and 1951. It was in that period that Gilbert Seldes proposed "a revaluation of the popular arts in terms of physics rather than aesthetics, in terms of social effects rather than private pleasure" (10). And it was then that Dallas W. Smythe (12) called attention to the

> ...ironic paradox that our teaching is so heavily—and worthily—weighted with critical evaluation of literature and drama which occupy a minuscule part of our population's attention, while the real 'literature' and 'drama' of our culture, as measured by the proportions of our resources which go into them, consists almost entirely of the content of radio, movies, magazines, newspapers—a now television. Is the educational objective for 'complete living' being served? Whose 'complete living' is to be attained: that of the teachers, or of the students?

Since that time "mass culture has reached into the Academy both by its pervasive influence and as a subject of serious study," Bernard Rosenberg observed in the recent successful compendium on *Mass Culture: The Popular Arts in America* (8). *Mass Culture* and its companion volume *Mass Leisure* (6) are themselves part of this trend. Gilbert Seldes' writing in the *Saturday Review* now calls for its extension all the way to the kindergarten (11).

The new type of academic attention devoted to mass-produced culture has also been noted in show business. The entertainment trade journal *Variety* devoted most of page 2 of its January 15, 1958, issue to the voices of the academy. It cited Patrick D. Hazard of the University of Pennsylvania suggesting that "the college teacher is an important factor in the new equation of show biz." And it observed with William D. Boutwell, director of Teenage Book Club: "If education is a process of preparing young people to do what they are likely to do anyway, isn't it the duty of the schools to teach the coming generation how to be masters, not slaves, of the mass media?"

Parents of youngsters often wondered how they spent their time "before children." Today they are equally apt to ask, "What did we do before television?" Their children hardly believe there even *was* such a time.

Television is only the latest of a snowballing series of cultural developments. The older discontinuity of cultural experience between first and second generation Americans may give way to a new and even more pervasive gulf between successive generations. The peer group and popular culture appear to gain importance in the primary context of socialization. The mass media of communications emerge as ever more authoritative socializing agencies.

As a nation we now devote more time to the consumption of mass-produced communications than to paid work, or play, or anything except sleep (and the "late show" is cutting into that, too). Television alone, only ten years old as a mass medium, now demands one-fifth of the average person's waking life. Comic books, twenty years old, can sell 1 billion copies a year at a cost of 100 million dollars—four times the budget of all public libraries, and more than the cost of the entire book supply for both primary and secondary schools. Movies, developed within a lifetime, reach 50 million people who still go to theatres each week, the same number who stay home and watch them on TV *each night*—a total of 400 million a week. Almost one-tenth of national income is invested in "leisure."

How do we manage that investment? What are the returns? What are the patterns, uses, and consequences of the mass-produced daydreams we share in common? What is the meaning of growing up, learning, and living in the new American culture?

These questions launch us on a curious journey. It is more exploration and discovery than "coverage" of a well-charted academic preserve. It brings together subjects traditionally separated. It touches closely upon some matters that have transformed the quality of life within a generation, yet have almost come to be taken for granted.

The main burden of the journey consists of ideas, reasons for holding them, and evidence supporting them. Activities include readings, discussions, demonstrations, and a group project involving joint study of a single subject such as science fiction, the Western, the image of Asia, or the portrayal of adolescents in the mass media. Individual student projects provide opportunities for probes in other directions.

The student does not require (nor should he expect to acquire) specialized skills in the manipulation of equipment, materials, or people. He will not prepare himself to "elevate" his tastes by criteria that never worked in the past, or to perform professional services required under conditions of employment in mass communications. He will be asked, rather, to *examine* conditions, to develop a way of *observing* circumstances of cultural mass production and consumption. This, we hope, will help him derive some insight into certain aspects of information, entertainment, and persuasion, and lead him to consider the formation of tastes, values, standards, and ways of professional conduct. Consideration of the role and functions of cultural industry in the life of a society might also enable him to speculate about what kinds of cultural aims can be fulfilled under what kinds of conditions.

We try to go beyond superficial or snob-classifications, such as hard cover vs. soft, slick vs. pulp, classical vs. popular, A. vs. B movie, spectacular vs. daytime serial, and so on, on the assumption that any representation of life to which millions expose themselves deserves serious study.

Respect for time, skills, energies, and lives spent in creating and consuming cultural products of all sorts should mean two things: On one hand, it should help us avoid the pose of sitting in judgment over people; on the other hand, it should encourage scrutiny of the circumstances of cultural creation and consumption undaunted by critical acclaim, popular clamor, or opprobrium: It should point the way to examination of sources, production, content, and social implications in terms of human values and uses.

The outcome of the journey can, perhaps, be measured most meaningfully in terms of progress toward three types of self-direction: (a) consumer self-direction—making choices in the light of considered interests and values; (b) professional self-direction—making choices in the light of the responsibility of the professional or producer in popular culture for providing the choices for the consumer; (c) self-direction as a citizen—making choices in the management and control of social institutions, in the creation of the conditions upon which the choices of both consumer and professional or producer depend.

Now for a descriptive outline of the journey itself. In a sentence, the course is designed to help develop ways of observing the mass media as social institutions producing images of man, life, and the world, and to reflect on the uses we make of them.

This nutshell description identifies four phases of the course. The first has to do with the development of observing "familiar" things in ways different from casual, everyday observations. The second involves the observation of the mass media of communications as social institutions and of popular culture as a function of society and of human development. The third phase of the course deals with that body of representations and points of view which provides the cultural time-space context and value orientation of behavior we consider characteristically human. The fourth phase explores the uses we make of our investment in "leisure time" and the range of alternatives that meet the criteria of democratic society.

Let us take a passing glance at each of these phases and note some of the problems and considerations that mark the course of the journey.

"TO DEVELOP WAYS OF OBSERVING..."

Analysis is acute observation from consciously varied points of view. It begins with awareness of one's position in relation to the thing observed, and goes on to search for the most valid point of view from which it can be observed to yield insight into its qualities and functions.

Assumptions, context, point of view, are key concepts in the discussion of observation and perception. They are involved in the ways we look at things, name things, use things; and, consequently, they are involved in the ways in which we represent things.

The analysis of communications is, therefore, compounded observation: In looking at a picture, for example, we do not merely observe a "thing"; we observe an observation.

What's in a picture? A "thing" viewed from a "built-in" point of view, in a certain context, and probably on the basis of some implicit assumptions about the nature of the object or event portrayed. For example, the angle of the camera and the position of the lights used to take a photograph (and used to convey, implicitly, a point of view) are just as much objective elements of the picture as is the "thing" portrayed. If we are unaware of the fact that we are observing the picture through the eye of a camera (or of an artist), we have lost some of our own power of observation; we fall in, unwittingly, with a "given" point of view.

Communication thus functions in several dimensions and on several levels. The terms of perception (the way people, life, and the world are "looked at") become built-in attributes of the way people, life, and the world are depicted through communication.

Each medium has its own terms of "perception" and system of observation. This is partly defined by the technical nature of the medium and partly by the social and institutional structure of the enterprise. The mass media of communications are not merely "windows" to a world of reality and dreams; they are active creators of synthetic images and observers of both reality and dreams from points of view, contexts, and assumptions historically structured, socially and technologically determined. To become analytical observers of these communications, and of the patterns of culture they weave, we need to study the position of the mass media in society, and the points of view their position imparts to their messages. Then we need to define and validate the position from which we observe their observations.

"THE MASS MEDIA AS SOCIAL INSTITUTIONS..."

The dreams of sleep are individual and private in any society. But the popular daydreams of our industrial culture are privately mass produced for a public market of shared desires. How did this arrangement come about? What are the communication requirements of mass production and the production requirements of mass communication? Are the media private business or public art?

Cultural (or any other) industry exists to produce at a profit. Regardless of the nature or quality of the product, if this bedrock requirement is not met, the enterprise goes out of business and investment goes elsewhere to seek returns. In the nature of commercial "free" enterprise, this is within the realm of private decisions. Any investor, corporation, large or small business, may decide to produce or underwrite the production of almost any cultural product. This right is protected under the assumption (born of an age before mass communications) that spontaneous, private competition in the marketplace is the best way to assure cultural diversity, the availability of all points of view, and freedom of speech essential for self-government.

By entering the cultural marketplace, the entrepreneur may or may not be governed by, or even concerned with, the original reasoning that protects his access to the facilities which now dominate that market. But he must be concerned, and governed, by another set of considerations. He has acquired a stake in the popularity of his product. He has risked his capital on the assumption that a certain market is large enough, or can be made large enough, to make mass production of his commodity profitable.

So far this is still a private matter.

Now there is no formula for popularity, but neither is popularity entirely accidental when the stakes are high. "At BBDO there is no room for guesswork in planning the TV special," announced the giant advertising agency in a trade paper (1). And it went on to explain:

> Everything begins with a marketing concept: a one-cent sale, a line introduction, a seasonal reason, a corporate profile to be etched indelibly in the public mind. This is the backbone of the event.
>
> Next comes selection of the right property....Then there's the clearance of the right time spot....Trade and consumer campaigns must be coordinated....Product and program promotion must be tied together....While this is all going on, one of the largest staffs of trained TV-research people helps us chart the show's course—they pre-test copy, analyze results and set ground rules for delivery of the next special.

The strategy of private enterprise mass production is geared to careful assessment, cultivation, and exploitation of marketable desires. A detachment of intelligence specialists probes public fancy; reconnaissance brings in the sales charts, cost-per-thousand figures, consumption statistics; corporate headquarters issues a series of battle orders; an army of popularity engineers prepares compelling messages designed to make the public want what it will get. Then vivid images of life roll out of the "dream factories," produced to exacting specifications to "give the public what it wants." These are the images and messages through which millions see, and judge, and live in the broader human context. They affect the tone of living and the pattern of society. They cater to an insatiable search for imaginative and informative representations of the human condition, for dreams that heal and restore, soothe and thrill, and bind men together across vast distances of space and time. They inevitably, and often unwittingly, help infuse life with direction, meaning, value.

This is a public matter.

"PRODUCING IMAGES OF MAN, LIFE, AND THE WORLD..."

At the private end of the transaction we observe problems of media ownership, control, and support, and we note market research gathering information about audiences and conditions of sale. At the public end we view social functions and controls and consider critical research inquiring into content. Then we see the two intertwined in the eyes of the beholder. We find the conditions of sale implicit in the content and quality of the dreams.

Beneath the overt forms of theme, plot characterization, reporting, description, even of light repartee, there are the covert elements of time, context, assumptions, point of view. In massive industrial enterprises such as the major communications media these elements are likely to be social rather than individual. A creator of mass cultural products who only wants to "express himself," a prominent screenwriter commented, "better go off to some other field where millions of dollars are not riding on his personal aspirations" (13).

Social content of media products becomes more discernible when large systems of output are studied and compared. Mass is part of the energy equation, and so is velocity. The atmospheric pressure of popular culture, as of gases, does not depend on the behavior of a single molecule. The laws of cultural dynamics, whatever they might be, will emerge from careful observations of the ways in which industrial and market conditions and the corporate positions of cultural enterprises—including their relationships to investors, agencies, sponsors, and their consequent approaches to audiences, to society, and to the world as a whole—implicitly shape the assumptions, contexts, and points of view imbedded in mass media products.

These covert elements of content are the "hidden messages" of popular culture—pervasive, subtle, yet obvious upon scrutiny. They spring from historical relationships and concrete circumstances of mass production. They are reflected in an ideological undertow expressed often through patterns of selection, omission, juxtaposition, through just the way things are looked at. Unwitting commitments to values, and to ways of perceiving, emerge from conditions of cultural production and consumption; they affect our assumptions about heroes and villains, love and sex, classes and professions, youth and old age, cooperation and conflict, past and future, ends and means. From these assumptions spring more mass-produced images of man, life, and the world.

"AND TO REFLECT ON THE USES WE MAKE OF THEM."

One way to measure the usefulness of a civilization is to trace the time it allows, and the provisions it makes, for activities that relate directly to a diversity of human aspirations.

Judged by the criterion of time, ours has been a useful civilization. The historic compromise between time committed to necessary labor on behalf of a ruler, an employer, or a society, and time spent on behalf of one's chosen aims, seems to be rapidly changing. But the change is a perplexing one.

Our industrial order was once attacked for subjecting man to wage slavery. It is now charged with operating a corporate "welfare state," exploiting the leisure-time markets it has brought into being, leaving little choice for individual self-direction between the dire alternatives of surfeit and boredom.

The building of markets has been among the prominent social uses of popular culture. Mass production requires mass markets. Mass markets are gained through mass audiences. Mass media of communication build mass audiences and, in the jargon of the trade, "deliver" them to mass producers through their ability to inspire and cultivate consumer desires for all types of goods and services.

But when consumer desires (or pocketbooks) appear to be drained, we find it difficult to flex our productive muscles to capacity except in war or in preparation for war. And we find it equally difficult to define creative tasks for the popular-culture arm of our industrial system.

So we use much of the leisure time gained through mass production to preach the gospel of more consumption right up to (and beyond) the limits of our ability to buy, use, or endure. And we tailor an increasing share of our popular cultural resources to the demands of salability, often irrelevant to creative purpose. This makes our machines more productive and our investments more profitable. To what extent, in what ways, and under what conditions can it also make lives more productive, and "leisure" time more creative?

"Pure entertainment" and "art for art's sake" are disguised merchandising slogans we use to evade examination of the human significance of what we want to sell, or buy. The uses of a pill are not disclosed in the taste of its sugar coating. The functions of cultural products are not revealed in the likes and dislikes that determine our selection from what is available. Our choices have far-reaching consequences beyond those registered at the box office or on the cash register. Study of these uses and consequences touches upon the terms of our own self-direction, and upon some hidden paradoxes that blur our vision of the good life.

Not least among the paradoxes confronting "people of abundance" "killing time" and the "affluent society" is the shadow of want, rather than boredom or surfeit, in our own midst and around the world. Some government reports speak of as many as 1 out of every 5 American families living in stubborn pockets of permanent poverty. Poor people, poor customers, are the forgotten people of our public arts. Out of sight in the selective mirror of the mass media, hidden from public consciousness, without power and without a voice, they are overlooked when the uses of popular culture are discussed.

All in all, the majority of human lives around the world are still spent in brutal labor not only machines but animals could do as well, if not better. Saving rather than spending, boosting production to build the foundations of a more human existence rather than titillating lethargic consumers—these are the worldwide material and cultural imperatives of our age.

The means that glut us (and at what price?) could also make human want obsolete. The alternatives we present thus involve the fate of others. But never "only" of the "others"; the American "way of life" as we know it today rests on the active (or at least passive) cooperation of half the world's peoples. Our decisions cannot long conflict with the needs and aspirations of the "others" without destroying the bases of any assumed benefits to us. The morality and usefulness of the alternatives we present, and of the decisions we make, can thus scarcely be shrugged off as a purely private matter of individual whim, taste, or enterprise.

Nor is that all of the paradoxes. The notion of self-government was predicated upon the existence of autonomous publics making conscious decisions in a cultural context of vigorous social criticism. This freedom and diversity was to be subject to no law, but guaranteed by law. The rise of cultural mass production, creating audiences, subjecting tastes, views, and desires to the laws of markets, and inherently tending toward the standardized and the safe rather than the diversified or critical, creates new problems in the theory and practice of self-government.

Considered in such a perspective, the value and uses of time, resources, and energies invested in mass communications take on new dimensions. Are thirsts exploited or quenched? Are sensibilities dulled or sharpened? Are vital resources spent in anxious, unreasoning drift, or invested in relevant exploration? Are the choices we make based on the real alternatives of our time presented in a representative context of all pertinent evidence? By what criteria and by what methods do we judge the market value of leisure time and the survival value of popular culture?

***

The journey ends, as it began, with a sense of discovering questions rather than of "covering" the answers. The issues explored do not require, or even permit, easy "solutions" arrived at in a classroom. They are permanent problems of personal judgment, professional conduct, communictnations research, social theory, and national policy. They have emerged as continuing responsibilities and challenge educational planning as the study of English or citizenship or science does. We have tried to indicate one possible response and to suggest that perhaps the time is ripe for more systematic planning. A good way to begin might be a series of experimental teachers workshops. The initiative could come from a number of fields. There are good reasons of past interest, current concern, and future professional orientation to suppose that it might come from those involved in the study and teaching of communications problems in education.

REFERENCES

1. *Advertising Age.* September 15, 1958. Full-page advertisement.
2. DeBoer, John J., editor. *Education and the Mass Media of Communication.* Research Bulletin of the National Conference on Research in English. Chicago: The National Council of Teachers of English, 1950.
3. Henry, Nelson B., editor. *Mass Media and Education.* Fifty-third Yearbook, Part II, National Society for the Study of Education. Chicago: University of Chicago Press, 1954.
4. Hutchins, Robert M. "Is Democracy Possible?" An address reprinted as a Bulletin of the Fund for the Republic, February 1959.
5. Inglis, Ruth. *Freedom of the Movies; A Report on Self-Regulation from the Commission on Freedom of the Press.* Chicago: University of Chicago Press, 1947.
6. Larrabee, Eric, and Meyersohn, Rolf. *Mass Leisure.* Glencoe, Ill.: The Free Press, 1958.
7. National Education Association and American Association of School Administrators, Educational Policies Commission. *Mass Communication and Education.* Washington, D.C.: the Commission, 1958.
8. Rosenberg, Bernard, and White, David M., editors. *Mass Culture: The Popular Arts in America.* Glencoe, Ill.: The Free Press and The Falcon's Wing Press, 1957.
9. Schramm, Wilbur, editor. *The Process and Effects of Mass Communication.* Urbana: University of Illinois Press, 1954.
10. Seldes, Gilbert. *The Great Audience.* New York: Viking Press, 1951.
11. Seldes, Gilbert. "What Can We Do?" *Saturday Review*, June 5, 1958.
12. Smythe, Dallas W. "A National Policy on Television?" *Public Opinion Quarterly* 14:461–74; No. 3, 1950.
13. *Variety.* September 10, 1958. Interview with Ernest Lehman.

CHAPTER 6

ON DEFINING COMMUNICATION

Still Another View

BY GEORGE GERBNER

Even the most reluctant scholars and researchers in the academic field of communications find it increasingly difficult to avoid defining their business, if only for the purpose of explaining it to others. Communicating among scholars of communication also requires some common conceptions of the field, and some consistency in the use of key terms.[1] The question can no longer be sidestepped by saying that we should just get on with significant work on important problems, and leave definitions to pedants. The implicit agreements of small groups at a few schools no longer suffice. Donald P. Ely found twenty universities offering communications programs of some sort in 1960 (1). Eleanor Blum listed at least eighteen formal university research organizations in the communications field (2). The Penn State team looked at fourteen interdisciplinary programs on the graduate level only (3). David Manning White's survey of research on a broad front (4), and the most recent inventory of behavioral science oriented research of the last decade (5), reveal vigorous activity of increasing scope and intensity.

In the limelight of growing attention, and in light of a diversity of approaches, these newer forms of academic organization and activity are called upon, quite legitimately, to demonstrate a rationale never demanded of the old. The choice of problems for study and research, the allocation of resources, and the assessment of the relevance of contributions depend on definitions. The continued viability of communications programs and the emergence of a recognizable field require efforts to identify a distinct problem area and center of intellectual concern.

The need to define, and the effort to strive for some integration amidst diversity, bring with them the temptation to talk of the best approach to a problem before agreement is achieved as to the problem to be solved. There is danger of seizing on the most convenient, and the most easily manageable, measurable, and fundable activities as being of the highest priority. These dangers, as I perceive them, are inherent in attempts to reduce communications study and research to an intelligence operation on behalf of any and all attempts to change behavior. I would like to argue that such a conception inhibits a workable definition of communication as a distinct form of social interaction, perpetuates the underlying confusion between effects and behavior change, and fails to do justice to the seminal contribution the study of communications can make to understanding some basic problems of life.

THE TACTICAL APPROACH

At the heart of the main line of inquiry in communications which was, according to Berelson, "playing out" in the 1950s (6), lay the explicit or implicit preoccupation with the tactics of power, persuasion, and manipulation. Correspondingly, there was a preference for research techniques which could yield "hard" and quick information for immediate administrative uses.

The tactical line of inquiry has made its contribution to our understanding of the mechanics of certain communication effects, uses, and gratifications. These insights, and their apparent applicability to a great variety of policy and management problems, gave rise to a great deal of research activity which undoubtedly will, and should, continue. But practical and theoretical limitations make it difficult to conceive of such study as the basic source of definitions and rationales for the field.

One reason for the "playing out" of the approach, even if not the activity, is that insight into the tactics of "making friends and influencing people" has limited significance for basic policymaking. The stake and role of an institution in the social order defines the total perspective in which it will view alternative policies. No institution will shrink from taking an "unpopular" decision when its vital interests are involved. Tactical intelligence will be called upon mainly to find the most suitable ways of "selling" (or disguising) policies which serve institutional objectives.

More crucial are the limitations the primarily tactical approach imposes on theory. Some of these limitations are inherent in approaching communications from a point of view which, as a historical phenomenon, is itself rooted in manipulative pressures of modern society. A recent formulation, prepared under a grant from an advertising agency, characteristically defined the study of communication as "the study of ways of arranging stimuli to produce desired responses by the organism" (7). This conception not only fails to define communication but defines it out of existence. It blurs the distinction between communication and other types of social interaction. The researcher might as well study pushing, pulling, shoving, or feeding, or any tactics intending to "produce desired responses." It becomes irrelevant whether or not the transaction involves communication. What really happens as a consequence of "arranging stimuli" is also secondary. The basic question is: did the tactic "produce desired responses," or did it not? As Dell Hymes pointed out, "To define communication as the triggering of a response...is to make the term so nearly equivalent to behavior and interaction in general as to lose its specific value as a scientific and moral conception" (8). Another theoretical difficulty is that the approach can, at best, yield a long and unwieldy list of "do's and don'ts" which must then be related to an almost infinite range of situations and objectives.

Attaching the criterion of internationality does not help to clarify matters. If the interaction involves a code or representation with recognized message properties, and if the nature and role of these properties in the interaction is the focus of the study, we are inquiring into a communication act which has consequences. To reduce the range of observation to those acts, aspects, or consequences which may have been "intended" as parts of a conscious communication effort is to place blinders on the researcher. The criterion would serve primarily those interested in measuring "effectiveness" by their own preconceived yardstick of intentions; it would inhibit inquiry into all aspects and consequences of communication, wherever such inquiry might lead.

"EFFECTS" OR "CHANGE"?

Underlying the confusion of the study of communications with that of assorted tactics has been the excessive concern with usually short-term, private, and personal effects, conceived as behavior change—such as the adoption of a new practice, the gaining of a vote, the sale of a new product. This preoccupation has obscured not only the concept of communication as a special type of social interaction, but also the meaning of effect. Equating effect with change tended to inhibit investigation of the massive historical and structural connections between communication behavior, the nature and composition of message systems, and corresponding system of social relations. What could be observed, and was indeed seized upon as something surprising and significant, was the complexity and difficulty of changing certain ideas and behavior patterns amidst generally unchanging social-cultural conditions. Such findings of complexity and difficulty were summarized in Klapper's comprehensive survey (9). But Klapper himself noted that much "effects" research may be inapplicable and misleading in regards to crucial issues and broader areas of influence upon life, thought, and values.

An image (or behavior pattern) must be sustained to exist at all. Once a pattern is established and sustained, it affects messages and tactics as much as (or more than) the other way around. Specific attitude or behavior "change" may be the least significant indicator of "effect" unless it is part of a general transformation of the message-production and image-cultivation process, and is, therefore, supported and reinforced by changing circumstances of life.

The cultivation of dominant image patterns is the major function of the dominant communication agencies of any society. There is significant change in that process when there is a change in the clientele, position, or outlook of the dominant agencies of communication. Such change, when it occurs, changes the relative meaning of existing images and behavior patterns even before it changes the patterns themselves. The history and dynamics of continuities, as well as of change, in the reciprocal relationships between social structures, message systems, and image structures are the "effects" of communication.

FIELD IS WHERE THE PROBLEMS ARE

Communication is social interaction through symbols and message systems. The production and perception of message systems cultivating stable structures of generalized images—rather than any tactic calculated to result in "desirable" (or any other) response—is at the heart of the communications transaction. Any definition or approach short-circuiting the distinguishing features of communication itself has no prospect of designating it as a recognizable field of study.

Social scientists in communication need to isolate and define something distinct and common about their work, but they also need to avoid the temptation of settling for the most convenient and salable service functions. The problems to be solved require fuller understanding of the types of message systems that tend to be produced under different cultural, institutional, and technological conditions; of the ways in which the composition of message systems tends to structure and weight issues and choices from the interpersonal to the international level; and of the ways in which information is processed, transmitted, and integrated into given frameworks of knowledge. Students of communication should not shrink from defining their field where the problems of communication are, rather than where solutions might be easiest to find.

NOTE

1. As a contribution to that end, and to explain my own usage of the term, let me suggest that "communication" (singular) be used in reference to (1) the act, and (2) the process, and "communications" (plural) in reference to (1) means, channels, media, and (2) programs, schools, and the field itself embracing a multiplicity of meanings.

REFERENCES

1. Ely, Donald P. "The Organization and Development of Communications Programs in Selected Institutions of Higher Education" (unpublished doctoral dissertation, Syracuse University, 1961).
2. Blum, Eleanor. *Communications Research in U.S. Universities. A Directory: 1965.* Urbana: Institute of Communications Research, University of Illinois, 1965.
3. Holtzman, Pauld, and Vendermeer, A.W. Interdisciplinary Graduate Programs in Communications: A Descriptive Study. A report of research under a U.S. Office of Education Contract No. E-3-16-029, College of Education, The Pennsylvania State University, Pennsylvania, 1965.
4. White, David Manning. "Mass Communications Research: A View in Perspective." In *People, Society and Mass Communications,* edited by L.A. Dexter and D.M. White. New York: The Free Press, 1964.
5. "A Symposium: 'Quantitative Group' Looks Back Over a Decade of Research," *Journalism Quarterly,* 42:591–622, Autumn 1965.
6. Berelson, Bernard. "The State of Communication Research," *Public Opinion Quarterly,* 23:1–6, Spring 1959.

7. Hartman, Frank R. "A Behavioristic Approach to Communication: A Selective Review of Learning Theory and a Derivation of Postulates," *Audio-Visual Communication Review,* 11:55–190 (156), September–October 1963.
8. Hymes, Dell. "Introduction: Toward Ethnographics of Communication," *American Anthropologist,* 66:1–33, December 1964.
9. Klapper, Joseph T. *The Effects of Mass Communications.* Glencoe, Ill.: The Free Press, 1960.

PART II

EDUCATION IN THE MEDIA AGE

Institutional Clashes and Symbolic Functions

CHAPTER 7

EDUCATION ABOUT EDUCATION BY MASS MEDIA

BY GEORGE GERBNER

It has never been wise to assume that the needs of education determine what goes on in the schools. "Ideas for educational innovation, which are being discussed today with high excitement among educators and the public, have actually been in the educational literature for many decades."[1] Studies of innovation in education indicate that neither demonstrations of need nor findings of research are, by themselves, sufficient causes for change. And the Brickell report on organizing New York State for Educational Change revealed that the rate of instructional innovation more than doubled within fifteen months after the firing of the Soviet Sputnik I on October 4, 1957.

It would be hasty to conclude that Moscow alone pulls the trigger of educational change in the United States, or that demonstration of needs and research on alternatives are wholly without effect. Change occurs against a background of the allocation of attention, values, and resources. Crises are made, and the shock of Sputnik was no exception. Nor was it accidental that its implications affected education rather than, say, the way industry is organized. The facts of Soviet scientific and technical development were available long before Sputnik, but it took a dramatic demonstration to make our media of communications direct public attention to them. And it was inherent in the industrial structure of our mass media that the finger of indignation should point away from, rather than toward, themselves and their clients.

A by-product of these institutional pressures was a belated, and perhaps only fleeting, recognition of the depth and magnitude of a crisis still in the making. The crisis relates both to education and to the technological imperatives of our age, but it is rooted in the system by which we allocate attention, values, and resources.

The industrial revolution and its extension into the field of communications and culture transformed the physical, social, and symbolic environment through which a member of the species Homo sapiens becomes some sort of a human creature. My purpose is to sketch the relationship between the two cultural offsprings of this transformation, and to trace the allocation of attention, values, and resources devoted to education. In attempting my task, I will be talking about how our society educates its citizens about education. This is a process conducted largely through the mass media, and it underlies the allocation decisions which ultimately determine whether the schools can meet the imperatives for investment in skill, responsibility, and enlightenment demanded of a viable civilization in a technological age.

When we discuss the amounts and trends in public attention the mass media direct to the formal educational enterprise, we are dealing with the way one cultural institution relates to and represents another. This is a complex and delicate relationship. It is the product of the historical development and of the institutional structures and vantage points of the two institutions.

Both institutions of public acculturation are offsprings of the industrial transformation. Public education, or formal schooling for all, was both out of the struggle for equality of opportunity (which is far from over), and is sustained by the demand for literacy, competence, and coherence in increasingly mobile, de-tribalized, de-traditionalized, and non-deferential industrial societies. Universal public education is feasible, of course, only when the availability of non-human energy makes it possible (as well as necessary) to invest human resources in their own further development.

The other major new branch of institutionalized public acculturation is the system of mass communication. Mass communication becomes possible when technological means are available and social organizations emerge for the mass production and distribution of message systems.

The mass media system is, then, the direct descendant of technology, mass production, mass markets, and corporate or collective organization. It is the cultural arm of the industrial order, well suited to its need for rapid, continuous, centralized, and standardized reproduction and distribution of cultural commodities to mass audiences. The revolutionary aspect of this technologically mediated communication system is its ability to mass produce and distribute messages beyond previous limitations of handicraft production and face-to-face interaction, and thus to form historically new bases for collective thought and action. Mass media use this "public-making" ability to pursue institutional goals of their own and of their clients. Mass media are in business to produce and sell publics, although their historic significance lies in their ability to allocate and channel public attention.

Constitutional commission and omission enabled both media and education to escape centralized public development and control. But, although partly exempt from the laws of the Republic, the mass media were fully subject to the laws of industrial organization and development from which they sprang. These "laws" required mechanization, concentration, and control—if not public, then private—and made mass media the cultural arms of the industrial order.

By comparison, public schools remain the last major folk institution of advanced industrial society. Schools are not easily mechanized, centralized, or even organized. Technological developments in instruction may release personal interaction for the less routine and more uniquely judgmental tasks of learning, but education requires individual attention at its most critical points, and thus large amounts of human investment. This makes it relatively expensive. But the amount of necessary or desirable expense—or investment—is not easily determined, because there is no convenient yardstick for measuring the product. A complex system of pressures and allocations of competing and often conflicting attentions and values determines how much of our resources will be invested.

In the following, I would like to report some fragments of a study I have recently concluded on this subject.[2] First I will compare the proportion of Gross National Product and the proportion of mass media content devoted to education. Then I will sketch some trends within these overall amounts. Finally I will attempt to place these trends and relationships in some historical perspective. My thesis is not only that our allocation of values needs some critical scrutiny, but also that our system of education about education has obscured the scope and depth of its underdevelopment.

The rate at which a proportion of Gross National Product is invested in education may be a basic index of knowledge development. Some contend that this rate is also related to growth of GNP (Gross National Product). At any rate, both the rate of increase in GNP and the percentage of GNP spent for all types of formal education in the U.S. fluctuated between 3 and 5 percent in the decade 1950 to 1960.

The proportion of mass media attention devoted to education bears some similarity to these figures. A fifty-year average of 2.5 percent of all privately published books (excluding textbooks) dealt with education; the 1960 figure was 3 percent. Various measures indicate an average of 4 percent of news content devoted to education news, schools, and teachers. Mass circulation popular magazines devoted about 2 percent of their nonadvertising space and three to four percent of all articles to education and teachers.

So much for the general magnitudes involved both in the allocation of resources and of mass media attention directed to the educational enterprise. Now let us look at *trends* in this allocation.

A few graphs will serve to establish general tendencies of mass media attention in the last fifty years. First, books about education, which, as we have noted, averaged 2.5 percent of all privately published titles (excluding textbooks). Figure 1 shows trends over a fifty-year period in comparison with similar data from Great Britain. The actual number of titles published in England is higher than in the United States, and the percentage of British books about education averages three times the U.S. percentage. But our concern here is with trends, and the graph does not show the differences in magnitude.

The trends are quite similar. From 1910 to 1960 (the last date for which comparable figures were available) the number of books about education and their percentage share of all titles declined. The deepest slumps were during wars and the sharpest gains in the immediate postwar periods. The postwar rise of the late 1940s was interrupted by a drop in the United States but not in Britain in the early 1950s. The post-Sputnik peak of the late 1950s in the United States contrasted with a relative decline in England about the same time.

The New York Times Index was used to obtain a measure of press attention over a fifty-year period in that newspaper. As we can see on Figure 2, both the number and proportion of news items about education increased considerably. However, the percentage share of these items exceeded 3 percent of all news items only in 1958 and 1961.

The slow increase in attention after World War I culminated in the spurt of 1930. In the 1930s, the decline in the proportion of attention was more prolonged than it was in the amount. After the slump of World War II, both rose sharply to a peak in 1950. The dip of the early 1950s turned to new heights in the number of stories by 1956, and in their percentage share by the post-Sputnik year of 1958. Attention leveled off after that.

Figure 1. Trends in Number and Percentage of New Books about Education (Excluding Textbooks) Published Annually in United States and Great Britain from 1910 to 1960

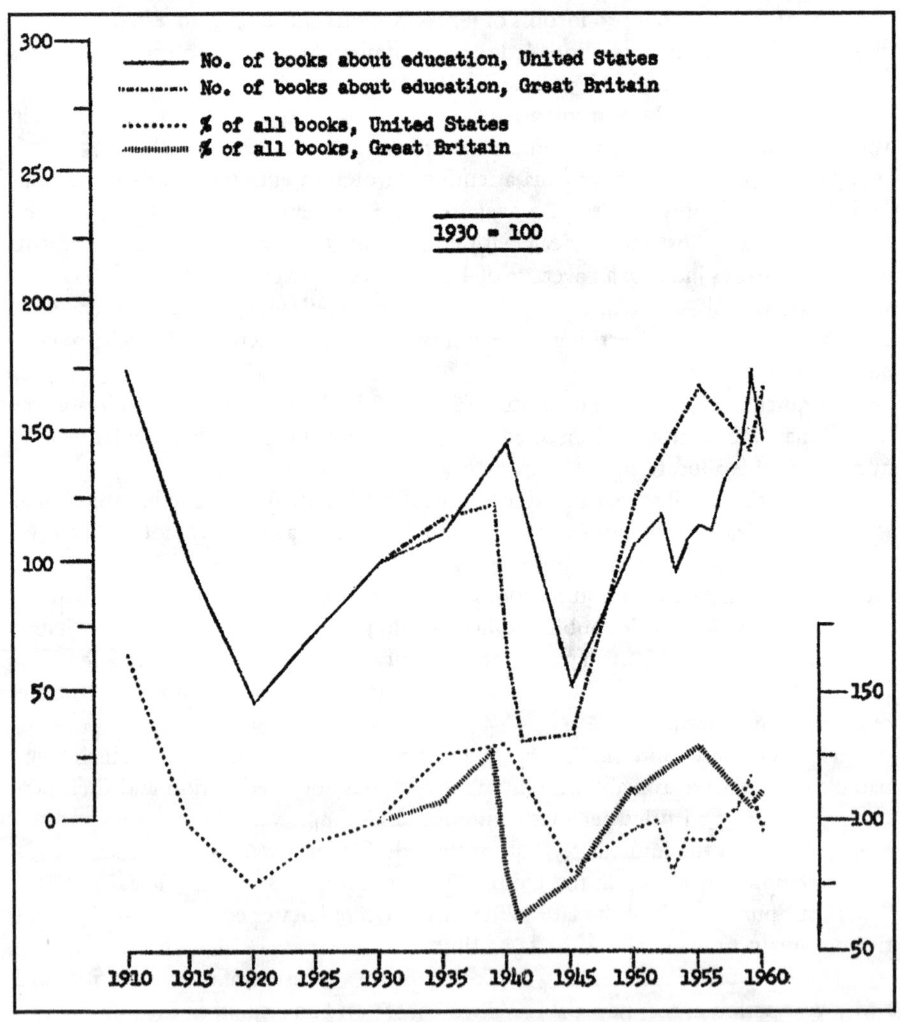

Figure 2. Listings Under "Teachers," "Schools," and "Education" Headings in the New York Times Index 1913–1962; No. of Columns and Percent of Total Index

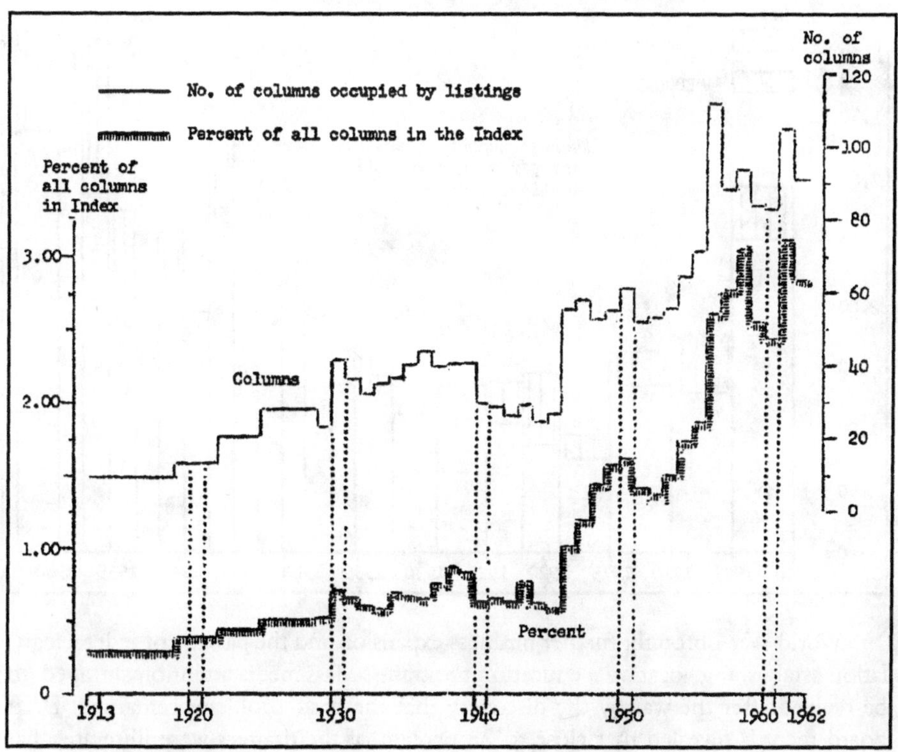

Similar trends were found in popular magazines. The most characteristic features of the pattern (shown on Figure 3) are the slumps of attention in depression and war, the sharp rise especially in the post–World War II period, the decline in the early 1950s, and the leveling off after Sputnik.

Without going into any detail, let me mention that we found similar trends in the portrayal of schools and teachers in Hollywood movies, in comic strips, and even on magazine covers. These trends cut across media. The magnitudes were generally below 5 percent of total media allocations. So was the percentage of GNP spent for education.

It may not be too far-fetched to suggest that the allocation of attention is related to that of resources, that media play a part in the process, and that the whole system of allocations may best be seen in the light of fundamental social developments.

We have observed a high level of media attention to education before 1910. Such attention reflected the peak of the vocational education and the progressive movements. Propelled by "muckraking" journalism, these movements resulted in the passage of federal grants for specific programs of most direct usefulness to the rapidly rising industrial forces.

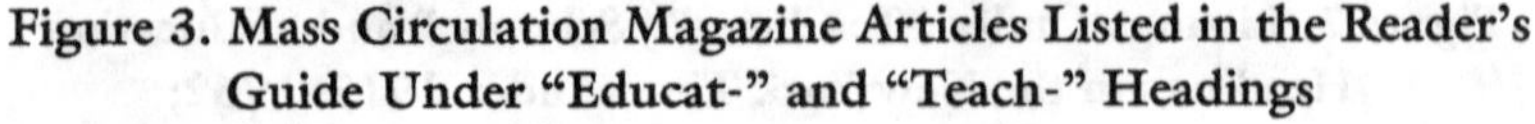

Figure 3. Mass Circulation Magazine Articles Listed in the Reader's Guide Under "Educat-" and "Teach-" Headings

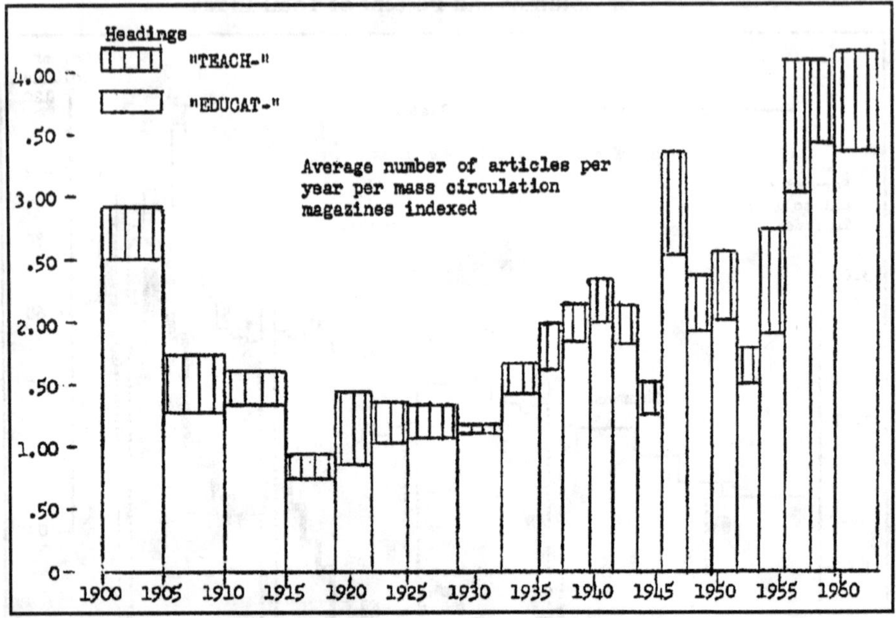

World War I brought further business expansion and the passage of federal legislation establishing vocational education programs. Mass media attention slumped, to be revived after the war by the discovery that the basic problems remained. Draft board records revealed that close to 25 percent of the draftees were illiterate, that surprisingly large numbers did not speak English, and that the great majority of the one-third who were physically unfit suffered from defects that could have been remedied if identified at school age. But the initial burst of enthusiasm faltered under the postwar counterattack against "radical" reform. Few of the remedial measures advocated, and none of the federal aid bills introduced, came to pass. Pressure was brought to bear to operate schools according to the principles of "scientific management" and "sound Business administration," despite the fact that education had no reliable measure of its "sales." A professional corps of public school administrators emerged. School public relations became a recognized specialty.

The crash of 1929 directed major mass media attention to the convulsions of the economic system and to their political repercussions. The proportion of news and magazine stories devoted to education declined to their lowest point since World War I. Educational expenditures also declined by one-fourth, although the drop in national incomes was even sharper. Public school systems in many states were near collapse. Over twenty-five emergency aid bills were introduced in Congress; none passed. Education had a depression but not a New Deal.

The gradual shift to war production accompanied and stimulated economic recovery, but also defeated attempts to allocate major new resources to the still depressed educational enterprise. Although dollar expenditures and mass media attention devoted to education increased slowly until the outbreak of World War II, both declined sharply during the war. Few new schools were built, and the school plant had further deteriorated. Teachers left the profession in droves. Inflation hit hard those who remained. The first wave of "war babies" began to flood the elementary schools. School systems expanded their community information activities. Listings under "Public Relations" in the *Encyclopedia of Educational Research* increased from four studies in 1941 to six pages in 1950. Mass media attention zoomed, as we have seen on the graphs, riding the crest of the general reformist zeal of the postwar years.

The watershed of high hopes appears to have been 1948. The G.I. Bill of Rights had given American higher education its biggest boost since the Land Grant and Morrill Acts of the last century. A federal aid bill had failed to clear the House Committee by a single vote and it was expected that favorable action could now be secured. Selective service rejections during the war had emphasized continuing illiteracy. The postwar teacher and classroom shortages and a rash of teacher strikes further dramatized the demand for action. But the confidence proved misplaced. As after World War I, the counterattack which was to dash hopes of fundamental reform had already begun. Tax and bond elections provided opportunities for attacks on weakened and vulnerable school districts. The governing groups of most communities were, by and large, unable to unwilling either to accept local solutions adequate to the needs or to share the burden—and possibly control over resource allocation (which is the critical issue, *not* curriculum)—with the federal government. The federal aid bill was defeated and the percentage of gross national income devoted to education actually declined.

The critical years between 1948 and 1953 saw the gathering and clashing of forces that were to shape American education, and perhaps national development itself, for decades ahead. The apparent promise—or threat—of the movement for a major redirection and reallocation of national resources brought forth a largely demagogic assault on "progressive education." The postwar reform movement collapsed under the counterattack of the combined political, economic, and military pressures which characterized the McCarthy era and the period of the Korean War.

The mass media played an ambivalent role. The proportion of attention directed to education declined, along with the relative allocation of financial resources in the early 1950s. Many newspapers became the primary vehicles for the attack, and other media either abetted or were intimidated by the onslaught. The turbulent "era" of the early 1950s first reduced the volume of attention and then changed the complexion of the coverage. After 1953–54, rising media attention reflected the controversies over school integration and the new criticism of the schools. This new criticism, for which the setbacks of the early 1950s provided ample ground, featured educators themselves in increasing numbers. The new criticism paved the way for the orgy of fingerpointing and pedagogical soul-searching released by Sputnik in 1957. But Sputnik seems to have signaled the culmination rather than the origin of a period of intense public attention. Special-purpose programs were launched again, and the rate of research and innovation may have been accelerated. But the massive reallocation of attention, values, and resources required to remedy the accumulated neglect that came to light, let alone to meet fully the imperatives of a technological age, was not forthcoming. Media attention leveled off again after 1958.

In my own city of Philadelphia, a recent survey found two-thirds of the city's public school pupils "culturally disadvantaged."[3] It has taken us since 1890 to triple the rate of investment in education. Dr. Jean Grambs suggests in her book on *Schools, Scholars, and Society* that this would have to be tripled again right now in order to do justice to every child in the schools and to utilize fully both human and technological resources available.[4] Before that day comes, however, we must understand more of education about education itself. I have tried to show that this is part of our general allocation of attention, values, and resources, a process which may well determine the future viability of our culture.

NOTES

1. Jean Dresden Grambs, *Schools, Scholars, and Society* (Englewood Cliffs, N.J.: Prentice-Hall, Inc., 1965), p. 8.
2. George Gerbner, "Mass Communications and Popular Conceptions of Education: A Cross-Cultural Study." U.S. Department of Health, Education, and Welfare, Cooperative Research Project No. 876, 1964.
3. The Philadelphia *Inquirer*, March 21, 1965.
4. *Supra.*

CHAPTER 8

EDUCATION IN NEWSPAPER ADVERTISEMENTS

BY GEORGE GERBNER

Attention often has been focused on the press as a medium through which the public learns about its educational enterprise. Yet, no one has asked how much of that image comes from news and how much from that other major feature of the American newspaper—advertising.

How much and what kind of advertising material relating to schools, students, teachers, or education in any way appears in leading American daily papers at the height of the "school news" and "back to school shopping" seasons? That was the question this pilot study attempted to answer.

We selected seven metropolitan newspapers, six of which were both on the list of "15 superior papers" picked by newspaper editors (*Editor & Publisher*, April 12, 1960, p. 14) and on the list of "the leading 15 dailies" chosen by a poll of professors of journalism (*Saturday Review*, May 13, 1961, p. 60). The *New York Herald Tribune*, also included in our study, was on the *Saturday Review* list only. The time period selected for the analysis was September 1–7, 1961.

All news, editorial, sports, and advertising items (excluding classified advertisements) dealing with or making reference to schools, students, teachers, or education in general were tabulated. The newspapers studied and the percentage of different types of items can be seen in the following table. While pre-season school and college sports accounted for only 10 percent of the items, advertising and news-editorial matter contributed about the same number of items to the image of education presented in all seven papers. The percentage of advertising items out of the total for each paper, however, ranged from 58.5 percent in the *New York Times* to 16.7 percent in the *St. Louis Post-Dispatch.*

Our sample of 591 advertising items was subjected to further analysis. Some 39 percent of the sample came from the *New York Times*, 20 percent from the *Kansas*

All Relevant Items Published in Seven U.S. Metropolitan Daily Papers							
	Number and Percentage of Types of Items						
Newspapers	Totals (100%)	News, Feature, Other Editorial Items		Sports		Advertising	
	N	N	%	N	%	N	%
ALL PAPERS	1336	609	45.6	136	10.2	591	44.2
New York Times	391	147	37.5	15	3.8	229	58.5
Chicago Tribune	228	110	48.2	38	16.7	80	35.1
Washington Post	124	80	64.5	17	13.7	27	21.8
Kansas City Star	205	78	38.0	6	3.6	119	58.6
St. Louis Post-Dispatch	120	78	65.0	22	18.3	20	16.7
NY Herald Tribune	165	69	41.8	10	6.1	86	52.1
Los Angeles Times	105	47	44.8	28	26.7	30	28.6

City Star, 15 percent and 13 percent from the *New York Herald Tribune* and *Chicago Tribune*, respectively, and the rest from the remaining three papers.

Most advertisements were placed by schools offering educational services. Only seventy (12 %) promoted the sale of products or related but non-educational services. Half of these were school supplies, one-fourth were school clothes, and the rest ranged from banks announcing student savings accounts to airlines featuring student rates.

A large illustrated bookstore advertisement described "a home training program" in book form "to improve your child's I.Q. showing" in taking intelligence tests "from elementary schools to college boards." The *Saturday Evening Post* announced that parents could "Learn how 'progressive' education can hold back your children. And how a gentle heiress is waging a crusade against leading educators."

In another advertisement, a brokerage firm called attention to the investment implications of "the impact of increased emphasis on education." Under the title, "Smart Money in Educational Texts?" the copy explained:

> A result of the exceptionally high post–World War II birth rates is currently making educational issues an extremely interesting growth area to investors. The first of this bumper crop of babies is now inundating the nation's high schools, giving the textbook field an ever-increasing momentum.

The 521 educational-service advertisements placed by schools offered instruction on the primary level (17%), on the secondary level (19%), and on the level of higher, specialized, and adult instruction (76%).

The majority of subjects advertised were non-academic, and most of the copy was straightforward and informative. Nearly half of all schools (49%) offered instruction in clerical, business, commercial, industrial, technological, and semi-professional skills. Most of them used the direct technique of simple announcement or of stress on quick results and employment opportunities. "An extraordinary 5 month course in piano tuning" vied with an offer of "Shorthand in 6 weeks" and even "A new career opportunity after only a few weeks" in "1401 Computer Programming." "Trained Men Get the Best Jobs" declared a school of automobile mechanics. "Make Big Money in Pleasant Real Estate Career" suggested a real estate school.

A chiropractic college advertisement showed a young male practitioner applying therapy to the back of a reclining half-nude female figure, but the copy stressed the business motive: "This is the age of the Specialist. Be in business for yourself. Enjoy the Prestige Hours and Remuneration of Your Own Professional Office....Get Education That Will Bring You Dividends on Graduation."

"Accountants Rise to Presidencies" declared the headline over copy giving names and dates to document the case of a school of accounting as "the best possible schooling for managerial positions."

Appeals in a more personal vein included such statements as "The Independence School of Hairdressing Is Interested in You!" and "Be a Nancy Taylor Secretary." The latter offered "Executive Secretarial Training Including the Nationally Famous Nancy Taylor Charm Course."

The lure of the "finishing school look," training in modeling, fashions, dancing, public speaking, "charm," and the arts came close to matching the commercial attention devoted to business and technological training. About 40 percent of all schools offered courses in personality improvement and the social graces. Largest and most colorful of these were the Arthur Murray and Dale (or Dorothy) Carnegie type advertisements. One of the former, for example, was directed at teenagers. "We have consulted with well-known Teen celebrities," the headline declared, "who have told us exactly what you need and want to learn." Typical of the latter (placed by a "Dorothy Carnegie Course in Personal Development for Women") was copy advertising a course "that deals not with charm, but with living at your best...a course that gives women direction for a more fulfilled, purposeful life."

Some 16 percent of the schools advertising in the seven papers offered courses in the liberal arts, sciences, and humanities in an academic setting. One-third of these included evening and correspondence courses.

Boarding schools, including military academies, accounted for about half of the "academic" offerings. The majority of these advertised in the newspapers of the East Coast, although some of the schools were located as far as Florida and Arizona. Of the thirty-six boarding schools running display ads on one page of the *New York Times Magazine* (Sunday), only two were in New York City. Twelve were located in New York State; six in New Jersey; four in Massachusetts; three each in Maine, Connecticut, and Florida; and one each in Rhode Island, Vermont, and Arizona. The special appeal of some of the more distant locations was stressed in such copy as "healthful, warm, dry climate," "on Beautiful Biscayne Bay," "study this year in the land of the Sun," and "strategically located near Cape Canaveral."

While the geographical appeal was stressed in only 14 percent of the boarding school advertisements, the attraction of sports activities and facilities was emphasized in 61 percent. In second place (53%) was the appeal of small classes and personalized instruction. This was followed (in 27%) by the appeal of psychological services expressed in such statements as "Individual attention and wholesome emotional guidance" and "expert guidance staff. Psychiatrists and psychologists."

College preparatory functions were pointed out also in 27 percent of the advertisements, and training in "study skills" and "study habits" was stressed in 22 percent. Qualities of military education ("Men in the Making"; "Builders of Men") were noted in 14 percent. Denominational auspices or religious instruction ("Bible study required") were announced in 11 percent. The "traditional" nature of the curriculum was stressed in 8 percent.

Few schools stressed specific subject matter of a more academic nature. The most frequently mentioned subjects of instruction were languages (noted by 6% of the "academic" institutions advertising in the seven papers), reading development and instruction (noted by 4%), training for the ministry (3%), and teacher training (3%).

Private and public colleges and universities advertised services ranging from the announcement of a single course to the listing of an entire curriculum. At one end of the range were such ads as that of "The New School, America's first university for adults. Famous faculty, new buildings, spirit to match." At the other end was the full-page illustrated announcement of New York University's Division of General Education and Extension Service listing 104 course titles (including 40 course descriptions) and tuition.

This was a pilot study on a limited sample and we shall avoid the temptation of drawing cosmic conclusions. The purpose was to establish the fact that advertising material relating to educational products and services plays a significant part—perhaps equal to that of all news—in presenting to the American public information and "images" of educational relevance. Most of this material is devoted to instruction itself. Implicitly and explicitly, it calls attention to educational facilities, purposes, opportunities, goals, and values. The range of appeals extends from the transparently fraudulent to the highly respectable, although there might be some dispute about which is which. Along another dimension, the appeals range from promises of quick and easy success for the backward to the prospect of special attention, prestige, or comfort for the well-to-do.

While most educational advertising is both straightforward and informative, many of the messages cultivate the twilight zone of instructional services. Regardless of the value and legitimacy of the services themselves, however, the steady emphasis on extravagant or fringe-type appeals makes a dubious contribution to the cultivation of public perspectives on learning

CHAPTER 9

TEACHER IMAGE AND THE HIDDEN CURRICULUM

BY GEORGE GERBNER

"The figure of the schoolteacher," wrote Richard Hofstadter in *Anti-Intellectualism in American Life*, "may well be taken as a central symbol in any society." But a symbol of what? Searching for an answer is like opening Pandora's box with its host of evils. My examination of the evidence suggests that teachers, schools, and scholars project a synthetic cultural image that helps to explain—and determine—the ambivalent functions and paradoxical fortunes of the educational enterprise in American society. The clues that point to that disquieting conclusion (which also raises questions about anticipated extensions of the present structure of culture-power) have led me to new reflections. These concern the illusions and reality of schooling, the nature of symbolic functions, the lessons of national and cross-cultural research on the teacher image, and the role of that "hidden curriculum" in social policy.

The basic features of American schools, as of our society, have been fixed for more than a century. Spectacular changes transformed the quality of life by unfolding and extending those features into every aspect of existence. Among the most dramatic of the changes has been the rise of institutions of cultural mass production—the mass media—exempt from the laws of public, but not of private, corporate development and authority. These institutions have taken over many functions performed in the past by the parent, the church, and the school. The media's chief impact stems from their universality as the common bond among *all* groups in our culture. The media manufacture the shared symbolic environment, create and cultivate large heterogeneous publics, define the agenda of public discourse, and represent all other institutions in the vivid imagery of fact and fiction designed for mass publics. Teachers and schools no longer enjoy much autonomy, let alone their former monopoly, as the public dispensers of knowledge. The formal educational enterprise exists in a cultural climate largely dominated by the informal "curriculum" of the mass media.

Many of those who would correct the evils of society slowly and painlessly have long argued for educational extension, improvement, and reform. And, for more than a century, schooling has been extended, improved, and reformed. Yet it is still compulsory, unequal, class-biased, racist, and sexist. From the Coleman report on *Equality of Educational Opportunity* (1966) through the Jencks report on *Inequality* (1972), study after study demonstrates that the schools, even when "equal," tend to justify rather than rectify the child's fate as defined by the culture of the home, the street, and the television.

Eminent public figures declare schools a "disaster area" and "a pathological sector of the economy," meaning that even money can't cure what ails them (although that remedy has never really been tried on a large national scale). A few call for their abolition. Instead of becoming the social corrective that idealistic reformers sought and democratic rhetoric promised, the more schools change the more they streamline their induction of young people into their places and roles in the existing social structure. The Mason-Dixon line has been abolished between the states, but its modern equivalent now rings every city, and the few bridges busing children across it may be dismantled. Schools still provide custodial drill for the poor, enrichment for the rich, and equal instruction for those with equal economic or political clout.

We are just beginning to understand that these harsh facts do not result from accidental aberration or cultural lag. A new generation of "revisionist" historians of education has exploded "The Great School Legend." Colin Greer's book by that title shows how the perennial "crisis" of the schools, like the perpetual "problem" of the slums, is in fact more functional to the existing social order than would be its elimination. Michael B. Katz's book, *Class, Bureaucracy, and the Schools: The Illusion of Educational Change in America*, documents the recurring phenomenon of school reform movements that engage the zeal and energies of those who would attack the iniquities of society, only to find each wave of "reform" harnesses their schools to the dominant interests of the times.

Nearly twenty years after the Supreme Court ordered school desegregation "with all deliberate speed," feeble efforts at enforcement bog down in political controversy, just as, before that, the parochial school aid controversy was used to defeat proposals for massive federal financing. Busing is claimed to threaten the fiber of society when it brings children of different races and social classes together, but not when used to keep them apart—its traditional use. If "campus unrest" is followed by recession and cutbacks, who is to blame? The schools that should redeem us teeter at the edge of bankruptcy. It seems that when citizens consider what is nearest and dearest to them, like children, they are most vulnerable to the deceptions of their culture.

SYMBOLIC FUNCTIONS

We are keenly aware that messages intended to persuade usually serve the purposes of those who create and disseminate them. Less obvious, but perhaps even more crucial, are the purposes served by news, fiction, drama, and other storytelling, designed with no other obvious or conscious intent than just to inform or to entertain. The social tasks to which presumably "objective" news, "neutral" fiction, or "nontendentious" entertainment lend themselves are what I call symbolic functions. They are the consequences inherent in the way things work in the symbolic world of storytelling.

Symbolic functions differ from those of nonsymbolic events in the ways in which causal relationships must be traced in the two realms. Physical causation exists outside and independently of consciousness. Trees do not grow and chemicals do not react on purpose, although human purposes may intervene or cause them to function. When a sequence of physical events is set in motion, we have only partial awareness and little control over the entire chain of its consequences.

The symbolic world, however, is totally invented. Nothing happens in it independently of man's will, although much that happens may again escape individual awareness or scrutiny. The reasons that things exist in the symbolic world, and the ways in which things are related to one another and to their symbolic consequences, as in a play or story, are completely artificial. That does not make their production any more arbitrary or whimsical than the events of the physical world. But it means that the laws of the symbolic world are entirely socially and culturally determined. A character in fiction dies not because he has lived but because it serves a purpose to have him die. Intended or not, that purpose is the only reality of the story. The causal life is not between life and death but between a creator's or producing organization's position in life and society and the significance of that death. No TV bad man ever dies a natural death, nor can the hero of a western serial be cut down in the prime of life. To be true to life in fiction would falsify the deeper truth of cultural and social values served by symbolic functions.

Whatever exists in the symbolic world is there because someone put it there. The reason may be deliberate and planned, or circumstantial, such as an unrelated marketing or programming decision, or a vague feeling that it will improve the story. Having been put there, things not only stand for other things as all symbols do, but also do something in their symbolic context. The introduction (or elimination) of a character, a scene, an event, has functional consequences. It changes other things in the story. It makes the whole work "work" differently. Dynamic symbol systems are not maps of some other "real" territory. They are our mythology, our organs of social meaning. They make visible some conceptions of the invisible forces of life and society. We select and shape them to bend otherwise elusive facts to our (not always conscious) purposes. Whether we know it or intend it or not, purposes are inherent in the way things actually work out in the symbolic world. Even when men and institutions lie, they cannot do so without giving off signs of the purposes of their lying, at least in the long run; otherwise why lie? More problems arise from communicating hidden purposes than from failing to communicate at all.

How things work out in mass-produced symbolic systems, as in all collective myths, celebrations, and rituals, is indicative of institutional interests and pressures. In the creation of news, facts impose some constraints upon invention; the burden of serving institutional purposes is placed upon selection, treatment, context, and display. Fiction and drama carry no presumption of facticity and thus do not inhibit at all the candid expression of social values. On the contrary, they give free reign to adjusting facts to the truth of institutional purpose. Fiction can thus perform social symbolic functions more directly than can other forms of discourse.

That is why in fiction and drama there is no need to moralize. The moral is usually in the facts themselves. For example, if a social inferior (lower-class, "native," black, etc.) usurps the place of a superior (through marriage, business deal, combat, etc.), he or she can have an unfortunate accident, thus avoiding overt bias and yet performing the symbolic function of enhancing the superior life chances of "superior" characters. Fiction can act out purposes by presenting a world in which things seem to work out as they "ought to," regrettable or even terrible as that might be made to appear.

Characters come to life in the symbolic world of mass culture to perform functions of genuine social import. These functions need not be planned or perceived as such. They need not even conform to any overt rationalizations or moralizing. The functions are implicit not in what producers and audiences think they "know," but in what they assimilate of what the characters of the symbolic world in fact are and do.

THE HIDDEN CURRICULUM AND ITS EFFECTS

The facts of life in the symbolic world form patterns that I call the "hidden curriculum." It is the framework that makes the notion of "effects" sensible as those changes that can be observed within a stable structure. The prior preoccupation with "effects" is misleading, however. It only betrays greater concern with marketing tactics than with the basic allocation of values in our society. As humanists have always known, no society designs its religions, or its customs, or its schools on the basis of a comparative assessment of the effects of various factual or philosophical statements. That would put the cart of tactics before the horse of basic aims and functions. Any assessment of effects must assume the existence of a standard of measurement against which different or changing quantities and qualities can be measured. That standard is implicit in the value structure of a culture. Should that be immune from inquiry? The contention that the existence or meaning of an action or communication should not be assessed until its effects are established is tantamount to the assertion that the structure of a culture should not be investigated; only its tactics are to be subjected to scientific inquiry. Far from being scientific, this is itself a symbolic tactic attempting to define what is scientifically reasonable and respectable in a way that serves only the most dominant, pervasive, and taken-for-granted social interests.

The hidden curriculum is a lesson plan that no one teaches but everyone learns. It consists of the symbolic contours of the social order. One cannot sensibly ask what its effects are any more than one can ask about the effects of being born Chinese rather than American. Culture-power is the ability to define the rules of the game of life that most members of a society will take for granted. That some will reject and others will come to oppose some of the rules, or the game itself, is obvious and may on occasion be important. But the most important thing to know is the nature and structure of the representations that most people will assume to be normal and inevitable. Having established some features of the hidden curriculum, one can then ask how its specific lessons are internalized and which of its functions serve what purposes.

Every culture, as any school, will organize knowledge into patterns that cultivate a social order. The fundamental lessons of the curriculum are not just what pupils learn in math, history, or physics, et cetera, but also the fact that those are its commonly required subjects, and not basket weaving, harmony, or Marxism-Leninism (except where that is required). One cannot ask about the effects of that pattern of required learnings except by comparing it with the functional dynamics of other patterns. The structures themselves and most of their symbolic functions are inevitably assimilated if there is to be anything like a relatively stable social order. Culture is that system of messages that makes human society possible. After grasping the implicit agenda of discourse, scale of priorities, spectrum of valuations, and clusters of associations that most members of a culture come to assume as the overall framework for most of their thinking and behavior, we can begin to observe the fluctuations and reversals within that structure. Only after that can we ask the "effects" question.

The prior need is to examine the framework implicit in the hidden curriculum. We must first go beneath the explicit and fragmented significance of individual images available to casual personal scrutiny, and find the symbolic patterns and functions that entertain (in every sense of that word) the collective morality, and the dominant sensibilities of the social order.

The image of schools and scholars is that part of the hidden curriculum in which all members of society learn about learning itself. Its symbolic functions relate images of learning, and of the formal institutions of learning, to basic human values and to the locus of power in society. I think that the figure of the schoolteacher is a central symbol of the uses and control of popular knowledge. Its most telling features touch upon questions of vitality and self-direction, social relations, morality, and power.

HISTORICAL IMAGES

When he is not the Ichabod Crane of literature (scared out of town by the virile males of the community, with a pumpkin smashed over his head), the typical teacher in American novels is "stooped, gaunt, and gray with weariness. His suit has the shine of shabby gentility and hangs loose from his undernourished frame" (Arthur Foff, in "The Teacher as Hero," *Readings in Education*). That is, until class is out and memory rings the school bell when we say a tearful "Good Morning Miss Dove," or bid a nostalgic "Goodbye Mr. Chips."

In his study of the college professor in the novel, Michael Belok noted that American fiction uses teaching to "unisex a woman." Even being a teacher's wife may be unenviable. Theodore Dreiser characterized Donald Moranville Strunk, A.B., Ph.D., professor of history, as having had "one of the homeliest women for a wife I ever saw." College students responding to a 1960 survey by Donald O'Dowd and David Beardsley characterized the schoolteacher as a person "who cannot even command an attractive wife." Love eludes even the attractive, eager "Our Miss Brooks" and the owlish, but smart, "Mr. Peepers"; sex degrades the neurotic, fascist Miss Brodie and destroys Professor Rath of *The Blue Angel.*

For Americans, the prestigious title "professor" resounds with mock deference. *The Century Dictionary and Cyclopedia,* 1899, gave as one definition of a professor "...any one who publicly teaches or exercises an art or occupation for pay, as dancing-master, phrenologist, balloonist, juggler, acrobat, boxer, etc." From there it was not too far to the piano player in a brothel, or as Henry L. Mencken euphemistically recorded in *The American Language,* "a house musician." In time the usage mellowed to permit any prominent orchestra leader to be called "professor," as those who remember Kay Kyser will recall. Recent media fare is replete with such phenomena as the movie *The Nutty Professor,* TV's "Professor Backward," the cartoon "Professor Wimple's Crossword Zoo," and Pat Paulsen's "Laugh-In" professor.

Belok could find only about two hundred novels since 1900 in which college professors appeared as characters. Major American novelists, wrote John Lyons, in *The College Novel in America,* either have avoided the academy or have written novels that are basically anti-intellectual. An English review of the American scene observed, however, that the college novel is not a "cottage industry." "And so it seems," commented Charles Shapiro, noting the entry of writers into the universities, "as book after book assaults us with tales of assorted hypocrisies committed under the name of higher education" (*Saturday Review,* October 19, 1963).

Hofstadter has also observed that the American teacher has not become an important national figure, worthy of emulation. Historical reasons may partly account for the fact that the scholar, as Dixon Wecter also noted in his *The Hero in America,* "has never kindled the American imagination."

Until the industrial and national revolutions that changed the map of Europe, teachers were likely to be recruited from among the misfits of society. When the common schools were established in Russia, the theological seminaries dumped their "undesirables" to be the teachers. In the Prussia of Frederick the Great, it was the army that disposed of its invalids by appointing them schoolmasters.

> The low opinion of the rank-and-file schoolmaster in Europe spread to the New World, and a seventeenth-century Rector of Annapolis recorded that on the arrival of every ship containing bondservants or convicts, schoolmasters were offered for sale but that they did not fetch as good prices as weavers, tailors, and other tradesman. (Alma S. Wittlin)

The national revolutions of Europe had a popular cultural character. Many of the leaders were writers and poets rising through the ranks of the intellectuals closet to the people, the teachers. W.G. Cove, the British teacher, strike leader, union president, and member of Parliament, once wrote that "At the head of every continental revolutionary movement, or near the head of it, stands an ex-teacher."

Until perhaps the emergence of the black liberation movement which, for reasons peculiar to American culture, seemed to propel clergyman rather than teachers into leadership, there has been no comparable historical force to add a heroic dimension to the traditional image of the American teacher. The forced pace of industrialization in the nineteenth century and the consequent pressure for extending public education created the monitorial schools, according to Wittlin, "to fit the early state of industrial civilization."

> Pupils were cheaply mass produced, down to $1 per year. The scholars, who first learned their lessons from the teacher, conveyed exactly the same lesson to other children, ten to a monitor....In 1916 a book appeared in Boston on *Public School Administration*, by E.P. Cubberley, in which it was stated that "...the schools are, in a sense, factories in which the raw materials are to be shaped into products to meet the various demands of life." According to this philosophy the educator was allotted the modest role of the copyist of patterns.

During the next fifty years, the cultural forces that shape the common images of society became largely mechanized, centralized, and commercialized. Teacher power emerged as an organized force, and education became a political battleground. But the social function of the teacher image in the new culture remained the traditional one: to cultivate mistrust of the intellect on the loose.

TEACHER AND SCHOOL IN UNITED STATES MEDIA

There are 2.5 million teachers in the public schools in the United States. They range from 22 to over 65 years of age, and come from all states, classes, religions and ethnic groups. Of course, they have some characteristics as a group: they average 39 years of age, 12 years of professional experience, and about $9,000 a year. Two out of every three are women. Teaching is the largest profession; its members run the gamut of human types.

But not in popular fiction and drama. The raw facts of life are not the truth of social and institutional purpose. Frequency of symbolic representation is not the reflection of census figures. The casting of the symbolic world has a message of its own.

Studies of occupational representation among mass media characters, celebrities, and even movie titles, agree that teachers, the largest profession in life, rank among the smallest in the media world. About 2 to 3 percent of all identifiable professional references or characterizations go to media teachers. Classifying occupational roles for the *American Sociological Review*, Lois and Melvin DeFleur found the same number of educators as taxi, truck, and bus drivers in the televised labor force.

Most of the literary studies delineate a teacher image created for elite audiences. Except when mellowed by misty memories of childhood, it is generally cruel and unsympathetic, as if in revenge for the intellectual and social pretensions of the hired hand. Much of that image found its way into the mass media, somewhat relieved by the populist fantasy of the good, if not too enviable, teacher.

Studies of media images were conducted by a group of researchers at the University of Illinois; the work is continuing at the University of Pennsylvania. For a number of years, our focus was the portrayal of teachers, students, and schools in the mass media. Some studies dealt with one medium, like Jack Schwartz's study of Hollywood movies and Roger Brown's study of magazine fiction; others ranged more widely. The United States Office of Education supported my analysis of over fourteen hundred feature films, television and radio plays, and popular magazine stories featuring twenty-eight hundred leading characters in the mass media of ten countries. The National Science Foundation, UNESCO, and the International Sociological Association jointly sponsored a study that I did of the film hero involving one year's feature film production in six countries. I will draw on the reports of these and other studies to piece together some basis for reflecting upon the symbolic functions and social role of the image of the teacher in mass culture.

Schwartz's study of Hollywood movies found that the presence of a teacher tips the odds three to one in favor of the movie being a comedy. Mass media teachers, creatures of private industry depicting public agents, suffer from signs of a cultural power conflict in which the media have the upper hand. The study's comprehensive review of research concludes:

> Teachers in books, drama, magazine cartoons, and films were depicted as tyrannical, brutal, pedantic, dull, awkward, queer, and depressed. The few attractive teachers remained in the profession only long enough to find a mate. Teachers had a difficult time getting and staying married. One investigator noted that two-thirds of the teachers were portrayed as emotionally maladjusted. Another writer noted that "to succeed as a teacher one must fail as a man or woman."

LOVE AND THE TEACHER

Love and sex are dramatic symbols of vitality and power. How a profession fares in love in the mass media is a good measure of its symbolic stature.

The mass media teacher pays a price for professional success. The price is impotence, and worse. The "schoolmarm" image hits women especially hard. Love and marriage are women's chief media specialties and typical reasons for existing in the stories at all.

Female characters in the world of mass fiction and drama are limited to a narrow range of parts; that is why media males not only dominate media females (except in the home, where males prefer to be incompetent), but also vastly outnumber them. The average ratio is four men for every woman, but the proportion varies by theme. Love, marriage, and bringing up children are themes that utilize women characters in parts that do not require special explanation.

Studies of school-related stories in all media found both women teachers and love playing prominent parts—but rarely together. Almost half of all media teachers are women; this is a high female ratio for the media, but still lower than the two-thirds of all real-life teachers who are women. The school stories are more likely to feature romance than are stories in general. But the romance rarely involves the teacher, and least of all the woman teacher. Typical is Miss Dove, who is so devoted, so self-less, so excruciatingly good, that she passes up her opportunity to marry in order to pay back the $11,430 her dead father had "borrowed" from the bank where he worked.

Nearly half of all media adults, but only 26 percent of male teachers and no more than 18 percent of female teachers, are married. Despite all the romance and happy endings in the stories, teachers rarely inspire love or fall in love, especially with each other. The most common condition of love is that the teacher find a partner outside education. The typical pattern has her quitting a New England high school and a biology teacher fiancé to "find herself" and a man in New York. Or it has him leaving a dull musical chair at a western college, along with a straitlaced professor girl friend, to be taught something about music and love in Tin Pan Alley.

Failure in love and defeat in life permit most media teachers to be fully dedicated to the profession. The media teacher leaving for another specific occupation knows the road to success in the media world. Five times out of six the road leads to show business.

POVERTY OF THE SCHOOLS

In the film study, 25 of the 470 movies portraying some aspect of education were found to show the financial plight of the schools. The deficiencies are usually in extracurricular activities such as entertainment and sports. There is never a need for more teachers or laboratories or classrooms. Profits from sports events, successful musical shows, and unexpected bequests of the rich are the usual solutions to academic poverty. Only two films show schools to be public responsibilities, publicly financed. One deals with support for West Point, and the other depicts the building of a school in a remote New Zealand village.

Only one film shows the financial problem as one of low salaries for teachers. A wealthy Texas rancher is shocked to find his son trying to raise a family on the meager salary of an instructor. He secretly negotiates with a local butcher to sell his son meat at half price. He also tries to prevent his son's promotion, confident that he will return to the ranch. When he does not, the father solves the problem by donating enough money to the school to provide a pay increase for all teachers.

An analysis of teacher characters in *Saturday Evening Post* fiction found them in more frequent financial pickles. This was usually explained by showing that they strive less than the other characters. About one-third of the magazine's teachers solve their financial problems by quitting the profession. No teacher is ever given a salary raise. No student is supported on a public scholarship. No community takes the initiative to raise taxes or to build or improve the schools. When there is a suggestion of improvement in the poverty of the schools it is likely to be a private solution, such as finding a rich donor or holding a fantastically successful show or sports event.

THE SCHOOL SPORTS STORY

Alan Booth, in "Sex and Social Participation," describes school sports as an arena of "early male socialization." Extensive friendship ties are linked to participation in games. The winning team is also a symbol of an institution's ability to attract talent and display power. Winning scores have been found to relate to legislative appropriations and certainly to alumni giving. An article in the *Philadelphia Magazine* (May 1972) quotes the head of the alumni society as saying that "The alumnus in Oregon or Texas is going to read about Penn's basketball team in his home town paper, not some professor's dingy old ruins in England."

There is no doubt that the most frequent appearance of schools and colleges in the American press is on the sports page. The magic words of American higher education are Ivy League and Big Ten. *Saturday Evening Post* readers loved the stories of George Fitch. The first of these, published in 1906, began:

> Yes, sir, it's been seven years now since old Siwash College has been beaten in football....We've shut out Hopkinsville seven times—pushed them off the field, off the earth, into the hospitals and into the discard. We've beaten six State universities by an average of seven touchdowns, two goal kicks, a rib, three jawbones and four new kinds of yells. We put such a crimp into old Muggledorfer that her Faculty suddenly decided that football developed the toes and teeth at the expense of the intellect and they took up intercollegiate bean-bags instead. And in all those seven years we've never really been scared but once.

The school sports story, with its violent terminology, strong group spirit, and concern over the rules of the game, is the most likely vehicle for community enthusiasm, teamwork, and the mixing of different classes and races in a common cause. It generally demonstrates the ethics of skill and power among those who achieve equal status. (This can be contrasted with the symbolic functions of the crime or spy story displaying the game of power among those of unequal status or those who do not play by the same rules.)

The film study shows sports to be the central theme in twice as many movies as deal with study, science, or research, and to depict virtues never seen in a portrayal of scholarly activity. The school sports story serves its symbolic functions in three ways: (1) as the means by which youths from different walks of life find acceptance in the group; (2) as the chief symbolic unifier of students, faculty, parents, and alumni; and (3) as teaching the importance of passing a realistic test of social and ethical "maturity."

The largest single group, nearly one-third of all films of school sports, concentrates on the third, the socio-ethical lesson. They warn that romantic illusions lead to cynicism and despair. They council realism and vigilance lest alien ideologies take advantage of and subvert "our" flexible rules for "their" purposes. "The most common presentation of sports," reported Schwartz, "was that it was a much less glamorous and honest activity than student-players were at first led to believe."

> For the sake of victory, schools were shown to sacrifice their honor by depending upon extra-collegiate sources for both personnel and financial support. This dependence upon outside sources was not portrayed as unethical in all films dealing with sports—in fact, several films portrayed this dependence in a vein of lighthearted comedy which, if not condoning the practice, did not take the unethical aspects of the situation seriously. However, in the films to seriously treat the unethical practices of the sport and their demoralizing consequences for students, the portrayal of school sports was likened to a rites de passage. Sports were shown as analogous to the battleground upon which a young initiate experienced teamwork and struggle, despair and disillusionment, victory and defeat.

The typical school sports story is a morality play that shows a sort of pragmatic "democracy in action." The rules will bend within reason, and anyone can play, as long as the game is just a game and the prime source of power is clearly understood. Abuse the rules and the tone changes. In a group of films, gangsters try to manipulate players and even faculty to reap large gambling profits. In another, radicals "disguised as students" (described in a contemporary *New York Times* review as "namby-pamby, bushy haired, and wearing tortoise-shell glasses") plan to overthrow capitalism, beginning with the college football team. The local hero falls briefly under their spell, but recovers in time to win the game of the year and the respect of normal healthy Americans.

COMMUNITY AND POWER

When they cannot relate to "the game," in which students play the lead, teachers usually do not "belong" at all. Typically presented as alien to the community in which they live and work, and often in conflict with its values, teachers may be seen as well meaning and kindly if impotent, or dangerous and evil if powerful, but rarely both good and effective.

Studies by Claude C. Bowman, Richard C. Boys, and Roland A. Springer trace community conflict and antagonism through fifty years of magazine publishing, general fiction, and Broadway drama. Brown's study of *Saturday Evening Post* fiction found that teachers "act differently" even when trying to conform. The film research concluded that all but six of the twenty-eight films touching upon relations between school and community portray a teacher as the target of hostility, ridicule, or ostracism. Schwartz found that the offending teachers are usually shown as "outsiders...with their own set of values often aiding in isolating them from the community."

Nonconformist media teachers usually come to see the error of their ways. One movie depicts a socialistically inclined economics professor striking it rich. He changes his mind about radical causes and returns to his job a millionaire.

Most instances of unreconciled conflict between teachers and community involve the cardinal sins of trying to change society rather than the schools (usually labeled "communism") or of finding a source of wisdom outside the approved community context (usually represented as "atheism"). Sex often appears as a malignant obsession when sought by such unlikely characters as teachers. A cynically explicit portrayal in a 1937 movie shows a southern mob lynching a "yankee" teacher convicted of assaulting an attractive student. The district attorney does not believe the teacher guilty, but prosecutes vigorously because of the political value of the case for his own career.

In casting about for occupations to delineate hero types who are both right and mighty, mass media authors rarely pick teaching. Dallas Smythe's analysis of television drama found teachers outstanding among all TV occupations in being the "cleanest" and the "kindest." But they were also rated the "weakest," the "softest," and the "slowest."

The more potent teacher risks turning into that symbol of evil intellect—the mass media scientist. On television, the scientist was rated as the most "deceitful," "cruel," and "unfair" of all professional types.

Personality ratings used to assess students' images of real-life teachers tapped mass-cultural stereotypes. O'Dowd and Beardsley found that the student image of the schoolteacher is that of an unselfish, uninteresting, unsuccessful, and effeminate person. The scientist, on the other hand, presents the image of the cool, cruel, hard-driving intellectual and often a loner who cannot be trusted.

Similarly, Joseph Gusfield and Michael Schwartz concluded in their 1963 article for the *American Sociological Review* that the teacher image presents "the sharpest contrast between elements of esteem and status, on the one hand, and those of power and income on the other." The teacher ranks as the most "honest" and second most "useful" of fifteen occupations, and also the "weakest" and "lightest." The scientist again appears to be cool, tough, and antisocial as well as "irreligious" and "foreign."

PUBLISH AND PERISH

It is not surprising that the dramatic uses of scholarship and research contrast sharply with those portraying sports and other entertainment. Academic research leads to murder in nearly half of the twenty-five films found to portray teachers conducting it. Film teachers invent poisons, revive prehistoric monsters, or train other creatures to do away with suspected enemies. One famous movie of the 1950s shows a psychology professor hypnotizing gorillas to murder the girls who reject his advances. The typical plot has some obsession drive the demented intellect to invent an instrument that gets out of control and destroys its maker, to the relief of all mankind.

In a group of nine films dealing with research, the experimenting teacher or professor falls victim to his own delusions and exposes the stupidity or hypocrisy of scholarship. Typical is the movie in which the professor of Egyptology incorrectly deciphers an ancient tablet and the false message sends him on a series of comic adventures.

Research and experimentation fare better in the hands of amateurs. Student scholarship is usually foolish but never evil or selfish. Incidentally, classroom scenes hardly ever exhibit learning or scholarship. They are used to display problems of authority and discipline.

The teacher struggling for discipline in the school is often brutal and sadistic. In films of more recent vintage, students (as if representing the avenging forces of society) strike back in kind. The "class struggle" is one in which the teacher rarely comes out on top.

IMAGES ACROSS CULTURES

Through a series of cross-cultural comparative studies we have tried to understand our own images better by comparing them with those of others. Four countries of Western Europe and five countries of Eastern Europe (including the Soviet Union) provided our comparisons. A plot sketch from each country's sample will give something of the flavor of the material:

> "Red Castle" is what townspeople call the new headquarters of the Teachers' Recreation Center. It was a baron's palace before the revolution. A priceless collection of jewels is still stored in the Castle. One day a precious stone is missing. The shadow of suspicion falls on Professor Zach, a frequent visitor at "Red Castle." But the clever deductions of his students (turned amateur detectives) vindicate the Professor, and the real culprits are caught. (Czechoslovakia)
>
> Word gets around that the attractive new teacher is carrying on with the well-known high school jock. And in the locker room, too. She is nearly ruined before it develops that the student, himself the victim of a psychopathic, scandal-mongering father, only tried to rape her in an unguarded moment. (United States)
>
> The tactlessness of a dry and dogmatic school director drives one of the students of the elementary school of Borsk into the clutches of a religious sect. The teachers' collective is dismayed. A timid young instructor is drawn into the struggle against the sect. Emboldened through her efforts to demonstrate that religious dogmatism defeats the goals of free education, she realizes the great role of the teacher in public life. (Russia)
>
> The humane methods of the new teacher in an East End slum school lead to disaster. "Spare the rod..." gloat the hardened old disciplinarians. The teacher is about to give up and leave when a glimmer of student response at the end of the term gives him second thoughts. (England)
>
> The impoverished peasants of a village refuse to work for starvation wages on the Count's estate. But the gendarmes have a firm grip on this treasonous activity. The peasants are ordered to the railroad station to welcome the arriving Count. They come. But they come to pay respects to the departing teacher who is being run out of town as the chief troublemaker. (Hungary)
>
> A utopian idealist teaching in a lycée becomes so involved in his pacifist schemes that he neglects his family. Reality finally deals him a tragic but sobering blow: his daughter has a lover, has taken part in a robbery, and is about to run away. (France)
>
> Orphaned, hungry and demoralized, a gang of boys terrorizes the countryside at the end of the war. A former partisan leader, now teacher, turns them into useful citizens. (Poland)

TEACHER GOALS AND FATES

We found that the Russian and other socialist media teachers are depicted as more "learned," "democratic," and "manly" than those of the West. Eastern mass media stories of schools and teachers stress the ideals of service to community and nation more than three times as frequently as U.S. and other Western media.

U.S. media portray a higher proportion of women teachers on all levels of education than do the media of other countries. Our media also depict a composite image of the teacher as less professional and less likely either to advance or to slip on the social ladder than the media teacher of other countries. The U.S. media teacher is more easily frustrated and victimized by the much higher level of violence and illegality prevalent in her world than is the media teacher of the other countries.

Teachers are quitting the profession in about 28 percent of U.S. and Western and 14 percent of Eastern media stories. The main reasons for giving up teaching in Western media are the frustrations and conflicts of the job, and marriage. Eastern media teachers leaving the field of education are most likely to be fired, retired at the end of their service, or advanced to positions of higher leadership.

Teachers stand out everywhere in seeking intellectual values more often than do the other adult characters in the same fictional environment. But Eastern European media characters, and especially teachers, are different from those of other countries in their much more frequent pursuit of goals of social morality (justice, honor, public service, a better world).

We analyzed the barriers that stand in the way of achievement and found that the one major difference between the problems of U.S. media teachers and those of the other countries lies in the teachers themselves. Only in U.S. media are teachers more likely than other adults to be depicted as handicapped by their own weaknesses and fears.

The fears maybe justified. Over one-third of all U.S. media teachers commit violence and nearly half fall victim to it. This is low by U.S. media standards, but it is roughly twice the mayhem found in Western media and about six times that found in the media world of education in Eastern Europe.

A happy ending is symbolic insistence that justice triumphs despite all troubles. American media stories are the most insistent. Conditions of success, however, are more indicative of its functions than frequency alone. We compared the goals of unambiguously successful characters with those who clearly fail.

Only in American media are successful teachers depicted as less likely to pursue aims of social morality than are teachers marked for failure. Many U.S. media teachers who do tackle social goals are naive, comic, and even mad, and most are crushed by some misfortune fictional fate throws in their paths.

THE ROLE OF STUDENTS

Being a student is a long and varied stage in life. The range of opportunities for portrayal is great. The institutional and social forces that shape the representation of teachers in the mass media also affect the depiction of students. But the potential diversity of the student image leads to extraordinary differences in scope and function.

American mass media are unique in not earmarking significant resources to young people. They treat children as a low-income, high-profit, quick-turnover market where the message of social power (police, violence) can be sold in its cheapest and crudest forms. As if to underline the analogy to the slum, the trade journals call the children's program segment on television the "kidvid ghetto."

Market considerations also account for the fact that children and youth (as well as old people) in leading roles make the product a "specialty story." They presumably fragment audience appeal and need special exploitation. American youths become universally employable for dramatic purposes (as in life) when they leave school.

An international study of the "film hero" which I wrote for *Journalism Monographs* classified students as an occupational group. Entertainers head the list of occupations, with 18 percent of all leading characters. Students are next to the last with 4 percent. (The last were laborers.) The Western European pattern is similar, although students are more numerous than in U.S. films.

The films of Eastern Europe offer striking contrast. Students are in first place on the same list of occupations, with percentages ranging from 20 percent in Poland to 24 percent in Yugoslavia, and 28 percent of all leading characters in Czechoslovakia.

The diversity of the portrayals permits few generalizations. Focus on childhood and adolescence in American media requires specialized story values. They are often found outside the regular social context. Several stories are about mentally ill, retarded, and physically handicapped youngetsrs. One revolves around a little boy "playing Cupid." Another deals with a sadistic teenage gang leader. A sociology student's research requires her to pose as a prostitute. Youngsters complicate life for attractive widowed fathers or mothers. A hard-boiled manager of a gambling house finds himself the guardian of a six-year-old orphan. A good-hearted mute befriends a homeless prostitute and her little daughter. Six homeless waifs camp out in an unused shack on the Connecticut estate where a glamorous but exhausted star seeks peace and quiet.

Students in the media of Eastern Europe are not only more numerous but also move in the thematic and moral mainstream of their symbolic world. This is a world in which a mountain youth pressed into hard labor by the lord of the manor joins the outlaws to fight injustice—as his father had done before him. A crippled and lonely student finds amusement in shooting birds from his wheelchair, until he downs a homing pigeon awaited by a little girl and her fishermen friends, and begins the slow, painful road to recovery for both the pigeon and himself. Three boys on a school outing steal away into the woods and come upon a partisan hideout; their teacher demands and explanation for their absence, but he is the local commander of the native fascist militia! A theft of puppets from the school theater sends a group of youngsters on a wild chase involving an unpopular boy who plays detective, unaware that his schoolmates suspect him of the crime. A schoolgirl's vacation love affair, her first, sets her on a course of competition and conflict with her attractive aunt. A school boy longing for a bicycle stumbles upon lost money—and discovers the difficulty of making a moral choice. A group of classmates decide to expose the hypocrisy and stealing going on at their collective farm—but what to do when they find some of their own parents among the culprits? A student poses as a German sympathizer in order to obtain information for the Resistance; the antifascist patriots are out to kill him, but his mission demands that he maintain silence. A young pupil is falsely accused of having stolen his classmate's pencil, and confesses to escape the ridicule of his accusers—only to make matters worse.

In these stories, school is often the center of social and moral struggle. Behind the authority of the teacher stands the power of the state. Analysts rated the media schools of Eastern Europe as "related to real life," and learning as "of immediate benefit" about twice as frequently as in the media schools of the West. Eastern European media students are shown as "interested in knowledge," as "leaders and organizers," and as "participating in community affairs" from two to three times as often as those of the West. Eastern European media students are depicted as taking examinations three times as frequently as U.S. media students, but the latter were observed "dominating classroom activity" four times as frequently as the former.

KNOWLEDGE AND ITS CONTROL

An episode of the television serial "Wild Wild West" features a geology professor who, imbued with noble if (naturally) impractical ideas, goes West in the employ of a rich prospector in order to alleviate his own genteel poverty. But the prospector lets him down. Feeling betrayed (with some justification), he becomes obsessed with thoughts of revenge. His knowledge, now out of control of an employer, becomes a menace to society. He plots to destroy the state through a series of earthquakes triggered by dynamite blasts at critical points in the fault line he mapped through the area. "I have turned the tide," he cries, "employed nature for my own use—now I want my reward." Brawny agent West and his brainy sidekick make sure that he gets it. We last see him scrawling equations on a chalkboard as he holds "class" alone in his jail cell.

All societies suspect what they need but cannot fully control. Symbolizing such uneasy symbiotic relationships are ambivalent images of oracles, eccentrics, witches, alchemists, and others "possessed' of independent knowledge, as well as teachers. The teacher image is likely also to fall short of the mandarin ideal or to suffer from the human tendency to denigrate "outgrown" authority.

Beyond such similarities, however, differences in mass-mediated symbolic functions reveal and cultivate significant social distinctions. As we go from West to East, teachers stand out in their own fictional environments as more distinguished in learning and in qualities of personal and social morality. The terms of this morality are not necessarily comparable across cultures. The ethic of individualistic liberalism is not the same as that of socialist morality of the Soviet concept of "the moral development of the child," even if some of the same terms are used. Nevertheless, the image of the teacher in the socialist media reflects a happier fate and more stable, purposeful, and socially meaningful existence in its own fictional world than it does in the West.

Differences in social organization account for some of these distinctions. Mass media are cultural organs of industrial society. Their ownership, management, and clientele—extending the institutional order into the cultural sphere—shape their outlook and functions. The organizational and client relationships of Eastern European media interlock with other public institutions, including the schools, the party, and the state itself. The hidden curriculum serves the same institutional interest as the overt one; both are agencies of planned social transformation. This places media images of schools, scholars, and the knowledge they symbolize in the mainstream of the symbolic world undergoing a cultural revolution. In performing their symbolic functions, socialist media can take advantage of their legacy of intellectual leadership in nationalist and proletarian movements in which teachers have had a prominent place for centuries.

Organizational and client relationships of American media also reward development of a particular selection from prevalent cultural patterns. The selection manifests the dual character of private enterprise views on public enterprise. On the one hand, schools are a necessary cost factor whose value is limited to its direct usefulness to the investment in current products, practices, and outlooks. On the other hand, schools represent political capital and popular aspirations for mobility, equality, and social reform. The concept of knowledge and its role in and control by society are caught in the crossfire. The most enduring and pervasive images of teachers in American mass culture are those that humiliate and depress them. Failure in love and impotence in life permit them to be "good." Or they can be vigorous but evil, or perhaps only ridiculous.

Poverty is normal and probably desirable for a dependent institution that should not develop a strong power base of its own. When we cut loose from corporate, military, law-enforcement, or other established power, even the miracles of science turn into "mad scientist" horrors.

No school or culture educates children for some other society. Giving teachers a messianic mission and having schools soak up all the dreams and aspirations citizens have for their children doom the enterprise to failure. No social order can afford to make good such a promise. The illusion itself contains the seeds of the noble-but-impractical image. It becomes only reasonable and realistic to show teachers full of goodness, but sapped of vitality and power. Turn on the power and the impotent figure becomes a monster, only confirming the doubts and suspicions inherent in the ambivalent image.

Unlike the army and the police, the schools do not appear to be a major public responsibility at all. They are shown as places of controversy and conflict, except when the goal is winning for "the team." The school sports story provides a dramatic framework for learning the rules of order and life in a community dedicated to skills directly applicable to competitive power.

American media scholars symbolize the promise of learning on behalf of noble and idealistic goals, and undercut that promise by being strange, weak, and foolish, and generally unworthy of the support of the community. The "hidden curriculum" cultivates the illusion of social reform through education and, at the same time, helps pave the way for the perennial collapse of its achievement. As things work out in the symbolic realm, the bankruptcy of the schools is their own fault. The invidious distinction between teaching and doing is maintained. The promise of a productive society to place the cultivation of a distinctly human self-consciousness highest on its scale of priorities is again betrayed.

American media are cultural arms of private enterprise in the public sphere. The images they project have a dual character. They attempt to be serviceable (or at least not inimical) to the commercial and other interests of private enterprise and, at the same time, represent those public ideals that give them universal attraction, currency, and credibility. That is why the study of capitalist mass media and their symbolic functions presents a particularly complex and challenging task. The task is to discover the actual laws of symbolic behavior in a field of conflicting institutional interests, and to assess their real contributions to the cultivation of human conceptions and social policy.

I doubt that the nature of education, the role of knowledge, and the prospect for real changes in school policy can be fully grasped until that assessment is well under way. New developments in communication technology have the potential of altering social patterns of knowledge, as did the old developments. The question is whether they will merely extend even further the scope and reach of the existing structures, or begin to change them. That, of course, is not a technological but an institutional question. Institutions use technology in communications and culture for their own purposes. The image of the schoolteacher in the hidden curriculum of the mass media may continue to be a useful indicator of those purposes.

Part III

MOVING TOWARD CULTURAL INDICATORS

Early Studies of Media Institutions and Content

Chapter 10

THE SOCIAL ANATOMY OF THE ROMANCE-CONFESSION COVER GIRL

BY GEORGE GERBNER

All mass media are market oriented, but popular magazines must also be *supermarket* oriented. Depending for the bulk of their circulation on single-copy sales through food, drug, and variety chains, they have a special task of salesmanship via magazine cover.

How do they tackle this task? How are editorial and distribution requirements reflected in the design and content of magazine covers? And how, in the light of these requirements, are the covers perceived? These questions furnished a starting point for a study of confession magazine covers, selected because of the curious way in which they express both the social appeal of the magazine and the pressures of supermarket distribution.

The market position of the confession industry shapes its content through an editorial prescription designed for working-class women with presumably middle-class pocketbooks, anxieties, and "behavior problems."[1] The social appeal of the confession pivots on the sympathetic heroine's human frailties in an inhospitable world she cannot fully understand. The heroine's "sinful" resistance, or desperate drift down the line of least resistance, brings further calamity, suffering, and the final coming to terms, but not to grips, with the punitive code of her world. Her inevitable "crime" becomes irrelevant as an act of social protest. She is rarely permitted to become conscious of the social origin of her personal troubles. This ingredient of unrelatedness appears to provide the editorial antidote to the risk of strong social medicine involved in evoking sympathy for victims of the brutal society of the confessions.

Figure 1. Four of the Twelve Covers
Used in the Experiment

The unique feature of the confession cover is the striking contrast between the "confession type" cover girl and the surrounding verbal context. She appears unrelated to the story titles and blurbs of her menacing verbal world. It is as if the editorial safety valve of social unrelatedness would find its outward manifestation in the structure of the confession cover. The mechanics of distribution also favor the development of such a cover design, and of a cover girl who has the specific function (as does the heroine) of being a reader-identification image.

The formal aspects of the romance-confession cover design have been surveyed through observation over a period of time and a study of all confession magazine covers on sale in the Champaign, Illinois, area in January 1957. These findings were amplified by soliciting policy statements regarding cover design from confession magazine art editors.[2]

There were twelve different titles on sale at the time, published by nine firms, and distributed by two wholesale news agencies.[3] Close-up pictures of eight blondes and four brunettes dominated the uniformly structured covers. (See Figure 1.) The eleven cover girls (two magazines happened to use the same model) displayed appealing features, flashing smiles, cosmetic perfection, and eye-contact with the viewer. There was nothing more "sexy" or revealing than one bare shoulder among them.

The verbal context surrounding the image of the radiantly poised, wholesome cover girl was anything but trouble-free. The story titles and blurbs spoke of women "attacked," "frightened and shamed," confessing "The Most Shameful Night of My Life," exclaiming "Oh, God, Don't Let Me Hurt Him," admitting that "We Didn't Know Our Love Was Abnormal," and so on.

About one out of every three cover titles dealt with sexual problems varying from apparent nymphomania to frigidity, and from taboos to sex-tests and tips. Another third reflected mainly marital and parental troubles such as adultery, bigamy, illegitimacy, miscegenation, etc. The remaining third focused on other forms of anguish, shame, terror, illness, and crime.

This is the dark and turbulent verbal world into which confession publishers insert, as a matter of policy, the dominant, concrete and colorful personification of clean-cut all-American girlhood. "There is virtually no relationship between the pictorial element and titles featured" on the cover, explains the art editor of one confession magazine. "The blurbs or cover titles have no relationship to the subject," writes another. Actually, they reason, each unit serves its own purpose, and combined they attempt to satisfy the multiple functions and requirements of the magazine.

THE MECHANICS OF DISTRIBUTION

In the women's field, the service and fan magazines have enough of a claim on a share of the romance-confession reader market to make competition a factor in cover design. Some outward manifestation of glamour and respectability helps the confession match its rivals' bright atmosphere of supermarket cheer.

The economics of magazine display space, and the rivalry among titles impose further requirements. Chain stores average about sixty magazine titles; but roughly 80 percent of the dollar volume comes from the top twenty magazines. Their total yearly sales from all general magazines put together just about equals that of chewing gums; but the magazines take up more space.[4]

Claims that confession readers spend more on some staples than do others are designed to attract advertisers;[5] they seem to have little effect on retail store managers who consider the magazine display space more a customer convenience than a major profit-maker. Although many of the racks are owned and serviced by the wholesale distributor, the floor manager often rules the display. His judgment, sometimes guided by customer comment, may result in preferential treatment for the magazines whose outward appearances conform to the widest variety of clientele sensibilities. Offenders, especially in the women's field, may suffer by being among those hidden from sight—and sale—behind their rivals on the crowded rack.[6]

There are other reasons, too, why the romance-confession magazine can ill afford to externalize its combustible editorial mixture. It is the only fiction group with both feminine *and* working-class readership. Under the soothing but transparent cloak of euphemistic names containing such words of presumably feminine appeal as "secrets," "love," "experience," the strong stuff of working-day life in its torrid aspects is the meat of the "romance-confession" diet. Its editorial formula hits closest to home, both literally and socially. Vivid cover pictures of its embattled and embittered heroine in action (as she *is* portrayed inside the magazine) would dramatize the editorial ingredient of incipient revolt—and by the supposedly more docile of the sexes—against the fabric of restraint of pseudo-middle class life.

So, all cannot be sweetness and light—not in the confessions. Their unique editorial appeal must find its way to the cover without inviting censorship. "Regulations enforced by chain store managements result in penalties to a publisher from banning one issue to losing forever the racks of that chain," writes an art editor. "Local censorship and religious black lists are also important in establishing [cover] format."

The compromise formula adopted by the confession relegates the explosive social appeal to the relatively abstract verbal form. Counterpointing this is the dominant pictorial image of the cover girl, conducive to identification and merchandising euphoria, and seemingly unrelated to the surrounding verbal context.

The confession cover may thus be seen as an objective record of the circumstances of its creation. Underlying the stimulus—whether so intended and recognized or not—is the social history of market-produced editorial functions and distribution requirements. But how does the cover girl actually perform her task of confession magazine salesmanship? How is the apparent contrast between the cover girl and her verbal setting resolved in perception? What *is* her image in the eyes of the viewer? How does her juxtaposition with the contrasting verbal context affect her assumed personality, status, functions?

The experiment discussed below attempted to provide some answers to these questions.

THE COVER GIRL EXPERIMENT

The experiment focused on the romance-confession cover girl, and on the influence of her position in the verbal context. Subject responses were elicited to the twelve covers described previously. There was no attempt to select confession readers as respondents. It was felt that more than average familiarity with the inside contents of the magazine would "contaminate" the judgment of the cover itself as a stimulus.

Each cover was prepared in three different forms to test the influence of the verbal context and the cover girl separately as well as together. One group of subjects received a form of the cover girl showing only the verbal material; the cover girl was cut out and replaced by a white sheet of paper. This will be referred to as the verbal form, and the group responding to it as Group V.

Another form showed only the cover girl's picture cut out of the verbal form, and pasted on cardboard. This is the pictorial form, shown to Group P.

The cover without any alteration, designated as the total form, was given to Group T. Figure 2 shows the three different forms of one cover.

Figure 2. Forms V, T, and of One of the 12 Covers Used in the Experiment. Stripes Below Form Correspond to Markings Used in Figure 3.

A total of 538 University of Illinois students from five different departments were used as respondents. Testing was done in class. A subject responded only once to one form of one cover. Subjects were told that they would be asked for their views and feelings about the girl's picture in front of them. (Group V subjects, who had the girl cut out from the cover, were instructed to respond to the test on the basis of their mental image of the girl whose picture might go on the cover.)

The testing was done in two stages, using two tests that had some features in common. The first stage included a total of 140 subjects in the three basic groups. The test used at this stage included a blank page for writing a personality sketch of the cover girl, and twenty-six "semantic differential" scales.[7] These are 7-point scales defined by contrasting adjectives such as good-bad, wise-foolish, active-passive, etc. Respondents mark their reaction to the stimulus (in this case their form of the cover girl) on these scales according to the intensity of their association with one or the other of the polar adjectives. If undecided, they check the middle.

The second stage of the testing, involving the balance of the subjects in the three basic groups, was confined to the semantic differential, and three questions asking about the cover girl's age, occupation, and "moral principles."

Although the findings reveal some differences *between* certain cover girls, these are fewer and no greater than differences between our forms V, T, and P. These and other underlying similarities justify lumping the data for the twelve cover girls together into a composite picture suggestive of the image of "the confession-type cover girl."

SEMANTIC DIFFERENTIAL RESULTS

The mean responses on the semantic differential for all subjects in the three groups are plotted on a summary form of the differential in Figure 3. This summary form includes the fifteen scales that appeared to represent the range of discriminating responses. The scales appear grouped into "combined characteristics" rather than in random order and direction as they appeared on the tests.

Figure 3. Mean Responses by Basic Group Plotted on Summary Form of Semantic Differential. Vertical stripes mark means for group V, horizontal stripes for group T, and diagonal stripes for Group P. Vertical bars indicate means of combined scales; profiles show means on individual scales. Line 4 represents dead center.

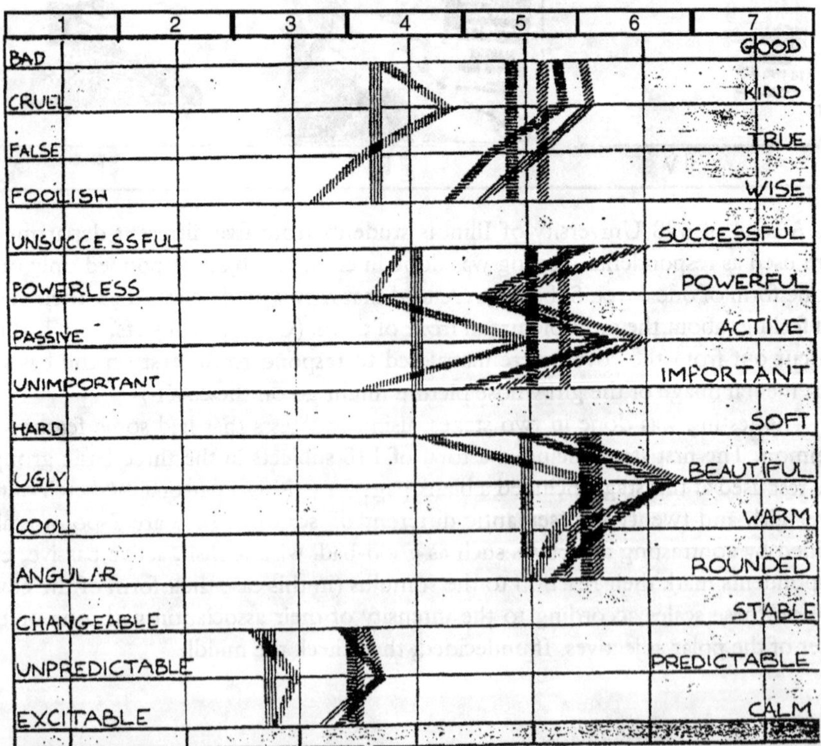

The results,[8] also shown in Table 1, suggest possible effects of illustrating, or matching with an overtly appropriate picture, the verbal material on these covers. Such practice would make the cover girl appear significantly more unfavorable on all but two of the fifteen characteristics, as she did appear to Group V in comparison with Group T. In other words, on the basis of story titles and blurbs alone, Group V conceived the cover girl as tending to be a "bad," "false," "foolish," "unsuccessful," "powerless," "unimportant," and almost "hard" creature. Group T, which saw the actual picture of the cover girl in the same verbal context, perceived her as "good," "kind," "true," "successful," "soft," and even a little "wise," "powerful," and "important."

Table 1. Mean Scale Positions on the Semantic Differential by Basic Groups

Scale	Group V (N-174)		Group T (N-185)		Group P (N-179)
bad—good	3.77	*	5.25		5.49
cruel—kind	4.39	*	5.32		5.53
false—true	3.64	*	4.67	+	5.06
foolish—wise	3.16	*	4.29		4.58
unsuccessful—successful	3.92	*	5.43	*	5.99
powerless—powerful	3.70	*	4.55		4.58
passive—active	4.97	*	5.61	+	5.98
unimportant—important	3.61	*	4.44		4.68
hard—soft	4.07	*	5.01		5.26
ugly—beautiful	5.59	*	6.13		6.20
cool—warm	5.22		5.58		5.40
angular—rounded	5.02		5.19		5.30
changeable—stable	2.49	*	3.29		3.53
unpredictable—predictable	2.99	*	3.69		3.68
excitable—calm	2.79	*	3.36		3.23

* The differences between the two means are significant at the 1% level.
+ The differences between the two means are significant at the 5% level.

She was rated quite "active" and "beautiful" whether seen or not, but a little more so when seen. She appeared "changeable," "unpredictable," and "excitable" to both groups, but less so when her picture was seen. The picture of the cover girl designed to the specifications of the romance-confession market thus transforms the impressions created by the supercharged verbal context of the cover.

Compared to the effects of her image on the verbal material, the effects of the verbal context on her image are subtle. These effects can be examined by comparing the responses of Group T to the actual cover with the responses of Group P, which saw only the cover girl's pictures.

This comparison reveals that Group P rated her slightly higher on all but two of the scales. However, only three of these differences are significant.

The implications of failure, trouble, and guilt in the verbal setting seem to depress significantly the cover girl's "successful" and "true" ratings, and—probably coupled with her apparent unawareness—make her appear less "active." The verbal context, on the other hand, does not injure significantly her other ratings, least of all her attractiveness. It even appears to enhance slightly her "warmness."

A separate analysis of responses by sex revealed that the appearance of the picture on the cover impressed men most as an indication of her success; it had its greatest effect on women in transforming her image from bad to good. When the verbal context was absent, the girl's success rating went up the most among both men and women.

OTHER PERSONALITY DATA

A further assessment of the cover girl's presumed personality was made on the basis of the questionnaire data. One-page personality sketches written by the 140 subjects were analyzed for straightforward assertions. Specific questions yielded additional information.

Analysis of the tabulation of personality assertions (see Table 2) reveals that those who saw only the verbal context wrote the least about the cover girl's personality, and most of that was unfavorable. Those who saw the picture alone wrote more, and most of that was favorable. But those who saw the confession cover girl in her "natural" verbal habitat wrote the most and came to her defense with the highest number of positive assertions. That this defense was felt necessary in view of her verbal setting is evident from the fact that in that setting she received more critical comment than in the absence of that setting (although not nearly as many as in the absence of her picture).

Table 2. Tabulation of Assertions by Basic Groups

Assertions	V (N-50)	T (N-40)	P (N-50)
Assertions about personality	196	322	306
Favorable	71	273	267
Average per respondent	1.4	6.8	5.3
Unfavorable	125	49	39
Average per respondent	2.5	1.2	0.8
Assertions about "sexiness," promiscuity	83	27	44
Average per respondent	1.7	0.7	0.9

The high number of favorable assertions in Group T is again indicative of the "contrast effect" of the cover design. For a number of subjects the confession-type cover girls appear "too good" for the confession. As one subject put it, "She has a smile on her face that shows contempt at the thought of the type of magazine that she appears in." Wrote another: "What I can't figure out is what a pleasant, clean-looking American girl is doing on the cover of a scandal sheet." In these cases the threatening implications of the verbal context did less to implicate the cover girl—

seemingly oblivious of her setting—than to make her appear perhaps vulnerable but the more virtuous by contrast.

Spontaneous statements about the cover girl's "sexiness" support this possibility. Such assertions occurred least often in Group T. Perhaps this "contrast effect" is also due to a feeling on the part of subjects that, in view of the girl's apparent innocence, there is little need to mention what is already vividly spelled out on the cover. But at any rate, it shows the effectiveness of her role in the cover design as a sop to moralists and censors.

CLASS STATUS, AGE, AND MORALITY

The confession market position requires the editorial prescription of "workshirt" social setting, and the woman's middle-class consumer status. The resulting "class structure" of the cover design appears in the responses to a question about the cover girl's socio-economic position. (See Table 3.)

Table 3. Questionnaire Responses on Class, Occupation

	V (N-50)	T (N-40)	P (N-50)
Class (socio-economic status)			
Middle and higher	55%	89%	84%
Lower	45%	11%	16%
Class status mean on 9 point scale	4.52	5.48	5.36
Occupation and activity			
"Higher type" (including model)	75%	100%	96%
"Lower type"	25%	—	4%

The verbal context alone suggested a "lower class" cover girl to four times as many subjects in Group V as did the cover girl when seen in the same context by Group T. Her contrasting verbal setting seemed to enhance her social position; the Group T girl on the cover rated slightly higher than did the Group P girl by herself.

The goal of identification may be served better if the cover girl does not seem too "professional." The test question about occupation or activity yielded a wide variety of guesses. But only about half of all respondents thought of the cover girl as a professional model. Occupational ratings were sorted into "higher type" (including model), such as student, secretary, career girl; and "lower type" ranging from waitress to prostitute. The verbal context alone suggested a lower occupational type to one in four Group V subjects. But none in Group T associated her image with a lower type occupation, and only a few in Group P.

All subjects were asked to judge the cover girl's age and morality. Analysis of these judgments shows that being on the cover enhances the cover girl's youth. More Group T subjects placed her in the 18-or-under and fewer in the 24-or-over category than those of the other groups. Both the verbal context and the appearance of her picture by itself yielded slightly higher mean estimated ages than the actual cover.

A breakdown of subject ages and age ratings by morality judgment indicates (1) that those who judged her to be of "low morality" (a minority, when her picture was seen) were generally younger themselves, and (2) that her moral critics rated her oldest of all groups when they saw only the verbal context, but youngest by a significant margin when they saw the actual cover girl in the same setting.

SUMMARY

The underlying contention is that mass media content reflects, in ways both explicit and implicit, the imprint of concrete circumstances of its production. This led to the hypothesis that the market-produced editorial and distribution requirements shape the functions of the confession cover design, and that these objective functions—whether consciously recognized or not—impart a subtle meaning to content which is implicitly reflected in the response.

The findings of the experiment, as far as they go, suggest that the image of the cover girl, and her juxtaposition with the contrasting verbal context, serve well the editorial and distribution specifications required of the cover girl. She resolves her apparent conflict with the lurid titles of the cover—suggestive of the brutal world of the confessions—to her favor. Her dominant image exhibits the human appeal of the heroine menaced by society, but in an overtly unrelated form, insulating her from most ill effects.

Her implicit involvement in the torrent of troubles raging verbally around her enhances, as if by contrast, some of her qualifications. It makes her appear both more immature and less active, hence probably less implicated by (or responsible for) that surrounding. It enhances her consumer and class status, yet preserves the "working-class" setting considered necessary for social appeal to the confession market. Her evident success is tinged with the verbally implied risks of failure, and her apparent virtue spiced with the basically innocent sexual attraction of the good-bad girl.

Art editors conceive of the romance-confession cover girl as a projection of the reader's self-image, "a composite of our reader type." Her function on the cover appears to be analogous to the inside heroine's function of identification. The editorial prescription calls for a heroine who may be outwardly plain and sinful, but not unsympathetic. The inherent human attractiveness of the heroine is reflected in the overt beauty of the cover girl; "badness" is implicit in the verbal background.

The confession story heroine—simple, trustful human being against a brutal world—sins, suffers, and repents, without consciously and actively grappling with the social meaning of her difficulties. The cover girl in carefree, suspended animation, her eyes gazing confidently into those of the viewer, appears innocent of insight into the tragic meanings around her.

NOTES

1. These conclusions are drawn from a report by this author on "The Social Role of the Confession Magazine," *Social Problems*, Summer 1958 (in press).

2. Letters were received from Edward Rethorn of Ideal Publishing Corporation, Mel Blum, Magazine Management Company, New York, and James B. Fitzpatrick, Fawcett Publications, New York.
3. The magazines are: *True Confessions, Revealing Romances, Life Confessions, Your Romance, Intimate Story, True Revelations, Personal Confessions, Secrets, Personal Romances, True Love Stories, True Romance,* and *True Experience.*
4. Chain store magazine sales have been reported by *Chain Store Age*, and summarized *in Advertising Age*, August 12, 1957. The figure on chewing gums can be found in the report on candy and gum sales, *Chain Store Age*, Grocery Edition, Product Study No. 3, September 1956.
5. Cf. *Supermarket Buying and Magazine Dollars*, a study by Crossley, Inc., 1954.
6. This general impression has been confirmed through interviews with 15 store managers in the Champaign-Urbana area.
7. These scales and their uses are described in Charles E. Osgood, "The Nature and Measurement of Meaning," *Psychological Bulletin*, 49:197–237, 1952, and in *The Measurement of Meaning*, by C. E. Osgood, G. J. Suci, and P. H. Tannenbaum (University of Illinois Press, 1957).
8. Space limitations preclude publication of all findings and tabular material. However, they may be obtained directly from the author.

CHAPTER 11

MENTAL ILLNESS ON TELEVISION

A Study of Censorship

BY GEORGE GERBNER

Somewhere along every production line stands a "gatekeeper" to see that products meet specifications. In cultural industry this "gatekeeper" is usually appointed by the industry itself as a matter of self-protection against "outside" or "political" control. He bears such titles as Code Administrator, Review Board Chairman, Continuity Acceptance Director, or Network Editor. Only one office door (at a movie studio) bore the straightforward title: CENSOR.

In this article the term censorship is used to designate the functions of a "gatekeeper" appointed to screen mass media output through a sieve of public relations, moral, political, marketing, and other specifications. The purpose is to illustrate some aspects of the dynamics of network censorship in one area of national concern: the treatment of mental illness and the mental health professions on television.

NETWORK CENSORSHIP AND MENTAL ILLNESS

Every program and commercial to be broadcast over a network goes through the office of the network "censor." Each network has its own codebook of standard practice which provides the broad context of censorship operation. Although administrative arrangements differ, censorship policies are similar among the networks. In the course of protecting the interests of industry network, censorship does, of course, reflect moral, political, scientific, and other considerations and may also express personal conviction or concern. "We're holding the line," one "censor" reported. "The airways would be drenched with blood and gore if we didn't." Another complained that "some producers are out for newspaper headlines, but controversy and sensational publicity hurt the network. We're here to protect it." "We are the conscience of the industry," commented a third network "censor," and added: "Conscience in our case means a nose for trouble."

Mental illness was found to be an area of "trouble" for network "censors." All network codes caution against the exploitation of mental (or physical) affliction for shock or comic effects. Previous studies have traced the development of the portrayal of mental illness into a "sensitive area" of public and censorial concern. This study reports the findings of an inquiry into the effects of this concern upon censorship performance and upon the images of mental illness and mental health professionals available to the public via television.

The study was based on the film clearance file at one network, and on other evidence of network censorship (including interviews) at the three major networks. The network film clearance file contains a record of every film program screened for telecasting over the network and its owned-and-operated stations. This record, going back to 1948, includes brief synopses of TV films, documentary films, and feature films, and it notes deletions, restrictions to "adult" viewing hours, rejections, or approvals for "family viewing."

This clearance file of over 6,000 cards was searched for relevant material. Every card making reference to mental illness themes or terms either in the synopsis or in the "censor's" comments or deletions was copied on McBee Keysort cards, coded, and sorted for analysis.

The search revealed no relevant films cleared through censorship before 1951, and only five relevant films between 1951 and 1953, four of which were documentaries. The mental illness "boom" started in 1954.

Table 1 traces the rise (and fall) of the frequency of references to mental illness themes, portrayals, and terms noted in the network film clearance file. It shows that the first advance ripple in 1954 was still dominated by documentary productions; this was the time of the "introspectaculars," as *Variety* termed them. They were soon swallowed up in a wave of feature films released for television and containing mental illness themes and terms spotted by increasingly sensitive "censors." Over the crest of this wave came in 1957 the swell of TV films apparently reflecting, among other things, the new "adult" or "psychological" programming concept in television drama. Relevant films dropped in 1958, with TV drama still increasing its share of the total.

Table 1. Films Containing Mental Illness Themes, Portrayals, or References as Noted in Network Film Clearance File

	1951–53	1954	1955	1956	1957	1958	1951–58
Total relevant films	5	27	39	124	170	73	438
Percent of total:							
Documentary films	80%	55%	5%	2%	1%	1%	6%
Feature films	20	37	54	67	43	30	48
TV films	—	8	41	31	56	69	46
	100%	100%	100%	100%	100%	100%	100%

Network censors rarely tabulate the contents of their own files. Their impressions of trends and of the application of their own standards are largely intuitive. "I have a mystic belief that censorship problems come in bunches," said the network "censor" when told of findings of a trend of mental illness material in the clearance file. "You see one extreme cleavage shot, you can be sure there will be two other Grand Canyons yawning at you very shortly; one 'hell' on the network seems to breed into five before the month is out. So, chances are that your marked increase is the result of purest coincidence plus the fact that more films were cleared in the first place."

Further analysis of the data and the findings of concurrent studies shed some light on these informal hypotheses. Trend studies in other media showed similar peaks of attention devoted to psychological and mental illness themes in popular magazines, motion pictures, and press coverage, with frequencies declining after 1957. No more likely than the "purest coincidence" theory is the possibility that the total number of films screened by censorship could account for the trends in the frequency of relevant films. Block purchases and screenings of old movies might have boosted the 1956 clearance figures but would not have produced similar trends in filmed programs for television. Yet the frequency of relevant TV films climbed from 2 in 1954 to 16, 39, and 96 in the three successive years. It dropped to 50 in 1958.

What does appear probable, however, is that actual changes in content, increasing censorial awareness of mental illness as a sensitive area, and consequently changing rates and forms of censorship applied to relevant films all contributed to the trends found in the analysis of the clearance file.

INCREASING AWARENESS

Increasing recognition of mental illness as a censorship "problem" appears to have contributed heavily to the frequency of relevant films. The effects of such recognition can be traced by comparing the number of films in which the mental illness theme was an integral part of the plot (as noted in the synopses) with those in which the relevant element was a minor or incidental reference not in the synopses but noted by the "censor."

Table 2 presents such a comparison. It shows that as the number of relevant films increased, the incidence of mental illness references spotted by the censor climbed more rapidly than did the incidence of mental illness themes mentioned in the synopses. With an overall decline of relevant films in 1958, major themes again predominated probably because of changes in the nature of the materials, as will be discussed below.

Table 2. Mental Illness Theme or Reference Noted in Synopses vs. Spotted by "Censor" But Not in Synopses

	1951–53	1954	1955	1956	1957	1958	1951–58
Noted in synopses	5	19	22	31	57	44	178
Spotted by censors but not in synopses	0	8	17	93	113	29	260
Totals	5	27	39	124	170	73	438

Discussions with network "censors" and the examination of some interoffice correspondence supported these evidences of rising censorial concern. "Censors" deplored the indiscriminate use of such terms as crazy, idiot, moron, and the frequent dramatic association of mental illness, psychologists, psychiatrists with comic, violent, or eerie situations. These concerns arose partly out of personal involvement and conviction and partly under the pressure of viewer complaints and of professional and organizational activities in the mental health field. A 1957 memorandum, founding the files of a network other than the one whose clearance records were studied, expressed sentiments (or rationalizations) voiced by most "censors":

> By comparison I think we, collectively, spend more time in the interests of MENTAL HEALTH than of any other group or organization of its kind. This may be the result of any one of a number or combination of reasons: (a) many officers of the Mental Health Association are those employed in the entertainment profession; (b) the media in itself and our ability to come into intimate contact with all members of a family and all classes of society; (c) our conscious moral responsibility to the viewing public; (d) our lawful responsibility to the various Federal Agencies (and consequently to local agencies and their offspring); (e) our own personal reaction to the great human tragedy.

CHANGING RATE OF CENSORSHIP

If it is true that during the current decade mental illness became an increasingly sensitive area in network censorship, films portraying mental illness during that period would be subjected to heavier censorship than other films. Such, indeed, appears to have been the case. If, from all relevant films those that contain mental illness as a significant story element (as noted in the synopses) are selected, thus eliminating those picked largely on the basis of censorship action in the first place, a conservative estimate of the level of censorship as applied to films portraying mental illness can be obtained. It was found that almost two out of seven such films (27%) were either cut or rejected from 1951 to 1958. Comparing that with the network "censor's" own tabulation of all TV and feature films censored through 1954 (the last date for which such figures were available) less than two out of ten (18%) of all films were cut or rejected.

When mental illness themes and references spotted by "censors" are combined for the entire period studied more than half of all relevant films (58%) suffered one or more deletions, and 3 percent were rejected entirely. Only 22 percent of all relevant films were approved for family viewing without any cuts; the rest were restricted to "adult" viewing hours.

Table 3 shows trends in types of clearance for the years of significant activity. As mental illness themes and references increased in number, the proportion of relevant films subjected to censorship increased. A decline in frequency in 1958 did not bring about slackening of censorial scrutiny; the percentage of uncut and unrestricted films further declined.

The shifts in rate and type of censorship over time reflected changes in the material itself, as well as the application of developing standards of censorship. These changes can be examined by observing the different types of films separately as shown (with the exception of documentaries) on Table 3.

Table 3. Types of Film Clearance Action as Percentage of Films in Which Network "Censor" Noted Reference to Mental Illness, 1954–58

	1954	1955	1956	1957	1958	1954–58
	%	%	%	%	%	%
Percent of all relevant films						
Cut*	21	41	65	65	52	58
Restricted to adult viewing*	19	26	27	28	44	29
Rejected	11	5	7	3	1	3
Approved for family without cuts	64	36	20	19	16	22
Percent of feature films						
Cut	40	48	76	81	77	73
Restricted to adult viewing	40	38	30	29	41	32
Rejected	10	9	2			2
Approved for family without cuts	20	10	11	11	14	11
Percent of TV films						
Cut	50	31	46	56	42	48
Restricted to adult viewing	50	31	46	56	42	48
Rejected				5	1	3
Approved for family without cuts	50	56	28	24	16	23

*Films may be both cut *and* restricted. Therefore, percentages do not necessarily add up to 100.

CENSORSHIP BY TYPE OF FILMS

Documentaries accounted for only two cuts and two rejections during the entire period. It is interesting to note that the two documentaries rejected outright for national telecast at the beginning of the era of rising sensitivity were both non-commercial educational ventures circulated by the National Association for Mental Health and the Mental Health Film Board. Queried about the rejections, the "censor" had this to say:

> You must remember that when one clears a film one does so with a specific time, day, audience and total program schedule in mind. Even though it would seem to bear the imprimatur of the NAMH I very much doubt if I would approve *Mental Hospital* for indiscriminate viewing without adequate explanation from an articulate expert....I cannot see that the cause of the NAMH is advanced, or public understanding broadened by showing close-ups of patients receiving shock treatments. Indeed, I should rather imagine it would have the opposite

> effect. *Man to Man*...here again, it seems to me in dubious taste to show mentally disturbed patients in as many scenes as were apparently included in this epic. I'd be very interested in what officials of the NAMH have to say on this count. What sort of film would I *approve* of on the subject of mental health? Something like was done on *Hemo the Magnificent*, or something like the excellent films produced by the American Cancer Society...in which the audio was very strong, very forceful, even brutal, but in which the video was either abstract or representational.

Feature films were generally subject to more cuts and restrictions than were films produced directly for television. The higher overall censorship rate of old movies can be attributed to the absence of reference to mental illness in the Hollywood Production Code, to the difference in markets between the media, and to the different standards of acceptability at the time the movies were produced. "Times have changed," remarked the "censor." "A brand new film in 1933 might be quite innocent, but that same film in 1953 is socially malodorous."

A special tabulation of feature films by date of original release bore him out. Every relevant film produced before 1938 was either rejected or cut upon screening for television. The proportion of cuts and rejections decreased with the recency of the film's original release. "Now," said the "censor," "we are dealing with much later second-hand models including the more realistic European post-war productions." This change in the nature of feature film material passing through the censorship gate shows up in the increased percentage of "adult" classifications in 1958.

TV films were less likely to be censored on "mental illness" grounds than were feature movies, but the rate was rising. The steady increase in the total proportion of TV films censored indicates that censorial vigilance has not been relaxed; and the shift from deletions to "adult" restrictions marks the change in the nature of TV programming likely to involve portrayals of mental illness. As one "censor" pointed out:

> In 1953 we had two Westerns; today we are lousy with Westerns plus other features of the so-called "adult" variety. Now, you are going to have more censorship problems with sophisticated fare like *Wagon Train* than you ever had with innocent old Hoppie. Alfred Hitchcock will give you more borderline situations to be handled with care than will the old *Schlitz Playhouse*.

A check on the content indicated that the proportion of TV films portraying mental illness as significant plot element was rising, and that these major themes, accounting for most of the restrictions, were most likely to occur in general TV drama and mystery, while verbal deletions were most frequently made in comedy. The words most often deleted from all types of films were, in order of frequency: crazy, idiot, moron, nuts, screwy, imbecile, psychiatry, feebleminded, lunatic, looney, and half-wit.

EFFECTS OF CENSORSHIP

The proportion of deletions (mostly verbal) dropped in 1958. The "censors" thought that this drop, especially pronounced in TV films, was due to more frequent prior review of scripts, and to greater awareness and better understanding on the part of writers and producers of the reasons for the verbal policy line. One "censor" commented:

> Obviously we would have avoided much time, trouble and expense had we reviewed more shooting scripts. In addition, fewer syndicated films would be floating around the country where they are shown unedited in the smaller markets, and where thoughtless and tasteless references to mental illness are repeated and repeated.

Some "censors" explained their policies in the form of bulletins, reports, or interoffice communication circulated to production units. The following is one of several attempts to clarify the views of one "censor" of *crazy*, taken from an interoffice bulletin:

> Could I try to clarify for those who seem to be misunderstanding it, our policy on uses of the word "crazy" and synonyms thereof? Of course many of us in spontaneous speech use the word and it naturally enough crops up in radio and television scripts. Our feeling is not that it is totally taboo, but that where it is so persistently and often equated with mental and emotional illness, it approaches being mercilessly tactless. We are trying to discourage this. We do not take the position that we refuse to take the word "crazy," but urge substitutions for it wherever feasible. Very few plots are in any way damaged if a line "you're crazy" or "you're insane" is changed to "you're a fool." Semantically speaking it is the latter that is meant anyhow and it injures no one who is mentally disturbed. Let's not have our network in a position of bearing a stigma that we don't know anything about the prevalent problem of mental illness in our country.

The rising percentage of restrictions to "adult" viewing hours marked the recent trend toward more "realistic" and "adult" presentations. Such restrictions are not necessarily uncomplimentary or harmful if the problem does not aim at a daytime or family audience. Rejections, on the other hand, are a different matter. Commenting on the 1957 figure of 5 percent of relevant TV films rejected, the "censor" said:

> I think your figures indicate a lack of liaison between us and some film producers. Let's look at what might result (believe me it did!) from this poor liaison. A guy spends $50,000 and three weeks producing a half hour film which utilizes some poor, mentally disturbed soul as the villain terrorizing the countryside. It is rejected by five major stations in markets over the country representing fifty percent of the potential American buying public. He has virtually kissed fifty thousand bucks "bye, bye," and next time around, he will make darn sure his film is going to be acceptable *before* he starts producing it.

The following year the rejection rate dropped to 1 percent.

On the whole, network censorship tends to discourage the flagrant and overt exploitation of mental illness or of mental health professionals, and the careless use of mental illness terms for purposes of dramatic effect. While—again, on the whole—there was little evidence of censorship blunting the edge of serious and responsible dramatic productions, there were many instances of censorship action based on the presumed context of television viewing rather than on the scientific or dramatic integrity of the material. The overall effects of network censorship upon the portrayal of mental illness on the television screen appear to be calculated to soften the impact of the more bizarre or potentially offensive images.

It is not known whether the apparent decline in the number of relevant films in 1958 reflected fear of censorship or even a real change in programming. While numbers declined, the portrayal of mental illness as significant plot element became more frequent. Associated Press feature writer Cynthia Lowry complained in the fall of 1959 that "Psychotics replaced villains, and neuroses have succeeded unbridled badness as motivating forces even in low budget high cliché weekly action tales."

Crudity and flamboyance could be toned down at the "gates," but "censors" and their files testified to increasing concern over the more subtle association of horror, crime, and violence with portrayals of mental illness. Attempts to reduce the amount of obvious gore or the number of careless references by judicious cutting might help avoid offending some viewers, but could have little effect upon the basic validity of approach built into the portrayal. As one of the informants said, "Censors can clean up the language but they can't clean up the motives." Some "gatekeepers" go to (and even beyond) the limits of the public relations functions delegated to them in striving for what they consider responsible portrayals. But the methods of censorship are hardly adequate to the task.

CHAPTER 12

PEACE, WAR, AND THE PRESS

Perspectives in Conflict

BY GEORGE GERBNER

In the realm of ideas it's finders keepers. I don't remember the source of this story, but (the way I tell it) it is a quaint tale of horror with an open ending, possibly tragic. In this it resembles almost any front page of almost any newspaper you might pick up these days. That is why I think it is relevant to the issue of press perspectives on peace and war.

Not long ago, the story goes, a sealed bottle drifted to our shores. There was an unfinished manuscript inside the bottle. The manuscript turned out to be a report from one of our communications researchers sent to survey the cultural habits, program preferences, and market potentials of far away countries. The people of these countries appeared to be the proud possessors of a flourishing culture much like that of some leading nations we know, with but one difference: they practiced cannibalism.

This combination of circumstances might have accounted for the fact that their most popular program was called "People are Yummy." The best-seller in the cannibal countries was a book entitled *How to Serve Your Fellow Men.*

The people inhabiting this thriving market were reported puzzled to find other countries having so little regard for humans that they would not consider eating them, no matter how well prepared. It was noted with some astonishment that other nations considering themselves democratic did not even permit free and open discussion on the subject.

They said (according to the report) that their system of chefs and balances was obviously the only truly pluralistic political system. Why, some of our best friends—said conservatives and liberals alike—believe in exactly opposite methods of preparation. So we clash, and we argue, and we carefully digest the matter. We let our party recipes compete for popular flavor. And we let the potato chips fall where they may—through free elections, of course. Our standard of living is high. Supply and demand never far out of balance. Hunger, needless to say, is unknown in the land. Few are so misguided as to think of subverting this happy order of things. And, sooner or later, they, too, serve the common good.

At this point the unfinished manuscript breaks off. Its author has not been heard from. We can only assume that he has been consumed by the attractive cultural perspective which, as any cultural perspective, tends to infect and protect those on the inside, and to insulate them from the irrational influences of other perspectives.

We must look at things from where we are. This simple fact involves selection, emphasis, point of view—a host of operations believed relevant to our position. These operations, in turn, lead to the *production* of images and points of view which *provide* ways of looking at the world and structuring its issues. And so the process goes on, interrupted only occasionally by inescapable reality "in the raw" breaking through the established perspectives.

Modern mass communication has made major national perspectives available on a global basis. Two American, one British, one French, and two Russian news agencies provide most of the international news for the entire world. An increasing number of world news readers and listeners are exposed to the competing and conflicting perspectives of different world systems.

In recent years I have become increasingly concerned with the limitations imposed by our own standards of reporting upon a realistic appraisal of the actual role news media play on the world scene. My concern is not so much with the propaganda we broadcast abroad as with the press perspectives we produce for ourselves but circulate abroad among an increasing number of world news readers, the politically significant elite of many countries.

> What do press perspectives do? How can we compare them? What do they mean to others and to us? These are the questions I would like to explore.
>
> This is what press perspectives do:
>
> They select their own set of significant events. They define what is "real" in the common culture, what is to be attended to, what is relevant to our purposes.
>
> They structure the agenda of common discourse. Thus they affect not only what gets talked about but how soon, how much, and how fast.
>
> They make available the dominant points of view from which to view our selection and priority of events.

Press perspectives may or may not decide the outcome of specific issues. They do something more important. They shape the collective outlook and climate in which the process of decision making goes on.

As instruments of *world* communication, national media represent dominant perspectives of their societies. But they can share the common basis necessary for world communication only to the extent that their definition of significant realities appears tenable, their priorities reasonable, and their points of view acceptable in the light of competing and conflicting perspectives *also available*.

How can we assess perspectives in conflict?

Obviously, we cannot use self-justifying standards to measure performance among those who do not share these standards. For example, our own rules of freedom and objectivity are more a hindrance than help in situations where freedom means the ability to marshal all resources on behalf of goals *we* have already achieved, and where objectivity means an intensely partisan preoccupation with the *objective requirements* of a needed reconstruction of life. Far from being universal yardsticks, such differential conceptions should themselves become weights on a scale of measurement.

The standard I propose as relevant to bases of communication with people around the world has two dimensions. The first is the dimension of procedure. From this point of view, strategy, conflict, and keeping the scoreboard up to date are the most significant aspects of newsworthy events. What the game is about is assumed to be known. Important items on the agenda concern matters of technique: how gains can be defended, rules utilized to best advantage, new points scored. The perspective is that of a contest. I call this dimension *procedural* and *conflict-oriented.*

The other dimension cuts the pie differently. The substance and promise of common issues occupy the center of the stage. Summit meeting, disarmament, colonial liberation are seen not so much as aspects of big-power strategy as aspects of everyday reality: bread and butter for tomorrow's table, a school for the children, a freer and more secure life for everyone *now.* From this perspective, conflict is seen as delaying and agreement as hastening the realization of all that really matters. I call this perspective *substantive* and *agreement-oriented.*

Now let us apply the yardstick.

I have recently concluded a comparative study of how two newspapers covered the fall 1960 "summit" session of the U.N. General Assembly. You recall that this was the session with President Eisenhower, Premier Krushchev, and other heads of state in attendance. The eyes of the world were focused on the conference coming on the heels of the U-2 fiasco, the Paris summit collapse, and the U.N.'s entry into the Congo. I wanted to compare the ways an American and a communist national newspaper highlighted that conference, as these perspectives might be seen by world news readers not necessarily committed to either side in the cold war.

In selecting the newspapers to be compared, I might appear to have stacked the deck in our favor. The American paper selected was *The New York Times*, and the communist daily was *Nepszabadsag*, the official organ of the Hungarian communist party.

Now, of course, the purpose was not to compare a giant of world journalism, as such, with a 12–14 page paper of a small European country, even though the latter is a fairly typical party organ with circulation about the same as *The Times.* The purpose was to compare *perspectives of emphasis* during Assembly. We tried to see what each paper selected as the *most significant* aspect of the sessions, how each paper structured the agenda, and from what point of view each paper viewed the events or aspects selected for emphasis.

Let me first give you a shortcut to our findings. Among other things, we classified every line of every major front page headline dealing with the Assembly in both papers—a total of about sixty lines in each paper. In the categories of both, procedural emphasis and stress on conflict fell 45 percent of the lines in *The Times* and 5 percent of the lines in the communist paper. In the categories of both substantive emphasis and stress on common goals fell 5 percent of all lines in *The Times* and 30 percent of the lines in *Nepszabadsag*. In other words, the substance of common aims which tend to unite mankind were highlighted in the communist paper five times as much as were the tactics of the cold war, and also five times as much as these common aims were given major emphasis in *The Times*. Conversely, procedural strategy and conflict were stressed in *The Times* nine times as much as were the goals the majority of mankind hold in common, and also nine times as much as these cold war tactics were emphasized in the communist paper.

The relatively subdued headlines and evenhanded treatment of cold war issues in *The Times* no doubt influenced the findings (in our favor). Let me hasten to repeat that this study ignored the major strength of *The Times*—its unequalled *record* of current events and its coverage in depth. In concentrating mostly on the selection of highlights and the priorities of emphasis, rather than on total coverage, we attempted to use *The Times* as an indicator of U.S. press perspective rather than to do justice to its unique qualities as a newspaper of record.

So the differences we found are indicative of perspectives of emphasis and of necessarily selective spotlighting of events, not of completeness or quality. Let me illustrate by describing the comparative highlights of the first two days of our study period, and then by sketching the treatment of three major issues before the Assembly.

The Soviet ship *Baltika* was still on the high seas with its retinue of Red dignitaries when the Security Council received a strong protest over the alleged role of the Secretary General as Commander-in-Chief of the U.N. army in the Congo. (You recall that this was shortly after Mobutu's military coup replaced the government of the late Premier Lumumba.) When our study period opened, *The Times* kept the spotlight on embattled Hammerskjold. Its September 18th top headline was "U.N. CHIEF WARNS/HE MAY QUIT POST OVER CONGO ROLE." This was followed by the reassuring top line the next day (when *Nepszabadsag* did not publish) that "ASIAN-AFRICAN BLOC AIDS U.N. CHIEF." Companion front page headlines asked for "restraint" in Khrushchev's TV coverage and related the hope of the State Department that the Assembly "will not become propaganda platform."

These procedural aspects of the conflict cast only a partial shadow on the back pages of *Nepszabadsag*. A page five headline in the September 18th issue of the communist paper declared "ILLEGAL ATTEMPT BY U.S. TO HAVE SPECIAL U.N. SESSION SANCTION AGGRESSION AGAINST CONGO." A companion piece claimed that "COLONIALIST'S AGENTS GRAB POWER IN LEOPOLDVILLE WITH U.N. ASSISTANCE."

Front page emphasis, however, was on peace, hope, and good wishes. "MAY SUCCESS FOLLOW YOUR WORK!" the two column headline cited one of the reportedly "hundreds of telegrams" pouring in from "workers, peasants, intelligentsia" to the passengers of the *Baltika* on their way to New York. The major three column spread was headlined "REPRESENTING PEACE." It was a long editorial sounding the keynote of the coverage for days to come. "Representing peace" were the socialist delegations soon to arrive at the world forum to battle for the overriding concern of all humanity, declared the editorial, and to engage in (what *The Times* warned about on *its* front page) propaganda for disarmament. The key portions of the lengthy piece are paraphrased below because they are necessary to an understanding of the communist press perspective.

> The West has defeated 40 disarmament proposals advanced by the socialist camp in the last 15 years. It has opposed, then scuttled the Summit. But the diplomacy of imperialism has suffered a setback: disarmament is on the Assembly agenda again and even a Summit is being realized. The world must listen now not only to our proposals but also to concrete unilateral steps that have been taken. In five years the Soviet Union reduced its armed forces from 5,763,000 to 2,423,000, and the Warsaw pact countries followed suit....
>
> And what does all this mean to mankind? Consider a few facts....Every single day a hundred million people spend almost a billion hours not to build houses, not to produce clothes and food and drugs and school implements but means of destruction!...Every year the world spends twice as much on armaments as on food for all mankind....
>
> Obviously, the success of disarmament cannot depend on those who profit from armaments. They are afraid; they say all our talk is propaganda. So be it; it is propaganda in the interest of humanity and of life itself!

When the *Baltika* reached New York, an elated *Nepszabadsag* devoted most of the front page to Khrushchev's arrival message. "WE MUST AGREE ON STRICTLY CONTROLLED DISARMAMENT" said the headline, alongside a smiling picture of the Soviet premier surrounded by friendly faces, captioned "Warm Reception." The arrival message itself sounded some of the key motifs: "All thoughts turn to peace....We must agree on the strictest international controls for disarmament....Unfortunately, those who pay lip service to strengthening the U.N. actually oppose its work for disarmament....They call our proposals propaganda....I am proud to conduct such propaganda until the last ounce of my strength."

The major *Times* headline of the same day was "U.N. CHIEF WINS 70–0 CONGO VOTE; KHRUSHCHEV RECEIVED COLDLY; ANGRY CASTRO SWITCHES HOTELS." The lead of the arrival story set a somber mood, noting that "The red carpet...was soggy, and rain streamed through the leaky roof of dilapidated Pier 73." The picture showed, according to the caption, "A well isolated Soviet Premier" stepping off the gangplank with head bowed.

And so on went our findings of the day-by-day highlights of news coverage in the two papers.

As seen from the two perspectives of emphasis, each newspaper highlighted its own set of significant realities from its own social and cultural vantage point. The standards we hold seem most applicable to reporting the progress of a game—business, political, athletic, personal, or atomic—with primary emphasis on the clash, the color, and the score.

The definition of significant realities in the communist paper appeared to be keyed to communication on a broader basis. Strategy, conflict, procedure were not neglected but treated as subordinate means to universal ends. The ends themselves were those generally accepted to be of major daily concern and hope to most people around the world. These ends were defined clearly, emphasized daily, and espoused enthusiastically. They implicitly swept aside the "game theory" of freedom and objectivity in preference to the claim that aspects of reality to be most freely objective about are the bread-and-butter promise and substance of the great issues of our time.

What do these perspectives mean to others? What do they mean to us?

Seldom do we have the disturbing privilege of taking a tough look at competing and conflicting perspectives available to politically significant elites in other countries. The rattle of atomic arms has a very special meaning for people obsessed with the actual use of these arms by a Western country upon a non-Western country a few days before the agreed upon Soviet entrance into the war against a collapsing enemy. The inescapable suspicion is that Hiroshima and Nagasaki were the monstrous opening shots of the *cold war*; that the cold war serves humanity upon the altar of big power frustration and ambition.

One of the most striking implications of our press perspective outside the West is the extent to which its cold war premises are seen as rationalizing hot wars against revolutionary movements in developing areas. A country which—the argument goes—with one-fourteenth of the world's population eats one-fifth of the world's foods and mines half of the world's resources to collect two-thirds of the world's income naturally derives its privileges from maintaining the present power structure. As this can best be done under the guise of anti-communism, the limited world supply of communists is carefully nurtured, rationed, even manufactured if necessary, and judiciously allocated to trouble spots in need of military attention. With an evacuation of bases and reduction of arms among the major powers, the armed shield of Western privilege would vanish, and the neo-colonial structure would collapse.

These are some of the assumptions and perspectives freely available to the non-Western news reader. He lives in a country of poor people, and in a climate of national fervor reacting to a colonial past. The din of big power conflict grates on the ears of hungry people impatient and determined to get on with the long-promised transformation of their daily lives.

Our perspective of emphases appears at best irrelevant, at worst running counter to a tidal wave of pent-up aspirations bursting the dams of the old power structure. Our vantage point appears to be that of a grim holding operation based on remnants of the established order and preoccupied with the mechanics of a fascinating—if deadly—game of power.

Our own structuring of issues in terms of cold war strategy does not help communicating with people to whom colonial freedom, racial equality, free medical care, free higher education, and care for the aged are much more brightly shining symbols of a good society than is the armed defense (often on their own territory) of a "free world" they have never known, of "free enterprise" they have never had, or of "dignity of the individual" they have never enjoyed.

In one of the few really tough appraisals of our encounter with other perspectives, Robert L. Heilbroner wrote in *The Future as History:* "Until the avoidable evils of society have been redressed, or at least made the target of the wholehearted effort of the organized human community, it is not only premature but presumptuous to talk of 'the dignity of the individual.' The ugly, obvious, and terrible wounds of mankind must be dressed and allowed to heal before we can begin to know the capacities, much less enlarge the vision, of the human race as a whole. In the present state of world history the transformations which are everywhere at work are performing the massive and crude surgery." What we need, wrote Heilbroner, is "a broad and compassionate comprehension of the history-shaking transformations now in mid-career, of their combined work of demolition and construction, of the hope they embody and the price they will extract."

What is the significance of our press perspective for the Russians themselves, and for others living in communist countries? This is more difficult to assess because most of them are prevented (one might say protected) by jamming and censorship from being exposed to it. The paradoxical consequence is that, as Ralph K. White of the United States Information Agency concluded on the basis of a number of studies, "they are basically very friendly to us, in spite of anti-American Communist propaganda." At the same time, these studies indicate that

> ...they think we are probably dangerous to them. They accept, though with some doubts, the Communist propaganda claiming that America is ruled by capitalists who profit from war....They find it hard to believe that we could be sincerely afraid of them....Even disaffected Soviet individuals are likely to think that their government would not risk war, and that their government's peacefulness must be evident to the rest of the world.

Studies of Soviet refugees by Harvard's Russian Research Center showed that their contact with the Western press and cheap literature produced the greatest negative effects, next to their surprise at the lack of free medical care and free higher education—features they had taken for granted as part of all civilized life.

A few months after completing my own study, I had the opportunity to discuss problems of the press with editors of communist newspapers in Eastern Europe. I would like to paraphrase the substance of their views for the sometimes unexpected light they shed upon the conflict of perspectives.

A high-ranking editor in Hungary had read my research report on *The New York Times* and the Hungarian paper (published in the *Journalism Quarterly*). When I asked him what he thought of it, he hemmed and hawed for a while. Then he gave me this view of the needs and pressures which shape their own press perspective.

"Your findings appear quite flattering," he said. "But right now we are more concerned with the other side of the coin. We are concerned with the ways in which *The New York Times* makes actually better propaganda abroad, even if not the kind you like.

"To our minds," the communist editor explained, "the Western private press is so brutally irresponsible that it becomes entirely credible. Who would question the sincerity of an opponent who shows himself in the worst possible light? Who would discount as 'propaganda' the kind of talk which can afford to shock and alienate people, which can look at the world with the callous and calculating eye of conflict and violence?

"We, on the other hand, have made the great mistake of looking at the world through rose-colored glasses. Living in a badly split society, we thought we could achieve greater unity by harping on glorious aims while ignoring the wide gap between promise and performance. We lost our credibility before we could close the gap. Our illusions were smashed in 1956, and so were our rose-colored glasses.

"Now we have a new policy. Unlike *The Times*, we still relate major events to the goals of peace and colonial freedom because these are also the needs and goals of socialist societies. But, like *The Times*, we no longer make secrets of our blunders, failures and shortcomings. This may lose us some friends, but it helps our credibility. So you see," he added with a rueful smile, "just when your study appeared I was trying to tell our reporters to act a little more like *The New York Times*!"

The foreign editors of a major Moscow daily paper also stressed their "new policy"—described as a more honest look at the outside world. When I asked them why they don't permit readers to look at the United States through the eyes of our own newspapers, they answered without hesitation:

"Because it would do both of us a disservice. Our readers are not accustomed to such reporting. They might think that we fabricated these papers just to discredit you. Or, if they believed them to be genuine, they might become panicky or lose the will to live and to work.

"We don't need your papers to frighten and discourage our people or to embolden our Stalinists. We say that capitalism is a bad system but not a mad system. When Walter Lippman writes something responsible we cite him or print him. When the State Department sends an important diplomatic note we print it along with our reply. When a responsible head of state gives us a special interview we print it. Our new policy is to convince our readers that we can plan and work for the future, that responsible people in the West do not want to commit suicide, that they are rational men."

My final question is: are we?

We were the first to usher in both the anti-imperialist and the atomic eras. We seem to be among the last to accept their ultimate implications. The challenge of anti-colonial revolutions seems as foreign to our press perspective as the futility of the arms race.

We are so busy refuting communist arguments and keeping the score in the cold war that we miss the opportunity of transforming a game no one can win to a contest no nation can lose.

While some may continue to profit from both, economic dependencies and weapons of mass destruction are neither national assets nor sources of real world power in the second half of the twentieth century. They pose their primary threat—and challenge—to the intelligence, courage, and imagination of people *possessing* them.

In the eyes of many, the cannibal may well be any cold warrior brandishing atomic boomerangs over the still bleeding body of mankind. Lacking from our press perspective is a compassionate view of the convulsions of this feverish body, and of the hope they embody as well as the price they will extract.

CHAPTER 13

IDEOLOGICAL PERSPECTIVES AND POLITICAL TENDENCIES IN NEWS REPORTING

BY GEORGE GERBNER

The basic editorial function is not performed through "editorials" but through the selection and treatment of all that is published. An earlier study on "Press Perspectives in World Communication"[1] indicated how this process of total selection and relative emphasis expresses and cultivates those aspects of national perspectives in world political communication which serve the industrial and social roles of media in their own societies. The subject of the present inquiry is the related proposition that, in fact, all news are views; that all editorial choice patterns in what and what not to make public (and in what proportion, with what emphasis, etc.) have an ideological basis and a political dimension rooted in the structural characteristics of the medium; that such ideological perspectives and political tendencies will be expressed and cultivated through presumably non-political news as much as, or perhaps even more than, through overtly political reporting, and in the commercial press as well as in the "party press."

Our case study inquired into the coverage of a criminal event in the French press. The French press is in the process of transformation from a "party press" to a commercially sponsored press system. Both types of newspapers exist side-by-side. They differ mainly in their criteria of news selection and editing. The party press select news and views according to standards relevant to its political clients' ideological perspectives. In a multi-party system, it creates and cultivates publics of different—and at times radically opposed—political tendencies. The commercial press selects material according to standards relevant to its clients'—the advertisers'—need for broad mass appeal. It creates and cultivates a public perspective which may cut across party lines.

The event was the probably unintended (but not entirely accidental) fatal shooting of a student by a teacher. The underlying political dimension of the reporting of any event, and especially an event involving education in France, found expression in the news coverage. Before giving an account of the coverage itself and of the "ideological dialogue" our analysis attempted to isolate and reconstruct, we shall consider the context of relevant circumstances and the tense and critical nature of the times.

PEOPLE AND EVENTS

Perpignan is a provincial town of over 70,000 in the foothills of the Pyrenees, at the southwestern edge of the winegrowing region along France's Mediterranean coast.

Jean Amiel, 37, teaches English at the Arago lycee of his hometown of Perpignan. His wife is also an English teacher at a local girls' school. They have a four-year-old daughter and lead a busy but quiet private life in their new house in the suburbs.

Alain Rolland, 16, is a good student at the Arago lycee. He has never had Amiel for a teacher. He divides his time between the Boy Scouts, his studies, and his family. The Rollands are recent arrivals in Perpignan. Alain's father is director of a local branch of a bank, the Algerian Credit Society. Alain has a brother also at the Aragon lycee.

It is the night of St. Jean, June 23, 1958. Bonfires and dancing on the streets celebrate the longest day of the year in the tradition of Catalonian youth. A group of boys, including Alain, heads toward the suburbs to engage in a familiar prank: lighting firecrackers in the mailboxes of the quiet and dignified residential district.

This is the third night the same prank (although not the same pranksters) plagues the Amiel house. Mme. Amiel does not feel well; the children cannot sleep. Jean Amiel has obtained a police permit for a gun to "scare off the vandals." Now he grabs the old revolver and fires three shots into the darkness.

Alain falls to the ground. "He's hurt, he's bleeding," a friend cries out. Amiel drives the wounded boy to the police station, then to the hospital. The intern pronounces him dead on arrival. *"Le coup du lapin,"* he says; a fatal blow to the spine, suffered in the fall.

Amiel drives the dead boy to his parents. He says he is responsible. But, despite their sorrow, the Rollands insist that only fate is responsible; a bad fall, *"le coup du lapin."* Amiel says nothing about the shots.

He arrives home pale, drawn, and still silent. His wife does not question him. Soon it's morning. Amiel calls his high school principal, says he will not meet his classes that day. He waits for the police. They arrive. The coroner has repudiated the intern's diagnosis. There is a small bullet hole in the back of Alain's neck.

Public emotion runs high in Perpignan. A crowd of 3,000 gathers around the Amiel house. The police delay the usual reconstruction of events at the scene of the crime to avoid a riot. For a while it seems that the trial itself has to be moved to another city.

Nearly a year goes by before the case comes to trial. The proceedings are held in Perpignan without incident. There is no denial of guilt. The defense pleads merely an accident, *"un cruel hazard."* The jury's verdict: two years in prison, two and a half million (old) francs damages.

Two years later the Amiels are gone, their house is sold, the crime is forgotten. A colleague is asked about the case, and about its political repercussions, if any, for purposes of this study. He says Amiel was a "moderate leftist," his wife "more outspoken and militant." Amiel's promotion, long delayed at the time of the crime (as noted in the press coverage, especially of the Left) had been going through channels at the Ministry and was announced while he was in prison (as pointed up by the indignant press of the Right). The right-wing provincial daily *Midi Libre* has been feuding with the teaching corps. An ultra-conservative radio commentator on the national network has been attacking "criminal professors." Anonymous threatening letters have been sent to some teachers. But instruction at the lycee goes on as usual. The name of Jean Amiel is no longer mentioned in Perpignan.

THE TIMES AND THE NEWS

The events reported in the materials of this study took place at a time of national crisis marking the end of the Fourth Republic. It was a time of war and revolt in Algeria, the establishment of rebellious Committees of Public Safety, rumors of impending paratroop landings in Paris. There were fears of right-wing dictatorship and civil war. A "legal coup d'etat" brought de Gaulle to power in May 1958. Labor unions, Left parties, many other organizations demonstrated in protest. Teachers called a one-day strike throughout France on May 30th. They continued to demonstrate (and suffer government sanctions) throughout the period. A new constitution reduced the power of the elected deputies and changed the basis of representation to the detriment of the Left. The strife over Algeria erupted in shocking terrorism and deepened the national trauma.

The crime of Jean Amiel shared the spotlight in the daily press not only with news of these climactic political and military developments but also with reports of industrial and commercial strides made despite all the turmoil, and with other sensational "affairs." Headlines of Alain's murder competed for attention with those of "L'affair Jaccoud" in which a famous Geneva lawyer killed the lover of his mistress; of the kidnapping of actress Michele Morgan's son by her ex-husband; and of the Tour de France bicycle race. During Amiel's trial, there was continuing coverage of the much longer Guillaume-Lacaze and the "Ballets Roses" affairs, implicating former ministers or other important personalities in corruption, extortion, and prostitution.

It was in this general context of the times and the news that the crime and trial of Jean Amiel stirred a modest sensation in the French press.

THE PRESS

We have noted that both "party" and commercial standards of news treatment operate side-by-side in the French press. Our analysis of the differential tendencies of news coverage included nine newspapers in three general groups: the Left press, the Right press, and the commercial press. Two Paris dailies and one provincial daily comprised each group. We did not include the unique "prestige paper" *Le Monde*, or the influential (and predominantly right-wing) Catholic press. Table 1 presents the available circulation and readership figures of all papers used in the analysis.

Table 1. Newspapers Studied and Space Devoted to l'Affair Amiel

			Space devoted the Amiel affair (in square inches)			
	*Circulation**	*Readership+*	*Total space (100%)*	*Percent on front page*	*Percent pictures*	*Number of stories on Amiel Affair*
Commercial Press						
France Soir	1,350,000	2,124,000	772	12%	17%	10
Parisian Libere	900,000	1,933,000	384	27%	19%	9
Independant	—	198,000	736	64%	29%	11
Left Press						
Humanite	200,000	283,000	336	19%	4%	6
Liberation	110,000	148,000	658	19%	5%	7
Provençal	205,000	690,000	520	43%	43%	7
Right Press						
Aurore	472,000	870,000	1,036	7%	27%	9
Figaro	480,000	1,018,000	252	28%	—	8
Midi Libre	—	577,000	1,120	27%	14%	10

*Circulation figures listed are those included in John C. Merrill, *Handbook of the Foreign Press* (Baton Rouge, La.: Louisiana State University Press, 1959).
+Readership estimates were obtained from unpublished 1958 data at the National Institute of Statistics, Paris.

It also indicates the total amount of space devoted to the Amiel affair in each newspaper (during the study period discussed below), and the allocation of that space to pictures and front page stories.

The "party press" of the Left and Right are not all political organs in the strict sense, although the Left press comes closest to a party-subsidized primarily by the business community as is the commercial press. But the two differ in the nature and extent of the subsidy, in reader appeal, and in the nature of their service to clients. The press of the Right appeals primarily to the more consciously conservative or reactionary readers. The commercial press serves the business community more as a merchandising vehicle of mass appeal; its overt political line must, therefore, be somewhat blander, broader, and more flexible within the limits compatible with the basic interests of its clients.

Following are some general characteristics of the papers of each group (at the time of the events reported):

LEFT PRESS

L'Humanite is the official Communist daily. About 40 percent of its circulation is outside of Paris. Its readers are primarily workers and lower middle class. Two-thirds are male, and three-quarters have not gone beyond primary school (which ends at age 14). *Liberation* is a socialist daily with readership concentrated in the Paris region. Two-thirds of its readers—mostly workers, clerical employees, and middle class—are male; about the same number have a primary school education only. *Le Provençal* is a widely read Marseilles daily. It is reported to have a readership about three times its circulation, mostly among workers of the southeast Mediterranean region. About 53 percent of its readers are male, and 71 percent have primary school education only.

COMMERCIAL PRESS

France Soir is the largest French daily. Three quarters of its circulation is concentrated in Paris. A little over half of its readers are women. It attracts all classes of readers, but nearly half have gone beyond primary school. *Parisien Libere* is the second largest French daily. Only 16 percent of its readers live outside Paris. More than half (53%) are male; 75 percent have primary schooling only. *L'independant* is a provincial daily read by farmers and others in the southwest Mediterranean (Midi) region. Its readership is 53 percent female and 71 percent primary school educated.

RIGHT PRESS

L'Aurore "is the daily of the big businessman; it is conservative almost to the point of being reactionary."[2] With a circulation of about 472,000, it also attracts a large readership of middle class, clerical, and other employees. More than half of them are women; three-fourths of them live in Paris. About 53 percent of its readers have completed primary school only. *Le Figaro* is the largest right-wing daily. Its proportion of national circulation (37% outside of Paris) is second only to *L'Humanite*'s. *Figaro*'s readers are mostly business and professional; 57 percent are women, and more than half are secondary school or university educated. *Midi Libre* is a Toulouse daily read by farmers and others (51% women) in the Midi region. The educational level of its readers is slightly higher than that of the other provincial dailies: 41 percent have gone beyond primary school.

THE METHOD OF ANALYSIS

A procedure we call "proposition analysis" was developed to provide a measure of the specific content composition of differential tendencies in the presentation of the same events by different sources. The procedure consists of the following steps:

Message samples produced by the different sources are screened sentence-by-sentence to develop a list containing all basic propositions advanced by each source. The form of a proposition may differ from the form of the statement advancing it in that the proposition incorporates the basic idea of the statement in a more general prepositional form.

A master list of propositions includes all essentially different propositions advanced in all statements of each source. A code following each proposition records the source or sources which advanced it in one or more statements. (The number of times a proposition was advanced was not recorded in this study.) These propositions are sorted into "balanced" and "differential" passages. The passages in which each source (or, in this case, press group) has about the same share of propositions are the "balanced" versions. Those in which some sources are represented more than others are the "differential" versions; they indicate the composition of differential tendencies in the message production of the different sources.

The newspapers listed above were screened from June 25 through July 1, 1958, and from April 10 through April 23, 1959. The crime was reported during the first period, and the trial was held during the second.

The material analyzed included every news and feature story dealing with the crime, the trial, the major participants, and the public repercussion of the case. (There were no editorials.) Every newspaper used in the study carried at least seven relevant stories, and at least two in each period. Stories from both study periods were lumped together to compose the sample for each paper.

It should be noted that the size of each sample affects primarily the total number of propositions advanced but not necessarily the number of *different types* of propositions. In other works, a paper may print a great deal of what is essentially common ground among all papers, or less but of a somewhat different slant.

Propositions were drawn from any and all kinds of statements in the relevant samples. They could be statements of the paper's own reporter, or they could be attributed to police, witnesses, lawyers, teachers—anyone the paper chose to cite. A large variety of potential news sources make a wide variety of statements; it is part of the editorial function of the press to select and compose from these some public representation of "the facts of the case" and of the views that shed light on the "facts."

A total of 642 separate propositions were listed as having been advanced in the statements of one or more of the newspapers studied. More than two-thirds of these propositions were "balanced" (advanced by papers of all three groups in about equal proportion), or were not strictly relevant to the events themselves, or both. (For example, there was much discussion about the general characteristics of modern youth in France and elsewhere.) About one-third of all propositions represented the differential aspects and versions. The passages were formed mainly from the differential propositions, or from 201 propositions out of a total of 642.

These propositions were grouped into eleven passages. Each passage dealt with a certain aspect or version of the events. The grouping of the propositions was done without reference to the stories themselves. The sequence of propositions does not necessarily represent any actual sequence of statements in the stories.

The passages represent sets of propositions abstracted from the total coverage. The focus and complexion of the account changes from passage to passage as the balance of representation shifts from one side of the political spectrum to the other.

THE FINDINGS

We shall now present each passage, and the measure indicating each newspaper's (and press group's) share of representation in the propositions of each passage. As the passages do not reconstruct any sequence of events or ports in a chronological order, they can be ordered at will. We shall first attempt to reconstruct the "dialogue of ideological perspectives" inherent in the press coverage of events in a multi-party press system. Later we shall discuss the passages in the order of the shifting ideological perspectives.

The passages and measures are presented as follows: A title and brief comment highlighting certain characteristics of each passage is followed by the propositions themselves (in somewhat abbreviated form) on the left hand side of the page. The propositions are divided by slashes; the total number of propositions contained in each passage is given in parentheses at the end of the passage.

The measures appear on the right hand side of the page, to the right of each passage. The first column of figures gives the number of different propositions each newspaper advanced out of the total number of propositions included in the passage. The second column is the percentage share of each paper (and each press group) in the total number of different propositions included in the passage and advanced by all papers.

The press group which has the largest share of representation in the passage is in capital letters like this: LEFT PRESS, etc. The reader can see at a glance which press group advanced the largest number of propositions in each passage.

Good man, terrible accident. The first passage is a relatively balanced version, recounting the story of a terrible accident that kills an innocent boy and ruins the life of a good man. The Left press leads in the number of propositions, but the differences are not very great and the individual papers rank in almost random order.

Propositions	*Propositions made by*	N	%
A good man / stable / intelligent / hard working / generally pleasant and friendly / opposite of a madman or murderer / with a serene life / beyond reproach / past without blemish / able educator / devoted husband / blessed with daughters he loves / a good sense of humor / fires into the air without thinking / intending to scare the pranksters / overwhelmed when sees a boy fall / seized by panic / consumed by remorse / lives a horrible calvary / will never get over it / cannot believe what happened / beyond himself / loses the will to live / calm at the trial / restrained, soft-spoken / weary / tearful / refuses to acknowledge any extenuating circumstances / almost indifferent to the fate that has befallen him (Total: 29)	LEFT PRESS		(37.6)
	Humanité	22	16.5
	Libération	17	12.8
	Provençal	11	8.3
	COMMERCIAL PRESS		(31.5)
	France Soir	18	13.5
	Parisien Libéré	14	10.5
	Indépendant	10	7.5
	RIGHT PRESS		(30.8)
	Aurore	13	9.8
	Figaro	14	10.5
	Midi Libre	14	10.5
	Total	133	100.0

Happy childhood, easy life. The second passage delves of into Jean Amiel's past. Its propositions paint a picture of a happy childhood and an easy life. The Right press is followed by the Commercial press in advancing these propositions. They provide a "psychological" rather than "social" context for the crime; the Left press takes scant notice of these propositions.

Propositions	*Propositions made by*	N	%
Comes from a family of civil servants / father held high government job / father was teacher / grandfather was also teacher / had happy childhood / no financial problems / student life without hardships / had only the normal money problems of all young couples / borrowed from parents / built beautiful villa (Total: 10)	LEFT PRESS		(10.0)
	Humanité	1	5.0
	Libération	—	—
	Provençal	1	5.0
	COMMERCIAL PRESS		(35.0)
	France Soir	3	15.0
	Parisien Libéré	3	15.0
	Indépendant	1	5.0
	RIGHT PRESS		(55.0)
	Aurore	4	20.0
	Figaro	4	20.0
	Midi Libre	3	15.0
	Total	20	100.0

Modest means, heavy burdens. The Left press leads in suggesting a very different context for the crime. The third passage points to the modest means and heavy financial burdens of the Amiel family. It notes the insufficiency of even two teachers' incomes to pay for the cost of a suburban home. The significance of the house for Jean Amiel, and his generosity and good humor amidst difficult circumstances, receive emphasis in this version.

Propositions

Comes from respectable family of modest means / father was customs inspector in small town / Jean wanted very much to own a nice home / his house cost more than he could afford / has been heavily indebted / even two teacher incomes in the family not sufficient / the house was his dream / his happiness / his success / the crowning point of his career / he decided to work double and triple time / still generous enough to give free English lessons to daughter of a colleague / looked to the future with optimism / and good humor (Total: 14)

Propositions made by	N	%
LEFT PRESS		(57.5)
Humanité	13	27.7
Libération	10	21.3
Provençal	4	8.5
COMMERCIAL PRESS		(27.6)
France Soir	8	17.0
Parisien Libéré	4	8.5
Indépendant	1	2.1
RIGHT PRESS		(14.7)
Aurore	1	2.1
Figaro	3	6.4
Midi Libre	3	6.4
Total	47	100.0

A defective personality. The fourth passage depicts Jean Amiel as a defective personality: pedantic, irascible, vindictive, provoking the wrath and revenge of students. The *France Soir* and the rightist *Aurore* take the lead in presenting or citing these statements.

Propositions

Often pedantic / inflexible / lacks warmth / takes refuge in rules / tried to gain respect through severity / lacks self-confidence / lacks real authority / tries to frighten students / rules by terror / beats students / brutal / loses temper in class / especially with younger students who offer less resistance / envies students for their youth and money / isolated from reality / worthless outside his field / students tried to take revenge / wanted to teach him a lesson (Total: 18)

Propositions made by	N	%
LEFT PRESS		(21.2)
Humanité	2	6.1
Libération	4	12.1
Provençal	1	3.0
COMMERCIAL PRESS		(45.3)
France Soir	7	21.2
Parisien Libéré	4	12.1
Indépendant	4	12.1
RIGHT PRESS		(33.4)
Aurore	7	2.1
Figaro	2	6.1
Midi Libre	2	6.1
Total	33	100.0

A "knight with a sad face." The fifth passage paints yet another portrait: a pitiful, harassed young man in a state of near collapse from worry and overwork, yet inspiring respect (though not a deserved promotion); a kind of *"chevalier a la triste figure"*—knight with a sad face. The Left press leads with nearly a half of all statements advancing such propositions.

Propositions

Still appears youthful / like a "knight with a sad face" / one of those "nice guys" with no strong personality / overworked / timid / sensitive about pranks and taunting / worried about financial problems / a plodder / students say he gave signs of fainting in class /

used stimulants to keep him awake / sleeping pills to make him sleep / no complaints were reported to the inspector / superiors generally commended his work / yet he was not promoted / gave private lessons to supplement his income / corrected papers of correspondence students / worked as interpreter at the airport / corrected baccalaureate exams at night / prepared the distribution of awards at the lycee / drafted the scholastic reports / attended meetings of the disciplinary council / colleagues held him in high esteem / wrote him in prison to assure him of their sympathy / offered financial help to Mme. Amiel (Total: 24)

Propositions made by	N	%
LEFT PRESS		(49.6)
Humanité	23	20.4
Libération	18	15.9
Provençal	15	13.3
COMMERCIAL PRESS		(28.3)
France Soir	15	13.3
Parisien Libéré	7	6.2
Indépendant	10	8.8
RIGHT PRESS		(22.1)
Aurore	12	10.6
Figaro	4	3.5
Midi Libre	9	8.0
Total	113	100.0

A contemptible wretch. The propositions brought together in the sixth passage counter the pathetic (and sympathetic) image of the "knight with the sad face" with a stark extension of the theme of defective personality: Amiel is a contemptible mental and physical wretch, a liar and a coward. He is indifferent to his (possibly intentional) crime, and is perhaps more concerned about bloodstains in his car than about the life of his innocent victim. The right wing ***Aurore*** is in the lead in citing these propositions, followed by ***France Soir*** and *Parisien Libere.*

Propositions

Weak / cowardly / introverted / suffering from a persecution complex / impulsive / heartless / lacking any sense of humor / having an exaggerated sense of pride / acting with unbelievable rashness / possibly even aimed his gun / grudgingly got his car to take the fallen boy / told the others not to let Alain's blood stain the seats / hid his act as long as possible / kept a cowardly silence / lied / became entangled in contradictions / a miserable physical specimen / ascetic features / tall and thin / long hands / prematurely aged / but does not appear particularly tormented (Total 22)

Propositions made by	N	%
LEFT PRESS		(23.8)
Humanité	7	11.9
Libération	7	11.9
Provençal	—	—
COMMERCIAL PRESS		(33.9)
France Soir	10	16.9
Parisien Libéré	9	15.3
Indépendant	1	1.7
RIGHT PRESS		(42.4)
Aurore	17	28.8
Figaro	5	8.5
Midi Libre	3	5.1
Total	59	100.0

A heart-rending affair. Counterpointing that hostile version is a heart-rending story of despair, pathos, and family devotion, advanced mainly by the Left.

Propositions
Amiel sobs when his parents enter the court / displays tender affection for his wife / dares not look at his mother during the trial / father dies, overcome with shame and grief / does not attend funeral to save his mother from sight of her son between gendarmes / Mme. Amiel (the wife) is beautiful / amazing / resembles tragic Antigone / pathetic in her attempt to defend her husband (Total: 9)

Propositions made by	N	%
LEFT PRESS		**(64.0)**
Humanité	7	28.0
Libération	8	32.0
Provençal	1	4.0
COMMERCIAL PRESS		(24.0)
France Soir	3	12.0
Parisien Libéré	1	4.0
Indépendant	2	8.0
RIGHT PRESS		(12.0)
Aurore	1	4.0
Figaro	1	4.0
Midi Libre	1	4.0
Total	25	100.0

A national disgrace. Another version, however, presents Mme. Amiel as a shrew, the family in discord, the trial unfair, Amiel's promotion while in prison a scandal. The whole affair is regarded as a national disgrace. The Right press reported nearly two-thirds of all such statements.

Propositions
Mme. Amiel has a harsh and cold face / she goaded her husband into taking action against the pranksters / she is heartless / quarrelsome and nagging / treats her husband cruelly during the trial / teachers testifying at the trial were biased / they concealed Amiel's abnormalities / the verdict was too lenient / spectators protested the leniency of the jury / many readers wrote indignant letters / Amiel was promoted while in jail / a teacher cannot be a killer / it is a national disgrace / invitation to anarchy / Amiel must leave France (Total: 15)

Propositions made by	N	%
LEFT PRESS		**(3.3)**
Humanité	1	3.3
Libération	—	—
Provençal	—	—
COMMERCIAL PRESS		(33.4)
France Soir	5	16.7
Parisien Libéré	3	10.0
Indépendant	2	6.7
RIGHT PRESS		(63.3)
Aurore	8	26.7
Figaro	7	23.3
Midi Libre	4	13.3
Total	30	100.0

Unjust conditions. The version favored by the Left press is very different. It dwells on conditions which frustrate the efforts and try the patience of teachers and other "intellectuals." No one, it is claimed, can judge or punish such a crime more than the teacher's own remorse. It is not the verdict that is seen as "disgraceful"; it is "the catastrophic situation in secondary education."

Propositions
It is difficult to judge such an extraordinary crime / it doesn't make sense / teachers like children / Amiel was interested in his students / he made them work / he gained their respect / now he has lost this respect / brought unhappiness to his family / must leave his

profession / his home / his own remorse is his greatest punishment / crime was unfortunate result of long exasperation / of taunting and pranks which followed him into his private life / he is to be pitied as are all intellectuals jeered at by nonentities / humiliated / working under great nervous strain / always watched, always supervised / underpaid / overworked / despite exacting preparation for their profession / forced to seek outside jobs / victims of unjust conditions / the trial failed to reveal the catastrophic situation in secondary education (Total: 23)

Propositions made by	N	%
LEFT PRESS		**(58.3)**
Humanité	15	19.0
Libération	19	24.1
Provençal	12	15.2
COMMERCIAL PRESS		(26.7)
France Soir	7	8.9
Parisien Libéré	7	8.9
Indépendent	7	8.9
RIGHT PRESS		(15.2)
Aurore	8	10.1
Figaro	3	3.8
Midi Libre	1	1.3
Total	79	100.0

Not a political case. All papers reported that the Amiels (like most teachers in France) had leftist political leanings. But only the press of the Right carried allegations that they really had no political convictions and did not take part, or at least not willingly, in the teachers' protest strike of May 30, 1958. Some of these propositions claim that neither politics nor conditions help explain the crime: others allege intimidation and class bias among teachers.

Propositions

Political explanations are out of place / religious motives are not involved / it has been claimed that the prankster was a Jesuit college student out to get a leftist public school teacher, but that was not the case / overwork and nervousness are no explanation / true causes are unknown / Amiel has no political opinion / he was never much concerned with politics / he did not join the teachers' strike on May 30 / he joined the strike but he didn't know why / he merely followed the instructions of the union / he went out of a feeling of solidarity, not of conviction / the teaching profession smothers differences of opinion / yet such differences exist even at the same school / the inspectors often have to arbitrate political quarrels / many teachers show hostility toward students from well-to-do families (Total: 15)

Propositions made by	N	%
LEFT PRESS		**(5.8)**
Humanité	1	2.9
Libération	—	—
Provençal	1	2.9
COMMERCIAL PRESS		(38.2)
France Soir	8	23.5
Parisien Libéré	2	5.9
Indépendant	3	8.8
RIGHT PRESS		(55.8)
Aurore	6	17.6
Figaro	8	23.5
Midi Libre	5	14.7
Total	34	100.0

Politics has much to do with it. In contrast with "non-political" explanations, the sociopolitical background is most explicitly invoked, again, in the Left press. The propositions of this passage expose the bitter conflict which beset France during this period.

Propositions

Political explanations are germane to this case / so are psychological explanations / Amiel was a man of the Left / his wife had leftist convictions / they were not sectarians or militants / took modest part in the activities of SFIO (Socialist Party) / went on strike May 30 to defend republican liberties / teachers are united in that cause / rich students and their families often feel superior to teachers / many of these students are spoiled and corrupt / they set themselves up as critics of the political convictions of teachers / sons of Algerian colons who settled in Perpignan show no respect for decency or democracy / are partisans of paratroop General Hassu / formed a Committee of Public Safety imitating the Algerian rebellion against the Republic / once they beat up the *concierge* of the lycee / threatened three teachers with death, including the secretary of the teachers union / wrote threatening letter to the local Communist weekly newspaper / instigated the formation of a "James Dean Club" of Perpignan / members were recruited from among the worst pranksters of the "rich kids" in town / inspired by the misdeeds of American youth / committed acts of vandalism in the school building to protest the teachers' strike of May 30 / made teachers with republican and anti-fascist ideas their major targets (Total: 22)

Propositions made by	N	%
LEFT PRESS		**(68.3)**
Humanité	21	35.0
Libération	14	23.3
Provençal	6	10.0
COMMERCIAL PRESS		(20.0)
France Soir	7	11.7
Parisien Libéré	3	5.0
Indépendant	2	3.3
RIGHT PRESS		(11.7)
Aurore	3	5.0
Figaro	1	1.7
Midi Libre	3	5.0
Total	60	100.0

THE SPECTRUM OF DIFFERENCES

Let us note again that this analysis was concerned with differences rather than with the considerable area of overlapping in the way the three press groups presented the events. The basic "facts" of the case were present in all accounts. The differential context of total propositions in which these "facts" were presented was the focus of this inquiry.

Figure 1 is an attempt to illustrate the order and magnitude of shifting perspectives from Left to Right. The boxed letters represent the newspapers of each press group. The number of letters and the size of the boxes indicate the approximate percentages advanced by each out of the total number of propositions advanced by all papers in each passage.

The Left press, as a whole, advances the most overtly "political" version of the case. It seizes the opportunity to make common cause with the left-leaning teachers of France in this "heart-rending" affair." It views the crime and personality of Jean Amiel against the background of "unjust conditions." Education itself is seen as the victim of the greater crimes of reactionary subversion, harassment, neglect. Mme.

Amiel becomes the "beautiful Antigone," victim of tyrants. Amiel himself is a victim; he is a modest man bearing heavy burdens, a "knight with a sad face," a symbol of the intellectual in a society ruled by wealth and privilege. Although the crime and the trial are fully reported, the differential accounts of the Left stress social injustice the root of personal tragedy.

Figure 1. The Shifting Ideological Perspective

Passages in order of percentage of representation in	Left press	Commercial press	Right press
Politics has much to do...	HHHHHHH LLLLL PP	SS P I	A F M
A heart-rending affair	HHHHHH LLLLLL P	SS P II	A F M
Unjust conditions	HHHH LLLLL PPP	SS PP II	AA F M
Modest means, heavy burdens	HHHHH LLLL PP	SSS PP I	A F M
"Knight with sad face"	HHHH LLL PPP	SSS P II	AA F MM
Good man, terrible accident	HHH LLL PP	SSS PP I	AA FF MM
A defective personality	H LL P	SSSS PP II	AAAA F M
A contemptible wretch	HH LL	SSSS PPP	AAAAAA FF M
Happy childhood, easy life	H P	SSS PPP I	AAAA FFFF MMM
Not a political case	H P	SSSSS P II	AAA FFFFF MMM
National disgrace	H	SSS PP I	AAAAA FFFFF MMM

KEY:

Left press	Commercial press	Right press
H L P	S P I	A F M
H-Humanite	S-France Soir	A-Aurore
L-Liberation	P-Parisien Libere	F-Figaro
P-Provencal	I-Independant	M-Midi Libre

Each letter represents approximately 5% of all propositions. The box devoted to each press group represents the approximate total percentage of that group.

With the theme of "defective personality," the balance of perspectives shifts to the Right. Hints of "abnormalities" and unknown "true causes" counter suggestions of mitigating circumstances. The alleged leftist convictions of the Amiels—and of all teachers—are refuted. The accounts merely observe Amiel's "contemptible" character, his dastardly deeds, and his wife's "harsh and cold face." After a "happy childhood" and "easy life," the crime must be outside the scope of social causation, or even reason. The right-wing perspective limits the scope of public discussion to a carefully circumscribed area. The crime is a mental rather than social aberration. Politics has nothing to do with it. The threat is not to liberty, learning, or justice, but to law and order.

The political strength of the French Left lies in the arena of popular political struggle. The political opportunity of the Right is usually in limiting that arena and exercising power outside or "above" politics. The differential aspects of news coverage in the "party press" reflected these political tendencies as parts of the respective ideological perspectives of reporting. The commercially dependent press occupied a position between the two groups of politically dependent newspapers, but, as we shall see, not in the middle.

The only passage in which the commercial press itself had the highest share of representation was the theme of the "defective personality." The order of representations of the commercial press, all following the lead of the Right, were in passages disclaiming political relevance, describing the Amiels' "easy life," observing their "contemptible" conduct, and protesting the leniency of the verdict.

The *distances* between the three press groups' percentage share of representation in each passage are indicated in Figure 2. The passages are again in order of representation from Left to Right. The letters L, C, and R represent the Left, commercial, and Right press groups. The bracketed letter marks the press group with the highest percentage of representation in each passage. The broken lines represent differences in percentage share of representation; each dash stands for one percentage point.

Figure 2. Relative Distances Between Left, Commercial, and Right Press Groups in Percentage Share of Representation in Each Passage

Politics has much to do...[L]- -C- - - - - - - -R
A heart-rending affair [L]- -C- - - - - - - - - - - - -R
Unjust conditions [L]- -C- - - - - - - - - - - - -R
Modest means, heavy burdens [L]- -C- - - - - - - - - - - - - -R
"Knight with a sad face" [L]- -C- - - - - - -R
Good man, terrible accident [L]- - - - - - -C-R
A defective personality L - - - - - - - - - - - - - -C- - - - - - - - - - - - -R
A contemptible wretch L- - - - - - - - - - -C- - - - - - - - -R
Happy childhood, easy life L- -C- -R
Not a political case L- -C- - - - - - - - - - - - - - - - - - - -R
National disgrace L- -C- -R

Each dash represents one percentage point difference.
The bracketed letter marks the press group with the highest percentage share of representation.

The commercial press shares more of the differential accounts of Left and Right than the two share of each other's. But the commercial press also shares more of the passages favored by the Right than it does of the versions advanced primarily on the Left. Furthermore, the greater the Left leadership in advancing the propositions of a passage, the closer the commercial press is to the Right press.

While the commercial press paves the way for certain types of propositions favored by the Right, and follows the lead of the Right in others, its most striking characteristic is a strong reaction *against* the perspective of the Left. In the passages advanced primarily on the Left, the commercial press is an average of 29 percentage points distant from the Left, and only an average of 9 percentage points away from the Right. If we take the passages advanced primarily on the Right, however, we find the commercial press more (but still not quite) centrally located: its average distance from the Left is 24, and from the Right, 19 percentage points. Across all passages the commercial press is an average of 26 percentage points distant from the Left, and 12 percentage points distant from the Right.

CORRELATIONS BETWEEN PAPERS

The percentage of different propositions each newspaper advanced out of all propositions contained in each passage was used to compute correlations between pairs of newspapers across all passages and thus determine the relative position of papers on the continuum of perspectives.

Table 2 presents the direction and magnitude of the correlations. The two highest correlations for each newspaper appear in italics. Figure 3 is a graphic representation based on the two highest correlations for each paper. The two highest positive correlations between each paper and two others are shown by lines leading from the former to the latter. The length of the lines represents the relative magnitudes of these correlations. It can be seen, for example, that the provincial *L'Independant* was the only commercial newspaper whose two highest correlations included one with an organ of the *Left*, the also provincial *Provençal*. It can also be noted that the provincial papers generally tended toward more central positions than their respective press groups, and that the commercial press interlocks with the press of the Right, while the Left press forms a fairly tight group of its own.

Table 2. Product Moment Correlations of Percents of Propositions Advanced by Each Newspaper Out of All Propositions in Each Passage

	Left Press			Commercial Press			Right Press		
	Human-ite	*Libera-ation*	*Pro-vencal*	*France Soir*	*Paris Libere*	*Inde-pendant*	*Aurore*	*Figaro*	*Midi Libre*
Left press									
Humanite		.92	.74	.32	.11	.31	.00 -	.54	.00
Liberation			.69	.15	.08	.39	-.49	-.67	-.27
Provençal				.38	.29	.70	-.18	-.30	.18
Commercial press									
France Soir					.45	.40	.17	.29	.67
Parisien Libere						.18	.53	.23	.38
Independant							.08	.00	.37
Right Press									
Aurore								.41	.27
Figaro									.73
Midi Libre									

Note: The two highest correlations for each newspaper are italicized.
P< .10—r = + or -.47
P< .05—r = + or -.55
P< .01—r = + or -.68

Figure 3. Corregram Showing Two Highest Correlations for Each Newspaper with Other Papers

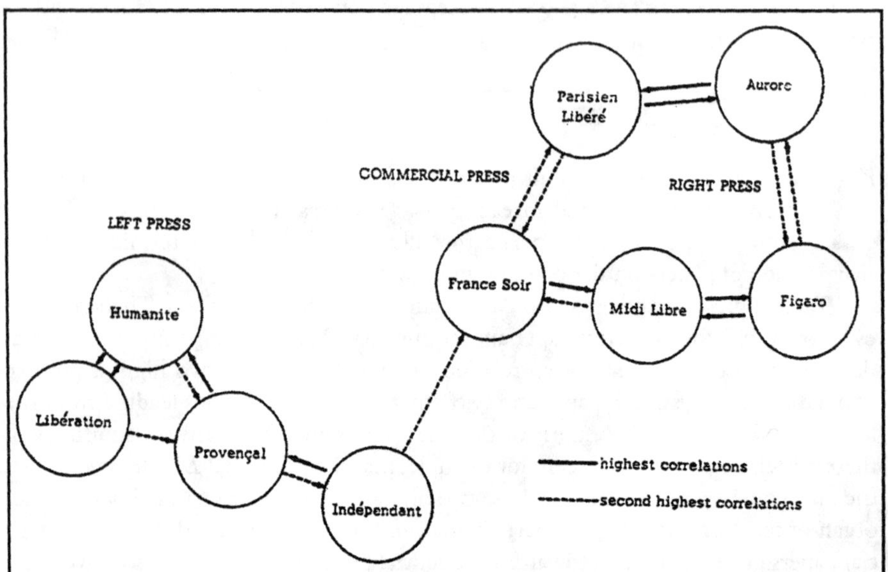

CONCLUSIONS: CHOICE OF PERSPECTIVES

The analysis focused on the differential aspects of the message systems produced by the different sources. The major cleavage was found to be between the perspectives of the Left and those of the commercial and Right press groups. The message systems produced in the French press differ from those of the English and American press systems in that they create and cultivate (rather than only represent through hostile sources) a radically left-wing reading public.

Under these conditions, the versions and accounts of events reported in the commercial newspapers make their appeal to the broadest range of publics. These perspectives indeed find an echo in the commercial press, even if only to be countered and refuted by a greater proportion of material seen from the perspective of the Right.

The analysis tends to support the proposition that there is no fundamentally non-ideological, apolitical, non-partisan news-gathering and reporting system. It also suggests that (at least under conditions of ideological plurality) the commercial press selects the broadest range of propositions concerning events to be made public, but weights its accounts and presents its news from a perspective countering that of the political Left, and close to that of the Right.

This study did not indicate what ideological and political role the commercial press might play in a system which does not cultivate ideological plurality and sharp political differentiation on a mass scale. Of course, no national press system is totally isolated from the basic currents of thought abroad in the world. And there is little doubt that the commercial press everywhere reacts most sharply against perspectives which challenge the bases of its existence and support as an institution. But when the challenge is not represented by competing mass publications in the same press system, the commercial press may be "freer" to ignore that perspective altogether, or to present it not only as a hostile but also as an "outside," foreign, alien view of the news.

At any rate, we find no support for the assumption that the commercial press is free of inherent ideological controls and political tendencies. Its appearance of political "non-partisanship" (if any) may be the result of its tendency to limit the scope of public decision making to carefully circumscribed and relatively marginal areas. Outside these areas, the terms "politics" and "government interference" are used mostly as epithets. The basic ideological and political choices are inherent not in party partisanship but in the total operation of "news values" and of standards of reporting. These choices are evident in press systems where ideological plurality is maintained through more than one source and method of press support. The choices are not so apparent, but they are made, nevertheless, without public debate, vote, and even often in the name of "freedom," where either the commercial press or a one-party press preempts the field of daily journalism.

NOTES

1. George Gerbner, "Press Perspectives in World Communication: A Pilot Study," *Journalism Quarterly*, 38:313–22 (Summer 1961).
2. John C. Merrill, *A Handbook of the Foreign Press* (Baton Rouge, La.: Louisiana State University Press, 1959), p. 58.

PART IV

CULTURAL INDICATORS

Theory and Method

CHAPTER 14

CULTURAL INDICATORS

The Third Voice

BY GEORGE GERBNER

Private and governmental commissions, congressional committees, and foundation-supported studies since the early 1930s have called for some surveillance of media performance and effects. But none of these proposals spelled out how that might be done or limited the scope to manageable proportions relevant to scientific purpose and public policy. Consequently, there is probably no area of significant social policy in which far-reaching decisions are made with as little reliable, systematic, cumulative, and comparative information about the actual trends and state of affairs as in the sphere of the mass production and distribution of the most broadly shared messages of our culture.

We are only vaguely aware of the fact that a decisive policymaking is going on, and that cultural politics is as much a part of the fabric of modern life as economic, welfare, or military politics. Abstract conceptions of "censorship" obscure the realities of direction, constraints, and controls in any mass production. Formal aesthetic categories derived from other times and places ignore social functions, relationships, and power, which lie at the heart of the cultural policy process.

We know very little about trends in the composition and structure of the mass-produced systems of messages that define life in urbanized societies. We know no more about the institutional processes that compose and structure those systems. Much of our research on how people respond and behave in specific situations lacks insight into the dynamics of the common cultural context in which and to which they respond.

Economists, anthropologists, and other social scientists have long been searching for measures of cultural differentiation and diversity. Citizens concerned with public issues such as health, education, delinquency, aging, generational conflict, group relations, drugs, and violence point to cultural "trends" to support their case. But there is no convincing evidence to support any case.

Educators increasingly wonder about the consequences inherent in the compulsion to present life in salable packages. We harness the process of acculturation to consumer markets of instant gratification. Is "Enjoy now, pay later" the prescription for healthy impatience with empty promises or for selfishness and irresponsibility?

Claims come from every vested interest in society. They generally fall into two categories. One is the voice of the political agent or agency staking a claim to "issues" dear to the heart of a political clientele. The other consists of media voices speaking for industrial and business clients. Lacking is a "third voice" of independent research building a continuing and cumulative factual basis for judgment and policy. That is what a scheme of cultural indicators is designed to do.

Cultural indicators will not resolve the issues. Policymaking is the task of citizen judgment and responsible authority. However, cultural indicators can illuminate the aspects that relate more to institutional policy than to personal choice or taste, more to general trends and configurations than to specific items, works, and qualities. In so doing, cultural indicators can assist those responsible for making and implementing policy, as well as the general public, in arriving at sounder judgments concerning the role of mass communications in the cultivation of public policy alternatives.

Cultural indicators will help close the "intelligence gap"' created by historic changes in institutionalized public acculturation. These are changes in the technologically based and collectively managed production of messages. To go McLuhan's half-truth one better, society is the message. Corporate, technological, and other collective processes of message production short-circuit former networks of social communication and superimpose their own forms of collective consciousness—their own publics—on other social relationships. The purpose of a scheme of cultural indicators is to monitor the aspects of our system of generating and using bodies of broadly shared messages that are most relevant to social issues and public policy decisions.

STOCK TAKING IN A CHANGING WORLD

Our progress as a nation depends today, as it has in the past, on meeting our national challenges with knowledge and reason," wrote the secretary of commerce in sending Americans their first census form by mail in 1970. "To do so, we must constantly take stock of ourselves."

But the ways in which "we must constantly take stock of ourselves: change as society changes. Article 1, Section 2 of the U.S. Constitution directed that "Representatives and direct Taxes shall be apportioned among the several States...according to their respective Numbers, which shall be determined by adding the whole Number of free persons...three-fifths of all other Persons." It took the Constitution one hundred years to recognize each and every person as a "whole Number," and the Census another one hundred years to publish, in collaboration with the Social Science Research Council, the first *Historical Statistics of the U.S.* In the meantime, the census went far beyond head counting. It became a chief source of regular, periodic, and cumulative demographic information essential to government, schools, business, and industry.

Economic accounting has also become a national responsibility. The President's Council of Economic Advisers prepared an annual report on the nation's economic health. The social and cultural transformations of our society have made economic and labor statistics and census information less than adequate to "meeting our national challenges with knowledge and reason." "Indeed," comments *Toward a Social Report* (1969), "economic indicators have become so much a part of our thinking that we have tended to equate a rising National Income with national well-being. Many are surprised to find unrest and discontent growing at a time when National Income is rising so rapidly.…Why have income and disaffection increased at the same time?"

Research that might shed light on such problems has been piecemeal, sporadic, uncoordinated, and rarely comparable over time and across cultures. Much of it has been conducted in response to "crises" and forgotten when interest (and funds) declined. Rarely have such studies made contributions to policy. Seldom did they continue long enough or in a broad enough framework to add much to the orderly accumulation of social intelligence.

The recognition of such deficiencies and waste has led social scientists and government officials to propose various remedies. Proposals call for a Council of Social Advisers, an annual social report, a National Institute for the Social Sciences, and other forms of "social accounting" or "social indicators." A review by Land (1971) argued for going beyond the accumulation of output data to gather intelligence about some "conceptualization of a social process."

President Johnson directed the Secretary of Health, Education, and Welfare "to search for ways to improve the Nation's ability to chart its social progress." The Department's response in 1969 illustrated the "intelligence gap" in health, mobility, public order and safety, learning, science, art, and in "information not only on objective conditions, but also on how different groups of Americans perceive the conditions in which they find themselves" (*Toward a Social Report*, 1969).

President Nixon set up a National Goals Research Staff charged with developing "indicators that can reflect the present and future quality of American life, and the direction and rate of its change." Although the group was disbanded without fulfilling its charge, another commission was appointed to review the information needs of government, and the National Science Foundation launched its problem-oriented program of Research Applied to National Needs (RANN). In 1972, the National Institute of Mental Health awarded the first research grant to Dr. Larry P. Gross and myself to conduct a pilot study leading to a full-fledged Cultural Indicator s project. This chapter is largely a discussion of assumptions and concepts underlying that project. It draws from and develops previous statements on that subject (Gerbner, 1966a, 1969a, 1969b, 1970).

AREAS AND TERMS OF ANALYSIS

The reliable observation of regularities in the production, composition, structure, and image-cultivation characteristics of large message systems is a specialized research enterprise. Selective habits of personal participation limit even the sophisticated practitioner to risky extrapolation about the cultural experience of different or heterogeneous communities.

The areas and terms of analysis leading to cultural indicators stem from a conception of communication and its institutionalized role in society. They were developed through prior studies (most of which are listed under my name in the bibliography). The studies demonstrated that the mass cultural presentations of many aspects of life and types of action teach lessons that serve institutional purposes. People do not have to accept these lessons but cannot escape having to deal with the social norms, the agenda of issues, and the calculus of life's chances implicit in them.

I have defined communication as interaction through messages bearing man's notion of existence, priorities, values, and relationships. Codes of symbolic significance conveyed through modes of expression form the currency of social relations. Institutions package, media compose, and technologies release message systems into the mainstream of common consciousness.

How is this massive flow managed? How does it fit into or alter the existing cultural context? What perspectives on life and the world does it express and cultivate? How does it vary across time, societies, and cultures? Finally, how does the cultivation of collective assumptions relate to the conduct of public affairs, and vice versa?

The questions designate three areas of analysis: how mass media relate to other institutions, make decisions, compose message systems, and perform their functions in society are questions for *institutional process analysis*; how large bodies of messages can be observed as dynamic systems with symbolic functions that have social consequences is the question of *message system analysis*; and what common assumptions, points of view, images, and associations do the message systems tend to cultivate in large and heterogeneous communities, and with what public policy implications, are problems for *cultivation analysis*.

INSTITUTIONAL PROCESS ANALYSIS

How do media managers determine and perform the functions their institutions, clients, and the social order require? What is the overall effect of corporate controls on the basic terms of symbolic output? What policy changes do, in fact, alter those terms and how?

Mass media policies reflect not only a stage in industrial development and the general structure of social relations but also particular types of institutional and industrial powers and pressures. Mass communicators everywhere occupy sensitive and central positions in the social network. They have suppliers, distributors, and critics. Other organizations claim their attention or protection. They have associations of their own. They have laws, codes, and policies that channel and constrain them. And they have patrons who, as in any industrial production, supply the capital, the facilities, and the authority (or at least opportunity) to address mass publics.

DECISION MAKING

Any enterprise may appear free to those who run it. But in a more objective sense, all mass production, including that of messages, is managed. Only a small portion of all potential messages can be formulated and even fewer can be selected for mass distribution. Therefore, research cannot realistically focus on whether or not there is "suppression"; selective suppression is simply the other side of the mass communication coin. The analysis must consider all major powers, roles, and relationships that have a systematic and generalized influence on how messages will be selected, formulated, and transmitted.

Some studies (e.g., Gerbner, 1961b, 1964) suggest that systems of messages produced by any institutional source, commercial as well as overtly partisan, have some ideological orientation implicit in selection, emphasis, and treatment. Other research, such as that by Warren Breed (1960), Pool and Shulman (1964), David Manning White (1964), and Walter Gieber (1960, 1964), show that most newsmen respond more to the pressures and expectations of the newsroom than to any generalized concept of audience or public interest. A study of newsroom decisions (Bowers, 1967) found that three out of four publishers are active in directing news decisions, with their influence greatest in news of the immediate market area, and in subjects that affect the revenue of the paper.

The systematic exercise of powers resides in institutional roles and in relationships to centers of power. A scheme designed to analyze this process needs to identify the power roles, suggest some sources of their powers, and specify those functions that affect what the media communicate. Power and its application become relevant to this scheme as they affect what is being communicated to mass media publics. Figure 1 outlines nine types of power roles or groups, and briefly notes the types of leverage and typical functions attached to each role.

1. *Authorities* possess legal powers to enact and enforce demands or impose sanctions on communicators. Legislative, executive judicial bodies, regulatory commissions, public administrators, the police, and the military may have such authority. Authorities may assume rights patrons ordinarily have, and may impose sanctions (such as for seditious or criminal acts) that patrons cannot. Authorities may also depend on the support of communicators for much of their authority; the "regulated" have been known to regulate the regulators.

2. *Patrons* are those who directly invest in or subsidize media operations in exchange for economic, political, or cultural benefits. Their clients are the media that provide such benefits in exchange for discretionary patronage. Media patrons may be banks, advertisers, other corporate or civic organizations, religious or military bodies, or governments. The principal types of patrons and the major client relationships determine the role of media management in the power scheme of every society. The client relationship also affects the institution's approach to most issues and problems, and permeates the climate of communicator decision making.

Figure 1. Major Power Roles, Types of Leverage, and Typical Functions Directing the Formation of Mass-Produced Message Systems

Power Roles (Groups)	Types of Leverage	Typical Functions
1. AUTHORITIES. Make and enforce legally binding decisions	Political and military	Arbitrate, regulate, legitimize power relations; demand service
2. PATRONS—invest, subsidize	Control over resources	Set conditions for the supply of capital and operating funds
3. MANAGEMENT	Control over personnel	Set and supervise policies; public relations
4. AUXILIARIES. Supplement and support management	Access to specialized services	Provide supplies, services
5. COLLEAGUES	Solidarity	Set standards; protection
6. COMPETITORS	Scarcity	Set standards; vigilance
7. EXPERTS. Talent, technicians, critics, subject specialists	Skill, knowledge, popularity, prestige	Provide personal creative, performing, technical services, advice
8. ORGANIZATIONS	Pressure through representation, boycott, appeal to authorities	Demand favorable attention, portrayal, policy support
9. PUBLICS. Groups created or cultivated (or both) by media	Individual patronage	Attend to messages; buy products

3. *Management* consists of executives and administrators who make up the chain of command in the organization. They formulate and supervise the implementation of policies intended to fulfill the terms of patron and other power group support. They engage and control all personnel. Management's chief functions are (a) to cultivate client relations and (b) to conduct public relations. From the management's point of view, the messages that the institution produces must serve these two functions.

4. *Auxiliaries* proved supplies and services necessary to management's ability to perform its tasks. They are distributing organizations, networks, agencies, and syndicates; suppliers of raw materials, talent, artistic properties, and logistical services; wholesale and retail outlets; related manufacturing and trade concerns, associations, unions; and trade concerns, associations, unions; and the holders of patents, copyrights, or other property rights.

5. *Colleagues* are communicators whose status, sense of direction or standards, and solidarity with one another can exert leverage on the formation and selection of messages.

6. *Competitors* are other professionals or media whose claims on scarce resources or ability to innovate can force the institution to exercise vigilance and either innovate or emulate in order to maintain its relationships with patrons and publics.

7. *Experts* possess needed personal skills, knowledge, critical abilities, or other gifts. They are writers, editors, creative talent, technicians, critics, researchers, subject matter specialists, consultants, and others who can give (or withhold) personal services necessary for communication.

8. *Organizations* are other formally structured or corporate groups that may claim attention, protection, or services. They may be business, political, religious, civic, fraternal, or professional associations. Inasmuch as some sort of public visibility has become a virtual requirement for organizational viability and support, the competition for attention is intense. Large organizational investments in public relations through the media exert pressure on media content and make media dependent on freely available (and self-serving) organizational resources.

9. *Publics,* finally, are the products of media output—groups created and cultivated through the messages. They are loose aggregations of people who may have little in common. But the symbols they share cultivate a community of meaning and perspective despite other differences. Management's task of "public relations" is to develop this sense of community into material value for the institution and its patrons.

THE EXERCISE OF POWER

Institutional power is exerted through the leverage built into power roles. Authorities can apply political or policy pressure; patrons can provide or withdraw subsidy; managements can hire and fire; auxiliaries can work overtime or quit servicing; colleagues can strike; competitors can raid, scoop, or corner the market; experts can refuse to serve; organizations can support, protest, or boycott; and publics can patronize or stop reading, viewing, buying, or voting.

These are forms of leverage rooted in the structure of intuitional roles and relations. Power applied to communications usually involves the demands that such and such be (or not be) communicated or altered in certain ways.

The demand may be ad hoc, that is, pertaining to a particular message, subject, or policy. When a system of "do's" and "don'ts" is to be regularly applied, it is usually *codified* (as in codes, regulations, and laws). The force or weight behind the leverage is a measure of institutional power. The test is what happens if the demand is not obeyed or the code not observed. That test is applied in what I call a critical incident.

If nothing happens, there has been no power, or at least no display of force to indicate power. (The ability and willingness to display force by applying sanctions is taken as an indication of institutional power.) Sanctions are *substantive* if they pertain to the substance or content of the communication itself, as in the order to revise or omit (or print) a story, add or delete a scene, withhold necessary information, or jam a broadcast. The force behind a substantive demand or sanction is procedural. Sanctions are *procedural* if they pertain to the procedure by which communication is created. Revoking a license, firing or blacklisting, denying equipment or raw materials, discriminatory taxation or rates, strikes, boycotts, and imprisonment are procedural sanctions.

While analytically distinct, neither power roles nor types of leverage are in reality separate and isolated. On the contrary, they often combine, overlap, and telescope in different configurations. The accumulation of power roles and possibilities of leverage give certain institutions dominant positions in the mass communication of their societies.

Institutional process analysis seeks, through interviews, participant observation, and the study of records, to amplify this scheme of power roles, functions, and leverage, and to apply it to the investigation of decision making in communications. (Gerbner, 1958a, 1958b, 1959, 1969a, 1972b.) Critical incidents (a clash of powers, when things "go wrong") may set the lines of powers and influence for more routine control of media content. The investigation contributes to cultural indicators in its accounts of the interplay of roles and powers that direct the formation of mass-produced message systems. These directions can then be related to the analysis of the message systems and to their cultivation functions. For example, how does management respond to the pressure of authorities or organizations concerning some sensitive aspects of content, and how does that response affect the frequency and symbolic functions of that particular content configuration across media and over time?

MESSAGE SYSTEM ANALYSIS

The material for analysis is taken from the massive flow of symbols produced by mass media for large and heterogeneous (usually national) audiences. Unlike most social science data, these are not symbols used to make inferences about largely hidden processes. They are visible and manifest sources of public acculturation. They provide direct access to the specific imagery, context, and content of a relatively centralized and institutionally managed release of symbolic materials into the common cultural environment.

THE SYSTEMS

The most popular products of mass-produced culture provide special opportunities for the study of socially potent message systems. In these systems-popular fiction, drama, and news—aspects of life are recreated in significant associations with total human situations. An area of knowledge or the operation of a social enterprise would appear only when dramatic or news values—that is, social symbolic functions—demand it.

Dramatic and fictional entertainment especially exhibit ritualistically repetitive social symbolic mechanisms that reveal conventionally cultivated approaches toward people and life. Unlike life, the bulk of popular fiction and dramas is an "open book." Facts do not get in the way of its reality, which is the reality of values. Characterizations are usually apt, motivations are transparent, problems and conflicts are explicit, and the interplay of forces that determines the outcome, and outcome itself, are usually clear. Of all the products of mass-produced culture, these appeal to the widest and most heterogeneous publics. Most people, especially the young and the less educated, encounter most subjects and ideas in the form of "incidental" treatment in the course of their relatively nonselective leisure time entertainment. In that way, "entertainment" can force attention to what most people would never seek out as "information."

The symbolic composition and structure of the message system of a mass medium defines its own synthetic "world." Only what is represented exists. All that exists in that "world" is represented in it. "Facts" reflect not opaque reality but palpable design. Focus directs attention, emphasis signifies importance, "typecasting" and fate accent value and power, and the thread of action or other association ties things together into dynamic wholes. The "World" has its own time, space, geography, demography, and ethnography, bent to institutional purpose and rules of social morality. What policies populate, actions animate, fates govern, and themes dominate this "world"? How do things work in it, and why do they change from time to time?

The "system" in message systems is that of institutional design and purpose. The systematic functions of and trends in the composite "message" can be made visible through the "decomposition" of the presentations into units and categories relevant to investigative purpose, and their "recomposition" in the form of social symbolic functions.

THE ANALYSIS

The analysis is designed to investigate aggregate and collective premises presented in samples of material. It deals with the "facts of life" and dynamic qualities represented in the systems. Its purpose is to describe the symbolic "world," sense its climate, trace its currents, and identify its functions.

The results make no reference to single communications. They do not interpret selected units of symbolic material or draw conclusions about artistic style or merit. The findings represent what large and heterogeneous communities absorb; they do not necessarily resemble what specific individuals or groups select.

The premises defining life in the symbolic world provide common imagery and a basis for interaction among separate and disparate groups. That common basis forms the agenda of public discourse and a starting point for individual conclusions and interpretations. The analysis of message systems pivots on the determination of those common terms and is limited to clearly perceived and reliably coded items.

The reliability of the analysis is achieved by multiple codings and the measured agreement of trained analysts. If one were to substitute the perceptions and impressions of casual observers, no matter how sophisticated, the value of the investigation would be reduced, and its purpose confounded. Only an analysis of unambiguous message elements and their separation from personal impressions left by unidentified clues can provide a baseline for comparison with the intentions of policymakers and the perceptions or conceptions of audiences. No such relationships can be established as long as the actual common terms and their symbolic functions are unknown, are derived from unexamined assumptions, or are inferred from subjective verbalizations of uncertain and ambiguous origin.

DIMENSIONS AND MEASURES

The study of a system *as system* notes processes and relationships expressed in the whole, not in its parts. Unlike literary or dramatic criticism, or, in fact, most personal cultural participation and judgment, message system analysis observes the record of intuitional behavior in message mass-production for large and heterogeneous communities. The reliable observation of that record of institutional behavior reveals collective and common instead of individual and unique features of public image formation and cultivation. The scheme and methods of analysis are designed to inquire into selected dimensions of the process composing and structuring message systems.

These dimensions stem from aspects of communication that we have previously identified as the cultivation of assumptions about *existence, priorities, values,* and *relationships.* Figure 2 summarizes the questions, terms, and measures of analysis relevant to each dimension.

Figure 2. Dimensions, Questions, Terms, and Measures of Message System Analysis

Dimensions:	EXISTENCE	PRIORITIES	VALUES	RELATIONSHIPS
Assumptions about:	WHAT IS?	WHAT IS IMPORTANT?	WHAT IS RIGHT OR WRONG, GOOD OR BAD, ETC.?	WHAT IS RELATED TO WHAT, AND HOW?
Questions:	What is available for public attention? How much and how frequently?	In what context or order of importance?	In what light, from what point of view, with what associated judgments?	In what overall proximal, logical, or casual structure?
	ATTENTION	EMPHASIS	TENDENCY	STRUCTURE
Terms and measures of analysis:	Prevalence, rate, complexity, variations	Ordering, ranking, scaling for prominence, centrality, or intensity	Measures of critical and differential tendency qualities; traits	Correlations, clustering; structure of action

The dimension of assumptions about existence deals with the question "What is?", that is, what is available (refereed to) in public message systems, how frequently, and in what proportions. The availability of shared messages defines the scope of public attention. The measure of attention, therefore, indicates the presence, frequency, rate, complexity, and varying distributions of items, topics, themes, and so on represented in message systems.

The dimension of priorities raises the question, "What is important?" We use measures of *emphasis* to study the context of relative prominence and the order or degrees of intensity, centrality, or importance. Measures of attention and emphasis may be combined to indicate not only the allocation but also the focusing of attention in a system.

The dimension of values inquires into the point of view from which things are presented. It rates certain evaluative and other qualitative characteristics, traits, or connotations attached to different items, actions, persons, groups, and so on. Measures of *tendency* are used to assess the direction of value judgments observed in messages.

The dimension of relationships focuses on the more complex associations within and among all measures. When we deal with patterns instead of only simple distributions, or when we relate the clustering of measures to one another, we illuminate the underlying *structure* of assumptions about existence, priorities, and values represented in message systems.

The four dimensions, then, yield measures of attention, emphasis, tendency, and structure. One or more of these measures can be applied to any unit of analysis. We have studied trends in the distribution of *attention* devoted to the subject of mental illness, of education, and of violence (Gerbner, 1961a, 1966b, 1972a). *Emphasis* was measured in the investigation of comparative press perspectives in world communication (Gerbner, 1961a). Research on political tendencies in news reporting and on the characterizations of violents and victims in television drama focused on measures of differential *tendency*. The study of the "film hero" utilized all dimensions of analysis (Gerbner, 1969c).

The analysis may record topics, themes, persons, and types of action represented in the material. It may touch on the history, geography, demography, and ethnography of the symbolic "world." The symbolic population and its interpersonal and group relationships may be observed. Themes of nature, science, politics, law, crime, business, education, art, illness and health, peace and war, sex, love, friendship, and violence may be coded. The roles, values, and goals of the characters that populate the symbolic "world" may be related to the issues with which they grapple and to the fates to which they are destined.

The scheme provides a conceptual framework and practical instrumentation for the systematic gathering and periodic reporting of comprehensive, cumulative, and comparative information about mass-mediated message systems. Content indicators can include measures specific to given issues, policies, or symbolic functions, such as the television "violence index" (Gerbner, 1972a). Or they can deal with general features of the symbolic world—census figures ranging over time, space, personality types, and social roles. Indicators can also trace the presentation of heroes and villains, victors and victims, fair means or foul, or the configuration of certain themes, actions, and values over time and across cultures.

Content indicators tell us not so much what individuals think or do as what most people think or do something *about* in *common.* They will tell us about the shared representations of life, the issues, and the prevailing points of view that capture public attention, occupy people's time, and animate their imagination. They will help us understand the impact of communication media development and social change on the symbolic climate that affects *all* we think and do. We can then inquire into the institutional aspects and the cultural consequences in sharper awareness of the currents that tug and pull us all.

CULTIVATION ANALYSIS

The most distinctive characteristics of large groups of people are acquired in the process of growing up, learning, and living in one culture rather than in another. Individuals make their own selection of materials through which to cultivate personal images, tastes, views, and preferences, and they seek to influence those available to and chosen by their children. But they cannot cultivate that which is not available. They will rarely select what is scarcely available, seldom emphasized, or infrequently presented. A culture cultivates not only patterns of conformity but also patterns of alienation or rebellion after its own image. Its affirmations pose the issues most likely to be the targets of symbolic provocation or protest.

The message systems of a culture not only inform but form common images. They not only entertain but create publics. They not only satisfy but shape a range of attitudes, tastes, and preferences. They provide the boundary conditions and overall patterns within which the processes of personal and group-mediated selection, interpretation, and image formation go on.

Cultivation analysis begins with the insights of the study of institutions and the message systems they produce, and goes on to investigate the contributions that these systems and their symbolic functions make to the cultivation of assumptions about life and the world. Style of expression, quality of representation, artistic excellence, or the quality of individual experience associated with selective exposure to and participation in mass-cultural activity are not considered critical variables for this purpose. What is informative, entertaining (or both), good, bad, or indifferent by any standard of quality are selective judgments applied to messages quite independently from the social functions they actually perform in the context of large message systems toughing the collective life of a whole community. Conventional and formal judgments applied to specific communications may be irrelevant to general questions about the cultivation of assumptions about what is, what is important, what is right, and what is related to what.

Message systems cultivate the terms on which they present subjects and aspects of life. There is no reason for assuming that the cultivation of these terms depends in any significant way on agreement or disagreement with or belief or disbelief in the presentations, or on whether these presentations are presumably factual or imaginary. This does not mean, of course, that we do not normally attach greater credibility to a news story, a presumably factual report, a trusted source, a familiar account, than to a fairy tale or to what we regard as false or inimical. It does mean that in the general process of image formation and cultivation both "fact" and "fable" play significant and interrelated roles.

THE PROBLEM OF EFFECTS

The bulk of experimental and survey research on communications "effects" has contributed little to our understanding of the mass cultural process. The reason is that most of it stemmed from disciplinary and theoretical perspectives that did not consider that process the principal criterion of relevance.

Mass communications research should be concerned with mass communications and not with assorted tactics of manipulating behavior. The preoccupation with such tactics is itself a reflection of manipulative pressures in a culture in which the "behavior" that ultimately counts (and pays most of the research costs) is that at the cash register, box office, or ballot box. But the concern with tactics at the expense of strategy has been self-defeating. It has neglected the steady cultivation of issues, conceptions, and perspectives that gives meaning to all ideas and actions. All animals "behave" but only humans act in a symbolic context. The tactical preoccupation has generally ignored that context and obscured the basic functions of communications—to cultivate, conserve, support, and maintain. The "effects" of communications are not primarily what they make us "do" but what they contribute to the meaning of all that is done—a more fundamental and ultimately more decisive process. The consequences of mass communications should be sought in the relationships between mass-produced and technologically mediated message systems and the broad common terms of image cultivation in a culture. If the citizens of a self-governing community do not like those terms, they cannot satisfy themselves by injecting a few messages of a different sort. They must attend to the structures and policies that produce most messages in ways functional to their institutional purposes.

THE QUESTION OF CHANGE

The principal "effect" of mass communications is to be found in coming to terms with the fundamental assumptions and premises they contain, and not necessarily in agreeing or disagreeing with their conclusions or in acting on their specific propositions at any one time. Communication is the nutrient culture and not just the occasional medicine (or poison) of mental life. The most critical public consequences of mass communications are in defining and ordering issues, and not just in influencing who will buy what in the short run.

Change can be evaluated and even noticed best in light of the massive continuities that systems of communications typically cultivate. "No change" may be a startlingly effective result of communications sustaining a belief against the cultural current. One cannot really compare a person swimming upstream with another drifting downstream and yet others straining in other directions. To compare and measure their "progress," all speeds and directions must be related to the current itself. If that were to change, all directions and even the meaning of "progress" would change without any change in "behavior" on the part of the swimmers. Similarly, the meaning and measure of communication "effects" are relative to the general flow, composition, and direction of the message-production and image-cultivation processes. It means little to know that "John believes in Santa Claus" until we also know in what culture, at what time, and in the context of what message system is cultivating or inhibiting such beliefs.

A culture cultivates the images of a society. The dominant communication agencies produce the message systems that cultivate the dominant image patterns. They structure the public agenda of existence, priorities, values, and relationships. People use this agenda—some more selectively than others—to support their ideas, actions, or both, in ways that, on the whole, tend to match the general composition and structure of message systems (provided, of course, that there is also other environmental support for these choices and interpretations). There is significant change in the nature and functions of that process when there is change in the technology, ownership, clientele, and other institutional characteristics of dominant communication agencies. Decisive cultural change does not occur in the symbolic sphere alone. When it occurs, it stems from a change in social relations that makes the old patterns dysfunctional to the new order. Such a change changes the relative meanings and functions of the existing images and practices even before these are actually altered. When altered, the new cultural patterns restore to public communications their basic functions: the support and maintenance of the new order.

The strategic approach to mass communications research considers an understanding of the mass cultural process, instead of other aspects of human behavior, the principal criterion of relevance. Institutional process and message system analyses generate the framework of terms and functions for cultivation analysis. Short-term or campaign-type "effects" studies, responses to messages elicited in unknown or uncertain symbolic contexts, or research concerned with "success" or "failure" of preconceived communication objectives are not adequate to the task. The dynamics of continuities, rather than only of change, need to be considered in the examination of mass-produced message systems and their symbolic functions. Such examination is necessarily longitudinal and comparative in its analysis of the processes and consequences of institutionalized public acculturation.

In a general sense there are not communication failures, only failures of intentions and campaigns. All systems of communications may cultivate terms and assumptions implicit in them whether or not those were intended or consciously recognized. We usually communicate more than we intend or know about, and often not what we wish. Many "communication failures" can be interpreted as the success of the receivers to understand the messages better than those who designed them, but in ways they did not intend. Message systems perform symbolic functions that may be apparent to *none* of the parties engaged in the communication. Communications research attempts to reconstruct these functions. Cultivation analysis seeks to discover their contributions to knowledge and meaning.

SYMBOLIC FUNCTIONS

Symbolic functions are intimately involved in and govern most human activity. The human meaning of an act stems from the symbolic context in which it is embedded. The significance of a person's life or death rests in some conception of role, personality, goals, and fate. When the symbolic context changes, the significance of acts changes. A structure may shift to accommodate the change and to preserve—or even enhance—the symbolic functions of the act. For example, in the TV violence study we found that as the proportion of violent characterizations was cut, the imbalance in the risks of victimization between groups of unequal social power increased, thereby strengthening the symbolic function of violence as a demonstration of relative social powers (Gerbner, 1972a). Such observations enable us to ask questions about what *that* message might cultivate in public conceptions and behavior. Thus we would relate the viewing of television violence to the cultivation of certain conceptions of goals, values, people, and power, instead of only to notions about "violent behavior."

In another study (Nunnaly, 1960), the opinions of experts on ten information questions concerning the mentally ill were compared with mass media (mostly fictional and dramatic) representations of mentally ill characters. The mass media image was found to diverge widely from the expert image. The "public image," as determined by an attitude survey along the same dimensions, fell between the expert and the media profiles. Thus, instead of "mediating" expert views, the media tended to cultivate conceptions far different from and in many ways opposed to those of the experts. What may be seen in isolation as "ineffective" communication was, on the contrary, powerful media cultivation "pulling" popular notions away from expert views. The reason is not necessarily ignorance or intentional obscurantism, but instead the difference between semantic labels for a certain type of behavior (such as "mental illness") and the symbolic functions of the dramatic representations of that behavior. The symbolic functions of mental illness in popular drama may be primarily those of indicating a dramatically convenient resolution of certain problems or of designating a morally appropriate "punishment" for certain sins. The dramatic associations with the personality traits that define mental illness *in the plays* should provide a basis for the further investigation of what that implicit message might cultivate in viewer conceptions.

The study of specific message structures and symbolic functions reveals how these communications help define, characterize, and decide the course of life, the fate of people, and the nature of society in a symbolic world. The symbolic world is often very different from the "real" world. Symbolic behavior usually bears little resemblance to everyday actions. The power and significance of symbolic functions rests in the differences. Fiction, drama, and news depict situations and present action in those realistic, fantastic, tragic, or comic ways that provide the most appropriate symbolic context for the emergence of some human, moral, and social significance that could not be presented or would not be accepted (let alone enjoyed) in other ways.

THE CULTIVATION PROCESS AND ITS ANALYSIS

Symbolic structures may cultivate certain premises about the world and its people and about the rules of the game of life. These premises are not necessarily embodied in overt prescriptions (which may, in fact, be quite different), but are implicit in the way things are presented, and in the way they function in the symbolic context. The same premises may lend themselves to a range of conclusions, depending on who draws them, why, when, and how. But the range of conclusions is held together by the definitions implicit in the premises. Should the premises change, the range and complexion of conclusions might also shift.

The cultivating effects of common communications patterns are typically those of selective maintenance on a certain level. General cultural patterns do not "cause" but support or weight or skew tendencies also functional to other (but not necessarily all) aspects of the social and institutional order.

Cultivation analysis starts with the patterns found in the "world" of public message systems. The common structures composing that world present images of life and society. How are these reflected in the expectations, definitions, interpretations, and values held by their "consumers"? How are the "lessons" of symbolic behavior derived from other times and places, and presented in synthetic contexts, applied to assumptions about life? In order to investigate the relationship between message systems and the views and expectations of audiences it is necessary to evolve and adapt a set of measures and investigative techniques.

The principal approaches employed in the cultivation analysis are projective techniques, depth interviews, and periodic questions on sample surveys. Adult and child panels provide subjects for projective and interview work. Projective techniques can structure situations in which respondents tend to reveal views, expectations, and values of which they may not be consciously aware, or which they would not verbalize if asked directly. Techniques of depth interviewing can isolate and highlight views, expectations, and values, and relate these to media exposure patterns and to demographic and other characteristics. Questions selected from the projective tests and interviews and others designed especially for survey use are to be submitted periodically to a national adult probability sample of respondents.

The impact of television and of its further development by cable and other technologies is of special concern, as is the cultivation of social concepts among children. For most people television *is* popular culture. Social, symbolic patterns established in childhood are the most easily cultivated throughout life. Longitudinal and cross-cultural research is needed to follow the lead of message analysis into the living laboratory of popular cultures.

We need to know general trends in the cultivation of assumptions about problems of existence, priorities, values, and relationships before we can validly interpret specific relevant facts of individual and social response. The interpretation of public opinion (i.e., published responses to questions elicited in specific cultural contexts), and of many media and other cultural policy matters, require cultural indicators similar to the accounts compiled to guide economic decisions and to other indicators proposed to inform social policymaking.

Technological developments in communications hold out the possibility of greatly enhancing culture-power on behalf of existing social patterns—or of their transformation. A modern Socrates might say, "know thy communications to know thyself." He would probably add that under conditions of symbolic mass production, the unexamined culture may not be fit to live in.

REFERENCES

Bowers, David R. "A Report on Activity by Publishers in Directing Newsroom Decisions," *Journalism Quarterly* (Spring 1967).

Breed, W. "Social Control in the News Room," in *Mass Communications*, Wilbur Schramm (ed.), Urbana, Ill.: The University of Illinois Press, 1960.

Gerbner, George. "The Social Role of the Confession Magazine," *Social Problems* (Summer, 1958a).

———. "The Social Anatomy of the Romance-Confession Cover Girl," *Journalism Quarterly* (Summer 1958b).

———. "Mental Illness on Television: A Study of Censorship," *Journal of Broadcasting* (Fall 1959).

———. "Psychology, Psychiatry and Mental Illness in the Mass Media: A Study of Trends, 1900–1959," *Mental Hygiene* (January 1961a).

———. "Press Perspectives in World Communications: A Pilot Study," *Journalism Quarterly* (Summer 1961b).

———. "Regulation of Mental Illness Content in Motion Pictures and Television" (with Percy H. Tannenbaum). *Gazette, 6* (1961c).

———. "Ideological Perspectives and Political Tendencies in News Reporting," *Journalism Quarterly* (Autumn 1964).

———. "An Institutional Approach to Mass Communications Research," in *Communication: Theory and Research*, Lee Thayer (ed.), Springfield, Ill.: Charles C. Thomas, 1966a.

———. "Education About Education by Mass Media," *The Educational Forum* (November 1966b).

———. Institutional Pressures Upon Mass Communicators," in *The Sociology of Mass Media Communicators*, Paul Halmos (ed.), *The Sociological Review Monograph* No. 13, pp. 205–248. University of Keele, England, 1969a.

———. "Toward 'Cultural Indicators'; The Analysis of Mass Mediated Systems," *AV Communication Review* (Summer 1969b).

———. "The Film Hero: A Cross-Cultural Study," *Journalism Monograph* No. 13, 1969c.

———. "Cultural Indicators: The Case of Violence in Television Drama." *The Annals of the American Academy of Political and Social Science*, March, 1970.

———. "Violence in Television Drama: Trends and Symbolic Functions," in *Television and Social Behavior*, G. S. Comstock and E. A. Rubenstein (eds.), Vol. 1. *Content and Control.* Washington: Government Printing Office, 1972a.

———. "The Structure and Process of Television Program Content Regulation in the U.S.," in *Television and Social Behavior*, G. S. Comstock and E. A. Rubinstein (eds.), Vol. 1. *Content and Control.* Washington: Government Printing Office, 1972b.

Gieber, Walter. "Two Communicators of the News: A Study of the Roles of Sources and Reporters," *Social Forces* (October 1960).

———. "News Is What Newspaper Men Make It," in *People, Society, and Mass Communications*, Lewis A. Dexter and David M. White (eds.), New York: The Free Press, 1964.

Land, Denneth C. "On the Definition of Social Indicators," *The American Sociologist* (November 1971).

Nunally, Jum C., Jr. *Popular Conceptions of Mental Health; Their Development and Change.* New York: Holt, Rinehart and Winston, 1960.

Pool, Ithiel De Sola, and Irwin Shulman. "Newsmen's Fantasies, Audiences, and Newswriting," in *People, Society and Mass Communications*, Lewis A Dexter and David M. White (eds.), New York: The Free Press, 1964.

Toward a Social Report, U.S. Department of Health, Education and Welfare, Washington: Government Printing Office, 1969.

White, David M. "The Gatekeeper: A Case Study in the Selection of News," in *People, Society and Mass Communications*, Lewis A. Dexter and David M. White (eds.), New York: The Free Press, 1964.

Chapter 15

GROWING UP WITH TELEVISION

The Cultivation Perspective

BY GEORGE GERBNER, LARRY GROSS, MICHAEL MORGAN, AND NANCY SIGNORIELLI

Television is the source of the most broadly shared images and messages in history. It is the mainstream of the common symbolic environment into which our children are born and in which we all live out our lives. Its mass ritual shows no signs of weakening and its consequences are increasingly felt around the globe. For most viewers, new types of delivery systems such as cable, satellite, and VCRs signal even deeper penetration and integration of the dominant patterns of images and messages into everyday life.

Our research project, Cultural Indicators, has tracked the central streams of television's dramatic content since 1967 and has explored the consequences of growing up and living with television since 1974. The project has accumulated a large database that we have used to develop and refine the theoretical approach and the research strategy we call cultivation analysis (see Gerbner, Gross, Morgan, & Signorielli, 1980a; Signorielli & Morgan, 1990). In this chapter we summarize and illustrate our theory of the dynamics of the cultivation process, both in the United States and around the world.

Television is a centralized system of storytelling. Its drama, commercials, news, and other programs bring a relatively coherent system of images and messages into every home. That system cultivates from infancy the predispositions and preferences that used to be acquired from other "primary" sources and that are so important in research on other media.

Transcending historic barriers of literacy and mobility, television has become the primary common source of socialization and everyday information (mostly in the form of entertainment) of otherwise heterogeneous populations. Many of those who now live with television have never before been part of a shared national culture.

Television provides, perhaps for the first time since preindustrial religion, a daily ritual that elites share with many other publics. The heart of the analogy of television and religion, and the similarity of their social functions, lies in the continual repetition of patterns (myths, ideologies, "facts," relationships, etc.) that serve to define the world and legitimize the social order.

Television is different from other media also in its centralized mass production of a coherent set of images and messages produced for total populations, and in its relatively nonselective, almost ritualistic use by most viewers. Exposure to the total pattern rather than only to specific genres or programs is what accounts for the historically new and distinct consequences of living with television: the cultivation of shared conceptions of reality among otherwise diverse publics.

We do not minimize the importance of specific programs, selective attention and perception, specifically targeted communications, individual and group differences, and research on individual attitude and behavior change. But primary concentration on those aspects and terms of traditional media effects research risks losing sight of what is most distinctive and significant about television as the common storyteller of our age.

Compared to other media, television provides a relatively restricted set of choices for a virtually unrestricted variety of interests and publics. Most of its programs are by commercial necessity designed to be watched by large and heterogeneous audiences in a relatively nonselective fashion. Surveys show that the general amount of viewing follows the style of life of the viewer. The audience is always the group available at a certain time of the day, the week, and the season. Viewing decisions depend more on the clock than on the program. The number and variety of choices available to view when most viewers are available to watch is also limited by the fact that many programs designed for the same broad audience tend to be similar in their basic makeup and appeal (Signorielli, 1986).

In the typical U.S. home the television set is in use for almost 7 hours a day. Actual viewing by persons over 2 years old averages more than 3 hours a day. And the more people watch, the less selective they can be (Sun, 1989).

The most frequently recurring features of television cut across all types of programming and are inescapable for the regular viewer (Signorielli, 1986). Researchers who attribute findings to news viewing or preference for action programs and so forth overlook the fact that most of those who watch more news or action programs watch more of all types of programs, and that, in any case, many different types of programs, including news, share similar important features of storytelling.

Various technocoligal developments such as cable and VCRs have contributed to a significant erosion in audience share (and revenue) of the three major broadcasting networks and have altered the marketing and distribution of movies. However, there is no evidence that proliferation of channels has led to substantially greater diversity of content. On the contrary, rapid concentration and vertical integration in the media industries, the absorption of most publishing houses by electronic conglomerates, the growing practice of producing the same material for several media markets, and the habit of time-shifting by VCR users (recording favorite network programs to play back more often and at more convenient times) suggest that the diversity of what is actually viewed may even have decreased.

Viewers may feel a new sense of power and control derived from the ability to freeze a frame, review a scene, and zip through commercials (or zap them entirely). The availability of prerecorded cassettes and films may also give viewers an unprecedented range of potential choices. But again there is no evidence that such a sense of power and choice has changed viewing habits or that the content that regular VCR users and heavy television viewers watch presents world views, values, and stereotypes fundamentally different from most network-type programs (Morgan, Shanahan, & Harris, 1990).

Given the tight links among the various industries involved in the production and distribution of electronic media content, and the fact that most of them are trying to attract the largest and most heterogeneous audience, the most popular program materials present consistent and complementary messages, often reproducing what has already proven to be profitable. For example, Waterman and Grant (1991) examined network and cable programming and Nielsen ratings and found that "broad-appeal programming" already aired accounts for "a major proportion of cable television menus, and a still higher proportion of cable viewing" (p. 138). Most of the variety we observe comes from novelty effects of styles, stars, and plots rather than from changes in program structure and perspective.

What is most popular naturally tends to reflect—and cultivate—dominant cultural ideologies. Certainly, the VCR allows selective (mostly light) viewers to seek out specialized, often "fringe" material (Dobrow, 1990). But most regular viewers use VCRs and cable to watch more of the most popular fare, which enhances rather than undermines established effects of television (Morgan, Alexander, Shanahan, & Harris, 1990; Morgan, Shanahan, & Harris, 1990).

What is most likely to cultivate stable and common conceptions of reality is, therefore, the overall pattern of programming to which total communities are regularly exposed over long periods of time. That is the pattern of settings, casting, social typing, actions, and related outcomes that cuts across program types and viewing modes and defines the world of television. Viewers are born into that symbolic world and cannot avoid exposure to its recurrent patterns, usually many times a day.

THE SHIFT FROM "EFFECTS" TO "CULTIVATION" RESEARCH

The bulk of scientific inquiry about television's social impact follows theoretical models and methodological procedures of marketing and persuasion research. Much time, energy, and money have been invested in efforts to change people's attitudes and behaviors. By and large, however, the conceptualization of effect as short-run individual change has not produced research that helps us understand the distinctive features of television we have just noted above. These features include massive, long-term, and common exposure of large and heterogeneous publics to centrally produced, mass-distributed, and repetitive systems of stories. But research traditions and ideological inhibitions both tend to produce resistance to the "cultivation perspective."

Traditional effects research is based on evaluating specific informational, educational, political, or marketing efforts in terms of selective exposure and measurable differences between those exposed and others. Scholars steeped in those traditions find it difficult to accept the emphasis of cultivation analysis on total immersion rather than selective viewing and on the spread of stable similarities of outlook rather than on the remaining sources of cultural differentiation and change.

Similarly, we are still imbued with the ideology of print culture and its ideals of freedom, diversity, and an active electorate. This ideal also assumes the production and selection of information and entertainment from the point of view of a variety of competing and conflicting interests. That is why many also resist what they assume to be the emphasis of cultivation analysis on the "passive" viewer and the dissolution of authentic publics that this emphasis implies. It seems logical to argue that other circumstances do intervene and can affect and in some cases even neutralize the cultivation process, that many, even if not most, viewers do watch selectively, and that program selections should make a difference.

We do not dispute these contentions. In fact, we account for them in our analytical strategies. But we believe, again, that concentrating on individual differences and immediate change misses the profound historical challenge television poses not only for research strategies but also for traditional theories of democratic government. That challenge is the absorption of diverse conceptions and attitudes into a stable and common mainstream. Cultivation theory is based on the results of research finding a persistent and pervasive pull of the television mainstream on a great variety of conceptual currents and countercurrents. The focus on broad commonalities of perspective among heavy viewers of otherwise varied backgrounds requires a theoretical and methodological approach different from traditional media effects research and appropriate to the distinct dynamics of television. Such an approach has been developed through the Cultural Indicators project.

CULTURAL INDICATORS

The project we call Cultural Indicators is historically grounded, theoretically guided, and empirically supported (Gerbner, 1969, 1970, 1972a). Although most early efforts focused primarily on the nature and functions of television violence, the Cultural Indicators project was broadly conceived from the outset. Even violence was found to be primarily a demonstration of power in the world of television, with serious implications for social control and for the confirmation and perpetuation of minority status as well as for disruption (Gerbner, Gross, Signorielli, Morgan, & Jackson-Beeck, 1979; Morgan, 1983). As it developed, the project continued to take into account a wider range of topics, issues, and concerns (Gerbner & Gross, 1976). We have investigated the extent to which television viewing contributes to audience conceptions and actions in areas such as gender, minority and age-role stereotypes, health, science, the family, educational achievement and aspirations, politics, religion, and other topics, all of which are increasingly also being examined in cross-cultural comparative contexts.[1]

The Cultural Indicators approach involves a three-pronged research strategy. The first prong, called institutional process analysis, is designed to investigate the formation of policies directing the massive flow of media messages. (For some examples see Gerbner, 1972b, 1988.) More directly relevant to our present focus are the other two prongs we call message system analysis and cultivation analysis. Both relate to—and help develop—theories about the most subtle and widespread impacts of television.

In the second prong, we have since 1967 recorded annual week-long samples of U.S. network television drama (and samples in other cooperating countries, whenever possible) and subjected these systems of messages to content analysis in order to reliably delineate selected features and trends in the world that television presents to its viewers.[2] We believe that the most pervasive patterns common to many different types of programs but characteristic of the system of programming hold the potential lessons television cultivates. We use these overarching patterns of content as a source of questions for the third prong, cultivation analysis.

MULTIDIRECTIONAL PROCESS

Our use of the term *cultivation* for television's contribution to conceptions of social reality is not just another word for "effects." Nor does it necessarily imply a one-way, monolithic process. The influences of a pervasive medium on the composition and structure of the symbolic environment are subtle, complex, and intermingled with other influences. This perspective, therefore, assumes an interaction between the medium and its publics.

The elements of cultivation do not originate with television or appear out of a void. Layers of social, personal, and cultural contexts also determine the shape, scope, and degree of the contribution television is likely to make. Yet, the "meanings" of those contexts and factors are in themselves aspects of the cultivation process. That is, although a viewer's gender, or age, or class makes a difference in perspective, television viewing can make a similar and interacting difference. Viewing may help define what it means, for example, to be an adolescent female member of a given social class. The interaction is a continuous process (as is cultivation) beginning with infancy and going on from cradle to grave.

Thus, television neither simply "creates" nor "reflects" images, opinions, and beliefs. Rather, it is an integral aspect of a dynamic process. Institutional needs and objectives influence the creation and distribution of mass-produced messages that create, fit into, exploit, and sustain the needs, values, and ideologies of mass publics. These publics, in turn, acquire distinct identities as publics partly through exposure to the ongoing flow of messages.

The question of "which comes first" is misleading and irrelevant. People are born into a symbolic environment with television as its mainstream. Children begin viewing several years before they begin reading, as well before they can even talk.

Television viewing both shapes and is a stable part of lifestyles and outlooks. It links the individual to a larger synthetic world, a world of television's own making.

Many of those with certain social and psychological characteristics, dispositions, and worldviews, and fewer alternatives as attractive and compelling, use television as their major vehicle of cultural participation. To the extent that television dominates their sources of entertainment and information, continued exposure to its messages is likely to reiterate, confirm, and nourish—that is, cultivate—its own values and perspectives (see Gerbner, 1990; Morgan & Signorielli, 1990).

Cultivation should not be confused with simple reinforcement (although, to be sure, reaffirmation and stability in the face of pressures for change is not a trivial influence). Nor should it suggest that television viewing is merely symptomatic of other dispositions and outlooks. Finally, it should not be taken as saying that we do not think any change is involved. We have certainly found change with the first "television generation" (Gerbner & Gross, 1976), and in studies that have followed viewers over time (Morgan, 1982; Morgan, Alexander, Shanahan, & Harris, 1990; Morgan & Rothschild, 1983). Change is also apparent as television spreads to various areas of the country (Morgan, 1986), and the world (Morgan, 1990).

When we talk about the "independent contribution" of television viewing, we mean that the development (in some) and maintenance (in others) of some set of outlooks or beliefs can be traced to steady, cumulative exposure to the world of television. Our longitudinal studies of adolescents (Gerbner et al., 1980a; Morgan, 1982, 1987; Morgan, Alexander, et al., 1990) show that television can exert an independent influence on attitudes and behaviors over time, but that belief structures and concrete practices of daily life can also influence subsequent viewing.

The point is that cultivation is not conceived as a unidirectional but rather more like a gravitational process. The angle and direction of the "pull" depends on where groups of viewers and their styles of life are with reference to the line of gravity, the "mainstream" of the world of television. Each group may strain in a different direction, but all groups are affected by the same central current. Cultivation is thus part of a continual, dynamic, ongoing process of interaction among messages and contexts. This holds even though (and in a sense because) the hallmark of the process, once television is established as the main cultural arm of a stable society, is either relative stability or only slow change. A radical change of social relations may, of course, lead to a change in the system of messages and consequently to the cultivation of new and different perspectives.

When studies of media campaigns advocating change found little or no change, conventional effects research wisdom concluded that media had no or only limited effects. In fact, however, cultivation analysis may lead to the opposite conclusion: "No change" often reflects the strength of the everyday cultivation process. In a relatively stable social structure, cultivation implies a commonality of outlooks and resistance to change.

As successive generations grow up with television's version of the world, the former and more traditional distinctions established before the coming of television—and still maintained to some extent among light viewers—become blurred.

Cultivation implies the steady entrenchment of mainstream orientations for most viewers. That process of apparent convergence of outlooks we call ***mainstreaming***.

METHODS OF CULTIVATION ANALYSIS

Cultivation analysis begins with message system analysis identifying the most recurrent, stable, and overarching patterns of television content. These are the consistent images, portrayals, and values that cut across most types of programs and are virtually inescapable for the regular (and especially the heavy) viewers. They are the aggregate messages embedded in television as a system rather than in specific programs, types, or genres.

We must emphasize again that testing "cultivation" on the basis of program preferences, short-run exposures, or claims of program changes or diversity (all of which have been tried as "replications") may illuminate some media effects but does not address fundamental assumptions of cultivation theory. That is that only repetitive, long-range, and consistent exposure to patterns common to most programming, such as casting, social typing, and the "fate" of different social types, can be expected to cultivate stable and widely shared images of life and society.

There are many critical discrepancies between the world and the "world as portrayed on television." Findings from systematic analyses of television's message systems are used to formulate questions about the potential "lesions" of viewing concerning people's conceptions of social reality. Some of the questions are semi projective, some use a forced-error format, and others simply measure beliefs, opinions, attitudes, or behaviors. (None asks respondents' views about television itself.)

Using standard techniques of survey methodology, the questions are posed to samples (national probability, regional, convenience) of adults, adolescents, or children. Secondary analyses of large-scale national surveys (e.g., the National Opinion Research Center's General Social Surveys) have often been used when they include questions that relate to potential "lessons" of the television world and viewing data are available for the respondents.

Television viewing is usually assessed by multiple indicators of the amount of time respondents watch television on an "average day." Because the amount of viewing is used in relative terms, the determination of what constitutes "light," "medium," and "heavy" viewing is made on a sample-by-sample basis, using as close to an even three-way split of hours of daily television viewing as possible. What is important is that there should be significant relative differences in viewing levels, not the actual or specific amount of viewing. The heaviest viewers of any sample of respondents form the population on which cultivation can be texted.[3]

The questions posed to respondents do not mention television, and the respondents' awareness of or beliefs in the sources of their information are seen as irrelevant. The resulting relationships, if any, between amount of viewing and the tendency to respond to these questions in the terms of the dominant and repetitive facts, values, and ideologies of the world of television (again, other things held constant) reflect television's contribution to viewers' conceptions of social reality.

The observable evidence of cultivation is likely to be modest in terms of absolute size. Even light viewers may be watching several hours of television a day and of course live in the same general culture as heavy viewers. Therefore, the discovery of a systematic pattern of even small but pervasive differences between light and heavy viewers may be of far-reaching consequence. It takes but a few degrees shift in the average temperature to have an ice age or global warming. A range of 3 percent to 15 percent margins (typical of our "cultivation differentials") in a large and otherwise stable field often signals a landslide, a market takeover, or an epidemic, and it certainly tips the scale of any closely balanced choice, vote, or other decision. A slight but pervasive (e.g., generational) shift in the cultivation of common perspectives may alter the cultural climate and upset the balance of social and political decision making without necessarily changing observable behavior. A single percentage point ratings difference in a large market is worth many millions of dollars in advertising revenue—as the networks know only too well.

VARIATIONS IN CULTIVATION

We have noted cultivation is not a unidirectional flow of influence from television to audience, but part of a continual, dynamic, ongoing process of interaction among messages and contexts. In many cases, those who watch more television (the heavy viewers) are more likely—in all or most subgroups—to give the "television answers." But often the patterns are more complex.

Cultivation is both dependent on and a manifestation of the extent to which television's imagery dominates viewers' sources of information. For example, personal interaction makes a difference. Parental co-viewing patterns and orientations toward television can either increase (Gross & Morgan, 1985) or decrease (Rothschild & Morgan, 1987) cultivation among adolescents. Also, children who are more integrated into cohesive peer or family groups are more resistant to cultivation (Rothschild, 1984).

Direct experience also plays a role. The relationship between amount of viewing and fear of crime is strongest among those who live in high crime urban areas. This is a phenomenon we have called *resonance*, in which everyday reality and television provide a "double dose" or messages that "resonate" and amplify cultivation. The relationships between amount of viewing and the tendency to hold exaggerated perceptions of violence are also more pronounced within those real-world demographic subgroups (e.g., minorities) whose fictional counterparts are relatively more frequently victimized on television (Morgan, 1983).

Television viewing usually relates in different but consistent ways to different groups' life situations and worldviews. A major theoretical and analytical thrust of many cultivation analyses has been directed toward the determination of the conditional processes that enhance, diminish, or otherwise mediate cultivation.

There are many factors and processes that produce systematic and theoretically meaningful variations in cultivation patterns. One process, however, stands out, both as an indicator of differential vulnerability and as a general, consistent pattern representing one of the most profound consequences of living with television. That is the process of mainstreaming.

MAINSTREAMING

Most cultures consist of many diverse currents. But there is typically a dominant set of attitudes, beliefs, values, and practices. This dominant current is not simply the sum total of all the cross-currents and subcurrents. Rather, it is the most general, functional, and stable mainstream, representing the broadest dimensions of shared meanings and assumptions. It is that which ultimately defines all the other cross-currents and subcurrents, including what Williams (1977) called "residual and emergent strains." Television's central role in our society makes it the primary channel of the mainstream of our culture.

This mainstream can be thought of as a relative commonality of outlooks and values that heavy exposure to the television world tends to cultivate. "Mainstreaming" means that heavy viewing may absorb or override differences in perspectives and behavior that ordinarily stem from other factors and influences. In other words, differences found in the responses of different groups of viewers, differences that usually are associated with the varied cultural, social, and political characteristics of these groups, are diminished in the responses of heavy viewers in these same groups. For example, regional differences, political ideology, and socioeconomic differences are much less influential on the attitudes and beliefs of heavy viewers.

As a process, mainstreaming represents the theoretical elaboration and empirical verification of television's cultivation of common perspective. It represents a relative homogenization, an absorption of divergent views, and an apparent convergence of disparate outlooks upon the overarching patterns of the television world.

Former and traditional distinctions (which flourished, in part, through the relative diversity provided by print) became blurred as successive generations and groups are enculturated into television's version of the world. Through the process of mainstreaming, television may have become the true twentieth-century "melting pot" of the American people—and increasingly of other countries around the globe.

Figure 1 illustrates some of the different models of the cultivation process that emerge when subgroups are compared. In Graph a, the subgroups show different baselines, but the associations are equivalent, and there is no interaction. Graphs b, c, and d show typical instances of mainstreaming, and imply that the light-heavy viewer differences need not point in the same direction or involve all subgroups. The pattern in Graph e depicts the kind of interaction we call resonance, and in Graph f there are no relationships within any subgroup. Except for Graph f, all these models reflect the cultivation process and relate to its center of gravity, the television mainstream.

Figure 1. Models of Civilization

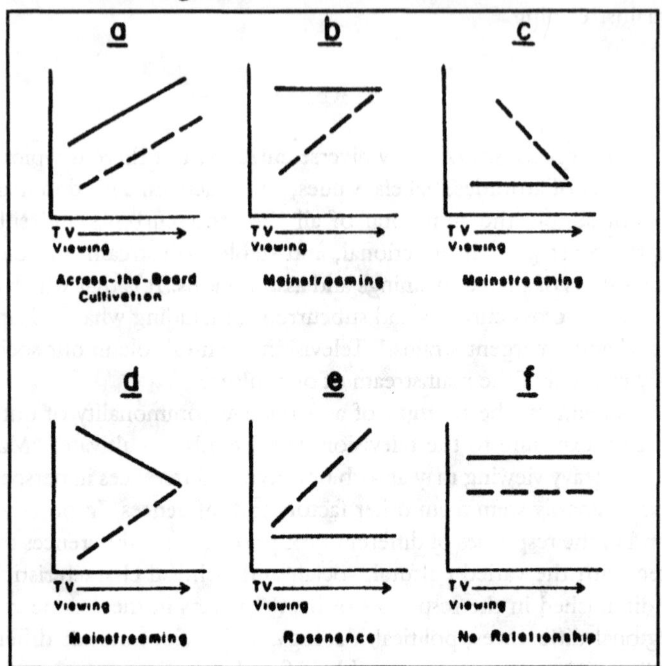

THE FINDINGS OF CULTIVATION ANALYSIS

Clear-cut divergences between symbolic reality and independently observable ("objective") reality provide convenient tests of the extent to which television's versions of "the facts" are incorporated or absorbed into what heavy viewers take for granted about the world. For example, we found that television drama tends to sharply underrepresent older people. Although those over sixty-five constitute the fastest growing segment of the real-world population in the United States, heavy viewers were more likely to feel that the elderly are a "vanishing breed"—that compared to twenty years ago, there are fewer of them, that they are in worse health, and that they don't live as long—all contrary to fact (Gerbner, Gross, Morgan, & Signorielli, 1980b).

As another example, consider how likely television characters are to encounter violence compared to the rest of us. Well over half of all major characters on television are involved each week in some kind of violent action. Although FBI statistics have clear limitations, they indicate that in any one year, less than 1 percent of people in the United States are victims of criminal violence. We have found considerable support for the proposition that heavy exposure to the world of television cultivates exaggerated perceptions of the number of people involved in violence in any given week

(Gerbner et al., 1979; Gerbner et al., 1980a), as well as numerous other inaccurate beliefs about crime and law enforcement.

To repeat what we have emphasized earlier, cultivation analysis centers on overarching patterns of casting and other characteristics that are common to most types of programming and that are long enduring. But the investigation is not limited to the lessons of television "facts" compared to real-world (or even imaginary but different) statistics. Some of the most interesting and important issues for cultivation analysis involve the symbolic transformation of message system data into hypotheses about more general issues and assumptions.

The "facts" of the television world are evidently learned quite well, whether or not viewers profess a belief in what they see on television or claim to be able to distinguish between factual and fictional presentations. (In fact, most of what we know, or think we know, is a mixture of all the stories we have absorbed. "Factual," which may be highly selective, and "fictional," which may be highly realistic, are more questions of style than function within a total framework of knowledge.) The repetitive "lesions" we learn from television, beginning with infancy, are likely to become the basis for a broader worldview, making television a significant source of general values, ideologies, and perspectives as well as specific assumptions, beliefs, and images. Hawkins and Pingree (1982) called this the cultivation of "value systems." (See also Hawkins & Pingree, 1990.)

One example of this is what we have called the "mean world" syndrome. Our message data say little directly about either the selfishness or altruism of people, and there are certainly no real-world statistics about the extent to which people can be trusted. Yet, we have found that long-term exposure to television, in which frequent violence is virtually inescapable, tends to cultivate the image of a relatively mean and dangerous world. Responses of heavier compared to matching groups of lighter viewers suggest the conception of reality in which greater protection is needed, most people "cannot be trusted," and most people are "just looking out for themselves" (Gerbner et al., 1980a; Signorielli, 1990a).

The Mean World Index, composed of violence-related items, also illustrates the mainstreaming implications of viewing (Signorielli, 1990a). For example, combining data from the 1980, 1983, and 1986 General Social Surveys, heavy and light viewers who have not been to college are equally likely to score high on the Mean World Index: 53 percent of both the heavy and light viewers agree with two or three of the items. However, among those who have had some college education, television viewing makes a considerable difference: 28 percent of the light viewers compared to 43 percent of the heavy viewers in this subgroup have a high score on the Mean World Index. There is thus a 25 percentage point difference between the two subgroups of light viewers but only a 10 point spread between the two subgroups of heavy viewers. The heavy viewers of otherwise different groups are both in the "television mainstream."

Another example of extrapolated assumptions relates to the image of women. The dominant majority status of men on television does not mean that heavy viewers ignore daily experience and underestimate the number of women in society. But underrepresentaion in the world of television means a relatively narrow (and thus more stereotyped) range of roles and activities. Most groups of heavy viewers—with other characteristics held constant—score higher on a "sexism scale" using data from the NORC General Social Surveys (Signorielli, 1989).

Several other studies have examined assumptions relating to gender roles in samples of children and adolescents. Morgan (1982) found that television cultivated such notions as "women are happiest at home raising children" and "men are born with more ambition than women." Rothschild (1984) found that 3rd- and 5th-grade children who watched more television were more likely to stereotype both gender-related activities (e.g., cooking, playing sports) and gender-related qualities (e.g., warmth, independence) along traditional gender-role lines. Although viewing seems to cultivate adolescents' and children's attitudes about gender-related chores, viewing was not related to actually doing these chores (Morgan, 1987; Signorielli & Lears, 1991).

Table 1. Television Viewing and Political Self-Designation, in the 1990 General Social Survey (N=885)

	Percent Who Call Themselves											
	Liberal				*Moderate*				*Conservative*			
TV viewing:	*L*	*M*	*H*	*Gamma*	*L*	*M*	*H*	*Gamma*	*L*	*M*	*H*	*Gamma*
Overall	28	29	25	−.04	33	35	45	.17	40	36	30	−.14
Males	24	31	23	−.03	32	32	43	.12#	42	37	34	−.09
Females	30	27	27	−.05	32	38	47	.20	38	35	27	−.17
Young	38	27	21	−.26	30	38	47	.23	32	35	32	−.00
Middle	26	34	28	.05	32	34	42	.11#	42	32	30	−.16
Older	18	15	25	.21#	39	33	49	.19#	43	52	26	−.32
Lo Educ.	19	29	22	−.00	42	39	49	.12#	39	32	29	−.13#
Hi Educ.	33	30	31	−.04	27	31	38	.15	40	39	31	−.11#
Lo Income	27	26	22	−.08	34	35	49	.21	39	39	29	−.16
Hi Income	31	31	28	−.04	30	34	40	.13#	39	35	33	−.09
Democrat	42	36	33	−.11	33	38	45	.15	25	26	22	−.06
Indep.	25	31	22	−.04	44	42	58	.18	32	28	20	−.19
Repub.	18	20	17	−.00	24	25	32	.13	59	55	51	−.10

# $p < .10$. *$p < .05$. **$p < .01$.

Note. TV Viewing: Light = 1 hour or less daily (*N* = 224); Medium = 2 or 3 hours daily (*N* = 418); Heavy = 4 or more hours daily (*N* = 243). Gender: Males (*N* = 394); Females (*N* = 491). Age: Younger = 18 to 30 years old (*N* = 203); Middle = 31 to 64 years old. (*N* = 515); Older = 65 years or older (*N* = 167). Education: Low = 12 or fewer years (No college; *N* = 449); High = 13 years or more years (at least some college; *N* = 435). Income: Low = less than $25,000 yearly (*N* = 368); High = $25,000 or more yearly (*N* = 433). Party: Democrats (*N* = 320); Independents (*N* = 268); Republicans (*N* = 287)

Other studies have dealt with assumptions about marriage and work. Signorielli (1990b, in press) found that television seems to cultivate rather realistic views about marriage but seemingly contradictory views about work. Heavy viewing adolescents were more likely to want high-status jobs that would give them a chance to earn a lot of money but also wanted to have their jobs be relatively easy with long vacations and time to do other things.

Other extrapolations from content patterns involve political views. For example, we have argued that as television seeks large and heterogeneous audiences, its messages are designed to disturb as few as possible. Therefore they tend to "balance" opposing perspectives, and to steer a "middle course" along the supposedly nonideological mainstream. We have found that heavy viewers are substantially more likely to label themselves as being "moderate" rather than either "liberal" or "conservative" (see Gerbner, Gross, Morgan, & Signorielli 1982, 1984).

We have observed this finding in many years of the General Social Survey (GSS) data. GSS data from 1990 reveal this pattern once again, as shown in Table 1. Heavy viewers in all subgroups tend to see themselves as "moderate" and avoid saying they are either "liberal" or "conservative." Figure 2 shows the patterns for Democrats, Independents, and Republicans. The percentage choosing the "moderate" label is again substantially higher among heavy viewers, regardless of party, and heavy viewing Democrats are less likely to say they are "liberal," whereas heavy viewing Republicans are less likely to call themselves "conservative." The general pattern shown in these data has appeared every year since 1975.

Figure 2. Comparisons of Political Self-Designation by Amount of Viewing within Parties

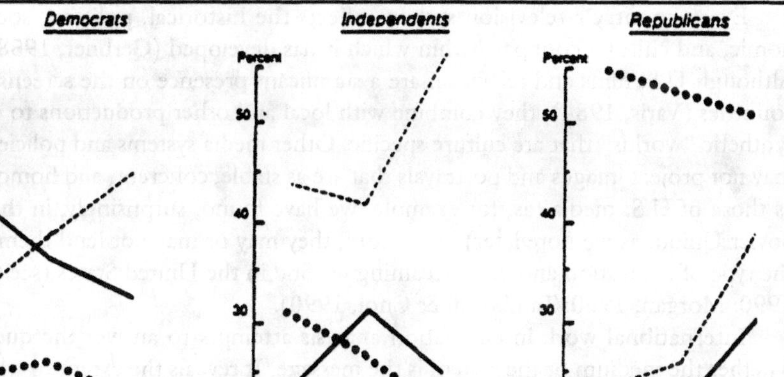

Yet, looking at the actual positions taken on a number of political issues shows that the mainstream does not mean the "middle of the road." When we analyzed responses to questions in the NORC General Social Surveys about attitudes and opinions on such topics as racial segregation, homosexuality, abortion, minority rights, and other issues that have traditionally divided liberals and conservatives, we found such division mostly among those who watch little television. Overall, self-styled moderates are much closer to conservatives than they are to liberals. Among heavy viewers, liberals and conservatives are closer to each other than among light viewers. We have also noted (Gerbner et al., 1982, 1984) that although mainstreaming bends toward the right on political issues, it leans toward a populist stance on economic issues (e.g., demanding more social services but lower taxes), reflecting the influence of a marketing orientation and setting up potential conflicts of demands and expectations.

Implications of cultivation for foreign policy were reflected in a study of attitudes toward the war in the Persian Gulf (Lewis, Jhally, & Morgan, 1991). Heavy television viewers were more familiar with the military terminology used and more supportive of the war but less informed about issues and the Middle East in general. Overall amount of viewing was far more important than specific exposure to news.

INTERNATIONAL CULTIVATION ANALYSIS

Cultivation analysis is well suited to multinational and cross-cultural comparative study (Gerbner, 1977, 1989; Morgan, 1990). In fact, such study is the best test of system-wide similarities and differences across national boundaries, and of the actual significance of national cultural policies.

Every country's television system reflects the historical, political, social, economic, and cultural contexts within which it has developed (Gerbner, 1958, 1969). Although U.S. films and television are a significant presence on the screens of most countries (Varis, 1984), they combine with local and other productions to compose synthetic "worlds" that are culture specific. Other media systems and policies may or may not project images and portrayals that are as stable, coherent, and homogeneous as those of U.S. media (as, for example, we have found, surprisingly, in the former Soviet Union, as we note later). Therefore, they may or may not lend themselves to the type of cultivation and mainstreaming we find in the United States (see Gerbner, 1990; Morgan, 1990; Tamborini & Choi, 1990).

International work in cultivation analysis attempts to answer the question of whether the medium or the system is the message. It reveals the extent to which, and the ways in which, each message system contributes to conceptions of social reality congruent with its most stable and recurrent messages and images. Of course, given the range of variations in susceptibility to cultivation even within the United States, there is no reason to assume that cultivation patterns will be identical or invariant across cultures.

Pingree and Hawkins (1981) found that exposure to U.S. programs (especially crime and adventure) was significantly related to Australian students' scores on "Mean World" and "Violence in Society" indices concerning Australia, but not the United States. Viewing Australian programs was unrelated to these conceptions, but those who watched more U.S. programs were more likely to see Australia as dangerous and mean. Weimann's (1984) study of high school and college students in Israel found that heavy viewers had an idealized, "rosier" image of the standard of living in the United States.

In England, Wober (1978) found little support for cultivation in terms of images of violence. (See also Gunter, 1987; Gunter & Furnham, 1984; Wober, 1984, 1990; Wober & Gunter, 1988.) But there was little violence in British programs, and U.S. programs only made up about 15 percent of British screen time. Piepe, Charlton, and More (1990) found evidence of political "homogenization" (mainstreaming) in Britain that was highly congruent with U.S. findings (Gerbner et al., 1982), as did Morgan and Shanahan (1991) in Argentina.

In the Netherlands, Bouwman (1984) found weak associations between amount of viewing and perceptions of violence, victimization, and mistrust. But the findings reveal the importance of cultural context in comparative cultivation research. Content analyses showed a good deal of similarity between U.S. and Dutch television (Bouwman & Signorielli, 1985; Bouwman & Stappers, 1984) and much programming was imported from the United States. Yet, it was found that both light and heavy viewers see about equal amounts of fictional entertainment, but heavy viewers see more "informational" programs, a situation quite different from that of the United States. (See also Bouwman, 1982, 1983, 1987; Bouwman, Nelissen, & Meier, 1987; Stappers, 1984.)

Cultivation analyses about conceptions of violence, sex roles, political orientations, "traditional" values, social stereotypes, and other topics have been conducted in numerous other countries, including Sweden (Hedinsson & Windahl, 1984; Reimer & Rosengren, 1990), Argentina (Morgan & Shanahan, 1991), the Philippines (Tan, Tan, & Tan, 1987), Taiwan and Mexico (Tan, Li, & Simpson, 1986), Japan (Saito, 1991), and Thailand (Tan & Suarchavarat, 1988). These studies show the complex ways in which the viewing of local or imported programming can interact with distinct cultural contexts. For example, in Korea, Kang and Morgan (1988) found that exposure to U.S. television was associated with more "liberal" perspectives about gender roles and family values among females. At the same time, more viewing of U.S. television among Korean male students correlated with greater hostility toward the United States and protectiveness toward Korean culture, suggesting a "backlash" of nationalism among the more politicized college students.

Most of these studies examined single countries. Comparative cross-cultural research typically requires complex joint development and collaboration. It takes longer, costs more, and is more difficult to fund. Nevertheless, recent research has begun to emphasize the comparative aspects of cultivation analysis. Morgan and Shanahan (1992) analyzed adolescents in Taiwan and Argentina. In Argentina, where television is supported by commercials and features many U.S. programs, heavy viewing cultivates traditional gender roles and authoritarianism. In Taiwan, where media are more state controlled, with fewer U.S. imports, and where overall viewing is much lighter, cultivation was much less apparent. Also, Morgan (1990) compared the cultivation of sex-role stereotypes in five different countries.

Large-scale comparative cultivation analyses involving many countries were under way or planned in the early 1990s. One of the first to be concluded, a study of U.S. and (what was then) Soviet television conducted in 1989 and 1990, found that television plays a different role in the two countries. In the United States, but not in the former Soviet Union, television heightens anxieties about neighborhood safety (including comparisons of light and heavy viewers in the same types of neighborhoods), perhaps as a result of frequency of violence on Soviet television. In both countries, but especially in the former Soviet Union, the more people watch television the more they are likely to say that housework is primarily the responsibility of the woman. General satisfaction with life is consistently lower among heavy than among light television viewers in the United States but not in the former Soviet Union (where it is relatively low for everyone).

In both places, greater viewing tends to reduce social and economic differences in attitudes, but this is especially so in the United States, where such differences are greater. Lacking regular prime-time dramatic series and relying more on movies, theater, documentaries, and the classics, Soviet television did, in fact, present more diversified dramatic fare than U.S. television. At any rate, television viewing seems to have greater mainstreaming consequences in the United States than was the case in the Soviet Union. The availability of different cultural and language programming in the different former Soviet republics may also have contributed to the relative diversity of their television—and to the centrifugal forces that tore the Union apart.

In summary, in countries in which television's portrayals are less repetitive and homogeneous than in the United States, the results of cultivation analysis also tend to be less predictable and consistent. The extent to which cultivation will occur in a given country will also depend on various structural factors, such as the number of channels available, overall amount of broadcasting time, and amount of time audiences spend viewing. But it will especially depend on the amount of diversity in the available content, which is not necessarily related to the number of channels. A single channel with a diverse and balanced program structure can foster (and, in fact, compel) more diversified viewing than many channels competing for the same audience, using similar appeals, and lending themselves to viewer selection of the same "preferences" most of the time.

Different media systems differ along all these dimensions, and complex interactions among these elements may account for substantial cross-cultural variations in cultivation. Imported U.S. programs can augment, diminish, or be irrelevant to these dynamics. The key questions are: (a) how important is television in the culture, and (b) how consistent and coherent is the total system of its messages? The more important, consistent, and coherent, the more cultivation can be expected.

CONCLUSIONS

Television pervades the symbolic environment. Cultivation analysis focuses on the consequences of exposure to its recurrent patterns of stories, images, and messages. Our theories of the cultivation process attempt to understand and explain the dynamics of television as the distinctive and dominant cultural force of our age.

Our explorations and formulations have been challenged, enriched, confirmed, and extended by studies of numerous independent investigators in the United States and abroad, and are still evolving especially as they are being applied in more and more countries.

Cultivation analysis is not a substitute for but a complement to traditional approaches to media effects. Traditional research is concerned with change rather than stability and with processes more applicable to media that enter a person's life at later stages (with mobility, literacy, etc.) and more selectively.

Neither the "before and after exposure" model, nor the notion of "predispositions" as intervening variables, so important in traditional effects studies, apply in the context of cultivation analysis. Television enters life in infancy; there is no "before exposure" condition. Television plays a role in the formation of those very "predispositions" that later intervene (and often resist) other influences and attempts at persuasion.

Cultivation analysis concentrates on the enduring and common consequences of growing up and living with television. Those are the stable, resistant, and widely shared assumptions, images, and conceptions expressing the institutional characteristics and interests of the medium itself.

Television has become the common symbolic environment that interacts with most of the things we think and do. Exploring its dynamics can help develop an understanding of the forces of social cohesion, cultural dependence, and resistance to change, as well as the requirements of developing alternatives and independence essential for self-direction and self-government in the television age.

NOTES

1. The Cultural Indicators project began in 1967–68 with a study for the National Commission on the Causes and Prevention of Violence. It continued under the sponsorships of the U.S. Surgeon General's Scientific Advisory Committee on Television and Social Behavior, the National Institute of Mental Health, The White House Office of Telecommunications Policy, the American Medical Association, the U.S. Administration on Aging, and the National Science Foundation. Cross-cultural comparative extensions of this work, involving long-planned international research coordination and cooperation, began in 1987 under a grant by the W. Alton Jones Foundation, and has continued with the support of the International Research and Exchanges Board (IREX), the Carter Center of Emory University, the Hoso Bunk Foundation of Japan, the Finnish Broadcasting Company, the Hungarian Institute for Public Opinion Research, Moscow State University, the National Center for Public Opinion Research of the USSR, and the Universities of Pennsylvania, Massachusetts, and Delaware.
2. The message system database accumulated detailed coded observations of over 26,000 characters and over 2,200 programs during the first two decades of its existence.
3. In all analyses we use a number of demographic variables as controls. These are applied both separately and simultaneously. Included are gender, age, race, education, income, and political self-designation (liberal, moderate, conservative). Where applicable, other controls, such as urban-rural residence, newspaper reading, and party affiliation, are also used.

REFERENCES

Bouwman, H. (1982). "Cultural Indicators": Die Gergnersche Konzeption der "message system analysis" und erste empirische Befunde aus den Niederlanden [Gerbner's conception of message system analyses and first empirical findings from The Netherlands]. *Rundfunk und Fernsehen*, 30(1), 341–355.

Bouwman, H. (1983). Een antwoord vanuit het cultural indicator perspectief. *Massacommunicatie, XI*(2), 68–74.

Bouwman, H. (1984). Cultivation Analysis: The Dutch case. In G. Melischek, K.E. Rosengren, & J. Stappers (eds.), *Cultural indicators: An Internaational Symposium* (pp. 407–422). Vienna: Verlag der Osterreichischen Akademie der Wissenschaften.

Bouwman, H. (1987). *Televisie als cultuur-schepper.* Amsterdam: VU Uitgeverij.

Bouwman, H., Nelissen, P., & Meier, U. (1987). Culturele indicatoren 1980–1985. *Massacommunicatie, XV*(1), 18–35.

Bouwman, H., & Signorielli, N. (1985). A comparison of American and Dutch programming. *Gazette, 35,* 93–108.

Bouwman, H., & Stappers, J. (1984). The Dutch violence profile: A replication of Gerbner's message system analysis. In G. Melischek, K. E. Rosengren, & J. Stappers (eds.), *Cultural indicators: An international symposium* (pp. 113–128). Vienna: Verlag der Osterreichischen Akademie der Wissenschaften.

Dobrow, J. R. (1990). Patterns of viewing and VCR use: Implications for cultivation analysis. In N. Signorielli & M. Morgan (eds.), *Cultivation analysis: New directions in media effects research* (pp. 71–84). Newbury Park, CA: Sage.

Gerbner, G. (1958). On content analysis and critical research in mass communication. *AV Communication Review, 6*(2), 85–108.

Gerbner, G. (1969). Toward "Cultural Indicators": The analysis of mass mediated message systems. *AV Communication Review, 17*(2), 137–148.

Gerbner, G. (1970). Cultural indicators: The case of violence in television drama. *The Annals of the American Academy of Political and Social Science, 388,* 69–81.

Gerbner, G. (1972a). Communication and social environment. *Scientific American, 227*(3), 152–160.

Gerbner, G. (1972b). The structure and process of television program content regulation in the U.S. In G. A. Comstock & E. Rubenstein (eds.), *Television and social behavior, Vol. 1: Content and control* (pp. 386–414). Washington, DC: U.S. Government Printing Office.

Gerbner, G. (1973). Cultural indicators: The third voice. In G. Gerbner, L. Gross, & W. H. Melody (eds.), *Communications technology and social policy* (pp. 555–573). New York: Wiley.

Gerbner, G. (1977). Comparative cultural indicators. In G. Gerbner (ed.), *Mass Media Policies in Changing Cultures* (pp. 199–205). New York: Wiley.

Gerbner, G. (1988). Violence and terror in the mass media. In *Reports and papers in mass communication* (No. 102). Paris: UNESCO.

Gerbner, G. (1989). Cross-cultural communications research in the age of telecommunications. In The Christian Academy (eds.), *Continuity and change in communications in post-industrial society* (Vol. 2). Seoul, Korea: Wooseok.

Gerbner, G. (1990). Epilogue: Advancing on the path of righteousness (maybe). In N. Signorielli & M. Morgan (eds.), *Cultivation analysis: New directions in media effects research* (pp. 249–262). Newbury Park, CA: Sage.

Gerbner, G., & Gross, L. (1976). Living with television: The violence profile. *Journal of Communication, 26*(2), 173–199.

Gerbner, G., Gross, L., Morgan, M., & Signorielli, N. (1980a). The "Mainstreaming" of America: Violence profile no. 11. *Journal of Communication, 30*(3), 10–29.

Gerbner, G., Gross, L., Morgan, M., & Signorielli, N. (1980b). Aging with television: Images on television drama and conceptions of social reality. *Journal of Communication, 30*(1), 37–47.

Gerbner, G., Gross, L., Morgan, M., & Signorielli, N. (1982). Charting the mainstream: Television's contributions to political orientations. *Journal of Communication, 32*(2), 100–127.

Gerbner, G., Gross, L., Morgan, M., & Signorielli, N. (1984). Political correlates of television viewing. *Public Opinion Quarterly, 48*(1), 283–300.

Gerbner, G., Gross, L., Morgan, M., & Signorielli, N. (1986). Living with television: The dynamics of the cultivation process. In J. Bryant & D. Zillmann (eds.), *Perspectives on media effects* (pp. 17–48). Hillsdale, NJ: Lawrence Erlbaum Associates.

Gerbner, G., Gross, L., Signorielli, N., Morgan, M., & Jackson-Beeck, M. (1979). The demonstration of power: Violence profile no. 10. *Journal of Communication, 29*(3), 177–196.

Gross, L., & Morgan, M. (1985). Television and enculturation. In J. R. Dominick & J. E. Fletcher (eds.), *Broadcasting research methods* (pp. 221–234). Boston: Allyn & Bacon.

Gunter, B. (1987). *Television and the fear of crime.* London: Libbey.

Gunter, B., & Furnham, A. (1984). Perceptions of television violence: Effects of programme genre and type of violence on viewers' judgments of violent portrayals. *British Journal of Social Psychology, 23*(2), 155–164.

Hawkins, R. P., & Pingree, S. (1982). Television's influence on social reality. In D. Pearl, L. Bouthilet, & J. Lazar (eds.), *Television and behavior: Ten years of scientific progress and implications for the 80's, Vol. II, Technical reviews* (pp. 224–247). Rockville, MD: National Institute of Mental Health.

Hawkins, R. P., & Pingree, S. (1990). Divergent psychological processes in constructing social reality from mass media content. In N. Signorielli & M. Morgan (eds.), *Cultivation analysis: New directions in media effects research* (pp. 35–50). Newbury Park, CA: Sage.

Hedinsson, E., & Windahl, S. (1984). Cultivation analysis: A Swedish illustration. In G. Melischek, K. E. Rosengren, & J. Stappers (eds.), *Cultural indications: An International Symposium* (pp. 389–406). Vienna: Verlag der Osterreichischen Akademie der Wissenschaften.

Jackson-Beeck, M. (1977). The non-viewers: Who are they? *Journal of Communication, 27*(3), 65–72.

Kang, J. G., & Morgan, M. (1988). Culture clash: U.S. television programs in Korea. *Journalism Quarterly, 65*(2), 431–438.

Lewis, J., Jhally, S., & Morgan, M. (1991). *The Gulf War: A study of the media, public opinion, and public knowledge* (Research Report). The Center for the Study of Communication, Department of Communication, University of Massachusetts/Amherst.

Morgan, M. (1982). Television and adolescents' sex-role stereotypes: A longitudinal study. *Journal of Personality and Social Psychology, 43*(45), 947–955.

Morgan, M. (1983). Symbolic victimization and real-world fear. *Human Communication Research, 9*(2), 146–157.

Morgan, M. (1986). Television and the erosion of regional diversity. *Journal of Broadcasting and Electronic Media, 30*(2), 123–139.

Morgan, M. (1987). Television, sex-role attitudes, and sex-role behavior. *Journal of Early Adolescence, 7*(3), 269–282.

Morgan, M. (1990). International cultivation analysis. In N. Signorielli & M. Morgan (eds.), *Cultivation analysis: New directions in media effects research* (pp. 225–248). Newbury Park, CA: Sage.

Morgan, M., Alexander, A., Shanahan, J., & Harris, C. (1990). Adolescents, VCRs, and the family environment. *Communication Research, 17*(1), 83–106.

Morgan, M., & Rothschild, N. (1983). Impact of the new television technology: Cable TV, peers, and sex-role cultivation in the electronic environment. *Youth and Society, 15*(1), 33–50.

Morgan, M., & Shanahan, J. (1991). Television and the cultivation of political attitudes in Argentina. *Journal of Communication, 41*(1), 88–103.

Morgan, M., & Shanahan, J. (1992). Comparative cultivation analysis: Television and adolescents in Argentina and Taiwan. In F. Korzenny & S. Ting-Toomey (eds.), *Mass media effects across cultures: International and intercultural communication annual* (Vol. 16, pp. 173–197). Newbury Park, CA: Sage.

Morgan, M., Shanahan, J., & Harris, C. (1990). VCRs and the effects of television: New diversity or more of the same? In J. Dobrow (ed.), *Social and cultural aspects of VCR use* (pp. 107–123). Hillsdale, NJ: Lawrence Erlbaum Associates.

Morgan, M., & Signorielli, N. (1990). Cultivation analysis: Conceptualization and methodology. In N. Signorielli & M. Morgan (eds.), *Cultivation analysis: New directions in media effects research* (pp. 13–34). Newbury Park, CA: Sage.

Piepe, A., Charlton, P., & More, J. (1990). Politics and television viewing in England: Hegemony or pluralism? *Journal of Communication, 40*(1), 24–35.

Pingree, S., & Hawkins, R. P. (1981). U.S. programs on Australian television: The cultivation effect. *Journal of Communication, 31*(1), 97–105.

Reimer, B., & Rosengren, K. E. (1990). Cultivated viewers and readers: A life-style perspective. In N. Signorielli & M. Morgan (eds.), *Cultivation analysis: New directions in media effects research* (pp. 181–206). Newbury Park, CA: Sage.

Rothschild, N. (1984). Small group affiliation as a mediating factor in the cultivation process. In G. Melischek, K. E. Rosengren, & J. Stappers (eds.), *Cultural indicators: An international symposium* (pp. 377–387). Vienna: Verlag der Osterreichischen Akademie der Wissenschaften.

Rothschild, N., & Morgan, M. (1987). Cohesion and control: Relationships with parents as mediators of television. *Journal of Early Adolescence, 7*(3), 299–314.

Saito, S. (1991). *Does cultivation occur in Japan?: Testing the applicability of the cultivation hypothesis on Japanese television viewers.* Unpublished master's thesis, the Annenberg School for Communication, University of Pennsylvania, Philadelphia.

Signorielli, N. (1986). Selective television viewing: A limited possibility. *Journal of Communication, 36*(3), 64–75.

Signorielli, N. (1989). Television and conceptions about sex roles: Maintaining conventionality and the status quo. *Sex Roles, 21*(5/6), 337–356.

Signorielli, N. (1990a). Television's mean and dangerous world: A continuation of the cultural indicators perspective. In N. Signorielli & M. Morgan (eds.), *Cultivation analysis: New directions in media effects research* (pp. 85–106). Newbury Park, CA: Sage.

Signorielli, N. (1990b, November). *Television's contribution to adolescents' perceptions about work.* Paper presented at annual conference of the Speech Communication Association, Chicago.

Signorielli, N. (in press). Adolescents and ambivalence towards marriage: A cultivation analysis. *Youth and Society.*

Signorielli, N., & Lears, M. (1991). *Children, television and conceptions about chores: Attitudes and behaviors.* Unpublished manuscript, University of Delaware, Newark.

Signorielli, N., & Morgan, M. (eds.). (1990). *Cultivation analysis: New directions in media effects research.* Newbury Park, CA: Sage.

Stappers, J. G. (1984). De eigen aard van televisie; tien stellingen over cultivatie en culturele indicatoren. *Massacommunicatie, XII*(5/6), 249–258.

Sun, L. (1989). *Limits of selective viewing: An analysis of "diversity" in dramatic programming.* Unpublished master's thesis, The Annenberg School for Communication, University of Pennsylvania, Philadelphia.

Tamborini, R., & Choi, J. (1990). The role of cultural diversity in cultivation research. In N. Signorielli & M. Morgan (eds.), *Cultivation analysis: New directions in media effects research* (pp. 157–180). Newbury Park, CA: Sage.

Tan, A. S., Li, S., & Simpson, C. (1986). American television and social stereotypes of Americans in Taiwan and Mexico. *Journalism Quarterly, 63*, 809–814.

Tan, A. S., & Suarchavarat, K. (1988). American TV and social stereotypes of Americans in Thailand. *Journalism Quarterly, 65*(4), 648–654.

Tan, A. S., Tan, G. K., & Tan, A. S. (1987). American TV in the Philippines: A test of cultural impact. *Journalism Quarterly, 64*(1), 65–72.

Varis, T. (1984). The international flow of television programs. *Journal of Communication, 34*(1), 143–152.

Waterman, D., & Grant, A. (1991). Cable television as an aftermarket. *Journal of Broadcasting & Electronic Media,* 35(2), 179–188.

Weimann, G. (1984). Images of life in America: The impact of American TV in Israel. *International Journal of Intercultural Relations, 8*(2), 185–197.

Williams, R. (1977). *Marxism and literature.* Oxford: Oxford University Press.

Wober, J. M. (1978). Televised violence and paranoid perception: The view from Great Britain. *Public Opinion Quarterly, 42*(3), 315–321.

Wober, J. M. (1984). Prophecy and prophylaxis: Predicted harms and their absence in a regulated television system. In G. Melischek, K. E. Rosengren, & J. Stappers (eds.), *Cultural indicators: An international symposium* (pp. 423–440). Vienna: Verlag der Osterreichischen Akademie der Wissenschaften.

Wober, J. M. (1990). Does television cultivate the British? Late 80s evidence. In N. Signorielli & M. Morgan (eds.), *Cultivation analysis: New directions in media effects research* (pp. 207–224). Newbury Park, CA: Sage.

Wober, J. M., & Gunter, B. (1988). *Television and social control.* New York: St. Martin's Press.

CHAPTER 16

ADVANCING ON THE PATH OF RIGHTEOUSNESS (MAYBE)

BY GEORGE GERBNER

Research rarely advances in a straight line. As I reflect on the journey cultivation analysis has taken so far, and suggest some guideposts for "advances" on its path, I must confess that I have also learned from the "deviations."

Cultivation is what a culture does. That is not simple causation, though culture is the basic medium in which humans live and learn. Cultivation rarely brings change except between generations and regions or among styles of life of which it is more or less a part. Cultivation is not the sole (or even frequent) determinant of specific actions, although it may tip a delicate balance, mark the mainstream of common consciousness, and signal a sea change in the cultural environment. Strictly speaking, cultivation means the specific independent (though not isolated) contribution that a particularly consistent and compelling symbolic stream makes to the complex process of socialization and enculturation.

Leading up to that special meaning, and to some desiderata for its study, I recall the original impetus and continuing concerns that gave rise to the development, definitions, and distinctions of the concept of cultivation. They stemmed from dissatisfaction with the narrowly conceived tactical emphasis of post–World War II communications research, incapable of addressing broader problems of culture. They continued with a concern over developments that challenged conceptions of democracy in communications. The two merged in long-term research under many different auspices but shared a common interest in addressing broader problems relevant to general acculturation and public policy.

The path of that research, I argue, should follow certain specific directions and touch on certain specific considerations. Other chapters in this volume may imply or demonstrate different conclusions. That internal dialogue cannot help but add the right note to this volume: "Advances" refers to the hypotheses we are advancing and not to final destinations. Nevertheless, in research, as in life, good hypotheses, euphemistically called theories, are the only testable guides to action and, therefore, more reliable than certainties.

I believe in magic. Unlocking incredible riches through music and dance, conjuring up visions of the unseen through art, creating worlds of imagination and fact through poetry, songs, and stories—that is the essential magic of human life.

Storytelling is my shorthand for that magic. It is what makes humans out of members of the species Homo sapiens. We are the only creatures I know of who live in a world much wider than the threats and gratifications of the immediate environment. It is a world erected through the stories we tell. These are stories called art, science, religion, law, statecraft, and many other things that have been excessively differentiated as if they all had totally different functions. They add up to a historically evolving, organically interrelated, seamless symbolic web called culture.

I was struck with (and have often quoted) the statement attributed to Scottish patriot Andrew Fletcher who said that if he were permitted to write all the ballads, he need not care who makes the laws of a nation. Ballads, songs, tales, gestures, and images make up the unique design of the human environment. All animals "behave" but only humans *act* in a world of towering symbolic constructions.

Culture is a system of messages and images that regulates and reproduces social relations. It introduces us into roles of gender, age, class, vocation; gives us models of conformity and targets for rebellion; provides the range of personalities, temperaments, mentalities said to be our "characteristics"; helps us rise to selfless acts of courage and sacrifice; and makes us accept (and perpetrate) repression and slaughter of unknown people assigned to the appropriate categories of barbarians and enemies.

Culture is a symbolic organization that cultivates our conceptions of existence, priorities, values, and relationships. We derive from it notions of what is; what is important; what is good, bad, or endowed with other qualities; and what is related to what. Its stories tell us how things work, what things are, and what we can or should do about them. Culture provides the overall framework in which we imagine what we do not encounter directly, and interpret what we do encounter directly. It is the context in which experience becomes consciousness. Culture, then, is a system of stories and other artifacts—increasingly mass produced—that mediates between existence and consciousness of existence, and thereby contributes to both.

The decisive transformation in the quality of human life was the industrial revolution. That was—and is—largely a cultural transformation. Printing begins the industrialization of storytelling. It makes possible the formation of the literate, press-based publics thought to be necessary for self-government. Freedom of expression and of selection is the key requirement for government reasonably representative of competing and conflicting interests. Democratic theory is thus based on the freedom of choice that print and other selectively used media make possible. That may be one reason why liberal and even some radical scholars cling to traditional notions of selective use and exposure even when new developments in telecommunications erode these processes and short-circuit conventional theories of democracy—and of research.

The mass production of messages exposes large and diverse groups to distant sources of stories produced to the specifications of industrial organizations for commodity and political markets. I wrote in 1958 that in the "quest for the *system* behind the facts and forms of mass communication, the media analyst regards content as expressive of social relationships and institutional dynamics, and as formative of social patterns." And: "...mass media content bears the imprint of concrete circumstances of its creation. This includes such things as the external outlook and internal dynamics of the producing industry; its relationship to competitors; its control over resources, facilities of production and distribution, the position of its decision makers in the industrial structure; their relationships to audiences, markets, advertising sponsors."

The analysis of mass-produced message systems then has three main objectives. First it yields clues about the outlook and de facto policies of social systems and industrial organizations in the cultural field. It scans the record of industrial behavior in culture. Second, it investigates that record as a system expressive of human potentials, social relations, and values. Neglecting full analysis of that system ("content analysis"), as behaviorally oriented communications researchers often do, limiting their search to measurable consequences of their uses ("effects"), ignores the richest revelations of what a particular culture considers important, relevant, and right, simply because it is not easily observed in action. The third objective, however, is to set the stage for eliciting action indicative of such consequences as can be observed. This objective is based on the belief that implicit in large and aggregated systems of messages are assumptions, contexts, and points of view indicative of cultural contributions to much of what we think and do. That is the task of cultivation analysis.

Trying to distinguish the study of communications as a basic cultural inquiry apart from the dominant research paradigm of persuasion and other forms of tactical manipulation, I stressed in 1966

> The limitations the primarily tactical approach imposes on theory. Some of these limitations are inherent in approaching communications from a point of view which, as an historical phenomenon, is itself rooted in the manipulative pressures of modern society. A recent formulation...characteristically defined the study of communications as "the study of ways of arranging stimuli to produce desired responses by the organism." This conception not only fails to define communication but defines it out of existence. It blurs the distinction between communication and other types of social interaction. The researcher might as well study pushing, pulling, shoving, or feeding, or any tactics intended to "produce desired responses." It becomes irrelevant whether or not the transaction involves communication. What really happens as a consequence of "arranging stimuli" is also secondary. The basic question is" did the tactic "produce desired responses," or did it not?...Another theoretical difficulty is that the approach can, at best, yield a long and unwieldy list of "do's and don'ts" which must then be related to an almost infinite range of situations and objectives....
>
> Underlying the confusion of the study of communications with that of assorted tactics has been the excessive concern with usually short-term, private, and personal effects, conceived as behavior change—such as the adoption of a new practice, the gaining of a

> vote, the sale of a new product. This preoccupation has obscured not only the concept of communication as a special type of social interaction, but also the meaning of effect. Equating effect with change tended to inhibit investigation of the massive historical and structural continuities between communications, the nature and composition of message systems, and corresponding systems of social relations. What could be observed, and was indeed seized upon as something surprising and significant, was the complexity and difficulty of changing certain ideas and behavior patterns amidst generally unchanging social-cultural conditions....
>
> An image (or behavior pattern) must be sustained to exist at all. Once a pattern is established and sustained, it affects messages and tactics as much as (or more than) the other way around. Specific attitude or behavior change may be the *least* significant indicator of effect unless it is part of a general transformation of the message-production and image-cultivation process and is, therefore, supported and reinforced by changing circumstances of life....The history and dynamics of continuities, as well as of change, in the reciprocal relationships between social structures, message systems, and image structures *are* the "effects" of communication.

From that distinction between change as a measure of communications effect and the broad historic continuities that stable cultural currents cultivate came a recognition of television's unique characteristics in contemporary America. Twenty years of research on these characteristics led to the formulation, refinements, and extensions of cultivation analysis, as illustrated by the chapters in this book.

Publication of initial results, and debates concerning methodology, discussed in Chapter 1, resulted in both proliferation and confusion. Both have continued to the present day, prompting me to develop these cautionary notes. Perhaps somewhat dogmatically, but more to advance than to limit debate, I offer the points that follow. They suggest for the path of our "advances" six general considerations:

1. Television is a unique medium requiring a special approach to study.
2. Television messages form a coherent system, the mainstream of our culture.
3. Those message systems (content) provide clues to cultivation.
4. Cultivation analysis focuses on television's contributions over time to the thinking and actions of large and otherwise heterogeneous social aggregates.
5. New technologies extend rather than deflect the reach of television's messages.
6. Cultivation analysis focuses on pervasive stabilizing and homogenizing consequences.

TELEVISION IS A UNIQUE MEDIUM REQUIRING A SPECIAL APPROACH TO STUDY

Television is the only medium that enters the home for over seven hours a day and provides the environment of symbols into which children are born. Literacy, mobility, prior tastes, and predispositions are less relevant than they are for other media.

Other media are introduced when some values, tastes, and habits have already been acquired in the home, and after parents and other family members have played the role of principal storytellers about life and the world. However, with television the process is reversed. It is the child who is "inserted" at birth into a television environment. Television competes, usually successfully, with all other storytellers. The extent and depth of the child's immersion in the world of television depends on the style of life of the family much more than on persons or programs.

Viewers watch by the clock. Despite the proliferation of VCRs and increased cable penetration, they watch whatever is offered to them. The size of audiences available for broadcasters to sell to advertisers is determined by the time of the day, the week, the season. Programs compete for socially marginal (though financially crucial) advantage in relatively stable markets. Demographic shifts, industrial consolidation, and new advertising outlets may erode old market contours (e.g., the major networks) but those are also marginal changes of little or no consequence for content (as opposed to channel) selection. Selectivity is necessarily reduced, especially compared to other media. Our studies have shown that the mix of programs and the relative coherence of the television world, including cable and even most videocassettes, is such that the average to heavy viewer (about three consecutive prime-time hours or more per day) cannot escape repetitive exposure to the same thematic and dramatic program elements day after day. There has not been a medium or institution like this since preindustrial religion.

Before television, "predispositions" resulted from the learning of tastes and values in the home and school, and led to selective exposure to media. But early childhood exposure to television can influence, and continuous cultivation maintain, the formation of those predispositions. This makes the usual research considerations of selectivity, "before-and-after" exposure, "intervening variables," and predispositions themselves, along with all other factors influencing communication effects, less relevant than they are for other media.

Unlike other media, television is in the home and readily accessible when the child arrives; there is no before exposure condition. The theory of cultivation thus applies to television but not necessarily to other media that do not have television's unique characteristics of early and repetitive exposure, simultaneous and pervasive involvement of total communities (providing a common basis for communication and interaction), and the relatively nonselective exposure to thematically and dramatically coherent, stable, and widely shared message systems. Other media may present some similar and complementary messages, but if their systems of messages do not fit these criteria, they are unlikely to cultivate prevalent conceptions in the same universal way.

TELEVISION MESSAGES FORM A COHERENT SYSTEM, THE MAINSTREAM OF OUR CULTURE

Cultivation as a cultural process relates to coherent frameworks of knowledge and to underlying general concepts revealed in responses to certain questions, rather than to isolated facts or beliefs. These general perspectives are cultivated by exposure to the total and organically related world of television rather than exposure to individual programs and selections. Whatever ripple effects or confirming (or disconfirming) tendencies discrete programs and program "preferences" may have, it would be difficult to reliably attribute them to the programs and selections that presumably gave rise to them. Heavier viewers watch more of the general mix of programming than light viewers, regardless of their preferences. Except for rare and freakish viewing patterns, those who watch three or more hours of prime time (i.e., the majority of regular viewers) see much of the same mix of basic dramatic ingredients whether they say they prefer comedy, crime, or news. That is why a measure of total viewing rather than particular favorites or selections is the most efficient for purposes of cultivation analysis.

Even to the extent that viewers feel that they are being selective in favoring or avoiding certain types of programs, the thematic and dramatic elements making up different types and genres of programs are often quite similar. In cultivation analysis we should ignore plot configurations and formal variety as—while perhaps aesthetically and morally satisfying—concealing by their surface novelty the underlying uniformity of the basic "building blocks" of the television world: thematic structure, interaction patterns, social typing, and fate (success-failure, violence-victimization, etc.) meted out to the different social types. These overarching elements expose large communities over long periods of time to a coherent structure of conceptions about life and the world. The investigation of this structure is the principal aim of cultivation analysis.

The coherence and stability of the symbolic structure of the television world is not due to the lack of creativity and talent producing. It is an expression of the coherence and stability of the commercial and sociopolitical constraints on the industry. "Congress shall make no law respecting an establishment of religion...or abridging the freedom of speech, or of the press" states the First Amendment to the U.S. Constitution. But commercial broadcasting rests on laws making advertising a tax-deductible business expense, thus both establishing the functional equivalent of state religion and surrendering the press to the plutocracy of market concentrations.

The broadcasting-advertising industries depend on the profitable marketing of commodities and the existence of enabling and protective legislation. The only abridgment they fight is of their freedom of unrestricted marketing. Despite much lip-service about First Amendment rights, a proposal to tax advertising in a state brings threats of a blackout depriving its people of that sacred right. The need to sustain favorable and preempt or counter any other form of legislation and pressure, and to serve the largest markets at the least cost in a competitive environment, makes program production conform to exacting specifications underlying its surface novelty. Many of these specifications were embodied in the television codes. Many more are pragmatically derived. Our annual monitoring has found striking stability and similarity among networks and across genres in the dramatic "building blocks" of thematic and action structure, demographic characterizations, and the associations of different social types with different outcomes of power vs. vulnerability, and so on.

Steady repetitive exposure to these structural components tends to cultivate stable images of society and the self. Some of these images may be held in common and some may vary among subgroups of the viewing population. For example, the relative vulnerability of minor groups as portrayed on television, compared to the relatively powerful portrayal of the dominant groups, may cultivate greater insecurity and dependence among the former. Such socialization into a power structure is more likely to stem from the coherent and interrelated symbolic structure to which most viewers are constantly exposed than from any specific programs, idiosyncratic viewing, or selective habits. The existence of this coherent, mainstream system of messages is thus the basic "medium" of cultivation. It can best be measured by total amounts of exposure to the prevalent interrelated program mix rather than partial exposure to presumed preferences and selections.

ANALYSIS OF TELEVISION'S MESSAGE SYSTEMS PROVIDES CLUES TO CULTIVATION

Survey questions used in cultivation analysis should reflect the overarching content configurations embedded in television's message systems presented to large groups of viewers over long periods of time, usually since infancy. Helter-skelter and exploratory questioning may be useful for a variety of theoretical and serendipitous purposes but do not test cultivation theory. The use of such data, or the comparison of responses of those who claim to prefer or view this and that type of programming, instead of measures of total viewing, is likely to yield confusing, contradictory, and misleading results.

Lines of questioning derived mainly from "real world" considerations, probing the cultivating characteristics of "informative" (i.e., realistic) styles, and interpreting content information fairly literally (sometimes called *first-order cultivation*) can lead to fruitful and interesting results. But I believe that equally important are the symbolic transformations (sometimes called *second-order cultivation*—a term that can be misleading) that exhibit the special power of symbolic life over and above verisimilitude. That is the special characteristic of terms of discourse to shift from specific cases to general classes and to be understood symbolically rather than literally. For example, in the television world, men outnumber women at least three to one. Taken literally, this would suggest that heavy viewers would underestimate the number or proportion of women in the world, which is not the case. Relative underrepresentation in the fairly rigidly structured symbolic world, however, is not only a question of numbers. It translates into differential "quotas" of life chances, ranges of activity, stereotyped portrayals, and levels of occupations. Questions dealing with these symbolic transformations of numerical deviations from statistical norms tap dimensions most relevant to cultivation.

CULTIVATION ANALYSIS FOCUSES ON TELEVISION'S CONTRIBUTIONS OVER TIME TO THE THINKING AND ACTIONS OF LARGE AND OTHERWISE HETEROGENEOUS SOCIAL AGGREGATES

Cultivation is a process driven by the common symbolic ritual engaging large communities over long periods of time. Other media uses and life circumstances interact with that process but do not counter or cancel the major thrust of its independent role in cultivating frameworks of knowledge. For example, our research has found that heavy viewers from different subgroups tend to share the television mainstream conception of science as a somewhat odd, risky, and ambivalent occupation. Those who also read science magazines have a generally more positive view of science. But the heavy viewers among them still share the relatively hostile mainstream conception. (This "convergence" of heavy viewers toward the dominant television image is what we call *mainstreaming*.)

Cultivation is usually revealed in such comparisons and correlations between those who watch more or less television within otherwise relatively homogeneous and comparable groups. The comparisons are with respect to patterns of responses elicited by questions relating to the most frequent common symbolic configurations of the television world. Largely irrelevant or confounding are surveys based on partial viewing, specialized groups such as college students, degrees of attention or intensity of viewing, beliefs about the presumed "reality" of the portrayals, reports about likes and dislikes or program preferences, and other mostly speculative qualities of viewing. Symbolic functions do not typically conform to received notions about long-term aggregate consequences of exposure. Not keenly or even consciously attended to background information may be more easily assimilated than the foreground. Fantastic stories from fairy tales to cartoons clearly demonstrate how things work behind the façade of appearances. Macho adventures and family comedies of prime time also convey a sense of reality (or at least realism) despite implausible plots and may be projected onto real life as much as factual and literally believable accounts of what things actually are. The crucial role of drama and fiction in socialization (and thus cultivation) may largely depend on the unique ability of contrived accounts to illuminate the otherwise invisible dynamics of human and social relationships. Accounts limited to events and facts believed to be real, and not just realistic, may become intelligible only in light of a tacit understanding of fictional dynamics. That is why controversies about and censorship of fiction have been historically so prominent and important in social control by cultural means.

However, emphasis on symbolic functions for large and enduring social aggregates does not necessarily imply across-the-board uniformity of the cultivation process. Again, the amount of viewing is an integral part of the style of life of the home and family. Therefore, factors other than programming or personal preference typically determine the amount of television watched. These factors must be controlled in the analysis before the responses of light and heavy viewers can be compared and related to the message systems of television.

When other controllable factors are kept constant, and total amount of viewing compared within fairly homogeneous subgroups of large and representative population samples, the results often reveal complex patterns. Clearly, conceptions of life cultivated by television relate as much to the demographic and social characteristics of large subgroups of viewers as to the characteristics of the message systems to which they are all exposed. The same portrayals are likely to cultivate different but interrelated sets of responses among viewers differentially related to images of life, including their own lives, regularly presented on television.

Researchers finding "no significant difference" between total populations of light and heavy viewers, with or without multiple controls, have at times failed to examine subgroups with those populations. Such subgroups have been shown to have different and even contrasting responses to the television questions, with heavier viewers of the different subgroups sharing a greater commonality of meanings than light viewers (mainstreaming).

Conversely, substantial light-heavy viewer differences can be spurious if other social and life-style factors to which they may be attributed are not held constant. Other chapters in this volume detail the varieties of cultivation. Here I only want to stress the importance of aggregate and appropriate measures related to the symbolic functions of television message systems, uncluttered by extraneous proofs and theories (possibly interesting for other purposes) as tests of *cultivation*.

NEW TECHNOLOGIES EXTEND RATHER THAN DEFLECT THE REACH OF TELEVISION'S MESSAGES

Cable systems, new independent stations, time shifting, and view through VCRs give viewers more control over program delivery. They may displace magazine reading and moviegoing. There is not evidence that they substitute for, rather than simply add to, overall television exposure. On the contrary, the evidence indicates that although new technologies and channels present alternative ways of delivering programs, movies, and commercials, and thus may cut into network revenues, they do not substantially alter audience exposure to network-type programs. In fact, they may extend such exposure into time periods that had been devoted to more diverse activities.

The most popular cable and video programs are even more sharply targeted at the most exploitable appeals than television can be. Networks must present some balance; they cannot repeat the same programs too often. Cable, VCR, and videocassette users can and do watch their favorite programs as often as they wish, and that is more often than they get it from the networks. Installing fancy new boutiques in the same old cafeteria, repackaging the same food supplied by the same old wholesalers, does not change the substance of what is consumed. New delivery techniques, none of which produces much new or original fare, provide the appearance of greater and more attractive choices but in fact promote grater concentration on fewer "block-busters" and other "best-sellers."

Always touted as the dawning of new freedoms, new technologies typically penetrate new markets and eventually concentrate money, power, and choices. To that extent, they may intensify rather than dilute the central thrust of the cultivation process.

CULTIVATION ANALYSIS FOCUSES ON PERVASIVE STABILIZING AND HOMOGENIZING CONSEQUENCES

Culture is the symbolic process that cultivates enduring conceptual and behavior patterns essential to human socialization. A central, cohesive, and pervasive cultural mainstream, which is what I believe television to be, is likely to cultivate relatively compact and cohesive conceptual and behavior patterns. That means that television's independent contribution to such patterns is most likely to be in the direction of homogeneity within otherwise different and diverse social groups, eroding traditional social and other distinctions. Again, this does not mean sudden change or bland uniformity. It means that large and otherwise comparable groups of regular television viewers from different walks of life share a stable commonality of meanings compared to the lighter viewers in the same groups, and the commonality reflects their exposure to the television mainstream, eroding other traditional group differences.

The patterns of exposure reflect the structure and constraints of a relatively stable society. Therefore, the building blocks of the symbolic world (rather than its shifting plots and surface novelties) are most likely to cultivate stable and lasting conceptions of social reality. These conceptions may well be more rigid than reality itself. The findings of cultivation analysis show not only a tendency toward homogeneity and conventionality but also the inclination to resist and reject such change as may be occurring in other aspects of life and culture.

I have characterized these dynamics as the 3Bs: cultivation implies the blurring of traditional distinctions, the blending of conceptions into television's cultural mainstream, and the bending of the mainstream to the institutional interests of the medium and its sponsors. Blurring, blending, and bending into increasingly massive, global, and comprehensive total cultural arenas of the transnational social order is what I see as television's fundamental challenge to democratic theory and practice.

The historical circumstances in which we find ourselves have taken the magic or human life—living in a universe erected by culture—out of the hands of families and small communities. What has been a richly diverse hand-crafted process has become—for better or worse, or both—a complex manufacturing and mass-distribution enterprise. This has abolished much of the provincialism and parochialism, as well as some of the elitism, of the pretelevision era. It has enriched parochial cultural horizons. It also gave increasingly massive industrial conglomerates the right to conjure up much of what we think about, know, and do in common.

The First Amendment to the Constitution has been used to protect practical monopoly control over that process. It now shields what is a virtual establishment of the functional equivalent of religion, forbidden by the same amendment. Better understanding of that process, its dynamics, and long-range social policy implications will make it at least accessible to rational public discussion. Advances in cultivation analysis can help move us toward that goal.

Most other civilized countries have already addressed crucial issues of democratic culture in the television age and are experimenting with various responses to its paradoxes and dilemmas. Comparative study across cultures, our next task, and better understanding of the cultivation process under different sociocultural circumstances, will help liberate us from an unwitting acceptance of our present and largely invisible but binding set of controls.

REFERENCES

Gerbner, G. (1958). On content analysis and critical research in mass communication. *Audiovisual Communication Review*, *6*, 85–108.

Gerbner, G. (1966). On defining communication: Still another view. *Journal of Communication*, *16*, 99–103.

Gerbner, G. (1973). Cultural indicators: The third voice. In G. Gerbner, L. Gross, & W. J. Melody (eds.), *Communications technology and social policy* (pp. 555–573). New York: John Wiley.

Part V

VIOLENCE

The Power and the Peril

CHAPTER 17

LIVING WITH TELEVISION

The Violence Profile

BY GEORGE GERBNER
AND LARRY GROSS

The environment that sustains the most distinctive aspects of human existence is the environment of symbols. We learn, share, and act upon meanings derived from that environment. The first and longest lasting organization of the symbolic world was what we now call religion. Within its sacred scope, in earlier times, were the most essential processes of culture: art, science, technology, statecraft, and public storytelling.

Common rituals and mythologies are agencies of symbolic socialization and control. They demonstrate how society works by dramatizing its norms and values. They are essential parts of the general system of messages that cultivates prevailing outlooks (which is why we call it culture) and regulates social relationships. This system of messages, with its storytelling functions, makes people perceive as real and normal and right that which fits the established social order.

The institutional processes producing these message systems have become increasingly professionalized, industrialized, centralized, and specialized. Their principal locus shifted from handicraft to mass production and from traditional religion and formal education to the mass media of communications—particularly television. New technologies on the horizon may enrich the choices of the choosy but cannot replace the simultaneous public experience of a common symbolic environment that now binds diverse communities, including large groups of young and old and isolated people who have never before joined any mass public. Television is likely to remain for a long time the chief source of repetitive and ritualized symbol systems cultivating the common consciousness of the most far-flung and heterogeneous mass publics in history.

Our long-range study of this new symbolic environment developed from, and still includes, the annual Violence Index and Profile of TV content and its correlates in viewers' conceptions of relevant aspects of social reality.

The research began with the investigation of violence in network television drama in 1967–68 for the National Commission on the Causes and Prevention of Violence (4) and continued through 1972 under the sponsorship of the Surgeon General's Scientific Advisory Committee on Television and Social Behavior (5). The study was broadly conceived from the beginning and both reports showed the role and symbolic functions, as well as the extent, of violence in the world of television drama. A conference of research consultants to the National Institute of Mental Health in the spring of 1972 recommended that the Violence Index developed for the report to the Surgeon General be further broadened to take into account social relationships and viewer conceptions. Implementing that recommendation, we issued the Violence Profile (fifth in our series of reports), including violence-victim ratios and eventually viewer responses. The then Secretary of Health, Education, and Welfare Caspar W. Weinberger reported to Senator John O. Pastore in the fall of 1973 that our research was "broadened to encompass a number of additional dimensions and linked with viewers' perceptions of violence and its effects, is recommended by NIMH consultants and as incorporated by Dr. Gerbner in his renewal research" (16).

The "renewal research" to which Secretary Weinberger referred is our present project, Cultural Indicators. Conducted under a grant from the National Institute of Mental Health, it consists of periodic study of television programming and of the conceptions of social reality that viewing cultivates in child and adult audiences. Although the study of violence is a continuing aspect of the research,[1] the project is also developing indicators of other themes, roles, and relationships significant for social science and policy.

The pattern of findings that is beginning to emerge confirms our belief that television is essentially different from other media and that research on television requires a new approach. In this article we shall sketch the outlines of a critique of modes of research derived from experience with other media and advance an approach we find more appropriate to the special characteristics, features, and functions of television. We shall illustrate the design and some contributions of the approach taken in the Cultural Indicators project by presenting the latest Violence Profile (no. 7 in the series), including indicators of some conceptions television cultivates in its viewers.[2]

The confusing state of television research is largely due to inappropriate conceptions of the problem.

The automobile that burst upon the dusty highways of the turn of the century was seen by most people as just a horseless carriage rather than as a prime mover of a new way of life. Similarly, those who grew up before television tended to think of it as just another in the long series of technological innovations in mass communications. Consequently, modes of thinking and research-rooted inexperience with other media have been applied to television. These earlier modes of study were based on selectively used media and focused on attitude or behavior change. Both assumptions are largely inadequate to the task of conceptualizing and investigating the effects of television.

We begin with the assertion that television is the central cultural arm of American society. It is an agency of the established order and as such serves primarily to extend and maintain rather than to alter, threaten, or weaken conventional conceptions, beliefs, and behaviors. Its chief cultural function is to spread and stabilize social patterns, to cultivate not change but resistance to change. Television is a medium of the socialization of most people into standardized roles and behaviors. Its function is, in a word, enculturation.

The substance of the consciousness cultivated by TV is not so much specific attitudes and opinions as more basic assumptions about the "facts" of life and standards of judgment on which conclusions are based. The purpose of the Cultural Indicators project is to identify and track these premises and the conclusions they might cultivate across TV's diverse publics.

We shall make a case for studying television as a force for enculturation rather than as a selectively used medium of separate "entertainment" and "information" functions. First, we shall suggest that the essential differences between television and other media are more crucial than the similarities. Second, we will show why traditional research designs are inadequate for the study of television effects and suggest more appropriate methods. Third, we will sketch the pattern of evidence emerging from our studies indicating that "living" in the world of television cultivates conceptions of its own conventionalized "reality."

The reach, scope, ritualization, organic connectedness, and non-selective use of mainstream television makes it different from other media of mass communications.

TV penetrates every home in the land. Its seasonal, cyclical, and perpetual patterns of organically related fact and fiction (all woven into an entertainment fabric producing publics of consumers for sale to advertisers) again encompass essential elements of art, science, technology, statecraft, and public (as well as most family) storytelling. The information-poor (children and less educated adults) are again the entertainment-rich held in thrall by the myths and legends of a new electronic priesthood.

If you were born before, say, 1950, television came into your life after the formative years as just another medium. Even if you are now an "addict," it will be difficult for you to comprehend the transformations it has wrought. Could you, as a twelve-year old, have contemplated spending an average of six hours *a day* at the local movie house? Not only would most parents not have permitted such behavior but most children would not have imagined the possibility. Yet, in our sample of children, nearly half the twelve-year-olds watch at least six hours of television every day.

Unlike print, television does not require literacy. Unlike the movies, television is "free" (supported by a privately imposed tax on all goods), and it is always running.

Unlike radio, television can show as well as tell. Unlike the theater, concerts, movies, and even churches, television does not require mobility. It comes into the home and reaches individuals directly. With its virtually unlimited access from cradle to grave, television both precedes reading and, increasingly, preempts it.

Television is the first centralized cultural influence to permeate both the initial and the final years of life—as well as the years between. Most infants are exposed to television long before reading. By the time a child reaches school, television will have occupied more time than would be spent in a college classroom. At the other end of the lifelong curriculum, television is there to keep the elderly company when all else fails.

All societies have evolved ways of explaining the world to themselves and to their children. Socially constructed "reality" gives a coherent picture of what exists, what is important, what is related to what, and what is right. The constant cultivation of such "realities" is the task of mainstream rituals and mythologies. They legitimize action along socially functional and conventionally acceptable lines.

The social, political, and economic integration of modern industrial society has created a system in which few communities, if any, can maintain an independent integrity. We are parts of a Leviathan and its nervous system is telecommunications. Publicly shared knowledge of the "wide world" is what this nervous system transmits to us.

Television is the chief common ground among the different groups that make up a large and heterogeneous national community. No national achievement, celebration, or mourning seems real until it is confirmed and shared on television.

Never before have all classes and groups (as well as ages) shared so much of the same culture and the same perspectives while having so little to do with their creation. Representation in the world of television gives an idea, a cause, a group its sense of public identity, importance, and relevance. No movement can get going without some visibility in that world or long withstand television's power to discredit, insulate, or undercut. Other media, used selectively and by special interests or cultural elites, cultivate partial and parochial outlooks. Television spreads the same images and messages to all from penthouse to tenement. TV is the new (and only) culture of those who expose themselves to information only when it comes as "entertainment." Entertainment is the most broadly effective educational fare in any culture.

All major networks serving the same social system depend on the same markets and programming formulas. That may be one reason why, unlike other media, television is used non-selectively; it just doesn't matter that much. With the exception of national events and some "specials," the total viewing audience is fairly stable regardless of what is on. Individual tastes and program preferences are less important in determining viewing patterns than is the time a program is on. The nearly universal, non-selective, and habitual use of television fits the ritualistic pattern of its programming. You watch television as you might attend a church service, except that most people watch television more religiously.

Constitutional guarantees shield the prerogatives of ownership. Technological imperatives of electronics have changed modern governance more than Constitutional amendments and curt decisions. Television, the flagship of industrial mass culture, now rivals ancient religions as a purveyor of organic patterns of symbols—news and other entertainment—that animate national and even global communities' senses of reality and value.

These considerations led us to question many of the more common arguments raised in discussions of television's effects.

An important example is the concern over the consequences of violence on television. The invention and development of technologies which permit the production and dissemination of mass mediated fictional images across class lines seems invariably to raise in the minds of the established classes the specter of subversion, corruption, and unrest being encouraged among the various lower orders—poor people, ethnic and racial minorities, children, and women. The specter arises when it seems that the lower orders may presume to imitate—if not to replace—their betters. Whether the suspect and controversial media are newspapers, novels, and theater, as in the nineteenth century, or movies, radio comic books, and television as in the twentieth, concern tends to focus on the possibilities of disruption that threaten the established norms of belief, behavior, and morality.

In our view, however, that concern has become anachronistic. Once the industrial order has legitimized its rule, the primary function of its cultural arm becomes the reiteration of that legitimacy and the maintenance of established power and authority. The rules of the games and the morality of its goals can best be demonstrated by dramatic stories of their symbolic violations. The intended lessons are generally effective and the social order is only rarely and peripherally threatened. The *system* is the message and, as our politicians like to say, the system works. Our question is, in fact, whether it may not work too well in cultivating uniform assumptions, exploitable fears, acquiescence to power, and resistance to meaningful change.

Therefore, in contrast to the more usual statement of the problem, we do not believe that the only critical correlate of television violence is to be found in the stimulation of occasional individual aggression. The consequences of living in a symbolic world ruled largely by violence may be much more far-reaching. Preparation for large-scale organized violence requires the cultivation of fear and acquiescence to power. TV violence is a dramatic demonstration of power which communicates much about social norms and relationships, about goals and means, about winners and losers, about the risks of life and the price for transgressions of society's rules. Violence-laden drama shows who gets away with what, when, why, how, and against whom.

"Real world" *victims* as well as violents may have to learn their roles. Fear—that historic instrument of social control—may be an even more critical residue of a show of violence than aggression. Expectation of violence or passivity in the face of injustice may be consequences of even greater social concern. We shall return to this theme with data from our studies.

The realism of TV fiction hides its synthetic and functionally selective nature.

The dominant stylistic convention of Western narrative art—novels, plays, films, TV dramas—is that of representational realism. However contrived television plots are, viewers assume that they take place against a backdrop of the real world. Nothing impeaches the basic "reality" of the world of television drama. It is also highly informative. That is, it offers to the unsuspecting viewer a continuous stream of "facts" and impressions about the way of the world, about the constancies and vagaries of human nature, and about the consequences of actions. The premise of realism is a Trojan horse which carries within it a highly selective, synthetic, and purposeful image of the facts of life.

A normal adult viewer is not unaware of the fictiveness of television drama. No one calls the police or an ambulance when a character in a television program is shot. "War of the Worlds"-type scares are rare, if they occur at all. Granting this basic awareness on the part of the viewers, one may still wonder how often and to what degree all viewers suspend their disbelief in the reality of the symbolic world.

Surely we all know that Robert Young is not a doctor and that Marcus Welby is an M.D. by only poetic license. Yet according to the *Philadelphia Bulletin* (July 10, 1974) in the first five years of the program "Dr. Welby" received over a quarter of a million letters from viewers, most containing requests for medical advice.

Doctor shows are not the only targets of such claims. A former New York City police official has complained that jury members have formed images and expectations of trial procedures and outcomes from television which often prejudice them in actual trials. In a courtroom incident related to us by a lawyer, the counsel for the defense leapt to his feet, objecting, "Your Honor, the Prosecutor is badgering the witness!" The judge replied that he, too, had seen that objection raised on the Perry Mason show, but, unfortunately, it was not included in the California code.

Anecdotes and examples should not trivialize the real point, which is that even the most sophisticated can find many important components of their knowledge of the real world derived wholly or in part from fictional representation.

How often do we make a sharp distinction between the action which we know is not "real" and the accumulation of background information (which is, after all, "realistic")? Are we keenly aware that in the total population of the television world men outnumber women four to one? Or that, with all the violence, the leading causes of real life injury and death—industrial and traffic accidents—are hardly ever depicted?

How many of us have ever been in an operating room, a criminal courtroom, a police station or jail, a corporate boardroom, or a movie studio? How much of what we know about such diverse spheres of activity, about how various kinds of people work and what they do—how much of our real world has been learned from fictional worlds? To the extent that viewers see television drama—the foreground of plot or the background of the television world—as naturalistic, they may derive a wealth of incidental "knowledge." This incidental learning may be effected by bald "facts" and by the subtle interplay of occurrence, co-occurrence, and non-occurrence of actors and actions.

In addition to the subtle patterns against whose influence we may all be somewhat defenseless, television provides another seductively persuasive sort of imagery. In real life much is hidden from our eyes. Often, motives are obscure, outcomes ambiguous, personalities complex, people unpredictable. The truth is never pure and rarely simple. The world of television, in contrast, offers us cogency, clarity, and resolution. Unlike life, television is an open book. Problems are never left hanging, rewards and punishments are present and accounted for. The rules of the game are known and rarely change. Not only does television "show" us the normally hidden workings of many important and fascinating institutions—medicine, law enforcement and justice, big business, the glamorous world of entertainment, etc.—but we "see" the people who fill important and exciting roles. We see who they are in terms of sex, age, race, and class and we also see them as personalities—dedicated and selfless, ruthless and ambitious, good-hearted but ineffectual, lazy and shiftless, corrupt and corrupting. Television provides the broadest common background of assumptions not only about what things are but also about how they work, or should work, and why.

The world of television drama is a mixture of truth and falsehood, of accuracy and distortion. It is not the true world but an extension of the standardized images which we have been taught since childhood. The audience for which the message of television is primarily intended (recall that an audience of about 20 million viewers is necessary for a program's survival) is the great majority of middle-class citizens for whom America is a democracy (our leaders act in accordance with the desires of the people), for whom our economy is free, and for whom God is alive, white, and male.

The implications for research are far-reaching and call into question essential aspects of the research paradigm stemming from historic pressures for behavior manipulation and marketing efficacy.

They suggest a model based on the concept of broad enculturation rather than of narrow changes in opinion or behavior. Instead of asking what communication "variables" might propagate what kinds of individual behavior changes, we want to know what types of common consciousness whole systems of messages might cultivate. This is less like asking about preconceived fears and hopes and more like asking about the "effects" of Christianity on one's view of the world or—as the Chinese *had* asked—of Confucianism on public morality. To answer such questions, we must review and revise some conventional articles of faith about research strategy.

First, we cannot presume consequences without the prior investigation of content, as the conventional research paradigm tends to do. Nor can the content be limited to isolated elements (e.g., news, commercials, specific programs), taken out of the total context, or to individual viewer selections. The "world" of television is an organic system of stories and images. Only system-wide analysis of messages can reveal the symbolic world which structures common assumptions and definitions for the generations born into it and provides bases for interaction (though not necessarily of agreement) among large and heterogeneous communities. The system as a whole plays a major role in setting the agenda of issues to agree or disagree about; it shapes the most pervasive norms and cultivates the dominant perspectives of society.

Another conventional research assumption is that the experiment is the most powerful method, and that change (in attitudes, opinions, likes-dislikes, etc., toward or conveyed by "variable X") is the most significant outcome to measure. In the ideal experiment, you expose a group to X and assess salient aspects of the state of the receivers before and after exposure, comparing the change, if any, to data obtained from a control group (identical in all relevant ways to the experimental group) who have not received X. No change or no difference means no effect.

When X is television, however, we must turn this paradigm around: stability may be the significant outcome of the sum total of the play of many variables. If nearly everyone "lives" to some extent in the world of television, clearly we cannot find unexposed groups who would be identical in all important respects to the viewers. We cannot isolate television from the mainstream of modern culture because it is the mainstream. We cannot look for change as the most significant accomplishment of the chief arm of established culture if its main social function is to maintain, reinforce, and exploit rather than to undermine or alter conventional conceptions, beliefs, and behaviors. On the contrary, the relative ineffectiveness of isolated campaigns may itself be testimony to the power of mainstream communications.

Neither can we assume that TV cultivates conceptions easily distinguishable from those of other major entertainment media. (But we cannot emphasize too strongly the historically novel role of television in standardizing and sharing with all as the common norm what had before been more parochial, local, and selective cultural patterns.) We assume, therefore, that TV's standardizing and legitimizing influence comes largely from its ability to streamline, amplify, ritualize, and spread into hitherto isolated or protected subcultures, homes, nooks, and crannies of the land the conventional capsules of mass-produced information and entertainment.

Another popular research technique which is inappropriate is the experimental or quasi-experimental test of the consequences of exposure to one particular type of television programming.

Much of the research on media violence, for example, has focused on the observation and measurement of behavior which occurs after a viewer has seen a particular program or even isolated scenes from programs. All such studies, no matter how clean the design and clear the results, are of limited value because they ignore a fundamental fact: The world of TV drama consists of a complex and integrated system of characters, events, actions, and relationships whose effects cannot be measured with regard to any single element or program seen in isolation.

How, then, should the effects of television be conceptualized and studied?

We believe that the key to the answer rests in a search for those assumptions about the "facts" of life and society that television cultivates in its more faithful viewers. That search requires two different methods of research. The relationship between the two is one of the special characteristics of the Cultural Indicators approach.[3]

The first method of research is the periodic analysis of large and representative aggregates of television output (rather than individual segments) as the system of messages to which total communities are exposed. The purpose of message system analysis is the establish the composition and structure of the symbolic world. We have begun that analysis with the most ubiquitous, translucent, and instructive part of television (or any cultural) fare, the dramatic programs (series, cartoons, movies on television) that populate and animate for most viewers the heartland of the symbolic world. Instead of guessing or assuming the contours and dynamics of that world, message system analysis maps its geography, demography, thematic and action structure, time and space dimensions, personality profiles, occupations, and fates. Message system analysis yields the gross but clear terms of location, action, and characterization discharged into the mainstream of community consciousness. Aggregate viewer interpretation and response starts with these common terms of basic exposure.

The second step of the research is to determine what, if anything, viewers absorb from living in the world of television. Cultivation analysis, as we call the method, inquires into the assumptions television cultivates about the facts, norms, and values of society. Here we turn the findings of message system analysis about the fantasyland of television into questions about social reality. To each of these questions there is a "television answer," which is like the way things appear in the world of television, and another and different answer which is biased in the opposite direction, closer to the way things are in the observable world. We ask these questions of samples of adults and children. All responses are related to television exposure, other media habits, and demographic characteristics. We then compare the response of light and heavy viewers controlling for sex, age, education, and other characteristics. The margin of heavy viewers over light viewers giving the "television answers" within and across groups is the "cultivation differential" indicating conceptions about social reality that viewing tends to cultivate.

Our analysis looks at the contribution of TV drama to viewer conceptions in conjunction with such other sources of knowledge as education and news. The analysis is intended to illuminate the complementary as well as the divergent roles of these sources of facts, images, beliefs, and values in the cultivation of assumptions about reality.

We shall now sketch some general features of the world of network television drama, and then report the latest findings about violence in that world.

As any mythical world, television presents a selective and functional system of messages. Its time, space, and motion—even its "accidents"—follow laws of dramatic convention and social utility. Its people are not born but are created to depict social types, causes, powers, and fates. The economics of the assembly line and the requirement of wide acceptability assure general adherence to common notions of justice and fair play, clear-cut characterizations, tested plot lines, and proven formulas for resolving all issues.

Representation in the fictional world signifies social existence; absence means symbolic annihilation. Being buffeted by events about, to act freely, boldly, and effectively is a mark of dramatic importance and social power. Values and forces come into play through characterizations; good is a certain type of attractiveness, evil is a personality defect, and right is the might that wins. Plots weave a thread of causality into the fabric of dramatic ritual, as stock characters act out familiar parts and confirm preferred notions of what's what, who's who, and who counts for what. The issue is rarely in doubt; the action is typically a game of social typing, group identification, skill, and power.

Many times a day, seven days a week, the dramatic pattern defines situations and cultivates premises about society, people, and issues. Casting the symbolic world thus has a meaning of its own: the lion's share of representation goes to the types that dominate the social order. About three-quarters of all leading characters are male, American, middle and upper class, and in the prime of life. Symbolic independence requires freedom relatively uninhabited by real-life constraints. Less fully represented are those lower in the domestic and global power hierarchy and characters involved in familiar social contexts, human dependencies, and other situations that impose the real-life burdens of human relationships and obligations upon freewheeling activity.

Women typically represent romantic or family interest, close human contact, love. Males can act in nearly any role, but rare is the female part that does not involve at least the suggestion of sex. While only one in three male leads is shown as intending to or ever having been married, two of every three females are married or expect to marry in the story. Female "specialties" limit the proportion of TV's women to about one-fourth of the total population.

Approximately five in ten characters can be unambiguously identified as gainfully employed. Of these, three are proprietors, managers, and professionals. The fourth comes from the ranks of labor—including all those employed in factories, farms, offices, shops, stores, mining, transportation, service stations, restaurants, and households, and working in unskilled, skilled, clerical, sales, and domestic service capacities. The fifth serves to enforce the law or preserve the peace on behalf of public or private clients.

Types of activity—paid and unpaid—also reflect dramatic and social purposes. Six in ten characters are engaged in discernible occupational activity and can be roughly divided into three groups of two each. The first group represents the world of legitimate private business, industry, agriculture, finance, etc. The second group is engaged in activity related to art, science, religion, health, education, and welfare, as professionals, amateurs, patients, students, or clients. The third makes up the forces of official or semiofficial authority and the army of criminals, outlaws, spies, and other enemies arrayed against them. One in every four leading characters acts out a drama of some sort of transgression and its suppression at home and abroad.

Violence plays a key role in such a world. It is the simplest and cheapest dramatic means available to demonstrate the rules of the game of power. In real life much violence is subtle, slow, circumstantial, invisible, even impersonal. Encounters with physical violence in real life are rare, more sickening than thrilling. But in the symbolic world, overt physical motion makes dramatically visible that which in the real world is usually hidden. Symbolic violence, as any show of force, typically does the job of real violence more cheaply and, of course, entertainingly.

Geared for independent action in loosely knit and often remote social contexts, half of all characters are free to engage in violence. One-fifth "specialize" in violence as law breakers of law enforcers. Violence on television, unlike in real life, rarely stems from close personal relationships. Most of it is between strangers, set up to drive home lessons of social typing. Violence is often just a specialty—a skill, a craft, an efficient means to test the norms of and settle any challenge to the existing structure of power.

The Violence Profile is a set of indicators tracing aspects of the television world and of conceptions of social reality they tend to cultivate in the minds of viewers.

Four specific types of indicators have been developed. Three come from message system analysis: (1) the context of programming trends against which any aspect of the world of television can be seen; (2) several specific measures of violence given separately and also combined in the Violence Index; and (3) structural characteristics of the dramatic world indicating social relationships depicted in it (in the present report, "risk rations"). The fourth type of indicator comes from cultivation analysis and will be shown in this report as the "cultivation differential." Although the violence Profile is the most developed, the Cultural Indicators project is constructing similar profiles of other aspects and relationships of the media world.

Before we present the indicators, let us briefly note the definitions, terms, and some procedures employed in generating the TV violence measures.[4]

Message system analysis has been performed on annual sample weeks of prime time and weekend daytime network dramatic programming since 1967 by trained analysts who observe and code many aspects of TV content. The definition of violence employed in this analysis is "the overt expression of physical force against self or other, compelling action against one's will on pain of being hurt or killed, or actually hurting or killing." The research focuses on a clear-cut and commonly understood definition of violence, and yields indicators of trends in the programming context in which violence occurs; in the prevalence, rate, and characterizations involved in violence; and in the power relationships expressed by the differential risks found in the world of television drama.

All observations are recorded in three types of units: the program (play) as a whole, each specific violent action (if any) in the program, and each dramatic character appearing in the program.

Program means a single fictional story presented in dramatic form. This may be a play produced for television, a feature film telecast during the period of the study, or a cartoon story (of which there may be one or more in a single program).

Violent action means a scene of some violence confined to the same parties. If a scene is interrupted (by flashback or shift to another scene) but continues in "real time," it is still the same act. However, if a new agent of violence enters the scene, that begins another act. These units are also called violent episodes.

Characters analyzed in all programs (whether violent or not) are of two types. Major characters are the principal roles essential to the story. Minor characters (subjected to a less detailed analysis) are all other speaking roles. (The findings summarized in this report include the analysis of major characters only.)

Samples of programming. Network dramatic programs transmitted in evening prime time (8 P.M. to 11 P.M. each day), and network children's dramatic programs transmitted weekend mornings (Saturday and Sunday between 8 A.M. and 2 P.M.) comprise the analytical source material.[5] With respect to four basic sample dimensions (network, program format, type, and tone), the solid week sample is at least as generalizable to a year's programming as larger randomly drawn samples (2).

Coder training and reliability. For the analysis of each program sample, a staff of twelve to eighteen coders is recruited. After about three weeks of training and testing coders analyze the season's videotaped program sample.

During both the training and data-collection phases, coders work in independent pairs and monitor their assigned videotaped programs as often as necessary. All programs in the sample are coded by two separate coder-pairs to provide double-coded data for reliability comparisons. Final measures, computed on the study's entire corpus of double-coded data, determine the acceptability of information for analysis and provide guidelines to its interpretation (11, 12).

Three sets of violence measures have been computed from the direct observational data of the message system analysis. They show the percentage of programs with any violence at all, the frequency and rate of violent episodes, and the number of roles calling for characterizations as violents, victims, or both. These measures are called *prevalence*, *rate*, and *role*, respectively. Each is given separately in all the tabulations that follow.

Figure 1. "Action" (Crime, Western, Adventure) Programs as Percentage of Cartoon and of Other General Programs Analyzed

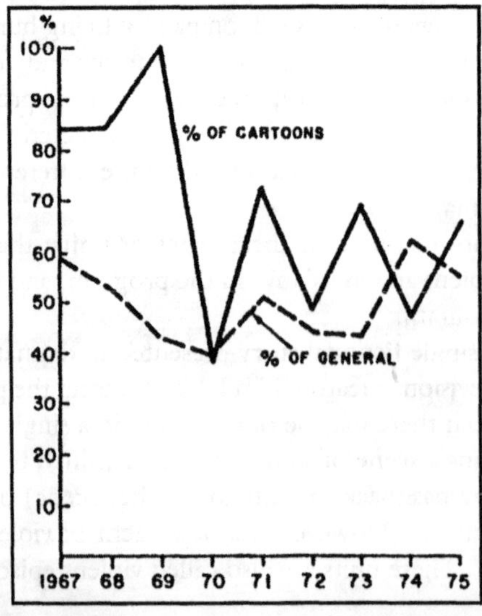

Figure 2. Violence Index for Different Hours of Dramatic Programming

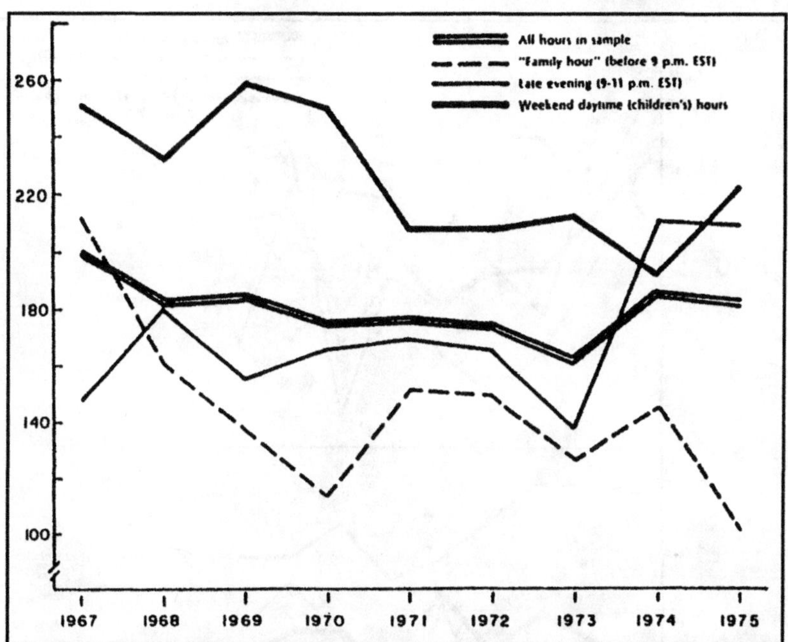

For ease of illustration and comparison, the three types of measures are also combined to form the Violence Index. The Index itself is not a statistical finding but serves as a convenient illustrator of trends and facilitates gross comparisons. The Index is obtained by adding measures of prevalence, rates (doubled to raise their relatively low numerical value), and roles. The formula can be seen on Tables 1 through 4 at the end of this chapter.

Before presenting the trends indicated by the measures just discussed, let us glance at the first indicator, that of program mix. "Action" programs contribute most violence to the world of television drama. Figure 1 shows that such programs comprise more than half of all prime time and weekend daytime programming, and their proportion of the total has not changed much in recent years. In fact, while general (non-cartoon) crime and adventure plays dropped from their 1974 high of 62 percent to 54 percent in 1975, cartoon crime and adventure rose in the same period from 47 percent to 66 percent of all cartoons.

These programming trends foreshadow the violence findings that follow. We can summarize them by noting that there has been *no significant reduction in the overall Violence Index despite some fluctuations in the specific measures and a definite drop in "family hour" violence, especially on CBS*, in the current season. The "family hour" decline has been matched by a sharp increase in violence during children's (weekend daytime) programming in the current season and by an even larger two-year rise in violence after 9 P.M. EST.

Figure 2 shows these trends in greater detail. Figure 3 provides similar information for each network separately, showing that late evening violence shot up on all

Figure 3. Violence Index for Different Hours by Network

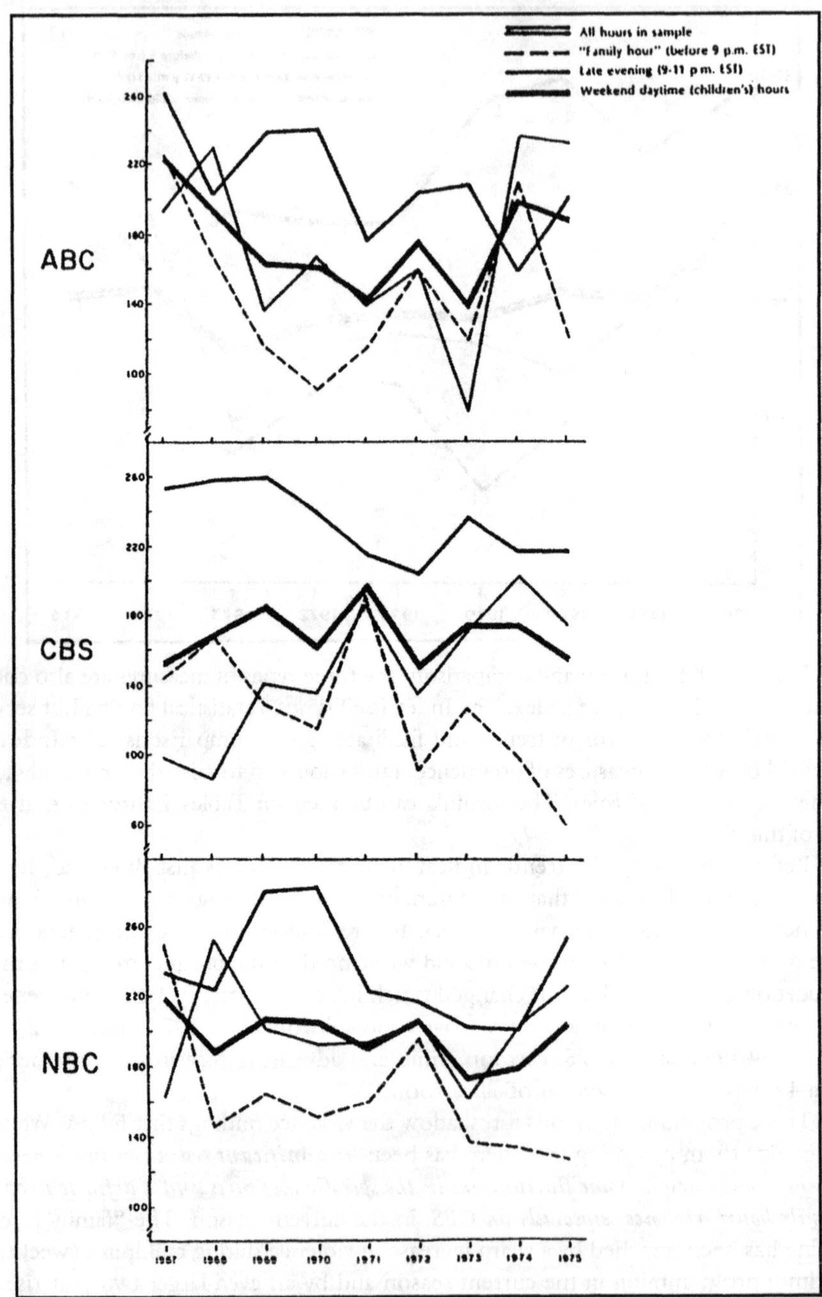

Figure 4. Violence Index for Each Network, All Programs in Sample

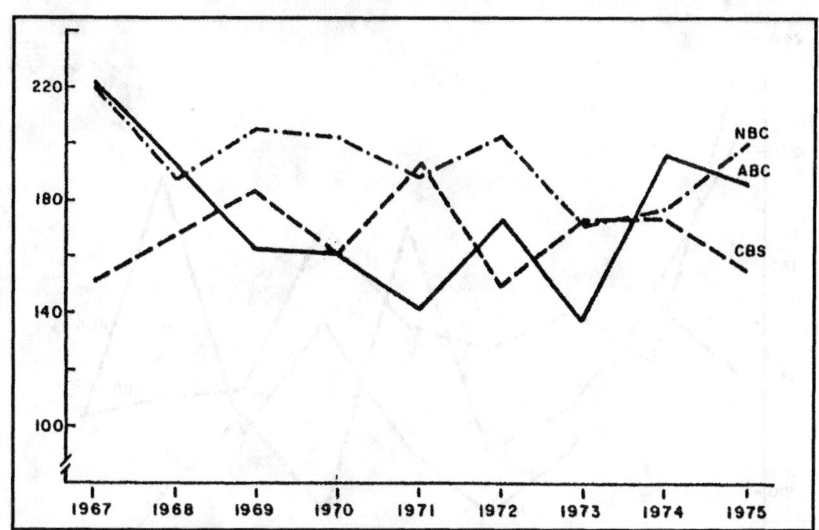

three networks in the past two or three years (with minor dips on CBS and ABC in 1975), and that children's (weekend daytime) programs became more violent on ABC and NBC in the past season. Figure 4 is a direct comparison of the Violence Index for each network, showing remarkable long-term stability and similarity among them. Figure 5 is a direct comparison of the "family hour" Violence Index for each network, showing little change over a two-year period for ABC and NBC, substantial reduction for the second year in a row for CBS.

Tables 1 through 4 (found at the end of the chapter) present all measures for the different hours of programming. They show how the specific measures of prevalence, rate, and role fluctuate and combine each year to make up the composite Violence Index. More complete tabulations, including network and format breakdowns, can be found in the Technical Report (3).

The indicators reflected in the Violence Index are clear manifestations of what network programmers actually do as compared to what they say or intend to do. Network executives and their censorship ("Standards and Practices") offices maintain close control over the assembly line production process that results in the particular program mix of a season (6). While our data permit many specific qualifications to any generalization that might be made, it is safe to say that network policy seems to have responded in narrow terms, when at all, to very specific pressure, and only while the heat was on. After nine years of investigations, hearings, and commissions (or since we have been tracking violence on television), eight out of every ten programs (nine out of every ten weekend children's hour programs) still contain some violence. The overall rate of violent episodes, eight per hour, is, if anything, higher than at any time since 1969. (The violence saturation of weekend children's programs declined from the 1969 high but increased from its 1974 low to sixteen per hour, double that of overall programming, as can be seen on Table 4.) Between six and seven out of every ten lead-

Figure 5. Violence Index for Each Network, Family Hour Only

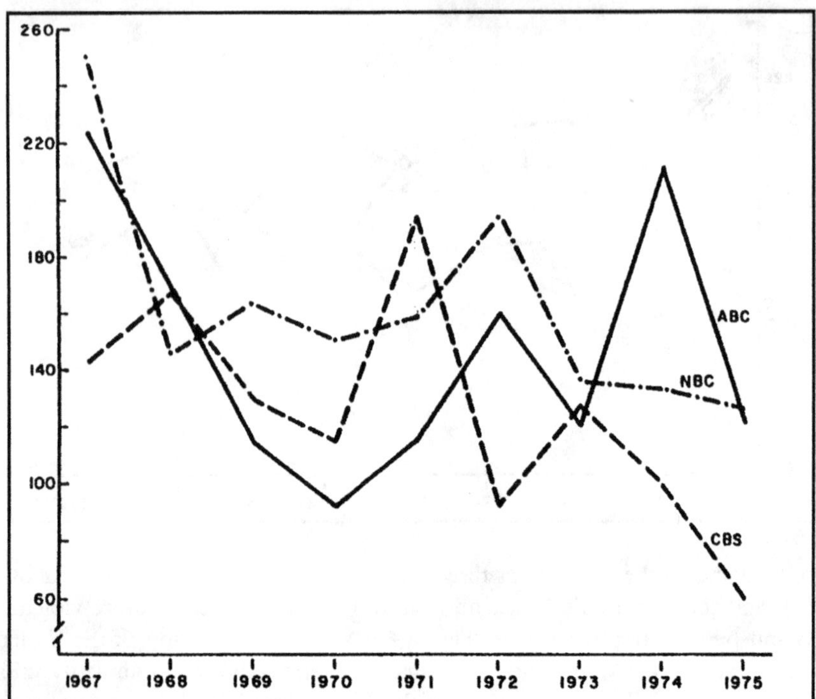

ing characters (eight and nine for children) are still involved in some violence. Between one and two out of every ten are still involved in killing.

Reductions have been achieved in the portrayal of on-screen killers (especially during weekend children's hours) and in "family hour" violence (especially by CBS), but, as we have noted, a sharp rise in late evening and general children's violence has canceled out any overall gains from the latter.

It is clear, at least to us, that deeply rooted sociocultural forces, rather than just obstinacy or profit-seeking, are at work. We have suggested earlier in this article, and have also developed elsewhere (9, 10), that symbolic violence is a demonstration of power and an instrument of social control serving, on the whole, to reinforce and preserve the existing social order, even if at an ever-increasing price in terms of pervasive fear and mistrust and of selective aggressiveness. That maintenance mechanism seems to work through cultivating a sense of danger, a differential calculus of the risks of life in different groups in the population. The Violence Profile is beginning to yield indicators of such a mechanism, and thereby also of basic structural and cultivation characteristics of television programming.

The structural characteristics of deletion drama are not easily controlled. They reflect basic cultural assumptions that make a show "entertaining"—i.e., smoothly and pleasingly fitting dominant notions (and prejudices) about social relations and thus demonstrating conventional notions of morality and power.

The most elementary—and telling—relationship involved in violent action is that of violent and victim. The pattern of those who inflict and those who suffer violence (or both) provides a differential calculus of hazards and opportunities for different groups of people in the "world" of television drama. Table 5 presents a summary of the scores of involvement and what we call risk ratios.[6] The character score is the roles component (CS) of the Violence Index; it is the percentage of all characters involved in any violence plus the percentage involved in any killing. The violent-victim and killer-killed (risk) ratios are obtained by dividing violents and victims, or killers and killed within each group. The plus sign means more violents or killers in the group; the minus sign means more victims (hurt) or killed.

We see that the 1967–75 totals show 1.19 male and 1.32 female victims for every violent male and female. Even more striking are the differential risks or fatal victimization. There were nearly two male killers for every male killed; however, for every female killer one woman was killed.

Table 5 also shows the differential risks of involvement and victimization attributed to other groups, projecting assumptions about social and power relations. Old men, married men, lower-class, foreign, and nonwhite males were most likely to get killed rather than to inflict lethal injury. "Good guys" were of course most likely to be the killers.

Among females, more vulnerable than men in most categories, both young and old women as well as unmarried, lower-class, foreign, and nonwhite women bore especially heavy burdens of relative victimization. Old, poor, and black women were shown *only* as killed and never as killers. Interestingly, "good" women, unlike "good" men, had no lethal power, but "bad" women were even more lethal than "bad" men. The victimization of the "good" woman is often the curtain-raiser that provokes the hero to righteous "action."

The pattern of relative victimization is remarkably stable from year to year. It demonstrates an invidious (but socially functional) sense of risk and power. We do not yet know whether it also cultivates a corresponding hierarchy of fear and aggression. But we do have evidence to suggest that television viewing cultivates a general sense of danger and mistrust. That evidence comes from the fourth and final element of the Violence Profile, the component we call the cultivation differential.

The cultivation differential comes, of course, from the cultivation analysis part of the Cultural Indicators research approach.

It highlights differences in conception of relevant aspects of social reality that television viewing tends to cultivate in heavy viewers compared to light viewers. The strategy is obviously most appropriate to those propositions in which television might cultivate conceptions that measurably deviate from those coming from other sources. Furthermore, the independent contributions of television are likely to be most powerful in cultivating assumptions about which there is little opportunity to learn first-hand, and which are not strongly anchored in other established beliefs and ideologies.

Figure 6. Percentage Giving the "Television Answer to a Question about the Proportion of People Employed in Law Enforcement

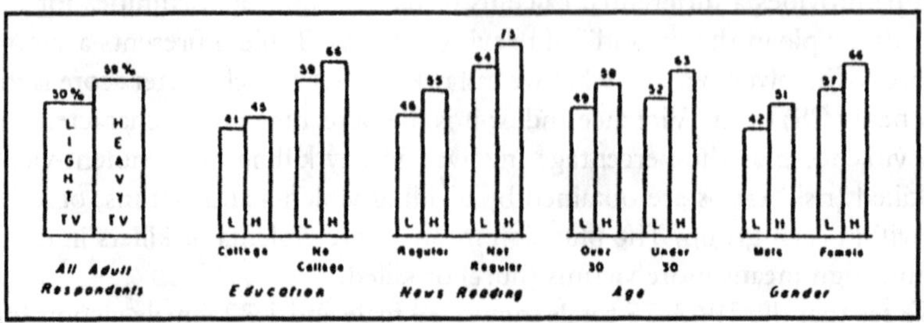

Figure 7. Percentage Responding "Can't Be Too Careful" to the Question "Can Most People Be Trusted?"

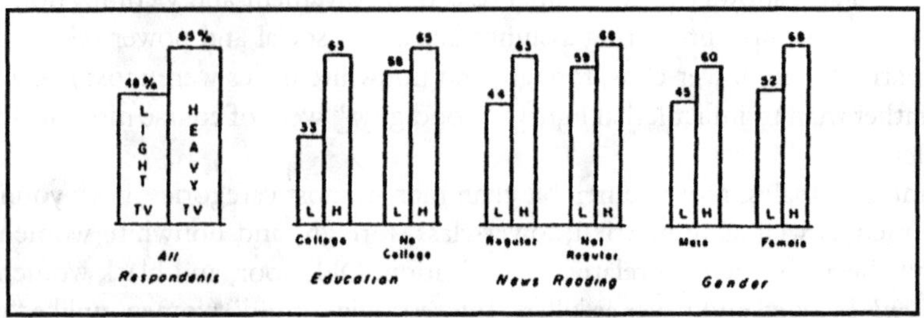

Figure 8. Percentage Giving the "Television Answer" (Exaggerating) Their Own Chance of Being Involved in Violence

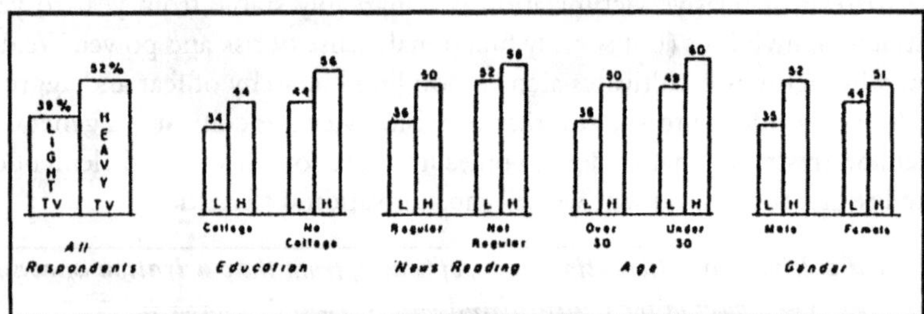

The obvious objection arises that light and heavy viewers are different prior to—and aside from—television. Factors other than television may account for the difference.

The point is well taken. We have found, as have others, that heavy viewing is part and parcel of a complex syndrome which also includes lower education, lower mobility, lower aspirations, higher anxieties, and other class, age, and sex related characteristics. We assume, indeed, that viewing helps to hold together and cultivate elements of that syndrome. But it does more than that. Television viewing also makes a separate and independent contribution to the "biasing" of conceptions of social reality within most age, sex, educational, and other groupings, including those presumably most "immune" to its effects.

Our study of TV's contribution to notions of social reality proceeds by various methods, each comparing responses of heavy and light viewers, with other characteristics held constant. Of the different methods used in cultivation analysis, only adult survey results are included in this report; the others are still in the process of development and summarization. These surveys were executed by commercial survey research organizations. For details of sampling, etc., the reader is referred to the Technical Report (3).

To probe in the direction of the pattern suggested by our message analysis, we obtained responses to questions about facts of life that relate to law enforcement, trust, and a sense of danger. Figure 6 presents the results of the first question asking what proportion of people are employed in law enforcement. The "television answer" (slanted in the direction of the world of television) was 5 percent. The alternative answer (more in the direction of reality) was 1 percent.

As Figure 6 shows, the heavy viewers (those viewing an average of four hours a day or more) were always more likely to give the television answer than the light viewers (those viewing an average of two hours a day or less). Figure 7 shows similar results for the question "Can most people be trusted?" and Figure 8 for the question "During any given week, what are your chances of being involved in some type of violence?" One in ten (the "television answer") or one in a hundred?

Let us take education as probably the best index of a complex of social circumstances that provide alternative informational and cultural opportunities. Those of our respondents who have had some college education are less likely to choose the "television answer" than those who have had none. But within each group, television viewing "biases" conceptions in the direction of the "facts" it presents. When we compared light and heavy viewers within the "college" and the "no college" groups, we got a typical step-wise pattern of the percentage of "television answers." Regular reading of newspapers makes a similar difference.

Both college education and regular newspaper reading seem to reduce the percentage of "television answers," but heavy viewing boosts it within both groups. This appears to be the general pattern of TV's ability to cultivate its own "reality."

An exaggerated impression of the actual number of law enforcement workers seems to be a consequence of viewing television. Of greater concern, however, would be the cultivation of a concomitantly exaggerated demand for their services. The world of television drama is, above all, a violent one in which more than half of all characters are involved in some violence, at least one-tenth in some killing, and in which over three-fourths of prime time hours contain some violence. As we have suggested, the cultivation of fear and a sense of danger may well be a prime residue of the show of violence.

Questions about feelings of trust and safety may be used to test that suggestion. The National Opinion Research Corporation's 1975 General Social Survey asked "Can most people be trusted?" Living in the world of television seems to strengthen the conclusion that they cannot. Heavy viewers chose the answer "Can't be too careful" in significantly greater proportions than did light viewers in the same groups, as shown in Figure 7. Those who do not read newspapers regularly have a high level of mistrust regardless of TV viewing. But, not surprisingly, women are the most likely to absorb the message of distrust.

Focusing directly on violence, we asked a national sample of adults about people's chances of being involved in violence in any given week. Figure 8 shows the patterns of overestimations in line with television's view of the world. It may explain why in recent surveys, such as the Detroit study conducted by the Institute of Social Research (13), respondents' estimates of danger in their neighborhoods had little to do with crime statistics or even with their own personal experience. The pattern of our findings suggests that television and other media exposure may be as important as demographic and other experiential factors in explaining why people view the world as they do.

Television certainly appears to condition the view of the generation that knew no world without it. All the figures show that the "under 30" respondents exhibit consistently higher levels of "television responses," despite the fact that they tend to be better educated than the "over 30" respondents. We may all live in a dangerous world, but young people (including children tested but not reported on here), the less educated, women, and heavy viewers within all these groups sense greater danger than light viewers in the same groups. College education (and its social correlates) may counter the television view, but heavy exposure to TV will counteract that too.

Fear is a universal emotion and easy to exploit. Symbolic violence may be the cheapest way to cultivate it effectively. Raw violence is, in comparison, risky and costly, resorted to when symbolic means fail. Ritualized displays of any violence (such as in crime and disaster news, as well as in mass-produced drama) may cultivate exaggerated assumptions about the extent of threat and danger in the world and lead to demands for protection.

What is the net result? A heightened sense of risk and insecurity (different for groups of varying power) is more likely to increase acquiescence to and dependence upon established authority, and to legitimize its use of force, than it is to threaten the social order through occasional non-legitimized imitations. Risky for their perpetrators and costly for their victims, media-incited criminal violence may be a price industrial cultures extract from some citizens for the general pacification of most others.

As with violence, so with other aspects of social reality we are investigating, TV appears to cultivate assumptions that fit its socially functional myths. Our chief instrument of enculturation and social control, television may function as the established religion of the industrial order, relating to governance as the church did to the state in earlier times.

NOTES

1. Several additional events influenced the further fate and development of the Violence Profile. Senator Pastore and Chairman Torbert Macdonald of the House Communications Subcommittee continued to take an active interest in it. The research director of the studies for the Surgeon General, Eli A. Rubinstein, continued to press for follow-up research (14). Douglass Cater and Stephen Strickland wrote a book on the report and argued for "ongoing research capable of undergirding large public inves-

tigations (1, p. 133). And finally, a committee of the Social Science Research Council especially formed and funded by NIMH to study the Violence Profile recommended continued use and further development (15).

2. A summary of the cultivation studies also appears in our article in the April 1976 *Psychology Today* (10).
3. For a more detailed description of the conceptual framework for this research see "Cultural Indicators: The Third Voice" (8).
4. For a more detailed methodological description and all tabulations not included here, see "Violence Profile: A Technical Report" (3), available for $12.00 (checks to be made out to the Trustees of the University of Pennsylvania) from The Annenberg School of Communications, University of Pennsylvania, PA 19174.
5. In 1967 and 1968, the hours included were 7:30 to 10 P.M. Monday through Saturday, 7 to 10 P.M. Sunday, and children's programs 8 a.m. to noon Saturday. Beginning in 1969, these hours were expanded until 11 P.M. each evening and from 7 A.M. to 2:30 P.M. Saturday and Sunday. As of 1971, however, network evening programming has been reduced by the FCC's prime time access rule. The effective evening parameters since 1971 are therefore 8 to 11 P.M. Monday through Saturday and 7:30 to 10:30 P.M. Sunday.
6. All tables appear at the end of the chapter.

REFERENCES

1. Cater, Douglass, and Stephen Strickland. *TV Violence and the Child; The Evolution and Fate of the Surgeon General's Report.* New York: Russell Sage Foundation, 1975.
2. Eleey, Michael F. "Variations in Generalizability Resulting from Sampling Characteristics of Content Analysis Data: A Case Study." Unpublished manuscript, Annenberg School of Communications, University of Pennsylvania, 1969.
3. Gerbner, George, and Larry Gross, with the assistance of Michael F. Eleey, Suzanne K. Fox, Marilyn Jackson-Beeck, and Nancy Signorielli. "Violence Profile No. 7: A Technical Report." Annenberg School of Communications, 1976.
4. Gerbner, George. "Dimensions of Violence in Television Drama." Chapter 15 in *Violence and the Media,* edited by Robert K. Baker and Sandra J. Ball, a staff report to the National Commission on the Causes and Prevention of Violence, U.S. Government Printing Office, 1969.
5. Gerbner, George. "Violence in Television Drama: Trends and Symbolic Functions." In G. A. Comtock and E. A. Rubenstein (eds.), *Television and Social Behavior*, Vol. 1. Washington, D.C.: U.S. Government Printing Office.
6. Gerbner, George, Gross, Larry, and Melody, William H. *Communications Technology and Social Policy.* New York: John Wiley and Sons, 1973.
7. Gerbner, George. "The Structure and Process of Television Program Content Regulation in the U.S." In G. A. Comstock and E. A. Rubinstein (eds.), *Television and Social Behavior*, Vol. 1. Washington, D.C.: U.S. Government Printing Office, 1972.
8. Gerbner, George. "Cultural Indicators: The Third Voice." In *Communications and Technology Social Policy.* New York: John Wiley and Sons, 1973.
9. Gerbner, George. "Scenario for Violence." *Human Behavior*, October 1975.

10. Gerbner, George, and Gross, Larry. "The Scary World of Television," *Psychology Today*, April 1976.
11. Krippendorff, Klaus. "Bivariate Agreement Coefficients for the Reliability of Data." In E. F. Borgatta and G. W. Bohrnstedt (eds.), *Sociological Methodology*. San Francisco: Jossey Bass, 1970.
12. Krippendorf, Klaus. "A Computer Program for Agreement Analysis of Reliability Data, Version 4." Mimeographed. Annenberg School of Communications, July 1973.
13. "Personal Safety a Major Concern: Public Perceptions of Quality of Life in Metropolitan Detroit Examined in ISR Study." *ISR Newsletter*, Winter 1976, p. 4.
14. Rubinstein, Eli A. "The TV Violence Report: What's Next?" *Journal of Communication*, Winter 1974, pp. 80–88.
15. Social Science Research Council. "A Profile of Television Violence." Report submitted by the Committee on Television and Social Behavior of the SSRC, July 1975.
16. Weinberger, Caspar W. Letter to Senator John O. Pastore dated November 13, 1973.

Table 1. Violence Measures for All Programs in Sample

	1967	1968	1969	1970	1971	1972	1973	1974	1975	TOTAL
SAMPLES (100%)	N	N	N	N	N	N	N	N	N	N
Programs (plays) analyzed	96	87	121	111	103	100	99	96	111	924
Program Hours Analyzed	62.0	58.5	71.8	67.2	70.3	72.0	75.2	76.0	77.3	630.2
Leading characters analyzed	240	215	377	196	252	300	359	346	364	2649
PREVALENCE	%	%	%	%	%	%	%	%	%	%
(%P) Programs containing violence	81.3	81.6	83.5	77.5	80.6	79.0	72.7	83.3	78.4	79.8
Program hours containing violence	83.2	87.0	83.2	78.3	87.2	84.2	79.7	86.8	83.0	83.6
RATE	N	N	N	N	N	N	N	N	N	N
Number of violent episodes	478	394	630	498	483	539	524	522	626	4694
(R/P) Rate per all programs (plays)	5.0	4.5	5.2	4.5	4.7	5.4	5.3	5.4	5.6	5.1
(R/H) Rate per all hours	7.7	6.7	8.8	7.4	6.9	7.5	7.0	6.9	8.1	7.4
Duration of Violent Episodes (hrs)	--	--	--	--	--	--	3.2	3.8	3.6	10.6
ROLES (% OF LEADING CHARACTERS)	%	%	%	%	%	%	%	%	%	%
Violents (committing violence)	55.8	49.3	48.5	52.0	46.0	39.3	34.5	40.8	43.1	44.6
Victims (subjected to violence)	64.6	55.8	58.9	56.6	50.8	49.7	48.2	51.2	53.8	54.0
(%V) Any involvement in violence	73.3	65.1	66.3	62.8	61.5	58.3	55.7	60.7	64.8	62.9
Killers (committing fatal violence)	12.5	10.7	3.7	6.6	8.7	7.7	5.8	9.8	6.3	7.7
Killed (victims of lethal violence)	7.1	3.7	2.1	4.6	3.2	4.7	3.3	5.8	3.8	4.2
(%K) Any involvement in killing	18.7	11.6	5.6	8.7	9.9	9.7	7.5	13.6	9.1	10.2
INDICATORS OF VIOLENCE										
Program Score: PS=(%P)+2(R/P)+2(R/H)	106.6	104.1	111.4	101.3	103.7	104.8	97.3	107.9	105.6	104.8
Character V-Score: CS = (%V) + (%K)	92.1	76.7	71.9	71.4	71.4	68.0	63.2	74.3	73.9	73.0
Violence Index: VI = PS + CS	198.7	180.9	183.3	172.7	175.1	172.8	160.5	182.2	179.7	177.8

Table 2. Violence Measures for Family Hour Only

		1967	1968	1969	1970	1971	1972	1973	1974	1975	TOTAL
SAMPLES (100%)		N	N	N	N	N	N	N	N	N	N
	Programs (plays) analyzed	38	36	38	35	28	27	32	29	31	294
	Program Hours Analyzed	30.0	27.0	27.3	26.0	25.0	23.5	29.0	27.0	21.5	236.3
	Leading characters analyzed	103	102	130	76	78	98	110	109	105	911
PREVALENCE		%	%	%	%	%	%	%	%	%	%
(%P)	Programs containing violence	78.9	75.0	63.2	57.1	75.0	74.1	56.3	69.0	51.6	66.7
	Program hours containing violence	86.7	83.3	74.3	67.3	86.0	85.1	70.7	77.8	60.5	77.1
RATE		N	N	N	N	N	N	N	N	N	N
	Number of violent episodes	240	123	122	86	110	122	147	108	77	1135
(R/P)	Rate per all programs (plays)	6.3	3.4	3.2	2.5	3.9	4.5	4.6	3.7	2.5	3.9
(R/H)	Rate per all hours	8.0	4.6	4.5	3.3	4.4	5.2	5.1	4.0	3.6	4.8
	Duration of Violent Episodes (hrs)	--	--	--	--	--	--	0.9	1.0	0.5	2.4
ROLES (% OF LEADING CHARACTERS)		%	%	%	%	%	%	%	%	%	%
	Violents (committing violence)	58.3	39.2	36.2	32.9	37.2	37.8	29.1	29.4	16.2	35.0
	Victims (subjected to violence)	68.9	46.1	40.8	39.5	38.5	40.8	33.6	36.7	27.6	41.4
(%V)	Any involvement in violence	75.7	56.9	49.2	40.8	50.0	50.0	40.9	45.0	36.2	49.5
	Killers (committing fatal violence)	22.3	10.8	6.2	3.9	9.0	4.1	6.4	12.8	1.0	8.6
	Killed (victims of lethal violence)	7.8	4.9	3.1	1.3	2.6	3.1	4.5	7.3	0.0	4.0
(%K)	Any involvement in killing	28.2	12.7	9.2	3.9	10.3	5.1	10.0	16.5	1.0	11.0
INDICATORS OF VIOLENCE											
	Program Score: PS=(%P)+2(R/P)+2(R/H)	107.6	90.9	78.5	68.7	91.7	93.5	75.6	84.4	63.7	84.0
	Character V-Score: CS = (%V) + (%K)	103.9	69.6	58.5	44.7	60.3	55.1	50.9	61.5	37.1	60.5
	Violence Index: VI = PS + CS	211.5	160.6	137.0	113.4	151.9	148.6	126.5	145.9	100.9	144.5

Table 3. Violence Measures for Late Evening (9-11 P.M. EST)

		1967	1968	1969	1970	1971	1972	1973	1974	1975	TOTAL
SAMPLES (100%)		N	N	N	N	N	N	N	N	N	N
	Programs (plays) analyzed	26	21	26	26	34	33	30	29	35	260
	Program Hours Analyzed	25.0	24.0	30.5	28.0	30.3	33.0	27.5	33.0	39.5	270.7
	Leading characters analyzed	75	60	88	56	91	119	104	115	133	841
PREVALENCE		%	%	%	%	%	%	%	%	%	%
(%P)	Programs containing violence	69.2	76.2	80.8	69.2	76.5	69.7	63.3	86.2	85.7	75.4
	Program hours containing violence	76.0	89.6	84.4	80.4	87.6	79.8	79.1	92.4	92.4	85.1
RATE		N	N	N	N	N	N	N	N	N	N
	Number of violent episodes	87	99	110	116	129	172	130	220	284	1347
(R/P)	Rate per all programs (plays)	3.3	4.7	4.2	4.5	3.8	5.2	4.3	7.6	8.1	5.2
(R/H)	Rate per all hours	3.5	4.1	3.6	4.1	4.3	5.2	4.7	6.7	7.2	5.0
	Duration of Violent Episodes (hrs)	--	--	--	--	--	--	1.3	1.8	1.9	5.0
ROLES (% OF LEADING CHARACTERS)		%	%	%	%	%	%	%	%	%	%
	Violents (committing violence)	38.7	55.0	34.1	46.4	44.0	37.8	32.7	56.5	51.1	44.0
	Victims (subjected to violence)	42.7	55.0	44.3	50.0	48.4	45.4	36.5	61.7	59.4	49.7
(%V)	Any involvement in violence	56.0	68.3	52.3	57.1	59.3	55.5	41.3	71.3	68.4	59.1
	Killers (committing fatal violence)	5.3	16.7	5.7	14.3	15.4	16.0	12.5	16.5	16.5	13.6
	Killed (victims of lethal violence)	4.0	5.0	2.3	12.5	5.5	8.4	6.7	10.4	9.8	7.4
(%K)	Any involvement in killing	9.3	16.7	6.8	21.4	17.6	19.3	14.4	24.3	23.3	17.6
INDICATORS OF VIOLENCE											
	Program Score: PS=(%P)+2(R/P)+2(R/H)	82.9	93.9	96.4	86.4	92.6	90.5	81.5	114.7	116.3	95.7
	Character V-Score: CS = (%V) + (%K)	65.3	85.0	59.1	78.6	76.9	74.8	55.8	95.7	91.7	76.7
	Violence Index: VI = PS + CS	148.2	178.9	155.5	165.0	169.5	165.3	137.2	210.4	208.1	172.4

Table 4. Violence Measures for Weekend Daytime (Children's) Hours

		1967	1968	1969	1970	1971	1972	1973	1974	1975	TOTAL
SAMPLES (100%)		N	N	N	N	N	N	N	N	N	N
	Programs (plays) analyzed	32	30	57	50	41	40	37	38	45	370
	Program Hours Analyzed	7.0	7.5	14.0	13.2	15.0	15.5	18.7	16.0	16.3	123.2
	Leading characters analyzed	62	53	159	64	83	83	145	122	126	897
PREVALENCE		%	%	%	%	%	%	%	%	%	%
(%P)	Programs containing violence	93.8	93.3	98.2	96.0	87.8	90.0	94.6	92.1	91.1	93.2
	Program hours containing violence	94.0	92.2	97.6	95.6	88.5	92.3	94.6	90.6	89.8	92.7
RATE		N	N	N	N	N	N	N	N	N	N
	Number of violent episodes	151	172	398	296	244	245	247	194	265	2212
(R/P)	Rate per all programs (plays)	4.7	5.7	7.0	5.9	6.0	6.1	6.7	5.1	5.9	6.0
(R/H)	Rate per all hours	21.6	22.9	28.4	22.5	16.2	15.8	13.2	12.1	16.2	18.0
	Duration of Violent Episodes (hrs)	--	--	--	--	--	--	1.0	0.9	1 2	3.2
ROLES (% OF LEADING CHARACTERS)		%	%	%	%	%	%	%	%	%	%
	Violents (committing violence)	72.6	62.3	66.7	79.7	56.6	43.4	40.0	36.1	57.1	54.8
	Victims (subjected to violence)	83.9	75.5	81.8	82.8	65.1	66.3	67.6	54.1	69.8	70.9
(%V)	Any involvement in violence	90.3	77.4	88.1	93.8	74.7	72.3	77.2	64.8	84.9	79.9
	Killers (committing fatal violence)	4.8	3.8	0.6	3.1	1.2	0.0	0.7	0.8	0.0	1.2
	Killed (victims of lethal violence)	9.7	0.0	1.3	1.6	1.2	1.2	0.0	0.0	0.8	1.3
(%K)	Any involvement in killing	14.5	3.8	1.9	3.1	1.2	1.2	0.7	0.8	0.8	2.3
INDICATORS OF VIOLENCE											
	Program Score: PS=(%P)+2(R/P)+2(R/H)	146.3	150.7	169.1	152.8	132.2	133.9	134.4	126.6	135.3	141.1
	Character V-Score: CS = (%V) + (%K)	104.8	81.1	89.9	96.9	75.9	73.5	77.9	65.6	85.7	82.3
	Violence Index: VI = PS + CS	251.2	231.8	259.0	249.7	208.1	207.4	212.3	192.1	221.1	223.4

Table 5. Risk Factors for all Programs Studies 1967–75

Groups	Male Characters				Female Characters			
	N	Character score	Violent–victim ratio	Killer–killed ratio	N	Character score	Violent–victim ratio	Killer–killed ratio
All characters	2010	80.0	−1.19	+1.97	605	48.9	−1.32	1.00
Social age								
Children-adolescents	188	64.9	−1.83	+0.00	77	46.8	−1.39	0.00*
Young adults	431	81.2	−1.21	+3.07	209	59.8	−1.67	+1.29
Settled adults	1068	80.8	−1.15	+1.98	267	37.8	1.00	1.00
Old	81	58.0	+1.03	−2.00	22	50.0	−2.25	−0.00*
Marital status								
Not married	1133	83.6	−1.16	+2.24	306	57.2	−1.51	−1.43
Married	462	66.9	−1.33	+1.57	252	39.3	−1.11	+1.40
Class								
Clearly upper	196	87.2	−1.28	+1.15	70	52.9	−1.64	+1.33
Mixed; indeterminate	1744	78.7	−1.19	+2.36	517	48.2	−1.26	1.00
Clearly lower	70	91.4	−1.11	−1.33	18	55.6	−2.67	−0.00*
Nationality								
U.S.	1505	75.0	−1.19	+2.39	503	46.1	−1.39	−1.08
Other	276	96.7	−1.22	+1.13	66	60.6	−1.55	+3.00
Race								
White	1533	77.6	−1.20	+2.12	541	49.9	−1.29	+1.07
Other	264	83.3	−1.27	+1.33	50	38.0	−2.43	−0.00*
*Character type***								
"Good" (heroes)	928	69.3	−1.26	+3.47	314	43.3	−1.56	−6.00
Mixed type	432	71.1	−1.31	+1.09	156	43.6	−1.37	1.00
"Bad" (villains)	291	114.1	−1.03	+1.80	41	82.9	+1.14	+2.00

* Group has neither violents nor victims. If 0.00 is preceded by a sign, group has either no violents or no victims; +0.00 means only violent(s) but no victims(s); −0.00 means only victim(s) but no violent(s).

** This classification was introduced in 1969.

Note: Character score is the percent of characters involved in any violence plus the percent involved in any killing. V-v ration is of violents (+) and victims (−). K-k ration is of killers (+) and killed (−).

Chapter 18

Death in Prime Time

Notes on the Symbolic Functions of Dying in the Mass Media

BY GEORGE GERBNER

Dying in the mass media—both news and entertainment (a distinction increasingly hard to make)—has a symbolic function different from death in real life but investing it—and life itself—with particular meanings. We can begin to consider what these might be by reflecting on the nature of representation.

A symbol system is an artifact par excellence. It is totally invented to serve human purposes. It can serve these purposes only if those interpreting it know the code and can fit it into a symbolic context of their own. They must share the rules of the invention and the interpretative strategies by which it should be understood.

Symbolic narrative, a story, has two basic elements of invention: fictive and selective. Selective invention is factual narrative such as news. Presumably true events (facts) are selected from an endless stream of events. A narrative is invented to convey some meaning about the selected facts as interpreted in a previously learned framework of knowledge.

Fictive invention is fiction and drama; the "facts" are invented as well as the narrative. (Selection is of course involved in both.) The function of fictive invention is to illuminate (literally to embody and dramatize) the invisible structure and dynamics of the significant connections of human life. It is to show how things *work*. Invention that can only select events but not create them must be more opaque; it can only show what things *are* but rarely why or how they work. The full development of the connections between events and human motivations and powers requires the freedom and legitimacy to invent the "facts" in a way that illuminates the otherwise hidden dynamics of existence.

In this totally invented world of symbols—selective and fictive—nothing happens without some purpose and function (which need not be the same). Let us use as example the world of television which we have studied for some years.[1] This discussion also applies to other media and cultural forms, with the difference that television is the generally non-selectively used universal storyteller of modern society. It is, therefore, more a symbolic *environment* than a traditional medium.

People are not born into the world of television. They are selected or created for a purpose. The purpose is usefulness to the symbolic world (called news values or story values) that the producing institutions and their patrons find useful for *their* purposes. More numerous in both news and drama are those for whom that world has more uses—jobs, power, adventure, sex, youth, and all other opportunities in life. These values are distributed in the symbol system as most resources are distributed in the society whose dominant institutions produce most of the symbols: according to status and power. Dominant social groups tend to be overrepresented and overendowed not only absolutely but also in relation to their numbers in the real population. (For example, men outnumber women at least three to one in television and most media content.)

Minorities are defined by having less than their proportionate share of values and resources. In the world of television news and drama, this underrepresentation means lower numbers, less usefulness, fewer opportunities, more victimization (or "criminalization"), more restricted scope of action, more stereotyped roles, diminished life chances, and general undervaluation ranging from relative neglect to symbolic annihilation.

DEATH IN NEWS AND DRAMA

Death in such a context is just another invented characterization, a negative resource, a sign of fatal flaw or ineptitude, a punishment for sins or mark of tragedy. It is always a reminder of the risks of life, cultivating most anxiety and dependence for those who are depicted as most at risk. In other words, death is one feature of the more general functions of social typing and control.

Obituaries are the Social Register of the middle class. Even a "nobody" of modest status and power (i.e., a person of no symbolic existence in the common culture) becomes a "somebody" if the flicker of his or her (and it's mostly his) life can leave its final symbolic mark of existence in the obituary column.

Death in the news is a tightly scripted scenario of violence and terror. Murders, accidents, "body counts," and catastrophes scatter a surfeit of impersonal corpses in ghoulish symbolic overkill across the pages of our family newspapers and television screens. By the time we grow up, we are so addicted to this necromania of our culture (and we are not alone) that its constant daily cultivation seems to add to a morbid sense of normalcy.

Yet it is all well (if unwittingly) calculated to cultivate a sense of insecurity, anxiety, fear of the "mean world" out there, and dependence on some strong protector. It is the modern equivalent of the bloody circuses in the Roman Empire's "bread and circuses" that were supposed to keep the populace quiescent.

At the center of the symbolic structure of death is the world of stories invented to show how things work—fiction and drama. The most massive and universal flow of stories in modern society (and history) is of course television drama, most of it produced according to the industrial formulas developed to assemble large audiences and sell them to advertisers at the least cost.

That is a world in which practically no one ever dies a natural death. Assembly-line drama generally denies the inevitable reality of death and affirms its stigmatic character. Violent death, on the other hand, befalls 5 percent of all prime time dramatic characters every week, with about twice as many killers (many of whom also get killed) stalking the world of prime time. The symbolic function of death in the world of television is thus embedded in its structure of violence, which is essentially a show of force, the ritualistic demonstration of power.

THE STRUCTURE OF VIOLENCE—AND POWER

Dominated as it is by males and masculine values, much of the world of prime time revolves around questions of power. Who can get away with what against whom? How secure are different social types when confronted with conflict and danger? What hierarchies of risk and vulnerability define social relations? In other words, how power works in society.

The simplest and cheapest dramatic demonstration of power is an overt expression of physical force compelling action against one's will on pain of being hurt or killed, or actually hurting or killing. That is the definition of violence used in our studies of television drama. Violence rules the symbolic world of television. It occurs at an average ten year rate of five violent incidents per hour in prime time and eighteen per hour in weekend daytime children's programming—a triple dose.

Violence as a demonstration of power can be measured by relating the percent of violents to the percent of victims within each social group. That ratio shows the chances of men and women, blacks and whites, young and old, to come out on top instead of on the bottom. Conversely, it shows the risks of each group to end up as victims instead of victors.

Table 1 is a summary of these "risk ratios" based on annual samples of prime time and weekend daytime (children's) programs' major dramatic characters, a total of 3,949, from 1969 through 1978. It shows for each of several demographic and dramatic groups the ratio of violents over victims (including killing) and of only killers over killed (or the other way around) within each group. It also shows the percent of characters in each group involved in any violence as either violents or victims (or both). For example, of the 415 children and adolescent characters studied, 60.5 percent (65.0 percent males and 49.1 percent females) were involved in violence. Of the males, victims outnumbered violents by 1.69 but killers outnumbered killed by 3.00. In other words, for every 10 child and adolescent violents there were about 17 victims, but for every 10 killed there were 30 killers in that group of characters.

Overall, 63 percent of all characters were involved in some violence. For every 10 violents there were 12 victims, but for every 10 killed there were 19 killers. However, as we have just seen, involvement in violence and its outcome—as with values and resources—is not randomly distributed.

Some features of the distribution of violence as a demonstration of power can be illustrated by selecting a few risk ratios from the table, showing how these victimiza-

Table 1. Risk Ratios[1]: Major Characters in All Programs (1969–1978)

	All Characters				Male Characters				Female Characters			
	N	Involved in Violence	Violent-Victim Ratio	Killer-Killed Ratio	N	Involved in Violence	Violent-Victim Ratio	Killer-Killed Ratio	N	Involved in Violence	Violent-Victim Ratio	Killer Killed Ratio
All Characters	3949	63.3	−1.20	+1.90	2938	68.4	−1.18	+2.02	956	46.1	−1.34	+1.20
Social Age												
Children-Adolescents	415	60.5	−1.60	+3.00	297	65.0	−1.69	+3.00	116	49.1	−1.33	0.00
Young Adults	813	64.5	−1.36	+2.00	539	69.6	−1.23	+2.17	270	53.7	−1.82	+1.33
Settled Adults	2212	59.8	−1.12	+2.07	1698	65.7	−1.12	+2.13	513	40.0	−1.12	+1.60
Elderly	106	47.2	−1.15	−1.75	80	50.0	+1.07	1.00	26	38.5	−3.33	−0.00
Marital Status												
Not Married	1873	65.6	−1.23	+1.90	1374	69.7	−1.18	+2.02	491	53.8	−1.44	+1.30
Married	987	45.5	−1.27	+1.67	626	52.9	−1.27	+1.82	361	32.7	−1.25	+1.11
Class												
Clearly Upper	269	59.5	−1.38	+1.50	182	67.6	−1.26	+1.57	87	42.5	−2.00	+1.25
Mixed	3549	63.4	−1.19	+2.07	2650	68.3	−1.17	+2.20	844	46.3	−1.29	+1.20
Clearly Lower	131	69.5	−1.25	−1.11	106	73.6	−1.20	−1.13	25	52.0	−1.71	1.00
Race												
White	3087	60.1	−1.19	+1.97	2235	65.1	−1.16	+2.11	852	46.9	−1.31	+1.26
Other	360	55.0	−1.33	+1.69	280	61.1	−1.27	+1.69	77	31.2	−1.83	0.00
Character Type												
"Good"	2304	58.4	−1.29	+2.93	1659	63.7	−1.24	+3.85	622	43.2	−1.51	−1.60
Mixed	1093	61.4	−1.22	+1.33	807	65.8	−1.21	+1.27	262	44.7	−1.31	+1.50
"Bad"	550	88.0	1.00	+1.84	471	89.4	−1.01	+1.86	71	77.5	+1.15	+1.67
Nationality												
U.S.	3100	58.1	−1.20	+2.06	2263	63.2	−1.16	+2.23	827	43.9	−1.38	+1.18
Other	264	73.5	−1.31	+1.31	203	80.8	−1.29	+1.27	61	49.2	−1.47	+2.00

[1] Risk Ratios are obtained by dividing the more numerous of these two roles by the less numerous within each group. A plus sign indicates that there are more violents or killers than victims or killed and a minus sign indicates that there are more victims or killed than violents or killers. A ratio of 0.00 means that there were no victims or killers or violents or killed. A +0.00 ratio means that there were some violents or killers but no victims or killed; a −0.00 ratio means that there were victims or killed but no violents or killers.

tion rates define a hierarchy of risks within which the depiction of dying (and killing) is embedded.

A HIERARCHY OF RISKS

Combining prime time and daytime characters, we find that victimization rates define a social hierarchy of risks and vulnerabilities. For every ten characters who commit violence within each of the following groups the average number of victims for

White men is .12
Nonwhite men is 13
Lower class women is 17
Young women is 18
Nonwhite women is 18
Old women is 33

If and when involved in violence, women and minorities, and especially young and old as well as minority women characters, are the most vulnerable.

Now let us look at dying (and its dramatic counterpart, killing) in that context. We can compute a lethal pecking order by relating the number of killers to the number of killed within each group. Unlike violence in general, killing eliminates a character and must be used more sparingly, either as curtain raiser or as the "final solution." Therefore, in most role categories, there are more killers than killed. "Good" men, the male heroes of prime time drama, are at the top of the killing order. For every 10 "good" men killed, there are 38 "good" men killers. Next are young men and American men; for every 10 young males killed, there are 22 young male and American male killers. The killed-killer ratio of all white males is only slightly lower: 21 killers for every 10 white males killed. In other words, if and when involved in some fatal violence on prime time television, "good," young, American and white males are the most likely to be the killers instead of the killed. They kill in a good cause to begin with or are the most powerful, or both.

Women do not fare so well. Their most favorable ratio is 20 killers for every 10 killed, and that goes to foreign women. The second highest female kill ratio goes to "bad" women: they kill 17 characters for every 10 "bad" women killed. Next are middle-aged women who kill 16 for every 10 killed. Thus women who tend to kill, kill much less than men, have relatively more lethal power when they are foreign, evil, or past the romantic lead age, than when they are "good," American, young, and white, as is the case with men. Their killing is more likely to be shown as unjust, irrational, and "alien" than is killing by men.

At the very bottom of the lethal pecking order are old women who get involved in violence only to get killed and "good" women who get killed 16 times for every 10 killers. Old and "good" women get into violence mostly as sympathetic (or only pathetic) victims, rousing male heroes to righteous (if lethal) indignation. Next in line are lower class men, lower class women, and old men. For every ten killers in each group there are, respectively, 11, 10, and 10 killed. Unlike those of greater ability to survive conflict or catastrophe, older and lower class characters pay with their lives for every life they take.

PROVOCATION AND RETRIBUTION

In general, then, as can be seen in Table 1, the pecking order of both mayhem and killing is dominated by men—American white, middle class, and in the prime of life. At the top of the general order of victimizers are "bad" women, old men, and "bad" men, in that order. The presence of evil at the top of the power hierarchy suggests the dramatic role of villains provoking heroes to violent action. Heading the ranking of killers over killed are "good" and other majority-type males. We can begin to discern not only the provocative role of the "bad" but also the retributive function of the "good" and the strong.

Lowers on the dramatic scale are women, lower class, and old people. Of the twenty most victimized groups (both total violence and killing), all but three are women.

Old women are at the bottom of the heap of both the battered and the killed. "Good" women are among the characters most likely to be both general and fatal victims of violence rather than the perpetrators. "Good" men have power as indicated by their heading up the killer-killed list; "good" women, on the other hand, end up near the bottom of the power hierarchy. When it comes to violence, "good" are the strong men and the weak women of the world of television.

Dying on television is a violent retribution for weakness, sin, or other flaw in character or status. It is part of the social typing and control functions of centralized cultural production. Our research has found that heavy viewers (compared to light viewers in the same social groups) derive from their television experience a heightened sense of danger, insecurity, and mistrust, or what we call the "mean world" syndrome. It can be conjectured that the symbolic functions of dying are part of that syndrome, contributing not only to a structure of power but also to the irrational dread of dying and thus to diminished vitality and self-direction in life.

NOTES

Originally published ANNALS, AAPSS, January 1980

1. The long range project was first described in my article on "Cultural Indicators: The Case of Violence in Television Drama: in the Annals, Vol. 388, March 1970. The most recent report, including a description of methodology, appears in George Gerbner, Larry Gross, Nancy Signorielli, Michael Morgan, and Marilyn Jackson-Beeck, "The Demonstration of Power: Violence Profile No. 10," *Journal of Communication,* Vol. 29 (Summer 1979).

CHAPTER 19

VIOLENCE AND TERROR IN AND BY THE MEDIA

BY GEORGE GERBNER

The purpose of this chapter is to examine the role of media violence and terror in provoking a siege mentality, and their more general functions in governance, research, and policy.[1]

Much of the controversy over press coverage of violence and terrorism revolves around who should control the news—public authorities, private media corporations, or information sources. Media are the cultural arms of any establishment. Private media relate to public authorities as church did to state in medieval times. It is a symbiotic relationship of mutual dependence and tension.

Western industrial societies relegate news control to private media as long as that poses no threat to established law and order. If, when, or whether it does is a political and legal issue. News sources have few rights in the game. At best, they trade control over information for visibility or notoriety.

Struggles for participation, representation, and power are shifting from military and political arenas to new cultural spheres. We have entered an era in which control by camera is gradually reducing the need for control by armed force.[2] "Arms control" and reduction become more feasible as cultural controls (often more efficient and certainly more entertaining) gain in effectiveness.

Highly publicized insurgent terrorism served to justify the imposition of military dictatorship, followed by even greater state terrorism in Argentina and Turkey. Onyegin's (1986) study of the Turkish case shows how killings were lumped together with legitimate strikes and protest demonstrations to criminalize and stigmatize political opposition and pave the way for the military. But the relatively crude and unpopular military rule may give way to cultural pressure. Anxious and insecure people lacking clear-cut political alternatives may accept, and appear to welcome, a crackdown even by "democratic" authorities if it can be presented as relief from a terrorist or other criminal menace.

Comparative studies of labeling and coverage of terrorism reveal unreliable statistics and blatantly political uses. The authoritative chronology of transnational terrorism by Mickolus (1980) showed that the frequency of incidents peaked in 1972 with 480 that year, and subsequently declined. Nevertheless, U.S. media and government policy put increasing emphasis on terrorism, justifying interventions in the strategic Middle East. Iraq was removed from the U.S. list of nations sponsoring terrorism in 1982 and given extensive credits and arms to use against Iran, until it invaded Kuwait. Syria was similarly rewarded for taking a stand against Iraq in 1990. There was no comparable consideration or coverage of equally widespread state terrorism in many countries of Africa, Latin America, or Asia.

Although international terrorism against states receives most attention, Bassiouni (1981, 1982) and others point out that terrorist acts by states and in a national context are far more numerous. "Disappearances," bombings, kidnappings and state violence in many countries, often unreported, claim thousands of times more victims than do well-publicized acts of anti-state and international terror.

While the physical casualties of highly publicized terrorist acts have been relatively few, the political and military uses have been far-reaching. Less than 1 percent of all casualties of international terrorism in 1986 were American, but they prompted the forcing down of an Egyptian airliner and the bombing of Tripoli (probably based, as it turned out, on false intelligence).

Wurth-Hough (1983) documented the role of U.S. network news coverage of terrorism in selecting events and defining issues according to political preference. Paletz et al. (1982) analyzed *The New York Times'* coverage of the IRA, the Red Brigades, and the Fuerzas Armadas de Liberacion Nacional (FALN) from 1 July 1977 to 30 June 1979 and found no basis for the charge that coverage legitimizes the cause of terrorist organizations. On the contrary, 70 percent of the stories mentioned neither the cause nor the objectives of the terrorists; almost 75 percent mentioned neither the organization nor its supporters; and the 7 percent that did mention names placed them in a context of statements issued by authorities.

In another study of U.S. network news, Milburn et al. (1987) noted the frequent omission of any causal explanation for terrorist acts, and the attribution of mental instability to terrorists and their leaders. (Similar acts directed against countries other than the United States were more frequently explained.) The implication, the researchers noted, was that "you can't negotiate with crazy people."

Knight and Dean (1982) provided a detailed account of how the Canadian press coverage of the siege and recapturing of the Iranian embassy in London from Arab nationalist "gunmen" served to assert the efficiency and legitimacy of violence by the British Special Forces. In the process of transforming crime and punishment into a selectively choreographed newsworthy event, the media "have to some extent assumed the functions of moral and political—in short, ideological—reproduction performed previously (and limitedly) by the visibility of the public event itself." It is not accidental, the authors claimed, that highly publicized and "morally coherent" scenarios of violence and terror have made public punishment unnecessary as demonstrations of state ideology and power.

Typically isolated from their historical and social context, denied legitimacy of conditions or cause, and portrayed as unpredictable and irrational, if not insane, those labeled terrorists symbolize a menace that rational and humane means cannot reach or control. Paletz and Dunn (1969) studied the effects of news coverage of urban riots in the United States and concluded that the attempt to present a view acceptable to most readers failed to illuminate the conditions in the black communities that led to the riots. News of civil disturbance shares with coverage of terrorist activity the tendency to cultivate a pervasive sense of fear and danger, and the consequent acceptability of harsh measures to combat it.

DeBoer (1979) summarized survey results in five countries and found that although terrorists claimed relatively few victims, the media coverage cultivated a sense of imminent danger that only unusual steps could overcome. Six or seven out of ten respondents in the United States, the United Kingdom, and the Federal Republic of Germany favored the introduction of the death penalty for terrorists. Similar majorities approved using a "special force" that would hunt down an kill terrorists in any country; placing them "under strict surveillance, even though our country might then somewhat resemble a police state"; using "extra stern and harsh action" unlike against other criminals; and "limitations of personal rights by such measures as surveillance and house searches in order to "combat terrorism."

The symbolic functions and political uses of "wars" on drugs and "drug lords" have joined images of violence and terror as highly selective and ideologically shaped portrayals. They serve as projective devices that isolate acts and people from meaningful contexts and set them up to be stigmatized.

Stigma is a mark of disgrace that evokes disgraceful behavior. Labeling some people barbarians makes it easier to treat them as barbarians would. Calling them aggressors justifies aggression against them, presumably to uphold the dictum that "aggression must not pay." Classifying some people as criminals permits dealing with them in ways otherwise considered criminal. Proclaiming them enemies makes it legitimate to attach and kill them. Naming some people crazy or insane makes it possible to suspend rules of rationality and decency toward them. Labeling a person or group terrorist seems to justify terrorizing them.

Stigmatization and demonization isolate their targets and set them up to be victimized. The cultural context in which that can precipitate social paranoia and political crisis is the historically unprecedented discharge of media violence into the mainstream of common consciousness. The ultimate victim is the community's ability to think rationally and creatively about conflict, injustice, and tragedy.

Humankind may have had more bloodthirsty eras, but none as filled with images of violence as the present. We are awash in a tide of violent representations such as the world has never seen. There is no escape from the massive infusion of colorful mayhem into the homes and cultural life of ever-larger areas of the world.

Of course there was blood in fairy tales, gore in mythology, murder in Shakespeare. It *is* a violent world. Systematic torture, "death squads" and other forms of terror rule many states. Wholesale violations of human rights keep Amnesty International busy. Media spotlight, selective as it is, makes massacres and genocides more difficult to hide.[3] Such facts are often invoked to argue that violent storytelling is not new and that it still did not make us into monsters.

Well, that may be debatable. The United States is the undisputed homicide capital of the world. It also leads all industrialized countries in jailing and executing people.[4] But if real life and cultural violence and terror stem from common cultural roots, the mechanism cannot be simple imitation. If it were, we would all be reeling under the blows of our children and stalking the streets as muggers rather than potential victims. Our research of over twenty-five years suggests that the dynamics of violence and terror are much more complex, even if not much less repressive.

Violence is a legitimate and necessary cultural expression. It is a dramatic balancing of deadly conflicts and compulsions against tragic costs. Even catering to morbid and other pathological fascinations may have its poetic or commercial license. Historically limited, individually crafted, and selectively used symbolic misanthropy is not the issue. That has been swamped by television violence with happy endings produced on the dramatic assembly line, saturating the mainstream of our common culture.

Audience appeal and broadcaster greed are said to play a part in the prevalence of violence on television. But neither these nor other historic rationalizations can fully explain, let alone justify, drenching nearly every home in the rapidly expanding "free world" with graphic scenes of expertly choreographed brutality.

The incremental profits of manufacturing and exporting such a troubling commodity as images of violence (as distinct from other dramatic qualities) is hardly worth its human and institutional risks and costs. Most highly rated programs are nonviolent. Using "sex and violence" appeals in program promotion has little effect on ratings (Williams, 1989). Economies of scale in cheaply produced violence formulas may have some financial advantages to program producers. But there is no general correlation between violence and the ratings of comparable programs aired at the same time.

Why would mainstream media, the cultural arms of established society, undermine their worn security for dubious and paltry benefits? Why would they persist in inviting charges of inciting to crime? Why would they suffer public and legislative criticism and face international condemnation? Halloran (1977) suggested an answer when he wrote that the conventional hand wringing about the media overkill, focusing only on imitation and incitation to crime, misses the point. His own research on protest demonstrations showed that in featuring even trivial or irrelevant violence, the media achieve certain "positive symbolic values."

A "positive" value equal to that of profits is, of course, power. A marketplace is an arena of control by power. Left to itself it tends toward monopoly, or total power. Violence is a demonstration of power. Images of violence project hierarchies of power—gender, racial, sexual, class, and national power—that the mass-cultural marketplace cultivates through its control of dramatic imagery rather than through consumer choice or commercial need alone. A marketable taste for a nightly quota of violence may be acquired more through assiduous cultivation from infancy rather than free and broad choice. The need for it may be political as much as commercial: to get, hold, and wield (or cater to) power. Media violence is its cheapest and clearest symbolic expression.

Violence in its most reliably observable form is a physical show of force. It is making one do or submit to something against one's will on pain of being hurt or killed. It demonstrates who has the power to impose what on whom under what circumstances. It illuminates the ability to lash out, provoke, intimidate, and annihilate. It designates winners and losers, victimizers and victims, champions and wimps.

In real life that demonstration is costly, risky, and disruptive. In storytelling it is usually clear, compelling, and instructive. Violent stories symbolize threats to human integrity and to the established order. They demonstrate how these threats are combated, how order is restored (often violently), and how its violators (though rarely its violent enforcers) are themselves victimized. Far from only inciting subversion, they display society's pecking order. In tragedy, rare in commercial entertainment, the hero dies unjustly but the idea lives on to triumph perhaps another day. The storyteller relinquishes control; s/he cannot help us any more; it's up to all of us to fight injustice. In formula violence with happy endings, offenders die but the hero lives on to protect good people another day. Who is who and what is what depends on who has the right looks and the badge; the storyteller keeps our fate under control. Things will turn out all right if we are on the right side (or look and act as if we were). Crime may not pay in the world of dramatic fiction, but violence always does—for the winner. A tragic sense of life—energizing, empowering—does not deliver viewers in the mood to buy.

The power to define violence and project its lessons, including stigmatization, demonization, and the selective labeling of terror and terrorists, is the chief cultural requirement for social control. The ability and protected right to mass produce and discharge it into the common symbolic environment may be a decisive (if unacknowledged) concentration of culture power in domestic and global policymaking.

Media violence is a political scenario on several levels. As a symbolic exercise, it is a demonstration of power: of who has it, who uses it, and who loses it. As a subject of media research, it has been a source of funding and ammunition for various positions in a debate purportedly about violence but really about media control and reform. The media themselves shape and manipulate the terms of the debate. Legislators milk the political juice in it.

In the United States, the assassinations of President John Kennedy, Senator Robert Kennedy, and the Reverend Dr. Martin Luther King, Jr. led to establishment in 1968 of the National Commission on the Causes and Prevention of Violence. Its Mass Media Task Force commissioned me to provide a reliable analysis of violence on television. That was the beginning of what has become the longest-running ongoing media research project, called Cultural Indicators. The project relates the analysis of television content to a variety of viewer conceptions and social consequences. It has provided research support for movements for media literacy, critical analysis and reform, and some protection to broadcasters against unjustified claims and scapegoating.

The Task Force Report by Baker and Ball (1969) presented our analysis. It established a standard format for tracking violence in network drama and revealed the high level of its frequency, a level that has not changed much over the years. Equally important was its systematic description of television violence not as a simple act but as a complex social scenario of power and victimization.

Media coverage of the report mentioned only the amount of violence, followed by charges and denials of violent imitation and incitation. The pattern of press reporting of media violence research, to which we shall return, focused on the potential threat individual acts of aggression and violence might pose to law and order. The social dynamics of violence and victimization, with its suggestion of power play and intimidation, were of no media interest.

The Task Force called for remedial action by government and the media, which, like many others that followed, went unheeded. But it moved Senator John Pastore to ask President Nixon for a larger investigation to safeguard public law and order. That investigation resulted in what are generally called the Surgeon General's Reports.

A Scientific Advisory Committee to the United States Surgeon General found indications of a causal relation between violence on television and "aggressive behavior" among some viewers (Comstock et al., 1972). In 1980, another Surgeon General's Advisory Committee was formed to review and summarize progress since the 1972 Report (Pearl et al., 1982). Both reported that television cultivates exaggerated beliefs about the prevalence of violence and heightens feelings of insecurity and mistrust among most groups of heavy viewers, and especially among women and minorities.

The Cultural Indicators research, the source of these conclusions (see Gerbner et al., 1986a, 1986b), also found that viewing cultivates a commonality of perspectives among otherwise different groups with respect to overarching themes and patterns found in many programs. That tends to erode traditional differences among divergent social groups. The outlooks of heavy viewers are closer to each other than are the outlooks of comparable groups of light viewers.

Research on the consequences of exposure to mass-mediated violence has a long and involved history. Most of it has focused on limited aspects of the complex scenario. It has been motivated (and dominated) by institutional interest in threats of individual imitation, incitation, brutalization, and subversion. Much research has concentrated on observable and measurable psychological traits and states—such as aggressiveness—that were presumed to lead to violence and could be attributed to media exposure.

Research on aggression has been the most prominent "media violence story." Although ostensibly critical of media, it may have been the preferred story because it is the easiest to neutralize and the least damaging to basic institutional interests and policies.

Aggressiveness is an ambivalent concept with positive as well as negative connotations. It is a traditional part of male role socialization. Its link to most real violence and crime, which is socially organized and systemic rather than personal and private, is tenuous, to say the least. It can even be argued that too many people submit too meekly to exploitation, injustice, indignity, and intimidation.

Approaches that focus on aggression and lawlessness view violence from the law enforcement point of view. They distract attention from official violence and state terrorism, and from economic and social conditions most closely related to individual violence and crime.

Traditional effects research models are based on selectively used media, messages, and campaigns. They focus on selective exposures "causing" attitude change, viewer preferences, etc. They miss the essential and unique feature of television culture: its universal, stable, and pervasive cultivation of conceptions about life and social relationships in large communities over long periods of time.

Television is a relatively non-selectively used medium. Virtually inescapable exposure to televised images of violence goes on from cradle to grave. The television answer to the age-old media cause-and-effects question "what comes first, the chicken or the egg?" is: the hatchery. Television is at the center of the new cultural hatchery.

The recurrent notions of "powerful" audiences "resisting" cultivation, producing their own "popular culture" and their own "uses and gratifications" are irrelevant to the new approach to television cultivation. They focus on differences in perception and response but ignore or minimize the commonalities television cultivates, commonalities decisive for broader issues in matters of public policy.[5]

Seldom asked and rarely publicized are these broader questions of policy. They deal with victimization and control, as well as with aggression. The key question is not what "causes" most violence and crime, as that goes far beyond media. It is: what contribution does constant exposure to certain scenarios of violence and terror make to different groups' conceptions of their own risks and vulnerabilities, to a society's approach to conflict, to the distribution of power, and to the likelihood of its abuse?

These questions do not fit the typical media violence story. They are more likely to challenge their assumptions and expose their social and political functions. It is not surprising, then, that they are seldom asked, rarely publicized, and sometimes strenuously resisted or distorted.

U.S. children are born into a symbolic environment of six to eight violent acts per prime time hour (where four-fifths of their viewing is concentrated), four times as many in presumably humorous children's programs, and two entertaining murders a night. Contrary to the hype that promoted them, most actual uses of cable, video, and other new technologies make the dominant patterns penetrate even more deeply (but not more cheaply) into everyday life.[6]

Television viewing is a time-bound activity. One must give credit to the creative artists and other professionals who seize opportunities—few and far between though they may be—to challenge and even counter the massive flow of formula programming. But most people watch by the clock, not by the individual program.

The overarching dramatic messages and images found in many programs tend to cultivate common conceptions most relevant to public policymaking. Violence is the most vivid and prominent of these inescapable presentations. Studies by Sun (1989) and Signorielli (1986) show that the average viewer has little opportunity to avoid frequently recurring patterns such as violence. Large audiences watch violent programs scheduled in time periods when large audiences watch television.

The world of prime time is cast for its favorite dramatic plays—power plays. Men outnumber women at least three to one. Young people, old people, and minorities have many times less than their share of representation. Compared to white American middle-class heterosexual males in the "prime of life," all others have a more restricted and stereotyped range of roles, activities, and opportunities, and less than their share of success and power. But they have more than their share of vulnerability and victimization.

The cultivation of conceptions of self and society implicit in these portrayals begins in infancy. For the first time in human history, major responsibility for the formative socializing process of storytelling has passed from parents and churches and schools to a small group of global conglomerates that have something to sell.[7]

The moderate viewer of prime time in the United States sees every week an average of 21 criminals (domestic and foreign) arrayed against an army of 41 public and private law enforcers. There are also 14 doctors, 6 nurses, 6 lawyers, and 2 judges to handle them. An average of 150 acts of violence and about 15 murders entertain us and our children every week, and that does not count cartoons and the news. Those who watch over 3 hours a day (more than half the people) absorb much more. Graze the channels any night for just 15 minutes. Chances are that you can linger over bodies (on or off screen) that had been threatened, terrorized, beaten, raped, killed, and perhaps mutilated. And they will not be just any bodies. Most likely they will be bodies of women, violated often just as curtain raiser to the real "he-man action."

The violence we see on television bears little or no relationship to its actual occurrence. Neither frequency nor type resemble trends in crime statistics. They follow marketing strategies that inject relatively cheap dramatic formulas into otherwise often dull "action programs." But, as we have suggested, the action goes far beyond markets and profits.

Our ongoing research (Gerbner, 1988, etc.) has found that exposure to violence-laden television cultivates an exaggerated sense of insecurity, mistrust, and anxiety. Heavy viewers buy more guns, locks, and watchdogs for protection than comparable groups of light viewers. A sense of vulnerability and dependence imposes its heaviest burdens on women and some minorities. For every 10 white males who commit violence in network television drama, 12 are victimized. For every 10 white women violents, 16 suffer victimization. For every 10 foreign or minority women, 22 become victims, doubling the ratio of vulnerability (Signorielli, 1990). The pattern of violence and victimization presents a mean world in which everyone is at risk (but some more than others). Happy endings assure the viewer that although evil and deadly menace lurks around every corner, strong, swift, and violent solutions are always available and efficient. Contrary to charges of liberal bias, our research shows that a political correlate of television viewing is the virtual collapse of a liberal orientation (Gerbner et al., 1982).

These are highly exploitable sentiments. They contribute to the irresistibility of punitive and vindictive demands and slogans ranging from "lenient judges" to capital punishment. They make the politics of a Willie Horton and a Willie Bennett hard to resist.[8] They lend themselves to the political appeal of "wars" on crime, and drugs, and terrorists that heighten repression but fail to address root causes.

Riding the wave of citizen activism and reformist zeal of the late 1960s, Senator John Pastore espoused television violence as his "issue" and held a series of legislative committee hearings on it. In a climactic session in 1974, I reported our findings on both the incidence of violence and an indication of what the most pervasive consequences of exposure might be. But the cultivation of insecurity and dependence seemed too complex and "academic" for Pastore. He kept pressing for an answer to the law-and-order question: "Does it lead to violent behavior?" Pastore's support was needed for the renewal of our research grant. I finally gave him the answer he wanted, which, while true, was not the most significant new research finding.

A decade of commissions, research reports, and committee hearings had produced no lasting policy change. A short-lived "family hour" (which only its originator, CBS, ever observed) resulted in an anti-trust legal challenge and quick retreat even from existing network program codes.

Upon Pastore's retirement in 1977, a House subcommittee headed by Lionel Van Deerlin took up the television violence cudgels and produced a draft report that called for an investigation of the structure of the television industry as the only way to get to the roots of the "violence problem." When the draft was leaked to the networks, the National Association of Broadcasters (NAB) threatened reprisals on other bills dear to Van Deerlin's heart, including a rewrite of the Communications Act of 1934, the basic law of American broadcasting. Due to these and other pressures, the report was delayed for months. Van Deerlin caved in and a watered-down version was passed.

The surrender was in vain. The rewrite bill was scuttled anyway. Van Deerlin was defeated in the next election. The broadcast reform movement collapsed. Foundation support for citizen action dried up. The coming era of market rule and private power, misnamed "deregulation," saw the dismantling of most public protections built up through many years.

The Young Turks of 1977, smarting from their defeat and dismayed at the collapse of the public constituency for broadcast reform, made another attempt in 1981. Under the leadership of then Congressman Timothy Wirth, a series of hearings attempted to revive the media violence issue. Many of the actors of 1977 were trotted out on the same stage. Our Cultural Indicators Violence Profile was introduced showing record levels and continued cultivation of insecurity and mistrust, the "mean world syndrome."

But this was the 1980s and the "public trust" concept of the Communications Act was in full retreat. Instead of all major networks, as at previous hearings, only CNN covered the hearing and only because its president, Ted Turner, was the lead-off witness. The hearing was billed "a forum for dialogue among interested parties," and went nowhere. There was no general press coverage, no report, and, of course, no bill.

Only one reference was made to our most telling basic findings. Representative Cardiss Collins, the only woman on the subcommittee, noted that our "research shows that when women and minority types encounter violence on television they are more likely to end up as victims than the majority types." Then she said: "You stated, 'The real questions that must be asked are not just how much violence there is, but also how fair, how just, how necessary, how effective, and at what price'." And she wondered aloud: "Are you saying that the price to the well-being of our society is much too high?" (United States Congress, 1982: 230–31). No one on the subcommittee followed up her question, or my answer.

The last substantive remark of the hearing was made by Representative Al Swift, who, recalling the fiasco of 1977, concluded that "We ought to be careful in our frustration of what television is doing to us that we do not take an axe to the tail of the tiger and think we have accomplished something. We may have accomplished a little bit, but it is the other end of the tiger that is ultimately going to get us" (United States Congress, 1982: 235).

The tiger is riding high. The cultivation of mistrust and paranoia in everyday life robs civilization of its civility. Hospitality and kindness to strangers seem quaint if not irresponsible anachronisms. Children learn early to beware of adults and, when they grow up, to stop for no one on the highway. When a six-year-old Italian girl whose father fell unconscious at the wheel ran bleeding and crying on the highway for thirty minutes while cars zipped by, the shock prompted a searching of souls, and of media. "We have begun to show the cold glacial face for which only recently we used to rebuke other countries that once were richer than ours," said an article in *Corriere della Sera*. *L'Unita* lamented that in the age of television, "A sheet of glass has been interposed between us and the world that once and for all eliminates real, tangible, and sensitive awareness of others" (reported in *The New York Times*, 19/7/90: A1).

A never-to-be-declared state of symbolic emergency is pitting white male heterosexual "prime-of-life" middle-class power against the majorities of humankind living in the ghettos of America and what used to be called the Third World before the Second collapsed into the First. The cold war may be winding down; the war on poverty has turned into a war on the poor. The cultural props for imperial policy are shifting from their anti-communist rationalizations to a sharp and selective offensive against real and concocted terrorists, narco-terrorists, petro-terrorists, and other dark demons. An overkill of violent imagery helps to mobilize support for taking charge of the unruly at home and abroad.[9]

Movies of the decade follow or lead and, in any case, cash in on the trend. With theatrical distribution dominated by a few chains, local cinema-goers have less and less to choose from. Escalation of the body count seems to be one way to get attention from a public punch-drunk on the global mayhem. *Robocop*'s first rampage for law and order in 1987 killed 32 people. The 1990 *Robocop 2*, targeting a 12 year-old "drug lord," among others, slaughters 81. The sick movie *Death Wish* claimed 9 victims in 1974. In the 1988 version the "bleeding heart liberal" turned vigilante disposes of 52. *Rambo: First Blood*, released in 1985, rambled through Southeast Asia leaving 62 corpses. In the 1988 release, *Rambo III* visits Afghanistan, killing 106. The daredevil cop in the original *Die Hard* in 1988 saved the day with a modest 18 dead. Two years later, *Die Hard 2* thwarts a plot to rescue "the biggest drug dealer in the world," coincidentally a Central American dictator to be tried in a U.S. court, achieving a phenomenal body count of 264.[10] But the decade's record goes to the 1990 summer children's movie and tie-in marketing sensation and glorification of the culture of martial-arts violence, *Teenage Mutant Ninja Turtles*. With its 133 acts of mayhem per hour, it was "the most violent film that has ever been marketed to children and given a 'PG' rating," reported the National Coalition on Television Violence.

As the cold war turns into a new Holy Alliance, the superpowers can concentrate on securing their ever more precarious hold on the remaining privileges and shrinking resources of a world liberated from some bankrupt forms of domination but increasingly free and open to symbolic invasion. The floodgates are opening for unrestrained penetration of media violence "Made in the USA" in the name of democracy. Few countries are willing or able to invest in a cultural policy that does not surrender the socialization of their children and the future of their language, culture, and society to "market forces." That is more likely to contribute to the resurgence of chauvinism, clericalism, and neo-fascism than to open, diverse, and humane democratic cultures around the world.

The mass production of images and messages of violence plays a perhaps small but pivotal part in the new imperial network. The questions we must ask are those of Congresswoman Collins: how and just and how necessary, not just how much? And how long can the "benefits" outweigh the costs and the risks? Isn't the price much too high already?

Bombarding viewers with violent images of a mean and dangerous world remains, in the last analysis, an instrument of intimidation and terror. This is not an isolated problem that can be addressed by focusing on media violence alone. It is an integral part of a market-dominated system of global cultural commercialism that permeates the mainstream of the common symbolic environment. Only a new international environmental movement, a cultural environmental movement dedicated to democratic media reform, can do justice to the challenge of violence and terror in and by media.

NOTES

1. For an extended summary and analysis of research on media violence and terror see Gerbner (1988). Parts of this chapter have appeared in an earlier version (Gerbner, 1991).
2. The "dominoes" of Eastern Europe fell ever more rapidly as television cameras, not guns, were turned the "wrong" way. Even in Romania where armed resistance was attempted, showing the execution of the Ceausescus on national and world television put an end to it.
3. Political priorities and media attention make reporting of loss of life around the world not only selective but also unequal. The CIA-assisted bloodbath of "communists" in Indonesia in 1965, "one of the worst mass murders of the twentieth century," received scant notice at the time (see, e.g., *Columbia Journalism Review* 12/90: 8–14). The "whole world witnessed" the "Tiananmen Square massacre"—or did it? (see Munro [1990] and Black [1990]). In any case, the similar crackdowns in Kwangju, South Korea, in 1980 (under U.S. tutelage), and in Burma in 1988, had no worldwide witness. Studies of disaster news conclude that in terms of media space and time allocated to it, the death of one Western European equals three Eastern Europeans, nine Latin Americans, and twelve Asians (Adams, 1986).

4. One of every 133 Americans will become a murder victim (U.C. Bureau of Justice Statistics Technical Report, 3/87: NCJ-104274). The U.S. rate of killings is 21.9 per 100,000 men aged from 15 to 24. The rate, for example, for Austria is 0.3, for England 1.2, and for Scotland (highest after the U.S.) 5.0 (National Center for Health Statistics study published in the *Journal of the American Medical Association* and reported in *The New York Times*, 27/6/90: A10). Between 1985 and 1989 the number of homicides in the U.S. nationwide increased 22 percent (Congressional hearings reported in the *Philadelphia Inquirer*, 1/8/90). The U.S. rate of incarceration is 407 per 1,000,000 citizens. This compares to 36 in the Netherlands, 86 in West Germany, and 100 in England. While the prison population in the United States doubled in the 1980s, the crime rate rose 1.8 percent, suggesting that the "need to incarcerate" is out of proportion with the actual crime rate but is a political response to culturally generated insecurity and demand for repression (see, for example, a study by criminologist Nils Christie reported in *The Philadelphia Inquirer*, 5/7/90). There is no evidence that capital punishment is a greater deterrent than a life sentence (Phillips and Hensley, 1984: 109), or that it relates to lower crime rates (Gartner, 1990). Cross-cultural comparative studies suggest that killing—both legal and illegal—and "the need to incarcerate" stem from common cultural roots. "Acts of violence," concluded criminologist Gartner (1990: 102) "may be part of a common cultural desensitization."
5. Todd Gitlin (1990: 191) writes: "Some of yesterday's outriders of youth culture have become theorists scavenging the clubs, the back alleys and video channels for a 'resistance' they are convinced, a priori, must exist. Failing to find radical potential in the politics of parties or mass movements, they exalt 'resistance' in subcultures, or, one step on, in popular styles, or even—to take it one step further—in the observation that viewers watch TV with any attitude other than devoted rapture. 'Resistance'—meaning all sorts of grumbling, multiple interpretation, semiological inversion, pleasure, rage, friction, numbness, what have you—'resistance' is accorded dignity, even glory, by stamping these not-so-great refusals with a vocabulary derived from life-threatening work against fascism—as if the same concept should serve for the Chinese student uprising and cable TV grazing."
6. Two-thirds of home video recording is of network programs. Video rentals bring movies rarely permitted on television and usually restricted (R-rated) in cinemas into the home for unrestricted viewing. Yang and Linz (1990) found that in a representative sample of 30 such videos only 1 did not portray violence, and 6 out of 10 included sexual violence.
7. Just as many intellectuals find it difficult to recognize the severe limitations media impose on concepts of pluralism and choice, many writers who see television as just another artistic outlet find it difficult to accept the responsibility of the creator for what is a native environment rather than a freely chosen artistic product. The biographer of Stephen J. Cannell, writer of some of the most violent television programs, complained that "It is difficult to imagine any other medium in which the artist is burdened with as much guilt and social responsibility by as many people as on television" (R. J. Thompson, 1990: 42).
8. Willie Horton was of course the "furloughed criminal" in the contrived Bush 1988 campaign commercial. Willie Bennett was a real near-victim of the "Stuart case" in Boston in 1989. When white suburban businessman Charles Stuart described a black

man as the murderer of his wife, the police quickly accepted and publicized his story. A small army of police invaded and terrorized black neighborhoods and picked up Bennett as a likely suspect, while demands for more jails and the death penalty echoed in the hysterical media coverage. Stuart identified Bennett in a police line-up as the killer. Later the killer turned out to be Stuart himself.

9. How selective the menace can be is suggested by the fact that the United States invades, bombs (the poor districts), takes control, and delivers to the old oligarchy an over-independent Panama (coincidentally, soon to take possession of the Canal), ostensibly to capture a head of state and former CIA-client charged with narcotics traffic, but releases an Orlando Bosch who blew up a Cuban airliner killing 73 civilian passengers aboard (*The New York Times*, 18/7/90: 1).
10. Count by Vincent Canby (*The New York Times* 7/16/90: C11). Canby observed that William Wellman's 1931 *Public Enemy* shocked viewers and critics (*The Times* reviewer noted its "general slaughter") despite the fact that each of its eight deaths takes place off screen. But, Canby observes, "death and mortal injury were treated with discretion than, at least in part because the then-new Production Code took a dim view of mayhem for its own sake."

REFERENCES

Adams, W. C. (1986) "Whose Lives Count? TV Coverage of Natural Disasters," *Journal of Communication*, Spring: 105–12.

Baker, R. K. and Ball, S. J. (1969) *Mass Media and Violence*, Report of the Task Force on Mass Media and Violence to the National Commission on the Causes and Prevention of Violence. Washington: U.S. Government Printing Office.

Bassiouni, M. C. (1981) "Terrorism, Law Enforcement, and the Mass Media: Perspectives, Problems, Proposals," *Journal of Criminal Law and Criminology*, 72(1).

Bassiouni, M. C. (1982) "Media Coverage of Terrorism: The Law and the Public," *Journal of Communication*, 33(2): 128–43.

Black, G. (1990) "A Myth That Lets Butchers Off the Hook," *Los Angeles Times*, 10 June.

Comstock, G. A., Rubinstein, E. A., and Murray, J. P. (eds.) (1972) *Television and Social Behavior*. Report to the Scientific Advisory Committee. Washington: U.S. Government Printing Office.

DeBoer, C. (1979) "The Polls: Terrorism and Hijacking," *Public Opinion Quarterly*, 43 (Fall): 410–18.

Gartner, R. (1990) "The Victims of Homicide: A Temporal and Cross-Cultural Comparison," *American Sociological Review*, 55: 92–106.

Gerbner, G. (1988) "Violence and Terror in the Mass Media," in *Reports and Papers in Mass Communication*, 102. Paris: UNESCO.

Gerbner, G. (1991) "The Politics of Media Violence: Some Reflections," in C. Hamelink and O. Linne (eds.), *Mass Communication Research: On Problems and Policies*. Norwood: Ablex.

Gerbner, G., Gross, L., Morgan, M. and Signorielli, N. (1982). "Charting the Mainstream: Television's Contributions to Political Orientations." *Journal of Communication*, 32(2):100–126.

Gerbner, G., Gross, L., Morgan, M. and Signorielli, N. (1986a) *Television's Mean World: Violence Profile, No. 14–15.* Annenberg School of Communications, University of Pennsylvania.

Gerbner, G., Gross, L., Morgan, M and Signorielli, N. (1986b) "Living with Television: The Dynamics of the Cultivation Process," in J. Bryant and D. Zillman (eds.), *Perspectives on Media Effects.* Hillsdale: Lawrence Erlbaum Associates Inc.

Gitlin, T. (1990) "Who Comunicates What to Whom, in What Voice and Why, About the Study of Comunications?", *Critical Studies in Mass Communication*, 7: 185–96.

Halloran, J. D. (1977) "Violence and Its Causes," Leicester: Centre for Mass Communication Research.

Knight, G. and Dean, T. (1982) "Myth and the Structure of News," *Journal of Communication*, 32(2): 144–61.

Mickolus, E. F. (1980) *Transnational Terrorism: A Chronology of Events, 1968–1979.* Westport: Greenwood Press.

Milburn, M. S., Bowley, C., Fay-Dumaine, J. and Kennedy, D. A. (1987) "An Attributional Analysis of the Media Coverage of Terrorism. Paper presented at the 10th Annual Meeting of the International Society of Political Psychology, San Francisco, July 6.

Munro, R. (1990) "Who Died in Beijing and Why," *The Nation*, 11 June.

Onyegin, N. (1986) "Construction of the 'Facts' of Political Violence: A Content Analysis of Press Coverage." Unpublished MA thesis, University of Pennsylvania.

Paletz, D. L. and Dunn, R. (1969) "Press Coverage of Civil Disorders: A Case Study of Winston-Salem," *Public Opinion Quarterly*, 33(3): 328–45.

Paletz, D. L., Fozzard, P. A. and Avanian, J. Z. (1982) "The IRA, the Red Brigades and the FALN in *The New York Times*," *Journal of Communication*, 32(2): 167–71.

Pearl, D., Bouthilet, L. and Lazar, J. (eds.) (1982) *Television and Behavior: Ten Years of Scientific Progress and Implications for the Eighties.* Rockville: National Institute of Mental Health.

Phillips, D. P. and Hensley, J. E. (1984) "When Violence Is Rewarded or Punished: The Impact of Mass Media Stories on Homicide," *Journal of Communication*, 34(3): 101–16.

Raboy, M. (1990a) *Missed Opportunities: The Story of Canada's Broadcasting Policy.* Montreal and Kingston: McGill-Queen's University Press.

Signorielli, N. (1986) "Selective Viewing: Limited Possibilities," *Journal of Communication*, 36(3): 64–76.

Signorielli, N. (1990) "Television's Mean and Dangerous World: Continuing the Cultural Indicators Perspective," in N. Signorielli and M. Morgan (eds.), *Cultivation Analysis.* Newbury Park: Sage.

Signorielli, N. and Morgan, M. (eds.) (1990) *Cultivation Analysis.* Newbury Park: Sage.

Sun, Lin (1989) "Limits of Selective Viewing: An Analysis of 'Diversity' in Dramatic Programming." Unpublished MA thesis, University of Pennsylvania.

Thompson, R. J. (1990) *Adventures on Prime Time: The Television Programs of Stephen J. Cannell.* New York: Praeger.

United States Congress (1982) *Hearing Before the Subcommittee on Telecommunications, Consumer Protection, and Finance of the Committee on Energy and Commerce, House of Representatives, Ninety-Seventh Congress, First Session, October 1981.* Washington: U.S. Government Printing Office.

Williams, G. A. (1989) "Enticing Viewers: Sex and Violence in TV Guide Program Advertisements," *Journalism Quarterly*, 66(4): 970–73.

Wurth-Hough, S. (1983) "Network News Coverage of Terrorism: The Early Years," *Terrorism*, 6(3): 403–521.

Yang, N. and Linz, D. (1990) "Movie Ratings and the Content of Adult Videos: The Sex-Violence Ratio," *Journal of Communication*, 40(2): 28–41.

CHAPTER 20

SCIENCE OR RITUAL DANCE?

A Revisionist View of Television Violence Effects Research

A BOOK REVIEW BY GEORGE GERBNER

The Politics of TV Violence: Policy Uses of Communication Research by Willard D. Rowland, Jr. Beverly Hills, CA: Sage, 1983. 320 pages. $25 (hard), $12.50 (soft).

Rowland's reading of the history of television American society "reveals how, in the violence effects issue and political concern about television's social impact, the mass communications research community found a vehicle to obtain identity and achieve legitimacy in the academy."

This book is not about violence. It is about the uses of violence effects research in the struggle for control, or authority, or at least influence, over television. "Violence effects research," writes Rowland, "has served both as a symbolic medium for public debate about the meaning of television in American society and as a means for accommodation among the interests of the principal parties to the policy debate" (p. 303). To put it more bluntly, he sees television violence research as a ritual dance in which academics were led by politicians looking for juicy issues, by industry looking for a safe legislative dead end, and by reformers looking for experts to support their claims and their illusions. The ritual fooled no one but the public. And all the dancers stepped to the music of "empirical social science" promoted by industry, infiltrating and eventually dominating the communications research community.

This is a provocative thesis and Rowland builds a strong case for it. If his focus on the academy tends to deflect his aim from more formidable targets, that is a small price to pay for this penetrating critique of the plays and players of thirty years of research (and not only violence research) on television. This book is required reading for well-informed students and scholars of the discipline.

I should reveal my personal involvements before I proceed. There are many good reasons for my reviewing—or not reviewing—this book. At one point in his academic career, Rowland was my student and also served on a (non-empirical) research project under my direction. I am one of the players in his Chronicle. *Caveat emptor!*

The book originated in a Ph.D. dissertation in communications at the University of Illinois, and a section dealing with the early history of research was published in *Communication Yearbook* 5. Accounts of television violence research by Barnouw, Cater and Strickland, Withey and Abeles, Comstock, Bogart, and others are fairly digested and referenced in this book. The only major relevant work that came too late for Rowland to acknowledge is the second edition of *The Early Window* by Liebert, Sprafkin, and Davidson (2), which gives a straightforward account of events and findings from a social science position. But that is the approach Rowland considers part of the problem and not the solution. His focus is not on the design and findings of research, but on the political implications and uses of social science applied to communications policy.

His story relies mostly on hearings records and the reports of committees and commissions. These documents and testimonies in Rowland's deft hands reveal as much about the interconnections, trade-offs, and accommodations of science politics as documents possibly can. But being there or interviewing some of the key actors can make a significant difference at certain times. A few well-placed telephone conversations judiciously triangulated can unravel many mysteries and supplement or correct many apparent certainties of the record. There is no evidence that Rowland gathered any such intelligence.

Rowland sets the stage with a critical account (long overdue) of the "received history" of effects research.

That story holds that once upon a time simple-minded researchers believed that communications worked like a "hypodermic needle," injecting people uniformly with the deadly venom of enemy propaganda or the life-saving serum of truth. Now, however, we are more sophisticated so we know very little for sure, except that there are many "intervening variables," "selective perceptions," "uses and gratifications," and other intricate mechanisms that limit whatever effect (if any) mass media may have. The agonistic view tends to absolve industry (and the researchers who serve it) from responsibility for consequences (except commercial) and shift that burden to the now "powerful" viewers. That history, as most received histories, serves to reveal for the uninitiated the inevitable unfolding of the glorious present as told by those who run it.

Rowland, in his welcome expose of this received gospel, attributes its force to the spread and authority or "empirical" social science. That attribution is not altogether false. But the exposition lacks comparative breadth against which different types of scientific endeavors can be judged. Rowland is silent on alternative methodologies, although he rightly urges greater consciousness of the political role of any social research.

He is, however, far from silent on an alternative view to the received history. In bold historical strokes, Rowland sketches the "capture" of communication studies by "the empirical sciences."

The "received history"—still taught in most schools of communications—is an invention, Rowland suggests. No responsible researcher ever proposed a "hypodermic needle" theory of mass media effects, or any theory that suggests universal, uniform, and irresistible effects. The enormous (but by no means universal, uniform, and irresistible) changes brought about by television after World War II "reenergized the debate about the impact of modern communications and ever-changing technology" (p. 23). The social, political, cultural, and commercial stakes were also enormous. As the television industry had no obligation to fulfill any responsibility but the commercial, it had everything to gain from reducing its accountability for other effects. The most successful tactic was to promote research that—and researchers who—would minimize any claim of effects. The most effective approaches were those that appealed to popular fears but formulated research problems in limited and ahistorical ways; that set up straw men to be easily knocked down; and that, while anxiety-provoking and emotionally arousing, and thus politically attractive, would not be likely to lead to any legislative action. If, in addition, the issue to be addressed could exploit public insecurities and mobilize support for defense of "law and order," thus strengthening rather than threatening established institutions, so much the better. The ideal candidate fulfilling these criteria was television violence research.

Having articulated his thesis, Rowland then turns the spotlight upon the ministrations of the newly canonized academic behaviorists.

Rowland tells the story of interaction among the mass communications research community, the broadcasting industry, the reformers, and the political process overseeing the introduction and advancement of television in American society. He traces this history from the motivations and findings of the Payne Fund studies of the effects of violence in film (1928–1933), moving through the successive phases of congressional and national-level commission investigations of television violence represented by the Harris hearings (1952), the juvenile delinquency investigations (Hendrickson-Kefauver, 1954–1955 and Dodd, 1961–1964), the inquiries of the National Commission on the Causes and Prevention of Violence (1968–1969), and the research of the Surgeon General's Scientific Advisory Committee on Television and Social Behavior, engendered and reviewed by the Pastore hearings (1969–1972).

Rowland's reading of this history reveals how, in the violence effects issue and political concern about television's social impact, the mass communications research community found a vehicle to obtain identity and to achieve legitimacy in the academy. Throughout the long process, and despite the findings of most research, the "limited effects" models tended to exonerate television, arguing that it did not have demonstrable negative effects (as in 1, pp. 27–28).

Rowland admits that "the critics retained the view that communication issues remained serious and substantial, and many of them therefore resisted the pressure to turn away entirely from the study of effects" (p. 28). But he says nothing more about these "critics" or their methodologies (which were as likely as not to be the same as those of the apologists). He continues to develop his thesis of the co-opted academy:

> ...But the new generation, trained during the postwar period with primary emphasis on methodology and technique, was not encouraged to reflect from a critical, self-conscious perspective upon the assumptions and the consequent implications of the contending scientific models. As a result, there was among many proponents of the expanding study of mass communications a rush to embrace the new approaches and to redefine communications research in terms of the new sociology and social psychology....In academic forums the critique of the media turned toward the rationalizations of functionalism and uses and gratifications; in popular debate it turned toward the McLuhanesque embrace of technology and the celebration of an electronic nirvana. (p. 28)

Rowland depicts the politicians as having found in effects research a way to project an image of concerned inquiry that would force them into little, if any, legislative action. The federal communications policymaking process associated itself with the popularly acceptable terms of scientific research. The research approach not only failed to address the underlying problems of institutional structure and control but served to mask and divert attention from such issues.

Rowland sees the broadcasting industry as avoiding outright opposition to governmental attention to the research, choosing instead to influence the process of decision making about appropriate and inappropriate lines of inquiry. Building on the prior relationships with university-based research centers, the industry continued to support and promote selected research efforts while overlooking or avoiding others (p. 30).

After stating this thesis in the first chapters, Rowland recounts in detail the rise of American social science and the early history of communication effects research to elucidate the relationships among the players.

Rowland names names and traces influences of applied research in marketing, at CBS, the army, the Bureau of Applied Research at Columbia University, and network-subsidized publications that became texts for generations of sociologists and communications researchers. By the time the story of the violence commissions and hearings begins, the reader can follow the moves played to familiar music. Rowland sounds the leitmotiv of the opportunistic agnosticism of behavioristic research, but he ignores the roles played by "critical" social scientists and notes instead the accommodations of researchers to money and power. On the report of the National Commission on the Causes and Prevention of Violence (the Eisenhower Commission), for example, Rowland observes:

> These recommendations are more remarkable for what they omit than for what they include. The commission carefully avoids offering measures that might raise questions about the basic structure or purpose of American television. At one level the Commission is willing to lament the commercial purpose of broadcast-

> ing: "Television entertainment based on violence may be effective merchandising, but it is an appalling way to serve civilization—an appalling way to fulfill the requirements of the law that broadcasting serve the "public interest, convenience and necessity." But in the end the Commission proves to be unwilling to confront the fundamental conflict between its implicit interpretation of that legal mandate and the programming imperatives of broadcasting's existence as a profit-making institution. (p. 132)

Rowland describes this pattern of political demagoguery, public catharsis, academic aggrandizement, and legislative paralysis many times over, in reference to the work and report of the Surgeon General's Scientific Advisory Committee and the hearings of the "Pastore era." Instructive and valid as much of his chronicle is, however, he obscures the fact that the "coming of age" of communications research did, after all, establish a disciplinary base capable of independent action and judgment, even if not from a position of power. The accommodations researchers make with power result more from their inclinations and dependencies than from their theories about evidence.

I can illuminate the pragmatics and power plays of research and politics from Rowland's account of my testimony before the Pastore Committee. By the 1974 Pastore hearings, our Cultural Indicators project had developed to the point where we could begin to try to change the terms of discourse from the conventional violence question to a more general problem of lessons about social relationships and power that exposure to violence cultivates in the minds of viewers. In fact, our violence effects research attempted to raise questions of institutional structure and control that Rowland found lacking in the Eisenhower report. Our study was supported by the Surgeon General's Scientific Advisory Committee of the National Institute of Mental Health (NIMH) largely because of Pastore's needs and would depend on the senator's further support. So in the climactic 1974 hearings I reported our first effects findings, along with the Violence Index. But the "cultivation analysis" showing violence to generate insecurity and possibly dependence seemed too complex and "academic" for Pastore. It did not suit his purposes and he kept pressing until I gave him the answer he needed, without of course compromising the report of our findings.

The hearings are, of course, pure theater. Research testimony is used as leverage to extract contrite public promises from network presidents as cover for less visible deals in more concrete areas of broadcaster interest, such as licensing. Having served its political purpose, the actual meaning and implications of effects research or the actual performance of the networks is of little importance. Rowland sums up the Pastore era:

> *The ritual had changed little over the years. Once more the senator invokes both common sense and the authority of science, reinforcing the impression that the problem is real, building up the image of conclusiveness, carefully introducing a few caveats, praising progress by the industry, reiterating the importance of self-regulation, and through it all taking credit both for stimulating progress and for doing nothing dangerous. (p. 224)*

One episode where Rowland's reading of documents falls short of revealing the full story is the 1977 culmination of a decade of commissions, research, reports, and hearings.

The House subcommittee headed by Lionel Van Deerlin, with more independent-minded and militant members and staff than previous committees, and well armed with critical effects findings of the kind Rowland tends to ignore, attempted to cut through the ritual. Dragging its reluctant chairman along, the subcommittee produced a well-documented draft report. It was the first time in all the years of congressional television violence hearings that a committee had even attempted to write a report. Furthermore, the draft called for an investigation of the structure of the television industry as the only way to get to the roots of the "violence problem" as a symptom of structural pressures affecting all programming.

However, a funny thing happened on the way to the final report. As Rowland duly notes, the final report made no mention of industry structure, and a minority report termed it a whitewash. But Rowland's account leaves out the struggle behind the scenes.

When the draft mentioning industry structure was leaked to the networks, all hell broke loose. Members of the subcommittee told me that they had never before been subjected to such relentless lobbying and pressure. Campaign contributors were contacted. The report was delayed for months. The subcommittee staffer who wrote the draft was summarily fired. The day before the final vote was to be taken, a new version drafted by a broadcast lobbyist was substituted. It ignored the evidence of the hearings and gutted the report, shifting the source of the problem from network structure to the parents of America. When the network-dictated draft came to a vote, members of the full committee (including those who had never attended hearings) were mobilized, and the watered-down version passed by one vote.

Research methodology had little to do with the debacle. The realities of institutional power set the terms of policy. Rowland knows those realities. He cites from the minority report that "the effect of the subcommittee's action is to reject out of hand the option of restructuring the industry as a way of solving the problem of televised violence. We find this rejection both incomprehensible and shocking" (p. 286). Then Rowland goes on to comment:

> *This persistent point in the minority reports cuts directly to the heart of this congressional strategy over the preceding decades. The entire process had become a well-rehearsed ritual—one of study, inquiry, review, research, debate and reports—but no congressional subcommittee had ever seriously contemplated major structural change in American broadcasting. In this light the dissenters in the 1977 House subcommittee should not really have been shocked. They must have understood the underlying realities that could not permit any substantial disturbance of the ritual. (p. 286)*

Those realities—the powers behind the political throne that deflect and defuse research and reports of research and defeat efforts at understanding and serving the public interest in and out of Congress—are given short shrift (at least until the end of the book) because of the methods-oriented blinders Rowland's thesis imposes on the interpretation of events.

> *But having said that, we can return to the unique and indispensable contribution Rowland makes to understanding the political uses and misuses of violence effects research and of the plays and players in that intricate game.*

They are all there. Network presidents and researchers strut and squirm and posture. The prestigious foundations such as Ford and Markle perform showy little charades whose consequences range from the timid to the disgraceful. The Aspen Institute and the Social Science Research Council nibble around the edges looking for risk-free visibility and credit. The Federal Communications Commission dodges a petition by Action for Children's Television for some simple guidelines for children's commercials (a common practice in most civilized countries) and finally rejects it. The Federal Trade Commission takes up the cause in a gesture to the growing anti-violence and reform movement; the backlash from industry and Congress subjects it to the sharpest vilification and budget cutting in its history. Even the National Citizen's Committee on Broadcasting can only rank "violent sponsors" and the American Medical Association can sponsor the violence Index, but neither can afford to attack industry structure. "There were always implicit understandings of the rules of the game," Rowland observes (p. 282).

A brief section describes the reception of the NIMH Surgeon General's "Update" report and summary of ten years of television research (3), attempting to broaden the issues and sharpen the conclusions just as the Rowland volume went to press. But Rowland correctly notes that "the more stridently the putative research findings were put, the more they seemed to be ignored in the climate of deregulation and marketplace appeals" (p. 289). The exceptions, too late for inclusion in this book, were the controversial NBC study of television and aggression (reviewed in the Spring 1984 issue of this journal) and ABC's bungled hatchet job on the NIMH Update report, a pamphlet entitled "A Research Perspective on Television and Violence." *The New York Times* report on July 31, 1983, headed "The Networks Shrug Off Violence," indicated that the ritual continues.

Rowland's summary of the symbolic and political uses of violence effects research consists of revealing portraits (some would say caricatures) of the four main "parties at interest": the academy, the industry, the government, and the reformers. The academy, Rowland's principal target, he sees as historically and philosophically compromised. It has accepted at face value the received history and false promise of the effects research tradition, "born of industrial need and nurtured in political ambivalence" (p. 292). Rejecting traditional authority as value-laden and institutionally inspired, "effects science" claims value-free analysis, unconscious of its own ideological and institutional relevance. "It has aligned itself with the mainstream of liberal reform in American social and economic thought, never comprehending that that affiliation implied commitment to certain forms of conceptualization and action that serve the very structure of political and industrial control that prompt the reform impulse in the first place" (p. 293).

While the academy uses effects research to climb the ladder of visibility, funding, and respectability, the broadcasting industry manipulates the resulting confusion to its advantage. It trots out its own research claims whenever needed to refute academics and thus perpetuate confusion mirrored in the media and even in the academy. It sponsors academic apologists and agnostics, thus giving the appearance of supporting self-examination. Industry's influence in establishing the original terms of scientistic reference and university bureaus makes such occasional continued support productive in achieving the aim of always rendering findings "inconclusive."

Building on that ambivalence and confusion, government discovered that "the science of effects proved to be just sophisticated enough to lend credibility to the political claims of serious scrutiny, while yet proving to be sufficiently inconclusive to prevent any draconian measures" (p. 297). When the public pressure for action gets strong enough to threaten to disrupt government's symbiotic relationship with industry, network clout or the rhetoric of new technologies and marketplace solutions serves to restore the equilibrium.

The reformers act out their role in the ritual by keeping alive the illusion of progress and technological or administrative rather than structural remedies to enduring social problems. Rowland is right on target in depicting reform groups as essentially pragmatic and opportunistic, using research (as did industry and government) only supporting rather than testing their claims. "If there were other attributes of communication science and the study of television, they were seldom considered by the reform mind. At best they were relegated to some secondary status of interesting but essentially useless academic fuzziness" (p. 301).

To be sure, that is also what Rowland appears to do. Social science research that does not fit his image of positivistic abstractions in the service of obfuscation or power is relegated to the unavoidable interstices of his elaborate chronicle. Only in the final section on "The Continuing Challenge to Communication Science" is there explicit recognition of several strands of empirical orientation, including critical communications scholarship. This needs to be said lest new generations of researchers are inhibited from learning and using the broadest repertory of methodologies, including empirical, for critical as well as other purposes.

What is missing? One looks in vain for a development of methodological or philosophical alternatives to social science research of equal real value, public credibility, and explanatory power. There is little appreciation of scientific efforts to understand, as well as explain, what happens when generations grow up with the experience of an average of thirty vivid and entertaining television murders per week. There is little balanced discussion of the gains as well as losses involved in the necessary trade-offs of television research politics. The development of a discipline of communications capable of some independent training and judgment is barely noted. And, most important for a book on communications, the role of the media as a "party at interest," shaping public discussion of research on violence in particular ways, is missing from the account. The net result of these omissions is to obscure the structure of powers that confront critical research and policy. Ironically, these blind spots deflect attention from that structure—a charge Rowland levels against violence effects research.

Strong theories historically and philosophically pursued can become blinders; that goes with the territory. Rowland has avoided most of those pitfalls. His is a subtle and rich account blazing paths in uncharted territory. The reviewer's task (much easier, by hindsight) is to point out whatever might round out and sharpen the reader's understanding—and the next attempt to assess the policy uses of communication research.

In the meantime—and Rowland's story is not likely to be improved upon for some time—we can take note of Horace Newcomb's prefatory observation (p. 11): "The 'play' is not yet done. Acts remain to be written in actions we will take.... The sure thing is that this book should make it impossible for us to step onto the stage without truly knowing our parts."

REFERENCES

1. Klapper, Joseph. *The Effects of Mass Communication.* New York: Free Press, 1960.
2. Liebert, Robert M., Sprafkin, Joyce N., and Davidson, Emily S. *The Early Window: Effects of Television on Children and Youth* (2nd ed.). New York: Pergamon, 1982.
3. Pearl, D., Bouthilet, L., and Lazar, J. (eds.). *Television and Behavior: Ten Years of Scientific Progress and Implications for the Eighties.* Washington, D.C.: U.S. Government Printing Office, 1982.

CHAPTER 21

THE HIDDEN MESSAGE IN ANTI-VIOLENCE PUBLIC SERVICE ANNOUNCEMENTS

BY GEORGE GERBNER

Despite the growing concern in the United States about the quantity and seemingly graphic portrayal of violence on television, such programming remains in place because of the commercial imperatives of programming in an international marketplace, from which more than one-half of U.S. media income is generated. In the international marketplace of television, violent programming needs no translation, is image-driven, and "speaks action" in any language and in any culture. Such factors help facilitate the sale of violence-laden television programs produced in the United States to countries abroad, and often at reasonable prices.[1]

If the television industry in the United States were solely a private entity, the commercial nature of television would not be a problem. In this situation, broadcasters would be under no obligation to meet anything but their own needs. But the industry is *not* a private affair. Under the Communications Act of 1934, U.S. broadcasters are licensed by the Federal Communications Commission (FCC) to use the public airways in "the public interest, convenience, and necessity." In other words, broadcasters receive a license free of charge in exchange for acting as public trustees. The notion of commercial broadcasters controlling the airways, in contrast to publicly supported systems such as the British Broadcasting Corporation, has become a standard practice of broadcasting in the United States.

However, some lingering notions exist of broadcasters' social responsibility, or of what the current chair of the FCC, Reed Hundt, calls "the social compact." The social compact to which Hundt refers allows broadcasters to have access to the public airwaves in return for the "quid pro quo" of service to the public. However, because the FCC has failed to provide any clear definition of the notion of service to the public, broadcasters often cite vague descriptions of educational programming and public service announcements (PSAs) as evidence of their fulfilling the quid pro quo.[2]

Simply put, many commercial broadcasters air educational programming and PSAs to give the appearance of serving the public and consequently to retain their broadcast licenses. Broadcasters are not reimbursed in any manner for airing PSAs, which effectively act as unpaid commercials. Furthermore, PSAs are aired at times of broadcasters' discretion, often not at times when they would target viewers who might most benefit from their messages, unlike regular commercials. The dismantling of most FCC rules against unrestricted commercial exploitation of the public airways (called deregulation) during the 1980s has exacerbated this situation.

Eyebrows must be raised, then, when media corporations produce PSAs to "educate the public," and when broadcasters claim that they are earning their right to retain their licenses specifically because of the PSAs they air. Recently, the world's largest media conglomerate, Time Warner, and two of its subsidiaries, Home Box Office (HBO) and Warner Music Group, the world's leading producer of recorded music, teamed up to produce a series of eight anti-violence PSAs, entitled "Peace: Live It Or Rest In It." The world, or at least the media world, took notice.

Released in June 1994, the commercial-length spots were featured on NBC's *Today* show, CNN (also controlled by Time Warner), and other media outlets. The news release accompanying the PSAs called them a campaign to combat gun violence. "The talent involved with this project," the release stated, "include hip hop performers...who will have a tremendous effect on their wide range of fans. The PSAs are at times dark and haunting...humorous...and hopeful...[and enlist] the creative energy of young and talented performers and directors of today's generation." *The New York Times* extolled "the unusually artistic and at times startling" series targeting urban youth, and cited Cornel West saying, "They are quite powerful....I think they can make a difference.[3]

PEACE: LIVE IT OR REST IN IT

The campaign of eight PSAs, five of which feature leading rap artists, captures scenes of urban violence amid fast-paced, creative, visually stunning imagery. By combining these images and the slogan "Peace: Live It Or Rest In It,' the PSAs depict graphically the horrors of urban violence. The next few paragraphs summarize the PSAs, not in an attempt to present individual critiques, but rather to set the stage for a broader discussion of the implications of the violent situations and characters depicted.

> "Stray Bullet"—Directed by Allen and Albert Hughes (the Hughes Brothers), "Stray Bullet" tracks the flight of a single bullet in great detail as it discharges in the hands of a White boy playing with the gun in his bedroom. The speeding bullet rips through walls, windows, a car, and a television set showing a baseball game about to come to a climax. The perspective shifts to a Black child peacefully eating a bowl of cereal on a kitchen highchair,

and—bang—in the final frames, the bowl, spoon, and meal crash to the floor in chilling slow motion.

"These Walls Have No Prejudice"—Also by the Hughes Brothers, this PSA is an equally chilling piece in which images appear only in shades of blue. Guns fire, barrels zoom, and triggers click at a frantic pace, followed by flashes of dead bodies, Black and White, laid out in the morgue.

"Chuck D."—Directed by Steve Conner and starring Chuck D., leader of the group Public Enemy, this PSA is an easy-going rap. The rapster exhorts the community to somehow get together and solve its own problems. "Save the drama and save the trauma" is his advice.

"Nikki and Khalif"—Directed by Nelson George and David Taylor, the PSA features rap artist Queen Latifa relating a poignant story of the lives of two urban Black adolescents—their love, stubborn independence, fear, vengeance, and death from a drive-by shooting.

"What Are You, Stupid?"—Directed by Peter Askin, this spot features the gallows humor of comedian John Leguizamo, who saunters down the streets of New York and taunts swaggering, macho-nerds with the words "the larger the gun the smaller the penis." The scene changes, and, inexplicably, he is hung on a meat hook in front of what seems like a butcher shop. Then suddenly he is at a cemetery, intoning "People should kill guns and not guns..." when a gun thrusts into his stomach, fires, and kills him. As he falls forward, the camera swings around to expose a masked and hooded figure towering over him.

"Good Kids"—Directed by Steve Conner, the piece features a young Black man in hooded black fatigues walking down the street on his way to a grocery store. A White matron crosses his path, stands petrified for a moment, and then walks on. The young man enters the grocery store, startling a Korean grocer who stands at the register as the young man proceeds down an aisle. The audience is set up to expect the worst. Then the young man emerges with a bag of potato chips and the money to pay for it, exchanges pleasantries with the grocer, and exits the store. "For every kid that carries a gun," says the voice-over, "there are thousands that don't. Let's not forget that."

"Hero"—Also directed by Steve Conner, this PSA is filmed in the directing style popularized by the television series ER and, in fact, was filmed in the Elmhurst Hospital in Queens. Real medics work frantically to save the life of a young Black man, shot by mistake, they are informed, by friends. The young man's last ghastly moan before dying reinforces the numbing, paralyzing effects of yet another tragic mistake.

"Et Tu Brutus"—Directed by Marcus Turner, the PSA features Sticky Fingaz and Fredro Starr from Onyx, a music group with the reputation of being both violent and raunchy. The slow-motion chase in this spot, the wild shooting, the dreadful recognition that a hooded Black youngster is out for vengeance, and a voice-over crying out, "Stop—you're only killing yourself," could be from any movie popularizing Black gangs.

THE HIDDEN MESSAGE

Two aspects of this series of anti-violence PSAs are problematic: the times the PSAs were actually aired, and their perpetuation of the kind of stereotyped violence seen in regular television programming. The PSAs were shown only on cable systems, some owned by Time Warner itself. Not all eight PSAs were aired, however. For example, MTV, usually innovative and irreverent, ran only "Good Kids," "Hero," and "Chuck D.," over a two-week period in June 1994. Apparently, squeamish MTV screeners (company censors) objected to actual guns firing in "Stray Bullet" and "Stupid." The PSAs that were aired did not necessarily appear at times when young people were likely to be in the audience. For example, ETV (Entertainment Television) showed "Chuck D." ten times during one week in July 1994—at 3:30 A.M., 4:30 A.M., and 5:30 A.M.!

The most obvious limitation of these PSAs, however, stems from the corporate structure of their production. The anti-violence content of the eight spots deals with symptoms of urban violence, while the PSAs ignore the wholesale manufacture of a media-generated culture of violence, Time Warner being a leading contributor to this culture. The PSAs do not confront television as a pervasive source of messages and images that can cultivate an acceptance of violence and a sense of victimization, vulnerability, and vengeance among viewers.

The PSAs overlook the complexity of violence, which in general involves a wide range of motivations, circumstances, and justifications. Violence depicted in the media sends out messages about power and vulnerability, problem solving, human relations, law enforcement, consequences of actions, and the rules of society. Many of these lessons may be interpreted differently by different viewers and different age groups. But on a more basic level, constant exposure to dramatic violence may cultivate similar assumptions about power and vulnerability, regardless of whether the violence is "gratuitous" or justified, as long as the social relationships involved are stereotyped, repetitive, or pervasive.

By not dealing with the way the media contributes to the culture of violence, the anti-violence PSA campaign actually reinforces television's negative messages and stereotypes about violence. The overt message in this series of PSAs is anti-violence, as reflected in the productions' words and actions. The PSAs' hidden message, whether intended or unintended, is in furthering the stereotypical context of media violence, and is accomplished by casting certain characters and selecting certain fates for them.

Upon closer examination of the cast of characters in these PSAs, violence is mostly a problem among Black male youths. Victims are disproportionately women (in fact, when involved at all, women are only involved as victims). Moreover, in these PSAs, a character from any minority group is more likely to encounter a violent situation, either as a perpetrator or as a victim. The PSAs' portrayals are congruent with the stereotypical characterizations of violence seen in general televised programming. In other words, these anti-violence PSAs may actually be perpetuating media images of violence. In regular television fare, the risk of violence to different categories of characters is not random. Women, children, poorer people, older people, and some minorities pay a higher price for violence on television than do males in the prime of their life.[4]

The Cultural Indicators research has shown that the symbolic overkill against such specific populations of characters may have strong impact on viewers' perceptions of reality. The data suggest that viewers who watch more television—controlling for factors such as age, gender, socioeconomic class, ethnicity, and neighborhood—are more likely to express feelings of insecurity and dependence.[5] In other words, "heavy" viewers of television express a greater sense of apprehension than do "light" viewers. Heavy viewers are more likely than comparable groups of light viewers to overestimate their chances of involvement in violence; to believe that their neighborhoods are unsafe; to state that the fear of crime is a "very serious personal problem"; and to assume that crime is rising, regardless of the facts of the case.

We have found that viewers who see members of their own group (race, ethnicity, age, gender, etc.) underrepresented but over-victimized develop a greater sense of apprehension, mistrust, and alienation—what the Cultural Indicators project calls the "mean world syndrome." Research from this project also suggests that insecure, angry people may be prone to violence, but that they are even more likely to be dependent on authority and susceptible to deceptively simple, strong, hard-line appeals. Further, they may accept and even welcome repressive measures such as more jails, capital punishment, harsher sentences—measures that have never reduced crime, but never fail to get the votes of an anxious and angry electorate. The cultivation of such beliefs is the deeper dilemma of violence-laden television.[6]

The splendid artistry of the production of these PSAs may have earned HBO/Time Warner brownie points with Congress, perhaps even with advertisers, and with the relatively few viewers who saw them at the obscure times they were aired. Unfortunately, in these PSAs, the complex roots of violence—its motivation, circumstances, and justification—remain unexamined. The structural constraints of the PSAs' being sponsored by one of the world's leading mass producers of violent images and messages and the requirements of mounting an effective campaign against violence in U.S. culture may be what inhibit a more accurate characterization of violence.

Nonetheless, the task of educators, parents, and other caring adults who spend significant time with children is not to deplore or ignore these anti-violence PSAs and other similar efforts. On the contrary, they should take the opportunity offered by these PSAs to use the broader context of their production and functions to illustrate for children the way that television perpetuates selective images of violence. For example, educators might require students to perform a content analysis of the violence present in scenes from prime time television programs. In such a content analysis, students would keep track of each character involved in any physical violence. Students would note the characters' gender, race, and class, as well as whether the characters perpetrate or suffer violence, or both. After students code the characters (30 to 40 characters should reveal the trends consistent in commercial television programs) in a number of scenes containing violence, they can calculate for themselves how nonrandomly victimization occurs on television. If the scenes the students code are at all typical, their results will reveal the "hidden message" of violent portrayals and relationships on television.

Despite the negative attributes inherent in the kind of PSAs produced by HBO/Time Warner, they can be used in similar ways as tools of analysis that teach, energize, mobilize, and organize, rather than as media agents that mostly terrorize and paralyze young audiences.

NOTES

1. For a more detailed discussion of the patterns and structural dynamics of television violence, from which some of these passages have been drawn, see my "Television Violence: The Power and the Peril," in *Gender, Race, and Class in Media: A Critical Text-Reader*, ed. Gail Dines and Jean M. Humez (Newbury Park, CA: Sage, 1995).
2. Public service announcements (PSAs) are 30- to 60-second messages on topics of social concern (e.g., encouraging the use of seat belts or discouraging cigarette smoking). Local broadcasters air PSAs voluntarily and do not receive financial compensation for the air time.
3. Sheila Rule, "A Message That Guns Are Lethal Weapons," *The New York Times*, May 31, 1994, p. 15C.
4. This information comes from the Cultural Indicators database, an ongoing research project updated on an annual basis that relates recurrent features of the world of television to viewers' conceptions of reality. The research began in 1967 with a study for the National Commission on the Causes and Prevention of Violence. It has continued under various sponsors, including the Surgeon General's Scientific Advisory Committee on Television and Social Behavior, the National Institute of Mental Health, the White House Office of Telecommunications Policy, the American Medical Association, the Administration on Aging, the National Science Foundation, the W. Alton Jones Foundation, the Screen Actors' Guild, the American Federation of Television and Radio Artists, the National Cable Television Association, the U.S. Commission on Civil Rights, the Turner Broadcasting System, the Center for Substance Prevention of the U.S. Public Health Service, and other reorganizations. This project is now based at the University City Science Center in Philadelphia, Pennsylvania.
5. This information is gathered from surveys from the Cultural Indicators project.
6. See, for example, George Gerbner, "Television Violence: The Art of Asking the Wrong Question," *The World and I: A Chronicle of Our Changing Era*, July 1994, pp. 385–397.

CHAPTER 22

TELEVISION VIOLENCE

At a Time of Turmoil and Terror

BY GEORGE GERBNER

Humankind may have had more bloodthirsty eras but none as filled with images of violence as the present. Even in ordinary times, TV's stress on crime and violence skews news priorities. Since September 11, 2001, however, the monopoly media have been carrying virtually no other major news.

Shocking and tragic as the attacks were on the World Trade Center and the Pentagon, they should not have come as a surprise. America bears some culpability for the conditions that provoked the murderous attacks. Rich countries should act to ease the global economic inequalities that provide a breeding ground for terrorism. French Prime Minister Lionel Jospin and German Chancellor Gerhard Schroeder said at a Franco-German discussion forum in Paris that more initiatives like the 1999 agreement on debt relief for poor nations were needed as well as a greater commitment to solving existing conflicts. Schroeder noted that "You have a situation which is favorable to terrorism if you do not deal with these problems.... Terror does not have poverty as its root cause "but the idea of sustainability has got to include the people of the Third World, otherwise these people become radicalized." As they do, the vicious cycle of fear, insecurity, prejudice, and hatred against people of color thrives in the white communities and helps drive crime reporting and its racist fallout.

Even before the recent escalation of violent rhetoric and imagery the *Des Moines Register* found that of the six top news events on Des Moines evening newscasts during February 1994, 118 stories dealt with crime and violence, 27 featured business, 17 dealt with government, 15 reported on racial relations, and 2 discussed schools. A recent study of local news by the University of Miami found that time devoted to crime ranged from 23 to 50 percent (averaging 32 percent) while violent crime in the city remained constant, involving less than one-tenth of 1 percent of the population.

Community leaders have often said that blacks, Hispanics, and now people of Middle Eastern appearance or Muslim religion are demonized by the choice of faces shown in crime stories. Evidence supports that charge. For example, a study for the

Chicago Council on Urban Affairs found that "a high percentage of African-Americans and Latinos are shown as victimizers of society, and few as social helpers." This distorted portrayal, the council said, contributes to the notion that "the inner city is dominated by dangerous and irresponsible minorities." Similarly, the *Journalism Quarterly* reported that Chicago newspapers carried stories on only one of every three homicides in the city and that the slayings most likely to be selected were those in which the victims were white, contrary to actual crime statistics.

We have been studying local news on Philadelphia television stations since 1967 as part of the Cultural Indicators monitoring project.[1] We found that crime and/or violence items usually lead newscasts and preempted balanced coverage of the city. Furthermore, only 20 percent of crime and violence on local news was local to the city, only 40 percent was local to the region, and since September 11, 2001, that proportion shrank even further. As also found in other studies, whites are more likely to be reported as victims and people of color as the perpetrators.

Crime and violence also play a prominent and pervasive role in TV entertainment. Scenes of violence occur an average three to five times per hour in prime time dramatic fiction, and between twenty and twenty-five times per hour in cartoons. We are awash in a tide of violent representations such as the world has never seen. Images of expertly choreographed brutality at home and half a world away drench our homes. There is no escape from the mass-produced mayhem pervading the life space of ever larger areas of the world.

The television overkill has clearly drifted out of democratic reach. Children all over the world are born into homes dominated by television's global monopoly of turmoil and terror. They are fully integrated into television's mean and violent world. The United States dominates that world, throwing its military weight around from Panama to Afghanistan. As Sam Smith, editor of the online *Undernews,* wrote: "Our leaders have failed us by creating a world so filled with hatred for our land."

TV's investment in mayhem was first reported by the National Association of Educational Broadcasters in 1951. The first Congressional hearings were held by Senator Estes Kefauver's Subcommittee on Juvenile Delinquency in 1954. Through several more rounds of hearings in the 1960s and '70s, despite the accumulation of critical research results, despite condemnation by government commissions and virtually all medical, law enforcement, parents', educational and other organizations, and in the face of international embarrassment, violence still saturates the airways (Gerbner et al., 1993).

Broadcasters are licensed to serve "the public interest, convenience, and necessity." But they are paid to deliver a receptive audience to their business sponsors. Few industries are as public relations conscious as television. What compels them to endure public humiliation, risk the threat of repressive legislation, and invite charges of visions that violence undermine health, security, and the social order? The answer is *not* popularity.

The usual rationalization that television violence "gives the audience what it wants" is disingenuous. As the trade knows well, violence is not highly rated. But there is no free market or box office for television programs through which audiences could express their wants.

Unlike other media use, TV viewing is a ritual; people watch by the clock and not by the program. Ratings are determined more by the time of the program, the lead-in (previous program), and what else is competing for viewers at the same time than by program quality or other attractions. Ratings are important only because they set the price the advertiser pays for "buying" viewers available to the set at a certain time, but they have limited use as indicators of popularity.

Therefore, it is clear that something is wrong with the way the problem has been posed and addressed. Either the damage is not what it is commonly assumed to be, or television violence and global mayhem must have some driving force and utility other than popularity, or both. Indeed, it is both, and more.

The usual question—"Does television violence incite real-life violence?"—is itself a symptom of the problem. It obscures and, despite its alarming implications and intent, trivializes the issues involved.

Television violence must be understood as a complex scenario and an indicator of social relationships. It has utility and consequences other than those usually considered in media and public discussion. And it is driven by forces other than free expression and audience demand.

Whatever else it does, violence in drama and news demonstrates power. It portrays victims as well as victimizers. It intimidates more than it incites. It paralyzes more than triggers action. It defines majority might and minority risk. It shows one person's, country's, race's, or ethnic group's place in the "pecking order" that runs the world.

Violence and now war, no matter how distant, is but the tip of the iceberg of a massive underlying connection of television's role as universal storyteller and an industry dependent on global markets. These relationships have not yet been recognized and integrated into any theory or regulatory practice. Television has been seen as one medium among many rather than as the mainstream of the cultural environment in which most children grow up and learn. Traditional regulatory and public-interest conceptions are based on the obsolete assumption that the number of media outlets determines freedom and diversity of content. Today, however, a handful of global conglomerates can own many outlets in all media, deny entry to new and alternative perspectives, and homogenize content. The common-carrier concept of access and protection applicable to a public utility like the phone company also falls short when the issue is not so much the number of channels and individual access to them but the centralized mass production of the content of all the stories we grow on in common.

Let us, then, preview the task of broadening a discourse that has gone on too long in a narrow and shallow groove. Violence on television is an integral part of a system of global marketing. It dominates an increasing share of the world's screens despite its relative lack of popularity in any country. Its consequences go far beyond inciting aggression. The system inhibits the portrayal of diverse dramatic approaches to conflict. It depresses independent television production and thereby diversity of choice, views, perspectives, and, not incidentally, political parties. No other country that calls itself democratic has such a monopoly on political expression and organization, while lacking socialist, communist, religious, and regional parties, and therefore, alternative views on how society might be organized.

Television's socio-political-cultural monopoly deprives viewers of more popular choices, victimizes some and emboldens others, heightens general intimidation, and invites repressive measures that exploit the widespread insecurities it generates.

The First Amendment to the U.S. Constitution forbade the only censors its authors knew—government—from interfering with the freedom of the press. Since then, large conglomerates, virtual private governments, have imposed their formulas of overkill on media they own. Therefore, raising the issue of overkill directs attention to the controls that, in fact, abridge creative freedom, dominate markets, and constrain democratic cultural policy.

Behind the problem of television violence is the critical issue of who makes cultural policy on whose behalf in the electronic age. The debate about the current tidal wave of mayhem creates an opportunity to move the larger cultural policy issue to center stage, where it has been in other democracies for some time.

The convergence of communication technologies concentrates control over the most widely shared messages and images. Despite all the technocratic fantasies about hundreds of channels, it is rare to encounter discussion of the basic issue of who makes cultural policy. In the absence of such discussion, cultural policy is made on private and limited grounds by an invisible corporate directorate whose members are unknown, unelected, and unaccountable to the public.

We need to ask the kinds of questions that can place the discussion of television violence as a cultural policy issue in a useful perspective. What creative sources and resources will provide what mix of content moving on the "electronic superhighway" into every home? Who will tell the stories and for what underlying purpose? How can we assure survival of alternative perspectives, regardless of profitability and selling power?

There are no clear answers to these questions because, for one thing, they have not yet been placed on the agenda of public discourse. It will take organization, deliberation, and exploration to develop an approach to answering them. What follows, then, is an attempt to draw from our research answers to some questions that can help develop such an approach. We will be asking: What is unique about television and about violence on television? What systems of "casting" and "fate" dominate its representations of life? What conceptions of reality do these systems cultivate? Why does violence play such a prominent, pervasive, and persistent role in them? And, finally, how can we as a society deal with the overkill while, at the same time, enhancing rather than further curtailing cultural freedom and diversity?

THE NEW CULTURAL ENVIRONMENT

Nielsen figures show that an American child today is born into a home in which television is on an average of over seven hours a day. For the first time in human history, most of the stories about people, life, and values are told not by parents, schools, churches, or others in the community who have something to tell but by a group of distant conglomerates that have something to sell.

Television, the mainstream of the new cultural environment, has brought about a radical change in the way children grow up, learn, and live in our society. Television is a relatively non-selectively used ritual; children are its captive audience. Most people watch by the clock and not by the program. The television audience depends on the time of the day and the day of the week more than on the program. Other media require literacy, growing up, going out, and selection based on some previously acquired tastes, values, predispositions. Traditional media research assumed such selectivity. But there are no "previously acquired tastes, values, predispositions" with television. Viewing starts in infancy and continues throughout life.

Television helps to shape from the outset the predispositions and selections that govern the use of other media. Unlike other media, television requires little or no attention; its repetitive patterns are absorbed in the course of living. They become part and parcel of the family's style of life, but they neither stem from nor respond to its particular and selective needs and wants. It is television itself that cultivates the tastes, values, and predispositions that guide future selection of other media. That is why television has a major impact on what movies, magazines, newspapers, and books can be sold best in the new cultural environment.

The roles children grow into are no longer homemade, handcrafted, community inspired. They are products of a complex, integrated, and globalized manufacturing and marketing system. Television violence, defined as overt physical action that hurts or kills (or threatens to do so), is an integral part of that system. A study of the "Limits of Selective Viewing" (Sun, 1989) found that, on the whole, prime time television presents a relatively small set of common themes, and violence pervades most of them.

Of course, representations of violence are not necessarily undesirable. There is blood in fairy tales, gore in mythology, murder in Shakespeare. Not all violence is alike. In some contexts, violence can be a legitimate and even necessary cultural expression. Individually crafted, historically inspired, sparingly and selectively used expressions of symbolic violence can indicate the tragic costs of deadly compulsions. However, such a tragic sense of violence has been swamped by "happy violence" produced on the dramatic assembly line. This "happy violence" is cool, swift, painless, and often spectacular, even thrilling, but usually sanitized. It always leads to a happy ending. After all, it is designed to entertain and not to upset; it must deliver the audience to the next commercial in a receptive mood.

The majority of network viewers have little choice of thematic context or character types, and virtually no chance of avoiding violence. Nor has the proliferation of channels led to greater diversity of actual viewing. (See, e.g., Morgan and Shanahan, 1991, Gerbner, 1993b, Gerbner et al., 1993.) If anything, the dominant dramatic patterns penetrate more deeply into viewer choices through more outlets managed by fewer owners airing programs produced by fewer creative sources.

MESSAGE SYSTEM ANALYSIS

Cultural Indicators is a three-pronged research effort. "Message System Analysis" is the annual monitoring of television program content; "Institutional Policy Analysis" looks at the economic and political bases of media decision making; "Cultivation Analysis" is an assessment of the long-range consequences of exposure to television's systems of messages.

Message system analysis includes every dramatic (fictional) program in each annual sample. It provides an unusual view of familiar territory. It is not a view of individual programs but an aggregate picture of the world of television, a bird's-eye view of what large communities of viewers absorb over long periods of time.

The role of violence in that world can be seen in our analysis of prime time network programs and characters. "Casting" and "fate," the demography of that world, are the important building blocks of the storytelling process. They have presented a stable pattern over the almost thirty years of monitoring network television drama and coding every speaking character in each year's sample. Middle-class white male characters dominate in numbers and power. Women play one out of three characters. Young people comprise one-third and old one-fifth of their actual proportions of the population. Most other minorities are even more underrepresented. That cast sets the stage for stories of conflict, violence, and the projection of white male prime-of-life power. Most of those who are underrepresented are also those who, when portrayed, suffer the worst fate.

The average viewer of prime time television drama (serious as well as comedic) sees in a typical week an average of 21 criminals arrayed against an army of 41 public and private law enforcers. There are 14 doctors, 6 nurses, 6 lawyers, and 2 judges to handle them. An average of 150 acts of violence and about 15 murders entertain viewers and their children every week, and that does not count cartoons and the news. Those who watch over 3 hours a day (more than half of all viewers) absorb much more.

About one out of three (31%) of all characters and more than half (52%) of major characters are involved in violence either as victims or as victimizers (or both) in any given week. The ratio of violence to victimization defines the price to be paid for committing violence. When one group can commit violence with relative impunity, the price it pays for violence is relatively low. When another group suffers more violence than it commits, the price is high.

In the total cast of prime time characters, defined as all speaking parts regardless of the importance of the role, the average "risk ratio" (number of victims per 10 violent acts) is 12. Violence is an effective victimizer—and characterizer. Its distribution is not random; the calculus of risk is not evenly distributed. Women, children, poorer and older people and some minorities pay a higher price for violence than do males in the prime of life. The price paid in victims for every 10 violent acts is 15 for boys, 16 for girls, 17 for young women, 18.5 for lower-class characters, and over 20 for elderly characters.

Violence takes on an even more defining role for major characters. It involves more than half of all major characters (58% of men and 41% of women). Most likely to be involved either as perpetrators or victims, or both, are characters portrayed as mentally ill (84%), characters with mental or other disability (70%), young adult males (69%), and Latino/Hispanic Americans (64%). Children, lower class, and mentally ill or otherwise disabled characters pay the highest price—13–16 victims for every 10 perpetrators.

Lethal victimization further extends the pattern. About 5 percent of all characters and 10 percent of major characters are involved in killing (kill or get killed, or both). Being Latino/Hispanic, or lower class means bad trouble: these characters are the most likely to kill and be killed. Being poor, old, Hispanic, or a woman of color means double trouble, a disproportionate chance of being killed; they pay the highest relative price for taking another's life.

Among major characters, for every 10 "good" (positively valued) men who kill, about 4 are killed. But for every 10 "good" women who kill, 6 women are killed, and for every 10 women of color who kill, 7 women are killed. Older women characters get involved in violence *only* to be killed.

We calculated a violence "pecking order" by ranking the risk ratios of the different groups. Women, children, young people, lower class, disabled, and Asian Americans are at the bottom of the heap. When it comes to killing, older and Latino/Hispanic characters also pay a higher-than-average price. In other words, hurting and killing by most majority groups extracts a tooth for a tooth. But minority groups tend to pay a higher price for their show of force. That imbalance of power is, in fact, what makes them minorities even when, as women, they are a numerical majority.

CULTIVATION ANALYSIS: THE "LESSONS" OF TELEVISION

What are the consequences? These representations are not the sole or necessarily even the main determinants of what people think or do. But they are the most pervasive, inescapable, and policy-directed common and stable cultural *contributions* to what large communities absorb over long periods of time. We distinguish the long-term cultivation of assumptions about life and values from short-term "effects" that are usually assessed by measuring change as a consequence of exposure to certain messages. Television tends to cultivate and confirm stable conceptions about life.

Cultivation analysis measures these "lessons" as it explores whether those who spend more time with television are more likely than comparable groups of less-frequent viewers to perceive the real world in ways that reflect the most common and repetitive features of the television world. (See Morgan & Signorielli, 1990, for a detailed discussion of the theoretical assumptions and methodological procedures of cultivation analysis.)

The systemic patterns in television content that we observe through message system analysis provide the basis for formulating survey questions about people's conceptions of social reality. These questions form the basis of surveys administered to large and representative national samples of respondents. The surveys include questions about fear of crime, trusting other people, walking at night in one's own neighborhood, chances of victimization, inclination to aggression, etc. Respondents in each sample are divided into those who watch the most television, those who watch a moderate amount, and those who watch the least. Cultivation is assessed by comparing patterns of responses in the three viewing groups (light, medium, and heavy) while controlling for important demographic and other characteristics such as education, age, income, gender, newspaper reading, neighborhood, etc.

These surveys indicate that long-term regular exposure to violence-laden television tends to make an independent contribution (i.e., in addition to all other factors) to the feeling of living in a mean and gloomy world. The "lessons" range from aggression to desensitization and to a sense of vulnerability and dependence.

The symbolic overkill takes its toll on all viewers. However, heavier viewers in every subgroup express a greater sense of apprehension than do light viewers in the same groups. They are more likely than comparable groups of light viewers to overestimate their chances of involvement in violence, to believe that their neighborhoods are unsafe, to state that fear of crime is a very serious personal problem and to assume that crime is rising regardless of the facts. Heavy viewers are also more likely to buy new locks, watchdogs, and guns "for protection." It makes no difference what they watch because only light viewers watch more selectively; heavy viewers watch more of everything that is on the air. Our studies show that they cannot escape watching violence. (See e.g., Gerbner, Morgan, Gross, and Signorielli, 1984; Sun, 1989.)

Moreover, viewers who see members of their own group underrepresented but overvictimzed seem to develop a greater sense of apprehension, mistrust, and alienation, what we call the "mean world syndrome." Insecure, angry people may be prone to violence but are even more likely to be dependent on authority and susceptible to deceptively simple, strong hard-line postures. They may accept and even welcome repressive measures such as more jails, capital punishment, harsher sentences—measures that have never reduced crime but never fail to get votes—if that promises to relieve their anxieties. That is the deeper dilemma of violence-laden television.

THE STRUCTURAL BASIS OF TELEVISION VIOLENCE

Formula-driven violence in entertainment and news is not an expression of freedom, viewer preference, or even crime statistics. The frequency of violence in the media seldom, if ever, reflects the actual occurrence of crime in a community. It is, rather, the product of a complex manufacturing and marketing machine.

Mergers, consolidation, conglomeratization, and globalization speed the machine. "Studios are clipping productions and consolidating operations, closing off gateways for newcomers," notes the trade paper *Variety* on the front page of its August 2, 1993, issue. The number of major studios declines while their share of domestic and global markets rises. Channels proliferate while investment in new talent drops, gateways close, and creative sources shrink.

Concentration brings denial of access to new entries and alternative perspectives. It places greater emphasis on dramatic ingredients most suitable for aggressive international promotion. Having fewer buyers for their products forces program producers into deficit financing. That means that most producers cannot break even on the license fees they receive for domestic airings. They are forced into syndication and foreign sales to make a profit. They need dramatic ingredients that require no translation, "speak action" in any language and fit any culture. That ingredient is violence and mayhem. September 11, 2001, was a striking example. (Sex is second but, ironically, it runs into more inhibitions and restrictions.)

Syndicators demand "action" (the code word for violence) because it "travels well around the world," said the producer of *Die Hard 2* (which killed 264 compared to 18 in *Die Hard 1*). "Everyone understands an action movie. If I tell a joke, you may not get it but if a bullet goes through the window, we all know how to hit the floor, no matter the language." (Cited by Ken Auletta in "What Won't They Do?," *The New Yorker*, May 17, 1993, pp. 45–46.)

Our analysis shows that violence dominates U.S. exports. We compared 250 U.S. programs exported to 10 countries with 111 programs shown in the United States during the same year. Violence was the main theme of 40 percent of home-shown and 49 percent of exported programs. Crime/action series comprised 17 percent of home-shown and 46 percent of exported programs.

The rationalization is that violence "sells." But what does it sell to whom and at what price? There is no evidence that, other factors being equal, violence per se is giving most viewers, countries, and citizens "what they want." The most highly rated programs are usually not violent. The trade paper *Broadcasting & Cable* editorialized (Sept. 20, 1993, p. 66) that "the most popular programming is hardly violent as anyone with a passing knowledge of Nielsen ratings will tell you." The editorial added that "Action hours and movies have been the most popular exports for years," i.e., with the exporters, not the audiences. In other words, violence may help sell programs cheaply to broadcasters in many countries even if audiences dislike such programs despite the dislike of their audiences. But television audiences do not buy programs, and advertisers, who do, pay for reaching the available audience at the least cost.

We compared data from over 100 violent and the same number of nonviolent prime time programs stored in the Cultural Indicators database. The average Nielsen rating of the violent sample was 11.1; that of the nonviolent sample was 13.8. The share of viewing households in the violent and nonviolent samples was 18.9 and 22.5, respectively. The amount and consistency of violence in a series further increased the gap. Furthermore, the nonviolent sample was more highly rated than the violent sample for each of the five seasons studied.

However, despite their low average popularity, what violent programs lose on general domestic audiences they more than make up by grabbing younger viewers the advertisers want to reach and by extending their reach to the global market hungry for a cheap product. Even though these imports are typically also less popular abroad than quality shows produced at home, their extremely low cost, compared to local production, makes them attractive to the broadcasters who buy them.

Of course, some violent movies, videos, video games, and other spectacles do attract sizeable audiences. But those audiences are small compared to the home audience for television. They are the selective retail buyers of what television dispenses wholesale. If only a small proportion of television viewers growing up with the violent overkill becomes addicted to it, many movies and games will be spectacularly successful.

PUBLIC RESPONSE AND ACTION

Most television viewers suffer the violence daily inflicted on them with diminishing tolerance. Organizations of creative workers in media, health professionals, law enforcement agencies, and virtually all other media-oriented professional and citizen groups have come out against "gratuitous" television violence. A March 1985 Harris survey showed that 78 percent disapprove of violence they see on television. A Gallup poll of October 1990 found 79 percent in favor of "regulating" objectionable content in television. A Times-Mirror national poll in 1993 showed that Americans who said they were "personally bothered" by violence in entertainment shows jumped to 59 percent from 44 percent in 1983. Furthermore, 80 percent in 1993 said entertainment violence was "harmful" to society, compared with 64 percent in 1983.

Local broadcasters, legally responsible for what goes on the air, also oppose the overkill and complain about loss of control. *Electronic Media* reported on August 2, 1993, the results of its own survey of 100 general managers across all regions and in all market sizes. Three out of four said there is too much needless violence on television; 57 percent would like to have "more input on program content decisions."

The Hollywood Caucus of Producers, Writers and Directors, speaking for the creative community, said in a statement issued in August 1993: "We stand today at a point in time when the country's dissatisfaction with the quality of television is at an all-time high, while our own feelings of helplessness and lack of power, in not only choosing material that seeks to enrich, but also in our ability to execute to the best of our ability, is at an all-time low."

Far from reflecting creative freedom, the marketing of formula violence restricts freedom and chills originality. The violence formula is, in fact, a de facto censorship extending the dynamics of domination, intimidation, and repression domestically and globally. Much of the typical political and legislative response exploits the anxieties violence itself generates and offers remedies ranging from labeling and advisories to even more censorship.

There is a liberating alternative. It exists in various forms in most other democratic countries. It is public participation in decisions about cultural investment and cultural policy. Independent grass-roots citizens organization and action can provide the broad support needed for loosening the global marketing noose around the necks of producers, writers, directors, actors, and journalists.[2]

More freedom from violent and other inequitable and intimidating formulas, not more censorship, is the effective and acceptable way to increase diversity, reduce the dependence of program producers on the violence formula, and reduce television violence to its legitimate role and proportion. The role of Congress, if any, is to turn its anti-trust and civil rights oversight on the centralized and globalized industrial structures and marketing strategies that impose violence on creative people and foist it on the children and adults of the world. It is high time to develop a vision of the right of children to be born into a reasonable free, fair, diverse, and non-threatening cultural environment. It is time for citizen involvement in cultural decisions that shape our lives and the lives of our children.

NOTES

Revised and updated version of an article that originally appeared in Gail Dines and Jean M. Humez (eds.), *Gender, Race, and Class in Media: A Text Reader.* Newbury Park, CA: Sage: 1995.

1. Cultural Indicators is a database and research project that relates recurrent features of the world of television to viewer conceptions of reality. Its cumulative computer archive contains observations on over 3,000 programs and 35,000 characters coded according to many thematic, demographic, and action categories. These form the basis for the content analyses cited in the references. The study is conducted at the University of Pennsylvania's Annenberg School for Communication in collaboration with Michael Morgan at the University of Massachusetts at Amherst and Nancy Signorielli at the University of Delaware. Thanks for research assistance are due to Mariaelena Bartesaghi, Cynthia Kandra, Robin Kim, Brian Linson, Amy Nyman, and Nejat Ozyegin.
2. One such alternative is the Cultural Environment Movement. CEM is a non-profit educational corporation, an umbrella coalition of independent media, professional, labor, religious, health-related, women's, and minority groups opposed to private corporate as well as government censorship. CEM is working for freedom from stereotyped formulas and for investing in a freer and more diverse cultural environment. It can be reached by writing to Cultural Environment Movement, P.O. Box 31847, Philadelphia, PA 19104.

REFERENCES

Bandura, A., Ross, D., & Ross, D. (1967). "Transmission of aggression through imitation of aggressive models." *Journal of Abnormal and Social Psychology*, 63, 575–582.

Bryant, J., Carveth, R.A., & Brown, D. (1981). "Television viewing and anxiety: An experimental examination." *Journal of Communication*, 31(1), 106–119.

Eleey, M. (1969). "Variations in generalizability resulting from sampling characteristics of content data: A case study." M.A. Thesis, The Annenberg School of Communications, University of Pennsylvania, Philadelphia.

Ellis, G. T. & Sekura, F., III. (1972). "The effect of aggressive cartoons on the behavior of first grade children." *Journal of Psychology*, 81, 7–43.

Gerbner, G. (1969). "Dimensions of violence in television drama." In R. K. Baker & S. J. Ball (eds.), *Violence in the Media* (pp. 311–340). Staff Report to the National

Commission on the Causes and Prevention of Violence. Washington, DC: Government Printing Office.

Gerbner, G. (1972). "Violence and television drama: Trends and symbolic functions." In G.A. Comstock and E. Rubinstein (eds.), *Television and Social Behavior, Vol. 1, Content and Control.* Washington, DC: U.S. Government Printing Office, 1972, pp. 28–187.

Gerbner, G. (1988). "Violence and terror in the mass media." *Reports and Papers in Mass Communication*, No. 102. Paris: UNESCO.

Gerbner, G. (1988). "Television's cultural mainstream: Which way does it run?" *Directions in Psychiatry*, 8(9). New York: Hatherleigh Co., Ltd.

Gerbner, G. (1993a). "Violence in cable originated television programs." A Report to the National Cable Television Association.

Gerbner, G. (1993b). "'Miracles' of communication technology: Powerful audiences, diverse choices and other fairy tales." In Janet Wasko (ed.), *Illuminating the Blind Spots.* New York: Ablex.

Gerbner, G. (1993c). "Women and minorities on television; A study in casting and fate." A report to the Screen Actors Guild and the American Federation of Television and Radio Artists.

Gerbner, G., Gross, L., Morgan, M. & Signorielli, N. (1980a). "Aging with television: Images on television and conceptions of social reality." *Journal of Communication*, 31(1), 37–47.

Gerbner, G., Gross, L., Morgan, M. & Signorielli, N. (1982). "Charting the mainstream: Television's contributions to political orientations." *Journal of Communication*, 32(2), 100–127.

Gerbner, G., Gross, L., Morgan, M. & Signorielli, N. (1984). "Political correlates of television viewing." *Public Opinion Quarterly*, 48(1), 283–300.

Gerbner, G., Gross, L., Morgan, M., & Signorielli, N. (1993) "Growing up with television: The cultivation perspective." In Jennings Bryant and Dolf Zillmann (eds.), *Media Effects: Advances in Theory and Research.* Hillsdale, NJ: Lawrence Erlbaum Assoc., Inc.

Gerbner, G. & Signorielli, N. (1990) "Violence profile 1967 through 1988–89: Enduring patterns." The Annenberg School for Communication, University of Pennsylvania.

Gross, L. (1984). "The cultivation of intolerance: Television, blacks, and gays." In G. Melischek, C. E. Rosengren, & J. Stappers (eds.), *Cultural Indicators: An International Symposium.* Vienna: Austrian Academy of Sciences.

Hawkins, R. P. & Pingree, S. (1982). "Television's influence on social reality." In D. Pearl, L. Bouthilet, & J. Lazar (eds.), *Television and Behavior: Ten Years of Scientific Progress and Implications for the 80's, Vol. 2, Technical Reports.* Washington, DC: Government Printing Office.

Lovas, O. I. (1961). "Effects of exposure to symbolic aggression on aggressive behavior." *Child Development*, 32, 37–44.

Morgan, M. (1983). "Symbolic victimization and real-world fear." *Human Communication Research*, 9(2), 146–157.

Morgan, M. (1984). "Heavy television viewing and perceived quality of life." *Journalism Quarterly*, 61(3), 499–504.

Morgan, M. & Shanahan, J. (1991). "Do VCRs change the TV picture?: VCRs and the cultivation process." *American Behavioral Scientist*, 35(2), 122–135.

Morgan, M., Shanahan, J., & Harris, C. (1990). "VCRs and the effects of television: New diversity or more of the same?" In J. Dobrow (ed.), *Social and Cultural Aspects of VCR Use* (pp. 107–123). Hillsdale, NJ: Erlbaum.

Morgan, M. & Signorielli, N. (1990). "Cultivation analysis: Conceptualization and methodology." In N. Signorielli & M. Morgan (eds.), *Cultivation Analysis: New Directions in Media Effects Research* (pp. 13–33). Newbury Park, CA: Sage Publications.

Pingree, S. & Hawkins, R. P. (1980). "U.S. programs on Australian television: The cultivation effect." *Journal of Communication*, 31(1), 97–105.

Signorielli, N. (1990). "Television's mean and dangerous world: A continuation of the cultural indicators perspective." In N. Signorielli & M. Morgan (eds.), *Cultivation Analysis: New Directions in Media Effects Research* (pp. 85–105). Newbury Park, CA: Sage Publications.

Signorielli, N., Gross, L., & Morgan, M. (1982). "Violence in television programs: Ten years later." In D. Pearl, L. Bouthilet, & J. Lazar (eds.), *Television and Behavior: Ten Years of Scientific Progress and Implications for the 80's, Vol. 2, Technical Reports* (pp. 154–174). Washington, DC: Government Printing Office.

Srole, L. (1956). "Social integration and certain corollaries: An exploratory study." *American Sociological Review*, 21, 709–712.

Sun, L. (1989). "Limits of selective viewing: An analysis of 'diversity' in dramatic programming." Unpublished Master's Thesis, The Annenberg School for Communication, University of Pennsylvania, Philadelphia.

PART VI

EXTENSIONS OF MESSAGE SYSTEM AND CULTIVATION ANALYSIS

CHAPTER 23

CHARTING THE MAINSTREAM

Television's Contributions to Political Orientations

BY GEORGE GERBNER, LARRY GROSS, MICHAEL MORGAN, AND NANCY SIGNORIELLI

Television is part and parcel of our daily life, investing it with particular meanings. This is a report of research on the political significance of these meanings. It is part of our ongoing project called Cultural Indicators[1] and develops our paradigm of "mainstreaming" first published in this *Journal* (6).

We shall first sketch the theoretical and research context in which we present our findings. Then we shall summarize our theory of television and apply our paradigm to political orientations. We shall use survey data to show television's contributions to political orientations and to attitudes on such issues as minority and civil rights, free speech, government spending, and taxes. The implications of our findings challenge conventional theories of the role of the "press" in the political process, and suggest new ways of thinking about television as well as political research.

Some conception of the role of the "press" has always been a central feature of modern political theory. A secular press of politics and commerce was instrumental in the rise of diverse mass publics independent of church and nobility. The press was (and is) a relatively specific and selectively used organ of the more literate of every class. Freedom of the press to advocate party and group (including class) interests and to cultivate competing and conflicting perspectives was supposed to sustain the political plurality presumably necessary for representative government in a complex society.

The decline of the party press and subsequently of political parties themselves as primary means of communication with voters limits the viability of the theory of the press as a pluralistic ideological advocate. The rise to dominance of a single, market-driven, advertiser-sponsored, and thus ideologically more coherent press system, claiming superior journalistic objectivity and invoking constitutional protection of its freedom to virtually preempt the mass marketplace of ideas, further strains the traditional concept of the role of the press in democratic political theory.

Nevertheless, the print-based and literacy-oriented culture from which our political assumptions stem still offers a possibility of a certain relative diversity of perspectives and selectivity of users. Compared to the historic strains and stresses qualifying the applicability of theories rooted in the print era, the challenge of television, and of the telecommunications system with television at its cultural center, is of a different order of magnitude.[2]

Television is a centralized system of storytelling. Its drama, commercials, news, and other programs bring a relatively coherent world of common images and messages into every viewing home. People are now born into the symbolic environment of television and live with its repetitive lessons throughout life. Television cultivates from the outset the very predispositions that affect future cultural selections and uses. Transcending historic barriers of literacy and mobility, television has become the primary common source of everyday culture of an otherwise heterogeneous population.

Many of those now dependent upon television have never before been part of a shared national political culture. Television provides, perhaps for the first time since preindustrial religion, a strong cultural link, a shared daily ritual of highly compelling and informative content, between the elites and all other publics. What is the role of this common experience in the general socialization and political orientation of Americans? That question of far-reaching social and political importance has not yet been fully addressed.[3]

The reasons for the lag are financial, methodological, and conceptual. The exigencies of social science research inhibit sustained theoretical development based on abundant and varied data collected over extended periods of time. Research methodologies dealing with selective exposure and specifically targeted communication effects have been inadequate to the study of pervasive symbol systems, broad continuities in the symbolic environment, and slow but massive cultural shifts. Research concentration on individual attitude and behavior change has inhibited the investigation of aggregate transformations in the lifestyles of generations (as those born before and after television, or into heavy and light viewing homes) that remain stable for individuals. Finally, focusing political communication research on explicitly "political" communications (or news) has obscured the complex nature of political socialization, especially in the television age, in which the entire spectrum of program types (the bulk of which is drama) plays an integral part.

Our opportunity to address the broader question comes after more than a decade of data collection and analysis mapping the world of television and tracing viewers' conceptions of reality.

The Cultural Indicators project employs a two-pronged research strategy. We call the first message system analysis and the second cultivation analysis. Both relate to—and help develop—a conception of television's historical and institutional position, roles, and functions.

For message system analysis we record and analyze weeklong samples of network television drama and have done so for each year since 1967. We subject these sample weeks of television drama to rigorous and detailed content analysis in order to reliably delineate selected features of the television world. We consider these the potential lessons of television and use them as the source of questions for the second prong of the inquiry. In this "cultivation analysis," we examine the responses of light and heavy viewers to these questions, phrased to refer to the real world. (Non-viewers are too few and demographically too scattered for serious research purposes.) We want to determine whether those who spend more of their time with television are more likely to answer these questions in ways that reflect the potential lessons of the television world (the "television answer") than are groups that watch less television but are otherwise comparable (in terms of important demographic characteristics) to the heavy viewers. We have used the concept of "cultivation" to describe the contributions of television to viewer conceptions. "Cultivation differential" is our term for the difference in the percentage giving the "television answer" within comparable groups of light and heavy viewers.[4]

On issue after issue we have found that the assumptions, beliefs, and values of heavy viewers differ systematically from those of light viewers in the same demographic groups. The differences tend to reflect both what things exist and how things work in the television world. Sometimes these differences hold across the board, meaning that those who watch more television are more likely—in all or most subgroups—to give "television answers" to our questions. But in many cases the patterns are more complex. We have found that television viewing may relate indifferent but consistent ways to different groups' life situations and worldviews. We have named the most general of these consistent patterns "mainstreaming."

The "mainstream" can be thought of as a relative commonality of outlooks and values that exposure to features and dynamics of the television world tends to cultivate. By "mainstreaming" we mean the expression of that commonality by heavy viewers in those demographic groups whose light viewers hold divergent views. In other words, differences found in the responses of different groups of viewers, differences that can be associated with other cultural, social, and political characteristics of these groups, may be diminished or even absent from the responses of heavy viewers in the same groups.[5]

Our concept of cultivation relates the process to those features and dynamics of television content that are the most stable and repetitive parts of the ritual, cutting across different program types. The reason is that heavy viewers watch more of all kinds of programs. Viewer availability determines program ratings and viewing patterns (2). Furthermore, our message system analysis finds such general features as demography, action structure, and fate of characters to be similar in most program types. Therefore, it is these general features and dynamics of the world of prime time, rather than specific programs, that would be likely to cultivate the most pervasive perspectives and orientations of heavy viewers. So to understand, and even to discover, the substance of issues involved in the cultivation process, we must know something about the nature of the mainstream and the institutional context of its creation.

Living with television means growing up in a symbolic environment shaped by service to client institutions.

The creation of that environment is a tightly controlled process. Commercial television is effectively insulated from public access; removed from public participation via direct consumer marketplace, box office, or ballot box; shielded from public governance by current interpretations of the First Amendment; and yet publicly licensed and protected on terms that render the medium dependent on private corporate governance.[6] The economic mechanism guiding that governance is advertising, a tax-deductible business expense, charged to all consumers regardless of their use of the medium. Sponsors pay television (and other media) for attracting and delivering customers and providing other services through news and entertainment. The occasionally unflattering portrayal of business people (probably useful for regaining credibility lost through advertising) only points up the fact that television serves its business clients through delivery, not flattery.

When many millions of dollars of revenue ride on a single ratings point, there are few degrees of freedom to indulge egos or yield to many other pressures. Competition for the largest possible audience at the least cost means striving for the broadest and most conventional appeals, blurring sharp conflicts, blending and balancing competing perspectives, and presenting divergent or deviant images as mostly to be shunned, feared, or suppressed. Otherwise, no matter how skewed or off-center a view might really be, it should be "balanced" by more "extreme" manifestations, preferably on "both sides," to make its presentation appear "objective," "moderate," and otherwise suitable for mass marketing.

These institutional pressures and functions suggest the cultivation of relatively "moderate" or "middle-of-the-road" presentations and orientations. More specific hypotheses can come from the results of the analysis of those features and dynamics of the television message system that may be relevant to the cultivation of those orientations.

Our summary of results is based on the Cultural Indicators message system data bank (unless otherwise noted) and focuses on prime time network programming. The world of prime time as seen by the average viewer is animated by vivid and intimate portrayals of over 300 major characters a week, mostly stock dramatic types, and their weekly rounds of dramatic activities.

Conventional and "normal" though that world may appear, it is in fact far from the reality of anything but consumer values and social power.

The curve of consumer spending, unlike that of income, bulges with middle-class status as well as in middle age. Despite the fact that nearly half of the national income goes to the top fifth of the real population, the myth of middle class as the all-American norm dominates the world of television. Nearly seven out of ten television characters appear in the "middle-middle" of a five-way classification system. Most of them are professionals and managers. Blue-collar and service work occupies 67 percent of all Americans but only 10 percent of television characters. These features of the world of prime time television should cultivate a middle-class or "average" income self-designation among viewers.

Men outnumber women at least three to one. Most women attend to men or home (and appliances) and are younger (but age faster) than the men they meet. Underrepresentation in the world of television suggests the cultivation of viewers' acceptance of more limited life chances, a more limited range of activities, and more rigidly stereotyped images than for the dominant and more fully represented social and dramatic types.

Young people (under 18) comprise one-third and older people (over 65) one-fifth of their true proportion in the population. Blacks on television represent three-fourths and Hispanics one-third of their share of the U.S. population, and a disproportionate number are minor rather than major characters. A single program like "Hawaii Five-O" can result in the overrepresentation of Orientals, but again mostly as minor characters. A study by Weigel and others (17) shows that while blacks appear in many programs and commercials they seldom appear with whites, and actually interact with whites in only about 2 percent of total human appearance time. The prominent and stable overrepresentation of well-to-do white males in the prime of life dominates prime time. Television's general demography bears greater resemblance to the facts of consumer spending than to the U.S. Census (9, 10). These facts and dynamics of life suggest the cultivation of a relatively restrictive view of women's and minority rights among viewers.

The state in the world of prime time acts mostly to fend off threats to law and order in a mean and dangerous world.

Enforcing the law of that world takes nearly three times as many characters as the number of all blue-collar and service worker characters. The typical viewer of an average week's prime time programs sees realistic and often intimate (but usually not true-to-life) representations of the life and work of 30 police officers, 7 lawyers, and 3 judges, but only 1 engineer or scientist and very few blue-collar workers. Nearly everybody appears to be comfortably managing on an "average" income or as a member of a "middle class."

But threats abound. Crime in prime time is at least ten times as rampant as in the real world. An average of five to six acts of overt physical violence per hour involves over half of all major characters. Yet, pain, suffering, and medical help rarely follow this mayhem. Symbolic violence demonstrates power; it shows victimization, not just aggression, hurt but not therapy; it shows who can get away with what against whom. The dominant white males in the prime of life score highest on the "safety scale"; they are the most likely to be the victimizers rather than the victims. Conversely, old, young, and minority women, and young boys, are the most likely to be the victims rather than the victimizers in violent conflicts.

What might be the "television answers" relevant for political orientations?

The warped demography of the television world cultivates some iniquitous concepts of the norms of social life. Except among the most traditional or biased, television viewing tends to go with stronger prejudices about women and old people (9, 10, 12, 14). Children know more about uncommon occupations frequently portrayed on television than about common jobs rarely seen on the screen (4). Viewing boosts the confidence rating given to doctors (16) but depresses that given to scientists, especially in groups that otherwise support them most (8).

Cultivation studies continue to confirm the findings that viewing tends to heighten perceptions of danger and risk and maintain an exaggerated sense of mistrust, vulnerability, and insecurity. We have also found that the prime time power hierarchy of relative levels of victimization cultivates similar hierarchies of fears of real-world victimization among viewers. Those minority group viewers who see themselves more often on the losing end of violent encounters on television are more apprehensive of their own victimization than are the light viewers in the same groups (13). Television's mean and dangerous world can thus be expected to contribute to receptivity to repressive measures and to apparently simple, tough, hard-line posturings and "solutions." At the same time, however, the overall context of conventional values and consumer gratifications, with their requirements of happy endings and material satisfaction, may suggest a sense of entitlement to goods and services, setting up a conflict of perspectives.

Thus we can expect the cultivation of preference for "middle-of-the-road" political orientations alongside different and at times contradictory assumptions. These assumptions are likely to include demographically skewed, socially rigid and mistrustful, and often excessively anxious or repressive notions, but expansive expectations for economic services and material progress even among those who traditionally do not share such views.

As most of our discussion revolves around differences among light, medium, and heavy viewers in otherwise comparable groups in giving "television answers," it will be useful to describe these groups.

The analyses presented here utilize data from the General Social Survey (GSS) of the National Opinion Research Center for 1975, 1977, 1978, and 1980. About 1,500 respondents took part in hour-long personal interviews each year, for a total of 6,020 respondents.[7] For purposes of analysis respondents have been divided into light viewers (24.6%) who said they watch a daily average of less than two hours; medium viewers (45.3%) who said they watch either two or three hours; and heavy viewers (30.1%) who said they watch four or more hours a day.[8]

Differences in amounts of viewing are of course rooted in the way people live. The heavy-viewing segment of the population includes a disproportionate number of women, young and old people, non-college-educated, and lower-income persons (see Table 1). Conversely, relatively more men and middle-aged, college-educated, and higher-income persons tend to be lighter viewers.[9]

It is evident, therefore, that simple comparisons of light, medium, and heavy viewers involve more than television. In order to isolate the independent contribution of television viewing to the cultivation of political orientations, it is necessary to control for other factors and to compare viewing-related differences in relatively homogeneous subgroups. All findings reported in this article include such controls.

Table 1. Relationship Between Amount of Television Viewing and Demographic Variables

	Television Viewing[a]					
	Light %	*Medium* %	*Heavy* %	*Gamma*	*Simple[b]* *r*	*4th order partial r*
Sex						
Male (N=2638)	50	46	37			
			.16***	.12***	.09***	
Female (N=3352)	50	54	63			
Age						
18–29 (N=1531)	24	24	31			
30–54 (N=2598)	51	46	34	.03	.02	-.06***
55+ (N=1834)	25	30	36			
Education						
No College (N=4077)	54	67	82			
			-.38***	-.19***	-.14***	
Some College (N=1893)	46	33	18			
Income						
Low (N=2060)	31	33	49			
Medium (N=1971)	35	37	33	-.23***	-.19***	-.12***
High (N=1543)	35	30	18			
Region						
Urban (N=2618)	45	43	43			
			.03	-.02	-.02	
Non-urbans (N=3372)	55	57	57			

***p <.001

[a] TV viewing: light=0–1 hours per day; medium=2–3 hours per day; heavy=over 4 hours per day

[b] Simple and partial correlations are based on continuous data; partials are based on simultaneous controls for all other demographic variables in table.

Subgroup differences in each viewing group enable us to specify the differential as well as the common dynamics of television viewing.[10]

In this article we refine and apply the paradigm of mainstreaming to political orientations.

We will advance and illustrate some propositions about television's contribution to class and political self-identification. We will examine the political dynamics of television through the analysis of the positions of heavy and light viewers of different political tendencies, simultaneously controlling for a wide range of other influences and factors.

Political party affiliation is traditionally related to social status. Therefore, it is not surprising that among heavy viewers, who tend to have lower status, we find more Democrats than among light viewers (45% to 35%), while proportionately more light than heavy viewers are Independents (41 to 34%) and Republicans (24 to 21% We will see, however, that television alters the social significance and political meaning of these and other conventional labels.

An example of this transformation is the blurring of class lines and the self-styled "averaging" of income differences. Table 2, illustrated on Figure 1, shows that low socioeconomic status (SES) respondents are most likely to call themselves "working class"—but only when they are light viewers. Heavy-viewing respondents of the same low-status group are significantly less likely than their light-viewing counterparts to think of themselves as "working class" and more likely to say they are "middle class." The television experience seems to counter other circumstances in thinking of one's class. It is an especially powerful deterrent to working-class consciousness.

Table 2. Relationship Between Amount of Television Viewing and Subjective Class Identification, and Perception of Family Income as Average

	Television Viewing				
	Light %	*Medium* %	*Heavy* %	*CD*[c]	*Gamma*
Subjective class identification[a] by actual SES[b] (N=5239)					
Low SES					
Working class	65	64	55	-10	.06*
Middle class	25	28	32	+7	
Medium SES					
Working class	55	58	55	0	-.07*
Middle class	42	39	38	-4	
High SES					
Working class	25	29	36	+11	-14***
Middle class	68	66	59	-9	
Percent who say their family income is "average," by actual family income (N=5541)					
Under $10,000	43	44	43	0	-.05*
$10-$20,000	62	65	66	+4	-.13***
Over $20,000	38	47	60	+22	-.26***

*p<.05
***p<.001
[a] "Lower" and "upper" class responses omitted because of small number of cases.
[b] Based on trichotomization of weighted factor scores of education, income, and occupational prestige.
[c] CD=Cultivation Differential: percent of heavy viewers giving response minus percent of light viewers giving response.

Figure 1. Class and Income Self-Designations by Television Viewing Within Actual SES/Income Groups

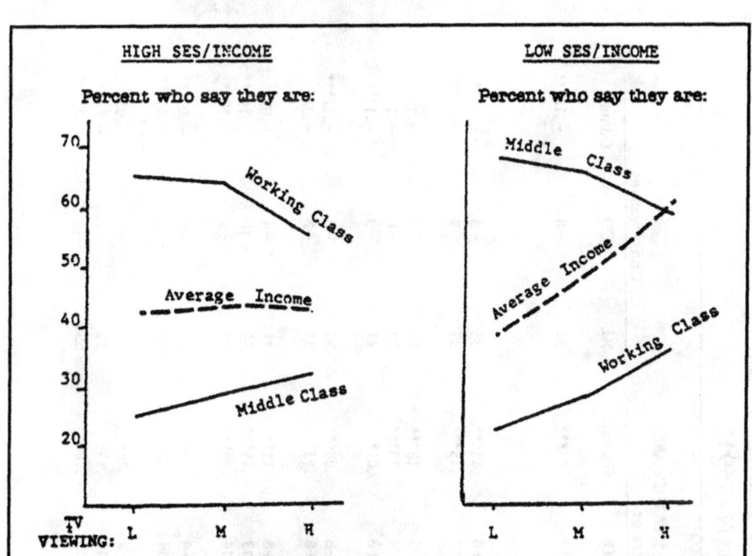

Middle SES viewers show the least sense of class distinction at different viewing levels. They are already "in" the mainstream. The high SES group, however, like the low SES group, exhibits a response pattern that is strongly associated with amount of television viewing. More high SES heavy viewers consider themselves to be "working class" than do high SES light viewers.[12] Television viewing tends to blur class distinctions and make more affluent heavy viewers think of themselves as just working people of average income.

These processes show up clearly when we relate television viewing to labels of direct political relevance. We used a relatively general and presumably stable designation of political tendency, most likely to structure a range of political attitudes and positions: the self-designations "liberal," "moderate," and "conservative."[13] We are assuming that the GSS respondents and, indeed, most of us, locate political positions on a continuum ranging from liberal to conservative (if not farther in either direction), owing in part to the generally accepted and commonplace use of these terms in interpersonal and mass media discourse. Consequently, unlike many things respondents might be asked about, we believe that these self-designations have a prior existence and are not created in response to the interview situation.

Table 3 shows the percentage of light viewers in each political tendency category and the percentage spread between them and heavy viewers both by demographic classifications and party affiliation. The most general relationship between television viewing and political tendency is that significantly more heavy than light viewers in all subgroups call themselves moderates and significantly fewer call themselves conser-

Table 3. Relationship Between Amount of Television Viewing and Political Self-Designation (N=5691)

	PERCENT WHO SAY THEY ARE:								
	Liberals			Moderates			Conservatives		
	%L[a]	CD[b]	Gamma	%L	CD	Gamma	%L	CD	Gamma
OVERALL	31	−3	−.04*	33	+12	.15***	36	−8	−.12***
Controlling for:									
Sex									
Male	33	−1	−.01	30	+8	.11***	38	−8	−.10**
Female	29	−3	−.05	36	+12	.15***	35	−9	−.13***
Age									
Under 30	45	−7	−.09*	30	+13	.18***	26	−7	−.13**
30–54	29	−5	−.09*	32	+14	.18***	39	−8	−.11***
55+	20	+3	.07	39	+6	.07*	41	−9	−.12**
Education									
No college	24	+2	.04	41	+6	.08**	35	−8	−.12***
Some college	38	−1	−.05	25	+8	.13***	37	−7	−.07*
Income									
Low	34	−4	−.06	35	+8	.11**	31	−4	−.07*
Medium	29	−3	−.04	35	+13	.16***	36	−10	−.14***
High	31	−5	−.10*	30	+14	.19***	39	−9	−.10**
Region									
Urban	36	−3	−.04	31	+9	.12***	33	−6	−.09***
Non-urban	26	−2	−.04	34	+14	.17***	40	−12	−.15***
Party affiliation									
Democrat	37	−6	−.06*	37	+7	.08**	27	−2	−.03
Independent	34	−7	−.11**	33	+14	.19***	33	−7	−.11**
Republican	16	+5	.11**	29	+13	.18***	55	−18	−.23***

* $p < .05$ (tau)
** $p < .01$ (tau)
*** $p < .001$ (tau)

[a] %L = percent of light viewers giving response.
[b] CD = Cultivation Differential: percent of heavy viewers giving response minus percent of light viewers giving response.

Figure 2. Political Self-Designation by Amount of Television Viewing, Within Party Categories

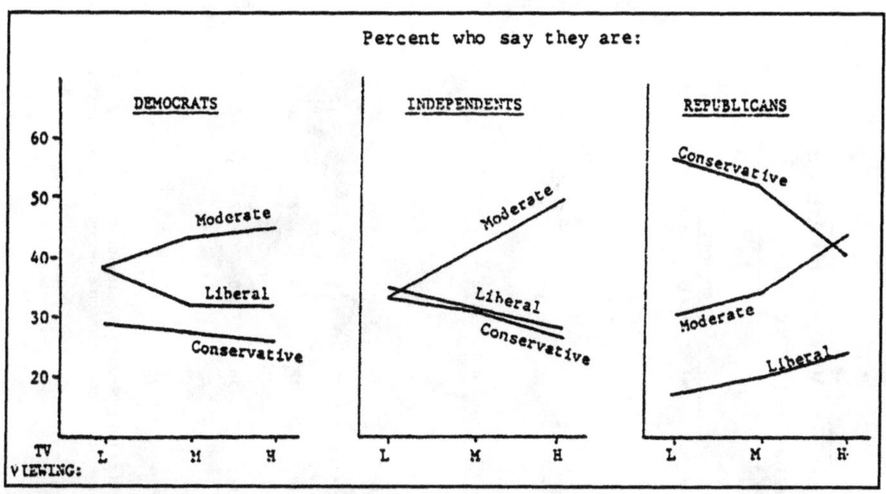

vatives.[14] The number of liberals also declines slightly among heavy viewers, except where there are the fewest liberals (e.g., among Republicans). Figure 2 illustrates the absorption of divergent tendencies and the blending of political distinctions into the "television mainstream."[15]

On the surface, mainstreaming appears to be a "centering"—even a "liberalizing"—of political and other tendencies. After all, as viewing increases, the percentage of conservatives drops significantly within every group (except Democrats), and the relationships of amount of television viewing with the percentage of liberals are generally weaker. However, a closer look at the actual positions taken in response to questions about political issues such as minorities, civil and personal rights, free speech, the economy, etc., shows that the mainstream does not always mean "middle of the road."

Eight questions about attitudes toward blacks were asked in at least two of the four GSS years analyzed here, and explicitly assess respondents; desire to keep blacks and whites separate.

Questions include, "Do you think that white students and black students should go to the same schools or to separate schools?" and "Do you think that there should be laws against marriages between blacks and whites?" Table 4 summarizes the relationships between amount of television viewing and these eight items, for self-designated liberals, moderates, and conservatives. Light viewing liberals are always least likely to endorse segregationist statements. Light viewing moderates and conservatives are, interestingly, often very close; in more than one instance, light viewing moderates are slightly *more* likely to support racial segregation than are light viewing conservatives.

Table 4. Summary of Relationships Between Amount of Television Viewing and Attitudes Toward Blacks, Controlling for Political Self-Designation (Whites Only)

	Liberals			Moderates			Conservatives			Int.
Percent who:	%L[a]	CD[b]	Gamma	%L	CD	Gamma	%L	CD	Gamma	beta[c]
Favor laws against interracial marriage (N = 3716)	13	+22	.38***	31	+10	.14***	32	+9	.12**	.15**
Would object if a black were brought to dinner (N = 2511)	13	+11	.24***	22	+7	.09*	26	+7	.10*	.02
Strongly agree: blacks shouldn't push where not wanted (N = 3715)	25	+15	,21***	43	+7	.10**	38	+12	.15***	.08
Strongly agree: whites have right to segregate neighborhood (N = 2474)	10	+9	.23**	14	+8	.15**	22	+1	.04	.17**
Are against open housing laws (N = 3743)	43	+12	.15**	63	−1	−.03	70	−1	−.01	.13**
Are against busing (N = 3670)	73	+6	.13*	87	−5	−.16**	93	−5	−.17**	−.11*
Would not vote for black for president (N = 3639)	8	+12	.29***	18	0	.01	17	+9	.17**	.03
Believe whites and blacks should go to separate schools (N = 2498)	6	+11	.35***	12	+1	.06	16	0	−.02	−.07

* $p < .05$
** $p < .01$
*** $p < .001$

[a] %L = percent of light viewers giving response.
[b] CD = Cultivation Differential: percent of heavy viewers giving response minus percent of light viewers giving response.
[c] Interaction beta = interaction of amount of viewing and political self-designation, with age, sex, education, income, region, and main effects of viewing and self-designation in equation.

Figure 3. Television Viewing and Attitudes About Blacks, by Political Self-Designation

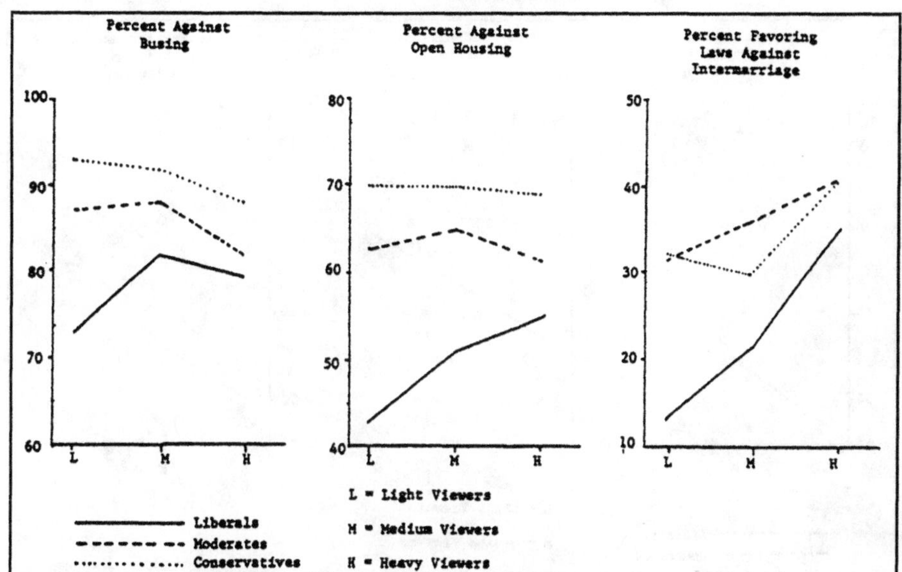

More importantly, associations between amount of viewing and these attitudes are sharply different for liberals, moderates, and conservatives. Liberals, who are least likely to hold segregationist views, show some dramatic (and always significant) associations between amount of viewing and the desire to keep blacks and whites separate. Among moderates and conservatives, in contrast, the relationships between viewing and these attitudes are smaller and inconsistent. (Four of the interaction terms are significant, showing the correlates of heavy viewing to be systematically different across political categories.) On busing, moderates and conservatives even show a significant negative association, indicating less segregationist attitudes among these heavy viewers; this is an instance of viewing bringing divergent groups closer together from both directions.

In general, these patterns vividly illustrate mainstreaming. There are, to be sure, some across-the-board relationships, but even these are markedly weaker for moderates and conservatives. Overall, these data show a convergence and homogenization of heavy viewers across political groups.

The differences between liberals and conservatives—i.e., the effects of political tendency on attitudes toward blacks—decrease among heavy viewers. Among light viewers, liberals and conservatives show an average difference of 15.4 percentage points; yet, among heavy viewers, liberals and conservatives differ by an average of only 4.6 percentage points ($t=4.54$, $p < .01$).

Figure 3 shows the mainstreaming pattern for three of these items. In the first, opposition to busing, we can see that heavy viewing conservatives are more "liberal" and heavy viewing liberals more "conservative than their respective light viewing

Figure 4. Television Viewing and Attitudes Toward Personal Conduct, by Political and Self-Designation

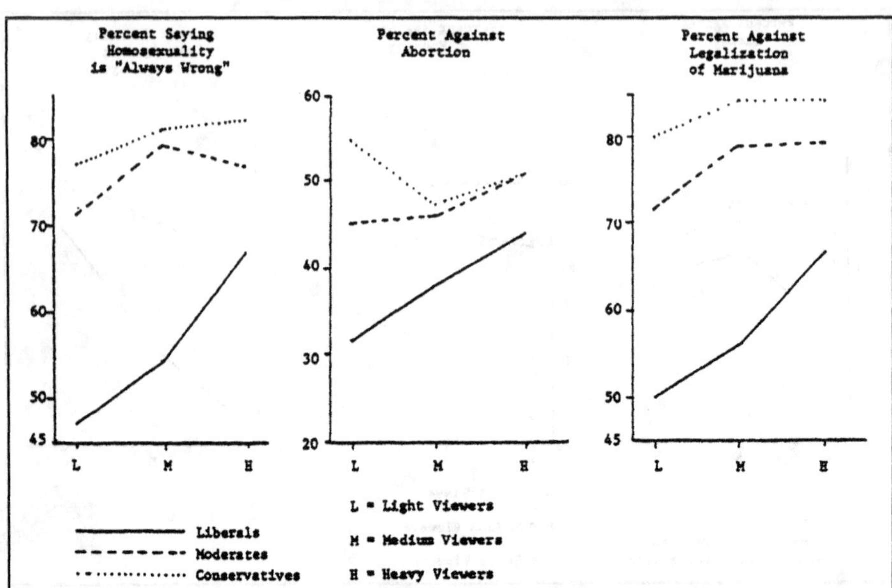

counterparts. In the second instance, opposition to open housing laws, viewing is not associated with any differences in the attitudes expressed by conservatives, but among liberals we see that heavy viewing goes with a greater likelihood of such opposition. Finally, in response to a question about laws against marriages between blacks and whites, we find that heavy viewers in all groups are more likely to favor these laws than are light viewers in the same categories, but this is significantly more pronounced for liberals.

In sum, the responses of heavy viewing liberals are quite comparable to those of all moderates and conservatives, and there is not much difference between moderates and conservatives. The television mainstream, in terms of attitudes toward blacks, clearly runs to the right.[16]

Many of the fiercest political battles of the past decade have been fought on the nation's "home front"—around a group of so-called moral issues which have sharply divided liberal and conservative forces.

We find liberals confronting conservatives over the propriety, morality, and even legality of personal behavior. The fights involving reproductive freedom, the rights of sexual minorities, and the Equal Rights Amendment have become a focus of that confrontation.

Our view of television is a stabilizing force, seeking to attract the largest possible audience by celebrating the "moderation" of the mainstream, which leads us to expect that heavy viewers, once again, will show a convergence of attitudes on issues of personal morality. We expect to find that self-designated moderates and conservatives are generally close together regardless of television viewing, and that heavy viewing liberals take up positions alongside moderates and conservatives.

Table 5 supports our predictions.[17] In the case of attitudes on homosexuality, abortion, and marijuana, there is considerable spread between light-viewing liberals and light viewing conservatives (an average of 28 percentage points); the latter are always much more likely to be opposed. And, once again, the attitudes of heavy-viewing liberals and conservatives are far closer together (an average of 13 percentage points; $t = 16.6$, $p < .01$), due primarily to the difference between light and heavy viewing liberals. (All interaction terms are significant.) In all instances, the self-designated moderates are much closer to the conservatives than they are to the liberals (see Figure 4).[18]

Table 5. Relationship Between Amount of Television Viewing and Attitudes Toward Personal Conduct, Controlling for Political Self-Designation

	Television Viewing					
Percentage of respondents:	*Light* %	*Medium* %	*Heavy* %	*CD*[a]	*Gamma*	*Int. beta*[b]
Saying homosexuality is always wrong (N=2736)						
Liberals	47	54	67	+20	.25***	
Moderates	71	79	77	+6	.08	-.19**
Conservatives	77	81	82	+5	.09	
Against abortion (N=5691)						
Liberals	32	38	44	+12	.16***	
Moderates	45	46	51	+6	.08*	-.18***
Conservatives	55	47	51	-4	-.05	
Against legalization of marijuana (N=4088)						
Liberals	50	56	67	+17	.22***	
Moderates	72	79	79	+7	.09*	-.18***
Conservatives	80	84	84	+4	.08	

*$p < .05$
**$p < .01$
***$p < .001$
[a]CD=Cultivation Differential percent of heavy viewers giving response minus percent of light viewers giving response.
[b]Interaction of amount of television viewing and political self-designation with age, education, income, race, sex, region, and amount of viewing and political self-designation in equation.

The narrowing of the political spectrum is also revealed in some more explicitly "political" findings.

Whatever its reasons and justifications, anti-communism has been used as the principal rationale for political repression since the first Red Scare of 1919–1920.

Responses to several GSS questions tap television's relationship to anti-Communist sentiments and to the tendency to restrict free speech.[19]

Table 6 shows the familiar pattern (illustrated on Figure 5). Five out of ten light viewing moderates and six out of ten light-viewing conservatives consider communism "the worst form [of government] of all." Heavy viewing moderates and conservatives nearly unite in condemning communism as "worst" by even larger margins (64 and 67%, respectively). But viewing makes the biggest difference among liberals: only one-third of light viewing but half of heavy viewing liberals agree that communism is "the worst form" of government (The interaction of amount of viewing with political self-designation is significant over and above all controls and main effects; beta = -.15, $p < .05$.) Responses on restricting free speech show similar patterns. Heavy viewers of all three political persuasions are more likely to agree to

Table 6. Relationship Between Amount of Television Viewing and Attitudes Toward Communism and Free Speech, Controlling for Political Self-Designation

	Television Viewing					
	Light %	*Medium* %	*Heavy* %	*CD*[a]	*Gamma*	*Int. beta*[b]
Communism is the worst form of government (N=2812)						
Liberals	34	45	49	+15	.19***	
Moderates	51	61	64	+13	.15**	-.15*
Conservatives	60	61	67	+7	.08	
Willingness to curtail freedom of speech of[c]	*Light* X	*Medium* X	*Heavy* X			
Left (N=2505)						
Liberals	2.04	2.66	3.95***			
Moderates	3.81	4.06	4.40			-.29***
Conservatives	4.24	4.42	4.29			
Right (N=2633)						
Liberals	1.71	2.07	2.83***			
Moderates	2.78	2.99	3.14			-.22***
Conservatives	2.79	3.01	3.03			

*p< .05
**p< .01
***p< .001
[a]CD=Cultivation Differential: percent of heavy viewers giving response minus percent of light viewers giving response.
[b] Interaction of amount of viewing and political self-designation with age, education, income, race, sex, region, and amount of viewing and political self-designation in equation.
[c] Scales for mean values of indices are explained in text footnote 19.

Figure 5. Television Viewing and Attitudes Toward Communism and Free Speech, by Political Self-Designation

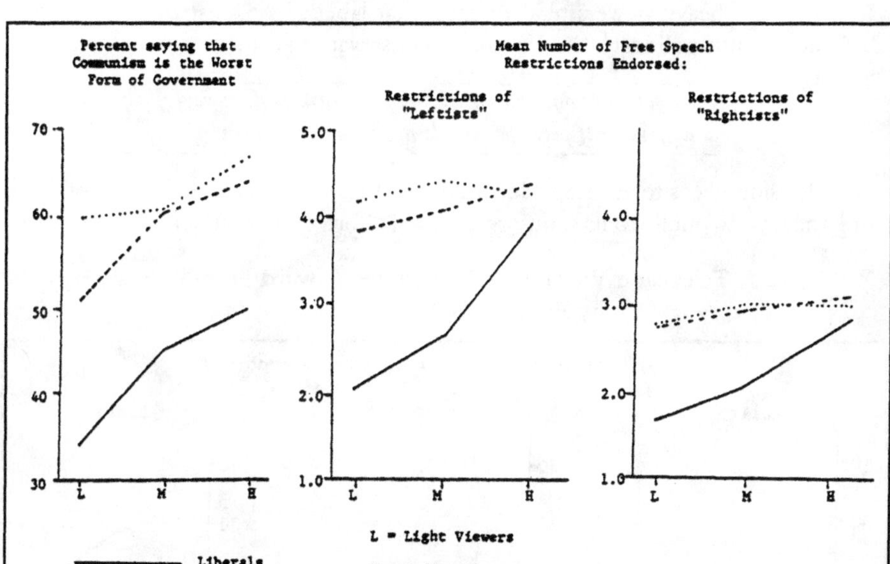

restrict, in various ways, the speech of "left" and "right" nonconformists than are their light viewing counterparts. There is little difference between conservatives and moderates. But, again, the most striking difference is between light and heavy viewing liberals.

In general, with respect to anti-communism and restrictions on political speech of the left and right, those who call themselves conservatives are in the "television mainstream." Those who consider themselves moderates join the conservatives—or exceed them—as heavy viewers. Liberals perform their traditional role of defending political plurality and freedom of speech only when they are light viewers. Mainstreaming means not only a narrowing of political differences but also a significant tilt in the political balance.[20]

But political drift to the right is not the full story. As we noted before, television has a business clientele which, while it may be politically conservative, also has a mission to perform that requires the cultivation of consumer values and gratifications pulling in a different direction.

A number of surveys have documented the tendency of respondents to support government services that benefit them while taking increasingly hard-line positions on taxes, equality, crime, and other issues that touch deeply felt anxieties and insecurities. The media interpreted (and election results seemed to confirm, at least in the early 1980s) these inherently contradictory positions as a "conservative trend" (5). Television may have contributed to that trend in two ways. First, as our Violence Profiles have demonstrated, heavy viewers have a keener sense of living in a "mean world" with greater hazards and insecurities than do comparable groups of light viewers (6, 13). Second, while television does not directly sway viewers to be conservative (in fact, heavy viewers tend to shun that label), its mainstream of apparent moderation shifts political attitudes toward conservative position.

When positions on economic issues are examined, however, a different if perhaps complementary pattern emerges.

Television needs to attract a wide following to perform its principal task of delivering the buying public to its sponsors. It could afford even less than most politicians

Figure 6. Television Viewing and Attitudes Toward Federal Spending, by Political Self-Designation

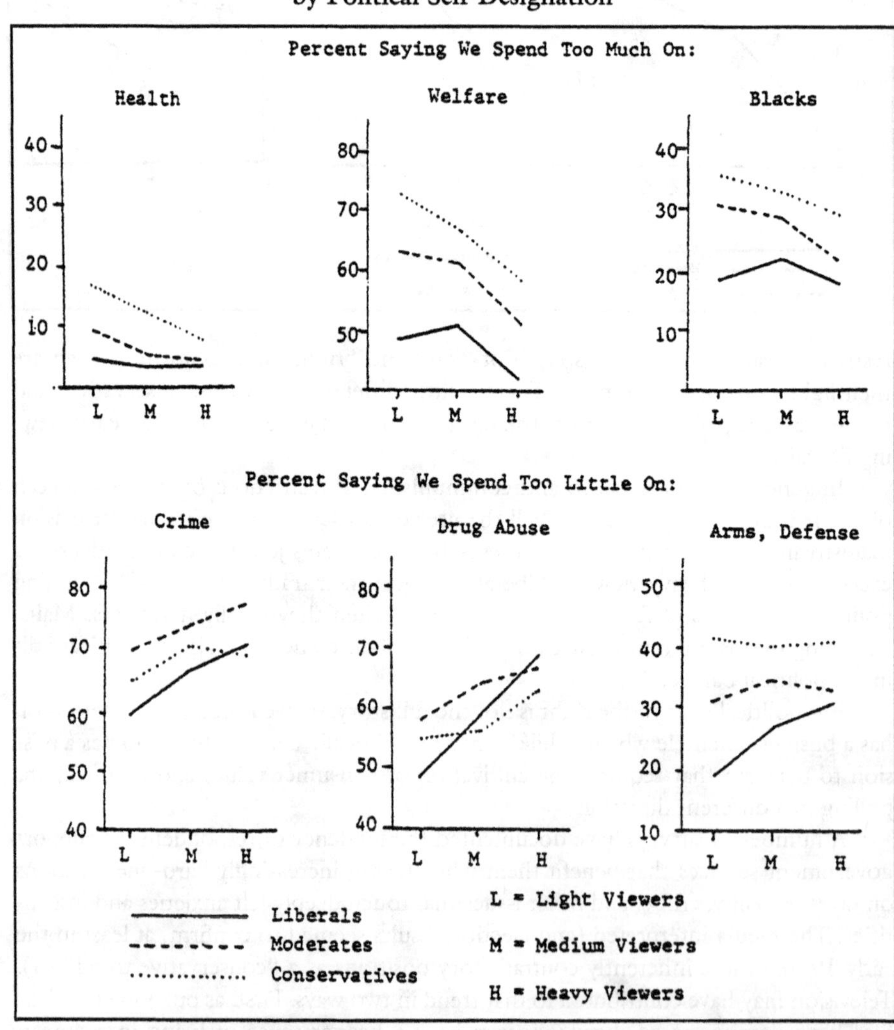

to project austerity, to denigrate popular bread-and-butter issues, or to urge saving instead of spending for goods, services, and security. The essential mission of the television institution—mass mobilization for consumption—would seem to dictate an economically popular and even populist stance.

We examined patterns of responses to questions about government spending on eleven programs. The results are shown in Table 7. Seven are traditional "liberal" issues: health, environment, cities, education, foreign aid, welfare, and blacks.[21] The percentages of light, medium, and heavy viewers in the three political categories who say the United States spends "too much" on health, welfare, and blacks are shown on the top of Figure 6.

Here, instead of heavy viewing liberals taking positions closer to conservatives, the opposite happens: heavy viewing conservatives, as well as moderates, converge toward the liberal position on six of the seven issues. The more they watch, the less they say the United States spends "too much." On these six issues, the average distance of 16 percentage points between liberal and conservative light viewers is only 9 percentage points for heavy viewers, with conservatives accounting for most of the convergence ($t=8.2$, $p< .001$). The exception is the relatively distant issue of foreign aid.

The remaining four issues are crime, drugs, defense, and space exploration. Percentages of respondents who say the United States is spending "too little" on the first three issues can be seen on the bottom of Figure 6. Here again, with the exception of space, heavy viewers generally want to spend more. As these are somewhat more "conservative" issues, it is the moderates and conservatives who are in the "television mainstream," taking a position toward greater spending, and heavy viewing liberals stand close to them. On these four issues, an average liberal-conservative spread of nearly 10 percentage points for light viewers compares with a gap of 4 percentage points among heavy viewers ($t=2.2$, $p< .12$).

To investigate further the populist streak in the otherwise restrictive political mix of the typology of the heavy viewer, we looked for questions that combine outlooks on both taxes and spending. The 1980 GSS permitted us to isolate those respondents who oppose reductions in government spending and yet feel their taxes are too high.[22] As shown in Table 8, heavy viewers are more likely to express this contradictory position in every subgroup (although the relationship remains significant at $p< .05$ only overall and within six of these groups). Figure 7 illustrates the political lineup.

As on the other economic issues, liberals and moderates are close together while heavy viewing conservatives join the liberal-moderate mainstream; the tilt is in the liberal (if conflicted) direction. Heavy viewing Republicans and Independents also express attitudes closer to the Democratic position than do their light viewing political counterparts. But all heavy viewers are more likely to want a combination of more social spending *and* lower taxes.

Is "commercial populism" the new American melting pot?

The cultural—and evidently political—television mainstream tends to absorb the divergent tendencies that traditionally shaped the political process and to contain its own cross-currents. Heavy television viewers tend more than comparable light viewers

Table 7. Relationship Between Amount of Television Viewing and Attitudes Toward Federal Spending, Controlling for Political Self-Designation

	Television Viewing					
% saying we spend too much on:	*Light* %	*Medium* %	*Heavy* %	*CD*[a]	*Gamma*	*Int. beta*[b]
Health (N=5478)						
Liberals	5	3	3	-2	-.16	
Moderates	9	5	4 -	5	.-22**	-.15**
Conservatives	17	11	8 -	9	-.25***	
Environment (N=5387)						
Liberals	7	7	8	+1	.03	
Moderates	14	10	9	-5	-.15**	-.19***
Conservatives	22	20	13	-9	-.16***	
Cities (N=4983)						
Liberals	13	15	15	+2	.06	
Moderates	23	20	16	-7	-.14**	-.11*
Conservatives	31	28	27	-4	-.07	
Education (N=5492)						
Liberals	7	9	7	0 -	.02	
Moderates	10	9	8	-2	-.11*	-.14**
Conservatives	20	16	14	-6	-.14**	
Foreign aid (N=5398)						
Liberals	70	70	69	-1	-.01	
Moderates	71	75	74	+3	.04	.08*
Conservatives	73	74	79	+6	.09*	
Welfare (N=5454)						
Liberals	48	51	43	-5	-.06	
Moderates	62	61	52	-10	-.15***	-.06
Conservatives	71	66	58	-13	-.17***	
Blacks (N=5275)						
Liberals	19	21	17	-2	-.04	
Moderates	30	28	22	-8	-.13**	-.06
Conservatives	35	33	29	-6	.07*	
% saying we spend too little on:						
Crime (N=5419)						
Liberals	58	66	70	+12	.17***	
Moderates	69	74	77	+8	.11**	-.09*
Conservatives	65	70	69	+4	.05	
Drugs (N=5317)						
Liberals	48	58	68	+20	.26***	
Moderates	57	64	67	+10	.12**	-.01
Conservatives	55	56	64	+9	.11**	
Arms (N=5328)						
Liberals	18	27	31	+13	.21***	
Moderates	32	35	33	+1	.00	-.15***
Conservatives	41	40	41	0	.01	
Space (N=5385)						
Liberals	20	16	10	-10	-.23***	
Moderates	10	10	8	-2	-.08	.04
Conservatives	18	15 9	-9	-9	-.21***	

*p< .05 **p< .01 *** p< .001

[a] and [b] : See definitions in Table 6.

Table 8. Percent of Respondents Who Oppose Spending Cuts and Reductions in Services But Feel Their Taxes Are Too High, by Television Viewing (N=1220)

	Television Viewing				
	Light %	*Medium* %	*Heavy* %	*CD*[c]	*Gamma*
OVERALL	29	31	38	+9	.13**
Controlling for:					
Sex					
Male	26	26	36	+10	.14*
Female	32	35	39	+7	.10 (p=.07)
Age					
Under 30	35	32	44	+9	.14 (p=.07)
30–54	27	35	41	+14	.19**
55+	26	22	29	+3	.08
Education					
No college	36	32	40	+4	.09 (p=.08)
Some college	23	28	29	+6	.12 (p=.08)
Income					
Low	31	32	37	+6	.10
Medium	28	29	40	+12	.18*
High	28	30	35	+7	.10
Region					
Urban	29	29	40	+11	.16*
Non-urban	29	32	36	+7	.10 (p=.07)
Party affiliation					
Democrat	40	35	4	2	+2 .04
Independent	24	31	38	+14	.19**
Republican	20	22	30	+10	.17 (p=.07)
Political self-designation					
Liberal	36	32	44	+8	.11
Moderate	32	33	37	+5	.07
Conservative	20	26	30	+10	.16*

*$p < .05$

**$p < .01$

[a]CD=Cultivation Differential: percent of heavy viewers giving response minus percent of light viewers giving response.

to call themselves "moderate" but take positions that are unmistakably conservative, except on economic issues.

Our analysis shows that although television viewing brings conservatives, moderates, and liberals closer together, it is the liberal position that is weakest among heavy viewers. Viewing blurs traditional differences, blends them into a more homogeneous mainstream, and bends the mainstream toward a "hard line" position on issues dealing with minorities and personal rights. Hard-nosed commercial populism,

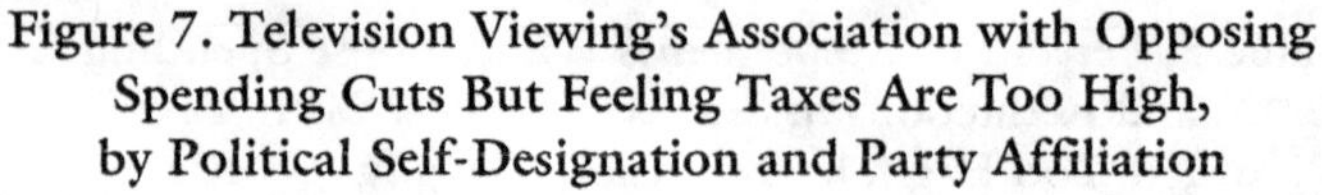

Figure 7. Television Viewing's Association with Opposing Spending Cuts But Feeling Taxes Are Too High, by Political Self-Designation and Party Affiliation

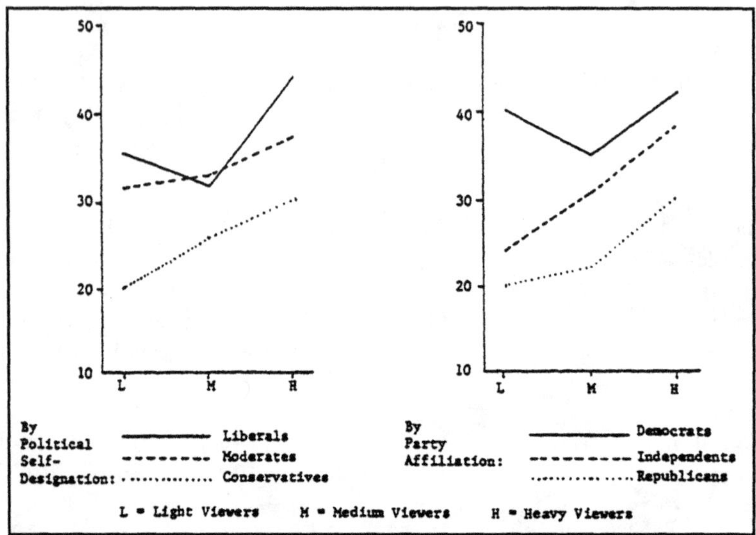

with its mix of restrictive conservatism and pork-chop liberalism, is the paradoxical—and potentially volatile—contribution of television to political orientations.

The "television mainstream" may be the true twentieth-century melting pot of the American people. The mix it creates is of central significance for the theory as well as the practice of popular self-government. If our charting of the mainstream is generally valid, basic assumptions about political orientations, the media, and the domestic process need to be reviewed and revised to fit the age of television.

NOTES

1. The project began in 1967–1968 with a study for the National Commission on the Causes and Prevention of Violence. It continued under the sponsorships of the U.S. Surgeon General's Scientific Advisory Committee on Television and Social Behavior, the National Institute of Mental Health, the White House Office of Telecommunications Policy, the American Medical Association, the U.S. Administration on Aging, and the National Science Foundation.
2. New communications technologies are more likely to extend than to transform that challenge. They will sharpen the aim and deepen the penetration of telecommunications culture-power into new areas now served mostly (and often less efficiently or more expensively) by print. The over-the-air mass ritual now called television has become essential to commerce, acculturation, and governance. It is most likely to remain basically intact alongside the resurgence of print by electronic means, and to become the object of increasingly sharp contest for control.

3. The work of Chaffee, Graber, Mannheim, Patterson, Robinson, and others (see, e.g., 11) has established the relevance of television to political orientations and provides a useful starting point for this study.
4. Earlier reports focused on dramatic demonstrations of social power and personal risk (the "Violence Profiles"). In recent years we have used our cumulative data bank of detailed observations based on the analysis of over 1,600 programs and 14,000 characters, and our own surveys, as well as the extensive archives of survey data available for secondary analysis, to investigate television portrayals and related viewer conceptions of women and minorities, aging, scientists and members of other professions, health and medicine, sexual depictions, family images and impact, educational achievement and aspirations, and other issues. Our data collection has been broadly conceived from the beginning so as to permit the analysis of many different trends and features of the world of television and their relationships to the conceptions and attitudes of various groups of viewers.
5. Mainstreaming has been found to explain differential within-group patterns in terms of the cultivation of images of violence, mistrust, and alienation (6); conceptions of science and scientists (8); health-related beliefs and practices (7); sex-role stereotypes (14); and other issues.
6. The work of Barnouw (1), Cantor (3), and Tuchman (15) describes in detail the institutional policy process.
7. The 1975 sample was drawn through a combination of block quotas and probability sampling; the samples for the other three years were full probability. The samples represent English-speaking, noninstitutionalized persons 18 years and older (see the GSS 1972–1980 cumulative codebook for full details on sampling and other issues).
8. The independent variable in these analyses is amount of television exposure, in hours. The actual question is, "On the average day, about how many hours do you personally watch television?" This measure is not interpreted as providing absolutely accurate reports of average viewing hours. Rather, we see it as an indicator of relative exposure to and immersion in the world of television. This distribution varies by no more than 3.5 percentage points within any of the four years. For the four years combined, respondents' mean amount of viewing is 2.92 hours (s.d.=2.17), and the median is 2.48. Thirty cases (0.5% of the entire sample) have missing data.
9. These patterns are generally independent of the other demographic factors, though they are slightly reduced under simultaneous controls. This also holds for the finding that younger and older respondents watch more. The simple correlation between amount of viewing and a middle-age dummy variable is -.14; controlling for the other variables in Table 1, the partial is -.09 (both $p<.001$).
10. Specifically, we will examine simple within-group differences to assess the shape of conditioning and mediating patterns, and enter multiplicative interaction terms in hierarchical regression equations following all background controls and main effects. This clarifies whether the observed simple differences among groups are significantly independent of all other factors.
11. Heavy viewers are more likely to say they are Democrats within each of the 12 subgroups shown in Table 1, and in all cases but one (respondents under the age of 30) the relationship is significant.
12. This result holds even when controlling for residual variation in actual SES within each of the actual SES groups.

13. Political tendency was measured by the question, "We hear a lot of talk these days about liberals and conservatives. I'm going to show you a seven-point scale on which the political views that people might hold are arranged from extremely liberal—point 1—to extremely conservative—point 7. Where would you place yourself on this scale?" Self-placements on this scale were recoded into three categories: "extremely liberal," "liberal" and "slightly liberal" (points 1, 2, and 3) respondents were treated as "liberals"; points 5, 6, and 7 were classified as "conservative"; and point 4 represents "moderate, middle of the road." The resulting groupings provide over the four years combined, 1,611 "liberals" (28.2%), 2,254 "moderates" (39.4%), and 1,849 "conservatives" (32.4%); 306 cases (5.1%) have missing data.
14. For purposes of space, medium viewers are omitted from Table 3. All the relationships in the moderate and conservative columns, however, are monotonic across all three viewing categories; eleven of the sixteen in the liberal column are monotonic. In addition, heavy viewers show significantly less dispersal around the mean of the seven-point political self-designation scale than do light viewers, overall and within most subgroups. In order to avoid curtailment of variance problems within subgroups, unstandardized regression coefficients reflecting the relationship between amount of viewing and the absolute value of respondents' deviations from the sample's political "center" (controlling for everything else) were computed within the major demographic subgroups. Without exception, all coefficients are negative, indicating that heavy viewers consistently show less dispersal around the sample mean. This is particularly true for college-educated respondents, those with medium incomes, younger and middle-aged people, noncity residents, females, and those of "Independent" party affiliation (all interaction terms except region and sex are significant). This shows that heavy viewers tend to choose "moderate" political self-designations over and above the effects of these powerful demographics.
15. The tendency for heavy viewers to designate themselves as "moderate" holds up within each of the four years analyzed here, although there are variations in the size of the association (it is weakest in 1977 and strongest in 1978). In addition, this moderating effect seems to be a specific correlate of television viewing, and not a general media exposure phenomenon: neither radio listening nor newspaper reading are associated with similar results. The percentage of moderates among light, medium, and heavy radio listeners (defined as for the viewing groups) is 38, 39, and 38, respectively; similarly, 39 percent of both daily and occasional newspaper readers call themselves moderates. Thus, it is television viewing, rather than general media use, that is associated with a self-ascribed "moderate" political disposition. Finally, this finding is replicated in a national survey conducted by Research and Forecasts, Inc., for the Connecticut Mutual Life Insurance Co. The percentage of moderates among light, medium, and heavy viewers in this survey is 41, 48, and 49, respectively. Controlling for party affiliation, the data are virtually identical to those in the GSS.
16. Besides these eight questions, the 1977 GSS contained twenty (mostly nonrepeated) items about attitudes toward blacks, and these were combined into six indices, each having acceptable internal homogeneity (with Cronbach's alphas from .50 to .60; all measures together produce an alpha of .82). Four of these indices measure support for racial segregation, in terms of interracial marriage, open housing, integrated schools, and avoidance of blacks. A fifth scale deals with respondents' tendencies to keep blacks "in their place," and a sixth measures respondents' agreement with

stereotypical explanations for blacks (social disadvantages). As with the eight repeated items, these indices show that, for liberals, greater viewing means greater support for segregation and related manifestations of racism toward blacks. Five out of six relationships are significant among liberals. Yet, none of the within-group comparisons are significant for moderates or conservatives; five out of six interaction terms are negative, two of them significantly. Once again, heavy viewing cultivates anti-integration and related opinions only among liberals—those who are "otherwise" least opposed to racial equality. Also, again, there is not much difference between moderates and conservatives.

17. For homosexuality, respondents indicated whether they felt "sexual relations between two adults of the same sex" are "always wrong," "almost always wrong," "wrong only sometimes," or "not wrong at all"; we focus on those who respond "always wrong." The question was asked in 1977 and 1980. Items measuring approval of legally obtaining an abortion under six specific conditions were included in each of the four GSS years that contained a television viewing question; these items produce a reliable Guttman scale (scalability=.80, reproducibility=.94). Respondents were treated as being "against abortion" if they agreed to legal abortions in less than three situations or only for the three "easiest" situations. Finally, a question on whether or not marijuana should be legalized was included in 1975, 1978, and 1980.
18. The same patterns hold for attitudes toward both premarital an extramarital sex. Light viewing liberals are much more unlikely to say that these behaviors are "always wrong," while the responses of heavy viewing liberals approach those of moderates and conservatives. As with busing, moderates and conservatives show significant negative associations between amount of viewing and disapproval of premarital sex—another instance of convergence from both directions (the interaction beta, with all other variables and main effects in the equation, is -.18, $p< .01$).
19. A single question (asked in 1977 and 1980) deals with respondents' feelings about communism, on a four-point continuum from "it's the worst kind [of government] of all," to "it's a good form of government." Fifteen questions (all asked in 1977 and 1980) deal with whether each of five types of people should be allowed to (a) make a speech in the respondent's community, (b) have a book in the community's library, and (c) teach in a local college or university. We subdivided the five types into "leftists" (atheists, Communists, homosexuals) and "rightists" (racists, militarists), and constructed two indices of respondents' willingness to curtail the freedom of speech of these groups. The antileftist items yielded an alpha of .90, and the antirightist alpha is .82.
20. The same basic patterns also hold in terms of attitudes toward the Equal Rights Amendment (asked only in 1977), but nonsignificantly. Among liberals, 17 percent of light but 20 percent of heavy viewers oppose its passage. For moderates and conservatives—who are more likely to be against the amendment—heavy viewing means greater support. Among moderates, 28 percent of light and 24 percent of heavy viewers are opposed; among conservatives, 40 percent of light and 32 percent of heavy viewers would not see it passed. A 23 percentage point spread between light viewing liberals and conservatives is cut in half (to 12 points) among heavy viewers.
21. These seven items yield an alpha of .65. The other four (space exploration, halting the crime rate, drug abuse, and the military/defense) share little common variance (alpha=.28) and clearly represent a different dimension.

22. In the 1980 GSS, respondents were asked their position on a seven-point scale, with point 1 equal to "government should provide many fewer services; reduce spending a lot" and point 7 labeled "government should continue to provide services; no reduction in spending." We combined respondents who fell on the upper three points with those who said the amount of taxes they pay is too high, in order to construct a typology of attitudes on spending and taxes. We focus on the one-third (32.1%) who takes the contradictory position of opposing reductions in spending while claiming their taxes are too high. Forty percent want less spending and lower taxes, 13.9 percent want reduced spending but do not feel their taxes are too high, and 13.9 percent want continued spending and do not feel their taxes are too high.

REFERENCES

1. Barnouw, Erik. *Tube of Plenty: The Evolution of American Television.* New York: Oxford University Press, 1975.
2. Barwise, T. P., Ehrenberg, A. S. D., and Goodhardt, G. J. Report on U.S. television viewing behavior. London Business School, 1982.
3. Cantor, Muriel G. *Prime-Time Television: Content and Control.* Beverly Hills, Cal.: Sage, 1980.
4. DeFleur, Melvin L. and DeFleur, Lois B. "The Relative Contribution of Television as a Learning Source for Children's Occupational Knowledge." *American Sociological Review* 32, 1967, pp. 777–789.
5. Entman, Robert M. and Paletz, David L. "Media and the Conservative Myth." *Journal of Communication* 30(4), Autumn 1980, pp. 154–165.
6. Gerbner, George, Gross, Larry, Morgan, Michael, and Signorielli, Nancy. "The 'Mainstreaming' of America: Violence Profile No. 11." *Journal of Communication* 30(3), Summer 1980, pp. 10–29.
7. Gerbner, George, Gross, Larry, Morgan, Michael, and Signorielli, Nancy. "Health and Medicine on Television." *New England Journal of Medicine* 305(15), October 1981, pp. 901–904.
8. Gerbner, George, Gross, Larry, Morgan, Michael, Signorielli, Nancy. "Scientist on the TV Screen." *Society* 18(4), May/June 1981, pp. 41–44.
9. Gerbner, George, Gross, Larry, Signorielli, Nancy, and Morgan, Michael. "Aging with Television: Images on Television Drama and Conceptions of Social Reality." *Journal of Communication* 30(1), Winter 1980, pp. 37–47.
10. Gerbner, George and Signorielli, Nancy. "Women and Minorities in Television Drama 1969–1978." The Annenberg School of Communications, University of Pennsylvania, 1979.
11. Graber, Doris A. *Mass Media and American Politics.* Washington, D.C.: Congressional Quarterly Press, 1980.
12. Morgan, Michael. "Longitudinal Patterns of Television Viewing and Adolescent Role Socialization." Unpublished Ph.D. dissertation, University of Pennsylvania, 1980.
13. Morgan, Michael. "Symbolic Victimization and Real-World Fear." Paper presented at the Symposium on Cultural Indicators for the Comparative Study of Culture, Vienna, Austria, February 1982.

14. Signorielli, Nancy. "Television's Contribution to Sex Role Socialization." Paper presented at the Seventh Annual Telecommunications Policy Research Conference, Skytop, Pennsylvania, April 1979.
15. Tuchman, Gaye. *The TV Establishment: Programming for Power and Profit.* Englewood Cliffs, N.J.: Prentice-Hall, 1974.
16. Volgy, Thomas J. and Schwarz, John E. "TV Entertainment Programming and Sociopolitical Attitudes." *Journalism Quarterly* 57(1), 1980, pp. 150–155.
17. Weigel, Russel H., Loomis, James W., and Soja, Matthew J. "Race Relations on Prime Time Television." *Journal of Personality and Social Psychology* 39(5), 1980, pp. 884–893.

Chapter 24

WHAT TELEVISION TEACHES ABOUT PHYSICIANS AND HEALTH

BY GEORGE GERBNER, LARRY GROSS, MICHAEL MORGAN, AND NANCY SIGNORIELLI

The U.S. Surgeon General's recent call for reordering health priorities (1) concluded that culturally sustained behavioral and lifestyle factors account for as much as half of U.S. mortality.

A shift in health priorities to cultural and behavioral research highlights the central role of television in socializing individuals and stabilizing lifestyles. The success or failure of educational and informational efforts depends largely on the cultural context into which they are injected. Few educators can succeed without knowing what the obstacles are. That means being aware of what other relevant patterns of messages and images television discharges into the mainstream of common consciousness.

Unlike other media, television is used relatively nonselectively. Most viewers watch by the clock rather than by the program. Television watching is like a ritual. It involves the average American household for 6.5 hours a day in a stable and repetitive world of shows, news, and commercials designed to hold and sell the largest possible public at the least possible cost. Its entertainment programs and commercials, with potential health (and other) lessons imbedded in them, reach tens of millions of viewers. Even more importantly, these messages reach viewers who otherwise do not expose themselves to such information.

While single programs and isolated messages or even campaigns may be submerged in the daily and weekly rhythm of the television ritual, the recurrent patterns of health information in regular programming become parts of the inescapable mainstream of our widely shared symbolic environment.

This is a review of what we know about these patterns and their lessons for viewers. The source of research results not otherwise cited or specifically identified as a pilot study we have conducted for the National Institute of Mental Health (2).

WHAT VIEWERS SEE

The world of prime time (8 to 11 P.M.) and of children's weekend-daytime 8 A.M. to 2:30 P.M.) network dramatic programming is by and large a man's world of action, power, and danger. Our annual analyses since 1967 of nearly 5,000 major and some 14,000 minor characters, in over 1,600 programs, reveal these consistent patterns: men outnumber women at least three to one; young people comprise one-third of their real numbers; characters over 65 years of age make up 2 percent of the television population but 11 percent of the real world's; professionals, lawbreakers, law enforcers, and entertainers greatly outnumber all other working people; crime is at least ten times as frequent as in the real world; and an average of five acts of violence per hour of prime time and eighteen acts per hour in children's weekend-daytime programs victimize half of the major characters of prime time and over two-thirds in children's time programs (3).

This violence is rarely followed by pain or suffering. On the average, only about 6 percent of major characters need any medical treatment. Specific diseases hardly exist in prime time. A special analysis of programs that include elderly characters indicated that such programs are not more likely to show ailments than the others. Of the specific health problems shown, digestive disorders led with 10 percent followed by heart disease with 7 percent, and stroke with 6 percent. A regular viewer of these programs would see an average of three illnesses of all types in one week of prime time viewing. The most frequent—stomach problem—would be seen once every three weeks. Infectious diseases, pneumonia, or diabetes were never shown in our analysis of 520 characters who appeared on dramatic programs that included elderly characters.

MENTAL ILLNESS

Our studies found that about 17 percent of prime time programs involve some significant depiction or theme of mental illness (4). About 3 percent of major characters are identified as mentally ill, as mental patients, ex-mental patients, and so on. In the late evening, with more violent programming, the percentage is twice as high.

In spite of their relatively small numbers, the mentally ill individuals on TV are the most likely to be portrayed as both perpetrators of violence and as victims. Out of all prime time dramatic characters, 40 percent of—if we may use the term—"normals" are violent but 73 percent of those characterized as mentally ill are violent. Forty-four percent of the "normals," as opposed to 81 percent of the mentally ill, become victims of violence.

TELEVISION PHYSICIANS

Professionals play a disproportionately large role in the world of television. Health professionals (primarily physicians and nurses) dominate the ranks of professionals, numbering almost five times their real-life proportions. Only criminals or law enforcers are more numerous than health professionals in the world of television, despite the paucity of sick characters.

The typical viewer sees about twelve physicians and six nurses each week on prime time alone, including three physicians and one nurse in major roles. By comparison, a scientist will be cast in a major role once every two weeks. Visible as health professions are in prime time, they are virtually absent from weekend-daytime (children's) programs.

About nine out of ten television physicians are male, white, and young or middle-aged. Nearly all nurses are female and young or middle-aged; nine out of ten are white.

Physicians probably fare best of all occupations on television. McLaughlin (4) found that they are easily accessible to patients, command nurses (who never disobey their orders), advise each other, but rarely receive advice from patients or orders from superiors and, when they do, often disregard them.

Warner's (5) study of another sample of prime time "doctor shows" confirmed these findings and also noted that 61 percent of the physicians' duties were performed during house calls or in the field. The television physician, Warner found, thrives on private relationships with patients, and wields absolute authority over auxiliary medical personnel, but is rarely shown at home or with a spouse or family of his own. Television physicians give advice and orders twice as frequently to female patients or to patients' wives as to male patients themselves.

NUTRITION IN PROGRAMS AND COMMERCIALS

The quantity and quality of food commercials on children's television were well documented in research conducted through the 1970s. During a year the average child viewer will see about 22,000 commercials, 5,000 of them for food products, over half of which are high calorie, high sugar, low nutrition items (6). Barcus found that 67 percent of Saturday morning commercials (7) and over half of general children's program commercials (8) were for sugared cereals, candy bars, and other sweets, usually presented as snacks to be eaten between meals. While dietary goals recommended by the U.S. Senate Select Committee on Nutrition and Human Needs (9) urged sugar reduction in the consumption of refined and other processed sugars, most food commercials directed at children promote the use of such sugars. Masover and Stanler's (9) 1978 report for the U.S. Senate Select Committee found that 70 percent of food ads promoted products high in fats, cholesterol, sugar, and salt, while only 3 percent were for fruits and vegetables. Another study by Mauro and Feins (10) found that only 7 percent of commercials promoted dairy products, fruits, and breads, and that most of the rest were devoted to the easily mass-produced and profitably marketed, but low nutrition, packaged products. A comprehensive review of much of the relevant research (11) concluded that "television advertising researchers have developed a sophisticated technology aimed not only at selling products to children, but also aimed at socializing these children to eventual consumer roles."

Food products, however, are not found only in commercial messages. Our pilot study (which examined the portrayal of eating, drinking, nutrition, and safety in a weeklong sample of prime time and weekend-daytime children's programming and is being reported in this paper) of a typical week's prime time network dramatic programs reveals that eating, drinking, or talking about food occurs nine times per hour. More than three-quarters of all dramatic characters, or some twenty-five each night, eat, drink, or talk about doing so, often more than once. Weekend morning programs present an additional eighty-four instances of eating and/or drinking, or nearly four per hour. (Interestingly, this is less than half the prime time rate, although food and drink commercials dominate "children's" advertising.)

Prime time nutrition is anything but balanced or relaxed. Grabbing a snack (39% of all eating-drinking episodes) is virtually as frequent as breakfast, lunch, and dinner combined (42%). In weekend-daytime children's programs, snacks go up to 45 percent and regular meals decline to 24 percent with "other meals" making up the rest. The snack is fruit in only four or five of these episodes.

In episodes involving drinking, the most prevalent beverages are alcoholic. Coffee and tea are next.

A similar analysis of a week's prime time programs by White and Sandberg (12) confirmed that one-third of the prime time program diet consists of alcohol and coffee.

Although most of the attention of nutritionists focused on television commercials, Kaufman's (13) comparative study found that, in fact, there are more representations in programs than in commercials. Furthermore, the nutritional value of program references is no greater than that of commercials.

Kaufman analyzed ten top-rated prime time programs and the commercials included in them. She found that by far most references to beverages (particularly alcoholic) and to sweets were in program content. On the other hand, commercial references to fruits and vegetables outweighed program references to these foods by a ratio of better than three to one. A point-by-point comparison of television eating behavior along nutritional guidelines exposed the contradictions between the dramatic requirements and motivations (such as reward, punishment, bribe), and recommended eating habits.

Breed and DeFoe (14) found that alcoholic beverages not only outnumber other beverages consumed on television but that the pattern of drinking on TV is virtually the inverse of the pattern in daily life. Alcohol drinking acts were more than twice as frequent as the second-ranking coffee and tea, fourteen times as frequent as soft drinks, and more than fifteen times as frequent as water. Of all identifiable alcoholic beverages, 52 percent were hard liquor, 22 percent were wine, and 16 percent were beer.

The most frequent reason given for drinking on television is a personal crisis, according to Breed and DeFoe. Drink was a means of dealing with crisis or tension in 61 percent of significant incidents. Leading guest actors in prime time series drank in a crisis 74 percent of the time. Lesser characters drank for social and other reasons. Only a few "bad" characters used alcohol to manipulate other people.

Our pilot study results show that although over one-third of all major characters are shown drinking, only about 1 percent are portrayed as having a drinking problem or being alcoholics. At any rate, drinking on television is not only prevalent, it is also generally condoned.

WHAT VIEWERS SAY AND DO

Jeffery et al.'s (15) comprehensive review of studies on the impact of television advertising on children's eating behavior concluded that advertising researchers have developed sophisticated techniques aimed not only at selling but also at socializing children to consumer roles that, stabilized by a lifetime of television reinforcement, may well resist attempts at modification.

It is essential, therefore, to learn what such attempts are up against. What are the health implications of television viewing per se and of exposure to health-related messages, such as those we have discussed above, embedded in daily television fare? What informational states, conceptions about health, and practices relating to health does television viewing tend to cultivate in different groups of viewers?

There are indications that exposure to television's portrayal of health matters contributes to the public's health-related knowledge and behavior. It should be stressed that although these findings are preliminary, they affirm the idea that television has tremendous potential impact on the public health status and that this problem merits concentrated and sustained research.

Among children, Leaman (16) found that fourth and sixth graders who watch more television have lower levels of nutritional knowledge. Moreover, the nutritional value of the children's diets seemed to vary inversely with amount of viewing.

Other, more indirect, pieces of evidence suggest that unhealthy practices may accompany reliance upon television for health information. In the General Mills study (17), respondents were given a list of sixteen information sources (e.g., physicians, friends, families, television programs, popular books on health, etc.), and asked which were their "two or three main sources" of health information. "Television programs" were the second most cited source (chosen by 31%), led only by "physicians and dentists" (chosen by 45%). All other sources were chosen by less than 30 percent of the sample.

More importantly, those who did choose television programs (vs. those who did not) manifest a distinct profile. Table 1 shows that in most demographic groups (defined by sex, social class, and place of residence), those who chose television programs are significantly more likely to be categorized as "complacent" (vs. "concerned") on health attitudes; as holding "old" (vs. "new") health values; as being "nonexercisers" in regard to physical fitness; and as being "poorly informed" (vs. "well" or "somewhat informed") in terms of health information. The latter two—not exercising and being less informed—show particularly strong and consistent associations with choosing television, across subgroups.

These data cannot support the argument that television contributes to poor health routines and lack of awareness of health information (although they are consistent with

Table 1. Health Values, Behaviors, and Information for Do and Do Not Select Television as One of Two or Three "Main Sources of Information," from a List of 16 Sources

	% who are complacent			*% with Old health values*			*% who are Nonexcercisers*			*% who are Poorly Informed*			
	TV not chosen	*TV chosen*	*gam*	*TV not chosen*	*TV chosen*	*gam*	*TV not chosen*	*TV chosen*	*gam*	*TV not chosen*	*TV chosen*	*gam*	*(+/-5)*
Social Class													
Lower	63	-0	.14	7	-11	24	62	60	-.04	24	48	49***	(380)
Middle	69	76	.1-**	14	18	14*	55	73	.38***	18	2	930***	(129-)
Upper	70	80	.27**	7	14	34**	50	60	.21**	13	24	36***	(539)
Residence													
Central													
City	70	72	.04	10	30	.57***	60	68	.18***	22	43	46***	(704)
Urban	68	77	.22***	15	16	.02	54	65	.22***	16	26	.28***	(978)
Rural	66	76	.22**	8	4	-.37*	56	73	.36***	13	21	.30***	(702)
Sex													
Male	73	72	-.04	13	20	.24***	51	69	.36***	23	33	.25***	(1026)
Female	64	78	.32***	11	13	12	60	68	.16***	13	26	.42***	(1359)

*p< .05
**p<.01
***p<.001
Data Source: General Mills/Yankelovich, Skelley and White, 1979.

such a notion). But they do suggest that those who credit television as a main source of information, even with other variables held constant, are not among the more health-minded segments of the population.

Other surveys, which include a measure of amount of daily television viewing, echo these patterns and provide more hints about the possible consequences of television viewing on health. A 1979 study conducted by the Roper Organization for Virginia Slims asked:

> Here are some statements different people have made about their weight and eating habits. Which one of these statements comes closest to being right about you?
>
> I'm not concerned about weight. I eat and drink whatever I want, whenever I want (31%);
>
> I'm not concerned about weight but I'm a little careful about what I eat and drink (31%);
>
> I diet occasionally to keep myself trim (23%);
>
> I pretty much stay on a diet all the time (15%).

The first choice clearly represents the most complacent outlook on diet and nutrition. Our analyses lend support to the notion that television may cultivate this perspective. Those who watch more television are significantly more likely to select the first response (see Table 2).

"MAINSTREAMING" HEALTH CONCEPTIONS

While this association holds up within most subgroups, there are interesting exceptions. The baselines and the intensity of the relationship do show some fluctuation across a range of groups, much of which may be explained by a process we call "mainstreaming" (18). "Mainstreaming" implies that some differences deriving from other factors may be reduced or even eliminated among those who watch more television (heavy viewers) (19). Groups who share a relative commonality of outlooks cultivated by television (the "mainstream" view) will often show weak or no associations between amount of viewing and a given perspective. But strong group relationships may be found for those groups whose lighter viewers do *not* share that outlook. Thus, cultivation may often imply a convergence into a more homogeneous "mainstream," rather than absolute, across-the-board increments.

Figure 1 presents graphic illustration of the concept of "mainstreaming" in this context. The figure shows the relationship between amount of viewing and being particularly unconcerned about diet and nutrition, by respondents' income levels. We see that the association is essentially zero for low-income respondents; if anything, they show a slight *negative* relationship. In other words, within the most complacent (i.e., low) income group, television may be associated with greater awareness.

Light viewers with middle or high incomes are relatively less likely to be complacent about their eating habits, yet we find a strong relationship with complacency for

Table 2. Relationship Between Amount of Television Viewing and Nutritional Complacency

	Television Viewing							
	Total		Light		Medium		Heavy	
		%	N	%	N	%	%	N
I'm not concerned about weight. I eat whatever I want, whenever I want.	31	(1142)	28	(284)	31	(510)	35	(348)
I'm not concerned about weight, but I'm a little careful about what I eat and drink.	31	(1132)	33	(335)	30	(489)	31	(308)
I diet occasionally to keep myself trim.	23	(842)	24	(242)	25	(408)	20	(192)
I pretty much stay on a diet all the time.	15	(535)	16	(166)	14	(234)	14	(135)
Total	100	(3651)	100	(1027)	100	(1641)	100	(983)

X^2=21.42, d.f.=6, p=.001
gamma=-.07, p=.001 (tau)
Data Source: Virginia Slims/The Roper Organization, 1979.

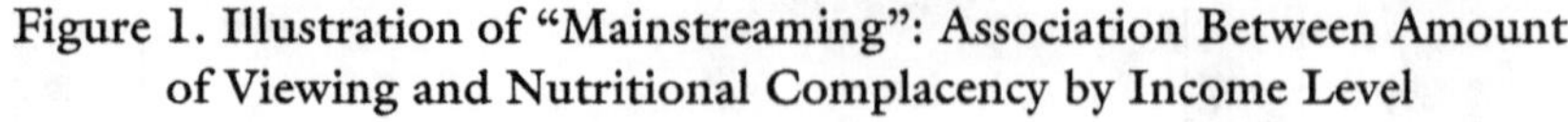

Figure 1. Illustration of "Mainstreaming": Association Between Amount of Viewing and Nutritional Complacency by Income Level

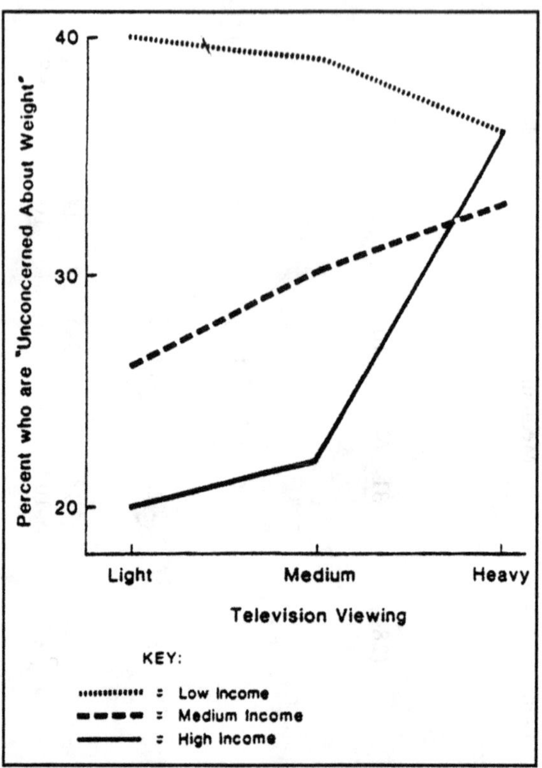

heavy viewers within the higher income groups. Clearly, heavy viewing goes with a more homogeneous "mainstream" of relatively strong nutritional complacency.

Our study of adolescents (20) found that about 83 percent say they "usually eat" while watching television. The tendency to eat while viewing increases as adolescents mature: 74 percent of sixth graders, 82 percent of seventh graders, 84 percent of eight graders, and 91 percent of tenth graders say they eat while watching television.

To conclude, television viewing is deeply integrated into different styles of life, with powerful implications for health practices. Television programs are a frequently cited source of health information: those who choose them, and/or heavier viewers, seem relatively neglectful and complacent about their physical well-being, are less informed about health, and exercise less.

The pattern of findings, including our own pilot study, indicates that television viewing is associated with a convergence of the heavier viewers upon paradoxical and disjointed "mainstream" conceptions and practices. Characteristic features are poor nutritional knowledge and behavior, general complacency about health, and high confidence in the medical community.

The cultivation of ignorance and neglect, especially among the otherwise relatively enlightened viewers, coupled with an unrealistic belief in the magic of medicine, is likely to perpetuate unhealthy lifestyles, hurt patients and health professionals, and frustrate efforts at health education. If culturally sustained health hazards are the new frontier in health promotion and disease prevention, there is a need for greater mobilization of effort and resources in a central sector of that frontier: television.

REFERENCES/NOTES

1. Healthy people. The surgeon general's report on health promotion and disease prevention. U.S. Department of Health, Education, and Welfare, Public Health Service. Washington, D.C.: U.S. Government Printing Office, 1979.
2. Gerbner, G., Morgan, M., and Signorielli, N. Programming health portrayals what viewers say and do. Prepared for: Television and behavior: ten years of scientific progress and implications for the 80s. (The National Institute of Mental Health update of the original report of the surgeon general's Scientific Advisory Committee on Television and Social Behavior.) Washington D.C.; in press. Also, parts of this study were reported in an article by Gerbner, G., Gross, L., Morgan, M., and Signorielli, N. Special report: health and medicine on television. NEJM 1981: 305(15): 901–904.
3. Gerbner, G., Gross, L., Morgan, M., Jackson-Beeck, M. The demonstration of power: violence profile no. 10. *Journal of Communication*. Summer 1979: 24.3: 177–196.
4. McLaughlin, J. The doctor shows. *Journal of Communication* 1975.
5. Warner, C. L. The world of prime time television doctors. Unpublished MA thesis. University of Pennsylvania, 1979.
6. Choate, R. B. Testimony before the Federal Trade Commission in the matter of a trade regulation rule on food nutrition. Advertising Council on Children, Media and Merchandising. Washington D.C., 1976.
7. Barcus, F. D., Wolkin, R. Children's television: an analysis of programming and advertising. New York: Praeger, 1977.
8. Barcus, F. E., McLaughlin, L. Food advertising on children's television: an analysis of appeals and nutritional content. Action for Children's Television. Newtonville, MA., 1978.
9. U.S. Senate Select Committee on Nutrition and Human Needs. Dietary goals for the United States. Washington, D.C.: Government Printing Office, 1977.
10. Mauro, F. L., Feins, R. P., Kids, food, and television: the compelling case for state action. Report for the Office of Research and Analysis Program and Committee Staff New York State Assembly, 1977 March.
11. Jeffrey, D. B., Bolin, D., Lemnitzer, N. B., Hickey, J. S, Hess, M. J., Stroud, J. M. The impact of television advertising on children's eating behavior: an integrative review. Unpublished research report. Department of Psychology. University of Montana, Missoula, MT, 1980.
12. White, M. A., Sandberg, B. The television prime time diet. Unpublished paper presented at APA Symposium. Montreal, Canada, September 1980.
13. Kaufman, L. Prime time nutrition. Journal of Communication. Summer 1975: 30.3: 46–48.
14. Breed, W., DeFoe, J. R. The portrayal of the drinking process on prime time television. *Journal of Communication*. Winter 1979: 29.4: 58–67.
15. Jeffrey, D. B., McLellarn, R. W., Hickey, J. S., Lemnitzer, N. B., Hess, M. J., Stroud, J. M. Television food commercials and children's eating behavior: some empirical evidence. *Journal of the University Film Association*. 1980 Winter-Spring: XXXII:41–43.

16. Leaman, F. A. Television's "fruitless" image: a cultivation analysis of children's nutritional knowledge and behavior. Unpublished MA thesis. Annenberg School of Communications. University of Pennsylvania, 1973.
17. General Mills Inc. The General Mills American family report 1978–79: family health in an era of stress. Minneapolis: General Mills, 1979.
18. Gerbner, G., Gross, L., Morgan, M., Signorielli, N. The "mainstreaming" of America: violence profile no. 11. *Journal of Communication.* 1980 Summer: 30.3: 10–27.
19. "Heavy," "medium," and "light" viewers represent relative rankings, according to the distribution of amount of viewing in a sample. In a report on health, it is worth noting that the term "heavy viewer" refers to the quantity of viewing, and not to the size of the viewer.
20. Morgan, M., Gross, L. Television viewing IQ and academic achievement. *Journal of Broadcasting* 1980. Spring: 24.2: 117–133.

Chapter 25

SCIENCE ON TELEVISION

How It Affects Public Conceptions

BY GEORGE GERBNER

We live in a scientific age. Yet cults, superstitions, pseudoscience, and hostility to science and technology are widespread and even show signs of new virulence. The giant conglomerate Proctor & Gamble abandoned its 103-year-old trademark, an art deco style face of the "man in the moon," after spending over $100 million on public relations in a vain attempt to dispel rumors that it was the mark of the Devil and promoted Satan worship. Creationists pressured at least two states to pass laws to teach "creation science" and some textbook suppliers to alter their treatment of evolution. Surveys show that only one in ten adults can provide a minimally acceptable definition of the meaning of scientific study; nearly one-third agree that "AIDS is a punishment God has given homosexuals for the way they live"; and nearly half believe that astrology is scientific.

Clearly, the reasons for contemporary obscurantism and misanthropy are many and complex. But their existence cannot be blamed on any information lag or gap. We live in an information-rich environment. Even illiteracy or isolation pose no barrier to the most pervasive source of information: television.

Science is a way of thinking and communicating that can both liberate and dominate. It can confer power on those who use it and devastate those who cannot. Its images and symbols inspire feelings of confidence and apprehension, authority and resistance, control and being controlled.

Communicators who deal with this ambivalence toward science do not have a simple task. The popular market for science (in contrast to the specialized market of users who know what they need) is a mixture of great expectations, fears, utilitarian interests, curiosities, ancient prejudices, and superstitions. Mass media appeal to all of these.

Under a grant from the National Science Foundation, my colleagues Larry Gross, Michael Morgan, and Nancy Signorielli, and I assessed the survey data to discover what contributions television and other media make to conceptions of science held by different groups of viewers. From our ongoing research project, called Cultural Indicators, we know that most U.S. citizens encounter science and technology most often on television. We also know that most of these encounters occur not through watching informative documentaries like "Nova"; they occur through watching prime time entertainment. Let me sketch the existing cultural context before I summarize what viewers see on prime time television and what they learn from it.

Science journalism caters to the most upscale information seeker. The field is dominated by a few dozen veteran reporters and their favorite contacts and sources. Although science news comprises only 1 percent of all news in daily newspapers (puzzles and horoscopes claim three times as much), science magazine publishing boomed in the late 1970s.

Publishers had reason to be optimistic. "After all," the trade paper *Advertising Age* reported on October 18, 1984, "the nation's 25-to-40-year-olds—that high profile demographic—had been reared on space walks, friendly computers, and organ transplants. As a group they were mostly well educated and had a more than passing interest in the problems of pollution, fuel shortages, and things nuclear." However, space walks, organ transplants, and things nuclear also gave rise to fearful visions.

Social researchers found, however, that being well informed results in greater wariness about science. The controversies surrounding fluoridation and nuclear power reflected a pattern of initial hope that turned to fear of the risks involved and of being manipulated and losing control. Researchers also found that new bursts of collective apprehension, energized by media stories about asbestos, animal experimentation, gene manipulation, and widespread pollutants, fueled anxieties about unrestrained science and technology.

Today these patterns mingle with alarmist sensationalism that appeals to three social types: those who hold the miracles and terrors of science in almost religious awe; those who have little use for or access to the bounties of science; and those who look at science with suspicion and mistrust. Curtis D. MacDougall's book, *Superstition and the Press*, details how newspapers carry reports on doomsday prophecies, exorcism, sea serpents and monsters, faith healers, psychics, gurus, subliminal persuasion, creationism, UFOs, and pseudoscientific cults and practices of all kinds.

This is the cultural context in which television plays its pivotal role. Unlike other media, television is used relatively nonselectively. The set is on daily in the typical U.S. home for an average of more than seven yours. It provides an abundance of information, mostly through entertainment, to all viewers, including those who seek no information. Television reaches the previously unreachable quickly and continuously.

To attract and sell to the largest audience at the least cost to the advertiser (the source of broadcaster income), television must cultivate the most common interests, hopes, and fears of the largest groups of viewers. These imperatives define television's role in society, guide its functions, and shape its contributions to public conceptions of science.

Our study of what viewers see was based on a detailed analysis of a ten-year sample of network prime time dramatic programs telecast between 1973 and 1983. A sample week from each season, stored in the Cultural Indicator's archive, showed 174 programs in which science, technology, or medicine were major themes, 410 programs in which they were minor themes, and 252 programs with no such themes.

The images of science and technology, including medicine, appear in seven out of every ten prime time dramatic programs. In addition to news and occasional documentaries, the average prime time viewer will see a dozen doctors and two other scientists each week.

Science and technology dominate all programs set in the future and are most likely to be featured in fast-moving globe-trotting adventure. Television doctors are among the most positively portrayed characters appearing on prime time. But other scientists, while on the whole positively presented, have a greater share of ambivalent and troublesome portrayals. They are a bit older and "stranger" than other professionals and are more likely to be foreigners. For every villainous scientist in a major role, there are five who are virtuous. But, for every "bad" doctor, there are nineteen "good"; for every "bad" law enforcer, there are forty "good."

This relative imbalance in the aggregate image of television scientists is also reflected in their success rate. For every scientist in a major role who fails, two succeed. But for every doctor who fails, five succeed, and for every law enforcer who fails, eight succeed. One reason for the higher rate of failure might be that about 5 percent of the scientists portrayed on television kill someone and 10 percent get killed. That is the highest victimization rate of all occupational groups on prime time television, including the army, police, and private investigators.

Scientific work on television is not all bad and certainly not "mad." Our trained analysts found that scientists were portrayed as stronger and smarter than other professionals and that they were quite rational. But of all occupational groups on television, scientists were observed as among the least sociable. They were the most likely to work alone and to hold jobs they considered "very important." Overall, they presented a negative image in comparison to doctors and other professionals, though not in absolute terms. And the image was somewhat foreboding, touched with a sense of evil, trouble, and peril.

Are the images of science on television reflected in the ideas and behaviors of viewers? To answer this question, our study used what we call cultivation analysis. This involves the examination of response patterns of light and heavy viewers, controlling for other demographic and media variables. The differences (if any) between the responses of light and heavy viewers indicate whether television makes an independent contribution to viewer conceptions. (There is no absolute measure of a "heavy viewer." The term designates the upper half of any distribution of amounts of viewing or correlations with amounts of viewing.) Our analysis was based on a telephone survey of a representative sample of 1,631 respondents conducted for us by the Public Opinion Laboratory of Northern Illinois University.

We combined the responses to five items into an index reflecting general orientations toward science. The items asked respondents to agree or disagree with propositions that science makes our way of life change too fast; makes our lives healthier, easier, and more comfortable; breaks down people's ideas of right and wrong; is more likely to cause problems than to find solutions; and that the growth of science means that a few people can control our lives.

We constructed a high versus low version of the index and analyzed the proportion of light, medium, and heavy television viewers holding positive responses to science in two groups divided by sex and by education. The pattern that emerges—heavy viewers are less likely than light viewers to be favorable about science—appears in groups divided by age, extent of newspaper reading, extent of viewing science documentaries on PBS, and extent of reading science magazines. The largest differences are in those groups whose light viewers are by far the most positive toward science.

In other words, exposure to science and technology through television entertainment appears to cultivate a generally less favorable orientation toward science, especially among higher status groups whose light-viewer members are its greatest supporters. Lower status groups have a generally low opinion of science, which television viewing only seems to confirm. Another pattern that emerges is one we call "mainstreaming": a relative similarity in outlooks reflecting greater exposure to the common mass ritual of television that overrides the influence of other important social factors. The result is that most group differences are larger among light than among heavy viewers.

Reading science magazines and watching science documentaries on television make a difference. Those who do (or even just read newspapers) are more likely to score high on the index of positive orientation. But mainstreaming is evident: the heavy viewing science readers and watchers are still less positive than their light viewing counterparts. Seeking out science documentaries or science magazines is a sign of more positive orientation, but heavy television viewing appears to counterbalance that positive tendency.

This basic pattern recurs, with some variations, in the responses to other questions. The more people watch television the less favorable they are about science, especially in groups (such as those who went to college) whose light viewers are the most favorable toward science. Some groups (such as older and lower-status respondents) are in the less favorable or more critical television mainstream. For them, viewing makes little difference. Reading and viewing nonfictional science materials relate to a generally more positive orientation toward science but do not prevent erosion of that view among heavy viewers. The cultivation of relatively critical and negative views and the blending of all views into the television mainstream are the usual correlates of viewing.

Respondents were asked to agree or disagree that scientists do dangerous work; don't get much fun out of life; usually don't get married; if married, don't spend much time with their families; are apt to be odd and peculiar; are apt to be foreigners; are not likely to be religious; have few interests outside their work; are mainly interested in knowledge for its own sake; and don't care much for its practical value. These items were combined into another index, showing television's contributions to the images of scientists held by different groups of viewers.

As before, in most comparisons television viewing is associated with a less positive view of science. In no case do heavy viewers within a particular group express views that are more positive, although in some instances (those age 55 and older, nonwhites, those with greater interest in religion), heavy and light viewers are equally negative. Again, groups whose light viewers are the least likely to offer positive views of scientists seem to be most in tune with the television mainstream. Reading science magazines and watching science documentaries raise the percentage of positive responses among light viewers but again yield to the mainstreaming pattern.

We combined the responses from six questions to create a factor-based index reflecting orientations toward technological innovation. The first of these questions noted, "These days, more and more things that people used to do are done by machines. Do you think that's a good thing or a bad thing?" The other five questions were addressed to specific technological developments, each to be labeled by respondents as good, a little of both, or bad. The technological developments included computers, industrial robots, electronic bank tellers, nuclear power plants, and video games. Overall, and in every subgroup, television viewing is associated with a less positive view of the new technologies.

We created an index from four items that were shown by factor analysis to reflect a desire to place restrictions on scientists' activities. Using this index we asked respondents whether they thought scientists should or should not be allowed to conduct studies that could enable people to live to be 100 or more; could allow scientists to create new forms of animal and plant life; could discover intelligent beings in outer space; and could allow parents to select the sex of their child.

The index revealed a consistent relationship to television viewing, with heavy viewers showing more willingness to place restrictions on science. Mainstreaming is evident in most groups. Among the light viewing respondents with some college education, for example, we find only 28 percent scoring high on this index, compared with 54 percent of the less educated light viewers. This difference of 26 percentage points compares with a difference of only 8 points between the heavy viewers of the two groups.

Dramatic images involve characters in action. We have seen that scientists in the world of television tend to be a bit older and stranger, are more ambiguous than most other characters, and lead lives that are more isolated and perilous. Are these images reflected in the ideas of viewers?

Respondents were asked to agree or disagree with the propositions that scientists are odd and peculiar people, that their work is dangerous, that they have few interests but work, that they spend little time with their families. We also asked them to rate the job of a scientist compared to "most other jobs." The results are similar to those we have seen before.

The more people watch television, the more they think that scientists are odd and peculiar. This is especially pronounced among males, nonwhites, those who do not watch science documentaries or read science magazines, and those who have a high interest in religion. The cultivation of a sense of danger in science is most striking among the higher status and younger viewers. Heavy viewers in most groups are more likely than light viewers to respond that scientists have few interests except work and that they spend little time with their families. Predictably, fewer heavy than light viewers believe that science jobs are better than most.

The final results deal with critical attitudes related to science. Does it make life change too fast? Pose more of a threat than a promise? What about nuclear energy? Space exploration?

The results show that most groups of heavy viewers believe that science makes life change too fast. Viewing also tends to enhance anxiety and erode or inhibit appreciation of the benefits of science. This is especially significant among groups that are otherwise the most supportive, such as those who are college educated, have higher incomes, and read science magazines.

Although most people disagree with the statement that science causes more problems than solutions, fewer heavy than light viewers do so, again, especially in groups otherwise most supportive. One of those problems may be nuclear power plants; heavy viewers in all subgroups are more critical of them. Space exploration is also in disfavor; almost all groups of heavy viewers would spend less money on it.

In sum, prime time television drama presents a steady stream of generally positive images and messages about science and scientists but they are less positive than the images and messages about other professions. Moreover, television drama tends to reflect and exacerbate public ambivalence and anxiety about science.

Television's contribution to popular conceptions of science and scientists blends with other social and cultural influences into a mainstream that tends to be more critical and negative than the views of comparable groups that watch less television. Foreboding images of odd and perilous activity seem to heighten fears, strengthen the desire for restraints, and inhibit the inclination for science as an occupation or an area of public participation. Reading science magazines and watching documentary programs about science make a significant positive contribution. However, even this does not completely overcome the cultivation of relatively critical and negative public conceptions, especially among those who are otherwise the most supportive of science. In other words, science readers and science documentary viewers are closer to the others.

Television did not invent the negative image of science. It only streamlines the image, puts it on the assembly line, and delivers it into every home. The image of science on television is only part of a broader problem: the skewed image television presents of the world. Television works well delivering to the advertiser the largest number of viewers at the least cost, but it does not necessarily do well at enlightening those viewers.

Television's portrayal of science deserves more focused attention by leaders in science, the community of scientists, and legislators. There is no quick or easy fix. The excellent information services of organizations such as the American Association for the Advancement of Science and the Scientists' Institute for Public Information make information available mostly to news media. Science writing programs, science museums, and more specialized science and technology promotional efforts are useful, but they are necessarily limited to those who elect to attend or seek information. Yet a single episode on a popular prime time program, or even a soap opera, reaches more people than all the other educational efforts put together. More important, television reaches those who receive no other information about science. The task is to make realistic information and imagery (not just flattery) not only available but inescapable. That means constant liaison with those who write, produce, and direct television programs of all sorts, especially dramatic series.

Academics often shun media opportunities because they know that they cannot control the content and context of what is presented or because of a misplaced distaste of "popularizing." The media, on the other hand, will always find the experts they need and feed the fears and anxieties in which the media seem to have a vested interest. Scientists seeking to make a contribution to public conceptions via media must accept a trade-off. They may lose something in transit, but increased visibility and public stature can be used to command more attention and to gain more opportunities to appear in contexts that they can control better.

Universities are increasingly turning to courses and programs in critical viewing or media analysis as an essential part of a general liberal education. Networks are increasingly concerned that the pendulum has swung so far in the direction of deregulation that, having dismantled many public protections against excessive and exploitive commercialism, they have become vulnerable to new legislative scrutiny when the pendulum starts swinging the other way. Senate bill 2323, introduced by Sen. Paul Simon (D-Ill.), would exempt the networks from the threat of antitrust prosecution if they agreed to restore parts of their old abandoned industry code, and especially if they ameliorate the corrosive effects of television mayhem (in which fictional scientists have more than their share).

Finally, a science media coordinating council to plan strategy, streamline national media liaison activities, and organize meetings with network executives and the handful of writers and directors who create most programs, would go a long way to synchronize other activities, reduce duplications, and avoid media projects working at cross purposes.

CHAPTER 26

LEARNING PRODUCTIVE AGING AS A SOCIAL ROLE

The Lessons of Television

BY GEORGE GERBNER

"Biology is destiny," but the course it takes is culturally shaped. Women and men, tall and short, skinny and fat, dark and light, gay and straight, disabled and able, young and old have not only physiological differences but also social and cultural distinctions that can confine and shame and hurt.

Age is one of these traps. Stereotyped roles of the life cycle are learned early and confirmed throughout life. Mass media are the most ubiquitous wholesalers of social roles in industrial societies.

Mass media, particularly television, form the common mainstream of contemporary culture. They present a steady, repetitive, and compelling system of images and messages. For the first time in human history, most of the stories are told to most of the children not by their parents, their school, or their church but by a group of distant corporations that have something to sell.

This unprecedented condition has a profound effect on the way we are socialized into our roles, including age as a social role. We learn to be children, pre-teens, adolescents, adults and parents, and old persons and to differentiate and often even segregate those roles from the messages and images around us. The world of aging (and nearly everything else) is constructed to the specifications of marketing strategies.

What is the contribution of television to the process of age-role socialization? More specifically, what does growing up and living with television have to do with productive aging, the central theme of this book ?

We have studied age-role portrayals in television drama and commercials and their association with conceptions of aging (Gerbner, 1980; Gerbner, Gross, Signorielli, & Morgan, 1980; Gerbner, Gross, Morgan, & Signorielli, 1981, 1986). Our ongoing research project, called "Cultural Indicators," builds a cumulative database of systematic and reliable coded observations. The samples of programs and commercials from which the data for this chapter were drawn includes prime time (8 P.M. to 11 P.M.) and weekend-daytime (children's) network television fictional programs in the late 1970s and the 1980s in this country and reflects trends through 1988. All speaking parts in such television programs were analyzed; major characters (those who portray leading roles) were given special attention. The analysis includes a total of 25,608 characters in dramatic programs (16,688 major characters) and 8,301 characters in commercials.

Sex, race, class, age, type of role (major or minor), and type of program were coded for all characters. Age was coded in terms of both chronological age and social age. Social age is a functional category scheme that was used to characterize life cycle as well as type of dramatic roles. The categories are children and adolescents, young adults (typically the age between adolescence and a more settled vocational and personal life and responsibilities), settled adults, and older adults. For major roles, we also coded various aspects of characterization including personality traits, success (whether or not the character achieves what he or she sets out to do or otherwise exhibits characteristics indicative of success), the type of role (comic, serious, or mixed) in which a character is cast, and a variety of other aspects of characterization. A reliability test was designed to insure that the observations did not reflect ambiguity in terms of our instructions or bias on the part of the observer.

Our analysis shows that age is a stable and strong determinant of who appears most and gains or loses most in the world of network television drama. In contrast to the distribution of age groups in the American population, the television curve demonstrates a pronounced central tendency; it bulges in the middle years and underrepresents both young and old people. Figure 1 shows the percentage age distribution in the actual population and in the "worlds" of prime time television dramas and commercials. More than half of all television characters in both samples were between twenty-five and forty-five years of age. Those sixty-five and over, comprising almost 12 percent of the U.S. population, made up less than 3 percent of the fictional television population. Commercials tend to further exaggerate these inequities.

The skewed pattern of age distribution reflects not real life but power, particularly purchasing power. The age profile of television characters resembles the distribution of consumer income by age. (Women may do most of the buying and older Americans may have significant purchasing and investment clout, but men earn and the middle-aged groups spend most of the money in this country.) On the whole, marketing strategies reflect a "prime time, prime-of-life" male orientation. Television's prime time viewer population is seen as a mirror of the audience referred to in the industry as the "prime demographic market."

Figure 2 compares the percentage distribution of characters in weekend-daytime dramas and commercials with the U.S. population distribution. Here we note the exaggerated overrepresentation of children and the virtual absence of older characters in children's programs and commercials. In children's programs, characters who are sixty-five years of age and older represented 1.4 percent of the fictional population. Characters in their twenties and early thirties, prominent in prime time, were reduced by half in children's programs and even more in the accompanying commercials. The

Figure 1. Age Distribution of U.S. Population, and Characters in Commericals and Dramatic Programs in Prime Time

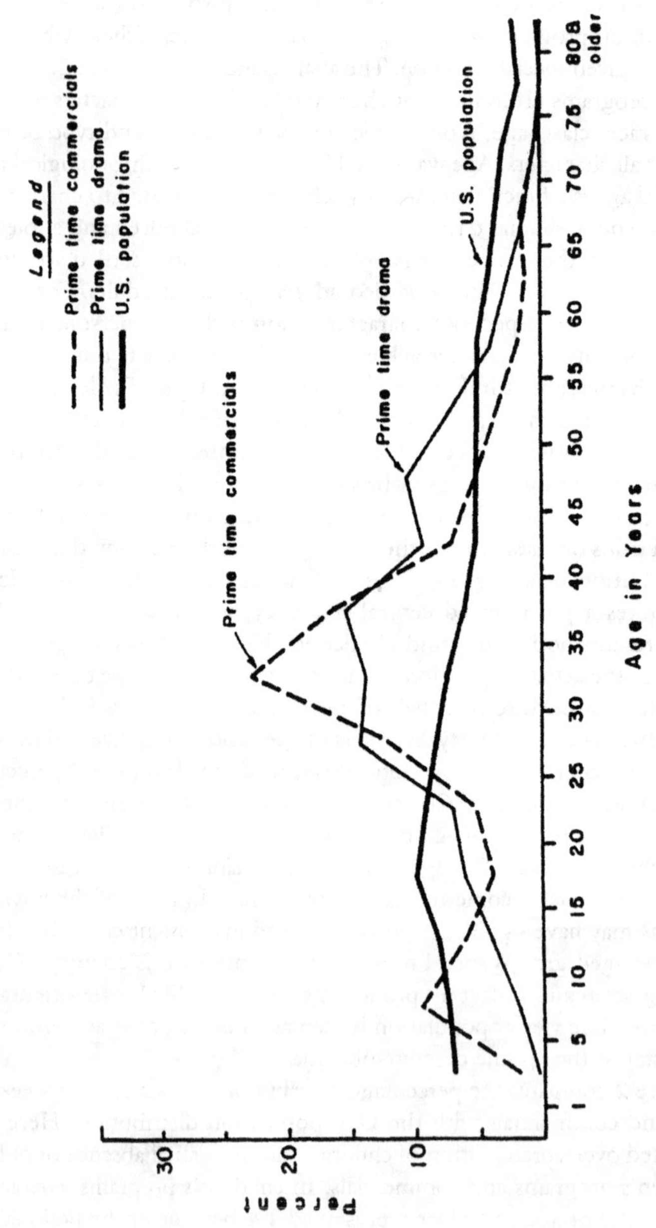

Figure 2. Age Distribution of U.S. Population, and Characters in Commericals and Dramatic Programs in Weekend-Daytime

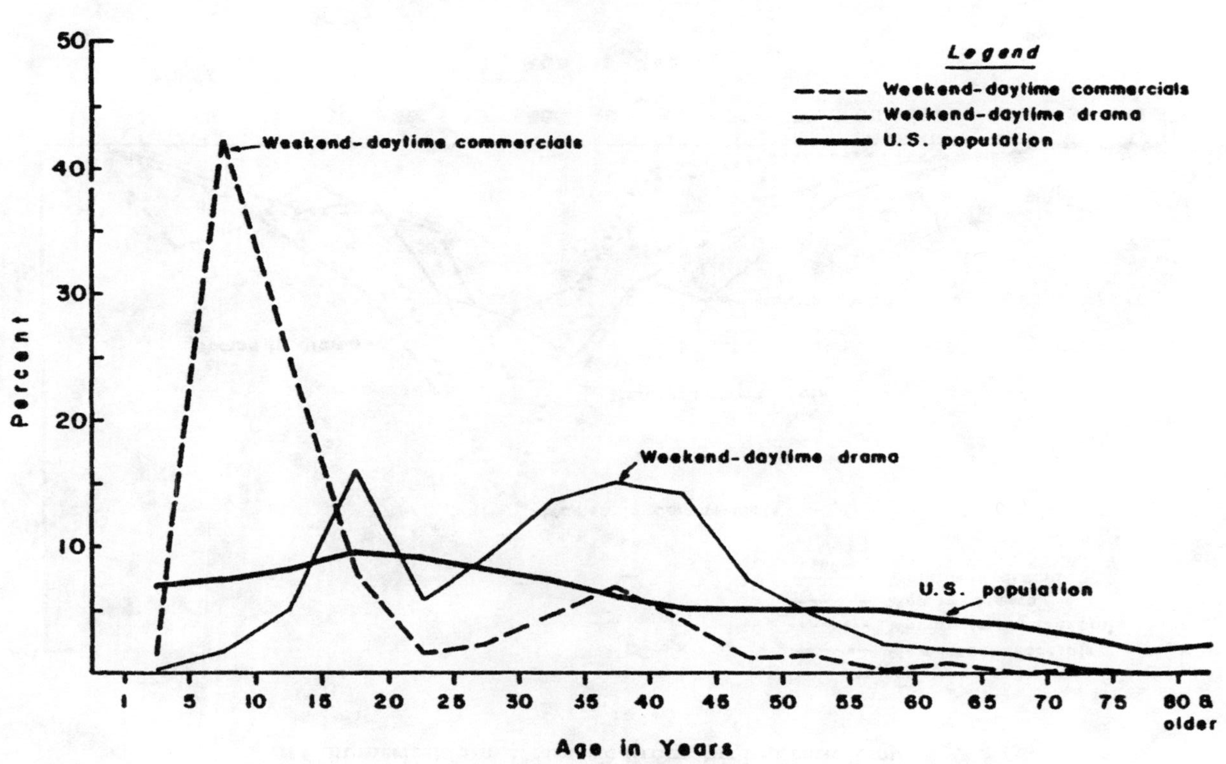

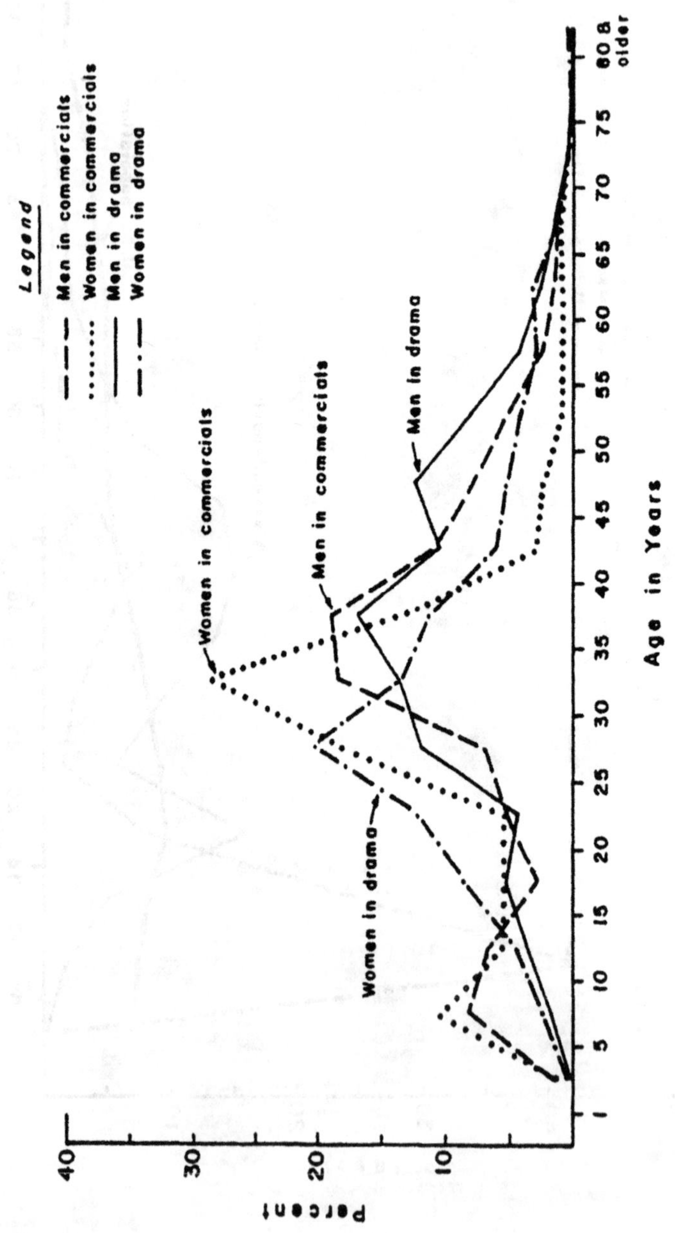

Figure 3. Age Distribution of Male and Female Characters in Commericals and Dramatic Programs in Prime Time

age group of the parents of young children had a low profile, as did the age group of their grandparents. A significant portion of the larger group in their forties provided most of the villains.

In the world of prime time television drama, as in most mass media, men outnumbered women about three to one. This act has profound consequences for all that happens in that world, from patterns of aging and employment to sex and violence. Given such a cast, the stories that can be told best are stories of power and conflict, stories in which older characters (especially women) are most likely to end up as victims.

Gender differences can be seen in Figures 3 and 4. Figure 3 shows the percentage age distribution of male and female characters in prime time dramatic programs and commercials. A larger percentage of women than men in their early twenties appeared in dramatic programs, when women's function as romantic partners and young housewives is supposed to peak, but then their numbers fall to four or five times below the number of men as their ages rise. (In commercials, there were more women than men in their early thirties.) As their usefulness in the world of television drama declined, their numbers shrank and their roles were constricted. While women were most concentrated—with almost a third of their total numbers—in the twenty-five to thirty-four years age bracket, men were most concentrated—also with almost a third of their numbers in the thirty-five to forty-four years age bracket.

The character population is structured to provide a relative abundance of younger women for older men, but no such abundance of younger men for older women. In other words, women age faster than men but both are barely visible in old age in the world of television. Television perpetuates an inequitable, if conventional, gender-age role.

Figure 4 shows the gender pattern in weekend-daytime children's programs (mostly cartoons). Over half of all females were under twenty-one, but only 28 percent of all males were under twenty-one. The most visible male age group was that between thirty-five and forty-five. Fully one-third of all men in weekend-daytime programs fell into that group. The pattern of aging reflected in prime time also is evident in weekend-daytime programs. Women over sixty-five, over 12 percent of the real female population, were 4 percent of the women in the world of children's television; older men accounted for only 3 percent of all male characters.

Weekend-daytime commercials showed a larger percentage of boys (71% of male characters) as well as girls (85% of females) under nineteen years of age. But older characters hardly existed; less than 1 percent of both genders were sixty-five and over.

Representation is, of course, not just a question of numbers or of fidelity to census figures. It is a question of the variety of roles, opportunities, life chances, and images most people see in common from infancy on and as they grow old. Those underrepresented in the world of television are necessarily more stereotyped and limited. Visibility is privilege in the symbolic world. Symbolic annihilation is the price paid for aging in our (and our children's) entertainment.

Figure 5 compares the percentage age distributions of white and non-white men and women in prime time drama. It shows that while white male characters

Figure .4. Age Distribution of Male and Female Characters in Commercials and Dramatic Programs in Weekend-Daytime

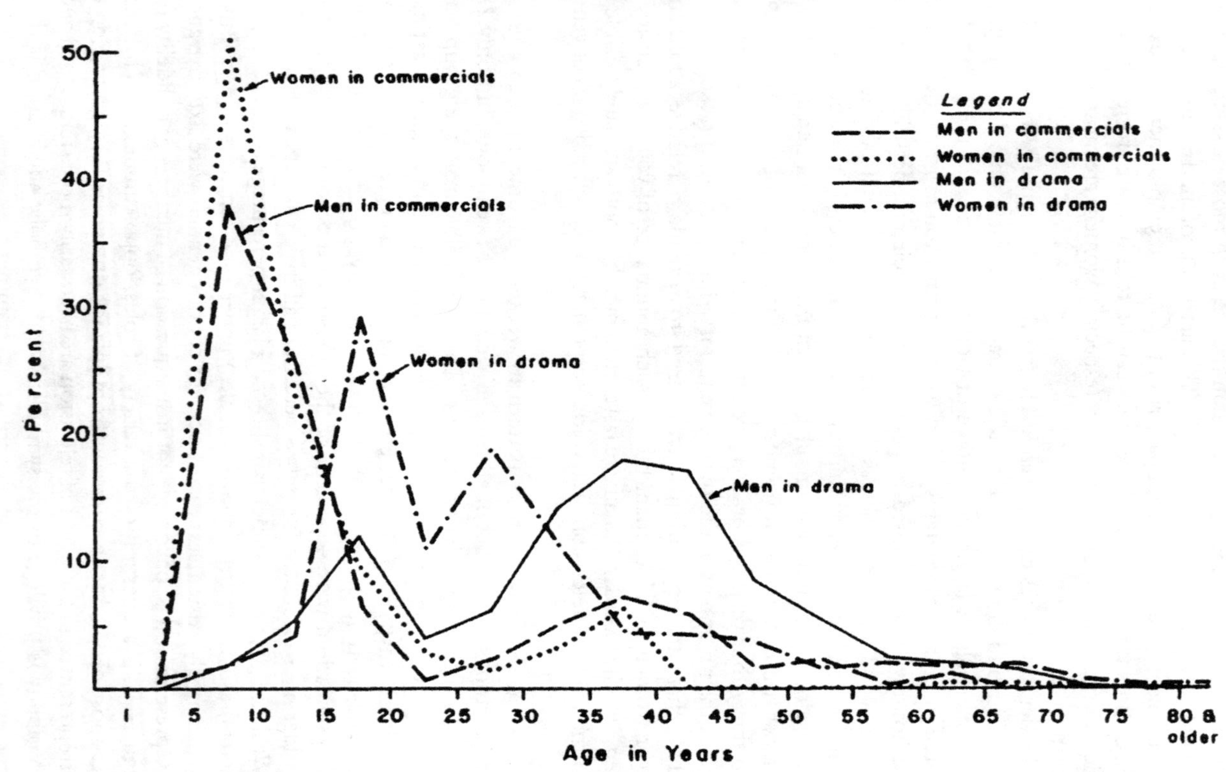

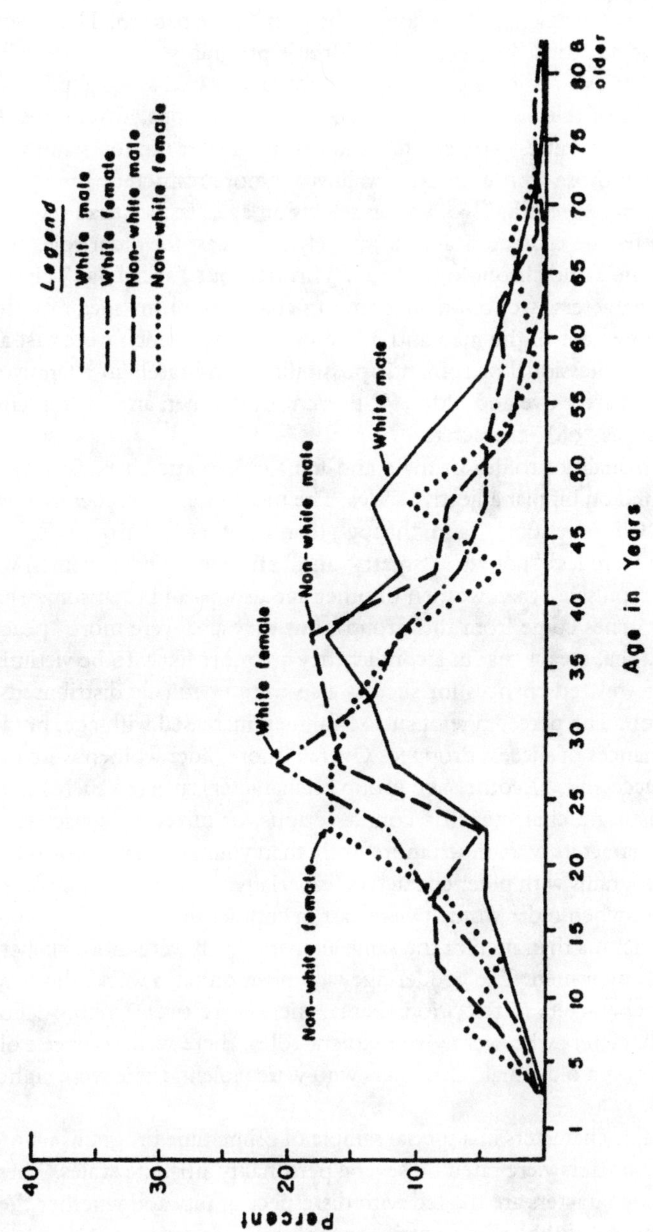

Figure 5. Age Distribution of White and Non-White Male and Female Characters in Prime Time Drama

dominated the age range between thirty-five and forty-five, both non-white men and all women tended to be younger than that. Minority males occupied an age-related power position between white males and all females. The pattern in commercials was a somewhat exaggerated version of the prime time pattern. There were no characters sixty-five and over in weekend children's programs or commercials who were not white. Age as a resource cuts two ways for race as well as for gender. Those for whom the world of television has more use—with more jobs, adventures, sex, power, and other opportunities—are created and cast in greater numbers and more potent positions than those whose dramatic values are more restricted.

We have seen that women on television age "faster" than men. This means that mature female characters are more likely to be cast for older roles than male characters of the same chronological age. Through our "social age" classification of dramatic characters, we found that among characters from ages fifty-five to sixty-four, only 22 percent of the men and 33 percent of the women were cast as old characters with no professional or romantic possibilities, and rarely in a family setting. Among characters sixty-five and older, 72 percent of the men and 90 percent of the women were cast as "old" characters.

Personality profiles of male and female dramatic characters by social age were delineated on bipolar adjective scales. The mean ratings of older men were less "attractive," "fair," "rational," and "happy" than of other age groups. The mean ratings of women were less "potent," "smart," and "efficient." Older women were significantly more "repulsive" than women of other age groups and even somewhat more so than men (witches come from this group); but they also were more "peaceful," which, as we shall see, means that in a conflict they are more likely to be victimized.

Age-related chances for success also were unequally distributed in the world of television. The percentage of successful men increased with age, but as women aged, their chances of success dropped. Overall, more older women were unsuccessful than were successful. No other age group of characters suffered such a fate.

Casting a character in a comic, serious, or mixed role also was related to age. Older characters were much more likely than younger characters to be cast in a comic role. Programs with older characters (especially women) were most likely to be comedies. But when older women were cast in conflict situations, they were more likely to be the victims than men of the same age, and both were more likely to be victimized than younger men. The gender-age victimization ratio works this way: For every ten violent characters in television drama, there were twelve victims. For every ten old male characters who were given violent roles, there were fourteen old male victims. For every ten old female characters who were violent, there were eighteen old women victims.

Major characters in a special sample of prime time programs whose casts included older characters were rated on several personality attribute scales. These scales include whether characters are treated with disrespect or pity and whether they are portrayed as nuisances, stubborn, eccentric, or foolish.

More older characters were treated with disrespect than were characters in any other age group. About 70 percent of the older men and more than 80 percent of the older women were not held in high esteem or treated courteously, a very different pattern of treatment than that found for younger characters. Similarly, a much larger proportion of older characters than younger characters were portrayed as eccentric or foolish. A greater proportion of older women than older men—two-thirds compared to about one-half—were presented as lacking common sense, silly, or eccentric.

What are the lessons viewers derive from television about growing old in our society? To investigate the conceptions of age among television viewers, we used data from the National Council on Aging's Myth and Reality of Aging survey, conducted by Louis Harris and Associates in 1974. We constructed an index of the conception of older people from responses to statements asserting that the number, the health, and the longevity of older people are declining. A high score on this index would reflect a generalized belief that old people represent a diminishing rather than growing segment of American society.

There is a significant positive relationship between the amount of television viewing and scores on this index. The more people watch television, the more they tend to perceive old people in generally negative and unfavorable terms. Heavy viewers believe significantly more than light viewers that old people are a vanishing breed. The correlation is not reduced by controls for education, income, sex, or age, and it is much stronger for younger people. Thus, even with important demographic variables held constant, heavy viewers are more likely than light viewers to believe that old people are disappearing. Furthermore, those who watch more television are more likely to believe that people (especially women) become old earlier in life than those who watch less.

Other and later survey findings also show that heavy viewers are more likely than otherwise comparable groups of light viewers to think that older people are not open-minded and adaptable, are not bright and alert, and are not good at getting things done. All of these relationships are stronger among younger respondents, those between the ages of eighteen and twenty-nine.

We found similar patterns in studies of adolescents. When we asked about 600 sixth- to ninth-graders, "At what age does a man become elderly or old?" light viewers gave the combined average as fifty-seven, while heavy viewers felt that people become old at fifty-one. Most of these adolescents believe women become old before men do.

We did not find watching television to be associated with *any* positive images of older people. Of course, there are notable exceptions of individual episodes and even series, such as the popular *The Golden Girls* (which, however, also conforms to the pattern of comedy format, age-sex humor, and the absence of normal family setting). But most viewers watch by the clock, not by the program, and heavy viewers watch more of everything. They cannot escape the overall portrayal of aging in the world of television, the composite view of which is revealed in our studies. Consequently, heavy viewers believe that the elderly are in worse shape both physically and financially than they used to be, not active sexually, close-minded, and not good at getting things done. At the same time, television is telling young people that old age, especially for women, begins relatively early in life.

The social goal of a medium that serves as the chief cultural arm of industrial society should be to mediate enlightened visions of aging, and of life in general, to the broadest and most diverse publics. However, the conflict between that goal and the function of efficient marketing tends to make productive aging and communication across age groups more difficult. Even with the proliferation of channels and the increasingly demographically targeted marketing strategies, the largest and most heterogeneous prime time and weekend children's audiences share in common a vision of aging that is anything but productive. It cultivates conceptions that trap the elderly in limited and unproductive roles and it fails to promote the kind of vitality that is, in fact, characteristic of a growing number of old women and men. The overall television image resists rather than assists efforts to increase the scope and speed of productive aging.

These patterns are parts of a system of broadcasting and of storytelling with deep historical and commercial roots. They compose the cultural environment into which children are born and in which we all grow and learn aging as a social role, shifting much of the battle for productive aging to the cultural frontier.

Despite progress on many fronts, the overall patterns of the mainstream of the cultural environment have been very stable over the quarter-century that we have been able to track them. The prospects for significant change depend on change in the environment in which these patterns are embedded. We need a new environmental movement, a cultural environmental movement, to place the issue of television policy on productive aging on the national agenda. The need is not to regulate the image of aging—or anything else—on television but to loosen the existing constraints distorting it.

Consciousness of the dynamics of how one learns about aging in a mass culture is necessary for liberation from its constraints. Old people and their organizations have good reasons to be in the forefront of that liberation movement. It involves coalition and constituency building, including media councils in the United States and abroad; groups concerned with children and youth as well as aging; women's groups; religious and minority organizations; educational, health, environmental, legal, and other professional associations; consumer groups and agencies; associations of creative workers in the media and in the arts and sciences; independent computer network organizers, and other organizations and individuals committed to loosening the constraints that now limit freedom and diversity on television.

Such a coalition will oppose domination of the airways by the limiting and exploitative formulas of marketing and work to abolish both concentration of ownership and censorship, public or private. It will expose use of the First Amendment only as a shield for power and privilege. It will seek to extend rights, facilities, and influence to interests and perspectives other than the most powerful and profitable. It will strive to include in cultural decision making the less affluent, more vulnerable groups which, collectively, are the majority of the population.

Waiting for advertisers to keep "discovering" the "age market," which they frequently do, is of limited use because it does not change the domination of the broad marketplace by the prime time perspective. Productive aging as asocial role is defined by the whole culture, not by the elderly or those who market to them. The best time to learn the meaning of productive aging is while one is growing up within a culture.

The cultural environment movement will support journalists, artists, writers, actors, directors, and other creative workers struggling for more freedom from having to present life in the most conventionally saleable packages. It will work with labor and other groups for diversity in employment and in media content. It will promote media literacy, media awareness, critical viewing and reading, and other media educational efforts as an essential educational objective on every level. It will place cultural policy issues on the social-political agenda. It will not wait for a blueprint; it will create and experiment with ways of community and citizen participation in local, national, and international media policymaking. A realistic democratic mechanism for broad public participation in cultural policymaking, unprecedented but ultimately inescapable, as that may be, is the way to make aging, starting with youth, as productive as it can be.

REFERENCES

Gerbner, G. (1980). Children and power on television: The other side of the picture. In G. Gerbner, K. J. Ross, & E. Zigler (eds.), *Child abuse reconsidered: An analysis and agenda for action* (pp. 239–248). New York: Oxford University Press.

Gerbner, G., Gross, L., Morgan, M., & Signorielli, N. (1981, June). *Aging with television commercials: Images on television commercials and dramatic programming*, 1977–1979. Philadelphia: The Annenberg School of Communications, University of Pennsylvania.

Gerbner, G., Gross, L., Morgan, M., & Signorielli, N. (1986, September). *Television's mean world: Violence Profile No. 14–15.* Philadelphia: The Annenberg School of Communications, University of Pennsylvania.

Gerbner, G., Gross, L., Signorielli, N., & Morgan, M. (Winter, 1980). Aging with television: Images of television drama and conceptions of social reality. *Journal of Communication*, 30(1), 37–47.

Part VII

HIGHLIGHTS, EXCERPTS, and BRIEF REPORTS

CHAPTER 27

CASTING AND FATE

Women and Minorities on Television Drama, Game Shows, and News

BY GEORGE GERBNER

INTRODUCTION

Casting and fate are the building blocks of storytelling. Ours is a bird's-eye view of what large communities absorb over long periods of time. It attempts to answer questions about the television all viewers watch but none see: What is the cast of characters that animates the world of television? How are women and minorities (seniors, racial and ethnic groups, poor and disabled persons, etc.) represented? And, finally, how do they fare in that world—what is their share of heroes and villains, winners and losers, violents and victims?

Our focus is on recurrent and inescapable images of the mainstream of the cultural environment in which we all live and which contribute to the shaping of power relations in society. These are features of the total programming structure that cultivate conceptions of majority and minority status and the corresponding calculus of visibility, power, and risk. Inescapable also are the implications citizens concerned with communication, culture, and community, and for the television industry—the people who sponsor it, run it, write, produce and direct its programs, and act in it. This report is based on ten years of monitoring and analyzing commercial television programs. Commercial television dominates American broadcasting with major networks capturing about 80 percent of the total audience. The report is based on the analysis of 19,642 speaking parts appearing in 1,371 major network (ABC, CBS, NBC) prime time and Saturday morning children's programs. One-season samples were used in daytime programs, game shows and news, cable-originated dramatic programs, and Fox network dramatic programs.

"Dramatic" was defined as fictional programs with a storyline or plot, including series, films, cartoons, and other clearly fictional programs shown on television. "Cable-originated" was defined as those programs, including feature movies, in whose production the eleven major cable networks had a substantial financial interest.

It is important to consider the strengths and limitations of the Cultural Indicators approach. It is intended to reveal features cutting across all types of programming and to bring out general patterns in a representative and comparative perspective. These are the patterns of conceptions and action television cultivates from cradle to grave.

In that perspective, the most remarkable finding is the relative stability of the patterns. We observe the cultural products of a robust industrial and marketing system whose structure changed little in the last decades.

This is not to underestimate the possibility and importance of change but, on the contrary, to emphasize the forces of resistance, both in deep-seated conceptions and in institutional policies. The most important contribution of these studies, therefore, is a realistic understanding of what efforts to change such conceptions and policies are up against. Understanding the cultural terrain in which corrective action is planned is the first requirement for successful intervention.

The studies were supported by the *Screen Actors Guild*, the *American Federation of Television and Radio Artists,* and the *Turner Broadcasting System* in 1992, and conducted by the *Cultural Indicators research team* at the *University of Pennsylvania's Annenberg School for Communication.*[1] All programs were screened and coded by trained analysts using an extensively tested instrument of analysis. The procedure requires the reliable observation by independent coders of programs and characters in the samples. Further methodological details can be found in publications in the list of references.

CASTING

Americans spend more time with television than the next 10 highest-ranked leisure time activities put together. During that time the average viewer of a major network station is exposed to an average of 355 characters playing speaking parts each week in prime time dramatic programs, 353 in daytime dramatic series, 138 in Saturday morning (children's) programs, 51 in game shows, and 209 news professionals (including repeated appearances) delivering the local and national news. About 1 out of 5 are "major characters."

A general demographic overview finds that women comprise one-third or less of characters in all samples except daytime serials where they are 45 percent and in game shows where they are 55 percent. The smallest percentage of women is in the news (28%) and in children's programs (23%). Even that shrinks to 18 percent as the importance of the role rises to "major character."

While all seniors are greatly underrepresented, visibly old people, roughly 65 and above, are hardest to find on television. Their representation ranges from none on the youth-oriented Fox network and about 1 percent on network daytime series to less than 3 percent in the other samples. In real life, their proportion is 12 percent and growing. African Americans are most visible on Fox and in game shows. On major network prime time programs they are 11 percent and on daytime serials 9 percent of all characters. They are least visible on Saturday morning children's programs. (Many cartoon characters cannot be reliably coded for race.)

Latin/Hispanic characters are rarely seen. Only in game shows do they rise significantly above 1 percent representation. Americans of Asian/Pacific origin and Native Americans ("Indians") are even more conspicuous by their absence. Less than 1 percent (in the case of Native Americans 0.3 percent) is their general representation.

Almost as invisible are members of the "lower class" (judged by a three-way classification of the socio-economic status of major characters). Although the U.S. census classifies more than 14 percent of the general population, 29 percent of Latino/Hispanics, and 33 percent of African Americans as "poor," and many more as low income wage earners, on network television they make up only 1.3 percent of characters in prime time, 1.2 percent in daytime, half that (0.6 percent) in children's programs, and 0.2 percent in the news.

We shall now take a closer look at the casts of prime time, daytime, children's, Fox and cable-originated dramatic programs, and news.

PRIME TIME DRAMATIC PROGRAMS

Despite changes in styles, stars, and formats, prime time network dramatic television presents a remarkably stable cast. As we have noted, two-thirds are men. The gender imbalance was virtually the same in 1982 as in 1992 (35% and 34%, respectively).

"Elderly" characters are 2.5 percent (the real life proportion is more than 12%). In the ten years included in the sample, they tended to decline in their proportion of the prime time population, a trend contrary to facts.

Women in prime time tend to be concentrated in the younger age groups. They "age faster" than men and lose more roles (and jobs) as they enter middle age. The percentage of young adult females exceeds that of males of the same age group by 12 percent. As "settled adults," however, women's roles are 13 percent fewer than men's. In the gender-bender world of television, there is a particular shortage of mature women. Contrary to any measure of reality, the average viewer will see 2.5 times as many mature men as women.

Romance may be rampant on prime time but marriage is not. Only one in ten characters is known to be married. Marriage is more of a defining circumstance for women than it is for men. For two-thirds of male characters we just don't know or care whether they're married or not. Knowledge of marital status, as of age, religion, or income, tends to place conditions on macho adventure. But we know that more than half of female characters are married. This results in the anomaly that nearly half of all married characters are women, despite the fact that prime time women are one-third of the cast and are concentrated in the younger age groups. Selective observers point to the high proportion of career women on television. They miss the fact that women are almost twice as likely to play the role of wife as men are to play the role of husband. Marriage is not only a more defining but also a more confining condition for women than for men.

As already noted, "lower class" characters make up only 1.3 percent of the prime time population. Women, who hold most of the lower paid jobs in real life, make up only 0.9 percent of the "lower class" of all characters and 0.5 percent of major characters.

Race and ethnicity are as skewed as gender, age, and class. The ten-year average of African Americans is 11 percent of the prime time population (12% in the 1991–92 season), fairly close to their actual proportion. But Latino/Hispanic characters, over 9 percent of the U.S. population, are 1.1 percent of the prime time cast. Americans of Asian/Pacific origin, more than 3 percent of the U.S. population, are 0.8 percent, and Native Americans ("Indians"), more than 1 percent in real life, are 0.3 percent in prime time. Most seasonal fluctuations are within 1 percent of the ten season averages, with no clear tendency in any direction.

The relative visibility of African American characters becomes a double-edged feature of casting. The mark of minority status is not only underrepresentation but also disproportionate deprivation. For example, in reality the poverty and unemployment rates of African Americans are two to three times those of whites. Arguably, a mass medium of universal appeal and some democratic pretension would pay special attention to that condition. On television it is hidden from view. On both prime time and Saturday morning, the black middle class is larger than the white (92 to 89%) but the "lower class" is about the same, around a minuscule 1 percent of each group.

Some form of disability strikes 11 percent of prime time major characters. Violence appears to be mostly painless because physical injury afflicts 8 percent of men and 7 percent of women, despite the fact that 49 percent of men and 31 percent of women suffer some violence. Physical illness strikes almost as many, and mental illness nearly 4 percent. We shall discuss their fate later.

Fox network programming targets young viewers. The average age of characters on Fox is 31—the youngest of all dramatic programs. Fox is also heavily comedy and action-oriented, as is cable-originated programming. Consequently, more men and fewer women are cast in major roles. Seniors are fewer and those cast play mostly minor roles. On Fox, and to a lesser extent on cable-originated programs, more characters are observed as unmarried and as injured than on other networks.

DAYTIME SERIALS

Daytime is serious business, mostly sexual and marital. Only 7 percent of daytime drama was judged to be "mostly humorous," far below the prime time 30 percent. Daytime is the only daypart where the number of women almost equals that of men (45 percent) and where almost as many women (49 percent) as men play major roles.

Male hegemony is preserved, if barely, in age-casting. Daytime, as prime time, favors men with longer mid-life span. However, daytime is a little more even-handed than prime time, and the cast is more clearly and evenly defined along marital lines. The world of daytime serial drama has less use for maritally undefined men and more need for married men and women.

The class and race structure of daytime is similar to that of prime time, and, if anything, even less poor and more "white." Handicaps, illness, and injury are rare and seem to afflict mostly men.

SATURDAY MORNING

Cartoon characters make up most of the Saturday morning cast. Women are less than one-fourth of that cast. As major characters, their percentage goes down to 18. Importance declines with age, as well as with gender. As age increases, the percentage of major compared to minor roles drops, especially for women.

Curiously for children's programs, married characters, potential father and mother images, are less than half their prime time proportions. Saturday morning shuns married women: they play 20 percent of major female roles in prime time but only 3 percent in children's programs.

Sex comes early on television, especially on cartoons, and most of all the women. Prime time romance involves a higher percentage of adolescent and young women than men, but more mature men than women. The disparity is even greater in Saturday morning children's programs. Only 22 percent of males but 49 percent of females involved in romance are adolescents. In all other age groups, the percentage of romantically involved males is greater than that of females. The child viewer may see three mature men involved in romance for every mature woman, and even a romantic old man every once in a while, but never a romantically involved old woman.

Social class, when it can be observed, is as skewed in children's as in prime time programs. The child viewer of Saturday morning major network programs would see, on the average, one lower class character every three weeks, usually in a minor role.

With more than half of all characters unclassifiable by race, African Americans average 3 percent, though their proportion varies greatly, reaching 7 percent in 1991–92. Hispanics are seen, on the average, once every two weeks (0.5%) and Asian/Pacific Americans once every three weeks (0.3%), and mostly in minor roles. In the nine Saturday morning three-network samples, only three Native Americans appeared (0.1%). Despite all the mayhem, only 3 percent of Saturday morning characters suffer any injury (in the 1991–92 sample none seemed injured) and less than 5 percent exhibit signs of any disability (in 1991–92 it was 2%).

Cable-originated children's programs present a slightly more equitable gender, race and disability character distribution, but otherwise they resemble the major network cast.

GAME SHOWS

Major network game shows feature a populist patriarchy. The contestants are more diverse than the casts of other programs. Women are 58 percent, African Americans 18 percent, seniors 7 percent, Latino/Hispanics 5 percent—more than on any other programs—and they tend to win more often than the majority types. The hosts, however, are middle-aged men. Women who are not contestants are young with assistants to the hosts, and three out of four assistants are seen but not heard.

MAJOR NETWORK NEWS

News items were classified into fifty different themes, including political, economic, and human interest. Topics judged to be the significant main themes in more than 15 percent of the items were issues of power: who has it, who uses it, who seeks it, and, most of all, who threatens it.

Criminal activities and health issues each attract major attention in 18 percent of the items; law enforcement and other legal issues in 16 percent each; and death and dying in 15 percent. Women's rights attract major attention only in connection with abortion, in 6 percent of the items. Other minority groups, people, or rights together are featured in only 3 percent.

The power-oriented thematic structure of television defines who delivers the news, who is cited in the news, and who make news. Next to game show hosts, the world of news is the most male-dominated. The mean age of those in the news is forty-one, the highest on television except for game show hosts. An article in *American Journalism Review* (September, 1993, p. 22) described the "classic anchor team" as "craggy veteran anchorguy; attractive, posed, perfect second-wife-for-the-anchorguy anchorgal; jolly weather fella; rugged sportsguy."

Men are 64 percent of those delivering the news, 80 percent of those cited as authorities, and 82 percent of those making news. Women are most visible (35%) as performers delivering the news. As authorities cited, they drop to 20 percent and as newsmakers to 18 percent. Productive aging in the news, even more than in other types of programs, is a privilege of men and majorities. Newsmakers over sixty are 12 percent of men, 6 percent of women, and 1 percent or less of minorities.

The most visible minority newscasters are African Americans. They make up 14 percent of those who deliver the news. But as their authority grows their number drops even faster than women's. Their proportion declines to 8 percent as newsmakers and to 4 percent of authorities cited in the news. Americans of Asian/Pacific origin are most likely to appear as sources cited (4%) and as delivering the news (2%). Latino/Hispanics make 1.5 percent of news, or less, in any category.

Three major groups dominate the stories in the news. Government officials (including law enforcement) are 43 percent of newsmakers and 12 percent of authorities cited. Private business makes up 11.5 percent of newsmakers and 8 percent of those cited. The next largest group making news (6.4%) is those suspected, arrested, or convicted of crimes. Women are more likely to make news as government officials (16%) than as private business persons (6%). Minorities have a proportionately even better chance to make news as government officials than as private business persons. African Americans in government (19%) are ten times as newsworthy and Latino/Hispanics (21%) four times as newsworthy as they are in business. Government is clearly more of an equal-opportunity newsmaker.

The disparities are even greater when we compare news of legitimate and illegal activity. Women make news in connection with legitimate activities 10 times as much as in crime. The same ratio for men is 8, for Latino/Hispanics 5, and for African Americans 2. The ratio of legitimate business-related vs. crime-related news shows still more striking contrasts. For every woman in crime news there are 3 in business news; for every man in crime news there are 2 in business news; for every Latino/Hispanic in crime news there is one in business news; but for every African American in business news there are 6.6 in crime news.

To look at this another way, crime claims 13 percent of African Americans in the news compared to 6 percent of all men, 5 percent of Latino/Hispanics, and 2 percent of women. The double-edged visibility of African Americans becomes clear when we consider that about 62 percent of real life criminals are white, African Americans are at least twice as likely to appear in crime news as any other group.

This brings us to the discussion of "fate" on television

FATE

"Fate" in this study means whether characters are destined to be clearly good or bad, to achieve success or to fail, and, if involved in violence, to be perpetrators or victims. We present the dynamics of fate in the multi-season samples of major network prime time and Saturday morning programs.

In the context of single programs and stores that we typically attend as viewers, these are of course complex matters of plot, reasoning, point of view, and interpretation. Simple counts cannot do justice to these complexities. But our methods are not designed to reflect subtleties, motivations, or justifications. Therefore, the validity of relatively simple counts should not be dismissed, nor their ability to illuminate crucial aspects of the dynamics of fate in television storytelling underestimated.

Close, detailed interpretations, such as those of television critics, may provide multiple intriguing and compelling insights about specific outcomes in specific dramatic contexts. But our analysis serves a different function. As the bird's-eye view of familiar territory, it shows not what individual viewers may or may not see at a particular time but the inescapable features large communities absorb over a lifetime. The repetitive daily systemic experience of who is who, who gets what, and who gets away with what against whom, regardless of reasons or justifications, has a message of its own: a message of value, effectiveness, vulnerability, and of social typing.

HEROES AND VILLAINS

Television seems to present a pre-ordained world. Positively valued outnumber evil characters between two and three to one in each of the years included in our samples. From half to two-thirds of the casts are mixed. Children's program characters are more sharply differentiated, with fewer mixed evaluations.

For every bad man there about two good men and for every bad woman about five good women in both prime time and Saturday morning programs. But while the ratio is generally favorable to women, the evaluations are reversed for elderly women. For every elderly male villain there are thirteen male heroes of the same age. But for every female villain, there is only one female hero. The proportion of bad old females is more than eight times that of bad old males.

A ranking of "goodness/badness" ratios has been constructed by dividing the number of positively valued by the number of negatively valued characters in each group. The results give us an order of "villainy."

For every 100 heroes in prime time there are, overall, 43 villains. The most favorable ratios are those of most minorities, women, and children. For example, for every 100 heroes, Asian/Pacific Americans have only 14, women and children 19, and African Americans 22 villains. Knowing the age, marital, and family status of characters generally means more favorable portrayal than not knowing. The least favorable ratios are those lower class, Latino/Hispanic, and foreign (or at least not identifiable American) characters. For every 100 heroes, lower class characters have 65, foreign characters of color 79, Latino/Hispanics 92, and foreign whites 119 villains.

Differences by gender shed further light on some of these ratios. For males, it is better not to be married than to be married. Among all male characters, foreign, young, and Latino/Hispanic men have the least favorable "hero/villain" ratios. Evil aliens of color are all men. Foreign white and mentally ill males provide a disproportionate ratio of male villains. The largest ratio of female villains comes from mentally ill and old women characters.

In Saturday morning children's programs, female, disabled, and older characters fare even worse than in prime time. Mother figures in leading roles—married, elderly, settled women—and major African American female characters, few as they are, are among the most evil. For every 100 African American female heroes in Saturday morning programs there are 33 villains, compared to 11 for African American men. For every 100 elderly women heroes there are 88 villains, compared to 8 for men—11 times the male "villainy" ratio. Looking at major characters only, wicked married, older, and African American women—but not men—actually outnumber positive characters.

WINNERS AND LOSERS

Characters who succeed in their aims we call winners and those who fail losers. Nearly half are "mixed" both in evaluation and success. Of those judged "good," 63 percent succeed and 6 percent fail. Of the "bad" characters, 10 percent succeed and 79 percent fail. Success, therefore, may be seen partly as a measure of effectiveness as well as of moral worth. In prime time, the average ratio is 40 failures for every 100 successes. Only foreign whites, Native Americans ("Indians"), and the mentally ill fail at least as often as they succeed. Mentally ill characters fail 1.5 times for every success.

Marriage hurts men but helps women. Men are more likely to succeed if not married. Unmarried men fail 32 times while married men fail 45 times for every 100 successes. Women, on the contrary, are more successful if married; their ratio is 29 failures if married and 42 failures if unmarried for 100 successes.

Latino/Hispanic and foreign males (but not females) are among those most likely to fail; 60 and 160 failures, respectively, for every 100 successes. Class, age, and health cut differently for men and women. Lower class men succeed 5 times as often as they fail but lower class women fail as often as they succeed. Elderly men are among the most successful with only 8 failures for every 100 successes, while elderly women fail over 6 times more, 50 for every 100 successes. Physically ill men fail 58 times but women 75 times for every 100 successes. Mentally ill men fail 147 times but women 160 times for 100 successes. Being cast Hispanic and foreign male, and poor, old, or ill female carry calamitous risks of failure in prime time.

The world of Saturday morning children's programs is more starkly, and darkly, defined. More than one-fourth of all characters fail, compared to 18 percent in prime time. Foreign, old, and ill characters fail more than they succeed. The mentally ill fail twice as often. All minorities run a higher rate of failure Saturday morning than in prime time.

While marriage hurts men and helps women in prime time, in children's programs it hurts more and it hurts both. Elderly women have 4 times the relative failure rate of elderly men. To be cast an older woman or a mentally ill character in children's programs is to run the highest risk of ill fate on all of television.

VIOLENTS AND VICTIMS

Mass-produced violence injected into formula-driven programs presents a consistent social structure. It occurs about 5 times per prime time and 25 times per Saturday morning hour. In prime time it involves more than 6 out of 10 programs and nearly half of all characters. In Saturday morning children's programs, more than 9 out of 10 programs and 8 out of 10 characters involve violence.

Of course, there is blood in fairy tales, gore in mythology, murder in Shakespeare. But the individually crafted, selectively used, and often dreadful violence of art and journalism, capable of balancing tragic costs against deadly compulsions, has been swamped by "happy violence" produced for general entertainment and sales on the dramatic assembly line. Happy violence is swift, cool, painless, and effective, employed by good guys as well as bad, leading to a happy ending. It is designed to deliver an audience to the next commercial in a receptive mood.

With a predominantly male cast, and given the typical action scenario, the stage is set for stories of power, conflict, violence. But violence and victimization are not evenly distributed. The relative risks of victimization are higher for women and for "lower class" characters. They are also higher, and even more uneven, in Saturday morning programs. Furthermore, as characters age, their risks tend to increase. Lethal victimization extends the pattern. Overall, about 10 percent of major characters are involved in killing. For every 10 killers 5 are killed. But for every 10 persons of color, 7 are killed; for Latino/Hispanic characters, 13 are killed; for disabled characters 15 are killed; and for every 10 women also 15 are killed. The most calamitous fatality ratio is reserved for the poor. For every 10 lower class characters who kill, 101 die a violent death, 20 times the general ratio.

CONCLUSIONS

Minorities are made, not born. The largest common process of their making is lifetime exposure to the world of television. That world seems to be frozen in a time warp of obsolete and damaging representations.

Women play one out of three roles in prime time television, one out of four in children's programs, and one out of five of those who make news. They fall short of majority even in daytime serials. They age faster than men, and as they age they are more likely to be portrayed evil and unsuccessful.

Seniors of both genders are greatly underrepresented and seem to be vanishing instead of increasing as in real life. As characters age they lose importance, value, and effectiveness. Visibly old people are almost invisible on television. Mature women seem to be especially hard to cast—and hard to take. They are disproportionately underrepresented, undervalued, and undersexed.

People of color are the vast majority of humankind, and African Americans are less than 11 percent of prime time and 3 percent of children's program casts, and mostly middle class. Latino/Hispanics, over 9 percent of the U.S. population, are about 1 percent of prime time and half of that of children's program casts. Americans of Asian/Pacific origin, more than 3 percent of the U.S. population, and Native Americans ("Indians"), more than 1 percent, are conspicuous by their virtual absence. The world of daytime serials is even more "white" than prime time. A child viewer sees the fewest minorities.

In the overwhelmingly middle-class consumer world of television, poor people play a negligible role. The low income 13 percent of the United States (and much larger percentage of minorities) is reduced to 1.3 percent or less on television. Women of low income, who hold most of the low income jobs in real life, are even more invisible.

As the 43 million disabled Americans gain legal rights of equal access and employment in real life, physical disability is visible in only 1.5 percent of prime time programs. Those shown as disabled fare relatively badly in Saturday morning children's programs. Mentally ill characters fare badly in all types of programs.

If prime time is a time of macho adventures, family comedies, and societal power plays, daytime is a time of interior turbulence. Its sexual and marital themes raise female representation but reduce social diversity below that of prime time.

Programs designed specifically for children's favorite viewing time, Saturday morning, present a world that is the harshest and most exploitive of all. The inequities of prime time are magnified Saturday morning. A child will see about 123 characters each Saturday morning, but rarely, if ever, a mature female as leader. The Saturday morning viewer sees an elderly leading character, if at all, about once every three weeks, and it is most likely to be a man. Married and parent images are curiously rare and gloomy in children's programs. Midlife and older women in Saturday morning children's programs are one of the least visible but most evil and, consequently, victimized group; this is where the witches come from.

All the mayhem in children's cartoons (32 acts per hour according to our studies) seems painless. Cartoon humor appears to be the sugar coating on the pill of cool, happy violence.

A disproportionate number of ill-fated characters comes from the ranks of poor, Latino, and foreign men, and both young and old, African American, and poor women. At the bottom of fate's "pecking order" are characters portrayed as old women and as mentally ill, perpetuating stigma of the most damaging kinds.

Casting and fate also affect those who deliver the news, who are referred to and cited in the news, and who are news. In most essential characteristics, news deals with the exercise of power: who has it, who uses it, who seeks it, and, most of all, who threatens it.

Women decline in representation from 35 percent as newscasters to 20 percent as authorities cited and 17 percent as newsmakers. Other minorities are also most visible delivering and least visible making news. When they do, they are most likely to appear as government officials or as criminals. African Americans make news as criminals at least twice as often as other groups do, despite the fact that 62 percent of criminals are white. No other minority suffers such fate.

These results show not what the U.S. television industry says or thinks it does but what it actually presents to the public. They provide a basis for judgment, policy, and citizen action. The cultural environment into which our children are born, just as the physical environment, is no longer a matter of individual choice but a matter of social policy and of human rights. A movement toward a free, diverse, and fair cultural environment has become a necessity to achieve media democracy in the telecommunication age.

NOTE

From Communication Culture Community, edited by Ed Hollander, Coen van der Linden, and Paul Rutten. Bohn Stafleu van Loghum. 1995

1. The Cultural Indicators project was initiated by the National Commission on the Causes and Prevention of Violence in 1969 and supported by the Surgeon General's Scientific Advisory Committee on Television and Social Behavior, the National Institute of Mental Health, the White House Office of Telecommunications Policy, the American Medical Association, the CEM Administration on Aging, the National Science Foundation, The Hoso Bunka Foundation, the National Cable Television Association, the Turner Broadcasting System, the American Association of Retired Persons, the Screen Actors Guild, and other organizations.

REFERENCES

Gerbner, G. (1985). Mass media discourse: Message System Analysis as a component of Cultural Indicators. In T. A. van Dijk (ed.), *Discourse and communication* (pp. 13–25). Berlin: Walter De Guyter & Co.

Gerbner, G. (1993). *Violence in cable-originated television programs. Research report.* Washington, D.C.: National Cable Television Association.

Gerbner, G., Holsti, O. R., Krippendorff, K., Paisley, W. J., & Stone, P. (eds.) (1969). *The analysis of communications content: Developments in scientific theories and computer techniques.* New York: John Wiley & Sons.

Gerbner, G., Gross, L., Morgan, M., & Signorielli, N. (1986). Living with television: The dynamics of the cultivation process. In J. Bryant & D. Zillmann (eds.), *Perspectives on media effects* (pp. 17–40). Hillsdale, N.J.: Lawrence Earlbaum Associates. [Reprinted in Halberstadt, A. G., & Ellyson, S. L. (eds.) (1990), *Social psychology readings: A century of research.* New York: McGraw-Hill Publishing Co.]

Gerbner, G., Gross, L., Morgan, M., & Signorielli, N. (1993). Growing up with television: The cultivation perspective. In J. Bryant & D. Zillman (eds.), *Media effects: Advances in theory and research* (pp. 17–41). Hillsdale, N.J.: Lawrence Earlbaum Associates.

Signorielli, N., & Morgan, M. J. (eds.) (1990). *Cultivation Analysis; New directions in media effects research.* Newbury Park, CA: Sage.

Chapter 28

EXCERPTS FROM ALCOHOL, TOBACCO, AND ILLICIT DRUGS IN ENTERTAINMENT TELEVISION, COMMERCIALS, NEWS, "REALITY SHOWS," MOVIES, AND MUSIC CHANNELS

BY GEORGE GERBNER
AND NEJAT OZYEGIN

We have noted in previous reports that the new frontier for health promotion and disease prevention is the cultural frontier. Most of what ails and kills us—such as alcohol, tobacco, and illicit drugs (ATID)—are culturally supported behavior patterns. They are sustained by the images and messages of a media-driven cultural environment.

Efforts to reduce the risk and prevent the abuse of addictive substances are up against the daily flow of "mixed messages" in that environment. This is an interim report of long-range research designed to track the direction and nature of that flow on prime time television, and in feature movies and music videos most popular especially with adolescents.

DESIGN OF THE RESEARCH

The research began in April 1995 and concludes in April 1997. Specific analytical issues to be addressed include (1) the frequency of portrayals over time, based on available trend data; (2) evaluative (positive, negative, neutral) and other tendencies and contexts of the representations; (3) the geography, demography, and action structure of substance use; (4) images, activities, appeals, and other associations found in alcohol commercials; (5) the frequency and content of tobacco and alcohol advertising, product placement, and use visible in television and movies; and (6) the association of alcohol, tobacco, and illegal drugs with particularly risky activities (e.g., driving, water activities, violence). This report focuses mostly on the first three objectives.

The Cultural Indicators (CI) database provides information about general trends on some items relevant to this investigation. An extended instrument of analysis was developed for this study. It includes many aspects of addictive substances presentation and characterization.

SAMPLES

The media samples used in this report are commercials on prime time television, news stories with alcohol, tobacco, and illicit drugs, and "reality shows" aired mostly during prime time.

The commercials sample consists of the 1,116 commercials aired during four weeks of dramatic programs on four major broadcast networks (ABC, CBS, NBC, Fox) from 7 P.M. to 11 P.M. The first week was sampled in April 1995, the second week in November 1995, the third week in April 1996, and the fourth week in October 1996. Of the commercials we analyzed, 1,003 are randomly selected. In addition, 144 commercials are coded because of their addictive substance content even though they did not fall into the random sample. The analysis is conducted by putting together all ATID commercials (including the 3.1% of the ATID commercials from the large random sample) and contrasting this group with the random sample of non-ATID commercials.

The news sample consists of the 151 news stories found by scanning a total of 1,985 stories in 124 local and national evening newscasts on four major broadcast networks (ABC, CBS, NBC, Fox). Selected stories are all of the news stories that deal with alcohol, tobacco, and illicit drugs during these newscasts. Local newscasts were from the Philadelphia area stations. The stories were aired during the last three of the sampling weeks mentioned in the preceding paragraph.

The reality shows sample consists of 51 episodes of programs that constitute a genre of television that uses documentary footage mostly for the dramatic purpose of telling a story of crime and law enforcement. The episodes aired mostly during prime time.

HIGHLIGHTS

A child is born into a home in which television is on an average of over 7 hours a day, four-fifths of it in prime time. It is a new cultural environment in which scenes containing alcohol, tobacco, or illicit drugs (ATID) are inescapable. They are present in 7 out of 10 prime time network dramatic programs, 38 of the 40 top-grossing movies, one half of the music videos, and many commercials and news stories.

ATID use is shown mostly as youthful, satisfying, and risk-free activity. Addicts are rare and evil rather than ill. While the wholesale distributor of ATID messages and images is prime time television, more selectively used media such as movies, news, and music channels extend similar patterns, exacerbate race and gender inequalities, and also ignore health implications but add associations with crime, destruction, and violence.

TELEVISION FICTION, FEATURE MOVIES, AND MUSIC CHANNELS

Alcohol, tobacco or illicit drugs are seen an average of every 15 minutes in prime time television drama. Alcoholic beverages lead with drinking scenes an average of every 22 minutes, smoking every 57 minutes, and illicit drugs every 112 minutes.

While there has been a general reduction of smoking on prime time dramatic television, the proportion of young and mid-life women who smoke has actually increased.

The use of addictive substances is shown as essentially risk-free. More than 9 out of 10 drinkers, more than 8 out of 10 smokers, and even 6 out of 10 illicit drug users experience either positive or no health effects. Although users are not as likely to be positive and successful characters as non-users, satisfied users are seen in at least one out of every 3 programs presenting illicit drugs.

The risk-free use of addictive substances isolates and reduces the reality of addiction to a small moral category. Addicts are presented as flawed characters, damned and doomed because they are evil rather than ill.

Popular movies extend the prime time pattern. In the sample of forty highest grossing titles, only two do not have any portrayal of alcohol, and six do not have any smoking. Illicit drug scenes are present in over one-third of the movies, three times their presence on prime time television.

Music videos present addictive substances even more frequently. A viewer of MTV sees alcohol use every 14 minutes compared to 17 in the movies and 27 on prime time television. Illicit drugs are seen every 40 minutes compared to 100 in movies and 112 on prime time television. There is also a close association between the presence of addictive substances and crime, violence, destruction, and sexual interaction.

COMMERCIALS

Commercials with alcohol scenes appear in 28 percent of all prime time programs. Half of them are beer commercials and another fourth advertise feature movies. Far beyond showing alcohol as merely risk-free, they associate drinking with a youthful lifestyle of romance, sports, fun, and sociability.

Commercials that feature alcohol scenes are 15 percent more likely to be "humorous," twice as much "fun," and 20 percent more "sexy" than other commercials. They are also twice as likely to suggest popularity as a result of drinking.

While young adults appear in 68 percent of all commercials, they are cast in 79 percent of commercials featuring alcohol. Nearly a fourth of all alcohol users, and a third of beer drinkers, engage in vigorous and often acrobatic activity. Only 6.4 percent of non-drinkers are presented as physically active.

Tobacco cannot be directly promoted on television, but smoking appears in commercials that advertise other products. Promotion for feature films constitutes 66 percent of smoking scenes in commercials.

NEWS AND REALITY SHOWS

About 8 percent of all news stories mention or show some addictive substance, half of the illicit drugs, most of them crime-related.

Four-fifths of those who make drug-related news are males, six out of ten are young, but only half of them white. Unlike in prime time fiction, only 3.7 percent of major characters in the news drink alcoholic beverages. However, the proportion of smokers, 4.8 percent, is higher than that of prime time. Furthermore, one out of every five underage persons in news stories is depicted as smokers.

Illicit drug users are 6.6 percent of the persons in the news. Most of them are young black males. The only female users of illicit drugs are young black women.

The use of alcohol and illicit drugs in the news, as in fiction, is more a matter of character than of health. Users usually appear as involved in crime and violence. Those identified as drinkers are three times as likely to be accused or convicted of criminal activity as non-drinkers. Over half of the alcohol drinkers are involved in violence, mostly as perpetrators.

Males identified as illicit drug users are twice as likely to be accused or convicted of criminal activity as non-users. Female drug users suffer an even worse fate; seven of the nine females who are mentioned as users are killed.

A negligible proportion of stories of alcohol and illicit drugs have health issues as their major focus (2.3% and 3.9% respectively). No negative health consequences are observed for 9 out of 10 drinkers and 8 out of 10 illicit drug users.

The health hazards of smoking are noted in 25.6 percent of news stories about tobacco; however, they are depersonalized. Eight out of ten smokers are shown as suffering no health consequences.

Reality shows (programs with multiple short episodes that use live footage showing law enforcers and criminals in action), as the news, depict addictive substances only because they are linked to crime rather than to negative health effects. As in prime time fiction, substance use emerges more as a matter of negative characterization than an accurate depiction of a social reality. Illicit drug users are young males of color who are social outcasts, deviates, and criminals.

CHAPTER 29

MIDLIFE AND OLDER WOMEN ON TELEVISION

BY GEORGE GERBNER

HIGHLIGHTS

Flying in the face of reality, television sends a disturbing and dangerous message to the mass audience. That is the conclusion of a comprehensive and representative twenty-year study of the image of midlife and older women in prime time and Saturday morning network television drama.

Women are concentrated in the younger age groups, and they "age faster" than men. After forty-five, their numbers decline, especially in major parts. Low income and most minority women are less visible than rich older women, thus obscuring a major social problem, and setting up older women as targets for easy scorn.

Although wealthier than other comparable groups, midlife and older women are less likely to be shown as mentally or physically sound, as gainfully employed, as professionals or leaders in business, or as active in anything—except crime. With this, the image of midlife and older women takes on a sinister tone.

Older women are cast in evil rather than benign roles three to six times as frequently as younger women or older men. They are losers rather than winners two to three times as often and suffer greater relative victimization than other groups. While older men are depicted mostly as killers rather than as being killed, older women mostly get killed.

An analysis of selected scripts illustrates some of the prime time findings and rounds out the picture. It shows older women on television not only physically and mentally unfit but also superficial, stubborn, and deservedly removed from the support of a community of family and friends. Older women's lives are laughable, their feelings unimportant, and their sexuality, if it exists at all, is trivial at best and exploitive at worst. With added burdens of physical and mental illness, as well as the presence of villainous predators and censorious family, television presents an ugly image of the aging process.

Programs designed specifically for children's favorite viewing time, Saturday morning, may be expected to present a world that is more tranquil and fair than the troubled world of prime time. However, the world of children's programming is, in fact, harsher and more exploitive. The inequities of prime time are magnified Saturday morning.

A child growing up with Saturday morning children's programs will see about 139 characters each week, but rarely a mature female as a valued person, a peacemaker, or a leader. Married and parent images are curiously rare and gloomy. Older women in children's programs are most likely to play the villain. That is where the witches come from.

The overarching formulas revealed in this study are those aggregate features of television that everybody watches but nobody sees. Understanding them makes it possible to inform viewers, alert organizations, and work with television professionals to change them.

CHAPTER 30

EXCERPTS FROM ANIMAL ISSUES IN THE MEDIA

A Groundbreaking Report

BY GEORGE GERBNER

Non-human animals appear in a variety of forms and functions. In some cases they are loved and admired, but often they are confined, hunted, exterminated, eaten, or worn on our bodies. Most often, however, they play all those and other roles in stories told by the mass media.

What kinds of animals do we see on television and in print media? What are the trends, themes, scenes, and contexts in which animals appear? How are they treated? What are the roles for which they are cast and the fate for which they are destined? What issues drive press and magazine coverage, and how do animal activism, legislation, science and other issues play out in the coverage? Finally, what are some implications for further research, activity, and policy?

These are questions we shall address in this report. The report presents the findings of a benchmark study that begins the task of systematically tracking the most pervasive sources that cultivate public conceptions of animals, and help shape behaviors, rules, and laws about the use and treatment of animals.

HIGHLIGHTS

Television is by far the largest single source of everyday information and imagery about animals, discharging, in prime time alone, an average of thirty-four animal images each week into the common cultural environment. Even though the average viewer will see more animals than old people, or poor people, or Latino and Asian Americans put together, television still underrepresents the animal world. A more adequate and diverse portrayal of animals as parts of life and nature would facilitate a more balanced representation.

Animals appear in their own habitat at their peril. Although most animals in prime time are treated well, many are treated badly, especially wild animals. In Saturday morning children's programs, wild animals are seen mistreated in twelve scenes for every one scene of good treatment.

Animal roles overplay villainy. While humans have many times more heroes than villains, animals have almost as many villains as heroes. They are more likely to be seen as a threat, thus seeming to justify their own victimization.

Animals suffer violence/victim overkill. Animals are more than twice as likely to be hurt or killed as humans are. In prime time more than one-third and in Saturday morning children's programs more than half of the animal cast suffers overt physical violence.

Animal rights activists are depicted as violent most of the time they are shown. Positive depictions of animal rights activists as calm, rational, and nonviolent were found in only three of thirty-two scripts featuring animals. In general, the disapproval of animal rights activism is at least twice as frequent as its approval.

Stories of activism and legislation account for nearly half of all news about animals. Violence, conflict, and opposition to animal rights claim much press attention. However, over time, news of activism stimulates policy, legislative, and other types of print media attention.

IMPLICATIONS

There is no doubt that the persistence and visibility of the animal rights movement has shifted the political, social, and scientific agendas, as well as some media priorities. We found that about 6 percent of prime time and nearly 60 percent of Saturday morning children's programs present animal themes and characters. Four out of the five prime time and more than half of the Saturday morning programs that contain animal themes also portray violence committed by or against animals.

The viewer of Saturday morning children's programs sees two-and-a-half times as many scenes of animals treated badly as animals treated well. Both animals and humans are more likely to act "bad" and violent than in prime time, but animals' share of villains is much higher, as is their share of victims of violence.

Script analysis reveals that while the majority of animal incidents and characterizations could be considered as positive, animal rights activities are frequently portrayed as violent and are disapproved of much more often than approved.

The analysis of print media shows that legislative and other policy considerations and animal rights activities dominate the news. There is frequent emphasis on discord among activists, litigation, violence, and criminal prosecution. Popular magazines publish more articles on scientific discoveries and animal biology and behavior, but animal rights and legislative activism begin to be reflected in magazines in the late 1970s. Over time, activism stimulates policy/legislative and other types of print media attention. The anti-fur campaign may have been the single most visible reflection of animal rights activity in print in the 1970s and '80s.

Any analysis of these representations inevitably confronts the problem of language. The terms we use are tainted by the history of their uses. "Human," with its connotation of humane, is often an antonym of "animal," with its connotation of beastly. A thriving industry of paraphernalia and cleansers helps us, as a Clorox ad instructs: "How to keep your pet from living like an animal."

Calling someone "an animal" is an insult. It conjures up images of uncontrolled savagery, despite the fact that only the human animal is capable of deliberate genocide. No other species plans and executes systematic slaughter of millions of its own kind simply for belonging to an abstract category of "enemy" or to a particular race, religion, or ethnic group.

A basic conflict exists between a definition of animals as mere instrumentalities of human wants and needs vs. a definition which sees animals as major players in an intricate ecosystem with many parts of inherent worth. The instrumental definition is buttressed by the projection onto animals, and especially of wild animals, the most representative—and lethal—characteristics of the human animal.

The language, imagery, and definitions we use have significant social, economic, legal, psychological, scientific, medical, and ethical implications. Our choices also define and test our own humanity, and perhaps even the long-term viability of our own species.

Agriculture and animal husbandry have changed our relationship to nature. Industrialization and urbanization transformed our storytelling. They ritualized and rationalized new systems of domination. Global agribusiness and the military-industrial-scientific-medical establishments are able to lobby for and subsidize media projections of their interests. The animal rights community has limited resources with which to overcome formidable obstacles in order to achieve a more balanced perspective. The first systematic study of animal issues in the media is part of the attempt to assess the problem and to define the challenge facing animal advocates.

The challenge is systemic, rather than a matter of isolated policies that can be easily altered. Systems change more slowly and require constant monitoring. The value of this benchmark study will be enhanced if periodically repeated. An annual "Animal Issues Index" can track changes in representation (if any) and guide further activity.

Priority should be given to achieving a more frequent and balanced representation of animals, and particularly wild animals, in prime time and, even more urgently, in Saturday morning children's programs. The violence-saturated portrayals are not only dangerous to animals but they are also misleading and detrimental to humane attitudes in general. Television shapes as well as reflects public attitudes about animals. For many nonhumans perhaps the future's best—or only—hope is a generation sensitized and enlightened by exposure to more diverse and positive images of animals in the mass media.

Chapter 31

THE ELECTRONIC CHURCH IN AMERICAN CULTURE

BY GEORGE GERBNER

The "fundamentalist" upheavals that have shaken large parts of the world seem to have found an echo in the rise of the "electronic church" on American television. With our legacy of Puritanism, populism, and evangelicalism, and our distinction as the world's heaviest users of television (7.5 hours a day in the average home and still rising), we may indeed be considered fertile ground for some sort of electronic revival.

My colleagues Larry Gross, Stewart Hoover, Michael Morgan, Nancy Signorielli, and I conducted a study in cooperation with the Gallup Organization, Inc., and funded by a committee on Electronic Church Research formed by the National Council of Churches, to address some basic questions about the electronic church in American culture. What is its audience? What effect does it have on the local churches? Is it more religion or more television? What is its general content? And what are the lessons—religious, social, and political—that its viewers seem to derive from the exposure?

The audience for religious programs on television is not an essentially new, or young, or varied audience. Viewers of religious programs are by and large also the believers, the churchgoers, the contributors. Their viewing of religious programs correlates with all important measures of religiosity. It appears to be an expression, confirmation, and cultivation of a set of religious beliefs and not a substitute for them.

The profile of the audience for religious programs tends to be fairly coherent and well defined. It is what religious audiences have always been: somewhat older, lower in education and income, more conservative, more "fundamentalist," and more likely to live in rural areas and in the South and Midwest than those who do not watch religious programs. The size of the audience is more stable and compact than has often been supposed. Our calculations indicate that the regular viewers of religious programs of all denominations number about 13.3 million, or 6.2 percent of the estimated total number of persons in television households.

Local religious programs do not extend the viewing audience. Those who watch local programs also watch the syndicated television ministries (defined as programs by denominations existing primarily through broadcasting). Cable viewing does not seem to extend the viewing audience; on the whole, viewers of religious programs are no more likely than non-viewers to have cable television in their homes.

The television ministries, therefore, serve a stable and coherent national constituency. They appear to reach a broader group mostly on Sundays when the most diverse viewing public is available for all television programs.

Viewers of religious programs are drawn by content they cannot find elsewhere on television. In fact, their dissatisfaction with the "prevailing moral climate" (much of which, of course, comes to them through and from television) may be one of the most distinctive bonds between religious programs and their viewers. The sermons, the preaching, the music, the experience of "having your spirits lifted" and "feeling close to God" are frequently expressed satisfactions that viewers derive from religious programs.

Those who do not watch religious programs on television—the majority of the younger and more "upscale" television viewers—are more likely to be disinterested than hostile. Only one in four express any objections (mostly to the emphasis on solicitation of funds), but three in four switch channels rather than watch religious programs.

The key distinctions between viewers and non-viewers of religious programs, besides the demographic, are religious and philosophical. Non-viewers are less likely to hold conservative, evangelical, or "fundamentalist" beliefs. Only a third (as opposed to half of the viewers of religious programs) express dissatisfaction with the prevailing moral climate. The same relative proportions consider evangelicalism and missionary work the main goal of the church. Conversely, only one-fifth of the viewers of religious programs, but one-third of the non-viewers, believe that the church should be "working for social justice."

The television ministries have been suspected of causing or at least contributing to the erosion of mainline church membership, financial contributions, and general participation. Our study has found no support for that charge. Viewers of religious programs, including the prominent television ministries, are no less likely than non-viewers to attend, contribute to, and participate in local church activities. Frequent churchgoers see little or no conflict between their participation and viewing. A personal "closeness to members" of one's local church is one of the few if not the only reason advanced for local church attendance that television ministries could not serve.

THE MESSAGES OF RELIGIOUS TELEVISION

In their essential features, the contents of evangelical and mainline religious programs do not present as much of a contrast as has been supposed. Discussion of political issues occurs in over half of both television ministry and mainline programs (but only one-third of general prime time drama television programs). The television ministries are more likely than mainline church programs to ask for money, with the prominent television ministries making the most numerous requests and asking for greater amounts.

Social and moral issues are discussed on both television ministries and mainline church programs. The most prominent of the television ministries are, however, more likely than the other groups to focus on these issues. Religious and theological issues are not discussed with any great frequency. When mentioned at all, they are most likely to be discussed on the prominent television ministries.

With regard to the participants in these programs, there are several important findings. First, men outnumber women by a considerable margin in all religious programs. In this and several other respects, the people who inhabit religious television are similar to the characters who populate the fictional world of prime time drama. Women are generally younger than the men. Minorities, especially minority women and all Hispanics, are underrepresented in these programs relative to their numbers in the general population.

"Women in religious programs have little authority or power, much like women in prime time drama."

About half of the women in major roles and one-fifth of all women participants are professionals. However, they are rarely, if ever, in the role of clergy and rarely quote the Bible. They are more likely than men to suffer from personal problems or physical ailments. Overall, women in religious programs have little authority and power, much like women in prime time drama. On the other hand, as on prime time, men are in charge. They have roles of authority, are the clergy, quote the Bible, and do not suffer from as many ailments and/or personal problems as women.

The conservatism of religious programs is also apparent in the condemnation, much more frequent than on commercial television, of abortion, homosexuality, and other behavior perceived as deviant. "Sinful sexual conduct," for example, was addressed in one out of every four religious programs.

The emphasis on personal problems and ailments (placing an unequal burden on women) focuses on family tensions, financial and health problems, unemployment, and physical handicaps. The most prominent television ministries tend to dwell most on these personal problems and ailments, and prescribe spiritual solutions or (in 1 out of 4 programs) financial contributions.

THE LESSONS OF TELEVISION—RELIGIOUS AND GENERAL

General commercial television viewing may supply or supplant (or both) some religious satisfactions and thus lessen the importance of religion for its heavy viewers. Demographic groups whose light viewers of television are most likely to find religion "very important" distance themselves the most as heavy viewers from that belief. Viewing general commercial television seems to displace, if not replace, religion as an important part of life.

The religious television mainstream tends to run conservative and restrictive rather than permissive. The general television mainstream tends to run politically "moderate," also more restrictive than permissive, and populist but not puritanical.

Heavy viewers of religious programs are more likely than non-viewers to describe themselves as conservatives, oppose a nuclear freeze, favor tougher laws against pornography, and report voting in the last general election. Heavy viewers of general television tend to describe themselves as political moderates, are more likely to favor a nuclear freeze, are not as concerned with pornography (or, as we have seen before, with the "moral climate"), and are far less likely to say they voted in a general election. The coherent mobilizing power of religious television, rather than its reach or scope, represents its political clout.

The "electronic church," with its prominent television ministries, expresses a fairly stable, coherent, and conservative worldview that serves more to rally believers than to recruit or convert others. Its regular viewers tend to be older, more "fundamentalist," and lower in income and education than non-viewers. They are greatly dissatisfied with what they perceive to be contemporary morality and interested in spreading the Gospel more than social justice. For them, watching religious television is an expression of belief and an experience that is not inconsistent with, and may even complement, local church attendance and contributions.

The world presented and the worldview expressed on the television ministries may compete more with commercial television than with mainline religion. Television itself may cater to needs that religion used to satisfy while presenting attractions and gratifications that counter some religious beliefs and absorb others in its broad and popular mainstream.

CHAPTER 32

ANGER ON TELEVISION

BY GEORGE GERBNER

Growing up and living with television exposes viewers to a wide range of people, situations, conflicts, attitudes, and emotions. Anger, one of the most volatile human expressions, involves all of these. What are television's contributions to the manifestations and management of anger? That is the question addressed in this study. The objective was to observe, classify, and record manifestations of anger in a sample of dramatic network programs (including action, "reality," comedy, general drama, etc.), in order to derive some implications useful for the professional, the parent, and the viewer.

THE ANALYSIS

The study on which this report is based involved the analysis of 121 prime time and 38 Saturday morning children's programs, a total of 159 entertainment programs aired on 4 television networks during the 1993–94 season. A total of 1,014 "anger scenes" were found and analyzed. Out of a total of 1,926 characters analyzed, 25.9 percent expressed anger. Their characteristics, violence and victimization, and ways of venting and/or managing anger were observed and tabulated.

Additional information came from the Annenberg School Script Archive, containing scripts of dramatic programs aired on television. Results of the script analysis are not included in the Appendix tables. The Script Archive was searched for illustrative material and some observations that could be best made from scripts. A random selection of thirteen scripts containing anger scenes and forty-eight angry characters (out of 306 total character population) was analyzed for those purposes.

Anger was observed as an overt expression affecting a character physiologically, cognitively, and/or behaviorally. Units of analysis were the program as a whole, the "anger scene," and every speaking part in the plays. The anger scene was action involving an angry character. The scene ended when a new character appeared, or the angry character left, or when the anger subsided, or when the scene shifted for other reasons. The overall reliability of observations was 96 percent agreement between coders.

RESULTS

The most important contribution of this study is a realistic understanding of what any therapeutic or counseling effort is up against. Understanding the general cultural territory in which any corrective effort takes place is the first requirement for success; without such understanding, even the most skillful intervention is likely to fail or have only short-lived success. Furthermore, when working with television professionals, only such an aggregate view can address problems that dramatic formulas pose for writers and directors, and can, therefore, discuss how to overcome them.

Anger is frequently seen on television. Almost three-quarters (72.7%) of all prime time programs, and all Saturday morning children's programs contain anger scenes. More than nine out of ten (94.1%) of prime time "action" programs, nearly as many (84.3%) situation comedies, and over half (52.9%) general drama programs contain anger scenes. There is probably no comparable source of information about expressions of anger in our culture.

In prime time, about one in four (24.7%) of all characters and more than half (54.6%) of major characters express anger. In Saturday morning children's programs, nearly a third (31.4%) of all characters and 65.2 percent of major characters express anger.

THE DEMOGRAPHY OF ANGER

Characters most likely to express anger are major rather than minor, men rather than women, upscale rather than lower class, whites rather than characters of color, and boys (male children and adolescents) rather than most other age and gender groups.

When angry women become violent, they pay a higher price in victimization than men. To extrapolate the findings to a larger scale, for every 100 angry women who hurt others, 162 angry women get hurt. But for every 100 angry men who hurt others, only 82 angry men get hurt. In other words, women bear a double burden of victimization for their violent anger.

Saturday morning children's programs are more stressful and stereotyped. They not only feature more anger than prime time, but the differences between males and females, whites and blacks, and the age groups also tend to be larger.

The exceptions and extensions are equally revealing. In prime time, young and elderly women are more likely to express anger than young and elderly men. Upscale characters are more often angered than others, but upper-class women are especially prone to anger. Angry women in cartoons are more likely to present a threatening criminal, and even lethal, menace than angry men. In fact, the relatively few females playing major roles in Saturday morning children's programs are the angriest group on television. Nearly seven out of ten (68.4%) express anger, compared to less than half (49.0%) of prime time women.

The script archive analysis suggests that the target of most anger is a stranger in a fleeting relationship. Most anger scenes (59%) involve male-to-male power struggles. Only 18 percent are between male and female, and 6 percent among females. Anger is directed at a friend or member of the family in only one-third of the scenes. Eight out of ten anger scenes involve new rather than previously existing issues; half escalate into violence; only one-third alter a relationship at all; and less than one in ten results in improvement.

EXPRESSING ANGER

Not all anger involves violence and not all violence involves anger, but six out of ten programs (61.6%) involve both. Of all anger scenes in prime time, 14.6 percent involve violence. Of the Saturday morning children's program anger scenes, 36.2 percent involve violence. Violence and/or anger occurs in 52.1 percent of prime time and 92.1 percent of Saturday morning children's programs. Male anger is consistently more violent than female anger.

However, most violence on television is "cool" and does not involve anger or perhaps any expression of emotion. Only a little over one-third (34.1%) of prime time violence and one-fourth (27.6%) of Saturday morning children's program violence involves expressions of anger.

Other manifestations of anger in prime time range from shouting (82.6%), blaming (53.3%), insulting (47.1%), saying "unfair" (41.4%), threatening (31.8%), crying (13.8%), cursing (12.1%), and breaking things (9.4%).

For example, in the sitcom "Blossom," Six and her mother are arguing because Six's mother does not approve of her boyfriend. Six's mother shouts at Six and demands that she not date him anymore.

Seeking revenge and blaming occurs in "Married with Children" when Kelly and Bud are angry that their dates left them. They blame their dates for the disappointment and devise a plan to take revenge; they lure a dog into their date's car.

Insulting is an expression of anger in "Melrose Place" as Michael and Jane are arguing about their divorce settlement. Michael believes Jane received too much money and accuses her of being a "greedy gold-digger." Insulting almost leads to blows in "21 Jumpstreet" from the Script Archive, when local boys confront two Asian college students getting in line at a local café. One of the locals says, "hey, they don't serve that Moo Goo Goo here." One of the students replies, "I see they serve idiots," to which the local retorts,"What did you say, zipperhead?" when the scene shifts.

Crying "unfair" happens when Harlan in "Evening Shade" discusses Ava's sex life in court. Ava is upset and insists that such invasion of privacy is unfair; Harlan has no right to discuss her personal life.

An example of threatening is in "Northern Exposure" when Joel gets angry at the electrician who is fixing his VCR. He does not believe the VCR was properly fixed and threatens to report it to the Better Business Bureau.

Crying is a way of venting anger in the TV movie *A Child Too Many.* Patty learns, after giving birth to twins, that the Davis family only wants to adopt the male twin, not the female. She is outraged that they would split up the infant twins and cries bitterly, hoping that Mr. and Mrs. Davis will reconsider.

Foul language (cursing) is heard (to the extent allowed on television) in "Murphy Brown" as Stuart, a lawyer, is offended when the FYI staff starts insulting lawyers. As Stuart reprimands the staff, he says "damn."

Hurting, breaking, destroying includes physical retaliation and taking out frustrations and anger on inanimate objects. In the show "Top Cops" a man is upset because his wife and daughter have locked him out of the house. He releases his anger by banging on the door. In the film *When Harry Met Sally,* the two main characters are bickering at their friends' wedding. Harry makes a comment that infuriates Sally and Sally slaps him.

There is substantial gender difference. Men are more likely to shout, break, threaten, hurt, and curse; women are more likely to blame, insult, say "unfair," and cry.

Every manifestation of anger is amplified in Saturday morning children's programs. Gender differences also tend to be wider. Angry women hurt, shut, break, threaten, as well as blame, more than men, and usually also more than in prime time.

MANAGING ANGER

In television drama, unlike perhaps in life, anger is not usually "managed" or "resolved." Only about six out of ten prime time and four out of ten Saturday morning children's program characters even attempt any resolution other than violence or just venting anger. About half of all characters in anger scenes listen to the target of their anger and try to discuss it, or just leave (12.2%), or reflect on their own anger (28.2%), or find humor in the situation (23.5%), or talk to themselves about it (10.2%), or the scene just dissolves into some other action. In four or five of all anger scenes, resolution, if any, remains to be suggested by the plot, but not shown.

When controlling or managing anger is allowed to slow the action, it is more likely to be done by women than men. More women listen to the target of their anger, recognize their own anger, and find humor in the situation. The only resolutions angry men exhibit slightly more than women are running away or talking to themselves.

Examples of managing anger include the recognition of one's own anger by apologizing, analyzing angry outbursts, and acknowledging fault. After Mike in "Saved by the Bell" yells at the "guys" for playing poker, he apologizes for his outburst. In a scene in "Murphy Brown," Miles yells at the staff for being uncooperative. Immediately afterwards, he worries aloud about the outburst. Jesse and Joe of the sitcom "Full House" are arguing about what name to give their radio call-in show. After a few minutes of bickering, they admit that their argument is petty and immature.

Talking to one's self is shown as a way of managing anger in the sitcom "Coach" when Kelly is upset because she did not get any job interviews. She talks to herself and tries to rationalize the situation to calm herself down.

Running away as a way of dealing with anger includes both walking out on the unpleasant situation and "running away" from the issue by changing the subject. In the TV movie *A Child Too Many,* a frustrated parent is arguing with an adoption agency representative. In the middle of the argument, the parent walks out of the representative's office. In the sitcom "Family Album," a husband and wife are quarreling when the wife, in order to end the debate, abruptly announces that it is time for bed. In an episode of "The Wonder Years" from the Script Archive, Kevin chides Jeff for his constant sarcasm and Jeff turns on him, angrily: "What are you, Ann Landers? The proper way to do this, the proper way to do that. It's not pretty, y'know." Kevin says, "Yeah, forget it," and walks away.

The most frequent way scripts call for managing anger is simply listening to its target and discussing how to deal with it or responding in a positive way. A police officer in "Cops" is talking on the phone with a suspect who refuses to leave his home. The officer calms the angry suspect by explaining why it is in his interest to cooperate. In "The Adventures of Brisco Country Jr.," as Brisco and his friend are roped together and stuck in quicksand, they become angry and argue with each other until they come up with an appropriate escape plan. In the same episode of "The Wonder Years," Kevin's father, Jack, is berating him: "Where the hell have you been?...You leave here six hours ago and come back with nothing? Where's your head?" To which Kevin replied, "I love you, Dad."

Finding humor in the situation as a way of managing anger occurs in the movie *She's Having a Baby* when Jake, upset with his wife for telling her mother private details, makes a joke about her parents now wanting to give them sexual pointers.

Saturday morning children's programs feature more anger and even less management than prime time. Most gender gaps are also wider. The major difference is that, despite the ostensibly humorous nature of cartoons, few men or women find humor in an anger scene. While nearly one-fourth (23.5%) of prime time characters can find humor in an anger situation, only 7.5 percent of cartoon characters can do so.

CONCLUSIONS

The television viewer sees expressions of anger in three out of four prime time programs and in all Saturday morning children's programs. Aggregate analysis brings out the pervasive features and overall configurations of those expressions. The lessons that dramatic formulas may hold for those exposed to them over long periods of time convey a sense of dynamic relationships: how things may work behind the scenes of everyday life, who are the winners and the losers, who can get away with what against whom. These are the lessons professionals dealing with anger on television confront in their work, and need to address.

In that sense, anger serves functions of dramatic stress and social typing. It projects power and places people into a hierarchy of powers dominated by major, male, upscale characters. The management of anger implies weakness or adjustment.

Anger often erupts in new situations and escalates into violence or leads to other disruptions but rarely to change. One out of four prime time and six out of ten Saturday morning children's program characters become violent when angry. Angry violent women bear a double burden of victimization, compared to men. When the manifestation is over, the scene often shifts without showing any consequences.

Venting and managing anger also varies by gender, class, age, and race. To oversimplify, men threaten, curse, and hurt; women complain, blame, and cry. In Saturday morning children's programs, however, women also present a fearfully angry image.

Only about half of angry characters, more women than men, use any type of anger management. Saturday morning children's programs involve more stress, violence, and stereotyping, and less anger management than prime time.

These are the inescapable images and messages that everyday exposure to television projects about anger, its expressions, counseling, and consulting professionals and those working with media professionals.

REFERENCES

Bandura, A., Ross, D., & Ross, D. (1967). "Transmission of aggression through imitation of aggressive models." *Journal of Abnormal and Social Psychology*, 63, 575–582.

Bryant, J., Carveth, R. A., & Brown, D. (1981). "Television viewing and anxiety: An experimental examination." *Journal of Communication*, 31(1), 106–119.

Ellis, G. T. & Sekura, F., III. (1972). The effect of aggressive cartoons on the behavior of first grade children." *Journal of Psychology*, 81, 7–43.

Gerbner, G. (1972). "Violence and television drama: Trends and symbolic functions." In G. A. Comstock and E. Rubinstein (eds.), *Television and Social Behavior, Vol. 1, Content and Control.* Washington, D.C.: U.S. Government Printing Office, pp. 28–187.

Gerbner, G. (1972). "The Violence Profile: Some indicators of trends in and the symbolic structure of network television drama 1967–1971." In *Surgeon General's Report by the Scientific Advisory Committee on Television and Social Behavior, Appendix A.* (Hearings before the Subcommittee on Communications of the Committee on Commerce, U.S. Senate, Serial No. 92–52.) Washington, D.C.: U.S. Government Printing Office, pp. 453–526.

Gerbner, G. (1988). "Violence and terror in the mass media." *Reports and Papers in Mass Communication,* No. 102. Paris: UNESCO.

Gerbner, G. (1988). "Television's cultural mainstream: Which way does it run?" *Directions in Psychiatry,* 8(9). New York: Hatherleigh Co., Ltd.

Gerbner, G. (1993). "Women and Minorities on Television: A study in casting and fate." A report to the Screen Actors Guild and the American Federation of Television and Radio Artists.

Gerbner, G., Gross, L., Morgan, M., & Signorielli, N. (1993). "Growing up with television: The cultivation perspective." In Jennings Bryant and Dolf Zillmann (eds.), *Media Effects: Advances in Theory and Research.* Hillsdale, N.J.: Lawrence Erlbaum Associates, Inc.

Gerbner, G., Morgan, M., & Signorielli, N. (1944). "Television Violence Profile No. 16: The Turning Point—From Research to Action." The Annenberg School for Communication, University of Pennsylvania.

Hawkins, R. P. & Pingree, S. (1982). "Television's influence on social reality." In D. Pearl, L. Bouthilet, & J. Lazar (eds.), *Television and Behavior: Ten Years of Scientific Progress and Implications for the 80s,* Vol. 2, Technical Reports. Washington, D.C.: Government Printing Office.

Lovas, O. I. (1961). "Effects of exposure to symbolic aggression on aggressive behavior." *Child Development*, 32, 37–44.

Morgan, M. (1983). "Symbolic victimization and real-world fear." *Human Communication Research,* 9(2), 146–157.

Morgan, M. (1984). "Heavy television viewing and perceived quality of life." *Journalism Quarterly,* 61(3), 499–504.

Morgan, M. & Shanahan, J. (1991). "Do VCRs change the TV picture?: VCRs and the cultivation process." *American Behavioral Scientist,* 35(2), 122–135.

Morgan, M. & Signorielli, N. (1990). "Cultivation analysis: Conceptualization and methodology." In N. Signorielli & M. Morgan (eds.), *Cultivation Analysis: New Directions in Media Effects Research.* Newbury Park, CA: Sage, pp. 13–33.

Signorielli, N. (1990). "Television's mean and dangerous world: A continuation of the cultural indicators perspective." In N. Signorielli & M. Morgan (eds.), *Cultivation Analysis: New Directions in Media Effects Research.* Newbury Park, CA: Sage, pp. 85–105.

CHAPTER 33

U.S. AND SOVIET ATTITUDES ABOUT LIFE AND INSTITUTIONS, AND TELEVISION'S CONTRIBUTIONS TO ATTITUDES

A Comparative Analysis

BY GEORGE GERBNER, ELLEN MICKIEWICZ, AND MICHAEL MORGAN

This is a report of the first large-scale comparative survey based on representative national samples in both the United States and the Soviet Union. Comparative findings are presented about attitudes and beliefs concerning security and safety, women's roles, general life satisfaction, and confidence in social institutions in the United States and the Soviet Union. We also compare the contributions of mass media, especially television, to these beliefs in both countries.

The perspectives we studied are deeply embedded in everyday life and culture. They reflect both life experience and lifelong exposure to widely shared media entertainment and news in the two countries. They may be more resistant to change than the political views revealed by typical polls, and yet they may be equally constraining of policy. They should, therefore, provide a basis for judging more ephemeral opinions and various official statements against the background of relatively enduring beliefs, seen from a comparative perspective.

The U.S. data come from a telephone survey employing a national probability sample of 1,496 respondents collected by the Roper Organization in June 1990. The

Soviet dataset is a national sample of personal interviews collected in the Soviet Union by the All-Union Center for Public Opinion Research under the direction of Boris Grushin and T. I. Zaslasvkaya at the end of 1989. This was the first large-scale personal interview survey involving a variety of nationalities in the U.S.S.R. It was conducted in Estonia, Belorussia, Georgia, Kazakhstan, Uzbekistan, and the Russian Republic. These republics represent 88 percent of the Soviet population. This report deals with overall national results only, based on a weighted sample of 2,006 Soviet respondents.

The results reveal striking differences but also a few similarities. Briefly, we found that Americans are much more concerned about domestic security and criminal violence than are Soviet respondents, but that Soviets feel less safe about walking in their own neighborhoods at night. The "traditional" view that women are happiest tending to the home is held by more Soviets than Americans, although large majorities in both countries express egalitarian beliefs about the roles of men and women. U.S. respondents seem to be much more satisfied with their lives than the Soviets. Education increases life satisfaction even further in the United States but depresses it in the Soviet Union. And class differences in attitudes (differences among different educational and income groups) are much sharper in the United States than they are in the Soviet Union.

Television plays a somewhat different role in the two countries. In the United States heavy viewing heightens anxieties about neighborhood safety while in the Soviet Union it leaves audiences relatively unaffected. In both countries, but especially in the Soviet Union, television projects the notion that housework is primarily the responsibility of the woman. The belief that women are happiest taking care of the home is more prevalent in the Soviet Union (especially among Soviet males!) than in the United States.

General satisfaction with life is consistently lower among heavy than among light television viewers in the United States but not in the Soviet Union. Overall, American television seems to contribute more to some apprehensions and dissatisfactions while Soviet television cultivates a higher degree of gender stereotyping.

More heavy than light viewers in both countries (but never more than 1 out of 2, and even fewer in the Soviet Union) express a "great deal" of confidence in social institutions ranging from government to education and the army. Both television systems tend to reduce class and group differences in attitudes; this is especially strong in the United States, where the homogenizing effect of television is greater.

More detailed findings follow.

SECURITY AND SAFETY

What people think about domestic security and how they feel about their own safety has become one of the most pivotal factors in personal and political orientations. We made a comparative assessment of these concerns in the United States and the Soviet Union by asking respondents how widespread they think violence is in their country, how serious they think the danger of their own personal victimization to be, and how safe they feel walking alone at night in their neighborhoods. We also assessed the contribution of cultural factors, mainly television and newspapers, to these conceptions of security and safety in both countries.

DOMESTIC VIOLENCE

Twice as many American (63%) as Soviet (31%) respondents say that "violence in our own country now" is "extremely widespread." Even though the incidence of violence and crime is increasing in the Soviet Union, the difference between U.S. and Soviet perceptions probably reflects actual differences in the amount of violence in the two societies. Moreover, Soviet media portray much less crime and violence than do U.S. media in both news and entertainment, and the reporting of domestic violence is a relatively recent phenomenon in Soviet media.

In the United States, the highest estimate of violence is given by low-income respondents (70% of them say violence is "extremely widespread") and the lowest is by college-educated respondents (55% give that response). U.S. gender and class comparisons show that 57 percent of men but 68 percent of women, and 59 percent of high but 70 percent of low income respondents believe that violence is "extremely widespread" in the United States. Lifestyles and conditions such as suburban living may be reflected in these perceptions.

There are fewer and smaller differences among subgroups in the Soviet Union. The largest difference (only 8 points) is between younger and older respondents; 27 percent of younger and 35 percent of older respondents say violence is "extremely widespread). Gender or income have even less impact on perceptions of violence in the Soviet Union.

Television viewing makes some contribution to Soviet estimates of violence (which are relatively low) but not to U.S. estimates (which are relatively high). For example, while only 25 percent of Soviet males who are light viewers consider violence "extremely widespread," 31 percent of Soviet male heavy viewers do. The same spread of 6 points also separates older and more highly educated light and heavy viewers. The corresponding figures for the American respondents show no evidence of television cultivating perceptions of violence. In fact, such a high number of low education and low-income light viewers believe violence is "extremely widespread" in the country (69 and 70%, respectively), that television viewing even reduces that figure somewhat. American television makes more of a contribution in the form of "mainstreaming," which is the cultivation of more homogeneous, common views among the heavy viewers of otherwise different subgroups.

DANGER OF CRIMINAL VICTIMIZATION

A similar pattern is evident in terms of the perceived personal danger of criminal victimization. When given four choices to express degrees of seriousness of the danger of such victimization personally, 21 percent of Americans but only 14 percent of Soviets select the highest degree, "very serious." Conversely, 14 percent of Soviets but only 9 percent of Americans chose the lowest category saying that such danger is "not serious at all."

In the United States it is again the low income and least educated respondents who express the highest level and the college educated respondents who express the lowest level of perceived personal vulnerability to criminal victimization.

Television viewing makes little consistent contribution to respondents' feelings of victimization but it shows a clear tendency to "mainstream" those feelings in both countries. Heavy viewing increases apprehensions in those demographic groups whose light viewers are the least apprehensive, and decreases apprehension in groups whose light viewers are the most apprehensive, thereby cultivating its own relatively high level of insecurity in the United States and a lower level of concern in the Soviet Union.

NEIGHBORHOOD SAFETY

While estimates of violence and vulnerability to criminal victimization are higher in the United States, a generalized feeling of fear in one's own neighborhood is more widespread in the Soviet Union. Responding to the question "Is it safe to walk alone at night on the street where you live," 41 percent of U.S. and 51 percent of Soviet respondents say it is "not safe." Soviet women and U.S. low income respondents express the most fear (54% say "not safe"); in the United States, college-educated and high income U.S. respondents are the least fearful (32 and 35%, respectively, say "not safe"). Group differences are insignificant in the Soviet Union.

U.S. television cultivates greater apprehension about neighborhood safety in almost every U.S. demographic category. This is especially pronounced among college educated and high income respondents who, as light viewers, express the lowest level of apprehension. For example, while 50 percent of low income light viewers feel unsafe, 58 percent of low income heavy viewers do. In the high income group, 27 percent of light viewers but 43 percent of heavy viewers feel unsafe. Viewing Soviet television makes much less difference. Its largest contribution is in the least educated group where 43 percent of light viewers but 53 percent of heavy viewers feel unsafe in their own neighborhoods.

WOMEN IN THE HOME

Gender-role conceptions were tested by asking "Do you think women are happier at home taking care of the family, or do you think that women are happier if they work outside the home?" and "Do you think that the husband and wife should share household tasks like cooking and cleaning equally or should that be mainly the responsibility of the wife?"

HAPPIER AT HOME?

In some respects, Soviet respondents are more traditional about gender roles than are U.S. respondents. While only about a quarter of U.S. respondents believe that women are happier staying at home taking care of the family than they are working outside the home, more than one-third of Soviet respondents (and 43% of Soviet males) tend to endorse that "traditional" view.

In the Soviet Union, the view that women are happier at home than at work undoubtedly reflects something more than simply a "traditional" or "patriarchal" view. Some respondents (male and female) bearing the double burden of housework (including standing for hours in line for the necessities of life) and full-time employment that is the fate of the vast majority of Soviet women may see the opportunity for women to stay at home as needed respite rather than denial of rights.

On the whole, however, the least convinced of female happiness in the home rather than on the job are Soviet women themselves; 30 percent endorse that choice. In the United Statesthere is no gender difference: only one-fourth of both men and women believe that women are happiest at home.

SHARING THE HOUSEWORK?

In terms of the division of labor within the home itself, however, respondents in both countries tend to claim egalitarian beliefs. Over 80 percent of both U.S. and Soviet respondents, overall and within demographic subgroups, respond that household tasks should be shared equally between husband and wife. Less than 20 percent in either country would relegate household chores mainly to the wife. The least supportive of the traditional role are again Soviet women. Only 12 percent of them (but 19% of Soviet men) believe that housework is mainly the wife's responsibility. In the United States, 15 percent of women and 17 percent of men express that view.

Income and education, even more than gender, mark differences in attitudes toward household chores in the United States. For example, 14 percent of high-income but 21 percent of low-income U.S. respondents believe that women should do all the housework. In the Soviet Union, the difference due to income is only 4 percent, and goes the other way: 18 percent of high-income but 14 percent of low-income respondents believe that housework is mainly the wife's responsibility.

LIFE SATISFACTION

Two somewhat different questions probed feelings of general satisfaction in the two countries. U.S. respondents were asked to pick one of four responses to the question: "All things taken together, how much satisfaction would you say you get out of life?" Soviet respondents were given a choice of five grades, as in their schools, to rate "the degree of satisfaction in your life in general." Because of the difference in wording and in rating, comparison should be made with caution and with special attention to the internal patterns of responses in each country.

DIFFERENT PATTERNS

U.S. respondents appear to be much more satisfied with their lives than are Soviet respondents. In the United States, 41 percent of respondents said they get "very much" satisfaction out of life, while another 42 percent said "quite a bit." Only 14 percent said "only some" and a mere 2 percent said "hardly any." The most satisfied were those with at least some college education (48%) and higher income (45%). Conversely, the low income and low education groups were the least likely to express "very much" satisfaction (35 and 37%, respectively).

Soviet patterns were quite different. Soviet respondents were asked to "grade" their lives, using the Soviet school grading system where 5 is the highest grade and 1 is the lowest. Overall, only 5 percent of Soviet respondents gave their lives the highest grade, 36 percent the second highest, 46 percent the third, and 9 percent the two lowest combined. If we combine the top two grades, however, we find that Soviets express satisfaction comparable to the "very much" category in the four-choice U.S. question. Nevertheless, the fact that so few Soviets selected the highest grade remains noteworthy.

Soviet subgroup differences range from a low of only 3 percent giving the most satisfied response (among those with the most years of education) to a high of 9 percent selecting the highest grade (among those with the fewest years of education).

It is striking that while education increases life satisfaction in the United States, it appears to depress satisfaction in the Soviet Union. Even more telling is the fact that while satisfaction climbs with income in the United States, higher income does not bring greater satisfaction with life in the Soviet Union.

TELEVISION AND LIFE SATISFACTION

In the United States, heavy television viewing consistently goes with lower levels of life satisfaction within all subgroups. Overall, 49 percent of light viewers but only 36 percent of heavy viewers say they get "very much" satisfaction out of life. U.S. heavy viewers are much less satisfied than light viewers in all subgroups, and this holds especially for males (52% of male heavy viewers but only 33% of male light viewers say "very much") and for those with lower incomes (for whom 48% of light but only 28% of heavy viewers say "very much"). In contrast, heavy newspaper readers are more satisfied than are those who read newspapers less often.

On the other hand, television viewing is at best only a weak indicator of lower life satisfaction in the Soviet Union. Overall, 42 percent of Soviet light viewers and 39 percent of heavy viewers give the two most satisfied responses combined, and only 7 percent of light and 5 percent of heavy viewers give themselves a grade of 5.

Heavy television viewing is as likely to be a symptom of lower levels of life satisfaction as it is to be a source of dissatisfaction. In any case, the difference between the two countries is noteworthy. Satisfaction is high in the United States, but sharply lower among heavy viewers. Life satisfaction is generally much lower in the Soviet Union, and so it is influenced less by demographic and social factors. Including television viewing, more education, more viewing, and more frequent newspaper reading tends to decrease satisfaction in the U.S.S.R. even further.

CONFIDENCE IN INSTITUTIONS

Analysis of American and Soviet confidence in political, social, and cultural institutions displays some of the most interesting differences and similarities between the two countries.

We asked respondents about roughly comparable institutions in the Soviet Union and in the United States. It is important to note the differences in the wording of the questions. The question on the American side was: "I am going to give you a list of institutions in our country. Please tell me as far as the following institutions are concerned, do you have a great deal of confidence, only some confidence, or hardly any confidence at all in them?" The question on the Soviet side was: "To what extent do each of the following organizations (agencies, organs) in our society make decisions in the interest of the people?" The response choices were: always, sometimes, never.

The institutions were as follows:

U.S.	U.S.S.R.
Churches	The church ("mosque" was added in Central Asia)
Educational institutions	Educational institutions
The government	Government offices (ministries, State Committees, etc.)
Labor unions	Labor union organs
Medical institutions	Medical institutions
Television	Television
Science institutions	Science institutions
Congress	Congress of People's Deputies or Supreme Soviet (two separate questions)
The armed forces	The army
Police	Organs of the Militia (name for police)
Newspapers	Newspaper editorial boards

By comparing attitudes toward these institutions in both countries, we do not imply that the organization and function of these institutions in their respective societies are the same or even, in many cases, similar. But the institutions we have named above do provide a reasonably parallel way in which to compare the level of trust and confidence in some of the key institutions in both countries.

COMPARATIVE RATINGS

American respondents express the highest levels of confidence in churches (48% say a "great deal"), the armed forces and educational institutions (39% each) followed closely by science, medicine, and the police (about 35% each).

The government, Congress, television, and labor unions rank lowest in receiving a "great deal" of confidence in the United States (between 10 and 15%).

Which Soviet institutions are said to act "always" in the people's interest? The largest number of Soviets (but still fewer than U.S. respondents) express such confidence in the Congress of People's Deputies (38%), the church (37%), and the Supreme Soviet (34%). Television is rated much higher than in the United States, with 28 percent saying the medium "always" makes good decisions for the people, but science is rated much lower than in the United States (only 14% say "always"). The army (28%), medical institutions (23%), education (23%), and the police ("militia organs," 19%), are rated relatively lower than in the United States, while labor unions receive higher rankings. Soviet government agencies receive almost as little confidence as in the United States (14%, compared to 12% in the United States).

There is a striking difference between the two countries in terms of the percentage who were unable (or unwilling) to state their degree of confidence in the various institutions. In the United States, only a small percentage did not answer for each institution, almost always less than 5 percent and usually less than 2 percent. In the Soviet Union, substantial numbers of respondents gave no answers. More than 20 percent did not respond in terms of the Congress of People's Deputies, educational institutions, or government agencies, and even more did not give confidence ratings for science institutions (33%) and the church (38% did not respond). Interestingly, the institution receiving an unusually high proportion (11%) of "Don't Know's" in the United States—labor unions—received the lowest proportion of no answers in the Soviet Union (9%).

Another major difference between the American and Soviet surveys is the effect of race and ethnicity. In the American survey, the differences between racial groups tend not to persist when other variables are controlled. For example, African Americans tend to be less confident in the police than the rest of the sample, although they are more positive toward television than are other groups. However, once education, gender, age, newspaper and television consumption are controlled, neither African Americans nor Hispanic Americans differ from members of other groups.

The situation in the Soviet Union is quite different. Ethnicity is among the most important factors explaining which Soviet citizens have confidence in their institutions. The greatest group differences in Soviet society are ethnic and national rather than racial.

The more satisfied with life people are, the more confidence they have in their institutions. On the other hand, the more education people have, the less satisfied they are. Education is one of the most important demographic factors that reduce respondents' confidence in institutions, especially in the Soviet Union. The more educated tend to be more critical, more aware of problems and alternatives, and expect more from their institutions. Age is not a significant contributor (when these other factors are taken into account) to the respondents' attitudes in either country. Differences due to income and gender disappear under controls.

TELEVISION'S CONTRIBUTIONS TO CONFIDENCE

Television viewing makes a positive contribution to institutional confidence in both countries. Heavy viewers are consistently and significantly more likely to give the highest ratings to a larger proportion of the institutions listed. In the United States, light viewers give the highest ratings to 25 percent of the institutions, compared to 30 percent of heavy viewers. This is particularly strong for females, older respondents, those with less education, and frequent newspaper readers.

Soviet responses are similar, although subgroup patterns are different. Overall, light viewers give the highest ratings to 21 percent of the institutions, compared to 27 percent for heavy viewers. This is especially strong for males and younger respondents.

In the Soviet Union, television is a fairly recent phenomenon; the penetration of television across all eleven time zones was effected only in the late 1970s and '80s. However, television has very rapidly captured the public there: by now most people get most of their information from television. Television, in both entertainment and news programming, has had a clear and articulated mission in the Soviet Union: to reinforce national policy. Right now, that means uncovering many of the abuses of power of all the previous regimes, as well as a good dose of investigative reporting about current domestic politics.

For specific institutions, other differences emerge. In the United States, amount of television viewing is positively and significantly related to confidence in the government, Congress, labor unions, and television itself (all of which receive low overall ratings), and also in the army and newspapers. Soviet heavy viewers give significantly higher overall ratings to the army, the police, education, medicine, the church, newspapers, and television. There is little overlap in these lists; confidence in the army, newspapers, and television are the only ones related to amount of viewing in both countries.

The pattern of confidence in institutions described above suggests that heavy consumption of television by Americans is related to support for the leading political institutions of the country. In the Soviet Union, heavy viewing has more effect on confidence in those institutions that are not directly political. Indeed, watching a lot of television has little effect on confidence in some of the pillars of the political system—the legislature, the labor unions, and the Communist Party.

Both television systems reduce class and group differences in attitudes, but this is especially strong in the United States where the homogenizing effects of television appear to be stronger. One of the most striking and consistent patterns in all comparisons was the similarity of Soviet responses across different groups in the population. In the United States, demographic factors such as age, sex, education, and income produced wide differences in people's attitudes. But Soviets express similar attitudes, even as light viewers, regardless of their demographic characteristics. Whatever accounts for the relative consistency of Soviet responses, television seems to serve similar functions in the United States.

Part VIII

CRITICAL CONTRIBUTIONS

CHAPTER 34

THE IMPORTANCE OF BEING CRITICAL—IN ONE'S OWN FASHION

BY GEORGE GERBNER

Communications as a discipline and its scholarly mission: some reflections.

A symposium is a dialogue of perspectives. Although the essays in this volume extend the discourse beyond the reach of any face-to-face encounter, frozen in print they leave the internal dialogue unvoiced. My purpose is to develop some aspects of that dialogue and to comment on them from my own point of view. My thesis is that the issues joined in this symposium help define the core and critical backbone of our discipline.

The study of communication revolves around the production, nature, and role of messages in life and society. Message making and storytelling capabilities provide the basic humanizing and evolutionary process of our species. A discipline that centers on that process makes distinctive contributions to the understanding of human problems.

In order to make such contributions, the discipline requires an intellectual domain, a body of theories and approaches that fits its subject matter, and professional organizations and journals that inform, socialize, and nurture its members.

A discipline also requires a sense of professional integrity. This means that its members are not just hired hands, but women and men prepared and free to scrutinize the ends as well as the means of any project. That, I believe, is the essence of the critical versus the administrative stance, a dichotomy that is expertly explored in this symposium.

Critical inquiry is the distinguishing feature of discipline and the hallmark of independent scholarship.

Social and symbolic structures cultivate tacit agreement on the terms of their existence. People growing up and living with these structures come to assume their existence as unwittingly as the proverbial fish in the ocean does salt water. Any scholarly inquiry that explicitly recognizes these structures and frameworks is inherently critical. It poses a challenge to unthinking acceptance. It extends the possibility of conscious control and deliberate change. It brings some degree of autonomy, self-direction, and development into the realm of human social possibilities. Posing that challenge is a unique task of an academic discipline and the only legitimate justification for its admittedly limited but still significant freedoms.

So the principal scholarly debate, as this symposium indicates, is not so much between "administrative" and "critical" research (as both are needed for different purposes) as among different approaches to the fundamentally critical functions of scholarship. The significant dialogue of perspectives is, as it should be, about how to make research most productive in illuminating the dynamics of power in communications and of communications in society. In other words, it is about ways to pursue the critical mission of the discipline.

Some scholars still see communications as an entry point to other and presumably broader fields and issues. They may find it a fresh approach to traditional concerns in sociology, economics, history, etc., or may use the study of communications to expose diverse social anomalies and inequities. But using communications study as a means to other ends gives short shrift to the discipline itself and reduces its ability to make significant contributions to the very problems those scholars may wish to address.

Those fixated on the "primacy" of such influences as "primary groups" or "opinion leaders" or economic and social relationships sometimes ignore data showing that mass media tend to weaken and short-circuit, rather than enhance, such influences. Those attributing complex behavior like violence primarily to media, particularly television, equally neglect the role communications study should play in understanding such behavior. As others point out, quite reasonably, unemployment, poverty, neocolonial wars, immorality in higher circles, and repressive activities of police and armies may be contributing "more" to social violence than the mass media. But that is like arguing about which is the most important section of the orchestra or which leg makes a three-legged stool stand up. If the implication is that the other sections (or legs) are somehow less significant or even dispensable, the statement becomes misleading and harmful.

In dealing with the confluence of complex social configurations, it is idle to claim primacy for any one set of forces and the field that addresses it. Each field offering seminal contributions to the understanding of any significant aspect of the constellation needs to develop its own critical discipline in order to play its appropriate role.

So the question is not whether mass media (or television) "cause" violence, but what common contribution, if any, do media make to viewers' otherwise diverse conceptions of the role of violence in life and society. Asking the question in that way opens the inquiry to a number or critical issues. What relationship does regular exposure to symbolic violence bear to one's own calculus of chances to use it successfully, and against what types of people? To one's feelings of mistrust, insecurity, and vulnerability, as well as aggression? To one's dependence on authority or force for protection? To the acceptance of repression if presented as a way of alleviating insecurity?

Posing questions in that way has made it possible to develop structural theories about symbolic violence as a demonstration of power and instrument of control rooted in the institutional order.

The question of "primacy" of social forces leads us to another underlying issue in communications study: the classical vs. a newly emergent line of materialist analysis.

The materialist line that originated with such Greek philosophers as Heraclitus and Democritus was eclipsed by the scholasticism of the Middle Ages. It was revived through the discoveries of Copernicus, Kepler, Galileo, Bacon, Newton, and Darwin; reformulated in different ways by philosophers such as Hobbes, Descartes, Spinoza, Locke, and the French Encyclopedists; and developed in the work of Marx and Engels into the theory of dialectical and historical materialism.

A central tenet (not to be confused with its vulgarized form of "economic determinism") is that social existence determines social consciousness. That means that the relationships of ownership and production provide an underlying coherence to political and cultural institutions, ideas, and modes of thinking. The dominant ideology is usually made invisible by being taken for granted and is disguised by religious, nationalistic, and pseudo-democratic trappings. That cultural "superstructure" reflects the more basic productive structure; both can be made visible through critical scrutiny and made accessible to action through agitation and the press. Thus aroused, class consciousness and struggle would be the prime movers of social change.

The classical conception was rooted in the print era. The era of telecommunications, with its mainstream culture of television, has witnessed a qualitative as well as quantitative shift away from reliance on the diversely and selectively used public-making instruments of the press. Instead of requiring, and building, more or less literate publics, mass media now saturate the life space of all Americans with a ritual serving the industrial establishment and presenting images of society and the world to which there is no equivalent challenge. At the same time, the productive "base" itself is shifting to the production of services and information. Study of the production, nature, and role of messages in social life becomes an integral part of the study of the material "base." It has been said, and not without reason, that if Marx were alive today, his principal work would be entitled *Communications* rather than *Capital.*

When common consciousness becomes a largely manufactured product and an integral part rather than only reflection of some other "base" of social existence, the concept of class or of any other authentic public consciousness may be obsolescent. Therefore, the investigation of industrial behavior in the cultural field—both policy formation and concept cultivation—becomes a central task of social analysis.

One's analysis of the cultural field defines the selection of the problems and definition of social tasks. Those who consider communications a relatively autonomous activity in a pluralistic society will seek media diversity, enlightenment, reform. Those who argue that media as cultural arms of established society cannot be expected to reform the body are more likely to suggest that the "basic" relationships of production must be altered before one can expect cultural industry to reflect the new order.

Plausible as that may seem, some contributors to this symposium question the separation of what used to be called the material "base" from its "reflection" in culture.

Those who see communications as an integral part and prime mover of both industrial and cultural structures point to the mass media ritual as the vital nexus between the two. Coming to grips with that ritual requires both the study of industry production (e.g., television program policy) and product (messages) and of what happens when a coherent mass-produced message system touches the lives of millions of otherwise diverse people directly and continuously. Understanding the dynamics of how particular industrial structures become part and parcel of our attempt to make sense of reality is also a prerequisite for making us aware of and involved in the shaping of policies that cultivate our common consciousness as national and transnational communities.

The new critique thus tends to stress those research tasks that can be seen (or used) to empower rather than control or even persuade people, to unmask rather than augment the established structure of power, and to reduce rather than exploit public vulnerabilities. It is no longer unusual to argue that a discipline should not condone the use of academic and research skills for purely tactical advantage without regard to ultimate social goals. Contributors using these lines of reasoning tend to suggest that some of the new research tasks are: demystifying culture-power; exposing languages (visual, verbal, systemic, etc.) of manipulation and repression (including the systemic role of themes and images that perpetuate inequity and injustice); revealing the dynamics of interdependence between industrial and cognitive structures; exploring how to cultivate resistance to persuasion and receptivity to the search for alternatives; and building, testing, and refining theories that make more visible and accessible the processes of power and control in industrial cultures.

The differences in perspectives about the appropriate goals and tasks of research are reflected in but not really illuminated by the debate over methodology.

Some scholars associate the rise and use of certain methodologies with social and ideological "bad company." But "guilt by association" may not be the best way to determine methodological merit. The proof of the methodological pudding is in the testing. Researchers should not be inhibited from selecting or developing and using any methodology suitable to a problem at hand.

It should not be necessary to point out that scientific thinking in general, and empirical methods requiring careful, representative observation and analysis in particular, have been humankind's chief intellectual weapons against arbitrary authority. The fact that the most effective tools are eventually taken over by those in power should attest to rather than diminish their utility.

Several contributors to this symposium note that the received history of research on communications effects tracing its progress from the "hypodermic needle" or "magic bullet" theories to the new and more sophisticated "active receiver" theories, should not be taken literally. No responsible communications researcher ever advanced a theory of helpless receivers falling under a hail of media bullets. That construction was advanced more to caricature exaggerated popular beliefs in the uniform efficacy of wartime (and other) propaganda and to call attention to research findings showing the greater complexity of the persuasion process. But it was elevated, with assistance from broadcast industry funds, publications, and researchers, to the stature of scientific ideology relating to media influence in general and not just to specific types of campaigns. As such, the formulation played a particular role at a particular time in postwar research history. Now that communications scholarship and research can be seen in a more balanced perspective, it is instructive to speculate about what that role might have been. Such reflection should also help us see the role of methodologies in less dogmatic ways.

Communications research has always had a critical thrust, even though it has also been used to justify almost any practice.

Perhaps the most comprehensive and—for its time—sophisticated and critical series of research projects was conducted in the 1930s under the title of Payne Fund studies. Concentrating on the then dominant entertainment medium, the movies, they advanced both a theory of centralized media power and the qualifications and modifications that later researchers were to refine and elaborate.

The traumatic sociocultural pathologies leading to World War II pushed the concern with media manipulation and centralized control to the forefront of political and academic attention. The reformist zeal following the war seemed to challenge the new concentration of industrial and media power about to achieve domestic and global hegemony. The reaction to that threat was twofold.

The explicitly political reaction was the attack on Hollywood, the blacklist, the so-called McCarthy era. The scholarly reaction, taking advantage of wartime and industry research on persuasion, was a new wave of agnosticism. The "hypodermic needle" and "bullet" formulations were set up as straw men with which to deride the concern about media power. The brilliant work of pioneers noted (and represented) in this symposium was diffused in a new wave of emphasis on traditional sociological and other "intervening variables" and "predispositions" deflecting media effects and channeling uses in audience-gratifying directions. These formulations were neither new nor wrong; they just ignored and distracted attention from what was new. That was a sea change taking place in the common symbolic environment involving directly, constantly, and systematically, though of course not uniformly, all who grew up in the new culture. That sea change was the rise of television. Unlike all previous media, campaigns, and propaganda, television is a relatively nonselectively used mass ritual into which children are born and which contributes, along with all other "variables," to the shaping of the very "predispositions" that are to structure subsequent media selections and effects.

Nevertheless, the "new wave" research came to dominate academic thinking for many years, and it still provides ammunition for media evasions of responsibility. Students trained in it learn valuable skills in applied work on communications campaign tactics and effects, needed by industries and governments alike. But the agnostic ideological implications of that training make it less likely that they will note, let alone challenge, the continuing concentration of media power. Even today, as some contributors note, scholarly as well as industry voices hail the march of new technologies as necessarily enhancing choice and pluralism, when in fact it can also signal further penetration of centralized electronic culture-power into every aspect of governmental, business, and personal life.

The emergence of communications as an independent and critical discipline using the full range of methodologies is beginning to right this imbalance. But the tendency of some scholars to associate empirical research only with administrative uses or evasive tactics blunts that critical thrust. It is a way of falling victim to history while attempting to explain it.

The danger is that the mixed bag of impassioned antiscientific arguments may congeal into a mystique that thwarts and trivializes the broadly critical thrust of the discipline.

Opposing science to art or humanistic scholarship presents a false dichotomy. The essence of humanism was its scientific (as well as artistic and linguistic) challenge to medieval scholasticism. In communications terms, science is the human attempt to penetrate the realities of existence, and art is the effort to express them. Science thus works to make statements true while art struggles to make them compelling and believable. The two complement rather than contradict each other.

Equally misleading is the qualitative-quantitative dichotomy. Qualitative distinctions and judgments (as in labeling or classifying) are prerequisites to quantitative measurements; the two are inseparable. To say that one can only measure what exists and, therefore, quantitative efforts can only support the status quo, is sophistry. The careful observation of existing conditions is necessary to support any judgment of or strategy for change, and judgment is not hurt by some attempt at precision.

Qualitative change cannot be understood, let alone achieved, without noting the accumulation of quantities. Add heat (quantity) to water and it changes to steam (quality). To consider quantification only mindless counting or number crunching is both a philosophical and a strategic fallacy.

Somewhat related to the question of counting is the issue of head counting. Methodological critiques of emphasis on individuals as units of analysis instead of social collectivities, and on collectivities instead of tangible human experiences, are both misplaced. Different levels and purposes of analysis require different focuses and units.

Those advancing sweeping historical claims should not, at the same time, disdain research on large collectivities, the proper testing ground for such claims, just because such research can also be used for other purposes. Critics who charge that mass-produced communications create impersonal bonds among otherwise diverse individuals or that they "atomize" and "privatize" individuals, loosen traditional bonds, dissolve authentic publics, increase alienation and dependence, etc., should not, at the same time, oppose the empirical testing and refinement of key aspects of these theories just because such research addresses individuals *as* individuals. The nature of the propositions makes that the proper focus. Only publicly accessible and replicable demonstrations, and the willingness to let the chips fall where they may, can make critical theories credible to those not already convinced.

While the long and checkered history of empiricism certainly produced fractured positivistic fantasies based on real data abstracted from their historical context, it also had a consistently critical line.

Its critical line is based on the assumption that freedom of action and protection against thought control depend on the ability to recognize salient aspects of reality existing independently of consciousness. No arbitrary power can make a false but testable proposition, no matter how widely believed, demonstrably true. Any recourse to publicly creditable procedures for testing significant propositions, rather than just professing them, provides legitimate leverage against arbitrary authority.

Those with little social power or dominant doctrine backing them have but one alternative for gaining attention and authority in rational public discourse. It is to be able to say: "If you don't believe it, here is how to ascertain key parts of it for yourself." Researchers who exclude that alternative from their repertory surrender authority to some critical mystique based on the assumption that methodological chastity and terminological purity are the best guarantees of truth. That ancient delusion makes for isolation and vulnerability to repression (or cooptation) when in opposition and the inclination to inquisition when in power—both unfortunate scholarly strategies.

The critical task of a discipline is to address the terms of discourse and the structure of knowledge and power in its domain and thus to make its contribution to human and social development. Those who search and struggle toward that end are critical scholars in the best and basic sense of the word. They should be able to search and struggle uninhibited by myths and mystiques that deprive them of opportunities or means at their disposal. The ferment in the field, and the expression of and response to it in this symposium, attest to the vitality of the discipline and to its ability to tackle the critical tasks ahead.

CHAPTER 35

"MIRACLES" OF COMMUNICATION TECHNOLOGY

Powerful Audiences, Diverse Choices, and Other Fairy Tales

BY GEORGE GERBNER

Trendy notions of audience empowerment through technology permeate promotional and even academic discourse. My analysis of trends, however, shows a different picture. New electronic communication patterns provide perhaps the clearest demonstrations of the rush toward cultural monopoly. Far from ushering a new age of media democracy and popular control, developments in mass media technology may reduce diversity and choice and extinguish all but the facade of democracy in the West, even as the floodgates to them are opening in the East.

Thomas Hughes, a leading historian of electrification, describes the logic of the monopolistic form in that industry in his book subtitled *A Century of Invention and Technological Enthusiasm* (1989). Huge grids dominated by single firms (permitting niches of independence for regulatory window-dressing) are needed to work the *loan factor,* that is, the ratio of average demand to peak demand. It requires very large reserve capacity, because electricity is hard to store. Similarly, electronic mass communications driven by advertising is also "hard to store." Maintaining or expanding market share depends on constant propagation of the sales message. Here a *risk factor,* the ratio of average marketing successes to total production capacity needed to sustain it, requires concentration, consolidation, large investments, and the pooling of resources through networking.

These imperatives create the impetus for what Hughes calls technological enthusiasm, that is, a cultural climate of swift and seemingly inevitable change propelled by inexorable forces of science, technology, and the "free market." Its speed and momentum tend to overwhelm public safeguards erected previously. Its sweep tends to disorient citizens who might form a constituency for democratic resistance and media reform.

The theoretical groundwork for confronting these trends has been laid by Dallas W. Smythe (see, e.g., 1977) in his work on the commodity form in advertising-driven mass-produced communications. The primary commodities created and sold in such production are not editorial or program content but audiences. Advertisers pay for media production according to the size and *quality* (i.e., propensity to consume) of audiences (called *markets*) mass media assemble and sell to them. Editorial and program content is the "free lunch," "loss leader," or "bait" that, in the argot of the trade, *delivers* the audience, preferably in the mood to buy.

Ads and almost everything sandwiched between them are designed to the specifications of a marketing plan built around the basic formula of *cost per thousand*, that is, the measure of the value of the commodity: how much does it cost to attract audiences in units of one thousand. That yardstick of value rewards cutting costs and boosting mass appeal; it punishes other qualities. The entire operation is funded by a levy hidden in the price of goods we buy, assessed on everyone who uses any advertised product (without representation, one must say), whether or not we need or use the media that it finances.

It is high time to distinguish our roles as commodities, markets, and consumers from that of citizens in self-governing society. In order to do that, we shall apply Smythe's theoretical contribution to the claims of technological empowerment and to look at the realities of availability and choice in mass communications.

CLAIMS

On the last day of 1989, in an editorial typical of the new media hype, the *New York Times* looked back at a decade of development in communications and pronounced it the Age of Speed. "Whatever else happened in this decade, the 1980s have been a time of acceleration, especially in America," *The Times* declared. Telephones have become portable. Microwave ovens speed labor in the kitchen. Computers drive business, industry, transport, government, and many professions to work ever faster. The videocassette recorder (VCR) appeared from nowhere to become a fixture in two-thirds of American homes. And more was still to come:

> Before cable, Manhattan residents could watch only seven channels.... Today's Manhattanite can graze among 37 channels, and others are on the way.[1]
>
> Because of cable, culture now travels faster. MTV provides throbbing music day and night. Three are channels for movies, channels for children, channels for talk, channels for sports. And, of course channels for news—news that seemed to sweep through living rooms at gale force.

All this, declared *The Times*, gave viewers "control over what was watched."

Similarly, *TV Guide* (December 9, 1989) looked back upon what it called a "Decade of Change, Decade of Choice" and declared that "two new technologies—

VCRs and cable—have forever changed the way we use our TV sets. And, indeed, the way we live."

If so, was it really in the direction of audience control and choice?

There is no doubt that the convergence of powerful new communications technologies speeds business, institutional, and professional life. But does the average home user who pays the extra price really gain and exercise greater control? Do new technologies promote freedom? Could it be (as I think the evidence seems to indicate) that the greatest acceleration in communications, in which *The Times* and *TV Guide* were both major participants, was the "age of speed" in global media concentration and hybridization? These are the questions we address in this chapter. First, we shall look at the actual diversity of media sources and materials available to the vast majority of people. Second, we shall review some evidence about the choices they make of them.

AVAILABILITY

Most people make their choices from what is made most readily available to them. The long-term trend in the availability of media materials—both information and entertainment—has been a rise in volume, a reduction in original sources, and a decline in the diversity of content.

The facts of media concentration and homogenization have been known for a long time. Yet they have been obscured or ignored by proponents of the new "powerful audience" theory. Media and academic voices both cheer and "revival" proliferation. They see "power" in whatever residual choices and interpretation audience members are able to make among media choices available to them. This apologia undermines analysis of the political economy of media and distracts attention from what is going on behind the scenes.

What is going on behind the scenes, unreported by mainstream media, is indeed a transformation of unprecedented speed and scope. The constant novelty of appeals and styles suggest content change and diversity. The relative stability of corporate names and logos implies constancy of structure. Together they help make the sea change in the manufacturing and control of the cultural environment not only unreported but virtually invisible.

The dismantling of public protections in banking facilitated the largest known financial rip-off in the country's history, the Savings and Loan (S&L) scandals. The same process called "deregulation" permits much less known, but for a democracy even more far-reaching, changes in the structure of cultural choices and the process of choosing.

CONCENTRATION

Many studies document the trend toward media concentration. Two wire services, one near bankruptcy, supply most world and national news. Chains dominate the daily and weekly press, with the top ten controlling more than one-third of circulation. Only 4 percent of cities have competing newspapers. Magazines and books provide the most varied fare, but electronically based conglomerates own the most and biggest publishing houses.

Broadcasting is of course the most concentrated. The top one hundred advertisers pay for two-thirds of all network television. Three networks, increasingly allied to giant transnational corporations—our private "Ministry of Culture"—control the bulk of production and set the trends for the rest of the cultural mainstream. Some fifty weekly series are cancelled every year, many without being given a chance to build a public. Many programs and films are made but never shown. A handful of huge conglomerates, probably not more than forty, manage most media operations. With the recent "merger mania," their numbers are shrinking and their reach is expanding every year. Other interests, minority views, and the potential of any challenge to dominant perspectives lose ground with every merger.

In one of the few studies of content diversity, Dominick and Pearce (1976) analyzed trends in network prime time programs over a twenty-year period—their "diversity index." Showing the number of program choices available to viewers declined from over sixty in 1953 to under twenty in 1974. Their "homogeneity index," tracing the similarity among network schedules, showed that the tendency to clone doubled "the symbolic structure has become more redundant and audiences have been presented with fewer and fewer alternatives" (p. 80).

The media proliferation of the 1980s strained some traditional client relationships (such as network advertising) and sharpened competition for existing markets. But it did not increase the supply of original sources of ideas or productions. On the contrary, the apparent market fragmentation was accompanied by an unprecedented new wave of mergers, acquisitions, cutbacks, and bottom-line pressures. The drive for ratings forced the same dramatic appeals on news as on fiction, and led to "reality shows" fronted by journalists and, ironically, involving dramatizations. Bizarre plot configurations popular on soap operas were recreated by "real people" on "trash TV." "The greatest threat to journalistic independence and integrity is not the Jesse Helmses," a network news executive was reported saying, "and it's not the libel suit—it's red ink."

Trying to finance their growth and still return a profit, giant conglomerates cut costs, reduced staffs, curtailed risky experimentation, and limited or totally abandoned specialized, minority, and public affairs programming (for a report, see Donahue, 1989). They seemed to be secure in the knowledge that large and otherwise diverse groups of media consumers exercise new media choices along existing lines. These are tastes and preferences cultivated mostly by television.

We have found that the cultural tidal wave that is television cultivates viewer conceptions of reality and shifts political orientations, and—vocal claims to the contrary—generates conformity and intolerance of differences. Provisions that had attempted to preserve fairness, plurality, and public participation in broadcast policy crumble under the impact of a shift of controls to ever larger industrial combinations. This process is called deregulation and is justified by an appeal to the free marketplace. The trade paper *Variety* announced in its September 11, 1985, issue (p. 45): "Diversity in the entertainment business, for decades the cornerstone of government policy and congressional oversight, seemingly has melted overnight into something akin to benign neglect." The last feeble remnant of broadcast fairness, the so-called Fairness Doctrine, is attacked by broadcasters as an infringement on their right to program as they (and their sponsors) please. The agency that is supposed to enforce the Doctrine decides to dismantle it because it "chills and coerces speech"—by requiring broadcasters to air controversy fairly. A survey of studies by Aufderheide (1990) shows that, while news and public affairs were cut for economic reasons, the Doctrine itself did not chill debate nearly as much as its absence does. Nevertheless, when Congress tried to restore the Doctrine, President Bush vetoed the bill, giving the same reasons.

When the state of Florida enacted a tax on advertising, industry's champions of the free marketplace of ideas threatened to blank out the state for national advertising, further confounding the distinction between free speech and profitable speech. Florida quickly reversed itself, and the experience slowed the desire of other states to tap a rich vein of potential revenue.

The Federal Communications Commission grants licenses free of charge in exchange for a promise to use the airways as a public trustee, broadcasting in "the public interest, convenience, and necessity." Never clearly defined or enforced, the concept of public trusteeship was virtually abandoned during the "deregulation era," largely because the FCC accepted the claim that new technologies make the license-holders' monopoly over scarce frequencies obsolete and diversity of content an inevitable consequence of market competition. Despite experience to the contrary, it has become increasingly difficult for community groups to challenge a broadcaster's failure to live up to any standard of public service and program diversity, or even of reporting. In turning down such a challenge to six commercial television stations serving Philadelphia, the FCC affirmed its elimination of quantifiable service or diversity requirements and only admonished a station for not even providing a publicly available file of its performance ("Memorandum Opinion and Order" released June 29, 1990).

OTHER TECHNOLOGIES

More than 60 percent of all American homes are wired for cable, but most cable companies do not engage in new production. Those that do compete for the most popular network-type fare. (And they also charge for it, and increasingly also carry advertising.) The more specialized channels appeal to upscale light viewers for whom they duplicate and compete with similar content on other (mostly print) media.[2]

Movie theaters, once an endangered species, now adjust to and reap record profits from the convergence of new technologies. Industry analysts report that "The box-office surge has been helped along by broadcast TV, cable TV and home video....Producers are using sales of foreign, cable TV and home video rights to virtually guarantee a film's profit before it even reaches theaters." Movie marketers are singing praises of the new technologies as efficient ways to promote movies that appeal to the largest audiences (Walley, 1990, p. 80).

Video production has of course been fully integrated into the new electronic system. Prerecorded videocassette buying, renting, and copying (illegal but widely practiced, costing the industry an estimated $500 million a year) concentrate on the most profitable titles. For example, more than half of VCR owners said they will buy, rent, or copy "Teenage Mutant Ninja Turtles" (*Variety*, June 27, 1990, p. 47). Videos also specialize in "adult" fare and other features that are more likely to imitate and even exceed some of the most exploitive aspects of standard productions than to offer alternatives or challenges to it.

It is, then, a political myth and intellectual conceit to assume that diverse audiences are clamoring for varied ideas, new knowledge, and fresh experiences. Often ignored by promoters of new technologies is the fact that cultural enrichment and diversity come from investment in education, art, science, and talent in general, and from resources devoted to the abolition of barriers to creative work such as minority status or assembly-line dramatic and news formulas. In the decade of media explosion, the proportion of resources devoted to such social investment declined.

While media outlets proliferate and consolidate, the numbers of writers, directors, journalists, and other creators of information and entertainment shrink. Media sociologist Muriel Cantor (1990) reported that, in the late 1960s, there were twenty-three program production companies; some twenty years later there were thirteen. During the same period, the eight major studios' share of all prime time programming increased from 40 percent to 75 percent (*Variety*, June 27, 1990, p. 60).

With the loosening of the long-standing FCC rule against the networks producing the syndicating of most of their own shows instead of contracting with the production companies (a rule nicknamed *finsyn*, for financial interest and syndication, designed to preserve a modicum of diversity), another wave of mergers and vertical integration is inevitable. "WALL ST. SEES FINSYN CHANGES TRIGGERING MEDIA MERGER SPREE" was the *Variety* headline of June 27, 1990 (p. 3). Michael Hill of the *Baltimore Evening Sun* foresees "A few media giants who would tower over all aspects of the entertainment and information business" (*The Philadelphia Inquirer*, July 4, 1990, p. 7D). Their expanding control over production would also enable these media giants and electronic conglomerates to enlarge their stranglehold over the global market and its extension into the hitherto limited territories of the Soviet Union and Eastern Europe.

CHOICES

Under these circumstances, the entry of new communication technologies into the home means, on the minority upscale information rich and the rest of the population, who may now be called the "entertainment rich." For them more channels means more time spent on the most popular types of electronic entertainment delivered by a greater variety of means. The new orchestration of mainstream media has fewer players handling more instruments playing fewer tunes for audiences who want more of what they already know and like.

Audience research from many countries confirms the fact that media diversification and novelty, as such, do not create new audience interests. On the contrary, they provide more means and styles (and markets) through which existing interests can be more single-mindedly exploited and pursued (see, for example, Becker & Schoenbach, 1989, p. 354).

Just as video rentals gravitate toward the "blockbuster" product, two-thirds of those who record programs on their VCRs tape popular network fare to view more often and at more convenient times. The A.D. Nielson Company reports that, instead of diversifying viewing patterns, most VCR users provide their own reruns. *Grazers* change channels frequently but relatively aimlessly. They are more creatures of chance than of choice. There is no evidence that their choices differ from those who watch by habit.

Viewer inertia and repeat viewing are the rule, eclectic and diverse choices the exception. These facts need not be interpreted as denigrating audiences as passive and powerless. Respect for audience choices comes from a recognition of the cultural context in which they are made. Given a particular cultural situation, audiences use their powers as they, not wishful thinkers, like to use them. In his summary of audience behavior, Comstock (1980, p. 11) concluded that "Viewers do watch programs they are familiar with and like, when they can."

Most cable homes watch more television and have more channels to pursue their preferences. Although VCR and remote control use led to a decline of viewer inertia (staying with the same channels through program changes), most cable and VCR users seek more of the same content types through a greater variety of outlets. Cable penetration even increased channel loyalty among those who stay with standard channels (Walker, 1988). A network-supported study reported in *Variety* (June 27, 1990, p. 52) also found that viewers are twice as likely to change channels when watching cable channels as when watching broadcast networks. By staying with regular station and network schedules, many of these loyal viewers may actually see a greater variety of programs than the volatile viewers, or *zappers*, who can pursue more limited preferences through the availability of more channels.

Evidence that this is indeed happening comes from several large-scale media market surveys. Neuman (1989) examined these data looking for diversity of viewer perceptions and choices. He was disappointed. Audience perceptions of program themes and motivations for viewing are strikingly similar across gender, income, educational, and age groups. Furthermore, the correlations of actual viewing patterns with perceptions are also similar in the different demographic categories. The highest positive correlation is with "relaxation" and the lowest (negative) correlation with programs perceived as "informative," or "sophisticated."

Our "cultivation analysis" of television viewing (Gerbner et al., 1986; Signorielli & Morgan, 1990) also shows the erosion of traditional differences in different generations born into television homes. The more viewers watch television, the more they share common conceptions of reality regardless of other group differences. Cable, VCR, news viewing, or other program preferences and selections do not significantly alter the basic "mainstreaming" pattern. Diversified media holdings and investments also imprint the book publishing business with their homogenizing tendencies.

All that does not mean the death of diversity. Credit should be given to the creative people who manage from time to time to produce thoughtful, challenging, magnificent works. Significant and restive pockets of resistance, alienation, and polarization also exist side by side with pervasive homogenization and mainstreaming. But it is clear that the global spread of mass marketing in all media, new or old, will not address, let alone satisfy, the human and public need for genuine diversity and choice.

The proliferating electronic discharge of evermore massive content configurations into the mainstream of the cultural environment, and of their ever deeper penetration into the dynamics of opinion formation and choice, confronts communities all over the world with a major new social policy problem. The mass production of evermore homogenized "masses" challenges any concept of popular self-government. A "revolt of the masses" as commodities, the building of an international constituency for democratic media reform, is needed to confront that challenge. A citizen constituency participating in and supporting the development of new and freer cultural policymaking is the imperative of the information age. A new environmental movement, dedicated to the cultural environment that will shape and guide those who survive the degradation of the physical environment, is needed to tackle that task.

NOTES

1. In fact, 1993 is the target date for 70 channels in Manhattan, operated by two large cable systems—both owned by the mega conglomerate Time Warner, Inc. The deputy mayor of New York when the first cable franchise was issued, Richard Aurelio, became the head of Time Warner Cable New York and negotiated the second franchise, running until 2003. "People who take cable, " Mr. Aurelio told the *New York Times* (July 2, 1990, p. B2), "have a love affair with television."
2. For example, *Broadcasting* magazine reported on June 18, 1990 (p. 53), that 40 percent of the viewers of four cable networks earn more than $40,000 a year, compared to one-third of broadcast network viewers. Over one-fourth of the Arts and Entertainment and Headline News networks earn more than $60,00, compared to about 13 percent of broadcast network viewers. Although the total number of cable viewers is still much less than that of the broadcast networks, and most cable viewers watch more television than non-viewers, the upscale character of a larger proportion of cable than broadcast viewers is used by cable operators to convince advertisers that putting together a commercial package aimed at four or five of the upscale cable networks is a good way to reach specialized audiences. That policy is most likely to drain advertising support from magazines (as well as from broadcasters) already hard hit by mergers and competitive media.

REFERENCES

Aufderheide, P. (1990, Summer). After the Fairness Doctrine: Controversial broadcast programming and the public interest. *Journal of Communication*, pp. 47–71.

Becker, B., & Schoenbach, K. (eds.). (1989). *Audience response to media diversification.* Hillsdale, N.J.: Earlbaum.

Cantor, M. (1990, June). Panel discussion at the International Communication Association Conference, Dublin, Ireland.

Comstock, G. (1980). *Television in America*. Beverly Hills, CA: Sage.

Dominick, J. R., & Pearce, M. C. (1976). Trends in network prime time programming 1953–74. *Journal of Communication, 26*, 70–80.

Donahue, J. (1989). *Shortchanging the viewers: Broadcasters' neglect of public interest programming*. Essential Information.

Gerbner, G., Gross, L., Morgan, M., & Signorielli, N. (1986). Living with television: The dynamics of the cultivation process. In Bryand & Zillman (eds.), *Perspectives on media effects*. Hillsdale, N.J.: Earlbaum.

Gerbner, G. (1990). Epilogue: Advancing on the path of righteousness (maybe). In N. Signorielli & M. Morgan, *Cultivation analysis*. Beverly Hills, CA: Sage.

Hughes, T. P. (1989). *American genesis: A century of invention and technological enthusiasm*. New York: Viking.

Neuman, W. R. (1989). *The future of the mass audience*. Unpublished manuscript.

Signorielli, N. & Morgan, J. J. (1990). *Cultivation analysis*. Beverly Hills, CA: Sage.

Smythe, D. W. (1977). Communications: Blindspot of Western Marxism. *Canadian Journal of Political* and *Social Theory, 1*, (3).

Walker, J. (1988). Inheritance effects in the new media environment. *Journal of Broadcasting and Electronic Media*, 32, 391–401.

Walley, W. (1990, January 30). Why movies are booming. *Advertising Age*.

CHAPTER 36

UNESCO IN THE U.S. PRESS

BY GEORGE GERBNER

The only official statement on mass media that UNESCO ever adopted was a consensus declaration supporting freedom of press and approved by the U.S. delegation and other Western countries in 1978. Nevertheless, American newspapers' depiction of UNESCO as an enemy of press freedom persisted and became increasingly strident though the withdrawal from UNESCO, and continues to be invoked in discussions of future relationships with the world organization. UNESCO coverage can thus be seen as an especially sensitive and problematic indicator of U.S. press coverage of global realities, especially in areas affecting the media's own interests.

This chapter presents two case studies exploring such coverage at strategically important points in time. The first deals with press performance before, during, and after the adoption of the Mass Media Declaration in 1978, based mostly on reporting in *The New York Times.* The second concerns general U.S. press coverage of the 1982 UNESCO conference that developed policies and programs (the "Fourth Medium-Term Plan") for the period before the U.S. withdrawal.

These studies should be read against the background of general paucity and selectivity in foreign news reporting. About 10 percent of total space in the average U.S. daily paper is devoted to general news, and a small proportion of that to news of the world. A comparative study of foreign news coverage ranked the American press last in the percentage of news space devoted to world news.[1]

A 1972 study already found U.S. press coverage highly selective, crisis-oriented, and increasing in factitiousness while decreasing in volume.[2] The media consolidation and bottom-line concentration of the 1980s resulted in further declines in both the amount and sources of foreign news. Within that sparse coverage, international organization news is the most likely to be dominated by a handful of usually like-minded agencies and correspondents. Press coverage of UNESCO bears the additional burden of special relevance to the interests of the press itself.

THE MASS MEDIA DECLARATION

On November 22, 1978, the 146 member states attending UNESCO's 20th General Conference in Paris approved by acclamation a "Declaration on Fundamental Principles concerning the Contribution of the Mass Media to Strengthening Peace and International Understanding, to the Promotion of Human Rights and to Countering Racialism, Apartheid, and Incitement to War." The Declaration was the first and only comprehensive official statement of principles regarding the mass media ever adopted by a UNESCO General Conference.

Contemporary accounts recorded a standing ovation and "thunderous applause" upon its passage. The chief American delegate called it "a triumph of the spirit of goodwill and international cooperation." A *Washington Post* story cited "the views of many" that UNESCO Director-General M'Bow's "role in today's unanimity opens the road for the former education minister of Senegal to make a serious bid to succeed U.N. Secretary General Kurt Waldheim."

The euphoria turned out to be short-lived. Five years later M'Bow would be discredited in the American press and decide not to run for a third term. The U.S. would pull out of UNESCO, charging attacks on the free press as an important reason.

How did this striking turnabout (if that's what it was) come about?

The *New York Times* Index provides an indication of general trends in that "newspaper of record." More than half (56%) of all listings of articles on UNESCO from 1960 through 1985 were in the three peak years of 1974, 1975, and 1984. The first two reflected the crisis over UNESCO condemnations of Israeli occupation policies and Zionism as a form of racism. In the third year, 1984, news of the U.S. withdrawal from UNESCO dominated the coverage. Most other years' listings occupied no more than 2 percent of the fifteen-year total.

The year the Declaration was approved, 1978, with barely 1 percent of fifteen-year listings, was one of the least newsworthy in the *Times*. The reasons can best be assessed in light of what preceded and followed it.

COVERAGE BEFORE THE DECLARATION

The *Times*' coverage of UNESCO in the 1960s was scant and bland, reflecting the organization's educational, scientific, and cultural work. No attention was paid to a resolution by the Byelorussian delegate to UNESCO's 16th General Conference in 1970. The resolution encouraged the use of information in the fight "against propaganda on behalf of war, racialism and hatred among nations." The 17th General Conference, two years later, passed a motion, opposed by the United States, to instruct the Director-General to draft a declaration embodying the principles of that resolution. The debate gave no warning of the storm this would eventually raise.[3]

The dispute first erupted briefly and obliquely at the 18th General Conference in 1974 where the crisis created by the anti-Zionist resolutions overshadowed and confused the mass media issues. While a committee of experts debated the mass media draft declaration, a resolution equating Zionism with racism was inserted into its preamble. The Western delegates left the meeting in protest. In their absence, the draft was approved and forwarded to the Director-General for submission to the 19th General Conference.

The *Times* reported on December 8, 1975, that an anti-Zionist resolution was included in "an official document" at "a conference on how the world news media should treat subjects such as racism and war propaganda." The rest of the story dealt only with attacks on the Israeli occupation. The next day an even longer story about the same session gave only three lines to the substance of the mass media resolution, noting only that it aimed to define "what the role of the news media should be in combating racism, war propaganda, and apartheid."

Not reported in the coverage focusing on the anti-Zionist passages were key provisions that were to figure prominently in later attacks on the Mass Media Declaration—even after they had been deleted from the document. These included Article 12 making "States…responsible for the activities in the international sphere of all mass media under their jurisdiction," and references to the U.N. declarations of human, civil, and economic rights, to free and balanced interchange of information, to the training and protection of journalists, to the development of an international code of journalistic ethics, and to the right of reply if "the circulation of erroneous news reports has seriously impaired" efforts to strengthen "peace and international understanding and to combat war propaganda, racism and apartheid."

The 19th General Conference met in Nairobi in 1976. Western pressure and withholding American contributions helped calm the anti-Zionist furor. The *Times* Index listings fell from 21 percent the year before to 7 percent of the fifteen-year total, most of it still devoted to Israel.

Wire services reported a Tunisian-initiated demand for a "new international information order" of more balanced flow of news.[4] Promises of American help for Third World media development and acknowledgment of a global information imbalance helped defuse what the *Times* called "the potentially explosive issue of press freedom."

A group of "wise men" [sic] was commissioned to study mass media issues. The draft declaration on mass media was referred to yet another group of experts for further consultation and submission to the next General Conference.

COVERAGE OF THE DECLARATION

The division and tactics of Nairobi were still in evidence when the 20th General Conference opened in Paris. Far from agreeing on a draft, Western, Socialist, Third World, and other factions submitted widely diverging versions and amendments of their own.

The *New York Times* published an editorial on November 8 which may have been the starting gun toward eventual withdrawal. "If it turns out to be impossible to reject this attempt to tamper with our basic principles," the *Times* declared in a bitter and prophetic blast, "there is always the alternative of rejecting Unesco itself."

Two weeks later, however, it seemed that the disagreements had been reconciled. Most objectionable features had been deleted and Western-oriented provisions inserted into the final draft. The Associated Press hailed the "unanimous consensus...endorsing the freedom of the press." It noted that the "consensus given in thunderous applause...represented...a significant diplomatic reversal in favor of the West and the moderate developing nations."

The *Washington Post* cited U.S. Representative Reinhardt saying, "We see no lingering hint of state control" in the Declaration. "In any case," he noted, "this declaration is unenforceable in the usual legal sense." Nevertheless, the *Post* story foreshadowed the eventual turnaround, observing that "Some Western editors and publishers say it was a mistake for the West to take part in any Unesco media negotiations at all." No mention was made of any virtues or moral, if not legal, obligations implicit in a document U.S. representatives fought hard and successfully to alter to their liking, and officially approved.

The *New York Times* carried the full text of the declaration. Under it was its story from Paris reporting approval of a "compromise declaration on world news coverage that eliminates all mention of government control of the news."

The façade of cautious optimism was shattered on November 27. On that day, by curious coincidence, both the *New York Times* and the *Washington Post* ran lengthy editorials on the Mass Media Declaration. Mocking Ambassador Reinhardt, the *Times* called the Declaration "a triumph of obfuscation," and "an affront to the very idea of communication." It observed that "Western diplomats are congratulating themselves on having turned a dangerous international declaration into an incomprehensible hodgepodge of slogans and prescriptions." And it declared that the American representatives who signed it "were not speaking for the free press of the United States."

The *Washington Post* editorial of the same day was equally critical. It said: "We don't wish to seem ungracious for official efforts undertaken in our, that is to say, the Western media's behalf. It is evident, however, that by helping to write and by approving even a moderate declaration like this one, the Western delegations condoned the idea that it is within the proper province of governments to call the media tune."

THE AFTERMATH

The report of the commission of "wise men," headed by Irish statesman Sean MacBride, compromised as it was[5] touched off more explosions in the U.S. press.[6] The American member of the MacBride Commission, veteran Elie Abel, was moved to comment that "the American press does not understand the Unesco communication decisions of recent years." His point was that the media construction of the issues, frozen in a cold-war "freedom vs. censorship" context, missed the historic shift of forces in global communications reflected in these documents.

Concerned about these developments, the National News Council, an independent organization dedicated to advancing the freedom and responsibility of the American press, undertook an examination of the U.S. press coverage of the 231st Belgrade General Conference, the session that received the MacBride report. The

News Council found the coverage so selective as to indicate "a strong correspondence between the judgment of editors on what constitutes news about Unesco and the fears that their papers express so unanimously on their editorial pages....The imbalance that characterized most of the Belgrade news coverage in the U.S. provided an inadequate foundation for independent judgment by U.S. readers of the correctness of the editorial positions their newspapers were taking on the Unesco communications issue."[7]

The report of the National Council attracted no press attention. Not long thereafter, the Council itself was disbanded for lack of media support.

THE FOURTH MEDIUM-TERM PLAN

UNESCO's general policies are set forth in six-year "Medium-Term Plans." They are developed by extraordinary sessions of the General Conference, to provide guidelines for specific programs to be voted on by the General Conference.

The Fourth Medium-Term Plan was debated at the extraordinary session held in Paris in the fall of 1982. Preliminary drafts had elicited 105 replies from member states, 19 from intergovernmental organizations, and 83 from nongovernmental organizations. Further consultations helped reduce the over 3,000-page document to a draft report of 256 pages which, as approved by the Paris conference, was to be the basis for UNESCO policy through the critical years of 1984–89.

Director-General Amadou-Mahtar M'Bow presented the draft Medium-Term Plan in two parts. The first part focused on the general tasks that world problems impose on the organization. The second part proposed fourteen major programs and budgets to support them.

The world problems M'Bow emphasized were the increasing "globalization" of human activities making nations vulnerable and dependant; the widening "fault lines criss-crossing the world" and "threatening to reduce vast numbers to despair"; massive violation of human rights; and the arms race draining resources while threatening total destruction.

Five tasks defined the substance of the fourteen major programs of the Medium-Term Plan. The first, tracking of world problems, was discussed in the first major program entitled "Reflection on world problems and future-oriented studies." The second task, achieving full participation in society, was addressed in the second major program on "Education for all" and in the third, entitled "Communication in the service of man."

The third task was the development of capabilities to use knowledge and the development of knowledge itself, giving rise to four major programs: "The formulation and application of education policies," "Education, training, and society," "The sciences and their application to development," and "Information systems and access to knowledge."

The fourth task before UNESCO was to facilitate change and transitions necessary in different societies. The three major programs addressing that need were "Principles, methods, and strategies of action for development," "Science, technology, and society," and "The human environment and terrestrial and marine resources."

The fifth task, the goals of understanding, peace, and mutual respect, was central to major programs on "Culture and the future," "The elimination of prejudice, intolerance, racism, and apartheid," and "Peace, international understanding, human rights and the rights of peoples." The last major program, entitled "The status of women," was defined as an area relevant to all tasks.

Delegates took the better part of two weeks to reach consensus on the fourteen major programs. Commenting on the debate, M'Bow stressed the complexity of the issues and urged moderation and conciliation. With regard to communication issues, M'Bow spoke of the wishes and aspirations of "many delegates, from all the regional groupings" for redressing the imbalance in world communication, but felt that "it was too soon for the General Conference to take a decision at the present session on the preparation of a declaration concerning the principles of a New World Information and Communication Order." Nevertheless, as we shall see, press coverage continued to focus on the NWICO.

Following adoption of the major program on "Communication in the Service of Man," M'Bow made some pointed comments about press coverage. He complained of the "tendentious character" of information in some member states. "I will go further," he said. "When the Director-General himself has sought to point out this tendentious nature and to give explanations, the newspapers or the media presenting Unesco cannot remain indifferent to the content of information about its own activities.…I intend…to have a study made of the way in which this General Conference has been covered by the information media.…If the information media have the liberty to say what they like, then others have the right to judge what they say." (Those remarks eventually led to the case study summarized here. For the full report, see note 4.)

Only one in about fifteen daily newspapers printed anything at all about the conference. The coverage was controlled by a few central organizations and sources, and was spread thinly across the country.

Wire service coverage began on November 20 with a comprehensive preview by Harry Dunphy of the Associated Press that no paper printed in full. Dunphy cited a "Western delegate" saying that "In paying attention to controversial areas such as communications and human rights, it's important not to overlook the important work Unesco does in many areas." Only one paper, the *San Diego Union*, carried that sentence.

The United Press International preview story went directly for the media angle. It began:

> Paris (UPI)—The tone was set Monday for a two-week special session on the future of Unesco with a senior official leveling harsh criticism at journalists who sensationalize the Unesco debate on establishment of a new information order.

The *New York Times'* preview story on November 22 began:

> The Western press is preparing for another confrontation with the developing countries and the Soviet Bloc over questions of press freedom.

On November 26, the AP reported:

> The United States clashed with developing nations Friday in a Unesco debate over a program that the Third World says will provide more balanced news coverage of their concerns and the U.S. government contends will foster state control of the press. [Guyana delegate Christopher A. Nascimento was cited as spearheading the move] to promote a proposed "world information and communication order." Among other things, it would establish systems for sharing technical facilities, create more regional news agencies and draft a code of ethics for journalists.

The UPI filed a similar account:

> Paris (UPI)—The United States and Britain Friday opposed adoption of an international agreement on world communications they say would endanger freedom of the press. Sharp debate opened between industrialized and developed countries on the United Nations Educational, Scientific and Cultural Organizations plan for a "new world information and communication order."

Typical headlines were "U.S., THIRD WORLD FEUD OVER PRESS PLAN," or "UNESCO STRATEGY FOR THE '80s CRITICIZED." An editorial in the *Baltimore News-American*, entitled "HIT 'EM WHERE IT HURTS," declared that "It's time to get tough" and cut off U.S. funds "if any freedom of press threat remains at the end of the Paris session."

By the time the session ran its course, the communications section, one out of the fourteen major programs of the Medium-Term Plan, emerged as the main, if not the only, issue of interest to the press. AP's final wrap-up story on December 3 led off with M'Bow's charge that "reporting by the Western media of the organization's activities amounted to a 'tendentious campaign' that he said he would challenge." The UPI story conceded that the final compromise resolution was satisfactory to and approved by the U.S. and Western delegations, but concluded: "Based on past experience with Unesco bureaucracy, some officials said they felt there could be cause for discouragement."

All twenty-one post-conference stories carried in the American press focused on communications. All editorials and columns focused on communications. No news story or editorial feature stressed any of the other thirteen major programs that occupied most of the time and over 94 percent of the space in the final report of the conference.

EDITORIALS

Twenty-six editorials provided the raw material for commentary printed in fifty-four different newspapers. All but one were negative.

Fifteen newspapers printed an editorial distributed by the Copley News Service. "By subtle rhetoric," it related, "the plan promulgated the doctrine long prevalent in Unesco that the press is an arm of government....It appeared that the West would be defeated in the censorship wrangle until the very end of the conference....For this unexpected victory, we must thank a little-noticed action by Congress. The so-called Beard Amendment warned the American funding of Unesco would cease if it took steps to control the news media."

Six newspapers, including the *Los Angeles Times* and the Minneapolis *Star and Tribune*, printed a feature by Xan Smiley (identified as "An editorial writer for the *Times of London*"). It concluded that although improving non-Western news services is commendable, "Unfortunately, the Third World nabobs who dominate the policy-forming vote at Unesco (while eight Western nations pick up nearly three-quarters of the check) have been demanding much more. Many of them want to keep out Western reporters altogether unless 'licensed' by the country in which they operate." (There was no such requirement in the resolution.)

An editorial in five newspapers, including the *San Francisco Examiner-Chronicle* and the *Seattle Post-Intelligencer*, warned: "How permanent the victory will be, no one knows, for Third Worlders and the Soviets have been persistent in their fight for managed news. They have made a temporary concession as a stalling tactic."

Another editorial in three newspapers sounded this (false) alarm:

> It may come as a surprise to some American taxpayers to discover that they're paying for elaborate plans for a new world information and communication order....Congress has threatened to cut off United States support for Unesco if that organization tries to limit press freedoms....Congress should most assuredly take this action.

An editorial in another three papers implied (erroneously) that the MacBride Commission report on communications was the basic "plan" of the Paris conference. It attacked the American delegation for conceding "that the Western 'monopoly' on news resources be balanced out. From this it follows that the West should not be allowed to report what isn't permitted to be known publicly in South Tsetse Fly or the Peoples Republic of Glorious Bloodshed."

Individually written editorial features follow many of the same themes. Several papers advocated cutoff of funds to UNESCO. Typical headlines were: "WHY GIVE OUR SUPPORT TO PRESS SUPPRESSORS?," "U.N. UNDERSTANDS MONEY," "HALT UNESCO POWER PLAY." A few worried about the threat of UNESCO broadcasting television programs through satellites. The *New York Post* of December 6 warned that "M'Bow's obsession with restricting freedom of the press—especially of Western news services—is only part of his much larger goal...to redistribute the West's industrial wealth to 100 underdeveloped countries."

Only one daily newspaper, the black-oriented 31,000 circulation *Chicago Defender*, viewed that prospect with equanimity. Its editorial of December 29 said:

> "...Right now the people of the Third World learn most about themselves—often incorrect information—from the highly technologized West. Multinational

> corporations, owners of many Third World papers now control much of the information and thinking of the Third World people....So Unesco is encouraging the Third World to set up its own news agencies, improve its own telex and communications generally. There should be more fairness in learning the truth of the world than now obtains, with the means of communication almost wholly centered in the self-interested West.

These case studies need little interpretation. The editorials about UNESCO only made what M'Bow called the "tendentious character" of the news coverage more explicit. A defensive, belligerent, and often paranoid tone pervaded most commentaries. There was little recognition of the actual consensus and compromise characterizing UNESCO'S positions, of the views of the U.S. delegation, or of any points of view other than that of the commercial press. When some of the handful of journalists reporting UNESCO tried to broaden the coverage, they were ignored. One correspondent (who asked to remain anonymous) wrote the author of the case studies that he was "trying to...show that there were other issues besides communications.... However, the desk felt that...that was the only reason editors would pay attention to a story about Unesco."

A few media sources, preempting the field of international information, paved the way for U.S. withdrawal from UNESCO, and prevented informed public discussion or even full awareness of the circumstances and consequences of the withdrawal.

One of the most strident of these voices, *The Wall Street Journal*, used the occasion of the 1989 General Conference to shed editorial "No Tears for Unesco." It lashed out at "the claptrap that passes for 'consensus'" at UNESCO, "One of the world's most corrupt organizations" and "a dreadful group," from which the U.S. has been "liberated." The editorial warned that "Unesco apologists are lobbying...to renege on...[the] decision to depart." It again conjured up visions of "ridiculous projects" such as "The Orwellian 'New World Information Order' [that] would give government officials rights against the press" and found, predictably, "plenty of reasons to stay out and none to rejoin Unesco."[8]

The U.S. media coverage of UNESCO is constructed more from selected bits and pieces to support prior assumptions than from actual resolutions and official actions. A speech, speculation, or even corridor talk that raises media hackles is real news, but a patiently hammered-out consensus statement is "hodgepodge" and "claptrap." That construction of facts shows a preoccupation with real and imagined threats to untrammeled private control of the press (interpreted as "freedom") to the virtual exclusion of other urgent world problems. It calls for a reexamination of the ability of media to deal with global information issues on terms other than their own self-interest.

NOTES

1. Gerbner, G. & Marvanyi, G. (1977, Winter). The many worlds of the world's press. *Journal of Communication.*
2. Szalai, A. (1972). *The United Nations and the News Media.* New York: Unitar.

3. Garbo, G. (1985). *A world of difference.* Paris: Unesco Documents on Communication and Society.
4. Harris. (1977). *News dependence: The case for a New World Information Order.* Centre for Mass Communication Research, University of Leicester.
5. Singh, K. & Gross, B. (1981, Autumn). Coverage of the Belgrade Unesco conference. *Journal of Communication.*
6. Mehan, J. (1981, Autumn). Unesco and the U.S.: Action and Reaction. *Journal of Communication.*
7. Raskin, A. H. (1981, Autumn). U.S. news coverage of the Belgrade Unesco Conference. *Journal of Communication.*
8. (1989 November 1). No Tears for Unesco. *The Wall Street Journal* (editorial).

CHAPTER 37

PERSIAN GULF WAR, THE MOVIE

BY GEORGE GERBNER

There comes a time in the accumulation of quantitative changes when a qualitative transformation takes place. Add heat to a pot of water, and at one point it begins to boil. A confluence of controls, technologies, and power reached that point in the war in the Persian Gulf. The change occurred not just in geopolitics. It also happened in the way we write—and make—history.

A scholar of media technology, Frederick Williams, compared the Gulf War to the first moon landing in 1969: "Its was one feat to put two astronauts on the surface of the moon, but another, perhaps just as amazing, to broadcast live that first human step on the moon's surface." Technology-based immediacy, Williams concluded, was a preview of the shape of things to come.[1] In 1991, the preview led to the main event.

When Mao Zedong was asked what he thought about the meaning of the French Revolution, he is reported to have said that it was too soon to tell.[2] Official history, written from the point of view of rulers, is typically the story of the inevitable unfolding of the glorious present. As written by losers, history is tragedy crying for redemption. When roles change, or when long-hidden facts come to light, it takes time to sort things out.

When that other astute observer of the world scene, Saudi financier of Irangate fame Adnan Khassoghi, was asked what he thought about the war in the Persian Gulf, he said that it was "like going to a movie: we paid our money, we went to the theater, we laughed, we cried, the movie ended and an hour later we had forgotten about it."[3]

Mao's and Khassoghi's observations marked a change that had come about after a long buildup. Cheap parchment had replaced rare papyrus. The printing press had replaced the quill. The telegraph and telephone had replaced the pony express. We had gone from oral to scribal, to literate, to audio-visual-digital-cybernetic mass-produced culture. The quantum leap had occurred when satellites connected them all around the world. The stage had then been set for centrally scripted real-time live global imagery, evoking instant reaction, feeding media events back into an ongoing crisis, and giving the deliberate sorting out of historical meanings a swift kick in the pants.

Historiography is a communicative activity that relates the past to the present and future.[4] But, as with any communicative activity, it depends not only on the events to be communicated about and the communicating parties but also on the means and modes of communication. When the means change, as Harold Innis, Marshall McLuhan, Elizabeth Eisenstein, and others have observed, access to and control over communications change, and the telling of stories, including history, also changes.

The boiling point is reached when the power to create a crisis merges with the power to direct the movie about it. Participation, witness, and confirmation hitherto limited to those on the scene can now be a vicarious global experience, and response, or cooptation, occurs while the event is still in progress. Having achieved the desired outcome, the movie ends, but the images remain in archives and memories.

The convergence of new communicative technologies confers controls, concentrates power, shrinks time, and speeds action to the point where reporting, making, and writing history merge. The "simultaneous happening," in which, as Ien Ang described it, "the whole world presumably participated through the electronic collapsing of time and space,"[5] usually occurs in crises, or tends to precipitate a crisis, as in climactic trials and hearings, disasters, uprisings, and wars.[6] These are situations when, one would think, deliberate speed and careful consideration are needed the most. Instead, however, past, present, and future can now be packaged, witnessed, and frozen into memorable moving imagery of instant history—scripted, cast, directed, and produced by the winners.

INSTANT HISTORY—IMAGE HISTORY

Instant history is made when access to video-satellite-computer systems blankets the world in real time with selected images that provoke immediate reactions, influence the outcome, and then quick-freeze into received history. Instant history is a magic lantern projecting images on a blank screen in a temporal void. The show has a clear beginning, middle, and end. It telescopes roles, parts, and outcome into the same act. It appeals to prior beliefs and predilections. It triggers familiar responses. It blends into our repertory of imagery. It is not easily dislodged, reinterpreted, or even attributed to one particular show. We have forgotten the title.

Films of Vietnam took hours or days to reach us after the fact. It may have been the first "living-room war," but not for the first few years and not in real time. Starting with the make-believe incident in the Gulf of Tonkin, it was a long, slow duplicitous buildup. It lasted eleven years, destroyed three countries, and left behind some 2 million dead and continuing economic sanctions for the living.

"Body counts" were in headlines but did not have public witness. The tide of public reaction turned after victory eluded policymakers and cameras began to record unsettling images: the Tet Offensive, a summary execution of an "enemy" suspect, naked "enemy" children fleeing napalm, thatched "enemy" huts being put to the torch. (When cameras turn to focus on the fallen, the war is lost, or soon will be. The press was barred from Dover Air Force Base, where Gulf War body bags landed.)

Instant history is image history. The crisis unfolds before our eyes, too fast for thoughtful consideration of antecedents, alternatives, or long-range consequences but just in time for conditioned reflex. The show is on, we are in it, and the deed must be done before second thoughts, counteracts, and regrets can derail the action.

The Iraq-Iran War, totally out of sight, dragged on for more than eight years, claimed more than 1 million casualties, and ended in exhaustion. Chaotic *perestroika*, made visible by *glasnost*, rolled into Eastern Europe, where each successive counter-revolution took half the time of the previous one. The long pent-up Soviet backlash led to the attempted coup of August 1991, or, as the plotters saw it, countercoup, which was intended to prevent disaster. But the plotters lost control. The magic lantern was snatched from their hands. Defiant imagery swamped their timorous stance. A tidal wave of domestic and world reaction swept them from power in seventy-two hours. Instead of victory, they fell victim to instant history.

Speed and controlled imagery give instant history its thrust—and its burden. When emphasis shifts to image, complex verbal explanations and interpretations, if any, switch into supporting and explanatory, rather than alternative, modes. Experiments have shown that dramatic imagery tends to inhibit both complexity and alternatives. Instant history preempts alternatives.

Neil Postman argued that pictures "have no difficulty overwhelming words and short-circuiting introspection."[7] He cited studies that found the complexity of diplomatic exchanges in international crises that ended in peace to be significantly higher than in crises that ended in armed conflict. Research by Tom Grimes concluded that words can influence the memory of imagery.[8] Thus, congruent narration will often be recalled as a part of actuality witnessed on the screen, even if it never occurred there.[9]

If, however, the voice-over conflicts with the image, the former may be ignored. Todd Gitlin recounted his four-hour interview for "The NBC Nightly News" in which he expressed the view that his opposition to the Gulf War did not conflict with donating blood for the troops. The few seconds selected for the news only showed him donating blood, with his opposition to the war briefly noted in the voice-over. Viewers who confronted him afterward recalled only the image of his apparent support for the war. "People who wouldn't be caught dead saying out loud that the news (to use the media's own favorite metaphor) mirrors reality, saw a media image and *assumed it not to be a construction, not a version, but the truth.*" And "when an image comes advertised as actuality, it raises the expectation of accuracy."[10]

Images of actuality appear to be spontaneous and to reveal what really happens. They do not need logic to build their case. Following William's observation, spontaneity and immediacy preclude time for reflection and evaluation. And if the audience response quickly becomes news, the effects of superficial responses to important world events can be exaggerated.[11]

"Image Industry Erodes Political Space" is the title of John M. Phelan's analysis of the uses of new technology. "The image's new role in organizing complex information is increasingly played out in dynamic interactive contexts," he wrote. In the cockpit of the latest automatically controlled aircraft, the pilot punches in this flight plan on a keyboard, and the flight management system on board calculates the route and flies the plane from takeoff to landing while he monitors the scenery. Phelan commented, "There is a running joke among pilots, who do not find it entirely comical, that the modern flight crew consists of a pilot and a dog. The dog's job is to bite the pilot if he touches any of the controls and the pilot's job is to feed the dog." "By a strange process, " Phelan observed, "the further one gets from the reality the more processed the information gets, the more authority it assumes."[12]

THE SCENARIO

The war in the Persian Gulf was an unprecedented motion picture spectacular. It crammed into its first month alone the entire imagery—and firepower—of four years of bombing in World War II. But unlike a carpet of explosives leveling cities and setting off firestorms, or of GI's "flushing out" Vietcong from their hiding places, we were shown "seeing-eye" bombs zooming in on their targets, followed by computer graphics tracing the ground offensive against an invisible enemy.

General Norman Schwarzkopf forbade casualty estimates, so sortie counts replaced body counts. Photographs of battle or of Iraqi (or U.S.) dead were censored. Sleek aircraft "sortied" over unmentionable people in unfought battles in an unseen country. The few unauthorized shots of bombs falling on civilian targets were attacked as treasonous or rationalized as "collateral damage." Never before were selected glimpses of actuality strung together with sound bites of photogenic crews, omniscient voice-overs of safari-clad reporters, and parades of military experts with maps and charts at the ready, so mesmerizing, so coherent, and so contrived.

Desert Storm was the first major global media crisis orchestration that made instant history. The Soviet coup six months later was the first attempt that miscarried. A year before the coup, Mikhail Gorbachev had signed a new press law that gave editorial staffs autonomy not known in the democratic West. This move made for a relatively fragmented and leaky communication system that may have saved his life, if not his job. When the coup came, the plotters could not shut down or conduct the increasingly cacophonous media orchestra. What happened then also made instant history, but that is another story.

Opportunities for making instant history may be few and far between, but when they come, they unloose a landslide that shifts the political landscape. ("I came back to another country," said Gorbachev returning from Crimean captivity.) George Bush grasped the opportunity and proclaimed his "new world order."

It takes a crisis and five strategic moves to seize (or possibly provoke) such an opportunity. They are control, orchestration, witness, feedback, and quick freeze. Here are instructions for successful crisis management by instant history as learned in the Persian Gulf War:

1. Gain access to and keep control of real-time global imagery. Speed the action, and develop a sanitized scenario to show how moral, decisive, necessary, and invincible the action is. One brief burst of saturation cov-

erage is all that is possible before unauthorized voices, costly network preemptions, and audiences missing their daily mayhem with happy endings blunt the momentum.

2. Orchestrate the main event with mainstream media events and other signs and symbols. Invent code names and terminology that fit the scenario, demonize the enemy, and wrap jarring realities in playful euphemisms. Encourage integration of supportive signs into everyday life, sports, and commerce (yellow ribbons on cars and Kent cigarettes, Super Bowl halftime prowar pageant with President and Mrs. Bush on tape and Peter Jennings live giving upbeat reports on the destruction in progress). Promote miracles. (The icon of St. Irene gained worldwide attention when congregants in a Chicago church reported that it wept "tears of grief" on the eve of the Persian Gulf War.)[13] Instant history requires a total environment of actuality, images, talk shows, slogans, and other evocative manifestations.
3. Offer the witness-audience a sense of "being there," including what appear to be spontaneous (but still stage-managed) occasions such as press conferences, panel, discussions, "briefings," and interpretations. This will suggest that alternative perspectives have been explored and exhausted. It will simplify and isolate the crisis from distracting complexities and unwanted alternatives.
4. Translate witness and participation into supportive feedback from polls, letters to the editor, driving with lights on, and horn honking. To evoke conventionally cultivated responses, make participation "like going to a movie." Let this feedback reverberate across all media, crystallize in public opinion (i.e., published opinion), and hasten the desired resolution.
5. Celebrate the outcome as the happy ending. Quickly produce and distribute videos, CD-ROM disks, paperback books, and lavishly illustrated texts to saturate the market for instant nostalgia and school use. Use the triumphant imagery to fight political opposition and resist revisionists.

PROLOGUE

The curtain rises on an operation long in preparation. Several U.S. administrations wanted to project U.S. power into the Middle East. Dwight Eisenhower landed troops there. Ronald Reagan landed troops there (only to have 241 Marines killed in one bombing attack), condoned Israel's invasion of Lebanon, and bombed Druse villages from the sea. After building up Iraq's war machine and also secretly arming Iran in its war with Iraq, U.S. diplomacy encouraged the Saudi and Kuwaiti economic offensive against Iraq. Iraq's historic claims, grievances, and offers to negotiate a settlement were ignored, as was Saddam Hussein's advance notice of his intentions. He finally took the bait and struck.

After the invasion, Hussein released parts of a transcript of his meeting with the U.S. ambassador in which she gave him no clear warning against the impending move. Ambassador April Glaspie related before an "informal" Senate committee meeting (not officially a "hearing" so she did not have to testify under oath) that she indeed warned Hussein in no uncertain terms. The State Department backed her up. When, under more congressional pressure, the diplomatic cables were declassified, the facts became clear: she and the State Department had lied.

No attention was paid to Hussein's brutalities until he marched on cue. Media "watchdogs" were still asleep when the U.S. head of Amnesty International complained that "there was no presidential indignation...in 1989, when Amnesty released its findings about the torture of Iraq children. And just a few weeks before the invasion of Kuwait, the Bush administration refused to conclude that Iraq had engaged in a consistent pattern of gross human-rights violation."[14]

When Hussein invaded Kuwait, however, gruesome atrocity stories filled the media. They were used in six speeches by Bush and were cited by seven senators as a reason for voting for the war resolution (which passed by six votes). A year later it was revealed that the story was hearsay told by the daughter of Kuwait's ambassador, whose appearance was arranged by Hill and Knowlton, the Washington public relations firm representing Kuwait. The *New York Times* also reported on December 20, 1991, "the discovery that the country suffered less damage than originally estimated" and was "recapturing its former affluence."

The first stage, Operation Desert Shield, was to stop Hussein from marching into Saudi Arabia, although there was no evidence he intended to do so and the United States had no treaty or prior policy to defend the Saudis. The mission of the troops, according to Bush, was defensive; they would not initiate hostilities.

Soon, however, the operation became a simple and unconditional offensive to rebuff "naked aggression." The U.S.-led military buildup proceeded swiftly with no consideration of the colonial and recent history of the shifting boundaries of Middle Eastern non-nations or of other invasions, occupations, and repeated violations of U.N. resolutions and international law by the United States and its allies.

The United Nations itself was brought out of media mothballs. The *New York Times*, after spearheading the successful campaign for U.S. withdrawal from UNESCO, and mostly ignoring U.N. actions, now editorially complimented the United Nations on September 11, 1990, for having "provided legal and political armor" for the operation.[15] Vague resolutions authorizing force were rammed through without significant opposition (absent on the world scene since the collapse of Soviet power). The resolutions concealed, but were later used to justify, the allies' ultimate objectives. Having achieved them, the allies exploded the equivalent in bombs of the next twelve to fifteen years of the entire U.N. global budget. Other resolutions condemning the invasion of Lebanon and continuing military occupation by Israel were ignored.

The United States was still withholding $720 million in overdue membership payments. This long-standing pressure tactic drove the United Nations to the brink of bankruptcy. Secretary General Javier Perez de Cuellar had to report in the fall of 1991 that "it is a source of profound concern to me that the same membership which sees it appropriate to entrust the United Nations Secretariat with unprecedented new responsibilities has not taken the necessary action to insure that the minimum financial resources required to carry out those responsibilities are provided on a reliable and predictable basis."[16]

A loose coalition was patched together, with the United States contributing most of the military might; the Arabs, the location; and the oil sheikhs, Germans, and Japanese, most of the cash. While preparation for was proceeded, diplomacy was faked for the media. Bob Woodward's book *The Commanders* described the panic in the White House when it seemed that the Saudis might "bug out" (in Bush's words) and accept some settlement.[17] King Fahd did not buy the excuse of a Iraqi threat to Saudi Arabia. (Neither did the satellite photos published in the *St. Petersburg Times* on January 6, 1991, which were refused by the U.S. wire services.) But then the White House sent Secretary of Defense Richard Cheney with an offer the king could not refuse, apparently a promise to push for favorable regional settlement after Hussein was safely out of the way. While Secretary of State James Baker went to Baghdad to "negotiate," national security adviser Brent Scowcroft told Saudi Ambassador Prince Bandar that the president had made up his mind and that diplomatic efforts were all exercises.

Exaggerated estimates of nuclear capability, "the world's fourth largest standing army," and Iraq's "crack Republican Guards" were fed to eager media. A vast and sophisticated U.S. intelligence community that five months later was able to warn Gorbachev of the impending coup in his own backyard (in vain, as it turned out) now seemed to be muted. Disinformation, rationalized as "confusing the enemy," confused everybody. Decision making was restricted to a small group headed by former CIA director (now President) George Bush. It was apparent even before the Gulf War, wrote Maureen Dowd in the *New York Times* (November 22, 1991, p. 1), that "this White House does not have a traditional policymaking process." Dowd cited a "top Administration official" as saying, "It's hard to debate decisions because there is a lot of secrecy."

In the preparation for Desert Storm, even the National Security Council was held at arm's length.[18] Woodward reported that the chair of the Joint Chiefs of Staff, Colin Powell, and other commanders advised "containment or strangulation" and found themselves excluded from decision making.[19] Later they complained of "faulty intelligence." The order to attack came from a White House apparently acting on superior intelligence.

Final planning for the attack was known to have begun in September but was not reported until much later. The *New York Times* published the "news" on March 3, after the war had ended. *Newsweek*'s account of the preparations, published on January 28, quoted "one of his closest advisers" as saying, "This is a fight George Bush has been preparing for all his life." Elizabeth Drew wrote in the *New Yorker* on January 25, "John Sununu...was telling people that a short successful war would be pure political gold for the President." Reporters who usually rushed on the air and into print with every scoop now held back. "The road from Watergate to the Gulf War is marked by ever greater cautiousness and opportunism on the part of the press," wrote Michael Massing. "Bob Woodward [who saved revealing details for his book] provides a particularly disquieting example of the change."[20]

The full history of the swift and massive military buildup still remains to be told. A nearly Vietnam-sized military force was built up over a period of months in the desert. Information, communication, and coordination were key elements. Williams reported that more communications networks were put into full use during the buildup and war than in all of World War II.[21] As late as December 1990, the Pentagon sent out a call for $30 million worth of computers to be shipped to Saudi Arabia in six weeks. A small and little-known Texas company called Compuadd got the contract and did the job. Its full reward came when, ten months later, it shared in the biggest Defense Department computer order ever awarded.

Forming the backbone of the new instant history-making machine were the portable uplinks, the global satellite network (including the collaborating Soviet satellite), the dedicated direct telephone lines, and the computer links. This tightly guarded system made it possible to provide controlled real-time simultaneous live global coverage in several selected sites, even when nothing much was going on. Suspenseful "live" boredom filled with breathless analysis and photo opportunities gave audiences around the world a realistic sensation of "being there." Donning gas masks enhanced the feeling of spontaneity even, or perhaps especially, when the alarm turned out to be false. At the height of the crisis, CNN's audience share rose more than five times its normal 3 percent.

The prologue ended with the U.S. ultimatum of January 15, 1991. The deception, suppression, misinformation, and disinformation that characterized the buildup overwhelmed and disoriented the public. Many watched in disbelief as the juggernaut assembled in the Gulf was set to strike. When the nonnegotiable ultimatum was about to expire, the public was still deeply divided: four out of ten responding to a *Times Mirror* poll thought sanctions should be given more time. The same number also wanted to hear more about the views of the 41 percent of the U.S. public that did not think Bush "did the right thing" sending troops to the Gulf.[22] Even though the congressional authorization had passed by only seven votes, once the war started, dissenting voices fell silent or were silenced, and the media-driven instant history blitz kicked in.

THE MAIN EVENT

"As the skies cleared…an American officer proclaimed it 'a beautiful day for bombing,'" wrote R. W. Apple, Jr., in the *New York Times* on February 12, 1991. Before the day was over, 750 bombing missions had been completed. "'There is more stuff up there than I'd see in 20 lifetimes,' said an Air Force pilot."

What may have been happening on the Iraqi ground could only be surmised from a safe distance. A British defense expert calculated that in the first month "the tonnage of high explosive bombs already released has exceeded the combined allied air offensive of World War II."[23] But the military terminology that permeated the reporting was more sports than slaughter. "Our team has carried out its game beautifully," exulted a military expert on NBC. "We ran our first play, it worked great," said a pilot interviewed on CBS. "We scored a touchdown."[24] Secretary of Defense Cheney told U.S. Air Force personnel that they had conducted "the most successful air campaign in the history of the world."[25]

The precision-bombing spectacular was, in fact, the dumping of the equivalent of five Hiroshimas on a small country of 18 million people. The targets were the life-sustaining infrastructure of water, power, and transportation facilities. When the bombing was over, the carnage of hunger and disease began. Western health authorities estimated 1 million children malnourished, and child mortality quadrupled within a year. Middle East Watch, an affiliate of the international Human Rights Watch organization, reported that allied decisions to drop unguided bombs in daytime over populated areas without warning civilians of imminent attacks violated generally accepted practice and international law "both in the selection of targets and the choice of means and methods of attack."[26]

The memorable Patriot missiles, costing $700,000 each, missed eight out of ten times. When they found their targets, the resulting debris caused more destruction than the Scuds might have done. MIT weapons expert Theodore Postol told the House Armed Services Committee that thirteen Scuds that fell unchallenged near Tel Aviv caused no deaths, fewer injuries, and less than half the property damage than the eleven Scuds in the same area that were intercepted by Patriots. Marc S. Miller, senior editor of *Technology Review* magazine, called Patriot "the anti-truth missile."[27] Roger N. Johnson concluded in his study of war damage that the Patriots were "successful mainly as psychological weapons used to fool the public."[28] Their public relations success was shown in the survey by Michael Morgan, Justin Lewis, and Sut Jhally: 81 percent of the respondents knew about the Patriots, while only 42 percent could identify Colin Powell.

The mighty armies that brutalized Kuwait and were supposed to march on to Saudi Arabia, if not beyond, could not be found. Poorly equipped and demoralized troops sitting in trenches, caves, bunkers without air cover were napalmed and "fuel-air bombed" to deprive those inside of oxygen, and then they were bulldozed; dead and alive alike were buried in some seventy miles of trenches. (Bodies of soldiers who "suffocated in their bunkers after U.S. tanks plowed them under" were still being discovered nine months after the war.)[29] Defenseless convoys fleeing in panic were bombed and strafed into oblivion in what pilots called a "turkey shoot."

There was much media concern expressed about Iraqi chemical and missile threats. The erratic Scuds and the even more erratic Patriots got extensive coverage. Missing were signs that the roughly four-week, $61 billion massacre inflicted on Iraq was more lethal than any nuclear, chemical, or biological warfare had ever been.[30]

One may question, as has Noam Chomsky, whether there really was a war, if by war we mean a conflict in which an enemy shoots back. The slaughter, as it is more properly called, claimed more than 100,000 lives in direct casualties alone. That is the official figure. In a secret report, former navy secretary John Lehman revealed a Pentagon estimate of 200,000.[31] The kill ratio of even about 100,000 to 150 U.S. soldiers, at least 35 of them, as it later turned out, killed by "friendly fire," was unprecedented in military history.[32]

The main facts of cost, casualties, and damage were carefully kept out of the briefings and were censored from the reports. U.S. and allied reporters were rigidly controlled, and few other journalists were even admitted into Saudi Arabia. The few independent reporters who managed to obtain information on their own, and the analysts who might have contributed more diverse perspectives, were excluded from the media mainstream.

NBC first commissioned, then refused to broadcast uncensored footage of heavy civilian casualties. (The broadcast was vetoed by NBC president Michael Gartner, who had led a media crusade for freedom of the press in the 1980s.) The video was then offered to CBS. The night before it was to air on the "CBS Evening News," the show's executive producer was fired and the report was canceled.[33]

Roger N. Johnson monitored CNN for the climactic twenty-seven-hour final prewar period when Iraq proposed conditional withdrawal and Soviet and Iranian peace initiatives were advanced.[34] His study revealed that thirty military experts but no peace experts were interviewed. George Bush, the most frequently shown, brushed aside peace talks. Others interviewed included mostly right-wing hawks, such as Oliver North, Robert McFarlane, Jeane Kirkpatrick, Pat Buchanan, Richard Allen, Richard Perle, Dan Quayle, and Ronald Reagan. And CNN may have been the most open to a diversity of views. (NBC is owned by General Electric, a supplier for every weapons system used in the Gulf. Major military contractors sponsor news programs and sit on the boards of directors of other networks and leading media, such as the *New York Times* and the *Washington Post.*)[35]

Instead of full and accurate reports and documentaries, network "docudramas" shot in sync sound on location and in Hollywood studios took audiences to the Persian Gulf War movie. Realistic shots of training, tanks maneuvering in the sand, simulated trench warfare, attacks on the enemy lurking in the darkness, scripted scenes of camp life and the "home front," patrols on a mission firing into the darkness, a full sequence of mission control launching a Patriot and scoring a "hit," and even "hostages" being beaten alternated with promos of *Die Hard 2* and *Terminator 2.* Spectacular explosions lit distant horizons, hurled vehicles, and blasted bodies in all three movies.

Deborah Amos, who covered the Gulf War for National Public Radio, scoffed at the adage that truth is the first casualty of war. "In this war," she wrote, "truth was more than a casualty. Truth was hit over the head, dragged into a closet, and held hostage to the public relations needs of the United States military." The docudrama's happy ending showed jubilant faces, while the voice-over spoke of "an outpouring of joy not seen since World War II." The real documentary footage of the conflict was locked in Pentagon vaults.[36]

THE CULT OF VIOLENCE

"It was a colossal failure of politics that plunged us into the war," said the *New Yorker* (January 28, 1991, 21). Then how did this failure become a triumph? How was the engineering of a vast and unnecessary human catastrophe made to seem not only acceptable but also politically advantageous, even triumphant? How did the war become a virtual breeding ground for presidential prospects?

The buildup, orchestration, saturation, and fabrications of the war provide only part of the answers to these questions. Another part comes from those characteristics of instant history that isolate critical events from their broader historical context and throw the spectator-witness back on conventional conceptions of how things work in the world. In our culture many of those conceptions stem from what we should recognize as the cult of violence.

Violence has many faces. Wholesale mass executions of people, otherwise known as war or genocide, have become increasingly technical, scientific, and deadly but not more precise.[37] They have killed an ever-increasing percentage of civilians, eventually far outnumbering military casualties. For instance, the German terror bombing of the small Spanish city of Guernica provoked worldwide outrage and Pablo Picasso's antiwar mural. But by the end of World War II—thousands of large-scale air raids and a genocide later—the calculated destruction of Dresden's historic center, the firebombing of Tokyo, and the pulverizing of Hiroshima and Nagasaki for little, if any, military advantage (but more likely to impress Joseph Stalin before the agreed upon entry of the Soviets into the war in the Pacific), numbed our senses.

The Vietnam War witnessed further escalation of firepower and the chemical poisoning of Vietnam's countryside, both which were met with rationalization. The trend toward increasingly skewed kill ratios has culminated, so far, in the Persian Gulf War. Recounting such facts of "cultural evolution and war," Roger N. Johnson observed that political bombing of civilians is no longer considered an act of barabarism.[38] Wholesale violence against basically innocent people is seen, if at all, as potentially embarrassing information to be sanitized and wrapped in euphemisms.

Retail violence is not far behind. The United States is the undisputed homicide capital of the world. We also lead industrialized countries in jailing and executing people.[39] Our streets, our schools, and our homes have become places of fear and brutality, widely publicized and profitably dramatized. Killings in the workplace doubled in the 1980s over the previous decade.[40] And yet the cult of violence is neither simply a reflection of these trends nor just a stimulus for them. It is more like a charged environment affecting many aspects of social relations, control, and power.

The facts of violence are both celebrated and concealed in the cult of violence that surrounds us. There has never been a culture as filled with images of violence as ours is now. We are awash in a tide of violent representations. There is no escape from the massive invasion of colorful mayhem into the homes and cultural lives of ever-larger areas of the world.

Of course, there was blood in fairy tales, gore in mythology, murder in Shakespeare, lurid crimes in tabloids, battles and wars in textbooks. The representation of violence is a legitimate cultural expression, even necessary to balance tragic consequences against deadly compulsions. But the historically defined, individually crafted, and selectively used symbolic violence of heroism, cruelty, or misanthropy has been swamped by violence with happy endings produced on the dramatic assembly line.

The violence we see on the screen and read about in our press bears little relationship in volume or in type, and especially in consequence, to violence in real life.[41] Yet much of it looks realistic, and we tend to project it onto the real world. This sleight of hand robs us of the tragic sense of life necessary for compassion. "To be hips," wrote Gitlin, "is to be inured, and more—to require a steadily increasing boost in the size of the dose required."[42]

Our children are born into a symbolic environment of six to eight violent episodes per prime time hour alone (four times as many in presumably humorous children's programs) and an average of at least two entertaining murders a night. Children are "the first to react to the environment around them," wrote playwright Steve Tesich.[43] "Unless we are willing to change that environment, we must accept the verdict that our children have become the victims of choice for most Americans."

The dominant portrayals of mayhem and crime misrepresent in important respects the actual nature, demography, and patterns of victimization of real-life violence. Contrary to promotional hype, most uses of cable, video, and other new technologies make the dominant patterns penetrate even more deeply (but not more cheaply) into everyday life. No historical, esthetic, or even commercial rationalization can justify drenching every home with images of expertly choreographed brutality.

Movies exploit the cult and increase the dosage. Escalation of the cinematic body count seems to be one way to get attention from a public punch-drunk on video mayhem. *Robocop*'s first rampage for law and order in 1987 killed 32 people. The 1990 *Robocop 2,* targeting a twelve-year-old "drug lord," among others, slaughtered 81. The sick movie *Death Wish* claimed 9 victims in 1974. In the 1988 version, the bleeding-heart liberal-turned-vigilante disposed of 52. *Rambo: First Blood,* released in 1985, rambled through Southeast Asia leaving 62 corpses. In 1988, *Rambo III* visited Afghanistan, killing 106. *Godfather I* produced 12 corpses, *Godfather II* put away 18, and G*odfather III* killed no less than 53. The daredevil cop in the original *Die Hard* in 1988 saved the day with a modest 18 dead. Two years later *Die Hard 2* thwarted a plot to rescue "the biggest drug dealer in the world," coincidentally a Central American dictator to be tried in a U.S. court, achieving a phenomenal body count of 264.

The decade's record goes to the 1990 children's movie and tie-in marketing sensation and glorification of martial arts, *Teenage Mutant Ninja Turtles.* Released as the Gulf War buildup began, with 133 acts of mayhem per hour, *Ninja Turtles* was the most violent film ever marketed to children. Undaunted by the outrage of trapped parents and overworked psychiatrists, *Turtles II,* appropriately subtitled *Secrets of the Ooze*, followed the success of the Ninjas (and of the Gulf War) as another nonstop punch-up and kick-in-the-teeth opera in which the martial artists continued their rampage.

The infamous "Faces of Death" videos, withdrawn from circulation in 1987, were quietly re-released in the fall of 1991.[44] The October 14, 1991, international edition of Variety featured 123 pages of ads for new movies, with pictures of shooting, killing, or corpses on every other page and a verbal appeal to violence, on the average, on every page. Leading the verbal procession were "kill," "murder," "death," "deadly," and "dead" (thirty-three times) and "terror," "fatal," "lethal," and "dangerous" (twelve times). Bringing up the rear were "rage," "frenzy," "revenge," "gun crazy," "kick boxer," "maniac," "warrior," "invader," "hawk," "battle," "war," "shoot," "fight," "slaughter," and "blood."

Terminator 2 dominated the list of box office blockbusters from fourteen major movie markets around the world. Its leading actor, promoter, and role model, Arnold Schwarzenegger, chaired the President's Council on Physical Fitness and Sports. The National Coalition on Television Violence named Schwarzenegger "the most violent actor" of 1987 and found that ten of Schwarzenegger's twelve movies averaged 109 often graphic and gruesome violent acts per hour.

Growing up in a violence-laden cultural environment cultivates aggressiveness in some people and desensitization, insecurity, mistrust, and anxiety in most people.[45] These are highly exploitable sentiments. They set up a scenario of violence and victimization in which some take on the role of violents but in which most adopt the role, and psychology, of victims. They demand protection and condone, if not welcome, violent solutions to domestic and world problems purported to save them from aggressors. This scenario contributes to the appeal of punitive and vindictive action against dark forces in a mean world, especially when the action is quickly and decisively presented as enhancing a sense of control and security.

The cold war is over, and the cultural props for imperial policy are shifting from anticommunist rationalizations to sharp and selective offensives against real and concocted terrorists, narco-terrorists, petro-terrorists, unauthorized aggressors, and other unfriendly (as opposed to friendly) demons of the Third World. The cult of violence is the ritual demonstration of brute power and its projection into sex, family, job, politics, and war.

An overkill of violent imagery helps train the military mind and mobilize support for taking charge of the unruly at home and abroad. Bombarding viewers with violent images of a mean and dangerous world without illuminating the real costs of violence and war is, in the last analysis, an instrument of intimidation and terror. It was indispensable to the triumph of instant history in the Persian Gulf. It is a preview of the shape of things to come in a unipolar world with no effective democratic opposition of geopolitical counterforce.

EPILOGUE

What was represented as a clean, swift, surgical strike to punish aggression, get rid of Hussein, and secure cheap oil, petrodollars, peace, jobs, and democracy became, in fact, a human and ecological disaster of "cataclysmic proportions" (in the words of the U.N. Inspection team) that achieved few of its purported aims. The war "changed almost nothing," concluded *Newsweek* on June 28, 1991. "Most of the same faces and the same tired policies remain....Internally, the regime's capacity for repression seems undiminished. Hussein was riding high. U.S.-inspired revolts of Kurds in the north and of Shiites in the south were crushed. A Palestinian settlement was as far from manifestation as ever.

At year's end, Human Rights Watch issued a comprehensive report saying that Washington had sacrificed principle to political interest, promoting rights "only when it is cost-free." "When competing interests arose," the report observed, "...maintaining warm relations with Saudi oil sheiks,...or avoiding politically embarrassing questions about why the United States went to war to restore the Kuwati Emir—human rights took a back seat at the White House."[46]

The war and its global imagery traumatized many Third World countries. It paralyzed the already weakened Nonaligned Movement, which "had done absolutely nothing to stop the war," observed the *Christian Conference of Asia News* in its November-December 1991 issue. "It is a cruel irony," the *News* noted, "that it took the blood bath of the Gulf War...to bring these cold realities home to the Non-Aligned Movement members." The disruption of trade and travel and the shutting of Iraq's pipelines deepened the Third World's economic distress and political paralysis.

The Middle East was left in turmoil, with Iran and widespread fundamentalist backlash gaining power. Arabs versus Arabs were arming faster than ever. (Saudi Arabia alone was getting twenty new Patriot batteries at the cost of $3.3 billion.)[47] Syria, invader of Lebanon and newfound U.S. ally, spent the $2 billion earned for good behavior in the Gulf on North Korean Scuds, Czech tanks, and Soviet MIGs.[48]

The full scope of nuclear disinformation was still unclear. Although Third World nuclear proliferation (generally unreported) was by no means limited to Iraq, and twenty Iraqi nuclear facilities were destroyed by U.S. bombers, the *Bulletin of Atomic Scientists* estimated in its March 1991 issue that Iraq was five to ten years away from producing a usable nuclear device. Since then, commission after commission has released widely publicized—and divergent—reports on hidden nuclear plants. The "nuclear story," not the story of misery the continuing blockade was inflicting on the people, became the largest single topic of postwar coverage. And yet the salient facts of even that story were missing from the sweep of instant history.

Not reported was the fact that the International Atomic Energy Agency (IAEA) had inspected the Iraqi facilities in November 1990 and had found them to be in compliance with IAEA safeguards, meaning that nuclear fuel was not being diverted to weapons use. Not reported were the further facts that Article 56 of the Geneva Protocols explicitly forbade the targeting of live reactors; that both IAEA and U.N. General Assembly resolutions had called for a ban on attacks on nuclear facilities; and that the IAEA had declared any such attack "a violation of the Charter of the United Nations and of the Statutes of [this] Agency." Many proliferation experts considered the targeted reactors to be of dubious military value and the bombing of operating reactors with probably "hot" cores to be potentially more harmful than either necessary or effective.[49]

The Western alliance had been strained. U.S. arm-twisting of Japan to contribute troops, in contradiction to the latter's U.S.-dictated constitution, divided Japan (which resisted, though agreed to contribute mine-sweepers and $13 billion) and started a political backlash. The backlash in the Muslim world led to the defeat of the Turkish government. The loss of trade and increased energy costs added to the trauma of the Third World. Kuwait's oligarchy was restored and proved more repressive than before. The Kurds had been abandoned again, as had the democratic forces in Iraq, which apparently posed a threat to the new world order.

The day the war ended, the Bechtel Corporation, from which U.S. secretaries of state and defense had been recruited, announced a multi-billion dollar contract for the reconstruction of Kuwait. Stock prices rose, but the economy slumped, and consumer confidence declined. The high costs and mounting deficits incurred to pay for the war and its aftermath contributed to recession in the United States. After an initial rise in the price of oil, friendly Gulf states boosted oil production. By year's end, falling prices (and revenues) plunged OPEC into a crisis and further postponed serious discussion of an effective U.S. energy policy.

The only clear successes have been the extension of U.S. power into an increasingly troubled region, the renewed flow of petrodollars propping up increasingly shaky economies, and the domestic "political gold." The quality of political (or any) thinking behind the celebration was suggested by George Bush's response to a question a year later: "If I had had to listen to advice from the United States Senate Leadership, the Democrats—or from the House, the leadership over there—to do something about the Persian Gulf, we'd have still been sitting there in the United States, Fat, dumb, and happy, with Saddam Hussein maybe in Saudi Arabia."[50]

Within weeks of the victory, Time Warner completed in record time the collection and compression of imagery that would fill five hundred floppy discs into a single CD-ROM history of Desert Storm and its speedy distribution to stores and school libraries. (The job ordinarily takes several months.) *CNN: War in the Gulf*, advertised as an "authoritative chronicle of the world's first 'real-time television war,'" was published soon thereafter. Pentagon-aided victory parades, the ABD-TV docudrama "Heroes of Desert Storm" (with a thirty-second introduction by President Bush), and the first deployment of Gulf War imagery in an election campaign rounded out the triumphant quick-freeze stage of instant history.[51]

In a fitting and perceptive tribute, *Time* magazine named CNN owner Ted Turner its Man of the Year for his influencing the dynamic of events and for his making viewers around the world into instant witnesses of history. (Time Warner is also one-fifth owner of Turner Broadcasting System.) A review of the year in *Modern Maturity*, the largest circulation magazine in the United States, was titled (appropriately to the promised "gentler, kinder nation") "The Gentle Giant." Sent to 32 million "mature" readers, the review summarized the war as "a stunning success in the Gulf" and concluded, "The Bush Administration's conduct of the crisis had been in the purest American spirit of respect for international law, winning the widest international support for joint action and the use of minimum force. It was a model of successful modern diplomacy."[52]

ANATOMY OF TRIUMPH

Let us now consider how this model of success played out on the home front. Once the saturation bombing had started, dissent had been marginalized, challenge had been suppressed, and the tide of saturation coverage had risen, most respondents to the *Times Mirror* poll were swept up in the flow. Their responses became news and sped the rush of events. Half the respondents, most of whom wanted more diverse views before, now said they heard too much opposition.[53]

As the operation entered its second full week, instant history found its true believers. Nearly eight out of ten believed that the censors were not hiding bad news; 57 percent wanted increased military control over reporting. Martin Shaw and Roy Carr-Hill report that in a British poll 82 percent agreed the sorties were "precise strikes against strategic targets with minimum civilian casualties."

The effect of television coverage can be gauged from the differences between responses of light and heavy viewers of otherwise comparable groups. The Morgan, Lewis, and Jhally survey showed that less than half (47%) of light viewers, compared to three-quarters (76%) of heavy viewers, "strongly supported" President Bush's decision to use military force against Iraq.

A panel conducted as part of the 1991 American National Election Study also revealed some gender differences. During the buildup, 61 percent of male light viewers but 71 percent of male heavy viewers approved "the way George Bush is handling the crisis in the Persian Gulf," a highly significant ten-point difference. For women, who were less supportive to begin with, viewing made no difference: About 50 percent of both light and heavy viewers "approved." After the war, however, with even the "light viewers" saturated with the images of the war, the approval rate for light and heavy male viewers rose to 83 and 86 percent and for light and heavy female viewers to 78 and 85 percent. Instant history almost closed the gender gap.

Heavy viewing also boosted the percentage of those who would vote for George Bush, especially among those who were otherwise the least likely to vote for him: Only 31 percent of low-income light viewers but 51 percent of low-income heavy viewers expressed an inclination to vote for Bush in 1992. And as Morgan, Lewis, and Jhally demonstrated, the more viewers saw, the more they remembered the misleading imagery, but the less they knew about the background and facts of the war.

Two months after the war, the public rated the coverage, military censorship, and general information about the war even higher. The *Times Mirror* percentage of "very favorable" rating of the military rose forty-two points from 18 to an unprecedented 60 percent. Secretary of Defense Dick Cheney's rating jumped from 3 to 33 percent (extraordinary for a secretary of defense). Desert Storm commander Norman Schwarzkopf's 51 percent was the highest "very favorable" score in more than 150 *Times Mirror* public favorability surveys conducted since 1985, stimulating instant speculation about his political future.

The war in the Persian Gulf is fading to a few flickering images: Scuds streaking through the sky and Patriots rising to intercept them, or so we thought; bombs falling down factory smokestacks with deadly accuracy, or so, too, we thought. But that was no movie. Its consequences will linger in the real world for a long time to come. When the balance sheet of critical events of the 1990s is finally tallied, the world will marvel at the mischief wrought by the new scenario of instant history.

Global immediacy gives us instant history, which is simultaneous, global, mass, living, telling, showing, and reacting in brief and intensive busts. Image driven and violence laden, as compelling as it is contrived, instant history robs us of reflection time, political space, and access to alternatives. The horror of a holocaust can now be managed with glorious efficiency.

This is not an isolated problem that can be addressed by focusing on media violence or crisis coverage alone. It is an integral part of a global cultural condition that increasingly permeates and poisons the mainstream of the common symbolic environment. Only a new international cultural environment movement, dedicated to democratic participation in cultural policymaking and an alternative media system, can do justice to the challenge, and terror, of instant history. But that, too, is another story.

NOTES

1. Frederick Williams, "The Shape of News to Come: The Gulf War as an Opportunity for TV News to Show Off, and to Raise Questions," *Quill* (September 1991): 15–17.
2. Cited in Timothy Garton Ash, "Poland After Solidarity," *New York Review of Books*, June 13, 1991, p. 57.
3. Cited in a book review by Tom Masland, *Philadelphia Inquirer*, September 1, 1991, p. 2F.
4. Ernst Briesach, "Historiography," *International Encyclopedia of Communications*, vol. 2 (New York: Oxford University Press, 1989), p. 280.
5. Ien Ang, "Global Media/Local Meaning," *Media Information Australia* (November 1991): 4.
6. Disaster relief has been particularly vulnerable to the vagaries of instant history. A 1991 report to the United Nations concluded that "far too often, thousands who are starving and uprooted in one part of the world receive the minimum of relief and succor, while aid pours forth for those who are suffering at the focus of international power politics and media attention." The highly politicized aid to the Kurds in Iraq was one case in point (*New York Times*, November 13, 1991, p. A9).
7. Neil Postman, *Amusing Ourselves to Death: Public Discourse in the Age of Show Business by Neil Postman* (New York: Penguin Books, 1985), p. 103.
8. Tom Grimes, "Encoding TV News Messages into Memory." *Journalism Quarterly* 67, no. 4 (Winter 1990): 757–766.
9. The Tianenman Square massacre, which many claim to have witnessed on television, did not take place on Tianenman Square; only the cameras were there, recording the clearing of the square by troops and tanks. The massacre took place off camera in another part of town.
10. Todd Gitlin, "On Being Sound-Bitten," *Boston Review* (December 1991): 16–17.
11. Williams, "The Shape of News to Come."
12. John M. Phelan, "Image Industry Erodes Political Space," *Media Development* 38, no. 4 (1991): 6–8.
13. The story of the weeping icon took on a life of its own when it was extensively described, then reported stolen, then recovered, and finally called a hoax and publicity stunt. (See, e.g., *New York Times,* December 29 and 30, 1991, January 1, 1992: and Associated Press stories during that time.)
14. Cited by Deborah Amos, "When Seeing Is Not Believing: Desert Mirage—the True Story of the Gulf War," *Nieman Reports* (Winter 1991): 61.
15. George Gerbner, "UNESCO in the U.S. Press," in George Gerbner, Hamid Mowlana, and Kaarle Nordenstreng (eds.), *The Global Media Debate: Its Rise, Fall,*

and Renewal (New York: Ablex, 1992).

16. "U.N. Asks Billion for Peacekeeper Fund," *New York Times*, November 25, 1991, p. A3.
17. Bob Woodward, *The Commanders* (New York: Simon and Schuster, 1991).
18. John B. Judis, "Twilight of the Gods," *Wilson Quarterly* (Autumn 1991): 55.
19. Woodward, *The Commanders.*
20. Michael Massing, "Sitting on Top of the News," *New York Times Review of Books*, June 27, 1991, p. 11.
21. Williams, "The Shape of News to Come."
22. "The 1990–91 Panel Study of the Political Consequences of War," in *American National Election Study* (Center for Political Studies, Institute for Social Research, University of Michigan, 1991).
23. Reported in the *Philadelphia Inquirer*, February 5, 1991, p. 6A.
24. For these and more examples, see Michael Parenti, "Media Watch: Now for Sports and Weather," *Z Magazine* (July-August 1991): 104.
25. *Philadelphia Inquirer*, February 9, 1991, p. A1.
26. Melissa Healy, "Group Faults U.S. on War Deaths," *Philadelphia Inquirer*, November 17, 1991, p. 9A. The law is a 1977 international treaty that has not been ratified by the United States.
27. Marc S. Miller, "Patriotic Blindness and Anti-Truth Weapons," *Index on Censorship* (November-December 1991): 32.
28. Roger N. Johnson, "Cultural Evolution and War: From Science to Social Science," *Bulletin of the International Society for Research on Aggression* 13, no. 2 (1991): 7–10.
29. Associated Press dispatch from Nicosia, Cyprus, November 5, 1991.
30. Pentagon estimate reported in the *Philadelphia Inquirer*, November 6, 1991, p. 3A.
31. *People* magazine reporter Dirk Mathison crashed the highly confidential Bohemian Grove encampment in northern California, where each year top male U.S. policymakers, including media chiefs, assembled. Mathison's story of what he heard (before he was discovered and ejected by an executive of Time Warner), including the Lehman speech entitled "Smart Weapons," was killed by *People* magazine, owned by Time Warner. It was published under the title "Inside the Bohemian Grove: The Story People Magazine Won't Let You Read," *Extra!* (November-December 1991): 1, 12–14.
32. David H. Hackworth, "Killed by Their Comrades," *Newsweek*, November 18, 1991, pp. 45–46.
33. Dennis Bernstein and Sasha Futran, "Sights Unseen," *San Francisco Bay Guardian*, March 20, 1991, p. 23.
34. Johnson, "Cultural Evolution and War."
35. See, for example, Martin E. Lee, "Arms and the Media: Business as Usual," *Index on Censorship* (November-December 1991): 29–31. Lee recalled that on the day U.S. bombs killed four hundred men, women, and children in a Baghdad shelter, *Newsweek* (owned by the Washington Post Company) featured a stealth bomber on its cover with the caption "How Many Lives Can It Save?" (30).
36. Deborah Amos, "Seeing Is Not Believing," *Neiman Reports* (Winter 1991): 61.
37. Wars in the twentieth century have killed 99 million people (before the Gulf War), twelve times as many as in the nineteenth century and twenty-two times as many as in the eighteenth century. Other hostilities, not counting internal state terrorism, are resulting in an estimated one thousand or more deaths per year (*World Military and Social Expenditures* [Washington, D.C.: World Priorities, 1986]).

38. Johnson, "Cultural Evolution and War."
39. One of every 133 Americans will become a murder victim. (*U.S. Bureau of Justice Statistics Technical Report*, NCJ-104274 [March 1987]). The U.S. rate of killings is 21.9 per 100,000 men fifteen through twenty-four. The rate, for example, for Austria is 0.3; for England, 1.2; and for Scotland (highest after the United States), 5.0 (National Center for Health Statistics study published in the *Journal of the American Medical Association* and reported in the *New York Times*, June 27, 1990, p. A10). Between 1985 and 1989 the number of homicides nationwide increased 22 percent (congressional hearings reported in the *Philadelphia Inquirer*, August 1, 1990). The U.S. rate of incarceration is 407 per 100,000 citizens. This compares to 36 in the Netherlands, 86 in West Germany, and 100 in England. While the prison population in the United States doubled in the 1980s, the crime rate rose 1.8 percent, suggesting that the "need to incarcerate" is out of proportion with the actual crime rate but is a political response to culturally generated insecurity and demand for repression. There is no evidence that capital punishment is a greater deterrent than a life sentence or that it relates to lower crime rates.
40. Associated Press dispatch by Fred Bayles reported in the *Philadelphia Inquirer*, November 15, 1991, p. 3A.
41. See, for example, Ray Surette, *Media Crime and Criminal Justice: Images and Realities* (Pacific Grove, Calif.: Brooks/Cole, 1992).
42. Todd Gitlin, "On Thrills and Kills: Sadomasochism in the Movies," *Dissent* (Spring 1991): 247.
43. Steve Tesich, "The Watergate Syndrome: A Government of Lies," *Nation*, January 13, 1992, p. 13.
44. *Variety*, October 14, 1991, p. 61.
45. See, for example, George Gerbner, "Violence and Terror in the Mass Media," Reports and Papers in Mass Communication, no. 102 (Paris: UNESCO, 1988).
46. Paul Lewis, "New U.N. Leader Is Taking Over at a Time of Great Expectations," *New York Times*, December 30, 1991, pp. A1, 6.
47. Eric Schmitt, "Saudis to Buy 14 More Batteries of Patriot Missiles from the U.S.," *New York Times*, November 9, 1991, p. 3.
48. Matthew d'Ancona, "All Eyes on the Armourer," *Index on Censorship* (November-December 1991): 2.
49. For more details, see Mel Friedman, "Too Little, Too Late: How the Press Misses the Proliferation Story," *Nuclear Times* (Winter 1991–1992): 27–31.
50. Andrew Rosenthal, "Bush Returns the Democrats' Fire, Pointing to Success Against Iraqis," *New York Times*, November 9, 1991, pp. A1, 9.
51. A "test run" by the National Republican Congressional Committee in a November 1991 race in central Virginia yielded positive results. A thirty-second spot superimposed a photo of the Democratic candidate over an antiwar demonstration showing a "Victory to Iraq" banner. Although it was acknowledged (after the election) that the candidate did not attend that rally, she lost the election 37 to 63 percent.
52. John Keegan, "The Gentle Giant," *Modern Maturity* (December 1991-January 1992): 52.
53. "The People, The Press and the War in the Gulf" (Washington, D.C.: Times Mirror Center for People and the Press, releases of January 10, January 31, and March 25, 1991).

Chapter 38

CHAIRMAN ZNAIMER'S "SENSUAL PAGAN TORRENT"

BY GEORGE GERBNER

The title scene, to which we periodically return, is a goose-stepping column of cardboard soldiers, marching, in mechanical cadence, with television sets under their arms. They seem to be storm troopers of television, off to do battle with print and the book people.

That, in brief, is the plot. Moses Znaimer, Toronto's maxi media mogul and mini guru, produced it, oddly enough, for the CBC. As Znaimer says, the telling is as important as the story, and the teller perhaps even more important, especially if the narrator is also the producer. Therefore, we can be assured that *TVTV: The Television Revolution* must be the very (single-minded) model of the walking, talking, moveable feast of sensual, liberating imagery that it claims television really is.

So let the plot unfold. "Unfold" may be a book word, so let it gush forth in a dazzling profusion of images and—inevitably—print in the form of subtitles with factoids and quotations from other gurus, and people just like me.

The saga's cosmic sweep begins in prehistoric times. Humanoids scamper about in a desert until they come upon a television set. They gawk and whimper and don't know what to do. Neither does the scene, so it shifts.

Enter Znaimer, with a quizzical expression and a tone at once imperious and querulous, suitable for all occasions. We who work in television, he explains, are the people of the image, "the eye." Deployed against us in this Wagnerian encounter are the critics, the "print people," the politicians, the regulators, and all those who whine about the scarcity of quality.

But now—Gotterdammerung!—no more scarcity. With the coming of "perhaps hundreds of channels" the very thing that was supposed to have ailed us has vanished. This is the revolution, Znaimer argues, "beyond the wildest dreams not only of those who, like me, love TV, but also of its critics." Yet the struggle continues because "they" just do not get it.

Cut to the "next generation"—MTV, rock, rap, and "the secret of TV's irresistible force" which is, "in one word, entertainment." Camille Paglia makes an early appearance to add the phrase "sensual pagan torrent" to the mix. Znaimer then announces, with a straight face, that "those of us in television have remained largely silent while the advocates of print damned TV." Well, no more Mr. Nice Guy., Now "we will have our say," and high time, too, because "print has become a medium of mistrust...inculcating cynical habits of mind, its visionaries replaced by constant carpers, notable mostly for mean-spiritedness."

Speaking of that, movie producer/director Oliver Stone also has scores to settle. He inveighs against "parasites" who "infest" the *New York Times* and the *Washington Post.* But no matter. The people of "the eye" who saw *JFK* know the truth. "What you saw you believe in your heart....Kennedy was killed by a conspiracy, no matter what the print people say...the picture speaks, it can't lie as you lie with the word." The subtitle says: "Neil Postman, Communication Scholar: 'Richard Nixon's dishonor was not that he lied but rather that he looked like a liar.'"

A long series of industry executives talk about the business of television. It boils down to: "Anybody who has a product to sell has got a chance in this country." So we cut to the best sell of all, graphic violence and expertly choreographed brutality all too familiar to viewers and, contrary to conventional wisdom, repugnant to most (of which more later). Appearing to justify the mayhem, the subtitle quotes me saying that "Heavy TV viewing does not increase violence, it increases our fear of violence." (More of that, too, later.)

Success stories of "hard-edged" investigative reporting are lovingly detailed. (There are no duds, invasions of privacy, entrapments, or other abuses of media power.) A subtitle cites Marshall McLuhan saying that "Television feels a revulsion to all centrist bureaucratic and political organization."

Predictably, the scene shifts to Moscow. The Znaimer party line on Soviet television is that is was not so much Party—as print-dominated. This must have been so because, on one occasion, a television program ran out of voice-over script when the Politburo was seven minutes late to a Party Congress. As the text was already in press for the next day's *Pravda*, and as print is sacred in Moscow, the commentator fell silent for seven minutes and picked up his script again when the Politburo arrived on the scene. (No mention is made of the spectacle of American presidential candidates engaged in TV debate standing like dummies, waiting for the sound to be restored. But that was, no doubt, in deference to the benign power of television, and not to the tyranny of print.)

"Print," we are told, "creates hierarchy, judgmental minds; TV seeks an opening to the heart." "It is immediate, inclusive, liberating, and democratic." "It is not controllable because humanity is not controllable." Hints that it might be just a bit controllable, after all, are swamped by the random cavalcade of "reality," such as Rin Tin Tin, World War II artillery barrages, Nixon, Sergeant Friday, Superman, an atomic mushroom cloud, and Marilyn Monroe—all in a dizzying, if hackneyed, succession of appropriately grainy black-and-white images. Carefully engineered illusions of informality and unrehearsed spontaneity are projected against backgrounds of bars, streets with shadowy passersby scurrying in the foreground, circus barkers and pitchmen, and even an interview in a café while the foreground figure seems to be carrying on another conversation. But I digress.

"The best TV tells me what happens to me here today in my own neighborhood." That, of course, is mostly crime. A news director at a Miami television station, notorious for its "if it bleeds it leads" formula, explains how to grab the grazing viewer before another channel does. Talk-show hostess Jenny Jones relates how she had to reveal her own personal secrets in her climb to success. Her producer tells the story of the inevitable side to lurid tabloid from the initial "kinder, gentler" format: "We had to play the game like everyone else."

At their Banff conference, public broadcasters confer and conspire on how to jettison their mandate in order to capture a bigger share of the market. Then on to a cathedral and a discourse on the origin of television imagery in medieval religious iconry. I am quoted again, via subtitle: "Sooner or later TV includes all the explanations of life we need. It is like the coming of a new religion."

Maybe we should become "showmen of God," a minister muses, as we switch to the real showmen of the global market, who exude much greater confidence. "We do business in 140 countries," says the president of Warner Brothers International, subsidiary of the Time Warner global mega-conglomerate. Now we are sailing on a yacht while the Warner chief explains: "The U.S. product has the largest market. The nets pay us 80 percent of our cost; I only have to generate the rest plus profit from the world market." Later we see how he wines and dines his international clients before he presents them with an irresistible business deal: high-cost programming at bargain basement prices.

There is talk about a "new brand of politics." Italian media baron Silvio Berlusconi "packaged himself well" on his way to power. But Znaimer assures us (again) that television "cannot be controlled because mankind cannot be controlled."

Marshall McLuhan's "probes" find television "an inner-directed depth-medium of all sorts of meditation." Camille Paglia returns, amidst sports, spectacle, rock, shock, smoke, drink, and fire, to extol, again, "the pagan sensual torrent that is television." Furthermore, this is no decline but "reversion to an earlier state of 'deep meanings.'" "So, if a grieving widow is interrupted by a commercial—well, that's life."

Henry Kissinger is summoned to warn that image politics can drive foreign policy. True enough, but the point is blunted when we are also told that "governments think television is a medium to be managed while it is an instrument to be played"—transforming the chairman into the conductor of an orchestra. A flag waves, a scroll unfurls. The ten sayings of Chairman Znaimer roll off, one by one, in print for weaker minds. The first, "The Triumph of the Image," also happens to be the title of our book on "playing the media" in the Gulf War.

Well, okay...now, let us see what have we here. The thrust of my quotation on violence, and of our TV violence studies, is that its contributions to desensitization and to a sense of insecurity and meanness are even more pervasive than its contribution to real-life violence. Our work also demonstrates that, far from being popular, violence depresses ratings; but it's still profitable because, being image-driven, it "travels well" on the world market where most of the industry's profits come from.

Therefore, violence is not an expression of freedom but part of a global marketing formula imposed on the creative people and foisted on the children of the world.

Second, my comment on "television as a new religion" is not meant to suggest deep spiritual meanings. I was comparing the medieval power-nexus of state and church with its modern symbiotic counterpart, the relationship between the commercial-political establishment and its chief cultural arm, television.

Tendentious use of quotations is, I suppose, part of trying too hard to construct a self-serving story that is, at the same time, just "entertainment." (The great emphasis Znaimer and other doggedly commercial entrepreneurs place on that word is significant. If "entertainment" as a singular concept has any meaning at all beyond the box office, it means stereotyped stories devoid of sharp edges and a tragic sense of life, mixed with sanitized violence and bland political mishmash. These stories are celebrations of the conventional.)

The main theme of *TVTV's* story collapses of its own pretentious weight. There is no battle of media, only competition for advertising moneys. The total cultural orchestration includes all media in complimentary and only partly distinctive roles. As sensory experience, print is as "visual" as pictures but, by abstracting, it can explain. By contrast, pictures "reveal," easily trapping the viewer in the illusion of witnessing "reality" rather than the inevitably selected and slanted bits of it.

The real media differences are institutional. All media are managed, involve a point of view, and confer great power to their owners. Increasingly, there are a few mega-conglomerates dominating the world market. This is not "an opening to the heart" so much as to the minds and pocketbooks.

While channels proliferate, ownership consolidates. Every merger denies entry to newcomers, reduces alternative voices, and shrinks jobs and freedom for creative people all over the world. But such mergers concentrate power to tap into the largest number of consumers at the least cost and to sell them to the largest constellations of bidders, people who have nothing to tell but lots to sell.

Television documentaries have become an endangered species. With cheaply obtained footage of crime and violence, balance in local news is hard to find. (Our own study of Philadelphia "local" television news found that eight out of ten stories of crime and violence were not even local.) Serving up fake "reality" is made to seem more authentic by turning the camera on the storytellers' fake reality of the working newsroom. Anchors and reporters sitting behind a desk and just reading the news might be suspected of presenting what actually happens in the world rather than a "reality show."

Far from telling "what happens to me here today in my own neighborhood," many local news, talk, tabloid, and "reality shows" present the most lurid, grotesque, and mean "real" people, acts, and events they can find, from wherever they can get them. They speak to a sense of fear and mistrust, arming and destroying, not liberating, communities. A University of Miami study of the very station Znaimer sets up as a model (and, no doubt, emulates) found that up to half of the stories involved crime (averaging 32%), while violent crime in the city remained constant, involving less than one tenth of 1 percent of the population. The price for grabbing a few viewers for marginal commercial advantage in both entertaining drama and news is the intimidation, alienation, and disgust of most viewers reflected in every poll about television violence, and the huge international embarrassment for the dumping of "action" programs on the rest of the world.

TVTV is an extended apologia for all that, perhaps seeking some latent mystical potential for the medium, but hiding its actually existing face behind a pagan sensual torrent of obfuscation and nonsense.

NOTE

Originally published in *Canadian Journal of Communication*, Vol. 21 (1996) 13–17

Part IX

OP-EDS AND SHORT TAKES

Chapter 39

It's 11:30. And Heeeeere's Justice

BY GEORGE GERBNER

PHILADELPHIA—Now that the United Sates Supreme Court has agreed to decide whether television trials may deny a defendant's constitutional right to a fair trial, it is time to call a moratorium on trials by television until the issues are fully explored.

Most of the public seems unaware that television is moving into the courtroom. This movement seems to fly in the face of the known risks of prejudice, the certainty of endless litigation, a prior Supreme Court decision opposing TV in the courtroom, resistance in federal courts to televised proceedings, and an American Bar Association vote last year to uphold its opposition to cameras in the courtroom.

Freedom of the press is not the issue. Journalists, both broadcast and print, are free to cover most trials, and cameras would not change any of the current limitations on such coverage. The only issue is the addition of actual sight and sound to coverage. We must ask: What price would justice have to pay for plugging courtrooms into a system geared to ratings?

Many states have already let cameras into state courtrooms without serious investigation of the effects that televised trials have on the administration of justice, and, equally important, on the image of justice held by viewers, who ultimately shape our system of justice.

We can infer such effects from research here at the University of Pennsylvania and from investigations of other social scientists.

Typical viewers of prime time and weekend daytime TV see an average of thirty police officers, seven lawyers, and three judges every week. What do they learn? Most action revolves around demonstrations of justice and power. Violence, the stock dramatic device of such demonstrations, provides the quickest lesson on who should get away with what against whom.

Two-thirds of all major dramatic characters are involved in violence. When women and minorities are involved, they are more likely to be victims than victimizers, and they are generally underrepresented and devalued in many ways.

Television characters are the targets of crime about ten times as often as people in the real world. Nearly 41 percent of all TV crimes are murders. A disproportionate number of victims are whites. (In the real world, property crimes are most common and a disproportionate number of victims are blacks.) Television policemen observe suspect's rights in about two in every ten cases.

Our research found that exposure to TV cultivates a heightened sense of living in a mean, violent world. Individuals, who watch more TV than others in their same age, sex and socio-economic groups, tend to exhibit a consistently higher degree of insecurity, mistrust, and question for protection. All in all, TV viewing appears to cultivate relatively anxious and hard-line attitudes among viewers of most types, particularly the young.

But if real trials are telecast, won't we get more accurate portrayals? No. Once in the courtroom, TV controls the message. Selected courtrooms become program-originating locations, transporting the sights and sounds of real courtrooms into millions of homes conditioned to a Perry Mason ritual of courtroom and crime drama. Trials will be picked and edited to fit and confirm that ritual.

A trial must proceed as independently as possible from conventional moral pressures and popular clamor. Televising trials can only erode judges' ability to do justice in each case. It would do nothing to ensure greater fairness that existing news media scrutiny could not do. We may be on the verge of drifting into a major institutional transformation while assuming that we are only making a few public-spirited adjustments.

Television is not neutral. It presents a coherent world of images and messages serving its own institutional interests. Plugging courtrooms into the TV system can make them appendages of that system. Once televised trials attract a large national following, the process will be irresistible, cumulative, and probably irreversible.

Neither history nor research support the contention that television coverage of courts would enhance fairness, protect freedom, increase public understanding, and promote needed court reform. Indeed, the evidence suggests the opposite. We need independent investigation, not self-serving demonstrations and uncontrolled "experiments." Only an immediate moratorium on televising trials can give us the time and the opportunity we need for responsible action.

CHAPTER 40

THE RISK OF PLAYING TO THE CAMERAS

BY GEORGE GERBNER

There seems to be no end to the O. J. Simpson media (excuse the expression) overkill. But in all the commentaries and interpretations of the apparently mesmerizing (and certainly inescapable) experience, and in all the self-congratulatory media effusions about the educational value of television trials, one thing seems to have gotten lost. And that is the only relevant and crucial issue. It is not information, education, or entertainment, important though they may be. It is whether televising criminal trials in real time helps or hinders the mission of the courts—namely, fair trial for a defendant—and, in general, assists or diminishes the integrity of the judicial process.

O. J. Simpson is not a typical defendant, but the great interest in his case is likely to increase the pressure for opening more courts to television, including federal courts that still bar the televising of criminal proceedings. Therefore, this is a timely occasion to review the issues and focus on the most sensitive area. The issue is not freedom of reporting, but transporting the sights and sounds of sensational criminal trials in "real time" to a global arena in which the spectacle—television's unique contribution to reporting by other means—can prejudice the outcome.

THAT'S ENTERTAINMENT

We start with a bit of history to see how the courts themselves have sorted out the issues.

In early frontier America, people traveled many miles to the county seat to be entertained by court proceedings. Later, the press brought to them sensational details of criminal trials. Court became the main circulation booster of many newspapers.

When radio was introduced, broadcasters looked to the courts as a source of programming. In 1925, Chicago station WGN broadcast the Scopes monkey trial to a large audience. In 1935, the trial of Bruno Hauptmann, convicted of kidnapping Charles Lindbergh's infant son, turned the tide. Reporters jostling each other and taking countless pictures with explosive flash devices created a carnival-like atmosphere in the courtroom that led to the American Bar Association's advocacy of a ban on cameras in court.

Most states and the federal judiciary observed the ban. Eventually, television came to be viewed by the courts as presenting additional dangers, different from the noise and physical disturbances caused by the older media. These were articulated in 1965 by the U.S. Supreme Court's decision in *Estes v. Texas,* 382 U.S. 875.

Billy Sol Estes, an associate of Lyndon Johnson, was convicted on swindling charges. Texas was one of the few states that had not adopted a ban on cameras in the courts, and Estes' highly publicized trial received extensive television coverage. Estes appealed the conviction to the U.S. Supreme Court, arguing that the televising of his trial had deprived him of his Fourteenth Amendment right to due process of law. A 5–4 majority of the Supreme Court agreed and voted to reverse his conviction.

Despite Estes, media organizations applied pressure and persuaded several states to admit cameras or at least conduct "experiments." By 1979, eighteen states permitted televising courtroom proceedings on either a permanent or an experimental basis. This prompted a judicial re-examination of the constitutionality of televised trials.

In general, the courts have focused on three issues: (1) whether a ban on coverage of trials violated the broadcast media's First Amendment right of free speech; (2) whether such a ban undermines the defendant's Sixth Amendment right to a public trial; and (3) whether camera coverage deprives the defendant in a criminal trial of this Fourteenth Amendment right of due process.

On January 26, 1981, the Supreme Court held in *Chandler v. Florida,* 449 U.S. 560, that a ban on television coverage of trials did not violate the broadcast media's First Amendment right of free speech; camera coverage (as distinct from reporting) is not protected by the First Amendment.

In Estes, the concurring justices had concluded that the Sixth Amendment does not confer upon the defendant a right to televise trials. In the words of Justice John Harlan:

> The "public trial" guarantee of the Sixth Amendment...certainly does not require that television be admitted to the courtroom....Its guarantee will be met as long as the court is open to those who wish to come, sit in the available seats, conduct themselves with decorum, and observe the trial process. It does not give anyone a concomitant right to photograph, record, broadcast or otherwise transmit the trial proceedings to those members of the public not present.

Likewise, Chief Justice Warren Burger observed in *Chandler* that "the requirement of a public trial is satisfied by the opportunity of members of the public and the press to attend the trial and to report what they have observed."

On the other hand, *Chandler* held that television coverage is not a per se denial of defendants' constitutional right to a fair trial; the lack of scientifically acceptable evidence bearing on the issue precluded such a conclusion. Therefore, states would be free to experiment in order to accumulate empirical evidence as to the actual effect of television coverage on trials.

But as a 1983 decision, *United States v. Hastings*, 695 F2d 1278 (11th Cir.), observed, in upholding the federal court ban, it is very difficult to detect the adverse impact of television coverage on trial participants. Indeed, at the Annenberg School for Communications, we studied the so-called experiments undertaken by the courts and found that none of them employed controls, none had specified criteria for "success," none tested effects on participants in scientifically acceptable ways, nor did any report the findings fully to the public. Most "experiments" were conducted by interested parties and came to the foregone conclusion that television coverage should be allowed to continue because it did not disturb the proceedings.

In contrast, a 1986 survey of participants and observers by a New Orleans researcher, William Henican, asked about a broader range of impacts and concluded that "the risks of allowing cameras into the trial courts of this country are very high" and that "when prejudice does occur, it will be very difficult to demonstrate." Paul Thaler's recent book, *The Watchful Eye: American Justice in the Age of the Television Trial* (Praeger Publishers, 1994), offers mixed but equally troubling evidence.

The situation, then is analogous to a pharmaceutical firm testing a new drug by distributing it to the public and, if nobody drops dead, declaring it a "success."

THE RIGHT TO DUE PROCESS

This murky factual situation is highly critical to the issue's most difficult legal question: Whether the televising of criminal proceedings violates the defendant's Fourteenth Amendment right to due process of law. Despite the rush to judgment and the relentless media pressure, the key question posed in *Chandler* remains unanswered.

Every student of communication (or public figure or actor) knows that if you change the audience, you change the performance. It is also clear that the addition of sight and sound, showing what participants look like and how they act—the most interesting parts of courtroom drama—are the least informative but potentially most misleading and prejudicial parts of trials.

Can judges ignore the fact that they are playing to a national or global audience? Or that their election or appointment may depend on how they appear on the screen? Likewise, prosecutors and defense attorneys know that television coverage presents career-making or breaking opportunities that may depend on how they look and sound on camera. Jurors become instant celebrities, recognized wherever they go, in a way that never happened before television. They return to communities aroused as only television images can arouse, facing hostility and even harassment from viewers who disagree with their verdict. Witnesses, like jurors, are catapulted into notoriety.

They can sell carefully tailored testimony ("cash for trash") to tabloids, destroying their usefulness in court.

Most defendants in criminal trials are not as handsome, rich, popular, and articulate as O. J. Simpson. Television is the new pillory exposing their close-up expressions and gestures to a public that will form judgments on that basis. What will form judgments on that basis? What about these presumed-to-be-innocent defendants' private rights and sensibilities, their public humiliation and personal anguish?

No research has been performed to properly answer these questions. It is time to put them to a genuine test before the court becomes fully integrated into a global entertainment system for purposes and in ways inimical to their mission. Good courtroom drama can best go behind the scenes and expose the invisible but all-important dynamics of justice.

If the networks are really interested in providing legal news, they should restore their regular Supreme Court beat. If we want legal education directly from the courtroom, we can record and broadcast or otherwise distribute on video the proceeding with appropriate explanations after the trial is over and all appeals have been exhausted. If we want live news from the courtroom, but still reduce, if not eliminate, the grave risk to lives and justice cameras may represent, we can extend to states the federal court practice of limiting television to civil cases.

Now that the Judicial Conference of the United States will soon consider whether to extend the federal "experiment" with cameras, it is a good time to answer the questions posed in *Chandler* in an independent and scientifically acceptable way. In the meantime, courts should take a more careful and critical view before dismissing appeals on grounds that camera coverage deprives defendants in a criminal trial of the Fourteenth Amendment right of due process. Let us stop using defendants as guinea pigs in live experiments that can have tragic consequences we would never know.

Chapter 41

ALL TOBACCO ADS SHOULD BE BANNED

BY GEORGE GERBNER

You may have seen the stunningly beautiful magazine ad featuring a wintry scene of rugged outdoorsmen in "Marlboro Country." You may also have noticed other ads and TV commercials celebrating the bicentennial of the Bill of Rights. Both were placed by Philip Morris Co. Inc., a tobacco, food and beer conglomerate and the largest advertiser in America.

What may have escaped you is the irony of the No. 1 manufacturer of the most lethal commercial product in the world masquerading as the benign patron of healthy living and a champion of free speech.

The tobacco industry spends more than $3 billion (Philip Morris alone spends $2 billion) to make sure that our children grow up in a culture in which they cannot escape vivid images of happy, daring, sexy, and healthy smokers.

These glowing visions of the "good life" counter and overwhelm all other information about an addiction that kills more than 1,000 people *a day*, more than heroin, crack, alcohol, fire, car accidents, homicides, and AIDS combined.

While smoking is down among the better educated, it is holding steady or even increasing among young people, minorities, and people of the Third World. It is fueled, reports the World Health Organization, "mainly by intensive and ruthless promotional campaigns on the part of the transnational tobacco companies."

This situation, and the lack of public awareness of its extent, has been made possible by a long history of news suppression by the very industry that now attempts to use the First Amendment to perpetuate its power.

The tobacco industry has used its advertising clout to impede the flow of information at least since 1938, when Raymond E. Pearl of Johns Hopkins University first presented large-scale data on smoking and early dying. An outpouring of studies and medical reports followed, confirming and elaborating the evidence linking smoking to cancer and other diseases.

But for a long time nothing happened. It took many years for the anti-smoking movement to gather momentum in the face of industry obstruction and often media complicity. The trial of Liggett Group Inc. for failure to advise of health risks (before warning labels were required in 1966) provided the first detailed information about the strategies of tobacco companies to evade, deny, and combat health research findings in the 1940s and 1950s.

Recent court cases revealed that tobacco industry tactics have become even more duplicitous and sophisticated.

While direct cigarette advertising is banned from television, one of the more successful of the tobacco industry's obfuscation tactics has been to hide under the cloak of "issue advertising." As findings of indirect hazards from cigarette smoke in public and work places began to appear, and studies showed the effectiveness of smoking restrictions, the R. J. Reynolds Tobacco Co. (now RJR Nabisco Inc.) launched an issue-advertising campaign that made legal history. One of its full-page ads entitled "Of Cigarettes and Science" declared that "the issue between smoking and health is an open one."

The Federal Trade Commission issued a complaint, but an administrative law judge ruled that the ad was an expression of corporate opinion, not sales talk, and thus outside of FTC jurisdiction.

Winning the battle on "issue advertising" provided a legal basis for pressing forward with a new campaign—that of joining the cause of tobacco with the cause of civil rights and freedom itself. The industry with its long history of suppression now claimed that it was victimized by zealots, bigots, and other enemies of liberty.

Philip Morris led the charge, with a series of full-page "issue" ads designed to look like a learned article. It portrayed smokers as victims of discrimination "forced to sit in the back of planes, trains and buses" by "violent anti-smokers and overzealous public enforcers."

"CENSORSHIP? HERE? IN THE U.S.A.?" asked a follow-up ad disguised as a scholarly article. It was the opening gun in a $15,000 Philip Morris competition for the best student essay that, in the words of the sponsor, "defines and defends the First Amendment's application to American business."

This brings us to the current $60 million Bill of Rights ad campaign, which can also be viewed as an attempt to skirt the ban on broadcast ads. It is clear that the ultimate goal of the "issue advertising" and "free speech" campaigns is protection of the cigarette sales pitch—and any sales pitch—from further restrictions, taxation or outright ban, all bills still pending in Congress.

The campaign could not halt moves to restrict smoking in many public and working spaces. But it succeeded in deflecting the national spotlight from America's premier health hazard and in defeating, diluting, or delaying every major attempt to blunt—let alone ban—the tobacco industry's power to fill print and outdoor media with lively images of rugged, happy, attractive, and healthy smokers.

Courts have ruled that there is no legal or constitutional basis for claiming unrestricted freedom for paid advertising that is harmful to health. Prohibition of tobacco would only drive the industry underground and out of control. But we should demand that Congress follow Canada's example and ban tobacco advertising on all media.

Our war on drugs is a sham until we at least stop pushing the most lethal of them all.

NOTE

Originally published in the *Philadelphia Inquirer* January 19, 1990: 19A

CHAPTER 42

THE TURTLES LIVE TO OOZE AGAIN

BY GEORGE GERBNER

It's October and the annual onslaught of holiday commercialism is creeping up on us. Or should I say oozing up on us, out of the sewers of our cultural environment. The principal targets, as always, are our children.

Oozing its way onto the screens and other holiday promotions is the record-breaking marketing sensation and glorification of the martial arts, *Teenage Mutant Ninja Turtles* and its sequel appropriately named *The Secret of the Ooze.* With 133 acts of mayhem per hour, they are the most violent films ever marketed to children and perhaps also the most appalling to adults who have the stamina, and stomach, to view them. A marketing survey of licensed cartoon characters found the Turtles by far the "LEAST favorite" (politely phrased) of both men and women.

Nothing can prepare the unaccustomed for the expertly choreographed brutality, wisecracking misanthropy, and rock-rap-rhythmic slashery crammed into one sick spectacle. Males fight, torture, gorge themselves on pizza (brand names prominently displayed), burn, crush, mutilate, and kill. One lone miniskirted sex object (intrepid reporter bossed by boorish editors) is assaulted, scared, victimized, and rescued at least three times. Finally she, too, kills and earns an appreciative "You're a natural, Sis!" The only other major woman character is the object of a long-ago rivalry that starts the blood feud now played out on the streets of New York's Little Tokyo. She appears briefly just to be brutally murdered.

Undaunted by the dismay of trapped parents, harried teachers, and overworked psychiatrists, *Teenage Mutant Ninja Turtles II: The Secret of the Ooze* is another punch up and kick-in-the-teeth opus in which the martial artists, indecently named for giants of the Renaissance, pursue their rampage into pseudo-scientific mysticism and blind obedience to the leader in a cult of violence and vengeance. (Britain, Germany, and Sweden are among countries that require cuts or age limits or both.)

The Secret of the Ooze has been oozing out of Burger King posters, toys, commercials, and ads in its *BK Kids Club* magazine. A thirty-second spot for the magazine (in addition to other promotions) should not surprise those who think they escape commercials when they buy the video for $22.95. Nor should it surprise anyone to find the Turtles show up in rival Pizza Hut and Nabisco Brands campaigns in time for the extended Christmas selling season.

Pizza Hut pumped $20 million into launching its campaign, despite the fact that more than 130 Ninja licenses already flood the country with over 500 Teenage Mutant Ninja Turtle products from T-shirts to yogurt. After a gala Radio City Music Hall Kick-off in New York, the Turtles went on a forty-city rock concert tour where rhythmically gyrating teenage Turtle groupies, many in Turtle costumes, personally helped set the stage for the sales campaign.

After the domestic blitz, global conglomerate PepsiCo, owner of Pizza Hut, hurtled the pizza-gobbling Turtles onto the international marketing circuit where retail sales of Turtle paraphernalia alone reached a record one billion dollars worldwide already by mid-1991. "Los Tortugas Ninjas" (and other dubbed versions) replaced Batman as the current global movie mania. There is concern that the list for pizza will replace tortillas or empanadas (and other local favorites) as the kids' new passion.

Not to be outdone, Nabisco Brands, part of another global conglomerate (tobacco and food), will offer four Tuttle gelatin molds on boxes of a new holiday flavor tastefully named "Royal Ooze." Oh yes, an unspecified "percentage of the profits" from the Turtles II video will be donated to Kids for Saving the Earth to remind us that, after all, the Turtles' mayhem is environmentally correct.

Saving the earth from the Turtles and their ilk may be a better idea. The environment most vital to our humanity is the cultural environment on which both physical survival and mental health depend. A Cultural Environmental Movement (CEM) could oppose domination of our holidays (and our children's minds) by storytellers who only have something to sell, and sell at any cost. CEM should help liberate creative energies from marketing strategies imposed on them, build a consistency for freer media, and develop ways of public participation in cultural policymaking. Wouldn't that be a more fitting gift for our children this holiday season?

NOTE

Originally published in *Advice,* Vol. 1, No. 3, October 1991

CHAPTER 43

THE BEST KEPT MEDIA SECRET OF NOVEMBER

Labor Day

BY GEORGE GERBNER

The mass media fill our cultural environment with affairs of the rich and famous. Our own Cultural Indicator study shows that low-income working people are virtually invisible; they account for only 1.3 percent of prime time characters. The Cultural Environment Movement, an international media-watch action coalition, is working for greater diversity on the public airways.

"Daily papers and hourly news broadcasts keep us well informed of stock market trends and outlooks for investors," writes syndicated columnist Norman Solomon. "But details aren't nearly as profuse when it comes to what directly affects most of the nation's employees: job security issues, eroding benefits and stressful working conditions."

It will come as no surprise, therefore, that November will pass without learning from the mainstream press about the international labor holidays of November 11, commemorating the Haymarket martyrs, and November 19, anniversary of the murder of labor organizer Joe Hill.

Every daily newspaper has a financial page but no labor page, or even a labor reporter. The U.S. Labor Party had its Founding Convention in Cleveland last June—but it was blanked out in the mainstream press. We celebrate Labor Day at a time that is the farthest removed from the international labor holiday on the first of May. Most Americans think that May Day is some kind of Soviet import, domesticated into a parade down Fifth Avenue.

In fact, however, Labor Day originated November 11, 1887, in Chicago, U.S.A. Chicago had gone through the devastating fire of 1871. Immigration from abroad and from the South doubled its population in a decade. Rapid growth and economic expansion brought unparalleled prosperity to property owners and unprecedented poverty to its polyglot working-class population.

The labor movement had been organizing and mobilizing workers through the 1870s and '80s. The Federation of Organized Trades and Labor Unions organized a rally that turned out some 90,000 demonstrators in Chicago's Haymarket Square.

The response was fierce. A bomb was thrown. The police riot that followed left eight demonstrators dead, seventy wounded, hundreds arrested. Thirty-one scapegoats were framed and indicted, and four hanged on November 11, 1887.

"Remember Haymarket" became a rallying cry of the labor movement. The International Socialist Congress meeting July 14–20, 1889, in Paris, resolved to honor the Haymarket martyrs by launching the annual international May Day as a demonstration for the eight hour day.

The reaction against union organizing struck again during and after both World Wars. Joe Hill, Swedish-born organizer of the Industrial Workers of the World (IWW), of whom Earl Robinson wrote one of his famous ballads, was framed on a trumped-up charge, tried in Salt Lake City, Utah, and, despite international protest, condemned to death and executed on November 19, 1915. The only memorial for Joe is in the Swedish town of Gavle where he was born in 1879 and grew up as Joel Emanuel Haglund. His ashes have been scattered under a cherry tree. About 10,000 visitors go through "Joe Hill Gardens" every year. There is no marker in the United States for whose workers Joe fought and died.

The infamous Palmer raids (named for Attorney General A. Mitchell Palmer) used the pretext of the Russian revolution of 1919 and the complicity of the mainstream press to incite the "red scare," leading to mass arrests, the deportation of another 556 scapegoats, and the rise of "red hunter" J. Edgar Hoover to head the F.B.I.

The cold war began while the Soviets were still our allies in World War II. During my service in the Office of Strategic Services (O.S.S.) of the U.S. Army, I was investigating war criminal suspects, until I was told by the colonel in command: "Lt. Gerbner, forget your charge. The real enemy is our ally, the Soviets." Soon the Truman Doctrine made the red hunt official. Loyalty hearings and wholesale firings of activists "purged" education and the labor movement.

I was subpoenaed before the California Un-American Activities Committee and asked if I ever showed a documentary film in my class entitled "Races of Mankind," based on anthropologist Ruth Benedict's book of the same title. As the Committee new well, I showed that film each semester. But during the "McCarthy era," named for infamous red-hunter Senator Joseph McCarthy of Wisconsin, any rational discussion of race was evidence of a communist conspiracy. I was fired from my teaching job.

The anti-red hysteria, fueled by the media, gave rise to Nixon, the Hiss case, and the execution, again despite worldwide protest, of the Rosenbergs. Its chilling effect persists to this date.

The way to counter the best kept secrets of November is to remember them in every home, school, and church, and to work with CEM for freedom, fairness, gender equity, general diversity, and democratic decision making in media ownership, employment, and representation.

CHAPTER 44

TV RATINGS' DEADLY CHOICE

Violence or Alcohol

BY GEORGE GERBNER

The much ballyhooed television program rating game is on. Signs like TV-G, TV-PG, TV-K, and TV-M have been flickering on the upper left corner of your screen since January 1, 1997. If you haven't noticed, or have been puzzled about what these little icons mean, or slack about providing PG (parental guidance), don't feel bad. That is how the system is supposed to work. Even if you have been observing the ratings, you may have traded violence for alcohol.

The movie-style rating system is an uninformative scheme that deceives the public and protects industries from parents rather than the other way around.

The *Chicago Tribune* reported on March 18, 1998:

> Yes, the hodgepodge of letters and numbers, instituted by the television industry under pressure from Congress and parent-advocacy groups, has been both ignored and derided since its debut in January 1997 and refinement last fall.
>
> One recent study, conducted by the Associated Press, found that 7 of 10 adults were paying it little or no mind. Many major newspapers, including this one, have not been publishing the ratings in their television programming guides.
>
> Parents at a congressional hearing in Peoria last spring ripped into the original ratings, which only labeled shows movie-style, based on recommenced ages for viewers. When the rest of the industry agreed after Peoria to add content indicators to the age-based ratings, the most popular network, NBC, refused to do so.
>
> But all of that has a chance to change with the news last week that the FCC has given the ratings...official seal of approval.

Well, fat chance. Most parents don't know about the ratings, or don't use them, or, if they did, don't know what they're getting instead. In any case, they assume that broadcasters, rather than the public, own the airways and that they air whatever is most popular.

Wrong again.

Mindless TV violence is not an expression of artistic freedom or of any measure of reality or popularity. On the contrary, it is the product of a de facto censorship: a global marketing formula and rating system imposed on program creators and foisted on the children of the world.

The political process that rammed through the business-as-usual rating system was orchestrated by Mr. Jack Valenti, president of the Motion Picture Association of America, Inc., one of the top Washington, D.C., lobbyists, and creator of the motion picture ratings that he cloned onto television.

The process included a series of "consultations" with parents' and children's advocacy groups. I attended one of these meetings as president of the Cultural Environment Movement, a coalition for equity and fairness in media.

All organizations present urged Valenti to design a system that provides reasons for the ratings so that parents can make informed decisions. Mr. Valenti first stonewalled; months later he gave in under pressure. But then syndicators reveled and refused to label cartoons, where of course most of the violence is.

The system that has now thus been patched up and rammed down the public's throats has four fatal flaws.

First, it confuses the choices made in moviegoing with the very different decisions of television viewing. You select a movie and go out to see it, or pick a video to bring home. By contrast, television comes into the home an average of seven hours a day. It is watched more by the clock than by the program. To monitor your child's viewing you have to be a full-time television watchdog. Opening credits (when the ratings flash on) are not the decisive choice points in television viewing.

Second, it results in inconsistencies in rating. With the number of programs on television, producers will rate their own programs. Therefore, inconsistencies are inevitable. "Tonight Show with Jay Leno" was given a TV-14 but "Late Show with David Letterman" a TV-PG. Without a common standard, "none of it will mean anything," says Warner Brothers network head Jamie Kellner. "A WB 'PG' will be different than a Fox 'PG,' and that will be a disservice to everybody."

Third, ratings designed by the industry and programmed into the V-Chip is like letting the fox (no pun intended) guard the chicken coop. Perhaps the best feature of the V-Chip is that no one knows how it works, and some of those who know think that it doesn't work well at all. One of these is Barry Diller, former ABC vice-president, Fox CEO, and Home-Shopping QVC chairman. "The whole idea of the V-Chip," he says, "is an absurd concept. It's simply unworkable. But it's nice to talk about, it's good to get a bunch of people to Washington and have their photo taken. It's good to stand there and say we're doing something for America. In fact, it won't work. But other than that, it's a lovely idea."

Fourth, even if the "family" (G) rating cuts down on one deadly substance, it opens the door to another: happy, risk-free alcohol. As shown in Table 1, G-rated shows still expose viewers to an hourly average of 2.4 acts of violence and 2.5 scenes of alcohol.

Table 1. Average Number of Alcohol and Violence Scenes

Rating label	TV-G	TV-PG	TV-14
% of sample with rating	18%	64%	18%
Alcohol scenes per hour	2.5	3.4	4.4
Violence scenes per hour	2.4	4.1	3.6

However, TV-PG rating increases the frequency of alcohol scenes to 3.4 per hour, and TV-14 rating increases the frequency of alcohol scenes to 4.4 per hour. There is more alcohol than violence in the most violent shows.

If age-grading is a mixed bag, content labeling has its problems as well. In response to lobbying by citizen action groups throughout 1996 and 1997, content labels are used in the ratings of most network programs. Shows are marked for violence (V), language (L), sex (S), and adult themes (D).

Prime time dramatic programming with a "V" label present scenes of violence every eleven minutes, compared to every thirty-eight minutes for shows without any content label.

In Table 2, shows are grouped into those with no content label, those with D or S or L (but no V), and those with the V (violence) label. (NBC, which initially opted out of content labeling, is not represented.) It can be seen that depictions of alcohol on prime time appear to be coupled with adult themes, adult language, and sex.

Table 2. Alcohol and Violence Scenes by Content Labels

Content labels (none)	V		
% of sample with label	41%	30%	30%
Alcohol scenes per hour	3.3	5.0	2.9
Violence scenes per hour	2.4	4.1	3.6

What shall we make of all that?

Our children are growing up in homes where television tells most of the stories. Before they go to school, which used to be the first time they encountered the larger culture, they are integrated into a television view of the world. That is not the view of parents, schools, communities, or even countries. Neither is it the view of creative people with something to tell. It is the view of a handful of conglomerates with something to sell.

The radical change has altered the socialization of children, transformed the mainstream of the cultural environment, and surrendered the public airways to a marketing operation. Paying for all that is a markup for all advertised goods and services, a form of taxation without representation.

Our Cultural Indicators (CI) research project has monitored and analyzed the world of prime time and Saturday morning television since 1967. This report about some features that ratings are supposed to reflect is taken from that database of more than 3,000 programs and 34,000 characters.

Humankind may have had more bloodthirsty ears, but none as filled with images of violence as the present. We are awash in a tide of violent representations the world has never seen. There is no escape from the massive invasion of colorful mayhem into the homes and cultural life of ever larger areas of the world.

We found prime time television saturated by an average of five scenes of violence per hour. Over twenty scenes of violence per hour fill Saturday morning cartoon programs.

Violence, whether serious or humorous, is essentially a demonstration of power. It shows who can get away with what against whom.

The ratio of violence to victimization defines the price to be paid for committing violence. When one group can commit violence with relative impunity, the price it pays for violence is relatively low. When a group suffers more violence than it commits, the price is high. In general, women, children, young people, lower income, disabled and Asian Americans are at the bottom of the television violence "pecking order."

We have also found that those who watch more television in every group express a greater sense of apprehension, mistrust, and insecurity than do light viewers in the same groups. We call this the "mean world syndrome." Whatever real dangers lurk outside people's homes, viewing violent television cultivates fears and dependencies that make some groups more vulnerable than others to exploitation and victimization. Ultimately, therefore, marketing mayhem contributes to domination and repression.

Ratings cannot alleviate the human, social, and political fallout of the "mean world syndrome." Can they at least keep viewers from flocking to violent programs? Wrong once again. Another well kept secret is that violence on television is not popular. Many studies have found that even though audiences are desensitized to violence, they don't like it. Our CI project has documented the fact that violence depresses the Nielsen ratings.

Why, then, all that violence? Here is the final secret, and challenge to conventional wisdom. What drives violence on the airways is not popularity but global marketing. This is how it works.

What you see on TV is not what the people want. What you see is what the advertisers think will attract an audience at the least cost. "Cost per thousand" is the unit of measurement, where the size of the audience is divided by the dollar cost of the time the advertiser pays to insert the commercial message. Viewers are the fish, programs the bait.

Production costs are climbing above what domestic advertising markets can support. Producers and syndicators reach for the global market.

What is the dramatic ingredient best suited to the global market? It is one that needs no translation, that is image-driven, that speaks "action" in any language, and that fits into any culture. That ingredient is violence.

What global programmers may lose domestically by saturating programs with violence they more than make up by selling it cheap to many countries. When you can dump a Power Rangers on 300 million children in 80 countries, shutting out domestic artists and cultural products, you don't have to care who wants it and who gets hurt in the process.

What shall we do?

Media watch groups, children's and parent's advocates, and other public interest organizations should make their voices heard on the real issues. They are issues of gender equity and general diversity in media ownership, employment, and representations. They are issues of marketing-driven media monopolization, homogenization, and globalization. In the last analysis, let us not get bogged down in rating system trivialities. Citizens own the airways. We should demand that it be healthy, free, and fair, and not just "rated."

CHAPTER 45

MASS MEDIA AND DISSENT

BY GEORGE GERBNER

Dissent is the lifeblood of the democratic process. It is the mark of a plurality of perspectives and a diversity of competing (and sometimes conflicting) interests.

At the same time, however, the right to dissent—although shielded by the First Amendment to the U.S. Constitution—is not unlimited and is always contested. Laws of libel, slander, defamation, and the protections extended to intellectual property are among obvious constraints on expression, including dissent.

But perhaps the principal limitation on political dissent is financial. It has been observed that the current cash-driven electoral system has a chilling effect on the nature and caliber of dissent. Furthermore, the market-driven and highly concentrated and conglomeratized media system has little room for ideological plurality—and thus dissent. There are no socialist, communist, or religious fundamentalist parties in the American mainstream. And even though the airways belong to the public, they have been largely given away to the same market forces that marginalize dissent in politics.

This marginalization of fundamental dissent in the cultural/political mainstream contributes to the low voter turnout and narrow range of debate where substantive issues are ignored and personalities (not to mention private personal affairs) often dominate.

It is one thing to assure individuals the right to dissent without fear of government regulation or worse. Anyone can find a street corner on which to pontificate. It is another thing to say that any individual has the right to establish a free press to disseminate dissent to a broader audience than could be reached by the spoken word. Moreover, those who own the media are in a position to determine who is empowered to disseminate which dissenting views to the mass public.

The basic argument about political dissent, then, is whether the First Amendment protects the rights of media owners to suppress fundamental dissent regardless of the implications for democracy. The alternative is to view the First Amendment's protection of a free press as a social right to a diverse and uncensored press with ample room for dissent. In this view the right of dissent to be heard is a right enjoyed by all citizens, not just by owners of media. Otherwise there is no more need for its inclusion in the First Amendment than it would be to guarantee individuals the right to establish a baking business or a shoe repair service. As Alexander Meiklejohn points out, those commercial rights are explicitly covered in the Fifth Amendment to the U.S. Constitution.

Modern advertising emerged in the past century and is conducted disproportionately by the largest corporations. This corporate media system has none of the intrinsic interest in politics or journalism that existed in the press of earlier times. If anything, it tends to promote depoliticization. Fundamental political positions are closely linked to elites. Dissent may exist on the margins, but the commercial system assures that these voices have no hope of reaching a mass audience.

There are two solutions to the crisis for democracy generated by a corporate-dominated media system. The most radical is to create a large nonprofit, noncommercial media system accountable to the public. In earlier times, John Dewey and the Hutchins Commission both proposed that newspapers be established as nonprofit and noncommercial enterprises, supported by endowments and universities, and managed through direct public election (or election by the media workers) of their officers.

The less radical solution is to tax the media giants or use public monies to establish a viable nonprofit and noncommercial media system that can serve the needs of citizens who are unable to own media corporations.

Of course, proposals such as these have met with significant corporate opposition and concerns that they would let the government control the media to an unacceptable extent, no matter how the nonprofit media system might be structured. From the Progressive Era to the present day, the corporate media giants have fanned the flames of this sentiment, using their immense resources to popularize the notion that a gulag-style, darkness at noon media system was the only possible alternative to the corporate, commercial status quo. Hence any challenge to their power was a challenge to democracy.

Broadcasting offers the best hope for those who wish to see the public airways committed to democratic media and reasonable opportunities for dissent. All Supreme Court decisions have affirmed the right of the government to regulate broadcasting in a manner that would be judged unconstitutional with the print media.

In the last 1920s and early 1930s, however, the government turned over the best parts of the broadcast spectrum to a handful of private commercial operators. There was no public or congressional debate on the matter. In the 1930s the ACLU was so alarmed by the explicit and implicit censorship in corporate and advertiser control of radio—especially against labor and the left—that it argued that the very system of commercial broadcasting was a violation of the First Amendment. For most of the 1930s the ACLU worked to have the government establish a nonprofit and noncommercial radio system that would foster more coverage of social issues and public affairs and greater opportunities for dissent. The ACLU backed off from this position when it became clear that the corporate power was entrenched and unchallengeable. After abandoning its commitment to structural reform, the ACLU went from being a proponent of regulation of commercial broadcasters in the public interest to being a defender of the commercial system without government interference. Finally, in the 1970s, the courts began to include corporate activities under the First Amendment, thereby eliminating or further weakening government regulation on behalf of an even playing field in the public airways.

Even political advertising is lame and devoid of fundamental dissent. It is commercialized political speech, indistinguishable from product advertising. Hence the content of political advertising generates apathy, cynicism, and mistrust, thereby reinforcing the depoliticizing aspects of the broader political culture.

It would be comforting to think that we could depend on the Supreme Court to reverse this situation. But members of the Court were placed in office by the politicians who benefit from the status quo. The task for advocates of the right and value of vigorous dissent is to make it a key component of social movement that links electoral reform with media reform. One such movement is the Cultural Environment Movement, founded in 1966, and dedicated to diversity in media ownership, employment, and representation.

Part X

LOOKING BACK, LOOKING FORWARD

CEM

CHAPTER 46

TELLING STORIES, OR HOW DO WE KNOW WHAT WE KNOW?

The Story of Cultural Indicators and the Cultural Environment Movement

BY GEORGE GERBNER

Most of what we know, or think we know, we have never personally experienced. We live in a world erected by the stories we hear and see and tell. It is a world of incredible riches of imagery and words, conjuring up the unseen through art, creating towering works of imagination and fact through science, poetry, song, tales, reports, and laws—the true magic of human life.

Through that magic we live in a world much wider than the threats and gratifications of the immediate physical environment, which is the world of other species. Stories socialize us into roles of gender, age, class, vocation and lifestyle, and offer models of conformity or targets for rebellion. They weave the seamless web of the cultural environment that cultivates most of what we think, what we do, and how we conduct our affairs.

How will future historians deal with that process? How will they be able to examine the common cultural environment of stories and images that shapes, every day, from infancy, on the shared action structure, thematic content, and representation of actions, places, and people? How will they trace the mainstream and the sweep of that environment of stories? And how will they know what to do about it?

Their source, possibly the only source, will be our Cultural Indicators (CI) database of media content and effects, and the action program based on it, the Cultural Environment Movement (CEM), an organization created to democratize media ownership, employment, and representation.

The historical inspiration for CI and CEM comes from the story of storytelling itself.

THE STORY OF STORYTELLING

Scottish patriot Andrew Fletcher once said: "If one were permitted to make all the ballads, one need not care who should make the laws of a nation." That was a time when "ballads"—the myths and stories of a culture—were handcrafted, homemade, community inspired. Today, they are the products of a complex global mass-production and marketing process.

The stories no longer come from families, schools, churches, neighborhoods, and often not even from the native countries, or, in fact, from anyone with anything to tell. Increasingly, they come from small groups of distant conglomerates with something to sell.

This is a profound transformation in human socialization and governance.

For the longest time in human history, stories were told only face to face. A community was defined by the rituals, mythologies, and imageries held in common. Writing was rare and holy, forbidden for slaves. Laboriously inscribed manuscripts conferred sacred power to their interpreters, the priests and ministers.

State and church ruled in a symbiotic relationship of mutual dependence and tension. State, composed of feudal nobles, was the political, economic, and military order; church was the cultural arm.

The industrial revolution changed all that. One of the first machines stamping out standardized artifacts was the printing press. Its product, the book, was a prerequisite for all other upheavals to come.

Printing begins the industrialization of storytelling. The machine-made book can be given to all who can read. Readers can interpret the book (at first the Bible) for themselves, breaking the monopoly of priestly interpreters, and ushering in the Reformation.

When the printing press is hooked up to the steam engine the industrialization of storytelling shifts into high gear. Rapid printing and distribution create a new form of consciousness: modern mass publics. Publics are loose aggregations of people who share some common consciousness but never meet face to face.

Stories can now be sent—often smuggled—across hitherto impenetrable or closely guarded boundaries to time, space, gender, race, class, and status. Books lift people from their traditional moorings as the industrial revolution uproots them from their local communities and cultures. They get off the land, go to far-away ports, factories and continents, form new communities and social classes, and find a bundle of common consciousness—the published book and journal, to cultivate their consciousness of class, culture, and status wherever they go.

People engage in long and costly struggles to be free to create and share stories that fit their competing and often conflicting interests. Publication becomes the key to and object of struggle and of democratic governance. A new form of rule emerges: rule by publics, res publica, or republic. The First Amendment to the U.S. Constitution protects that rule by forbidding Congress to make laws abridging the freedom of the press.

The second great transformation, the electronic revolution, ushers in the telecommunications era, changes the old rules, and challenges the concept of democracy itself. The mainstream of the new cultural environment, television, is superimposed upon and reorganizes print-based culture. Unlike the industrial revolution, the new upheaval does not uproot people from their localities but transports them in their homes and transforms them into audiences. Audiences are not publics with some consciousness of their basic interests. Their interests are promoted by publicity and advertising. They are markets to be exploited. They are created and traded by broadcasters and sold as markets for advertisers to exploit. Advertisers, in turn, subsidize the private broadcasters to whom the public airways have been licensed. The corruption of the First Amendment has come full circle.

Children are born into homes where a few mass-mediated storytellers reach them on the average more than seven hours a day. Most waking hours, and often dramas, are filled with these mass-produced stories. Giant industries discharge their messages into the mainstream of common consciousness. The historic symbiotic nexus of church and state is replaced by television and state.

Broadcasting is the most concentrated, homogenized, and globalized medium. The top one hundred U.S. advertisers pre-empt the public airways. They subsidize two-thirds of all network television. Four networks, allied to giant transnational corporations—our private "Ministry of Culture"—control the bulk of production and distribution and shape the cultural mainstream. Other interests, minority views, and the potential of any mainstream alternative to the dominant perspective, lose ground with every merger.

While channels proliferate, the basic features of their storytelling, casting, and fate become more and more similar. For most viewers, new types of delivery systems such as cable, satellite, and the Internet mean even deeper penetration and integration of the dominant patterns of images and messages into everyday life.

Technological developments such as cable, VCR, and the Internet have contributed to a significant erosion in audience share (and revenue) of the major broadcasting networks and have altered the marketing and distribution of movies. However, there is no evidence that proliferation of channels has led to substantially greater diversity of content. On the contrary, rapid concentration and vertical integration in the media industries, the absorption of most publishing houses by electronic conglomerates, the growing practice of producing the same material for several media markets, and the habit of time-shifting by VCR users (recording favorite network programs to play back more often and at more convenient times) suggest that the diversity of what is actually viewed has decreased.

Formula-driven assembly line produced programs mean a homogenization of outlooks and limitation of alternatives. For media professionals, the changes mean fewer opportunities and greater compulsions to present life in saleable packages. Creative artists, scientists, and humanists can still explore and enlighten and occasionally even challenge, but, increasingly, their stories must fit marketing strategies and priorities.

What is most likely to cultivate stable and common conceptions of reality is, therefore, the overall patterns and formulas of programming to which total communities are regularly exposed over long periods of time. That is the pattern of settings, casting, social typing, actions, and related outcomes that cuts across program types and viewing modes and defines the world of television. That is the pattern observed, coded, recorded, and analyzed in the Cultural Indicators project.

THE CULTURAL ENVIRONMENT MOVEMENT (CEM)

CEM was launched in response to the challenge for democratic culture implicit in the findings of the Cultural Indicators project. Its Founding Convention was held in St. Louis, Missouri, March 15–17, 1996. It was the most diverse representation of leaders and activists in the field of culture and communication that has ever met.

CEM is a non-profit coalition of independent organizations and individual supporters in every state of the United States and fifty-seven other countries on six continents, united in working for gender equity, general diversity, and democratic decision making in media ownership, employment, and representation.

Its objectives are:

> Building a new coalition involving media councils in the U.S. and abroad; teachers, students and parents; groups concerned with children, youth and aging; women's groups; religious and minority organizations; educational, health, environmental, legal, and other professional associations; consumer groups and agencies; associations of creative workers in the media and in the arts and sciences; independent computer network organizers and other organizations and individuals committed to broadening the freedom and diversity of communication.
>
> Opposing domination and working to abolish existing concentration of ownership and censorship (both of and by media), public or private. It involves extending rights, facilities, and influence to interests and perspectives other than the most powerful and profitable. It means including in cultural decision making the less affluent more vulnerable groups who, in fact, are the majority of the population. These include the marginalized, neglected, abused, exploited, physically or mentally disabled, young and old, women, minorities, poor people, recent immigrants—all those most in need of a decent role and a voice in a freer cultural environment.
>
> Seeking out and cooperating with cultural liberation forces of other countries working for the integrity and independence of their own decision making and against cultural domination and invasion. Learning from countries that have already opened their media to the democratic process. Helping local movements, including in the most dependent and vulnerable countries of Latin America, Asia, and Africa (and also in Eastern Europe and the former Soviet Republics), to invest in their own

cultural development: opposing aggressive foreign ownership and coercive trade policies that make such development more difficult.

Supporting journalists, artists, writers, actors, directors, and other creative workers struggling for more freedom from having to present life as a commodity designed for a market of consumers. Working with guilds, caucuses, labor and other groups for diversity in employment and in media content. Supporting media and cultural organizations addressing significant but neglected needs, sensibilities, and interests.

Promoting media literacy, media awareness, critical viewing and reading, and other media education efforts as a fresh approach to the liberal arts and an essential educational objective on every level. Collecting, publicizing and disseminating information, research and evaluation about relevant programs, services, curricula, and teaching materials. Helping to organize educational and parents' groups demanding preservice and in-service teacher training in media analysis, already required in the schools of Australia, Canada, and Great Britain.

Placing cultural policy issues on the social-political agenda. Supporting and if necessary organizing local and national media councils, study groups, citizen groups, minority and professional groups and other forums of public discussion, policy development, representation, and action. Not waiting for a blueprint but creating and experimenting with ways of community and citizen participation in local, national and international media policy making. Sharing experiences, lessons, and recommendations and moving toward a realistic democratic agenda.

CEM offers the liberating alternative, working for freedom, fairness, gender equity, general diversity, and democratic decision making in media ownership, employment, and representation.

VIEWER'S DECLARATION OF INDEPENDENCE

This Declaration originated at the Founding Convention of the Cultural Environment Movement (CEM) in St. Louis, Missouri, U.S.A., on March 17, 1996. It was revised following suggestions by a committee elected at the Convention.

We hold these truths to be self-evident:

That all persons are endowed with the right to live in a cultural environment that is respectful of their humanity and supportive of their potential.

That all children are endowed with the right to grow up in a cultural environment that fosters responsibility, trust, and community rather than force, fear, and violence.

That when the cultural environment becomes destructive of these ends, it is necessary to alter it.

Such is the necessity that confronts us. Let the world hear the reasons that compel us to assert our rights and to take an active role in the shaping of our common cultural environment.

1. Humans live and learn by stories. Today they are no longer handcrafted, homemade, community inspired. They are no longer told by families, schools, or churches but are the products of a complex mass-production and marketing process. Scottish patriot Andrew Fletcher once said: "If one were permitted to make all the ballads, one need not care who should make the laws of a nation." Today most of our "ballads"—the myths and stories of our culture—are made by a small group of global conglomerates that have something to sell.
2. This radical transformation of our cultural environment has changed the roles we grow into, the way we employ creative talent, the way we raise our children, and the way we manage our affairs. Communication channels proliferate but technologies converge and media merge. Consolidation of ownership denies entry to newcomers, drives independents out of the mainstream, and reduces diversity of content. Media blend into a seamless homogenized cultural environment that constrains life's choices as much as the degradation of the physical environment limits life's chances.
3. This change did not come about spontaneously or after thoughtful deliberation. It was imposed on an uninformed public and is enshrined in legislation rushed through Congress without any opportunity for public scrutiny or debate about its consequences and worldwide fallout. The airways, a global commons, have been given away to media empires responsible to no one but their stockholders.
4. In exchange for that give-away, we are told, we get "free" entertainment and news. But in truth, we pay dearly, both as consumers and as citizens. The price of soap we buy includes a surcharge for the commercials that bring us the "soap opera." We pay when we wash, not when we watch. And we pay even if we do not watch or do not like the way of life it promotes. This is taxation without representation. Furthermore, the advertising expenditures that buy our media are a tax-deductible business expense. Money diverted from the public treasure pays for an invisible, unelected, unaccountable, private Ministry of Culture making, behind closed doors, decisions that shape public policy.
5. The human consequences are also far-reaching. They include cults of media violence that desensitize, terrorize, brutalize and paralyze; the promotion of unhealthy practices that pollute, drug, hurt, poison, and kill thousands every day; portrayals that dehumanize, stereotype, marginalize and stigmatize women, racial and ethnic groups, gays and lesbians, aging or disabled or physically or mentally ill persons, and others outside the cultural mainstream.

6. These distortions of the democratic process divert attention from the basic needs, problems, and aspirations of people. They conceal the drift toward ecological suicide; the silent crumbling of our vital infrastructure; the cruel neglect of children, poor people, and other vulnerable populations; the invasions of privacy at home and in the workplace; the growing inequalities of wealth and opportunity; the profits made from throwing millions of people on the scrap heap of the unemployed; the commercialization of the classroom; and the downgrading of education and the arts.
7. Global marketing formulas, imposed on media workers and foisted on the children of the world, colonize, monopolize, and homogenize cultures everywhere. Technocratic fantasies mask social realities that further widen the gaps between the information rich and the information poor.
8. Repeated protests and petitions have been ignored or dismissed as attempts at "censorship" by the media magnates who alone have the power to suppress and to censor. No constitutional protection or legislative prospect will help us to loosen the noose of market censorship or to counter the repressive direction the "culture wars" are taking us. We need a liberating alternative.

We, therefore, declare our independence from a system that has drifted out of democratic reach. Our CEM offers the liberating alternative: an independent citizen voice in cultural policymaking, working for the creation of a free, fair, diverse, and responsible cultural environment for us and our children.

REFERENCES

Gerbner, George. "The Social Role of the Confession Magazine." *Social Problems*. Summer 1958.

———. "Mental Illness on Television: A Study of Censorship." *Journal of Broadcasting*. Fall 1959.

———."Toward 'Cultural Indicators,' The Analysis of Mass Mediated Systems." *AV Communication Review*. Summer 1969.

Pool, Ithiel De Sola, and Shulman, Irwin. "Newsmen's Fantasies, Audiences, and Newswriting." In *People, Society and Mass Communications*, edited by Lewis A. Dexter and David M. White. New York: The Free Press, 1964.

Toward a Social Report. U.S. Department of Health, Education, and Welfare. Washington: Government Printing Office, 1969.

White, David M. "The Gatekeeper: A Case Study in the Selection of News." In *People, Society and Mass Communications*, edited by Lewis A. Dexter and David M. White. New York: The Free Press, 1964.

CHAPTER 47

AN INTERVIEW WITH PROFESSOR GEORGE GERBNER

BY RAMESH CLOSEPET
AND LAI-SI TSUI

George Gerbner, the doyen of research on television violence in the United States, is Dean Emeritus of the Annenberg School of Communications at the University of Pennsylvania, Philadelphia. He is best known for his theory of the "social construction of reality" and his work on the "Cultural Indicators" project (1972–1980), designed to study television content and effects. This influential work followed a three-year study (1968–1970) of the portrayal of violence in network television drama. His studies have been oriented toward uncovering the cultural homogenization of TV programming and advertising—the portrayal of violence, abuse of power, sexism, and racism.

While Gerbner's works have gained popular and academic recognition, his research methodology, or more specifically his use of multivariate statistics to interpret data from the "Cultural Indicators" project, has been severely criticized. Reanalyses of Gerbner's data by other researchers (Doob and MacDonald, 1979; Hirsch, 1980; Hughes, 1980) have found little or no influence of television viewing on social reality variables and therefore Gerbner's findings have often been dismissed as spurious, or it has been claimed that television has no effect at all. Yet, while Gerbner's research methodology may be open to question, one should not dismiss the validity of his theory and the theoretical value of his view on cultural homogenization of TV programming and advertising both in the United States and the world.

From being a social scientist and researcher, Dr. Gerbner has increasingly assumed the role of a political activist. In the following wide-ranging interview, he expostulates on his new initiative, the "Cultural Environmental Movement."

In the article "The Challenge Before Us" (1986), you indicate that television images perpetrate/perpetuate sexism, racism, and violence, and that the socializing function of television is more like that of a tribal religion. Your claim seems to be that television fare leads to a sort of cultural homogenization. Could you elaborate/substantiate this?

Well, for the first time in human history a child is born into a home in which the television is on, in the U.S., on average seven hours a day. It provides the total cultural environment for the child. It's not the parents, nor the school, nor the church who tell most of the stories but distant, global corporations who have something to sell. That has profoundly affected the way our children are socialized.

When most of the stories are designed for a global marketing strategy, and when storytelling is highly centralized, and where exposure to the same set of stories is how a wide set of otherwise heterogeneous groups receive stories, when so many of the stories that children hear do not even originate in their own country, the tendency is towards uniformity and homogenization. We've done research on this for over twenty-seven years. It continues to show that indeed such homogenization, what we've called "mainstreaming," takes place. It erodes traditional distinctions among human groups—gender, class, nationality, location.

Homogenization takes place in terms of overarching building blocks of storytelling. The principal building blocks are what I call "casting" and "fate." Casting means what kind of people are involved in the stories that you tell. In the U.S., for example, men outnumber women three to one in television programming. You put a cast on the stage, and you've to tell a story that fits the cast. This means that there is a severe limitation on the stories TV can tell.

Next, what is the systematic association between the cast and what happens to the cast? Who succeeds, who fails? Who can put what over on whom? Who can force whom to behave the way they want?—which is a demonstration of power. That's where our interest in violence comes from. Violence is a demonstration of power, a form of social control. It indicates to people their chances of winning or losing: their "fate." So, our aim is to analyze social typing (casting), and fate. Then we go on from there to look at the occupations, the action structure, the semantic structure, and storytelling that cuts across all kinds of presentations. They're designed to sell goods, and to sell people. The products that television sells are the people it collects and presents to the advertiser.

It seems that this building block has certain characters that are important, certain people who win and certain others who lose. Could you make those more explicit?

Men outnumber women three to one. The young and the old are not represented in their true proportion. Minorities are underrepresented because representation is a cultural resource, and the definition of minorities is that they don't get their share of resources, including power and all their values. Now if you are overrepresented you see yourself having a wide variety of opportunities, you think you can go anywhere, do anything, you can have any kind of adventure, you are not dependent, you are powerful. Who are these people? They're usually white males.

If you're a woman, you see yourself in a much more restricted light. You're more stereotyped. You need women for romantic stories, to be grandmothers, or to be victims. So you see yourself as having limited life chances. Representation goes down in terms of status from white males in their prime of life to older people, to minorities, to foreign born, then a combination of these, as they get more and more underrepresented. But they get more and more victimized, compared with their ability to inflict violence on somebody else. For example, overall on television, for every ten violent characters there are twelve victims. For every ten women written into the script there are sixteen women victims.

If you grow up in this environment, and if you're a woman or minority, or a woman *and* a minority, you not only think of yourself as more limited in life chances but also as a victim. You're more insecure, more afraid, more dependent. So this becomes training in dependence. This is training to seek protection from the "stronger" members in society. And this is often training in approving repression of other people if you consider that it enhances your security. This represents itself in increasing demands for capital punishment, in approving police action, in approving the army, even foreign wars because they're considered to enhance your chances of survival. This homogenization then represents an expression of insecurity. Even among white males a sense of danger is cultivated, what we call the "mean world syndrome."

In the chapter "Teacher Image and the Hidden Curriculum," you argue that "any assessment of 'effects' must assume the existence of a standard of measurement against which different or changing quantities and qualities can be measured. That standard is implicit in the value structure of a culture." You compare U.S. media with those of some Eastern European countries. What, at present, is your assessment of the symbolic functions of mass media? Are you optimistic or pessimistic of the role media may now play, especially after the recent changes in Eastern Europe? Do you have any particular model of media ownership/structure to advocate to these newly "liberated" countries?

The recent collapse of governments, and government policies, especially in Eastern Europe and in the Soviet Union, paid lip service to socialist ideas of international cooperation, quality, and attempted to reduce inequality in society, to have some equitable sense of economic development, and a great deal of attention was paid to the cultural needs of people. They had a very inexpensive theater, gave strong support to the motion picture industry, publishing industry, and so on. However, much of it turned out to be lip service. Reality turned out to be quite different. It came as a shock to people, here and elsewhere. The communist party/orthodox thinkers thought news was a key instrument of information and propaganda, and was therefore fairly strictly controlled. In terms of entertainment, most of them basically ignored it or considered it as less important. In Eastern Europe and in the Soviet Union you could see films from all over the world, and motion pictures took up to 60 percent of television time. While not very diversified, it was much more so than American television where much of the programming consists of soap operas, series, and so on. In terms of entertainment, therefore, the ideological controls were relatively loose.

Now there are peculiar and perplexing changes taking place. Changing old policies and guidelines is done chaotically. Opportunism and resurgence of all kinds of ideas, good, bad, and indifferent is leading to neo-fascism, parochialism, and chauvinism. So, while diversification is taking pace, it is not just in a democratic direction.

To the next part of your question, they have to develop their own direction. But I am going to warn them of uncritical acceptance of international monopolies and conglomerates. For example, in Hungary, many of the major newspapers and magazines are owned by Rupert Murdock, Axel Springer, and, until recently, Robert Maxwell. In effect they're mortgaging the socialization of their children to global conglomerates. To many people it seems this is a fresh, new, and exciting development. I want to caution them because they seem to be moving in a reckless way.

In your concluding essay in the "Ferment in the Field" issue of the *Journal of Communication* you say that "When common consciousness becomes a largely manufactured product and integral part rather than only reflection of some other 'base' of social existence, the concept of class or of any other authentic public consciousness may be obsolescent" (p. 358). Is the concept of class obsolescent in poor countries that are struggling to join the "global village"? What are the theoretical implications of your claim that the "investigation of industrial behavior in the cultural field—both policy formation and concept cultivation..." and not class relations becomes the "central task of social analysis"?

The concept of class is a major category of social analysis. But if there is class and no class consciousness, then class becomes an unknown and non-functional fact of life. Now class consciousness is mainly a print-based notion. The industrial revolution begins with printing. Printing makes it possible for people to start telling stories from their point of view and their own interests. Printing makes it possible to build a consciousness, a community among people who never meet.

When television comes in, it blurs that picture. Everybody is watching the same thing, it's designed as a marketing concept, to cultivate people's notion as consumers, of being middle class in a large market. The more a working-class American watches television the more he doesn't know where he belongs. We've succeeded in raising two or three generations of poor people with the mentality of millionaires!

What has to replace the notion of class? Class is still there, but the notion of class consciousness is not. It has to be replaced by the question of cultural environment in which we grow up. I advocate a cultural environment movement. I think that if Marx were alive today, he would say, "electronic mass media are the opiate of the people." In his day, even a century or so after him, it was the church that could act as the cultural arm of the state. Today it is television, and to an extent other media. When you've that kind of a consciousness machine that diffuses and denies the facts of life, that indeed blurs differences and advocates consumption, you're faced with a new cultural mechanism. We have to develop a kind of cultural environment which is sufficiently diversified, in which the marketing strategy, if not totally replaced, has only a small role to play, and which does not monopolize the development of consciousness.

Until we do that it is idle to speak about class. It is no longer a situation that most people become aware of reality from their own life but from stories, and from the culture in which they live. Class circumstance never communicates itself by itself. You've got to hold up a symbolic context in your mind to interpret it. So that symbolic context by which we interpret the circumstances of our life becomes an instrument of giving meaning to the circumstances in life. If you grow up with the idea of actually being a millionaire, you are then against higher taxes even though you would benefit from them. You've no ideas, you're told a lot of stories, you're against politics, you give up your democratic participation. Everything you are told denies in many ways, betrays the objective interest you may have in life. Therefore, it becomes idle to talk about class.

The last part, that's a big question. The theoretical implications are several. First of all, culture has to be included in what used to be called a basic, fundamental, material culture. The notion of culture as a superstructure that mainly reflects society is a print-based notion. When many different groups can get their own printing press—print-based culture reflects different segments, contradictions, and conflict in society—it becomes a principal agent of social change, or propaganda, and illumination of one's own interest. When this dissolves into a total coherent mythology that reorganizes the whole function, the principal industry that shapes the way we think and act, then that becomes part of the material base. It's not superstructure.

Culture becomes part of the material base, the arm of the state, of the establishment. I don't mean the establishment only as a political state. In the U.S. we have two governments, one private, one public. Commercial media, which is the dominant media, is a cultural arm of private government. We have a ministry of culture, and we don't even know we have one! We have a tightly organized private government with enormous public functions, that is not accountable, and that democratic decisions and participation cannot even reach.

I advocate a movement in which public groups, unions, guilds, professional organizations, and minority organizations have some role in the construction of the cultural environment in which infants are born and learn from day one. I see a cultural environment movement as a restructuring without which no other institutional restructuring is possible.

What kind of vision do we have for social development, restructuring of society? We are so politically inexperienced that at this point it is difficult to even begin thinking of that kind of vision for a new society. This does not come out of people's minds. It comes from long, slow, and sometimes painful political experience. We are just beginning on that road.

Since a large number of readers of Media Development are Third World scholars, could you talk about the strategies you suggest, and the obstacles you foresee in "extending cultural liberation to other countries…(and) helping local movements" in Third World countries "against cultural domination and invasion" to which you allude in your proposal "The Cultural Environmental Movement: A Prospectus, 1991"?

No country in the world, except the U.S., has appreciated the kind of investment that they ought to make in their own mass media culture. U.S. products can be had cheap, and by and large they are popular because they're designed for a global market. Where the state has to allocate money for television, it competes with roads, transportation, social services, defense, and everything else. It becomes very tight. In the U.S., our investment in television represents the true value for the huge mobilization that we employ to bring people to the market.

Individuals think they pay nothing for television. In fact, the price we pay for goods includes the cost of advertising—about $200 per household per year. It's a large amount. No other country is willing to make that kind of investment. My only advice is, if you value the culture of your children, if you value the notion of your own sovereignty, if you value any sense of independence in the future, you make a serious investment in your own television programs and motion pictures to compete with the American products and, if necessary, place limits on the American products.

American commercial products have one great advantage: they go for immediate gratification. They don't say "save for the future," "invest for social development." They say "spend right away." The sense of immediate gratification, in effect the glorification of selfishness, is something that appeals to individuals. Therefore, the idea of competing with American products is a difficult idea.

One has to do more than say "let the market decide." The market doesn't usually make humanly and humanely correct decisions. The market is a plutocracy, not a democracy, and it will always favor those who spend more. Therefore, you've to have a cultural policy, you've to know that a cultural policy is difficult to maintain. These are tough choices, but if you can persuade your own people to make an investment in culture, you can look forward to being as independent as any country can be in a world which is increasingly dominated by global conglomerates.

You say that the most productive research is that which illuminates the dynamics of power in communications and of communications in society (Ferment in the Field, p. 356). In your own quest to do such critical work, were there any pressures (explicit or implicit) from the university system, funding agencies, and the media to tone down your criticism, or make your conclusions more palatable to them?

Well, of course there are always pressures if you're not with the mainstream. Your chances of getting grants are much more limited. I've been lucky though. I've worked with various government commissions on the violence issue, and our work has been well funded, and we've been able to establish a line of research that provides a useful service.

Once you interpret things in certain critical ways, your opportunities shrink, your opposition grows, and you are up against more and more formidable obstacles. I expect that. If nobody screams, you are not doing anything. If nobody opposes you, you have so well disguised what you're doing that it doesn't mean anything. However, I try to be of some service to a much broader spectrum of ideological perspectives than my own. But at the same time, I am also advocating a social environment movement which is an activist thing, for I'm not just a social scientist but also a human being and a citizen.

But a social scientific basis is a good approach to enhance "authority." That is my opinion. However, as I become more politically active, that posture of a neutral and generally agreeable social scientist recedes into the background. That means my research funding also declines. I have to depend more and more in the future on the movement itself to generate its own income. I have been lucky for a long time. I don't expect to be so lucky, I don't think it's an accident, for that's how our society works. If you are not a mainstream scholar, you don't get certain resources. And getting resources, to an extent, is an indication of success.

In your writings there is a surfeit of "water," "stream,' and "ocean" metaphors. Is the use of these metaphors conscious? What are your reasons (aesthetic, philosophical, metaphysical) for using them?

No, they've been quite unconscious until you brought them to my attention. You're absolutely right, because I think of television as an environment, as a tidal wave, a flood, an ocean in which we are swimming without knowing or being aware of the nature of the ocean. Therefore, this to me is a good analogy. Individual stories, programs, are like a drop in the ocean. So, when you're dealing with a total environment you're looking for environmental analogies. It's easier, somehow more dramatic, to talk about life as a movement of water. I talk about the river, about mainstreaming, and currents. We're all swimming in the same river, most going in the same direction, but some people are in the center and going faster, others are maneuvering around the sides, and some even try to go against the current, or against the tide. So, I find it a useful analogy, and I like water...

To extend this question, do you think that you're going against the tide now?

In a sense, I have always been going against the tide. From my experience in the 1930s in Central Europe, and where I grew up under fascism, I've got an anti-fascist mentality. I'm against many tendencies in modern societies that go in the direction of fascism. I've been going against the tide first as an analyst and a researcher, and now as a more politically active person.

The idea is not just to go against the tide. The idea is to know that the tide is our own creation. This is where the natural analogy breaks down. We're not dealing with physical nature, we're dealing with our own creation. What's happening today could not be foreseen even five or ten years ago. Therefore the element of unpredictability in history is so strong that even though it may seem you are going against the tide, you may be part of the buildup of an alternative course of change, in a sense building a counter-tide.

Because of the major difficulties we're now facing, environmentally, in terms of resources and so on, people are longing for alternatives. In effect, we are laying the ground for an alternative tide, so to speak, that'll go in the direction of greater equality, greater diversity, and greater respect for human aspiration, more civilized life, less manufactured human brutality, which I think is appalling. Therefore, you must have alternatives to make a claim for a better human, social, and political direction. I think that's a good note on which to end.

NOTE

This interview took place in Chicago, Illinois, U.S.A., on 26 May 1991.

REFERENCES

Gerbner, G. (1983). The importance of being critical—In one's own fashion. *Journal of Communication*, 33:3, 355–362.

Gerbner, G., Gross, L. P., and Melody, W. H. (1973) (eds.). *Communications technology and social policy*. New York: John Wiley & Sons.

Doob, A. M., and MacDonald, G. E. (1979). Television viewing and fear of victimization: Is the relationship causal? *Journal of Personality and Social Psychology*, 37:2, 170–179.

Hirsch, P. M. (1980). The "scary world" of the non-viewer and other anomalies: A reanalysis of Bergner et al.'s findings on cultivation analysis, part I. *Communication Research*, 7, 403–456.

Hughes, M. (1980). The fruits of cultivation analysis: A re-examination of some effects of television watching. *Public Opinion Quarterly*, 44:3, 287–302.

APPENDIX

PUBLICATIONS BY GEORGE GERBNER

BOOKS

2000 *A Media Rejtett Uzenete.* (In Hungarian.) Budapest: Osiris Kiado.

1996 *Invisible Crises: What Conglomerate Media Control Means for America and the World.* With Hamid Mowlana and Herbert Schiller (eds.). Boulder, CO: Westview Press.

1993 *The Global Media Debate: Its Rise, Fall, and Renewal.* With Hamid Mowlana and Kaarle Nordenstreng (eds.). New York: Ablex.

1992 *Triumph of the Image: The Media's War in the Persian Gulf. An International Perspective.* With Hamid Mowlana and Herbert Schiller (eds.). Boulder, CO: Westview Press.

1991 *Beyond the Cold War. Soviet and American Media Images.* With Everette E. Dennis and Yassen N. Zassoursky (eds.). Newbury Park, CA: Sage Publications.

1989 *The Information Gap: How Computers and Other Communication Technologies Affect the Distribution of Power.* With Marsha Siefert and Janice Fisher (eds.). New York and London: Oxford University Press.

1988 *Violence and Terror in the Media: An Annotated Bibliography.* With Nancy Signorielli. Westport, CT: Greenwood Press.

1988 *International Encyclopedia of Communications.* 4 volumes. (Chair, Editorial Board). New York and London: Oxford University Press.

1984 *World Communications: A Handbook.* With Marsha Siefert (eds.). New York and London: Annenberg/Longman Communication Books.

1981 *Communications in the Twenty-First Century.* With Robert W. Haigh and Richard B. Byrne (eds.). New York: John Wiley & Sons.

1980 *Child Abuse: An Agenda for Action.* With Catherine J. Ross and Edward Zigler (eds.). New York: Oxford University Press.

1980 *Mass Media Policies in Changing Cultures* (ed.). New York: Wiley Interscience, 1977. Translated into Italian in De Donato (Editore), *Le Politiche dei Mass Media.* Bari, Italy: S.P.A.

1973 *Communications Technology and Social Policy.* With Larry P. Gross and William H. Melody (eds.). New York: John Wiley & Sons.

1969 *The Analysis of Communications Content: Developments in Scientific Theories and Computer Techniques.* With Ole R. Holsti, Klaus Krippendorff, William J. Paisley, and Phillip Stone (eds.). New York: John Wiley & Sons.

PAPERS, REPORTS, ARTICLES, CHAPTERS

In press "Use Of Alcohol, Illicit Drugs, and Tobacco among Characters on Prime-Time Television." (With Judith A. Long, G. O'Connor, and John Concato.) *Journal of Substance Abuse.*

In press "Growing Up with Television: Cultivation Processes." (With Larry Gross, Michael Morgan, Nancy Signorielli, and James Shanahan.) In Jennings Bryant and Dolf Zillmann (eds.), *Media Effects: Advances in Theory and Research* (2nd ed.). Hillsdale, NJ: Lawrence Erlbaum Associates.

2000 "Mass Media Discourse: Message System Analysis as a Component of Cultural Indicators." In John Hartley and Roberta E. Pearson (eds.), *American Cultural Studies: A Reader.* Oxford: Oxford University Press.

2000 "Ki Mondja El a Torteneteket?" In *Media az Ezredfordulon.* Budapest: Szegedi Tudomanyegyetem.

1999 "The Scenario of Media Violence." In Erika Gabos (ed.), *A Media Hatase a Gyermekekre es Fiatalokra.* Budapest: Nemzetkozi Gyermekmento Szolgalat Magyar Egyesulet.

1999 "What Do We Know?" Foreword to James Shanahan and Michael Morgan, *Television and Its Viewers: Cultivation Theory and Research.* Cambridge: Cambridge University Press.

1999 "Profiling Television Violence." (With Michael Morgan and Nancy Signorielli.). In Kaarle Nordenstreng and Michael Griffin (eds.), *International Media Monitoring* (pp. 335–365). Creskill, NJ: Hampton Press.

1999 "Casting and Fate: Women and Minorities on Television Drama, Game Shows, and News." In Kaarle Nordenstreng and Michael Griffin (eds.), *International Media Monitoring* (pp. 219–240). Creskill, NJ: Hampton Press.

1999 "Mass Media and Dissent." In L. R. Kurtz (ed.), *Encyclopedia of Violence, Peace and Conflict* (pp. 375–376). New York: Academic Press.

1998 "The Ratings Rant, V-Chip Gyp, and TV Violence Shuffle: What Are the Real Issues?" *Peacework,* November, pp. 16–17.

1997 "Gender and Age in Prime Time Television." In Diana Adile Kirschner and Sam Kirschner (eds.), *Media Psychology.* Washington, DC: American Psychological Association.

1997 "Media, Violence and Health." *New Jersey Medicine.*

1996 "Chairman Znaimer's 'Sensual Pagan Torrent.'" *Canadian Journal of Communication,* 21, 13–17.

1996 "The Story-Telling Animal." Foreword to Garth S. Jowett, Ian C. Jarvie, and Kathryn H. Fuller, *Children and the Movies: Media Influences and the Payne Fund Controversy.* Cambridge: Cambridge University Press.

1996 "The Invasion of the Story Sellers." Foreword to Roy F. Fox, *Harvesting Minds: How TV Commercials Control Kids.* Westport, CT: Praeger.

1996 "Fred Rogers and the Significance of Story." In Mark Collins and Margaret Mary Kimmel (eds.), *Mister Rogers' Neighborhood: Children, Television and Fred Rogers* (pp. 3–13). Pittsburgh: University of Pittsburgh Press.

1995 "Terrorism: A Word for All Seasons." *Peace Review,* 7(3/4), 313–319.

1995 "The Cultural Frontier: Repression, Violence, and the Liberating Alternative." In Philip Lee (ed.), *The Democratization of Communication*. Cardiff: The University of Wales Press.

1995 "Cameras on Trial: The O.J. Simpson Show Turns the Tide." *Journal of Broadcasting and Electronic Media*, 39(4), 562–568.

1995 "Casting and Fate: Women and Minorities on Television Drama, Game Shows, and News." In Ed Hollander, Coen van der Linden, and Paul Rutten (eds.), *Communication, Culture, and Community*. Houten, The Netherlands: Bohn Stafleu van Loghum.

1995 "Animal Issues in the Media." Research report to the Ark Trust, Inc. Philadelphia: The Annenberg School for Communication, University of Pennsylvania.

1995 "Bringing the Nicotine Cartel to Justice." *Adbusters Quarterly*, Summer, 89–93.

1995 "Alcohol in American Culture." In Susan E. Martin (ed.), *Alcohol and the Mass Media: Issues, Approaches and Research Directions* (pp. 3–29). Washington, DC: National Institute on Alcohol Abuse and Alcoholism, U.S. Public Health Service.

1995 "Marketing Global Mayhem." *Javnost/The Public*, 2, 71–76.

1995 "What's Wrong with This Picture?" Foreword to Yahya R. Kamalipour, *The U.S. Media and the Middle East: Image and Perception*. Westport, CT: Greenwood Press.

1995 "Television Violence: The Power and the Peril." In Gail Dines and Jean M. Humez (eds.), *Gender, Race, and Class in Media: A Critical Text-Reader* (pp. 547–557). Newbury Park, CA: Sage Publications. French translation ("Pouvoir et Danger de la Violence Televisee") in *Les Cahiers de la Securite Interieure*, Paris, No. 20, 2.

1995 "The Hidden Message in Anti-Violence Public Service Announcements." *Harvard Educational Review*, 65(2), 292–298.

1994 "Growing Up with Television: The Cultivation Perspective." (With Larry Gross, Michael Morgan, and Nancy Signorielli.) In Jennings Bryant and Dolf Zillmann (eds.), *Media Effects: Advances in Theory and Research* (pp. 17–48). Hillsdale, NJ: Lawrence Erlbaum Associates.

1994 "There Is No Free Market on Television." *Hofstra Law Review*, 22, 879–884.

1994 "Instant History/Image History: Lessons from the Persian Gulf War." In Roy F. Fox (ed.), *Images in Language, Media & Mind* (pp. 123–140). Urbana, IL: National Council of Teachers of English. Also in *The Velvet Light Trap*, # 31, Spring 1993, pp. 4–13. Also in Finnish translation: "Pikahistoria/Kuvien Historiaa: Persianlahden Sodan Ja Neuvostoliiton Vallankaappauksen Opetukset." *Tiedotustutkimus*, 15(4), 1992, 6–25.

1994 "Television Violence Profile No. 16: The Turning Point—From Research to Action." (With Michael Morgan and Nancy Signorielli.) Research report. Philadelphia: The Annenberg School for Communication, University of Pennsylvania, January.

1994 "The Risk of Playing to the Cameras." *Legal Times*, July 25, pp. 21–22.

1994 "Television Violence: The Art of Asking the Wrong Question." *The World & I: A Chronicle of Our Changing Era*, July, 385–397.

1994 "Learning Productive Aging as a Social Role: The Lessons of Television." In Scott A. Bass, Francis G. Caro, and Yung-Ping Chen (eds.), *Achieving a Productive Aging Society* (pp. 209–219). Westport, CT: Auburn House.

1993 "Who Tells All the Stories?" *Media Competency as a Challenge to Schools and Education: A German–North American Dialogue*. Gutersloh, Germany: Bertelsman Foundation Publishers.

1993 "Women and Minorities in Television: Casting and Fate." Research report to the Screen Actors Guild and the American Federation of Television and Radio Artists. Philadelphia: The Annenberg School for Communication, University of Pennsylvania, June.

1993 "Brave New Cultural Environment." *Adbusters Quarterly*, Winter, 69–70.

1993 "Challenging the Mythology of the Television Courtroom." *Governing*, 6(9), 11.

1993 "Violence in Cable-Originated Television Programs." Washington, DC: National Cable Television Association, January.

1993 "TV Violence in Context: Movies Produced for Television by the Turner Broadcasting System." Philadelphia: The Annenberg School for Communication, University of Pennsylvania, March.

1993 "Instant History: The Case of the Moscow Coup." *Political Communication*, 10, 193–203.

1993 "UNESCO in the U.S. Press." In George Gerbner, Hamid Mowlana, and Kaarle Nordenstreng (eds.), *The Global Media Debate: Its Rise, Fall, and Renewal*. New York: Ablex.

1993 "'Miracles' of Communication Technology: Powerful Audiences, Diverse Choices and Other Fairy Tales." In Janet Wasko (ed.), *Illuminating the Blind Spots*. New York: Ablex.

1993 "The Politics of Media Violence: Some Reflections." In Cees Hamelink and Olga Linné (eds.), *Mass Communication Research: On Problems and Policies* (pp. 133–145). Norwood, NJ: Ablex.

1992 "Persian Gulf War, The Movie." In George Gerbner, Hamid Mowlana, and Herbert Schiller (eds.), *Triumph of the Image: The Media's War in the Persian Gulf—An International Perspective*. Boulder, CO: Westview Press. (A previous version was delivered as the first Wayne A. Danielson Award for Distinguished Achievement in Communication Scholarship lecture at the University of Texas at Austin and published in *Representative American Speeches 1991–92*. New York: H.W. Wilson Company.)

1992 "Violence and Terror in and by the Media." In Marc Raboy and Bernard Dagenais (eds.), *Media, Crisis and Democracy*. London: Sage Publications.

1992 "Violence in the Mass Media." In Lucien Sfez and Francis Balle (eds.), *Dictionnaire Critique de la Communication*. Paris: PUF.

1991 "The Image of Russians on American Media and 'The New Epoch.'" In George Gerbner, Everette E. Dennis, and Yassen N. Zassoursky (eds.), *Beyond the Cold War: Soviet and American Media Images* (pp. 31–35). Newbury Park, CA: Sage Publications.

1991 "Führt Kanalfülle zu mehr Programmvielfalt?" ("Does Channel Proliferation Promote Program Diversity?"). *Media Perspectiven* (Frankfurt), January.

1990 "The Second American Revolution." *Adbusters Quarterly*, Winter.

1990 "Stories That Hurt: Tobacco, Alcohol and Other Drugs in the Mass Media." In *Youth and Drugs: Society's Mixed Messages* (pp. 53–127). OSAP Prevention Monograph-6. Washington, DC: U.S. Department of Health and Human Services.

1990 "The Crack in the Tobacco Curtain, or the Bill of Rights Disinformation Campaign." In *Free Speech.* Speech Communication Association, Spring.

1990 "A New Environmental Movement in Communication and Culture." *Media Development*, April, 13–14.

1990 "Epilogue: Advancing on the Path of Righteousness (Maybe)." In Nancy Signorielli and Michael Morgan (eds.), *Cultivation Analysis: New Directions in Media Effects Research.* Newbury Park, CA: Sage Publications.

1990 "Violence Profile 1967 through 1988–89: Enduring Patterns." (With Nancy Signorielli.) Research report. Philadelphia: The Annenberg School for Communication, University of Pennsylvania, January.

1990 "Communications, Study of." (With Wilbur Schramm.) *International Encyclopedia of Communications* (pp. 358–368). New York: Oxford University Press. Reprinted as "The international development of communication studies." *Communicatio*, 1990, 16(1).

1989 "Media Coverage of the Declaration." In Hamid Mowlana (ed.), *Aspects of the Mass Media Declaration of UNESCO.* International Association for Mass Communication Research Occasional Papers No. 9. Budapest: Hungarian Institute for Public Opinion Research.

1989 "Cross-Cultural Communications Research in the Age of Telecommunications." In Christian Academy (ed.), *Continuity and Change in Communications in Post-Industrial Society. Volume 2 in The World Community in Post-Industrial Society.* Seoul, Korea: Wooseok Publishing Company.

1989 "Waiting for Prime Time: The Outlook for Women in TV News." *New Choices*, 29(3), 74.

1988 "Violence and Terror in the Mass Media." *Reports and Papers in Mass Communication*, No. 102. Paris: UNESCO.

1988 "Television's Cultural Mainstream: Which Way Does It Run?" *Directions in Psychiatry*, 8(9), 3–7.

1988 "Symbolic Functions of Violence and Terror." *The Terrorism and the News Media Research Project.* Boston: Mass Communication and Society Div., AEJMC, Emerson College, July.

1988 "Telling Stories in the Information Age." In Brent D. Rubin (ed.), *Information and Behavior.* New Brunswick, NJ: Transaction Books.

1987 "Ministry of Culture, the USA, and the Free Marketplace of Ideas." *National Forum*, Fall, 15–17.

1987 "The Electronic Church in American Culture." *New Catholic World*, May/June, 133–135.

1987 "Science on Television: How It Affects Public Conceptions." *Issues in Science and Technology*, Spring, 109–115.

1987 "Television's Populist Brew: The Three Bs." *et cetera*, 44, 3–7.

1987 "Televised Trials: Historic Juncture for Our Courts?" Introduction to Susanna Barber, *News Cameras in the Courtroom.* Norwood, NJ: Ablex.

1986 "Television's Mean World: Violence Profile No. 14–15." (With Larry Gross, Michael Morgan, and Nancy Signorielli.) Technical research report. Philadelphia: The Annenberg School for Communication, University of Pennsylvania, September.

1986 "Living with Television: The Dynamics of the Cultivation Process." (With Larry Gross, Michael Morgan, and Nancy Signorielli.) In Jennings Bryant and Dolf Zillmann (eds.), *Perspectives on Media Effects* (pp. 17–41). Hillsdale, NJ: Lawrence Erlbaum Associates. Reprinted in Amy G. Halberstadt and Steve L. Ellyson (eds.), *Social Psychology Readings: A Century of Research.* New York: McGraw-Hill Publishing Co., 1990.

1986 "The Symbolic Context of Action and Communication." In Ralph L. Rosnow and Marianthi Georgoudi (eds.), *Contextualism and Understanding in Behavioral Science.* New York: Praeger Publishers.

1985 "Children's Television: A National Disgrace." *Pediatric Annals*, December, 822–827. Reprinted in Owen Peterson (ed.), *The Reference Shelf: Representative American Speeches, 1985–1986.* New York: H.W. Wilson Company.

1985 "Dreams That Hurt: Mental Illness in the Mass Media." Presented at the First Rosalynn Carter Symposium on Mental Health Policy, Emory University School of Medicine, Atlanta, November.

1985 "Mass Media Discourse: Message System Analysis as a Component of Cultural Indicators." In Teun A. van Dijk (ed.), *Discourse and Communication* (pp. 13–25). Berlin: Walter de Gruyter & Co.

1985 "Television Entertainment and Viewers' Conceptions of Science." (With Larry Gross, Michael Morgan, and Nancy Signorielli.) Research report to the National Science Foundation, Philadelphia: The Annenberg School for Communication, University of Pennsylvania, July.

1985 "Le Colonialisme de la Television: Les Fonctions Symboliques de la Violence." In *TViolence: Actes du Colloque.* Montreal: Association Nationale des Telespectateurs.

1984 "The Mainstreaming of America: Television Makes Strange Bedfellows." *TV Guide*, October 20, pp. 20–23.

1984 "Gratuitous Violence and Exploitive Sex: What Are the Lessons? (Including Violence Profile No. 13)." Statement prepared for the Study Committee of the Communications Commission of the National Council of Churches hearing, New York, September 21.

1984 "Facts, Fantasies and Schools." (With Larry Gross, Michael Morgan, and Nancy Signorielli.) *Society*, September/October, 9–13.

1984 "Defending the Indefensible." (With Steven H. Chaffee, Beatrix A. Hamburg, Chester M. Pierce, Eli A. Rubinstein, Alberta E. Siegel, and Jerome L. Singer.) *Society*, September/October, 30–35.

1984 "The Impact of the 'Electronic Church' on the Local Church." (With Larry Gross, Michael Morgan, and Nancy Signorielli.) *Ministries*, Fall, 58–61.

1984 "Defining the Field of Communication." *ACA Bulletin*, April.

1984 "Religion on Television." (With Harry E. Cotugno, Larry Gross, Stewart Hoover, Michael Morgan, Nancy Signorielli, and Robert Wuthnow.) Research report, 2 volumes. Philadelphia: The Annenberg School for Communication, University of Pennsylvania, and the Gallup Organization, Inc., April.

1984 "Health, Medicine, and Violence on TV." *Transactions and Studies of the College of Physicians of Philadelphia*, March, 33–40.

1984 "Political Correlates of Television Viewing." (With Larry Gross, Michael Morgan, and Nancy Signorielli.) *Public Opinion Quarterly*, 48(1), 283–300.

1983–84 "Liberal Education in the Information Age." *Current Issues in Higher Education*, 39(1), 14–18.

1984 "Political Functions of Television Viewing: A Cultivation Analysis." In Gabriele Melischek, Karl Erik Rosengren, and James Stappers (eds.), *Cultural Indicators: An International Symposium.* Vienna, Austria: Osterreichischen Akademie der Wissenschaften.

1983 "The Importance of Being Critical—In One's Own Fashion." *Journal of Communication*, Summer, 355–362.

1983 "The American Press Coverage of the Fourth Extraordinary Session of the UNESCO General Conference, Paris 1982." Research report to UNESCO. Philadelphia: The Annenberg School for Communication, University of Pennsylvania, August.

1982 "The World According to Television." (With Nancy Signorielli.) *American Demographics.* October, 15–17.

1982 "Television in the Courtroom." In *Americana Annual/Encyclopedia Year Book.* Danbury, CT: Grolier, Inc.

1982 "What Television Teaches about Doctors and Health." (With Larry Gross, Michael Morgan, and Nancy Signorielli.) *Mobius: A Journal for Continuing Education Professionals in Health Sciences*, April, 44–49.

1982 "Charting the Mainstream: Television's Contributions to Political Orientations." (With Larry Gross, Michael Morgan, and Nancy Signorielli.) *Journal of Communication*, Spring, 100–126.

1982 "The Gospel of Instant Gratification." Symposium on advertising. *Business and Society Review*, Spring.

1982 "TV's Changing Our Lives." *Presbyterian Survey*, January, 11–13.

1982 "Programming Health Portrayals: What Viewers See, Say and Do." (With Michael Morgan and Nancy Signorielli.) In David Pearl, Lorraine Bouthilet, and Joyce Lazar (eds.), *Television and Behavior: Ten Years of Scientific Progress and Implications for the 80's.* Washington, DC: U.S. Dept. of Health and Human Resources Publication No. (ADM) 82–1196.

1982 "TV Professions." (With Michael Morgan.) In Meg Schwartz (ed.), *TV & Teens: Experts Look at the Issues.* Reading, MA: Action for Children's Television, Addison-Wesley.

1981 "Health and Medicine on Television." (With Larry Gross, Michael Morgan, and Nancy Signorielli.) *The New England Journal of Medicine*, October 8, 305(15), 901–904.

1981 "Television as Religion." *Media & Values*, Fall, No. 17, pp. 1–3. Reprinted as "Society's Story-Teller: How Television Creates the Myths by Which We Live," in the 15th Anniversary Issue, Fall 1992.

1981 "Final Reply to Paul Hirsch." (With Larry Gross, Michael Morgan, and Nancy Signorielli.) *Communication Research*, July, 259–280.

1981 "A Curious Journey into the Scary World of Paul Hirsch." (With Larry Gross, Michael Morgan, and Nancy Signorielli.) *Communication Research*, January, 39–72.

1981 "Aging with Television Commercials: Images on Television Commercials and Dramatic Programming, 1977–1979." (With Larry Gross, Michael Morgan, and Nancy Signorielli.) Research report to the Administration on Aging. Philadelphia: The Annenberg School for Communication, University of Pennsylvania, June.

1981 "Scientists on the TV Screen." (With Larry Gross, Michael Morgan, and Nancy Signorielli.) *Society*, May/June, 41–44.

1981 "Television: The American Schoolchild's National Curriculum Day in and Day Out." *PTA Today*, April, 58–59.

1981 "Education for the Age of Television." In Milton E. Ploghoft and James A. Anderson (eds.), *Education for the Television Age* (pp. 173–178). Athens, Ohio: The Cooperative Center for Social Science Education, College of Education, Ohio University.

1980 "TV: The New Religion Controlling Us." Feature article in *Long Island Newsday*, "Ideas," November 9. Also published in the *Miami Herald*, "Viewpoint" (as "TV as the New Religion"), November 30. Also published in the *Free Press* (London, Ontario, Canada), November.

1980 "Television's Contributions to Public Understanding of Science: A Pilot Project." (With Larry Gross, Michael Morgan, and Nancy Signorielli.) Research report to the National Science Foundation. Philadelphia: The Annenberg School for Communication, University of Pennsylvania, October.

1980 "The 'Mainstreaming' of America: Violence Profile No. 11." (With Larry Gross, Michael Morgan, and Nancy Signorielli.) *Journal of Communication,* Summer, 10–24. Reprinted in *Mass Communication Review Yearbook II.* Beverly Hills, CA: Sage Publications, April 1981; also in Jarice Hanson and David J. Maxcy (eds.), *Sources: Notable Selections in Mass Media.* Guilford, CT: Dushkin Publishing Group/Brown and Benchmark Publishers, 1996.

1980 "Television Violence, Victimization and Power." (With Larry Gross, Michael Morgan, and Nancy Signorielli.) *American Behavioral Scientist*, May, 705–716.

1980 "Media Portrayal of the Elderly." Statement in *Hearing Before the Select Committee on Aging*, House of Representatives, Los Angeles, CA, April 26. Washington DC: U.S. Government Printing Office, Comm. Pub. No. 96–231.

1980 "Media and the Family: Images and Impact." (With Larry Gross, Michael Morgan, and Nancy Signorielli.) Research report presented at the National Research Forum on Family Issues sponsored by the White House Conference on Families, Washington, DC, April 11.

1980 "Trial by Television: Are We at the Point of No Return?" *Judicature*, 63(9), 117–126. (Winner of the Media Award of the Philadelphia Bar Association, 1981.) Reprinted in *National Shorthand Reporter*, June 1980. Also published in two parts in a different version in *Louisville Law Examiner*, "Brandeis Brief" series of "Emerging Legal Issues," Louisville, KY: University of Kentucky, March 6 and April 14.

1980 "Violence Profile No. 11: Trends in Network Television Drama and Viewer Conceptions of Social Reality 1967–1979." (With Larry Gross, Michael Morgan, and Nancy Signorielli.) Technical research report. Philadelphia: The Annenberg School for Communication, University of Pennsylvania, April.

1980 "Interpreting The TV World." *Irish Broadcasting Review*, Spring, 7–11.

1980 "Sex on Television and What Viewers Learn from It." Paper prepared for the National Association of Television Program Executives Annual Conference, San Francisco, February 19.

1980 "Death in Prime Time: Notes on the Symbolic Functions of Dying in the Mass Media." *The Annals of the American Academy of Political and Social Science*, 447, 64–70.

1980 "Aging with Television: Images on Television Drama and Conceptions of Social Reality." (With Larry Gross, Nancy Signorielli, and Michael Morgan.) *Journal of Communication*, Winter, 37–47.

1980 "Children and Power on Television: The Other Side of the Picture." In George Gerbner, Catherine J. Ross, and Edward Zigler (eds.), *Child Abuse: An Agenda for Action*. New York: Oxford University Press.

1980 "Electronic Children: Will the New Generation Be Different?" In Al Klose (ed.), *Democracy—Technology...Collision!* Indianapolis: Bobbs-Merrill.

1980 "Stigma: Social Functions of the Portrayal of Mental Illness in the Mass Media." In J. Rabkin, L. Gelb, and J. B. Lazar (eds.), *Attitudes Toward the Mentally Ill: Research Perspectives*. Washington, DC: U.S. Government Printing Office.

1980 "The Violent Face of Television and Its Lessons." (With Larry Gross.) In Edward L. Palmer and Aimee Dorr (eds.), *Children and the Faces of Television: Teaching, Violence, Selling*. New York: Academic Press.

1979 "The Demonstration of Power: Violence Profile No. 10." (With Larry Gross, Nancy Signorielli, Michael Morgan, and Marilyn Jackson-Beeck.) *Journal of Communication*, Summer, 177–196. Reprinted in *Mass Communication Review Yearbook I*. Beverly Hills, CA: Sage Publications, 1980.

1979 "Editorial Response: A Reply to Newcomb's Humanistic Critique." (With Larry Gross.) *Communication Research*, April, 223–229.

1979 "Violence Profile No. 10: Trends in Network Television Drama and Viewer Conceptions of Social Reality 1967–1978." (With Larry Gross, Nancy Signorielli, Michael Morgan, and Marilyn Jackson-Beeck.) Technical research report. Philadelphia: The Annenberg School for Communication, University of Pennsylvania, March.

1979 "On Wober's 'Televised Violence and Paranoid Perception: The View from Great Britain'." (With Larry Gross, Michael Morgan, and Nancy Signorielli.) *Public Opinion Quarterly*, Spring, 123–124.

1979 "The Role of Media in Citizen Perception of Crime." In *Crime and People: Fears and Realities*. Forum Proceedings published by the Maryland Conference of Social Concern.

1978 "The Image of the Elderly in Prime-Time Television Drama." (With Nancy Signorielli.) *Generations*, Fall, 10–11.

1978 "Uber die Angstlichkeit von Vielsehern." ("About the Anxiousness of Heavy Viewers.") *Fernsehen und Bildung*, 12:1/2.

1978 "The World of Television News." (With Nancy Signorielli.) In W. Adams and F. Schreibman (eds.), *Television News Archives: A Guide to Research*. Washington, DC: George Washington University.

1978 "Cultural Indicators: Violence Profile No. 9." (With Larry Gross, Marilyn Jackson-Beeck, Suzanne Jeffries-Fox, and Nancy Signorielli.) *Journal of Communication*, Summer, 176–207.

1978 "Deviance and Power: Symbolic Functions of 'Drug Abuse.'" In Charles Winick (ed.), *Deviance and Mass Media*. Beverly Hills, CA: Sage Publications. Also in *Studies in the Anthropology of Visual Communication*, Fall 1978.

1978 "Violence Profile No. 9: Trends in Network Television Drama and Viewer Conceptions of Social Reality 1967–1977." (With Larry Gross, Marilyn Jackson-Beeck, Suzanne Jeffries-Fox, and Nancy Signorielli.) Technical research report. Philadelphia: The Annenberg School for Communication, University of Pennsylvania, March.

1978 "Television's Influence on Values and Behavior." *Weekly Psychiatry Update Series* (Lesson 24, Vol. 2). New York: Biomedia, Inc.

1978 "Women in Public Broadcasting: A Progress Report." (With Nancy Signorielli.) Research report. Philadelphia: Institute for Applied Communication Sciences, The Annenberg School for Communication, University of Pennsylvania.

1978 "The Dynamics of Cultural Resistance." In Gaye Tuchman, Arlene Kaplan Daniels, and James Benet (eds.), *Hearth and Home: Images of Women in Mass Media* (pp. 46–50). New York: Oxford University Press.

1978 "Television as New Religion." (With Kathleen Connolly.) *New Catholic World*, March/April, 52–56.

1978 "Fernsehen und Familie." (With Suzanne Jeffries-Fox.) *Fernsehen und Bildung* 11, 222–234.

1977 "Controller of Our Fears." Symposium on "The War against Television Violence." *Business and Society Review*, Fall.

1977 "Popular Culture: Who Pays?" *Popular Culture* ("Courses by Newspaper," University of California, San Diego, distributed by United Press International.) Del Mar, CA: Publishers, Inc., pp. 8–10.

1977 "The Real Threat of Television Violence." In Judy Fireman (ed.), *TV Book: The Ultimate Television Book*. New York: Workman Publishing Company.

1977 "Proliferating Violence." *Society*, September/October, 8–14.

1977 "Comparative Cultural Indicators." In George Gerbner (ed.), *Mass Media Policies in Changing Cultures* (pp. 199–205). New York: Wiley Interscience.

1977 "'The Gerbner Violence Profile'—An Analysis of the CBS Report." (With Larry Gross, Marilyn Jackson-Beeck, Suzanne Jeffries-Fox, and Nancy Signorielli.) *Journal of Broadcasting*, Summer, 280–286.

1977 "One More Time: An Analysis of the CBS 'Final Comments on the Violence Profile.'" (With Larry Gross, Marilyn Jackson-Beeck, Suzanne Jeffries-Fox, and Nancy Signorielli.) *Journal of Broadcasting*, Summer, 297–303.

1977 "Television: The New State Religion?" *et cetera*, 34(2), 145–150. Reprinted in Larry Hickman (ed.), *Philosophy, Technology, and Human Affairs*. College Station, TX: Ibis Press, 1985.

1977 "Institutional Forces and the Mass Media." In Mary B. Cassata and Molefi K. Asante (eds.), *The Social Uses of Mass Communication*. State University of New York at Buffalo: Department of Communication, Communication Research Center.

1977 "Violence Profile No. 8: Trends in Network Television Drama and Viewer Conceptions of Social Reality, 1967–1976." Testimony and report printed in *Sex and Violence on TV*, hearing before the Subcommittee on Communications of the Committee on Interstate and Foreign Commerce, House of Representatives, Serial No. 95–103. Washington, DC: U.S. Government Printing Office.

1977 "TV Violence Profile No. 8: The Highlights." (With Larry Gross, Marilyn Jackson-Beeck, Suzanne Jeffries-Fox, and Nancy Signorielli.) *Journal of Communication,* Spring, 171–180.

1977 "The Many Worlds of the World's Press." (With George Marvanyi.) *Journal of Communication*, Winter, 52–66. Reprinted in Jim Richstad and Michael H. Anderson (eds.), *Crisis in International News: Policies and Prospects.* New York: Columbia University Press, 1981.

1976 "Television Violence: Measuring the Climate of Fear." Impact, *American Medical News,* December 13.

1976 "The Family Hour and Beyond." *Human Behavior*, November, pp. 70–71.

1976 "IAMCR Assembly." *Intermedia*, October.

1976 "Living with Television: The Violence Profile." (With Larry Gross.) *Journal of Communication*, Spring, 172–199. Reprinted in Horace Newcomb (ed.), *Television: The Critical View*, 2nd ed. New York: Oxford University Press, 1979.

1976 "Violence Profile No. 7: Trends in Network Television Drama and Viewer Conceptions of Social Reality, 1967–1975." (With Larry Gross, Michael F. Eleey, Suzanne Fox, Marilyn Jackson-Beeck, and Nancy Signorielli.) Technical research report. Philadelphia: The Annenberg School for Communication, University of Pennsylvania, April.

1976 "The Scary World of TV's Heavy Viewer." (With Larry Gross.) *Psychology Today*, April, pp. 41–45. Reprinted in David Manning White and John Pendleton (eds.), *Mirror of American Life.* Del Mar, CA: Publisher's, Inc., 1977. Reprinted in M. Cummins and C. Slade (eds.), *Writing the Research Paper,* 1988.

1975 "The World of Television: Towards Cultural Indicators." (With Larry Gross.) *Intermedia: Journal of the International Broadcast Institute*, 3(3), 2–3.

1975 "Scenario for Violence." *Human Behavior*, October, 64–69. Reprinted in Robert Atwin, Barry Orton, and William Vesterman (eds.), *American Mass Media: Industry and Issues* (pp. 102–107). New York: Random House, 1978.

1975 "Violence Trends in Television." (With Larry Gross.) *Journal of the Producers Guild of America*, March, 9–12.

1974 "Teacher Image in Mass Culture: Symbolic Functions of the 'Hidden Curriculum.'" In David R. Olson (ed.), *Media and Symbols: The Forms of Expression, Communication, and Education* (pp. 470–497). Chicago: The University of Chicago Press.

1974 "Violence Profile No. 6: Trends in Network Television Drama and Viewer Conceptions of Social Reality." (With Larry P. Gross, and with the assistance of Michael F. Eleey, Nancy Signorielli [Tedesco] and Suzanne Fox.) Technical research report. Philadelphia: The Annenberg School for Communication, University of Pennsylvania, December.

1974 "Symbolic Functions of 'Drug Abuse': A Mass Communication Approach." *Studies in the Anthropology of Visual Communication*, 1(1), 27–34.

1974 "Communication: Society Is the Message." *Communication*, 1, 57–64.

1974 "Statement on Violence Profile." Hearings before the Subcommittee on Communications of the Committee on Commerce, United States Senate, Serial No. 93–76 (pp. 56–105). Washington, DC: U.S. Government Printing Office.

1974 "The New Media Environment." In *New Perspectives in Communication.* Boston University, School of Public Communication.

1973 "Violence Profile No. 5: Trends in Network Television Drama and Viewer Conceptions of Social Reality." (With Larry P. Gross, and with the assistance of Michael F. Eleey and Nancy Signorielli [Tedesco].) Technical research report. Philadelphia: The Annenberg School for Communication, University of Pennsylvania, June.

1973 "Cultural Indicators: The Third Voice." In George Gerbner, Larry P. Gross, and William H. Melody (eds.), *Communications Technology and Social Policy.* New York: John Wiley & Sons.

1973 "Teacher Image and the Hidden Curriculum." *The American Scholar*, 42(1), 66–92. Also in George Gerbner, Larry P. Gross, and William H. Melody (eds.), *Communications Technology and Social Policy.* New York: John Wiley & Sons.

1972–73 "Apples, Oranges, and the Kitchen Sink: An Analysis and Guide to the Comparison of Violence Ratings." (With Michael F. Eleey and Nancy Signorielli [Tedesco].) *Journal of Broadcasting*, 17, 21–31.

1972–73 "Validity Indeed!" (With Michael F. Eleey and Nancy Signorielli [Tedesco].) *Journal of Broadcasting*, 17, 34–35.

1972 "Communication and Social Environment." *Scientific American*, September, 153–160. Reprinted in *Communication: A Scientific American Book.* San Francisco: W.H. Freeman & Company, 1972.

1972 "The Violence Profile. Some Indicators of Trends in and the Symbolic Structure of Network Television Drama 1967–1971." In *Surgeon General's Report by the Scientific Advisory Committee on Television and Social Behavior, Appendix A.* Hearings before the Subcommittee on Communications of the Committee on Commerce, U.S. Senate, Serial No. 92–52 (pp. 453–526). Washington, DC: U.S. Government Printing Office.

1972 "Violence in Television Drama: Trends and Symbolic Functions." In G.A. Comstock and E.A. Rubinstein (eds.), *Television and Social Behavior 1: Content and Control.* Washington, DC: U.S. Government Printing Office.

1972 "The Structure and Process of Television Program Content Regulation in the U.S." In G.A. Comstock and E.A. Rubinstein (eds.), *Television and Social Behavior 1: Content and Control.* Washington, DC: U.S. Government Printing Office.

1970 "Cultural Indicators: The Case of Violence in Television Drama." *The Annals of the American Academy of Political and Social Science,* 388 (March), 69–81.

1970 "La Politica Culturale e lo Studio delle Commicaziona de massa." In Giovanni Bechelloni (ed.), *Politica Culturale? Studi, Materiali, Ipotesi.* Bologna, Italy: Guaraldi Editore.

1969 "The Film Hero: A Cross-Cultural Study." *Journalism Monographs*, No. 13.

1969 "Pouvoir Institutionnalise et Systemes de Messages." *Communications*, 14, Paris, 116–128.

1969 "Dimensions of Violence in Television Drama." In Robert K. Baker and Sandra J. Ball (eds.), *Violence and the Media*, Chapter 15. Staff report to the National Commission on the Causes and Prevention of Violence. Washington, DC: U.S. Government Printing Office.

1969 "Toward 'Cultural Indicators': The Analysis of Mass Mediated Message Systems." *AV Communication Review,* 17 (Summer), 137–148. Also in George Gerbner, Ole R. Holsti, Klaus Krippendorff, William J. Paisley, and Phillip Stone (eds.), *The Analysis of Communications Content: Developments in Scientific Theories and Computer Techniques.* New York: John Wiley & Sons, 1969.

1969 "Institutional Pressures Upon Mass Communicators." In Paul Halmos (ed.), *The Sociology of Mass Media Communicators.* The Sociological Review Monograph No. 13 (pp. 205–248). University of Keele, England.

1968 "McLuhan, Herbert Marshall." *The Encyclopedia Americana.*

1968 "Bibliography of Studies on the Representation of Education and Educators in the Mass Media." *AV Communication Review,* 16 (Summer), 210–217.

1968 "Communication." *The Encyclopedia Americana.*

1967 "The Press and the Dialogue in Education: A Case Study of a National Educational Convention and Its Depiction in America's Daily Newspapers." *Journalism Monographs* 5.

1967 "Newsmen and Schoolmen: The State and Problems of Education Reporting." *Journalism Quarterly,* 44 (Summer), 211–224.

1967 "Mass Media and Human Communication Theory." In Frank E.X. Dance (ed.), *Human Communication Theory: Original Essays.* New York: Holt, Rinehart & Winston. Reprinted in Denis McQuail (ed.), *Sociology of Mass Communications.* New York: Penguin Books, 1972.

1966 "Education about Education by Mass Media." *The Educational Forum,* 31 (November), 7–15. Also in Ralph A. Smith (ed.), *Criticism and Mass Communications.* Urbana: University of Illinois Press, 1967.

1966 "On Defining Communication: Still Another View." *Journal of Communication,* 16(2), 99–102.

1966 "Images Across Cultures: Teachers in Mass Media Fiction and Drama." *The School Review,* 74 (Summer), 212–229.

1966 "Mass Media and the Crisis in Education." In *Technology and Education* (pp. 99–109). School of Education, Syracuse University.

1966 "An Institutional Approach to Mass Communications Research." In Lee Thayer (ed.), *Communication: Theory and Research* (pp. 429–445). Springfield, IL: Charles C. Thomas, Publisher.

1965 "Communication and Social Science: A 'Strategic' Approach." *The Japanese Annals of Social Psychology,* 6, 161–174.

1964 "A Communication Approach." In Robert O. Hall (ed.), *The Content and Pattern for the Professional Training of Audiovisual Communication Specialists.* Washington, DC: Educational Media Branch, U.S. Office of Education, Department of Health, Education and Welfare.

1964 "Ideological Perspectives and Political Tendencies in News Reporting." *Journalism Quarterly,* 41 (Autumn), 495–509.

1964 "Mass Communications and Popular Conceptions of Education: A Cross-Cultural Study." Cooperative Research Project No. 876. Report of 10-nation international research project. Washington, DC: U.S. Office of Education.

1964 "The Role of Media in Communicating Results of Research." In W. C. Meierhenry (ed.), *Media and Educational Innovation.* Lincoln, NE: University of Nebraska Press.

1964 "Education in Newspaper Advertisements." *School and Society,* 92 (November 28), 363–365.

1963 "'Mr. Novak': Young Man to Watch." *Phi Delta Kappan,* 45 (October), 13–19.

1963 "Teachers vs. the Machine: The Headline Battle of Atlantic City." *AV Communication Review,* 11, 10–18.

1963 "Un Modele de la Communication." *Etudes de Radio-Television,* 1, 13–19.

1963 "Mass Communication and the 'Humanization' of Homo Sapiens." *The AAUW Journal,* 56 (3), 102–104.

1963 "A Theory of Communication and Its Implications for Teaching." In *The Nature of Teaching.* Milwaukee, WI: University of Wisconsin–Milwaukee, School of Education. Reprinted in Ronald T. Hyman (ed.), *Teaching: Vantage Points for Study* (pp. 18–31). Philadelphia and New York: J.B. Lippincott, 1968.

1963 "Smaller Than Life: Teachers and Schools in the Mass Media." *Phi Delta Kappan,* 44 (February), 202–205.

1962 "Mass Media Censorship and the Portrayal of Mental Illness: Some Effects of Industry-Wide Controls in Motion Pictures and Television." (With Percy H. Tannenbaum.) In Wilbur Schramm (ed.), *Studies of Innovation and of Communication to the Public.* Stanford, CA: Stanford University Press.

1962 "How Teachers Can Respond to the Challenge of Video." *Professional Growth for Teachers,* 6.

1962 "Technology, Communication, and Education: A Social Perspective." In *Tomorrow's Teaching.* Oklahoma City, OK: Frontiers of Science Foundation.

1962 "Instructional Technology and the Press: A Case Study." Occasional Paper 4. Washington, DC: National Education Association, Technological Development Project.

1961 "Press Perspectives in World Communications: A Pilot Study." *Journalism Quarterly,* 38, 313–322.

1961 "Regulation of Mental Illness Content in Motion Pictures and Television." (With Percy H. Tannenbaum.) *Gazette,* 6, 365–385.

1961 "Psychology, Psychiatry and Mental Illness in the Mass Media: A Study of Trends, 1900–1959." *Mental Hygiene,* 45 (January), 89–93.

1960 "The Individual in a Mass Culture." *Saturday Review,* 43 (June 18), 11–13, 36–37. Also (abridged) in *The Executive,* 4 (1960), 14–16 and *The National Elementary Principal,* 40 (February 1961), 49–54.

1960 "Mass Communications and the Citizenship of Secondary School Youth." In Franklin Patterson and others (eds.), *The Adolescent Citizen* (pp. 179–205). Glencoe, IL: The Free Press.

1960 "The Interaction Model: Perception and Communication." In John Ball and Francis Byrnes (eds.), *Research, Principles, and Practices in Visual Communication* (pp. 4–15). East Lansing, MI: National Project in Agricultural Communications.

1960 "Social Science and the Professional Education of the Audio-Visual Communication Specialist." *AV Communication Review,* 8, 50–58.

1960 "Visual Communication Training: Philosophy and Principles." In *Communication Training* (pp. 29–34). East Lansing, MI: National Project in Agricultural Communications.

1959 "Education and the Challenge of Mass Culture." *AV Communication Review,* 7 (Fall), 264–278.

1959 "Popular Culture and Images of the Family." *The Chicago Theological Seminary Register,* 49 (November), 31–37.

1959 "Mental Illness on Television: A Study of Censorship." *Journal of Broadcasting*, 3, 292–303.

1958 "The Social Anatomy of the Romance-Confession Cover Girl." *Journalism Quarterly*, 35, 299–306.

1958 "The Social Role of the Confession Magazine." *Social Problems*, 6, 29–40.

1958 "On Content Analysis and Critical Research in Mass Communication." *AV Communication Review*, 6, 85–108. Reprinted in L. A. Dexter and D. M. White (eds.), *People, Society and Mass Communications*. Glencoe, IL: The Free Press, 1964.

1956 "Toward a General Model of Communication." *AV Communication Review*, 4, 171–199.

Sut Jhally & Justin Lewis
General Editors

This series will be publishing works in media and culture, focusing on research embracing a variety of critical perspectives. The editors are particularly interested in promoting theoretically informed empirical work using both quantitative and qualitative approaches. Although the focus is on scholarly research, works published in the series will appeal to readers beyond a narrow, specialized audience.

www.ingramcontent.com/pod-product-compliance
Lightning Source LLC
Chambersburg PA
CBHW060125280326
41932CB00012B/1431